Archaeology of Mountain Landscapes

THE INSTITUTE FOR EUROPEAN AND MEDITERRANEAN ARCHAEOLOGY
DISTINGUISHED MONOGRAPH SERIES

Peter F. Biehl, editor-in-chief
Sarunas Milisauskas and Stephen L. Dyson, editors

The Magdalenian Household: Unraveling Domesticity
 Ezra Zubrow, Françoise Audouze, and James G. Enloe, editors

Eventful Archaeologies: New Approaches to Social Transformation in the Archaeological Record
 Douglas J. Bolender, editor

The Archaeology of Violence: Interdisciplinary Approaches
 Sarah Ralph, editor

Approaching Monumentality in Archaeology
 James. F. Osborne, editor

The Archaeology of Childhood: Interdisciplinary Perspectives on an Archaeological Enigma
 Güner Coşkunsu, editor

Diversity of Sacrifice: Form and Function of Sacrificial Practices in the Ancient World and Beyond
 Carrie Ann Murray, editor

Climate and Cultural Change in Prehistoric Europe and the Near East
 Peter F. Biehl and Olivier P. Nieuwenhuyse, editors

Water and Power in Past Societies
 Emily Holt, editor

Coming Together: Comparative Approaches to Population Aggregation and Early Urbanization
 Attila Gyucha, editor

The Early Bronze Age in Western Anatolia
 Laura K. Harrison, A. Nejat Bilgen, and Asuman Kapuci, editors

The Archaeology of Inequality
 Orlando Cerasuolo, editor

Homo Migrans: Modeling Mobility and Migration in Human History
 Megan J. Daniels, editor

Archaeology of Mountain Landscapes
 Arnau Garcia-Molsosa, editor

ARCHAEOLOGY OF MOUNTAIN LANDSCAPES

Interdisciplinary Research Strategies of Agro-Pastoralism in Upland Regions

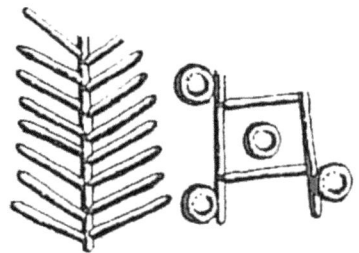

IEMA Proceedings,
Volume 12

EDITED BY
Arnau Garcia-Molsosa

STATE UNIVERSITY OF
NEW YORK PRESS

Logo and cover/interior art: A vessel with wagon motifs from Bronocice, Poland, 3400 B.C. Courtesy of Sarunas Milisauskas and Janusz Kruk, 1982, Die Wagendarstellung auf einem Trichterbecher aus Bronocice, Polen, *Archäologisches Korrespondenzblatt* 12: 141–144.

Published by
State University of New York Press, Albany

© 2023 State University of New York

All rights reserved

Printed in the United States of America

No part of this book may be used or reproduced in any manner whatsoever without written permission. No part of this book may be stored in a retrieval system or transmitted in any form or by any means including electronic, electrostatic, magnetic tape, mechanical, photocopying, recording, or otherwise without the prior permission in writing of the publisher.

For information, contact
State University of New York Press, Albany, NY
www.sunypress.edu

Library of Congress Cataloging-in-Publication Data

Names: University of Buffalo. Institute for European and Mediterranean Archaeology. Conference (10th : 2017 : Buffalo, N.Y.) | Garcia-Molsosa, Arnau, 1983– editor.
Title: Archaeology of mountain landscapes : interdisciplinary research strategies of agro-pastoralism in upland regions / [edited by] Arnau Garcia-Molsosa.
Description: Albany : State University of New York Press, [2023] | Series: SUNY series, The Institute for European and Mediterranean Archaeology distinguished monograph series | "This volume dedicated to the Archaeology of Mountain Landscapes is the result of the 10th edition of the International Conference organised by the Institute for European and Mediterranean Archaeology at the University at Buffalo."—Introduction. | Includes bibliographical references and index.
Identifiers: LCCN 2022005757 | ISBN 9781438489872 (hardcover : alk. paper) | ISBN 9781438489896 (ebook) | ISBN 9781438489889 (pbk. : alk. paper)
Subjects: LCSH: Mountain people—Antiquities—Congresses. | Landscape archaeology—Congresses. | Pastoral systems, Prehistoric—Congresses. | Human ecology—Congresses.
Classification: LCC GF57 .U64 2022 | DDC 304.20914/3—dc23/eng20220528
LC record available at https://lccn.loc.gov/2022005757

10 9 8 7 6 5 4 3 2 1

Contents

ILLUSTRATIONS ix

CHAPTER ONE *Arnau Garcia-Molsosa*
Mountain Landscapes: The Archaeological Perspective 1

CHAPTER TWO *Felipe Criado-Boado*
Steps Lost: Mountains as Sacred Topographies? *(with Ana Ruíz-Blanch in section 4)*
19

CHAPTER THREE *Phillips Stevens Jr.*
Toward an Anthropology of Sacred Mountains 37

CHAPTER FOUR *Cecilia Dal Zovo*
An Integrated Approach to the Archaeology of a Sacred Mountain:
Sacred Geography, Mobile Pastoralism, and
Longue Durée in the Mongolian Altai Mountains 51

CHAPTER FIVE *Mercourios Georgiadis*
The Mountainscape of the Peak Sanctuary at Leska on Kythera 77

CHAPTER SIX *Robert H. Brunswig and*
Exploring Seasonal Transhumance of Hunter-Gatherers and *Pawel Valde-Nowak*
Neolithic Pastoralists in Poland's High Tatras and Foothill
Lowlands: Applying Landscape Archaeology Methodologies
from the Colorado Rockies to the Western Carpathians 93

CHAPTER SEVEN *Klaus D. Oeggl, Daniela Festi,*
The Onset of Alpine Pastoral Systems in the Eastern Alps *and Andreas Putzer*
117

CHAPTER EIGHT — *Franco Nicolis*
Central Alpine Environments as Mountain Cultural Landscapes
from Prehistory to Contemporary Past — 139

CHAPTER NINE — *Sabine Reinhold, Andrey B. Belinskiy, and Dmitrij S. Korobov*
Mountain Archaeology of the Bronze Age Caucasus: From Vertical Pastoralism to Combined Mountain Economy and Mountain Farming — 153

CHAPTER TEN — *Josep M. Palet, Hèctor A. Orengo, Arnau Garcia-Molsosa, Tania Polonio, Ana Ejarque, Yannick Miras, and Santiago Riera*
Landscape Archaeology in Eastern Pyrenees High Mountain Areas (Segre and Ter Valleys, Northeast Iberian Peninsula): Human Activities in the Shaping of Mountain Cultural Landscapes — 179

CHAPTER ELEVEN — *Christopher Prescott and Lene Melheim*
Southern Norway's Mountain Landscapes: Between National Romantic Legends and the Political Economy of Agropastoralism — 197

CHAPTER TWELVE — *Emilie Gauthier*
Comparison between Medieval and Modern Landscape: The Impact of Pastoral Activities in South Greenland — 219

CHAPTER THIRTEEN — *Pawel Valde-Nowak*
Neolithic Penetration of the European Mid-Mountains — 233

CHAPTER FOURTEEN — *Yannick Miras, Michela Mariani, Florian Couderc, Marlène Lavrieux, and Paul M. Ledger*
Addressing the Complexity of the Paleoenvironmental Impact of Prehistoric Settlement and Protohistoric Urbanism in the Auvergne Mountains (Massif Central, France) — 253

CHAPTER FIFTEEN — *Michael R. Coughlan, David S. Leigh, Ted L. Gragson, and Mélanie Le Couédic*
Holocene Anthropization of Mid-elevation Landscapes around Pic d'Orhy, Western Pyrenees — 277

CHAPTER SIXTEEN — *Ralf Vandam, Eva Kaptijn, Patrick T. Willett, and Jeroen Poblome*
Highlands and Lowlands—Different Landscapes, Different Archaeologies? A Diachronic Micro-regional Case Study from the Western Taurus Mountains (Southwest Turkey) — 303

CHAPTER SEVENTEEN *Martijn van Leusen, Wieke de Neef,*
Developing a Systematic Approach to the *and Jan Sevink*
Archaeological Study of Mountain Landscapes:
The Raganello Basin Experience 325

CHAPTER EIGHTEEN *Michael L. Galaty*
Agropastoralism in a Dispersed Village, Mountain Economy:
Results of the Shala Valley Project, Northern Albania 343

CHAPTER NINETEEN *José Alejandro Beltrán-Caballero*
The Inka Landscape of Cusco and the Watanay Valley: *and Ricardo Mar*
Territorial Patterns in Andean Cities 361

CHAPTER TWENTY *Hèctor A. Orengo*
On the Supposed Marginality of Mountain Areas 385

CONTRIBUTORS 399

INDEX 401

Illustrations

FIGURES

Figure 1.1 Location of the mountain areas addressed in the different chapters of this book: 1 Central Andes and 2 Galician Massif (Criado-Boado); 3 Northern Andes (Beltran-Caballero and Mar); 4 Eastern Altai (Dal Zovo); Rocky Mountains (Brunswig and Valde-Nowak); 6 Greenland (Gauthier); 7 Scandinavia (Prescott and Melheim); 8 Western Pyrenees (Coughlan et al.); 9 Eastern Pyrenees (Palet et al.); 10 French Massif Central (Miras et al.); 11 Central Alps (Nicolis); 12 Eastern Alps (Oeggl et al.); 13 Carpathians (Brunswig and Valde-Nowak, Valde-Nowak); 14 Southern Apennines (Van Leusen et al.); 15 Northern Albania (Galaty); 16 Kythera (Georgiadis); 17 Western Taurus (Vandam); 18 North Caucasus (Reinhold et al.)   3

Figure 1.2 Picture taken during early spring in the Catalan Pyrenees (Northeastern Spain). From this image is possible to do a first sketch of the different landscape zones: The alpine and subalpine zones situated over the timberline (1) are dominated by extensions of grass historically exploited on a seasonal basis as summer pastures. Slopes are mainly covered by forests (2), which were the principal source of energy but also complemented the pastures, and they might be subject to clearance for the construction of terraces where forage could be grown. Permanent settlements (3) are founded in different altitudes through the southern slopes but never above the timberline, usually taking advantage of small plains and accompanied by areas dedicated to agriculture. The village in the image, at 1,400 m, is the highest permanent settlement in a valley where the highest peak is 2,900 m high. Down the valley, the landscape is characterized by narrow mountain rivers (4). Settlements in the junctions of different

	rivers act as small regional centers, while the hydraulic power of the watercourses have played a major role powering protoindustrial and early industrial facilities. 5
Figure 2.1	Topographical profile of the case studies referred to in this text, showing the relationship between them. 22
Figure 2.2	Panorama of the inner part of the Sierra de Barbanza, with prehistoric tumuli overlooking the entire landscape. 24
Figure 2.3	Profile of the mountain range of Sierra de Barbanza, as seen at a distance of 20 km from the southwest. The megalithic necropolis is in the highest part of the topography, in the central part of the mountains. 25
Figure 2.4	Distribution of the tumuli in the Sierra de Barbanza, with the main necropolis in the center of the highest part of the peninsula. 26
Figure 2.5	The tumuli of the Barbanza Peninsula in relation to the network of routes that organize the most effective movement throughout the region. The main megalithic necropolis marks the focal point of all of the different routes. 27
Figure 2.6	Profile of the Pico Sacro, a prominent and distinguishable feature in the landscape around Santiago de Compostela. 28
Figure 2.7	There are early medieval remains (ca. seventh–tenth century AD) located on the very top of the Pico Sacro. While proper archaeological research is still lacking, it is remarkable that these remains highlight the connection between the mountain with "the above" (the sky) and "the below" (the chthonic) by carving into the natural bedrock to create steps (*left*) marking a "stairway to heaven" and digging a tunnel (*right*) marking the steps that lead. The image on the left also gives a good idea of the vast panorama that is visible from the Pico Sacro. 30
Figure 2.8	The visual catchment of the Pico Sacro (marked with a pentagon) comprises a vast area of land in the center of Galicia and around the city of Santiago de Compostela. 31
Figure 3.1	Representation of a system of religious beliefs as operating along two dimensions. 39
Figure 3.2	Photo from promotional literature issued by the Balinese tourist company CV.Balinicho (balinicho.com). 47
Figure 4.1	Research area, place names, and geographic terms mentioned in the text. 52

ILLUSTRATIONS   XI

Figure 4.2   The flat summit of IBU Mountain and Orog Nuur Lake viewed from the north, on the paleo-terraces of Tuyn Gol River south of Bogd Village.   53

Figure 4.3   Abandoned winter pastoral campsite with corral for animals (*left*) next to late prehistoric funerary mound (*right*) and guide B.D.'s car as scale, in the inner mountain valley of Koshuun Ulzii, IBU Mountain.   55

Figure 4.4   Traditional Mongolian *ovoo* cairn on Zaisan Hill, at the foot of Bogd Khan Uul Mountain, a sacred elevation protected by official decree since 1783, south of Ulaanbaatar city center (Mongolia).   57

Figure 4.5   Mongolian Late Bronze Age *khirigsuur*: a round-fenced mound with deer stone stela on the top of Puntsag Ovoo Hill, overlooking a mountain pass in the high-pastures area of Ikh Bogd Uul.   59

Figure 4.6   Late prehistoric mound adapted as an ovoo, at the entrance of Ikh Bogd Uul Regional Park (road sign in the background).   60

Figure 4.7   View to the east from Tsagaan Övdög, with Orog Nuur and Valley of Lakes in the background. In the foreground, a late prehistoric mound and a track running along midway the northern slope of Ikh Bogd Uul, in a location also known as a former Chinese post station.   61

Figure 4.8   Baga Shiree: abandoned winter campsite with rock art carvings on IBU Mountain, with a herd of goats from a neighboring camp. View from the southwest, October 2010.   63

Figure 5.1   Sites discussed in text: 1: Kastri; 2: Ayios Yeoryios sto Vouno; 3: Leska peak; 4: Katafygadi cave; 5: Drymonas top (contours at 100 m). Adapted from Coldstream and Huxley 1972.   78

Figure 5.2   Leska top, view from east.   82

Figure 5.3   A: North Path; B1: Northeastern Path; B2: Southeastern Path; C: Southwestern Path; 1: Leska peak; 2: Katafygadi cave; 3: Lazarianika grave; 4: Merm.1; 5: Merm.2; 6: Merm.3; 7: Merm.4; 8: Merm.5 (HGMS, scale 1:5,000).   84

Figure 6.1   Earth image showing relative locations of the authors' mountain research regions (baseline planet image from GoogleEarth™ Pro).   94

Figure 6.2   Chart of the cultural/archaeological timeline for Northeastern Europe and Poland based on a review of current literature. Column 3 (*far right*) provides a very broad estimate of human site (and by inference population) density in the Tatra Mountain region (high and mid mountains, foothills, and Upper Vistula River "foreland").   99

xii   Illustrations

Figure 6.3   Locations of Late Upper Paleolithic Late Magdalenian and descendent culture Federmesser and Świderian) sites and proposed river corridor transhumance routes from Tatra Park through the Spisko-Gubalowskie Foothills and Orawa-Nowy Targ (Podhale) Basin. Later Early Holocene Mesolithic sites are also shown. Upper Paleolithic culture sites within 30 km (a 1–2 day walk) of Tatra Park's lower (north) boundary are captioned with a white background. (The figure's base map is composed over a GoogleEarth™ Pro Satellite Image.)   103

Figure 6.4   Map showing Beskidy and Bieszczady mountain range areas with concentrations of lower river valley and foothills located Neolithic through Bronze Age farming settlements and related open camps and isolated artifacts in higher mountains thought to represent pastoral transhumance. Stars indicate locations of bog sites that have produced prehistoric Neolithic-era botanic (including pollen) evidence of mountain ecosystem changes interpreted as reflecting transhumant domestic animal grazing effects.   107

Figure 7.1   Topographic map of the investigation area: the small black square of the inserted rectangle in the right corner shows the location of the study area at the Austrian/Italian border; dotted line = ancient track; asterisk = discovery site of the Neolithic glacier mummy Ötzi; ○ = investigated sites; □ = settlements; ▼ = Neolithic findings; A = Austria; CH = Switzerland; D = Germany; I = Italy; 1 = Lake Vernagt; 2 = Schwarzboden mire; 3 = Lagaun mire; 4 = Penaud mire.   121

Figure 7.2   Relative pollen diagram of the Penaud mire. The prehistoric sequences are displayed and only taxa of significance are given. Iron A = Iron Age, T = type   125

Figure 7.3   Relative pollen diagram of the Lagaun mire. The prehistoric sequences are displayed and only taxa of significance are given.   126

Figure 7.4   Relative pollen diagram of the Schwarzboden mire. The prehistoric sequences are displayed and only taxa of significance are given.   128

Figure 7.5   Relative pollen diagram of Lake Vernagt. The prehistoric sequences are displayed and only taxa of significance are given. Bronze = Bronze Age   129

Figure 7.6   Compilation of the grazing indicators: for each investigated site the direct comparison of the z-scores of our specific grazing indicators (in gray) and the percentage values of the classical pasture indicators are given. The asterisk indicates the evidence of archaeological structures related to pasture activities.   131

Figure 8.1	The Trentino region in the context of the Italian Peninsula. 1. Storo Dosso Rotondo site. 2. Luserna Pletz von Mozze site. 3. Punta Linke site.	143
Figure 8.2	Storo Dosso Rotondo: general view of the area (arrow indicates the archaeological site) and excavation area with postholes.	143
Figure 8.3	Storo Dosso Rotondo: fragments of strainers. Drawings by Livia Stefan.	145
Figure 8.4	Luserna Pletz von Mozze: general view of the excavation area and detail of a fire structure, probably a roasting bed.	146
Figure 8.5	Punta Linke: view of the site from east and exterior view of the transit station.	148
Figure 8.6	Punta Linke: the final part of the tunnel.	149
Figure 8.7	Punta Linke: interior view of the transit station today with the engine on its original base.	149
Figure 8.8	Punta Linke: the overshoes made of rye straw found during excavation and a pair of overshoes after restoration.	150
Figure 8.9	Presena glacier: remains of uniforms of Austro-Hungarian soldiers emerging from the ice and remains of two Austro-Hungarian soldiers during the excavation.	151
Figure 8.10	Presena glacier: part of the uniform of one of the two Austro-Hungarian soldiers.	151
Figure 9.1	The Caucasus mountain system and sites mentioned in the text. 1 Dzudzuna, Kotis, Tsona Klde, 2 Cmi, 3 Arukhlo, 4 Unakozovskaya, 5 Meshoko, 6 Zamok, 7 Novosvobodnaya-Klady, 8 Chobareti, 9 Sakdrisi, 10 Dzdaghi salt mines, 11 Zagli Barzond, 12 Koban, 13 LBA case study area.	155
Figure 9.2	Meshoko, view from the settlement on the nearby gorge.	158
Figure 9.3	Archaeological sites in the Kislovodsk area from the fifth to the third millennium BC. A. Eneolithic and Maykop sites, late fifth/fourth millennium BC. B. Middle Bronze Age burial mounds.	159
Figure 9.4	Late Bronze Age sites at high altitudes. 1 Gumbashi pass, 2 Ransyrt 1, 3 Kabardinka 2.	162
Figure 9.5	Aerial image and sketches of settlement layouts: A. Linear settlement Pokunsyrt 38. B. Linear and symmetric sites Pokunsyrt 10 and 11. C. Symmetric-oval settlement Pokunsyrt 23.	163

Figure 9.6   Kabardinka 2, MBA mounds, and LBA settlements.   164

Figure 9.7   Cost-weighted buffer zones around the Kabardinka micro-region sites: demands versus available terrains.   168

Figure 9.8   Settlement dynamics in the central North Caucasus from the third millennium BC to the sixth century BC.   169

Figure 10.1   Map with indication of the studied areas in the Eastern Pyrenees.   181

Figure 10.2   Archaeological map of Coma de Vaca and Coma del Freser valleys (upper Ter), with indication of the structures subjected to test pit digging.   183

Figure 10.3   General view of Aigols Podrits I and II sites in the upper Freser valley. Photo by J. M. Palet.   185

Figure 10.4   Ortophotography of the Roman hut 114 in Coma de Vaca I site, with detail of Roman occupation levels 214–215 and the early medieval reoccupation. Photo by A. Garcia and H. A. Orengo.   187

Figure 10.5   Pitch kiln M157 at the Riu dels Orris III site in the Madriu valley (Andorra). Photo by J. M. Palet.   189

Figure 10.6   Archaeological map with the situation of the seven pitch kilns attested in MPCV (Andorra). Map by H. A. Orengo.   189

Figure 10.7   Iron kilns at the El Goleró site in the Cadí Range (upper Segre valley). Photo by J. M. Palet.   190

Figure 11.1   Map of southern Scandinavia indicating topographical features. The Sumtangen, Nyset-Steggje, and Skrivarhelleren site complexes are indicated. Map by Håkon Glørstad and Christopher Prescott.   199

Figure 11.2   Photograph of the Sumtangen Peninsula (Lake Finsbergsvatn, Hardangervidda). The Sumtangen site has been central to mountain archaeology since the 1830s, and remains so today. The peninsula is to the left in the small sound in the middle of the picture. To the right is the Hardangerjøkulen glacier (1,876 masl). Reindeer were chased or herded down from the glacier and into the water. Hunters rowed out to kill them, pull them onto land at Sumtangen, and butcher them. The ruins of two large stone-built huts (that could accommodate ten to fifteen people) from around AD 1200 are visible on the surface, though deposits extending back to the Neolithic are found here, too. Middens from the Middle Ages with the remains of several thousand reindeer are found outside the huts (Indrelid and Hufthammer 2011). Photo by Svein Indrelid, University of Bergen.   201

Figure 11.3   The Urutlekråi site (970 masl, Vikadalen, Årdal). The standing hut is a shieling built in the 1870s and was in use for nearly one hundred years. Before being flooded in connection with hydroelectric development, sites associated with summer shielings from the Late Bronze Age to the Middle Ages were excavated here as part of the Nyset-Steggje project (1981–1987). The upland meadows exhibit a vegetation pattern typical of upland landscapes subjected to long-term intensive grazing. Photo by Christopher Prescott.   208

Figure 11.4   The Skrivarhelleren rock-shelter site (790 masl, Moadalen, Årdal). The rock-shelter is under the lenticular-shaped rock face in the middle of the picture. Excavations were conducted 1987–1989, 2013–2015. Cultural deposits up to 2 m in depth span much of the period from the Nordic Late Neolithic (2350 BCE) to the modern era. Photo by Christopher Prescott.   210

Figure 11.5   A Bronze Age shoe from the melting ice patch at Kvitingkjølen, Lom, Oppland. Numerous organic objects preserved in the ice for centuries and millennia are recovered as ice patches melt in response to a warmer climate. Photo by Ann Christine Eek, Museum of Cultural History. © 2018 Kulturhistorisk museum, UiO / CC BY-SA 4.0.   212

Figure 12.1   Localization of Lake Igaliku. A. Map of the Eastern settlement in South Greenland. Black dots represent Norse archeological sites and black triangles, recent farms. B. Map of the catchment of Lake Igaliku (drawn in dotted line). C. Bathymetry of Lake Igaliku and localization of the coring.   220

Figure 12.2   Synthetic figure of the different proxies analyzed over the last two millennia: A. Simplified pollen diagram (in percentage) of the period of the last two millennia. B. Evolution of pastoral pressure markers with the desoxycholic acid and Sporormiella influx (Guillemot et al. 2015). C. Soil erosion and the main historical events of the Norse period (Massa et al. 2012a and b). D. The trophic status of the lake with the curve (in percentage) of mesotrophic diatoms (Perren et al. 2012). E. Climate change with PCA axis 1 of chironomids and changes in summer Arctic temperatures (Millet et al. 2014).   225

Figure 13.1   Nieznajowa, distr. Krosno, Lower Beskidy Mountains. General view of the Cergowa Mount, 716 masl (1) with the topography (2) and localization (arrow) of stray finds of hammer axes (3) of Funnel Beaker Culture and small stone artifacts (4–6) found close to the axe.   237

Figure 13.2   Zawoja-Przysłop, distr. Sucha Beskidzka, High Beskidy Mountains. General view of the Babia Góra massif, 1,725 masl (1) with the topography (2) and localization (dotted ellipse) of stray finds of hammer axes (3) of Corded Ware Culture and small stone artifacts (4–6) found close to the axe.   238

Figure 13.3   Łoniowa, distr. Brzesko, site 18—West Carpathians Wiśnicz Foothill. Model (1), topographic position (2), and aerial view of Linearbandkeramik long house no. 2 during excavations.   241

Figure 13.4   Jaroszowice, distr. Wadowice, Lower Beskidy Mountains. General view of the Skawa River valley (1) with the localization (arrow) and topography (2) of stray finds of shoe-last celts (3) of Late Linearbandkeramik; small stone artifact series have been found in the vicinity during verification.   243

Figure 13.5   Dąbrówka, distr. Wadowice, Lower Beskidy Mountains. General view of the Skawa River valley (1) with the localization (arrow) and topography (2) of stray finds of shoe-last celts (3) of Linearbandkeramik; small stone artifact series have been found in the vicinity during verification.   244

Figure 13.6   Durfeld, distr. Viechtach, Bavarian Forest. Topography in the range of a half-hour walk (1) and agricultural evaluation of soil (2) in the localization (black diamond) of a Late Neolithic axe found during survey. A. Half-hour actualized range (Bailey and Davidson 1983). B–D. Agricultural soil categories (B = best, D = worst). E–F. Green land (E = meadow, F = forest).   247

Figure 14.1   A. Location of Auvergne and the study region within France. B. Paleoecological sites and oppida in the drainage basin of the River Veyre.   255

Figure 14.2   Current landscapes in the lower Auvergne mountains and the studied sequences. Photo by B. Dousteyssier and Y. Miras.   256

Figure 14.3   Complementarity of the paleoecological bioindicators.   258

Figure 14.4   Summary percentage pollen and non-pollen palynomorphs diagram of Lake Aydat (837 masl, analysis by Y. Miras), and rarefaction index. + indicates ≤ 1% of the total pollen sum.   260

Figure 14.5   Comparison between pollen and vegetation cover percentages (data processing by M. Mariani): summary of Aydat and Espinasse pollen data.   261

Figure 14.6   Summary percentage pollen diagram of Espinasse fen (1,160 masl, analysis by Y. Miras), charcoal proportions, and rarefaction index. • indicates ≤ 1 percent of the total pollen sum.   262

Figure 14.7   Phases of human impact revealed by pollen data in the lower Auvergne mountains compared to climatic oscillations.   263

Figure 14.8   Locations of Early Bronze Age settlements in the lower Auvergne. GIS by F. Couderc.   265

Figure 14.9   Summary percentage pollen diagram of Espinasse fen (1,160 masl) and Lac du Puy/Corent pond (550 masl, analysis by P. M. Ledger): different landscape patterns revealed by pollen data in mountain and lowland areas in Auvergne.   268

Figure 14.10   Overview of the paleoenvironmental impact in the lower Auvergne during prehistory and protohistory.   269

Figure 15.1   Impact-pulse hypothesis at catchment level showing hypothesized charcoal accumulation (CHAR) and archaeological site patterns. Symbols courtesy of the Integration and Application Network, University of Maryland Center for Environmental Science (ian.umces.edu/symbols/).   280

Figure 15.2   Press-coevolution hypothesis with catchment-level alternative stable states (circles), basins of attraction, and feedbacks aligned with hypothesized charcoal accumulation (CHAR) and archaeological site patterns. Symbols courtesy of the Integration and Application Network, University of Maryland Center for Environmental Science (ian.umces.edu/symbols/). Adapted from McWethy et al. 2013.   281

Figure 15.3   Location of project area, colluvium sample sites, archaeological sample areas, and prehistoric sites located in the literature review.   283

Figure 15.4   Colluvial catchments, archaeological sample area, and radiocarbon-dated archaeological sites.   284

Figure 15.5   Pastoral fire at tree line with Pic d'Orhy in the background. Photo by M. Coughlan, 2011.   287

Figure 15.6   Charcoal accumulation (Log scale) with the number of radiocarbon dates from archaeological contexts by probability distribution.   288

Figure 15.7   Mulhedoy charcoal accumulation (CHAR) black bar graph, showing the probability distributions (99.7% CI, dark gray and 68.2% CI, light gray) for archaeological radiocarbon from nearby sites.   289

xviii   Illustrations

Figure 15.8   Ibarrandoua charcoal accumulation (CHAR) showing the probability distributions (99.7% and 68.2% CI) for archaeological radiocarbon from nearby sites.   291

Figure 15.9   Ihitsaga charcoal accumulation (CHAR) showing the probability distributions (99.7% and 68.2% CI) for archaeological radiocarbon from nearby sites.   292

Figure 15.10   Three-way plot of colluvial catchment "climate space" and relative topographic flammability.   293

Figure 16.1   A. Overview of Turkey including the Taurus and Pontus Mountains. B. Locations of the two survey research areas in relation to the ancient city of Sagalassos. C. Burdur Plain landscape. D. Dereköy Highlands landscape.   304

Figure 16.2   Applied survey methodology in the Burdur Plain and Dereköy Highlands. In addition to our tract-walking surveying method (A), an undulating transect walking (B) and gridded survey (C) were implemented within the Dereköy Highlands in areas with less visibility.   308

Figure 16.3   Artifact distributions of the Burdur Plain (*above*) and the Dereköy Highlands (*below*).   310

Figure 16.4   Distribution of the chronology of the collected sherds from the Dereköy Highlands and the Burdur Plain.   311

Figure 16.5   Slope inclination map with indication of suitable farming land. Note the wide variety across the territory of ancient Sagalassos (black line).   313

Figure 16.6   Calculated least-cost path from the Burdur Plain to Sagalassos with the main late antique secondary centers.   315

Figure 16.7   Calculated least-cost paths from the surrounding ancient centers to Sagalassos. Many of the newly identified sites in the Dereköy Highlands were founded along these paths.   316

Figure 16.8   Middle Paleolithic lithic artifacts were discovered in areas (e.g., Field 117) with active erosion process.   319

Figure 17.1   Topography and morphology of the Maddalena basin, with locations of coring transects and (selected) protohistoric sites.   328

Figure 17.2   Protohistoric scatter RB73 after the initial survey in 2005—field photo, survey map, assemblage photo.   329

Figure 17.3	Results of the magnetic gradiometer and magnetic susceptibility surveys conducted in 2013, after De Neef et al. 2017, fig. 11. Locations of scatter, mound, and corings indicated.	330
Figure 17.4	Section drawings across the mound and lower terrace bank based on our understanding of the situation in late 2013 (A, B). A: interpretation by De Neef, original drawing; B: interpretation after Sevink et al. 2016, fig. 39. Locations of 2013/2014 test pits indicated by block arrows. Sections of the two test pits showing tilted stratigraphy (C, D). After De Neef 2016, figs. A80 and A82.	314
Figure 17.5	Additional gradiometer and coring data collected in 2015 indicate the presence of an erosional gully, in existence since at least the EBA and still not completely filled by settlement debris in the Early Imperial period. Inset (*top right*): A modern parallel to the protohistoric situation at RB73 is shown here, with spring water buffered in the basin at the top of the slope used to irrigate garden crops in the foreground.	333
Figure 17.6	Cross section showing slope processes and soils around site RB175 (A). Landscape-scale coring transect through the Maddalena upland, showing diverse composition of flysch basin fills, resulting in different relief and soils (B). Source Sevink et al. 2016, figs. 32–34.	335
Figure 17.7	Peroni's models for the Recent and Final Bronze Age settlement in the Sibaritide (after Peroni and Trucco 1994, figs. 229 and 232). A significant reduction in the number of tribal territories takes place in the northern half of the area by the end of the Recent Bronze Age. Closed circle: new site; open circle: site continuing from previous period; cross: abandoned site.	338
Figure 18.1	Modern northern Albania and surrounding countries showing major cities, rivers, lakes, and the SVP's study region. Map by Jill Seagard.	344
Figure 18.2	Map of northern Albanian tribal territories. Map by Jill Seagard.	345
Figure 18.3	Map of Shala showing villages, roads, rivers, and sites identified by the SVP. Map by Jill Seagard.	346
Figure 18.4	Houses and terraces, looking south down the valley of the Shala River. The Ulaj and Kolaj neighborhoods are in the foreground, Grunas neighborhood in background. Photo by Ann Christine Eek.	347
Figure 18.5	Satellite image of Theth with streams, neighborhoods, and churches marked. Map by Jill Seagard.	348

Figure 18.6	Largest, westernmost terrace wall at Grunas. Photo by Ann Christine Eek. 352	
Figure 18.7	Map of site of Grunas. Dashed numbers indicate excavation units; individual terraced platforms enumerated in boldface; single-digit numbers not in boldface refer to individual structures. Map by Christopher T. Fisher and Jill Seagard. 352	
Figure 18.8	Map of Theth transposed and overlaid on a satellite image of Pylos, from the palace to the coast. Map by Michael L. Galaty. 354	
Figure 18.9	Scaled comparison of Structure 221, ground floor, in Theth, a large joint-family house (line drawing by Jill Seagard), to a Late Helladic IIIA2 house from Unit III-2, Nichoria (McDonald and Wilkie 1992:384). The latter image is used by permission of University of Minnesota Press. 355	
Figure 19.1	Aerial view of the virtual image of the ceremonial center of Inka Cusco with Saqsaywaman compound (*foreground*), San Blas agricultural terraces (*top left*), and the ceremonial center between the Tuyumayo and Saphi Rivers (*top right*). For the first time ever we have an image that brings us closer to what could be the capital of the Tawantinsuyu and its interpretation. Drawing by R. Mar and J. A. Beltrán-Caballero. 363	
Figure 19.2	Virtual view of some of the most representative compounds of the ceremonial center: Hatun Rumiyoq (*foreground left*), Awkaypata square (*foreground right*), Hatunkancha (*center*), and Cusikancha and Korikancha compounds (*background*). Drawing by R. Mar and J. A. Beltrán-Caballero. 364	
Figure 19.3	Evolution of Cusco Valley before the Inka expansion, drawing by R. Mar and J. A. Beltrán-Caballero. A. Extension of the valley covered by Morkil Lake. Formed at the end of the Pleistocene after the last glaciation, the lake emptied at some point due to the collapse of the cap that contained it at Angostura. As a result, a number of lagoons/wetlands remained as the last vestiges of the great lake. B. Perimeter of the two main wetlands. The refounding of Cusco as the imperial capital accomplished by Pachacuti required their drainage and desiccation. 366	
Figure 19.4	1. Reconstruction of wetlands in pre-Inka times. 2. Distribution of the sixty main *killke* (pre-Inka) settlements published by Bauer (2004:Figure 8.4). 3. Courses of rectified rivers, new Inka channels for the drying up wetlands, road system, and ceremonial center of the Inka capital. Drawing by R. Mar and J. A. Beltrán-Caballero. 367	

Figure 19.5	Roads, terraces, canals, *wakas*, and settlements in the great capital of Tawantinsuyu, drawing by R. Mar and J. A. Beltrán-Caballero. The idea of Cusco as a constellation of settlements was described by Santiago Agurto over thirty years ago (Agurto 1987:80–81). The road network organized both neighborhoods of the city and the surrounding towns. Agurto drew as a "puma" shape the politico-religious center settled between the Saphy and Tullumayo Rivers. This was surrounded by a buffer zone without buildings and peripheral settlements described by Garcilaso de la Vega. 368
Figure 19.6	DIRAF aerial photos of 1956 of the valley of Cusco have allowed drawing the slopes and platforms that distributed agricultural fields. They coincide with the position of Inka retaining walls, not always well preserved, and their relation with Inka roads. If we complete the layout of the retaining walls (dashed lines), a system of curved terraces like that known in Urubamba Valley in Pisac and Ollantaytambo is drawn. In 1956 the valley lands had a complex irrigation system consisting of canals and reservoirs. The more complicated and irregular paths are the most modern. It is also possible to identify a system of regular layout of parallel channels that define elongated crop fields too. It is a unitary system that extends from the Avenida Collasuyu to the Watanay River. Its layout is conditioned by Inka roads and the retaining walls of the terraces. Both circumstances show that the remains of the original Inka irrigation system were partially preserved until 1956. Drawing by R. Mar and J. A. Beltrán-Caballero. 370
Figure 19.7	Aerial photograph between San Blas and Qencomayo River in 1956 (DIRAF) and its interpretation in a drawing by R. Mar and J. A. Beltrán-Caballero. *Wakas*, roads, terraces, and Inka planning from Illapa temple (San Blas) to Patallacta. 373
Figure 19.8	Aerial photography from 1956 DIRAF flying (*top*), and its interpretation in a drawing by R. Mar and J. A. Beltrán-Caballero. Between the neighborhood of San Blas and Kachimayo River an extensive network of agricultural terraces stretched. Retaining walls were prolonged over several kilometers forming an integrated layout with the old roads and some large sacred rocks (*wakas*) that were the focus of several religious centers. Inka builders transformed the upper part of the slope using curved terraces adapted to the terrain. Curved terraces start at the top of San Blas and continue, following a wavy line along 3 km to reach Kachimayo River and the town of Salinas. Aerial photographs make it possible to reconstruct a sequence with twenty stepped terraces. In 1956 photographs it is possible to identify an Inka settlement of polygonal enclosures surrounded by curved platforms (*left*, A). 375

Figure 19.9   Reconstruction of the urban layout of the ceremonial center of Cusco between Saphi and Tullumayo Rivers. Drawing by R. Mar and J. A. Beltrán-Caballero.   378

Figure 19.10   Virtual reconstruction of Inkilltambo. Drawing by R. Mar and J. A. Beltrán-Caballero.   379

Figure 20.1   Territorial boundaries around the Albufera coastal lagoon (Valencia) and in the Garraf mountain range (Barcelona).   392

Tables

Table 6.1   Examples of Inferred Transhumant Cultural Traditions in the Eurasian Mid-Late Pleistocene and Early-Mid Holocene   98

Table 7.1   Pollen Types Used as Grazing Indicators by Bortenschlager (2000); Their Pollen Transfer, Dispersal, and Indicator Values according to Oeggl (1994): L = local, R = regional, O = overrepresented, U = underrepresented, x = indifferent, + = indicative, − = not indicative.   123

Table 7.2   Weighting Average Values (WA_{opt}) of Pasture Indicators in Order of Importance: The Higher the Value the Higher the Preference for Pasture according Festi et al. (2014)   132

Table 9.1   Hypothetical Economic Range of the Bronze Age Mountain Economies at the Mountain Plateaus   167

Table 14.1   PPEs (with Their Standard Errors) and Fallspeed of Thirteen Taxa according to Mazier et al. (2012).   259

Table 15.1   Previously Published Archaeological Chronologies for the Project Area   285

Table 15.A.1 Uncorrected Radiocarbon Age for Archaeological Sites   295

Table 15.A.2 Corrected Radiocarbon Dates for Archaeological Sites. Years CE Are Positive and Years BCE Are Negative   297

Table 16.1   Overview of the Total Number of Collected (or Counted; Tiles) Artifacts per Material Category and Sites   309

Table 16.2   The Percentage of Surveyed Area per Visibility Score   318

Table 18.1   Spatial Statistics Related to Theth Neighborhood Size and Configuration   350

Chapter One

Mountain Landscapes

The Archaeological Perspective

Arnau Garcia-Molsosa

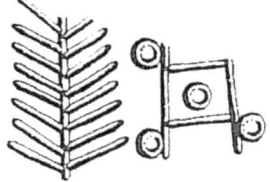

Abstract   *This introductory chapter explores mountain landscapes as a subject of study within the archaeological disciplines. Mountains are part of the geography of human societies: places to transit and to inhabit, and sources of sustaining resources and symbolic meanings. In that perspective, present mountain landscapes contain the material traces of long-term human–environment interactions.*

The vision of archaeologists over mountain landscapes is in a radical process of change, due to the incorporation of archaeological fieldwork in multidisciplinary research programs carried out in mountain environments. Research assembled at the tenth IEMA conference represents a significant sample of studies that are changing our perspective of mountain landscapes as archaeological documents, resulting in critical contributions for the understanding of the history of mountain environments and creating new archaeological datasets to use in the interpretation of human societies.

Mountains: An Archaeological Subject

This volume dedicated to archaeology of mountain landscapes is the result of the tenth convening of the international conference organized by the Institute for European and Mediterranean Archaeology at the University at Buffalo. The main aim of IEMA conferences is to offer to the participants a comprehensive perspective on how the research on a subject is currently developing, including research questions, methodological approaches, and final results. The same objectives apply to this book, whose chapters have been elaborated from the presentations given by the authors, incorporating the results of the debates held during the two days of the meeting in April 2017.

With the word "mountain" we define primarily topographical features on Earth's surface. To choose an element of the physical geography as a central topic is not strange in archaeological practice, although it takes a different perspective than most common and traditional geographical and chronological compartmentalization of the archaeological research. In the ensemble of the archaeological discipline, the perspective adopted in this book can be grouped together with other archaeologies of environments (e.g., archaeology of islands, rainforests, deserts, rivers). The interest of archaeologists in this type of focus departs from the fact that the processes involved in the different stages of the formation of the archaeological record, including its documentation, occur in the context of a local and regional environment, and, in consequence, cannot be understood outside of it. On the other hand, the different categories for environmental and topographical units are based on shared characteristics, which might comprise human interactions.

Those factors have established the framework for comparative approaches about how societies separated by time, space, and cultural background have related to their environment in broadly equivalent circumstances, and, at the same time, to test how different techniques and methodological approaches perform in similar conditions. It has also been a framework exploited by multidisciplinary teams to establish research questions and integrate data from different sources in a common subject of interest. Besides that, it directs the research to the analysis of the archaeological record as a part of the present, which is critical in the conception of archaeology as a live heritage and a tool to help to understand the present world, in opposition to a subject of interest only for antiquarianism.

The results of the intertwined human–environment relationships are often conceptualized in academic and nonacademic practice through the term "landscape." In the use of this concept, there is always implicit the idea of environment as it is modified by humans. It can include all sorts of actions, and, among them, how it is thought, represented, and perceived. From this point of view, landscapes can be understood within the archaeological disciplines as a cultural production, shaped through long-term socioenvironmental interactions. It is from that perspective that mountain landscapes are conceptualized as the topic of this volume.

The case made for the Scandinavian mountains by Christopher Prescott and Lene Melheim (Prescott and Melheim in this volume) illustrates how the study of mountain landscapes has contributed to the development of Scandinavian archaeology beyond the specific case of high-altitude areas. New ideas on methods and theoretical approaches and on heritage conceptualization and management accompanied new data that transformed previous ideas about past societies and present landscapes. The long tradition of studies in Scandinavian uplands provides the authors of that chapter with the necessary historical perspective, but the same ideas can be extended to the other case studies analyzed here.

The assemblage of works on mountain archaeology collected in the present volume has the intention of providing the broader archaeological community with an introduction to new sets of archaeological data. Those are significant for the geographic areas presented here, but also for the understanding of historical processes in the near lowlands and, in a larger perspective, as an example of the potential information that mountain areas around the world can provide for the study of past societies and present landscapes and heritage. Connected to that, a second specific objective of this volume is to present how these new data sets have been created in each case, through sources and methods that have been adapted to the constraints of mountain environments. In that sense, the collected case studies can be used as a guide to undertake new research in mountain areas but, at the same time, the theoretical and methodological approaches of the different projects have elements of interest for the study of other environments.

Mountains Nowadays: Physical and Cultural Landscapes

Mountains are a consequence of the long-term geological forces that shape earth surface. In Figure 1.1 it is possible to observe that most of the case studies addressed in this book are situated in one area of convergence of tectonic plates: in a series of ranges aligned east to west in southern Eurasia. However, in a global perspective, irregularities on earth surface defined as mountains can be found in almost every part of the planet. The idea of "moun-

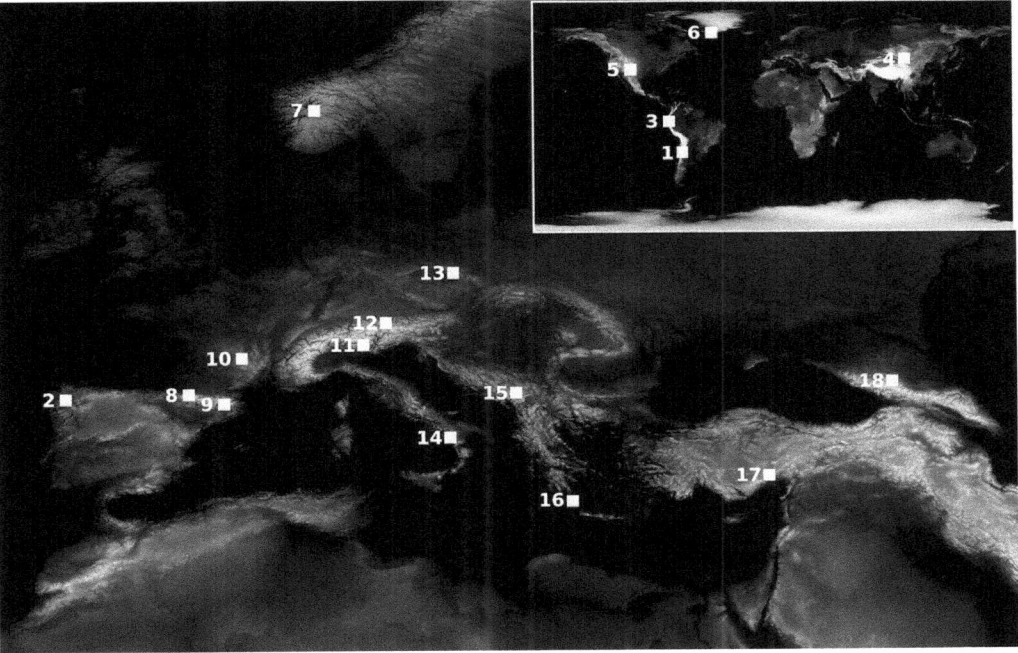

Figure 1.1. Location of the mountain areas addressed in the different chapters of this book: 1 Central Andes and 2 Galician Massif (Criado-Boado); 3 Northern Andes (Beltran-Caballero and Mar); 4 Eastern Altai (Dal Zovo); Rocky Mountains (Brunswig and Valde-Nowak); 6 Greenland (Gauthier); 7 Scandinavia (Prescott and Melheim); 8 Western Pyrenees (Coughlan et al.); 9 Eastern Pyrenees (Palet et al.); 10 French Massif Central (Miras et al.); 11 Central Alps (Nicolis); 12 Eastern Alps (Oeggl et al.); 13 Carpathians (Brunswig and Valde-Nowak, Valde-Nowak); 14 Southern Apennines (Van Leusen et al.); 15 Northern Albania (Galaty); 16 Kythera (Georgiadis); 17 Western Taurus (Vandam); 18 North Caucasus (Reinhold et al.)

tain" then evokes a general recognizable object, although it is more difficult to summarize it in a universal definition. Mountain in the singular can refer to an individuality, represented through the iconic image of the lonely peak appearing isolated from its surroundings. But when we speak of mountain landscapes, the focus is on the diverse composition of both biogeographical and cultural features.

Both as individuals or as a landscape, mountains are defined by a combination of characteristics based on local relief, slope, steepness, geology, and vegetation; but—since the relationship between these elements depends on local combinations—there are no universal criteria to differentiate mountains from other elevated landforms (Price 1986:1–5). The definitory elements of a mountain depends on the context (height from the surrounding area), the perception (conspicuousness), and comparison (larger than a hill, steeper than a plateau).[1] Geographers also point to the importance of cultural and social values in the definition of mountains. As is illustrated in the plot of "The Englishman who went up a hill but came down a mountain," the definition of a singular feature as mountain can be relative.

Distinctive parts of the mountain are the foot, slope, and summit. Environmental conditions define alpine, subalpine, and montane zones as characteristic mountain ecosystems, but not all mountain landscapes are defined by them. It is very common to distinguish between high, middle, and low mountains, depending on the character of the topography and environment analyzed, although the limits between them are not clearly delimited. Finally, the concept of mountain landscapes embraces a much larger set of landforms than the singular mountain: ranges and massifs are formed by groups of mountains. Uplands or highlands are often used as a synonym for mountainous areas, although they have a less precise meaning and could contain any mountain, narrowly speaking. Plateaus and valleys are in a literal sense antonyms of mountains, but they are essential parts of mountain landscapes.

Figure 1.2 provides an example of the main characteristic of a mountain landscape: its vertical specialization that results in the formation of niches or zones that are cultural and biologic at the same time. Being shaped by complex interactions between climate, geology, biology, and human uses and ideas, the resulting landscapes can vary a lot between different mountain ranges and, also, between neighboring valleys.

The diversity of environments that mountain areas play host to are recognized by the UN in Agenda 21 (Agenda 21, Chapter 13). The inclusion of a chapter entitled "Managing Fragile Ecosystems: Sustainable Mountain Development" recognized mountains as a global subject of political attention (Debarbieux and Price 2008; Messerli and Ives 1997). Sustainability of mountain environments is considered in that document as essential for preserving the planet's biodiversity and improving human welfare. Biological diversity and key resources (with water and energy in the forefront) are mentioned as the main contributions of mountain ecosystems in a global perspective. The document also states the value of indigenous knowledge and traditional practices in the maintenance of mountain ecosystems and identifies poverty as one of the main problems of mountain communities. A key aspect of the document is the admission that there is "a lack of knowledge of mountain ecosystems," encouraging the development of regional studies. One example is the report elabo-

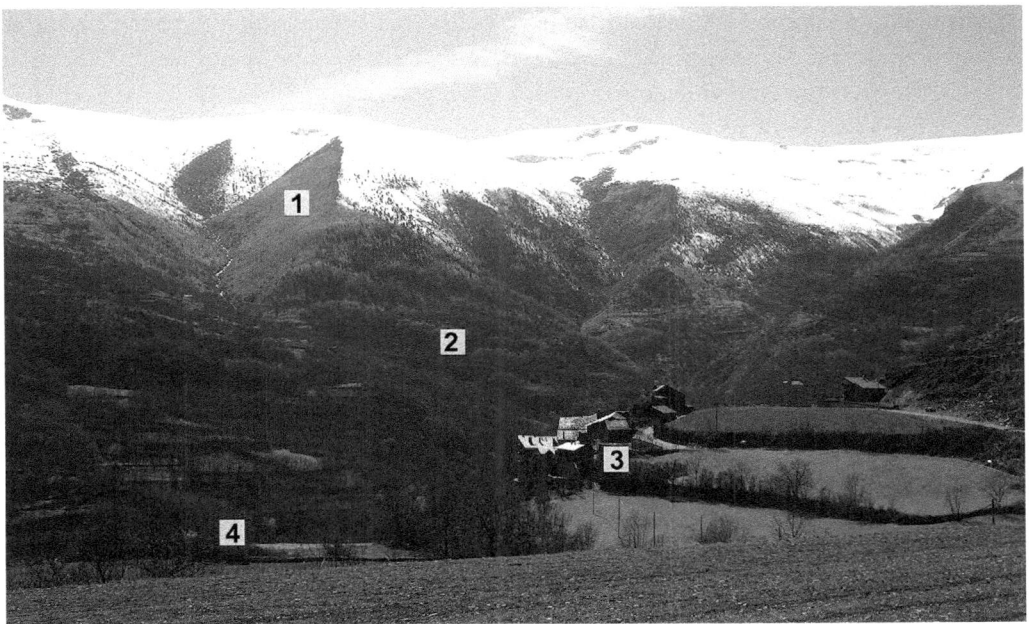

Figure 1.2. Picture taken during early spring in the Catalan Pyrenees (Northeastern Spain). From this image it is possible to do a first sketch of the different landscape zones: The alpine and subalpine zones situated over the timberline (1) are dominated by extensions of grass historically exploited on a seasonal basis as summer pastures. Slopes are mainly covered by forests (2), which were the principal source of energy but also complemented the pastures, and they might be subject to the construction of terraces where forage could be grown. Permanent settlements (3) are founded in different altitudes through the southern slopes but never above the timberline, usually taking advantage of small plains and accompanied by areas dedicated to agriculture. The village in the image, at 1,400 m, is the highest permanent settlement in a valley where the highest peak is 2,900 m high. Down the valley, the landscape is characterized by narrow mountain rivers (4). Settlements in the junctions of different rivers act as small regional centers, while the hydraulic power of the watercourses have played a major role powering protoindustrial and early industrial facilities.

rated at the request of the European Commission to first delimit and then obtain specific data of European mountains (Schuler et al. 2004). This document, largely based on Agenda 21 principles, points out four main aspects for why mountains are of vital importance to the European continent: "1) as 'water towers' supplying much of the continent's water, especially in summer, and as sources of hydroelectric power; 2) as centers of diversity, both biological and cultural; 3) for providing opportunities for recreation and tourism, based on natural attributes and cultural heritage; and 4) because of their sensitivity to environmental change, as manifest in the melting of glaciers" (Schuler et al. 2004:2). Another significant statement in the same document observes, "In the context of European cohesion and enlargement, mountain regions are considered as having permanent natural handicaps, due to topographic and climatic restrictions on economic activity and/or peripherality" (Schuler et al. 2004:2). At the same time, the results of this report point to the diversity of European mountain regions, with no common trends regarding demography, economic activities, or access to services.

The conceptualization of mountain landscapes outlined in these documents, and particularly in Agenda 21 for its worldwide scope, has an important impact on fixing the ideas of how we understand mountains. As a guide for designing polities, it has a strong influence in funding calls for research projects or regional and local economic development initiatives. It also influences political and environmental activism seeking the attention of global actors over local conflicts. At the same time, the writing of these documents is a product of a particular historical moment (Debarbieux and Price 2008). For instance, the apparent contradiction between high biodiversity and key resources on one side and "natural handicaps" on the other has to be understood in the context of the debates of late twentieth-century society trying to address how environmental and cultural diversity should be integrated into a global economic system, which the available data show as particularly destructive toward both sides.

In that sense, in the analysis of mountain landscapes it is important to consider how the subject is influenced by the perspective of modern Western societies. In 1936, in the introduction of his book dedicated to mountain geography, Roderick Peattie (1936:5–7) distinguished between two contemporary approaches to the mountains: the climber and the scientist (identified basically as a naturalist). This vision is very representative of how mountain landscapes have been perceived by nineteenth- and twentieth-century urban societies. Even nowadays, mountains are largely imagined and promoted as unlimited, free, and wild spaces where people participate in sports and activities in contact with pristine nature. It is important to note that this modern "nature tourism" is practiced in social contexts and needs a well-established and controlled network of infrastructures: from roads and parking lots to apartments, hotels, restaurants, stores, or ski lifts. This economic activity can be very intensive in some areas and requires a reshaping of the environment, creating new landscapes associated to that type of tourism. The impact on the inherited landscape is important, sometimes quite disruptive, but perceived as a necessary toll for the economic sustainment of mountain communities.

On another side, people working in the primary sector tend to see the landscape as a mosaic of limited spaces where nature is manipulated through agropastoral activities to obtain resources. Mountains are not different in that sense. From the perspective of the agropastoral and industrial activities, mountains are territories delimited by social, political, and economic interactions, which regulate the access to the resources and define the identity of the inhabitants. The contrast between the visions from the service sector on one side and the primary sector on the other is in conflict within contemporary mountain region societies. This is especially true because services are increasingly dominant in mountain economies. Responses to this background conflict vary from direct confrontation to different degrees of coexistence and compatibility, since in many mountain areas the inhabitants usually combine the two activities.

The idea of "natural handicaps" that caused "poverty" to populations is commonly applied to mountain areas and it has a long history since antiquity (Price 1986; Walsh 2005). This idea is based on less productivity of cereals and that main communication nodes tend to concentrate in coasts and alluvial plains. However, it can be misleading, since mountains can provide high-value products, precisely thanks to their "natural handicaps." The poverty among mountain communities, historically and today, must be understood from the perspective of the inequality in the access to the resources and its role within socio-economic structures.

In fact, mountain economies are integrated into superregional contexts through differentiation and specialization, as historians have noticed (see, e.g., Braudel 1972). It takes advantage of the environmental diversity, directing mountain economy to the exploitation of resources not available in lowlands and cities: selected agropastoral productions, forestry, extraction of minerals, industrial processes related to those products, and tourism are examples of both traditional and modern fields of specialization for mountain communities in local products. Several chapters in this book analyze the role of those products in the development of past economies, which have gone unnoticed in many models about past economies.

In a different perspective, this differentiation also has an impact on the social and political identity of mountain communities. More than isolation, it is the combination of the involvement in specific and differentiated economic activities together with historical processes and geopolitical circumstances that are the factors that influenced the development of different sorts of alternative identities in mountain regions, embodied through language, distinctive cultural features, and particular institutions or political positioning.

In that aspect, mountain communities are often represented and/or self-represented either as a sort of uncontaminated version of lowland and urban populations or as alien, often a menace, to the main national identities. One way or the other, they have shaped an image of rebellious populations and areas difficult to control from the perspective of central states. These ideas have been analyzed through anthropological narratives (Scott 2009), fueled romanticized visions of mountain communities (Fermor 1966), and have also been present in archaeological literature (Prescott and Melheim in this volume; Orengo in this volume).

Archaeologists and Mountains

Mountains have provided some iconic archaeological finds: the mummy of Ötzi, the necropolis of Hallstatt, or the city of Machu Pichu are three examples of high-impact discoveries in mountain environments. Although the discovery of sites has triggered questions regarding their local and regional contexts, the general perception among archaeologists remained that mountains are areas of secondary interest, less occupied and without an interesting archaeological record to address big questions such as the adoption of agriculture or the development of complex societies. In that sense, archaeology is influenced by the more general ideas about mountains commented on in the previous section. Another factor to consider is that the important contribution of rescue excavations in some countries has been concentrated in urban centers and around big infrastructures going through lower valleys. Thus, a general overview results in the strong correlation between blank areas in archaeological maps and mountain areas.

Before the 1990s there were few archaeological programs directed to understanding how elevated areas were settled by past human populations. We previously mentioned the case of the Scandinavian mountains that have been the object of surveys since the 1950s (Prescott and Melheim in this volume). In North America there is a long tradition of studies in the Rocky Mountains (Bender and Wright 1988; Benedict 1992; Brunswig 2004).

Regional surveys have been one of the traditional gateways to the study of mountains since the late 1980s. Initially, those surveys were concentrated in the plains. In the case of classical studies, the central role of the city in antiquity literature pushed the initial questions toward the immediate hinterland of well-known ancient settlements. Also, for prehistoric and, in fewer cases, medieval archaeology, the departing point was the immediate context of well-known lowland settlement systems. On the other hand, that research focused on the documentation of surface pottery made visible by the plowing of agricultural fields, concentrating the surveys on this type of land cover. In a second stage, archaeologists observed the high integration of urban, lowland, and highland rural economies, considering that mountain areas should be integrated in the regional economic models and proposing the implementation of regional survey approaches in upland areas. The interest in pastoral practices was a key aspect of this approach. Some significant examples that had a large impact on further research were the works directed by Graham Barker in the Italian Apennines in the late 1980s (Barker et al. 1991) or the research that has been developed since the early 1990s by researchers based in the Maison Méditerranéenne des Sciences de l'Homme (Aix-en-Provence) in the lower and high Provençal mountains (Leveau 2014; Leveau and Segard 2004; Mocci et al. 2005). Ethnoarchaeology was another field explored in this context (Halstead 1998).

In some cases external factors have had a definitive influence in the initiation of mountain archaeological surveys. This is the case in the hydroelectrical reservoirs flooding Norwegian valleys. Forest fires in Southern Europe have been, in singular occasions, the starting point of intensive research programs (D'Anna et al. 1992; Passarrius et al. 2009).

A second main contribution to the interest in the mountainous archaeological record comes from paleobotanical studies. In the context of the studies about mountain vegetation niches the role of human activities has been acknowledged as a factor crucial to understanding the ecological dynamics. Moreover, some mountain areas host a rich paleoenvironmental record. That's particularly true for high mountain subalpine zones, where the existence of glacial lakes and peat bogs can provide good sequences to address questions such as the evolution of timberland, the creation and evolution of pastures, and the impact of fire, grazing, and climate change. Pollinic diagrams of mountain sites have been produced during the twentieth century and integrated in early regional approaches (Beaulieu et al. 1990; Biagi and Nandris 1994; Galop 1998; Moe et al. 1988; Richard 1997). Initial works in this field focused mainly on natural history and progressively integrated human activity both as a research interest and a proxy to study vegetation changes. The confluence with archaeological teams working on regional surveys has been very productive since the 1990s and early 2000s. The incorporation of archaeological data has been accompanied by the development of multiproxy approaches and the increase of spatial and chronological resolution (Oeggl et al.; Palet et al.; Gauthier; Miras et al. in this volume). It defines an "archaeology of pasturelands," which has been often used as a synonym of "mountain archaeology," and in which the research focus is the environmental and cultural history of subalpine pastures.

Works from the 1990s have been consolidated and extended during the decades of the twenty-first century. The proliferation of published research can be observed through the bibliographical references included in the different chapters. This scientific activity has also been the ground for continued academic exchanges. Sessions about mountain areas have been organized in many major international conferences, and specific meetings gathered research groups on international and regional bases. That resulted in the publication of several collective works and monographs that can be used as gateways to the subject (Collis et al. 2016; Della Casa 1999; Della Casa and Walsh 2007; Gerling et al. 2018; Leveau and Rémy 2008; Lozny 2013; Pelisiak, Nowak, and Astaloş 2018; Rendu 2003; Stirn 2014; Tzortzis and Delestre 2010; Walsh 2013).

The ensemble of subtopics that emerges from the present-day researches places the study of mountain environments in the middle of conceptual and methodological debates concerning the archaeological disciplines. From the archaeologist point of view, knowing the ongoing researches in mountain areas and embarking in new investigations cannot be dismissed anymore, since it is an area where the research is active and is providing significant contributions in the ambits of new data, methodological innovation, interpretative tools, and case studies for comparative analysis. Moreover, the role that mountain areas, seen by contemporary societies as potentially protected ecosystems, has to be critically addressed from a historical perspective. In that context the long-term perspective is important, in which the interpretation of archaeological data is a key aspect. Those questions have been important in the historical development of archaeological research in and about mountain environments and they are among the main aspects that justify the present interest on the topic.

Mountain Archaeologies: Overview of Chapters

The Symbolic and Sacred Character of Mountains

The first chapters of this book address the integration of mountainous topographies in human cultural systems through its ideological dimension. The concept of "sacred mountain" is at the center of the discussion here. Mountains are prominent landmarks, and the sacred character of individual mountains is documented in different cultural contexts around the world. In that perspective, sacred mountains are an excellent case study for the symbolic, ideological, and spiritual uses of landscapes.

The conference's keynote lecture delivered by Felipe Criado-Boado introduces these central concepts and offers specific examples to approach this ideological dimension of mountains within prehistoric cultural landscapes. Phillips Stevens presents in his chapter a comprehensive overview of the key concepts used by cultural anthropology to define and study the sacred character of mountains and to conceptualize it in the framework of religious beliefs.

The other two chapters in the first group in the volume are dedicated to case studies in which material culture is used to address the sacred dimension of singular mountain landscapes. Long-term cultural uses in Ikh Bogd Uul in the Eastern Altai Mountains (Mongolia) are addressed in the case study by Cecilia Dal Zovo. The case study presented by Mercourios Georgiadis focuses on Mount Leska on the Aegean island of Kythera (Greece), interpreted as a Bronze Age peak sanctuary, with parallels within the Minoan world.

Global Warming and Archaeology of Mountain Snow Line

The snow line has only recently attracted the attention of archaeologists. The retreat of mountain glaciers and the melting of ice patches, a phenomenon in expansion due to actual climate change, is revealing material culture long trapped in the ice. In those conditions, organic materials are well preserved, sometimes for thousands of years. It offers extraordinary insight on past material culture, but it is also a fragile record that disappears soon after it is revealed on the surface. The challenges associated with this unexpected snow line archaeology are addressed through the case of World War I battlefields in the high Alps (Nicolis) and the newly defined "ice patch archaeology" in the Scandinavian Mountains (Prescott and Melheim).

Subalpine Pastures as High-Altitude Archaeological Sites

Subalpine pastures are one of the most characteristic ecocultural landscapes of mountain areas. The research developed has taken advantage of the characteristics of the environment to develop specific methodological approaches, adapted to those environments. That includes the analysis of a multitemporal dry-stone architecture, often visible through high-resolution aerial images. Although surface material assemblages are scarce, the incorporation of test excavations and C14 dating allows for a chronostratigraphic approach to those elements. Integration of archaeological with high-resolution multiproxy paleoenvironmental studies of lake sediments and peat bogs is a common practice in those projects that tend to have a strong multidisciplinary character.

Early human presence in higher altitudes is documented since the Paleolithic (Efstratiou et al. 2006). It is interpreted as part of the seasonal movements of hunter-gatherer groups first and, beginning in the Neolithic, later incorporating domestic animals. The prehistoric seasonal movement in the high Tatras (Western Carpathians, Poland) since the Late Paleolithic to the Bronze Age is analyzed by Robert Brunswig and Pawel Valde-Nowak in this volume.

There is a consensus that points to a prehistoric onset of the practices that led to the development of high-altitude pasturelands in the long term. The identification of the chronology and process of creation of extensive grasslands and its subsequent maintenance and/or abandonment have been an important focus of the research in mountain areas. Beyond prehistory, the analysis of antiquity and medieval periods in those areas has provided insight about the diversification of activities, documenting minero-metallurgical activities and forestry activities alongside pastoralism.

The case studies included in this volume introduce examples from the main European subalpine environments and are based on projects that combine archaeological and paleoenvironmental analysis. The chapters include research in the Eastern Alps (Oeggl et al.; Nicolis), the North Caucasus (Reinhold et al.), and the Eastern Pyrenees (Palet et al.).

A part of altitude, latitude also determines the extension of alpine conditions. Northern and circumpolar regions share characteristics with environments that, in other latitudes, are exclusive of high mountain valleys. Moreover, they also document similar agricultural practices (seasonal grazing) and similar archaeological and paleoenvironmental archives. They represent outstanding case studies to explore the relationship between climate, grasslands, and human activities. In this volume they are illustrated by research programs in Norwegian mountains (Prescott and Melheim) and Greenland (Gauthier).

Euro-Mediterranean Middle and Low Mountain Landscapes

The next group of chapters address the archaeological context of the middle and lower altitude mountain landscapes. In temperate areas of the northern hemisphere, it defines slopes and mountain formations where the highest points rarely surpass 2,000 masl. It defines extensive areas of the European subcontinent and the circum-Mediterranean regions. Those landscapes are characterized by a higher anthropization, represented by patched landscapes combining montane forests and deforested areas of eroded soils occupied by grasslands and shrubs. Cultivation, usually in terraces, is also present. Lower mountains have historically been a source of building material for nearby urban centers, charcoal and other forestry products, metallurgical materials, and many other resources. Permanent settlements can be present in those areas, and, in some contexts, they have been historically favored locations for settlements that prioritize defensive, strategic, and symbolic functions.

Middle and lower elevations represent a complicated challenge for archaeological research. High slopes and dense vegetation cover make the archaeological record less perceptible. At the same time, high-quality, long-term paleoenvironmental archives are less available than in high-mountain contexts, especially as the latitude increases. On the other hand, those areas can present a historical mix of uses combining cultivation, grazing, forestry, and mining, providing different specialization and complementarity of uses during overlapping time frames. Despite the interest in those environments as historical landscapes, they are complex and difficult to interpret. The development of specific survey techniques to understand the archaeological and paleoenvironmental records, together with analysis of this area in regional perspective, is the focus of the chapters included in this volume.

Representative examples of European mid-mountain contexts are the focus of the chapters dedicated to the Carpathian (Valde-Nowak), the Massif Central (Miras et al.), and the middle slopes of the Atlantic Pyrenees (Coughlan et al.). The development of archaeological surveys in Mediterranean uplands is a subject addressed through case studies in the Taurus Mountains (Vandam et al.) and in the Southern Apennines (Van Leusen et al.).

Valley Architecture

In the context of mountain regions, valleys can have an important structuring role. They concentrate the arable land available in mountain contexts. At the same time, they can function as socioeconomic units and network nodes. The next two chapters explore the relationship between social structures and the formation of settlements in mountain valleys in two very different case studies: in one case, the tribal community of a valley enclaved in the Northern Albanian mountains (Galaty); the second case focuses on the valley of Cuzco (Beltrán-Caballero and Mar). Probably more than any other ancient state, the Inka territory exemplified the incorporated control of diversified landscapes, here defined by the steep slopes of the Andean range.

The volume closes with a review that addresses a series of modern preconceptions of mountain communities and economies (Orengo). The author analyzes how these ideas, although much more critically considered than in the past, are still influential when we interpret the archaeological record in high altitudes.

Final Remarks: Base Camps and New Questions for the Archaeology of Mountain Landscapes

As with any other part of the Earth's surface, human societies have been part of the history of mountain regions: moving through, settling, fighting, exploiting their resources, incorporating them into social ideological and belief systems and, as is underlined by this volume, doing archaeological research.

Surveys conducted in different mountain environments have seen a quantitative and qualitative increase since the beginning of the twenty-first century, expanding the results obtained by sparser previous work and making mountain archaeology a relatively new dataset in the context of archaeological disciplines. There is currently strong consensus among archaeologists that have developed projects in mountain areas since the 1980s to reject or nuance the image of upland regions as empty areas in terms of archaeological interest. On the other hand, combined paleobotanical, geomorphological, and archaeological approaches underline that mountain landscapes have an undoubted cultural character and human actions are part of the historic ecology of montane environments.

In that sense, a series of consensual points must be considered in light of the research developed up to this point and exemplified by the different chapters collected here: First, mountain areas harbor a large and singular archaeological record. It represents an archive that archaeologists can identify, register, and interpret using the appropriate conceptual and methodological tools. Secondly, human activities have been documented since prehistory in all sorts of mountain environments. Those activities represented a significant factor in landscape shaping and landscape conceptualization that integrated archaeological, anthropological, and paleoenvironmental studies can explore. Third, mountain environments provide outstanding case studies to address highly spatialized and specialized exploitation of resources. In that sense seasonal transhumance, intensive and extensive pastoral practices, forestry, and metallurgy could be considered the formation of symbolic topographies and landscape narratives. Finally, it emerges that the idea of a natural isolation of mountain communities must be critically reconsidered. Economic practices and social structures of past communities inferred from material traces in mountain environments need to consider its multiscale regional connections. In that sense, the assumption that mountains are "secondary" areas or "archaic strongholds" can obscure key aspects of historical processes such as the emergence of complex societies and diversified economies.

Those points, as well as other ideas that can be extracted from the combined lectures of the different chapters of this volume and other similar works, represent features of what we can define, using alpinist vocabulary, as "base camps" for archaeological research in mountain areas. In our current state, archaeologists have at our disposal a basic infrastructure developed and systematized by recent research: an ensemble of tested methodological approaches, developed conceptual frameworks, and models to explore in comparative perspectives.

Those base camps, among them those we consider in this volume, provide a preliminary guide to approaching the archaeology of mountain areas and offer support from which to develop new questions. Among those new questions we can consider a multitude of perspectives: new specifically directed projects could provide data to study the still-not-very-well-known traces of Paleolithic hunter-gatherer societies in high altitudes. Why, how, when, and in what extension prehistoric societies change mountain environments to adapt them to specific productions such as herding are questions currently open, particularly in light of the studies conducted in subalpine pastures. Settlement dynamics have a decided micro-regional character, but some trends can be documented in different areas. In that sense, the Bronze Age appears as a moment of intensification in grazing proxies in high altitudes, while in some cases there is an apparent reduction in the archaeological record available for different moments of the Iron Age.

Mountain products, specialization, and landscape diversification have an intense relationship with the emergence of complex societies and state formation that can be explored in many different contexts. Pastoralism emerges as a key factor in landscape dynamics and, thus, the study of the complexity of herding practices appears as a challenge for future researches. The absence of zooarchaeology in the following chapters is not an intentional omission but a consequence of the absence of consumption contexts in the grazing areas. In that respect there is great potential if effective interdisciplinary strategies can be established between high-mountain archaeology, ethnographical research, zooarchaeology, and the application of isotope analysis.

Other activities that have defined the largest areas of mountain landscapes, such as forestry, are much less well known and specific methodological approaches to those areas have yet to be developed. Multidisciplinary, multiproxy analysis has been a key aspect used to understand upland landscape dynamics. Its potential as well as its limits and obstacles are questions addressed in several of the following chapters. On the other hand, multiproxy studies in mountain areas have focused on the advancement and retreat of high-mountain grasslands and have been less effective addressing other aspects like prehistoric and historic woodland management or the environmental and cultural processes involved in the history of mixed cultivation and herding practices in lower altitudes. The continued discussion among multidisciplinary teams stands, as it has been through the history of the discipline, as a foundation stone in the archaeological studies of mountain landscapes.

In another focus, acknowledgment of the cultural character of mountain landscapes poses the question of its heritage dimension. That aspect is addressed in the following chapters from the experience and point of view of different research programs. In that sense, a commonly expressed idea in the final discussion of the conference pointed to the challenge to reach the agents involved in heritagization processes (authorities, local communities, and visitors). In fact, most of the archaeological record presented in the following chapters is largely unnoticed as historic cultural heritage, not only by nonspecialists but also by the archaeological discipline and, as a consequence, by the public bodies in charge of maintaining and promoting historic cultural heritage. Mountain archaeological records contain, in a general perspective, few remains that are likely to be perceived as archaeological monuments. That doesn't imply that mountain material cultural heritage lacks interest or explanatory potential, even those beyond local aspects. Perhaps the most illustrative case included in this volume is the intervention in the alpine during World War I, 3,629 masl, at the Austro-Hungarian post of "Punta Linke" (Nicolis in this volume). The (re)materialization of the place where soldiers would guard and fight in the highest landscapes of Western Europe is an outstanding testimony to the geopolitics, technology, human costs, and consequences of the Great War. Its value is, in that aspect, the same as the fortifications of Verdun or the monuments erected throughout European geography.

In considering a heritage perspective, the long-term human–environment relationship is as much a part of the present of mountain landscapes as it was part of its past. As will be developed in the next chapter (Criado-Boado), mountains can be considered agents participating in human lives. That character can be traced in different cultural systems, both historical and contemporary, including contemporary Western societies, as described, for example, by the characters of the novel *The Eight Mountains* (Cognetti 2018). In a general perspective, therefore, mountain landscapes are a present issue. As discussed in a previous section, this notion is underlined by the inclusion of mountain landscapes as a subject of global, regional, and local politics.

Consequences of climate change, sustainability of economic activities, or the resilience of local cultures in the context of globalized societies are among the central points that will define the future of mountain landscapes and their inhabitants. The long-term historical dimension of these phenomena makes them an area in which the research included in this volume can present a necessary and critical contribution.

Acknowledgments

The author wants to thank IEMA and the SUNY Departments of Anthropology and Classics for the opportunity to organize the tenth visiting scholar conference and edit this volume, and for support in all stages of the work. This gratitude is personally directed to Peter F. Biehl and Stephen L. Dyson as heads of the departments and codirectors of IEMA, as well as to all the faculty, staff, and students, with a special mention of the students who volunteered to participate in the organization of the conference. The notes taken by Ashlee Hart and Nathan Dubinin during the discussion that closed the conference have been of great use to elaborate this introduction. Heather Rosch has provided inestimable support during the compilation of chapters for this volume and proofreading this chapter.

The ideas contained in this introduction have been developed thanks to the work performed by the author in the context of the projects carried out by the Landscape Archaeology Research Group of the Catalan Institute of Classical Archaeology under the direction of Josep M. Palet and Hèctor A. Orengo. Their comments on the first draft of this introductory text provided many insights to improve the final text.

A final thanks to all the researchers who participated in the conference and contributed to this volume with the result of their outstanding scientific work.

NOTE

1. As reflected in the dictionaries: "A high area of land that rises steeply above its surroundings, usually has a sharply pointed top, and is larger than a hill" (Park and Allaby, mountain); "A landmass that projects conspicuously above its surroundings and is higher than a hill. b: an elongated ridge" (Merriam-Webster); "A raised part of the earth's surface, much larger than a hill, the top of which might be covered in snow" (Cambridge Dictionary Online).

REFERENCES

Barker, G., A. Grant, P. Beavitt, N. Christie, J. Giorgi, P. Hoare, T. Leggio, and M. Migliavacca 1991 Ancient and Modern Pastoralism in Central Italy: An Interdisciplinary Study in the Cicolano Mountains. *Papers of the British School at Rome* 59:15–88.

Beaulieu, J. L. D., J. L. Edouard, P. Ponel, C. Roando, L. Tessier, M. Thinon, and A. Thomas 1990 Timber Line and Human Impact in the French Alps: The State of the Art and Research Programs. *Pact* 31:63–80.

Bender, S. J., and G. A. Wright 1988 High-Altitude Occupations, Cultural Process, and High Plains Prehistory: Retrospect and Prospect. *American Anthropologist* 90(3):619–639. DOI: https://doi.org/10.1525/aa.1988.90.3.02a00060.

Benedict, J. B. 1992 Footprints in the Snow: High-Altitude Cultural Ecology of the Colorado Front Range, U.S.A. *Arctic and Alpine Research* 24(1):1. DOI:https://doi.org/10.2307/1551315.

Biagi, P., and J. Nandris (eds.) 1994 *Highland Zone Exploitation in Southern Europe*. Monografie di "Natura bresciana"; no. 20. Museo Civico di scienze naturali di Brescia, Brescia, Italy.

Braudel, F. 1972 *The Mediterranean and the Mediterranean World in the Age of Philip II*, vol. 1. University of California Press, Berkeley.

Brunswig, R. H. 2004 Paleoindian Colonization of Colorado's Southern Rockies: New Evidence from Rocky Mountain National Park and Adjacent Areas. In *Ancient and Historic Lifeways of North America's Rocky Mountains: Proceedings of the 2003 Rocky Mountain Anthropological Conference*, 264–281. Department of Anthropology, University of Northern Colorado, Greeley, Colorado.

Cambridge Dictionary Online. Mountain. https://dictionary.cambridge.org/dictionary/english/mountain.

Cognetti, P. 2018 *The Eight Mountains*. Harvill Secker, London.

Collis, J., M. Pearce, and F. Nicolis 2016 *Summer Farms: Seasonal Exploitation of the Uplands from Prehistory to the Present*. JR Collis and Equinox, Sheffield.

D'Anna, A., P. Leveau, and F. Mocci 1992 La montagne Sainte-Victoire de la Préhistoire à la fin de l'Antiquité: Les rythmes de l'occupation humaine (prospection-inventaire 1989–1992). *Revue archéologique de Narbonnaise* 25:265–299.

Debarbieux, B., and M. F. Price 2008 Representing Mountains: From Local and National to Global Common Good. *Geopolitics* 13(1):148–168. DOI:https://doi.org/10.1080/14650040701783375.

Della Casa, P. 1999 *Prehistoric Alpine Environment, Society and Economy: Papers of the International Colloquium PAESE'97 in Zurich*. R. Habelt, Bonn, Germany.

Della Casa, P., and K. Walsh (eds.) 2007 Interpretation of Sites and Material Culture from Mid-High Altitude Mountain Environments. Proceedings of the 10th annual meeting of the European Association of Archaeologists 2004. *Preistoria Alpina* 42:5–8. Museo delle Scienze, Trento.

Efstratiou, N., P. Biagi, P. Elefanti, P. Karkanas, and M. Ntinou 2006 Prehistoric Exploitation of Grevena Highland Zones: Hunters and Herders along the Pindus Chain of Western Macedonia (Greece). *World Archaeology* 38(3):415–435.

Fermor, P. L. 1966 *Roumeli: Travels in Northern Greece*. New York Review of Books, New York.

Galop, D. 1998 *La forêt, l'homme et le troupeau dans les Pyrénées: 6000 ans d'histoire de l'environnement entre Garonne et Méditerranée—contribution palynologique*. Geode, Toulouse.

Gerling, C., C. Knipper, L. Martin, and T. Doppler 2018 Editorial: Casting a Glance over the Mountain—Multi-proxy Approaches to the Understanding of Vertical Mobility. *Quaternary International* 484:1–2. DOI:https://doi.org/10.1016/j.quaint.2018.05.030.

Halstead, P. 1998 Ask the Fellows Who Lop the Hay: Leaf-Fodder in the Mountains of Northwest Greece. *Rural History* 9:211–234.

Leveau, P. 2014 Occupation et modes d'exploitation de la montagne dans les cités romaines de Gaule Narbonnaise orientale. *Atti del IV Convegno Internazionale di Studi Veleiati: Veleia-Lugagnano Val d'Arda, 20–21 Settembre 2013*:471–486.

Leveau, P., and B. Rémy (eds.) 2008 *La ville des Alpes occidentales à l'époque romaine*. Les Cahiers du CRHIPA 13, CRHIPA, Grenoble.

Leveau, P., and M. Segard 2004 Le pastoralisme en Gaule du sud entre plaine et montagne: de la Crau aux Alpes du sud. *Pallas* 64:99–113.

Lozny, L. R., ed. 2013 *Continuity and Change in Cultural Adaptation to Mountain Environments: From Prehistory to Contemporary Threats*. Springer.

Merriam-Webster. n.d. Mountain. Merriam-Webster.com; accessed March 22, 2018.

Messerli, B., and J. D. Ives 1997 *Mountains of the World: A Global Priority—A Contribution to Chapter 13 of Agenda* 21, edited by B. Messerli and J. D. Ives; editorial advisory committee, Jayanta Bandyopadhyay . . . [et al.]. Parthenon, New York.

Mocci, F., J. M. P. Martinez, M. Segard, S. Tzortzis, and K. Walsh 2005 Peuplement, pastoralisme et modes d'exploitation de la moyenne et haute montagne depuis la Préhistoire dans le Parc National des Écrins. In *Territoires et paysages de l'âge du Fer au Moyen Âge. Mélanges offerts à Philippe Leveau*, edited by A. Bouet and F. Verdin, 197–212. Presses universitaires de Bordeaux, Bordeaux.

Moe, D., S. Indrelid, and A. Fasteland 1988 The Halne Area, Hardangervidda: Use of a High-Mountain Area during 5000 Years—An Interdisciplinary Case Study. In *The Cultural Landscape: Past, Present and Future*, 429–444. Cambridge University Press, Cambridge.

Park, C., and M. Allaby 2013 Mountain. In *A Dictionary of Environment and Conservation*. Oxford University Press, Oxford. http://www.oxfordreference.com/view/10.1093/acref/9780199641666.001.0001/acref-9780199641666-e-5165.

Passarrius, O., A. Catafau, and M. Martzluff 2009 *Archéologie d'une montagne brulée: Massif de Rodès, Pyrénées-Orientales*. Trabucaire, Perpignan.

Peattie, R. 1936 *Mountain Geography: A Critique and Field Study*. Harvard University Press, Cambridge.

Pelisiak, A., M. Nowak, and C. Astaloş (eds.) 2018 *People in the Mountains: Current Approaches to the Archaeology of Mountainous Landscapes*. Archaeopress, Oxford.

Price, L. W. 1986 *Mountains and Man: A Study of Process and Environment*. University of California Press, Berkeley.

Rendu, C., ed. 2003 Avant-propos au dossier spécial: La montagne—Habitats et systèmes pastoraux d'altitude (Pyrénées, Massif Central, Alpes)—L'occupation de la haute montagne, premiers acquis et perspectives. *Archéologie du Midi médiéval* 21:142–145. Association Centre d'Archéologie Médiévale du Languedoc (C.A.M.L.), Carcassonne.

Richard, H. 1997 Indices polliniques de néolithisation du massif jurassien aux VIème et Vème millénaires [Pollen evidence of an early Neolithic presence on the Jura range at the sixth and fifth millenia]. *Quaternaire* 8(1):55–62.

Schuler, M., E. Stucki, O. Roque, and M. Perlik 2004 *Mountain Areas in Europe: Analysis of Mountain Areas in EU Member States, Acceding and Other European Countries*. European Commission contract No. 2002.CE.16.0.AT.136.

Scott, J. C. 2009 *The Art of Not Being Governed: An Anarchist History of Upland Southeast Asia*. Yale University Press, New Haven.

Stirn, M. 2014 Why All the Way Up There? Mountain and High-Altitude Archaeology. *SAA Archaeological Record* 14:7–10.

Tzortzis, S., and X. Delestre 2010 *Archéologie de la Montagne européenne*. Actes Table Ronde Internat (Gap, 29 sept.–1 er oct. 2008), coll. Biama.

Walsh, K. 2005 Risk and Marginality at High Altitudes: New Interpretations from Fieldwork on the Faravel Plateau, Hautes-Alpes. *Antiquity* 79(304):289–305. DOI:https://doi.org/10.1017/S0003598X00114097.

Walsh, K. 2013 Mountain Economies and Environmental Change. In *The Archaeology of Mediterranean Landscapes: Human-Environment Interaction from the Neolithic to the Roman Period*. Cambridge University Press, Cambridge. DOI:https://doi.org/10.1017/CBO9781139024921.

Chapter Two

Steps Lost

Mountains as Sacred Topographies?

Felipe Criado-Boado
(with Ana Ruíz-Blanch in section 4)

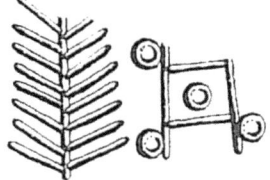

Abstract *In many cultural traditions, mountains are considered privileged, sacred topographies that connect the earth and the heavens, the underworld and the upper world, the landscape and the skyscape. Due to empirical limitations, this aspect of mountains has scarcely been explored in landscape archaeology, despite their service as visual markers, as focal points for orienting and permitting movement throughout a territory, through areas with special resources, part of major herding routes, or destinations. Although this aspect is very much alive in certain parts of the world, such as the Andes, they have fallen into disuse in Europe, and this could be the reason behind this relative lack of awareness of and interest in research about this dimension of mountains. This text will focus on a series of evidence that suggests that mountains were also used to materialize ancient cosmological landscapes.*

Step One: The Sacred Is Ever Something Else

Mountains are focal points, powerful attractors, magnets. Mountains draw our attention, in a challenging way: we cannot stop looking at them. Mountains are pure *actants* in the truest meaning of this Latourian term: they make things happen, influence interaction with humans, and affect the way that humans perceive them.

In Mexico or the Andes, mountain peaks continue to be cultural objects that mark human life. This is a phenomenon that is well known and has been studied in depth (Broda et al. 2007; Loera Chávez et al. 2007; Reinhard 2012; Vitry 2012). It is impossible to travel across the snowy peaks of Mexico or high plateaus of the Andes, live in their valleys, or journey along the road of the Incas, the Qhapaq Ñan, without the presence of mountains marking the rhythm, the sense of place, and the orientation within the territory and toward the world. In the Andes, travelers know they are walking toward the west and the sea because the mountains are behind them, and they know they are heading toward the south because the mountains are on their left. The mountains (called *cerros* in American Spanish) connect daily life with the world of myth, the space occupied by human beings with that of their ancestors, and social time with that of the gods. They embody different senses and principles of rationality, and they materialize mythical characters. Stories are told about them. Basically, they are said to be sacred.

However, the "sacred" is always something more. Despite the fact that I constantly refer to "the sacred" in this text, this is simply a surrogate term to refer to certain features of a number of prominent mountains that have been traditionally considered as "sacred." However, this attribute mainly reveals the lack of a proper understanding of what was behind the special character of these mountains by those who interact with them—generally Westerners—without having any relationship with them. The best way of understanding this "sacred" character would be by adopting an emic approach, a term relying on the meaning of the same cultural context. *Huaca*, for instance, is a much better term for the "sacred," as shown later. It would be wrong to consider the sacred as something isolated. It was the process of secularization of the modern age, and previously the specialization of differentiated functions of Western culture, that separated the sacred from other spheres of human activity. In other societies, the sacred is a dimension that constitutes and complements all human activity; nothing can be done without first offering it to the divinity, although this does not necessarily mean that this activity is sacred. We miss steps on the stairway when we consider the sacred as being a special, unique quality. But we also miss them when we forget that, among other things, mountains may well have been a stairway to heaven.

Step Two: Mountains as *Huacas*

Mountains comprise a complex semantic system, which also includes a sacred aspect. They constitute a ritual landscape that includes the symbolic, the intangible, meaning, rituals, and tales. Through narratives that consider mountains their starting point, where the genealogy of each social group is defined, the sense of belonging to each domestic group and to each specific social group derives. In Mexico and the Andes, these tales are told against the backdrop of a mythical time, of stories that describe how a community was founded, and how it developed. They often describe a mountain that "is the ancestor who rivaled another mountain for the love of a woman, who was another mountain; they fought, hurling stones, and on landing, each stone formed another small mountain; they joined together, and had mountains as children." The mountains then captured the clouds and snow, and made water; the water that irrigates the fields, and makes life possible; in part, this is the source of their sacred nature (Castro Pérez 2007).

The *cerros* are alive, and have their own biographies or life stories. They are appeased or pacified by making offerings to them, praying before them, and creating sanctuaries (Troncoso et al. 2012). Their existence forms a space that is full of meaning for the social group: their life creates a social cartography, by turning the episodes of their life into topographic locations.

To some degree, the mountains are "wild monuments" (cf. Criado-Boado 1995:197), natural entities that society has endowed with specific meaning, and which, thanks to their formal characteristics (height, size, visibility at a great distance, and of course, their intransience over time), meet all of the conditions of a monument in the strictest sense: they are visible in both space and time, and also from a great distance away. Their specific shape or profile is always easily recognizable: this is why they serve as a reference point and as a landmark. They define a network of coordinates that include the physical space within a pattern of human order, legitimized by gods, naturalized in the environment, and essentialized by their continuity over time. In addition, they are a space that is both used and exploited.

The wisdom of the native Andean peoples, including the Aymara, Quechua, and Atacameños (or Lincan Antai), states this in a much clearer way. To a certain extent, the *cerros* are a type of *huaca*, a concept that belongs as much to the Quechua as it does to the Aymara, used to identify physical objects, whether natural or human-made, which have sacred attributes and function as the main organizational elements of space and time in the Andes. All of the ancient sites, dating back to deep time, including archaeological sites, are *huacas* (see Alejandro Beltrán-Caballero in this volume). A *huaca* is not the same as a sacred site: once again, it is more complex. A *huaca* is a place where there is an intimate connection between an ancient time (the tradition) and a space: it is time converted into space, or space extended in time. For this reason, archaeological sites are *huacas*. Also, the mountains are *mayllkus* for the Lican Antai of Atacama, tutelary beings "who represent the dwelling of the ancestors, the controllers of weather phenomena, the place that is the source of the waters, the riches of the Inca, certain illnesses, and all of it connected with the mythical past" (Moyano 2012:103).

However, this general meaning calls for a more precise definition. Each *cerro* has its own particular significance for the community that lives in its shadow, largely because the community exists thanks to it. When the mountain soars to heights of more than 5,000 m, above the snowline, its melt waters produce the water for the communities that live in the valleys below.

All of this means that the Andean peaks are "earth beings" (*cerros tutelares*) for their local communities. The tutelary mountain is an attribute of the identity of the community, and each member of it. It is a powerful example of Latour's actant: an inanimate agent that has real effects on human and social agents. It is not only alive in people's fantasies but is also recognized as playing an active role in the social world, as well as influencing people's attitudes. One looks at it constantly, and at the same time is feeling observed.

In the salt flats of San Pedro de Atacama, at an altitude of 2,500 m, each settlement has its own tutelary mountain at its rear, toward the east, in the central range of the Andes, which generally reaches heights of 5,500 m or more (Figure 2.1). In this way, the local identity is created. However, the regional supra-local identity is created by looking to the west, toward the Domeyko range, which encloses the salt flats to the west. It is crowned by a single mountain, Quimal (4,278 masl), the region's main peak. Quimal is the woman who the men from the other side lusted after and was finally betrothed to the mountain of Likancabur (5,920 masl), the highest peak in the area, and the guardian mountain of San Pedro de Atacama, the central settlement of the region.

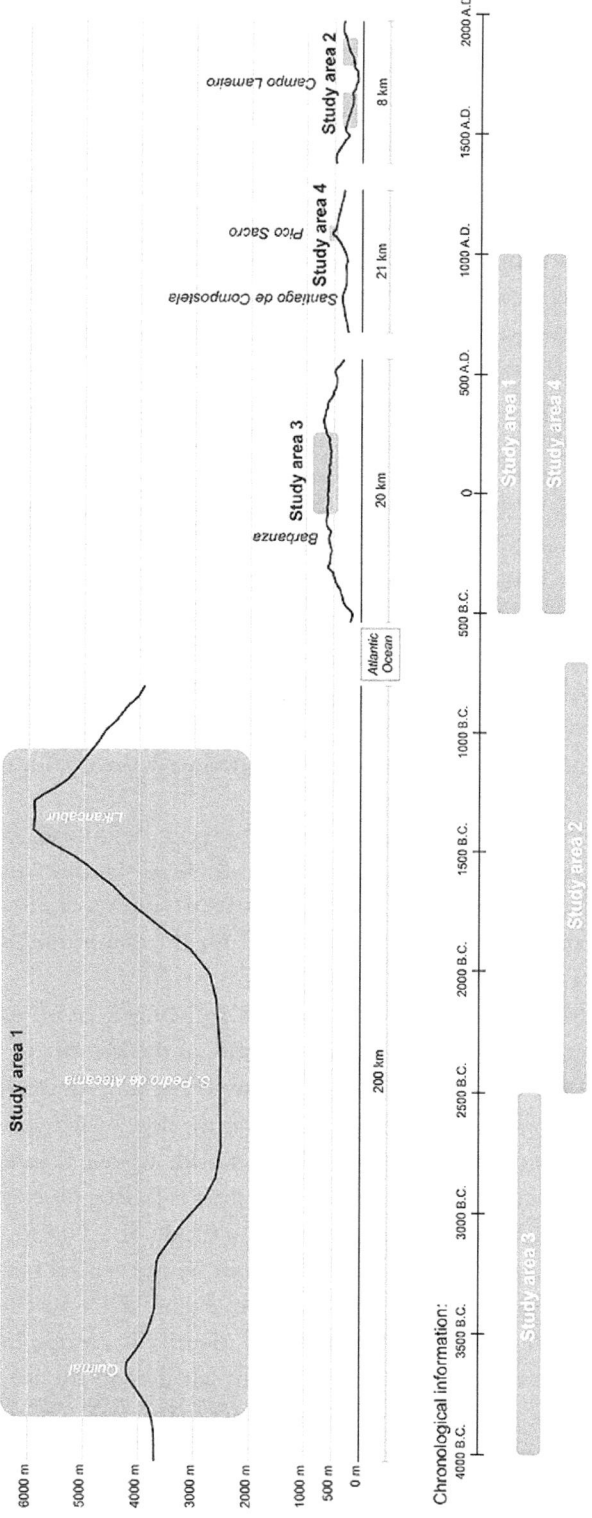

Figure 2.1. Topographical profile of the case studies referred to in this text, showing the relationship between them.

Here the question we must ask is, in the same way South American landscape archaeology has considered the archaeology of the mountains, introducing this complex sacred anthropology into the study of these mountain landscapes (Iwaniszewski and Vigliani 2011): Can we, or should we, do the same in other areas, and in particular in relation to European prehistory and protohistory? Of course I do not mean directly transposing this complex cultural belief. Instead, I refer to whether we can identify in the cultural landscapes of late prehistory in Europe, and the value of mountains as sacred topographies and cultural principles for organizing the world: as spatial and temporal devices used to construct the social landscape.

The study by Cecilia Dal Zovo included in this volume presents an example in Mongolia. Dal Zovo shows how the mountain of Ikh Bogd Uul, in the Eastern Altai Mountains, functions in the longue durée as the main organizing feature of a sacred landscape that connects livestock routes with rock art, tumuli (*khirigsuur*) from the Bronze and Iron Ages, and later on, *oboos* (Buddhist stupas). The tumuli and rock art mark the routes and buffer zones (or interface areas) that connect the valley and the steppe with the high mountains and the sacred peaks (Dal Zovo 2016). There are many similar examples throughout all of Asia, in the Himalayas (McKay 2015), and in the Indian subcontinent (Aas 2008). But what can we say about Europe?

Data that associates events and archaeological sites with mountains point toward their importance as sacred spaces. And yet, this association has been partly lost, as it would seem that the layer of traditional folklore that initially gave a sense of meaning to the spaces where our family events took place (i.e., the narrations, tales, chronicles, and myths of the traditional peasant societies that lived throughout the whole of Europe, until the expansion of modernity), has lost sight of this special, sacred quality of the mountains.

Step Three: Prehistoric Conjectures

Archaeological evidence can help to fill in this gap. Concentrations of archaeological elements are frequently found on peaks and prominent outcrops. The engagement between significant sites and mountainous landscapes means that the former, by being located on the latter, adopt their special physical features, making them visible and permanent: they create their meaning in continuity with the previously existing "wild" monuments. There are many examples of this, but I will focus on two highly relevant cases (Figure 2.1).

High concentrations of rock art are normally found in buffer zones that connect lowland areas with high mountain peaks. We find similar cases, adapted to the local geography, to those Dal Zovo found in the Eastern Altai of Mongolia. The large concentration in Valcamonica, one of the most relevant areas of rock art from the Bronze and Iron Ages in Western Europe, occupies a valley that forms a long corridor connecting the Padan Plain in Northern Italy with the Alps, and through them to the lands that lie beyond.

On a smaller scale, determined by the lower average altitudes of the territory, the same occurs in Galicia, a small region in the northwestern Iberian Peninsula, in the southwest corner of Eurasia. It does not matter whether we refer to low or medium mountains in comparison to the high mountains; the important aspect in this case is that the same effects of mountains can be experienced in the region, due to the rugged, highly fragmented nature of its geography. In particular, the large concentration of Atlantic rock art from the Bronze and Iron Ages found in Campo Lameiro occupies a valley that serves as a transition point between the coastal and precoastal lowlands and the medium-altitude mountain ranges of the central part of Galicia. As stated by Bradley et al. (1995:364), it is an ecological frontier that marked the transition point between densely populated coastal lands, with a gentler climate and land suitable for agriculture, and the less populated mountainous regions of the interior, with less fertile land. The sacred landscape that was created through rock art, apart from other social uses and functions (Criado-Boado et al. 2013), would have served as an interface between very different regions, substantiating in this way the process of accessing and climbing into the mountains. Valcamonica and Campo Lameiro, like many other parts of Atlantic Europe with rock art, would have had a very similar role to the sacred landscape of Rishikesh (India), the valley through which the Ganges crosses from the great Indian plain toward the sacred mountains of the Himalayas.

We find even better examples of this in Megalithic structures. Throughout the whole of Western Europe (in Carrowmore, the largest megalithic cemetery in Ireland [Bergh 1995], Sedano, in Burgos, Central Spain [Delibes de Castro 2000], or in the Serra da Abobeira, in Northern Portugal), we find large groups of tumuli engaged with dominant topographies that are highly visible at a great distance (Figure 2.2). The artificial monumentality of these

Figure 2.2. Panorama of the inner part of the Sierra de Barbanza, with prehistoric tumuli overlooking the entire landscape.

megalithic structures, making them visible at a close distance, took advantage of the wild monumentality of the topographic features on which they were erected, which, in comparison, are visible from dozens of kilometers away (Figure 2.3).

Analyzing these types of ensembles, the density of monumental activity, and the complexity of the type of cultural landscape they created, makes it difficult to avoid thinking that they shaped spaces that included a dimension that we now refer to as sacred, closely linked to the mountain, to the heights, the skies, and the heavens. This connection with the heavens is highlighted in studies focusing on megalithic archaeoastronomy (González-García and Belmonte 2014; González-García et al. 2017). The creation of a cultural landscape that materializes a structural model for conceiving space (Criado-Boado 2014) is something that I have been able to analyze in different case studies. In the Barbanza Peninsula, in Galicia, the greatest concentration of tumuli is found in the middle of the interior mountain ranges (Figure 2.4), with all of them marking the routes that made this territory accessible in every sense of the word (Figure 2.5), and making it easier to cross the peninsula from side to side, and from it toward the hinterlands of the region (Criado-Boado and Villoch Vázquez 2000). However, this concentration is also located in the highest point of the mountains of the Barbanza Peninsula, halfway between the sea, the earth, and the skies (Figure 2.2). The complexity of this megalithic landscape is easier to demonstrate by means of animation (available at this address: http://hdl.handle.net/10261/154985).

Figure 2.3. Profile of the mountain range of Sierra de Barbanza, as seen at a distance of 20 km from the southwest. The megalithic necropolis is in the highest part of the topography, in the central part of the mountains.

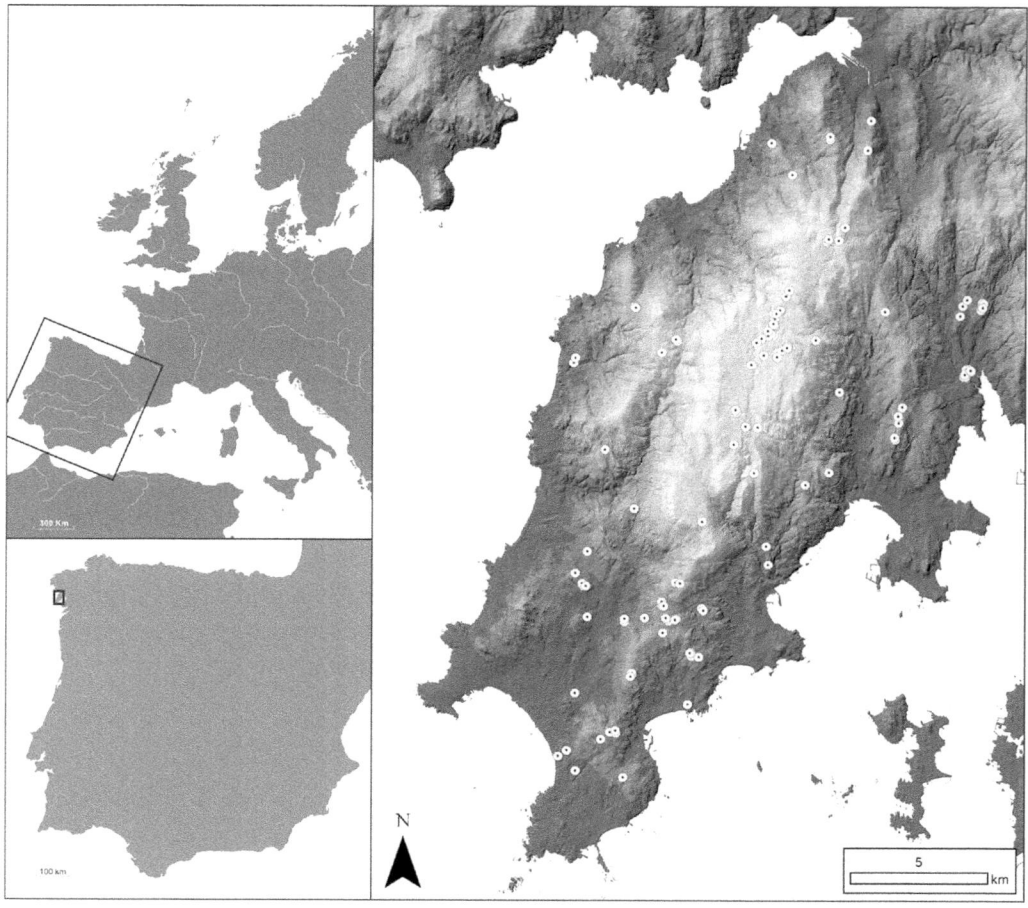

Figure 2.4. Distribution of the tumuli in the Sierra de Barbanza, with the main necropolis in the center of the highest part of the peninsula.

Step Four: The Reason Lost (coauthored with Ana Ruíz-Blanch)

We do not have data in any of these cases that would explain the type of symbolic character the mountains once had, and what type of cultural meaning was attributed to them in support of human activity. There is no longer any living mythology that, as in the Andes or Mongolia, reveals to us today what the mountain once meant, and how it was understood. But I believe that the mountain, its altitude and difficulty in scaling, provided a special symbolic component to the cultural landscape that grew up around it. I suggest this not only because of the relationship revealed by relevant archaeological features, but also because, in some exceptional cases where the folk and traditional values of the mountain have survived until the present, its symbolic aspect can still be perceived. There are still examples such as Mount Olympus, a huge amount of ethnographic references to sacred mountains, place

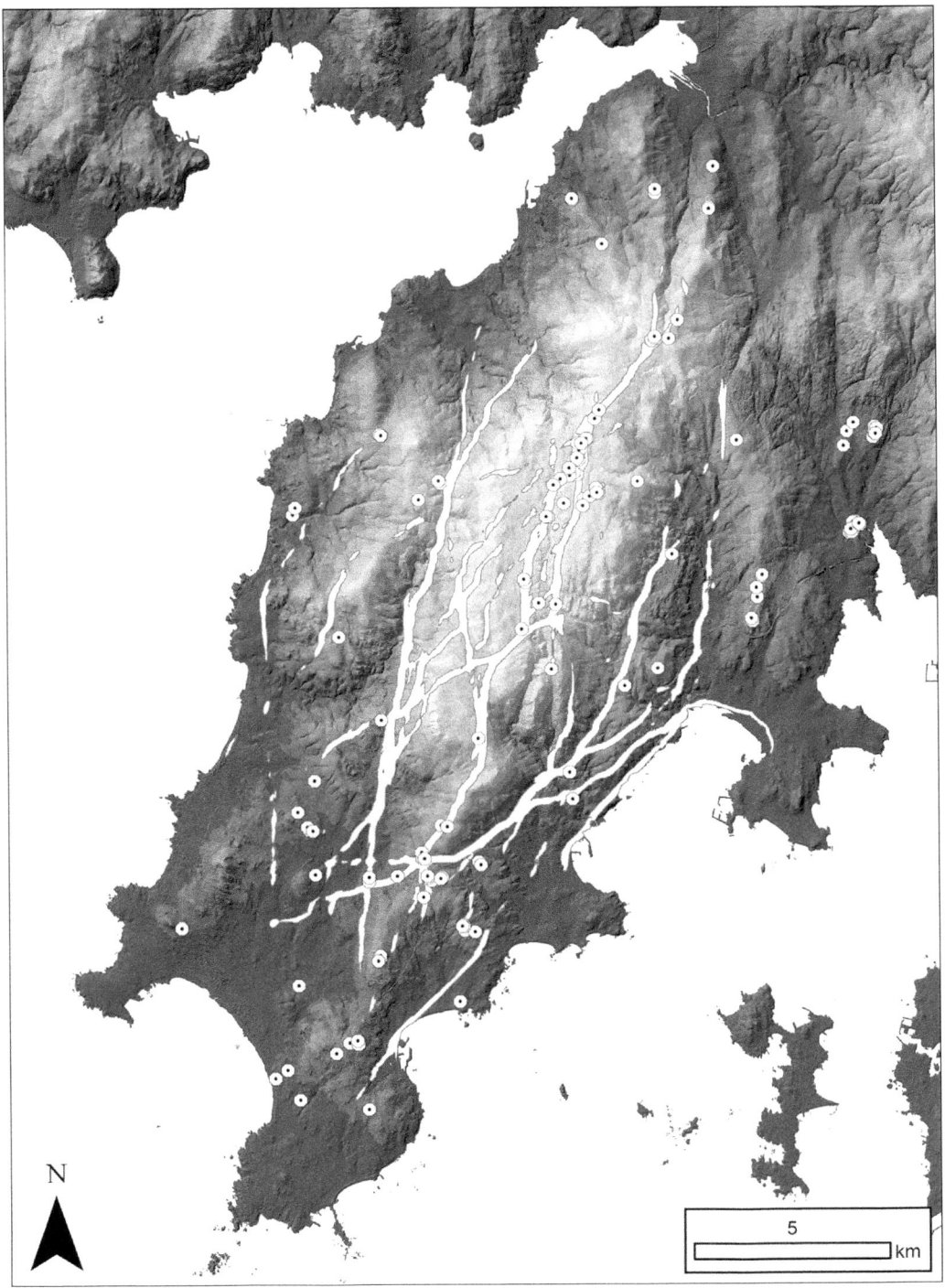

Figure 2.5. The tumuli of the Barbanza Peninsula in relation to the network of routes that organize the most effective movement throughout the region. The main megalithic necropolis marks the focal point of all of the different routes.

names, and indirect traditions. But they are not frequent, or highly obvious. If we compare it with America and Asia, the traditional European landscape has lost the power of its ancient semantic layer. This is undoubtedly due to modernization, to the disappearance of traditional rural societies, and the wholesale capitalist domestication of the environment. This absence should serve to remind us that the "Capitalocene" (i.e., the Anthropocene by another name), like the Neolithic, is not only an economic way of life, but instead a state of mind that quashes the ancient significance of the landscape, subjecting it to capitalist dominion.

Returning to Galicia, in the westernmost corner of Europe, we find the mountain known as the Pico Sacro ("Holy Peak"), closely related to the tradition of Santiago de Compostela and the tomb of the Apostle St. James the Elder. The city of Compostela is the final point on the pilgrims' routes that wind their way through Western Europe until reaching the sea, the true Land's End of Eurasia.

At a distance of 12 km to the southwest of what is now the city of Santiago de Compostela (at an altitude of 360 m) there is a mountain 534 m high that stands out in the landscape for its height and characteristic shape (Figure 2.6). What also makes it special is

Figure 2.6. Profile of the Pico Sacro, a prominent and distinguishable feature in the landscape around Santiago de Compostela.

the fact that it is comprised of white quartz and offers sweeping views from its summit over the surrounding landscape (Figure 2.7 left). It is different from any other peak or geographic feature in the area, and is one of the protagonists of the legend describing how the city was founded.

Saint James the Apostle was beheaded by Herod in Jerusalem, in the middle of the first century AD. His disciples rescued his remains, which had been thrown to the animals, and took them to a beach, seeking a place to give them a Christian burial. There a divine sign sent them a boat that carried them, together with the remains, to the port of Iria Flavia, in Galicia, in just seven days. They were told to bury Saint James there, and to spread the Christian faith. When they asked who ruled the area, they were taken before Queen Lupa (*lupa* means wolf and also prostitute in Latin), a pagan widow, whom they asked to destroy her temples and idols, and allow them to bury Saint James and build a mausoleum on the site. The queen attempted to deceive them several times and have them killed, although they were always saved by divine intervention. And so they traveled on a route through some of the most significant parts of the territory that can be seen from the Pico Sacro (Padrón, Iria Flavia, Castro Lupario, Finisterre, Monte Pindo, the Pico Sacro itself, and finally the city of Compostela). Finally, they were sent to the hill of Monte Ilicino, a Latin name that refers to the god Jupiter and to the holm oak—a sacred tree, dedicated to Jupiter—and which can also be interpreted as meaning attractive or seductive, perhaps referring to its special shape, crowned by glittering quartz. They were told that they would find oxen there who would be capable of drawing the cart to the burial place. This was yet another trick, as the hill was known for being a place of evil. On arriving, a fire-breathing dragon charged toward them, but when the saint's disciples made the sign of the cross, it exploded and vanished. The oxen also turned out to be wild bulls, but after making the sign of the cross once again, they became tame. From that moment on, having cleansed the hill of its evil aura, it became known as the Pico Sacro. Once the queen heard about these miraculous events, she converted to Christianity and destroyed her greatest temple, smashing it to pieces, burying the apostle on the site, and building a beautiful mausoleum where the cathedral of Santiago now stands.

The tomb remained hidden and forgotten until the ninth century: around the years 820–830 CE, legend tells that a hermit named Paio saw a series of lights that led him toward the apostle's tomb. Paio notified the Bishop of Iria Flavia, who in turn contacted King Sancho II, instigating the legend of Santiago de Compostela.

This same tale appears in different versions between the ninth and twelfth centuries, although despite a large number of studies (mainly from a linguistic perspective), we still do not know exactly how old it is (Díaz y Díaz 2010:112; Guerra Campos 1961; Rey Castelao 2006). The episode on the Pico Sacro appears in all of these versions from the beginning, but despite its importance, there is a notable lack of specific, modern studies about the mountain. There are some community-based studies that have compiled the large number of legends and beliefs about the Pico Sacro, which range from the curing powers of the area, through to the "Palace of Queen Lupa," built by giants and dragons (Groba González and Vaqueiro Rodríguez 2004). As occurs with all folklore, these legends seep into the official history and give it a new meaning. The tradition of the Pico Sacro is still very much alive today: the remains of rituals, such as candles, flowers, and other offerings, can still be found on the hill (Figure 2.7). This image can also be taken as a graphic metaphor of the concept of hierophany developed by Eliade (1998:15), locations that break the profane homogeneity to get in touch with the immanent, be it heaven or the underworld (or both) and that we can understand as sacred.

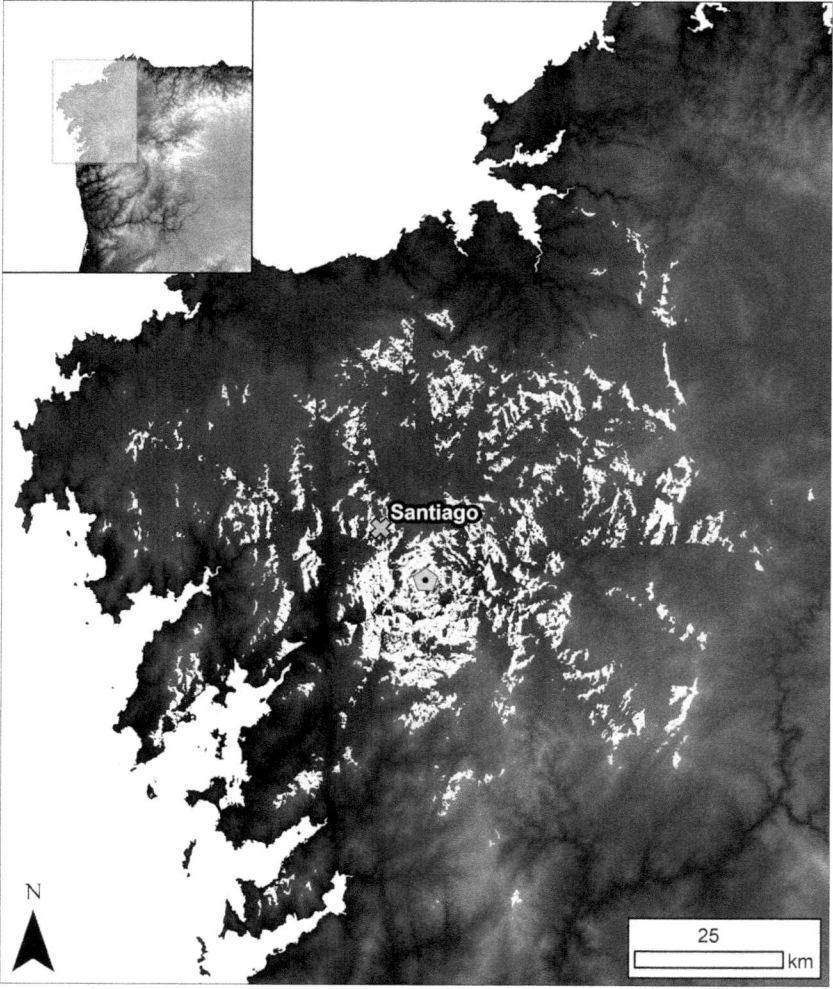

Figure 2.7. There are early medieval remains (ca. seventh–tenth century AD) located on the very top of the Pico Sacro. While proper archaeological research is still lacking, it is remarkable that these remains highlight the connection between the mountain with "the above" (the sky) and "the below" (the chthonic) by carving into the natural bedrock to create steps (*left*) marking a "stairway to heaven" and digging a tunnel (*right*) marking the steps that lead. The image on the left also gives a good idea of the vast panorama that is visible from the Pico Sacro.

At the same time, recent archaeological investigations have shown that the Pico Sacro was significantly connected to protohistoric sites and monuments in the area. Actually, the visual catchment of the Pico Sacro is huge and commands a vast area of central Galicia; the mountain itself is seen and distinguished from a very far distance (Figure 2.8). In some cases, these date from the Bronze Age, such as Devesa do Rei, a cultural area located 3 km to the south of the Pico Sacro, and which has a special relationship of intervisibility with it (Aboal et al. 2010). However, the most interesting example is the large rock art panel from O Castriño de Conxo, a Bronze Age site that was subsequently incorporated into an Iron Age hill fort. Situated on the panel, and after making the necessary archaeoastronomic corrections, sunrise at the winter solstice creates a spectacular effect, as the sun appears out of the darkness over the western slopes of the Pico Sacro, then commences its journey across the skies from its summit (Bouzas Sierra 2013). This rock art panel was suggested to have been a supra-local ritual area for Bronze Age communities, part of a network of equidistant points that would have been comprised of the large petroglyphs with images of weapons in Galicia (Güimil Fariña and Santos Estévez 2013).

No data are available that would help us to identify the age and origin of the legend of the Pico Sacro. But if we consider that it dates back to the ninth century, and its connection with protohistoric sites, then we cannot rule out that it dates back to at least this time. These legends only survived as a result of being reused in the tradition of the Apostle Saint James. This is possibly a reused prehistoric mythical cycle to invent a tradition with which the Christian kings legitimized the emerging monarchy of Asturias and León, and the formation of a Christian kingdom in the northwestern confines of Iberia and the known world, which forged cultural and commercial relations with the rest of Western Europe via the Way of Saint James, at a time when most of the peninsula was under the control of the Moors. García Quintela studies the tradition of Saint James as a part of his research by analyzing the formation of the Christian cultural landscape based on the Roman world, and by incorporating previous cultural traditions (García Quintela 2015; García Quintela and González-García 2017).

Figure 2.8. The visual catchment of the Pico Sacro (marked with a pentagon) comprises a vast area of land in the center of Galicia and around the city of Santiago de Compostela.

And so, without conserving this step, the significance of the Pico Sacro would have been lost. This is a further case of reason lost in archaeological hermeneutics. As was argued in Criado-Boado (2012:208–209), without a pattern of rationality that makes it possible to translate the logic of the archaeological record, the possibility of interpretation is lost.

We have seen how, in the Andes, the mountains serve as earth beings that give shape to social territories and landscapes of identities, connecting local and regional identities, against the backdrop of agropastoral land uses and water management. We have seen in other cases (in Galicia, on the Atlantic coast of Europe) that mountains served as the basis for megalithic, Neolithic, and rock art Bronze Age ceremonial landscapes, landscapes of movement and ceremonialism, connected to routes that permeated the territory, made resources accessible, and linked the hinterlands with the shoreline, the mountains with the sea. We have seen in the case of the Pico Sacro that the mountain is associated with the mythology of Saint James the Apostle, forming part of a political landscape that is related to protohistoric traditions of appropriating the land and establishing social dominance.

So, were mountains sacred, or not? (cf. Stevens in this volume). Obviously, in the case of premodern societies, this single question does not make any sense. Mountains are no more sacred than any other place in premodern societies. The case of the Andes serves to remind us that mountains were *huacas* in one sense or another. This "sacred" worldview became lost in modern societies because of their (and indeed our) secularization. But when one considers the possibility of living in a traditional society, this sense of the world can still be experienced. In fact, this sacred dimension is what archaeologists, anthropologists, or philosophers now understand as the active power (i.e., the agency) of the things in the world. What the new ontology now understands as the agency of things was understood in premodern societies as the soul (the spirit) of things, which was then reused by state religions as being of a religious nature, and then reinterpreted by us as sacred. The sacred quality of the mountains forms a part of wider systems, of greater human landscapes that usually went beyond the mountains themselves, involving relationships with the lowlands, long-distance movements, and economic relationships over vast territories (almost every chapter in this volume refers to this aspect, such as the studies by Prescott or Palet). This also means that we can expect this special characteristic of mountains to be attributed by outsiders, and not their local people.

Because the importance of mountains arose from a wider perspective (as a source of particular resources, frontiers, passing points, or whatever), they embodied specific meanings and obtained a symbolic preeminence and power. This symbolism took the form of place names, narratives, mythologies, heavenly spheres, and places where it was possible to come into contact with other worlds, with divinities, death, and so on. This was often materialized or monumentalized by special sites, sanctuaries (see Georgiadis in this volume on this aspect), or ceremonial landscapes.

The fact that mountains have a special, symbolic dimension cannot be denied, whether it is referred to as "sacred" or otherwise. And yet it is often something more complicated, which comes together with many other dimensions, interweaving functionality with economic, social, political, and ritual aspects. Mountains form a part of the wider, complete landscape; they are not isolated elements but are contained within complex network of elements and meanings. Mountains are active cultural objects. What is more, they are agents amid agents. Mountains become pure actants.

Acknowledgments

The author would like to sincerely thank Arnau Garcia-Molsosa and Peter Biehl for inviting him to read the keynote lecture of this seminar. I am grateful for the comments and material from the other contributors. As ever, I am obliged to the Incipit (Institute of Heritage Sciences, CSIC) for providing a rich intellectual environment. The figures were created by Anxo Rodríguez-Paz, Jorge Canosa-Betés, and Iñaki Villa-Indurain. The video cited in this text was made by Rubén Vuelta Santín. As ever, Marco García Quintela was a superb interlocutor in exploring the longue durée of the Pico Sacro.

References

Aas, L. R. 2008 Rock Carvings of Taru Thang: The Mountain Goat—A Religious and Social Symbol of the Dardic Speaking People of the Trans-Himalayas. MPhil dissertation, Faculty of Humanities, University of Bergen, Bergen.

Aboal Fernández, R., X. Ayán Vila, and P. Prieto Martínez 2010 Un espacio cultual de la Prehistoria Reciente: el yacimiento de Devesa do Rei (Vedra, A Coruña). In *Reconstruyendo la historia de la comarca del Ulla-Deza (Galicia-Spain): Escenarios arqueológicos del pasado*, edited by P. Prieto-Martínez, 63–70. Editorial CSIC, Madrid.

Bergh, S. 1995 *Landscape of the Monuments: A Study of the Passage Tombs in the Cúil Irra Region, Co. Sligo, Ireland*. Riksantikvarieämbetet, Stockholm.

Bouzas Sierra, A. 2013 Espacios paganos y calendario céltico en los santuarios cristianos de Galicia. *Anuario Brigantino* 36:43–74.

Bradley, R., F. Criado-Boado, and R. Fábregas Valcarce 1995 Rock art and the Prehistoric Landscape of Galicia: The Results of Field Survey, 1992–1994. *Proceedings of the Prehistoric Society* 61:347–370.

Broda, J., S. Iwaniszewski, and A. Montero (eds.) 2007. *La montaña en el paisaje ritual*. Escuela Nacional de Antropología e Historia, Mexico.

Castro Pérez, F. 2007 Las montañas: locus sagrado y fábricas de agua. In *Páginas en la nieve: Estudios sobre la montaña en México*, edited by M. Loera Chávez y Peniche, S. Iwaniszewski, and R. Cabrera, 119–129. Instituto Nacional de Antropología e Historia, Mexico.

Criado-Boado, F. 1995 The Visibility of the Archaeological Record and the Interpretation of Social Reality. In *Interpreting Archaeology: Finding Meaning in the Past*, edited by I. Hodder, M. Shanks, et al., 194–204. Routledge, Oxford.

Criado-Boado, F. 2012 *Arqueológicas: La Razón Perdida—La construcción de la inteligencia arqueológica*. Edicións Bellaterra, Barcelona.

Criado-Boado, F. 2014. Archaeologies of Space: An Inquiry into Modes of Existence of XScapes. In *Paradigm Found: Archaeological Theory—Present, Past and Future. Essays in Honour of Evžen Neustupný*, edited by K. Kristiansen, L. Smejda, and J. Turek, 61–83. Oxbow Books, Oxford.

Criado-Boado, F., A. Martínez Cortizas, and M. García Quintela (eds.) 2013 *Petroglifos, paleoambiente y paisaje: Estudios interdisciplinares del arte rupestre de Campo Lameiro (Pontevedra)*. Editorial CSIC, Madrid.

Criado-Boado, F., and V. Villoch Vázquez 2000 Monumentalizing Landscape: From Present Perception to the Past Meaning of Galician Megalithism (Northwest Iberian Peninsula). *European Journal of Archaeology* 3(2):188–216.

Dal Zovo, C. 2016 Archaeology of a Sacred Mountain, Mounds, Water and Mobility of Ikh Bogd Uul, Eastern Altai Mountains, Mongolia. PhD dissertation, University of Santiago de Compostela, Santiago de Compostela. http://hdl.handle.net/10261/130643.

Delibes de Castro, G. 2000 Itinerario Arqueológico de los dólmenes de Sedano (Burgos). *Trabajos de Prehistoria* 57 (2):89–103.

Díaz y Díaz, M. 2010 *Escritos Jacobeos*. Universidade de Santiago de Compostela, Santiago de Compostela.

Eliade, M. 1998 (1957) *Lo sagrado y lo profano*. Paidós, Barcelona.

García Quintela, M. 2015 La construcción del paisaje cristiano en Galicia: hacia la definición de un modelo de transformación. *Estudos do Quaternario* 12:143–159.

García Quintela, M., and C. González-García 2017 Archaeological Footprints of the "Celtic Calendar"? *Journal of Skyscapes Archaeology* 3(1):49–78.

González-García, C., and J. A. Belmonte 2014 Sacred Architecture Orientation across the Mediterranean: A Comparative Statistical Analysis. *Mediterranean Archaeology and Archaeometry* 14(2):95–113.

González-García, C., F. Criado-Boado, and B. Vilas-Estévez 2017. Megalithic Skyscapes in Galicia. *Culture and Cosmos* 21(1).

Groba González, X., and M. Vaqueiro Rodríguez 2004 A cova do Pico.

Guerra Campos, J. 1961 *El Pico Sacro*. El Eco Franciscano, Santiago de Compostela.

Güimil Fariña, A., and M. Santos Estévez 2013 Territorialidad en la Edad del Bronce del noroeste de la Península Ibérica. *Revista d'Arqueologia de Ponent* 23:9–26.

Iwaniszewski, S., and S. Vigliani (eds.) 2011 *Identidad, paisaje y Patrimonio*. Instituto Nacional de Antropología e Historia, Mexico.

Llobera, M. 2015 Working the Digital: Some Thoughts from Landscape Archaeology. In *Material Evidence: Learning from Archaeological Practice*, edited by R. Chapman and A. Wylie, 173–188. Routledge, Oxford.

Loera Chávez y Peniche, M., S. Iwaniszewski, and R. Cabrera (eds.) 2007 *Páginas en la nieve: Estudios sobre la montaña en México*. Instituto Nacional de Antropología e historia, Mexico.

McKay, A. 2015 *Kailas Histories: Renunciate Traditions and the Construction of Himalayan Sacred Geography*. Brill, Leiden.

Moyano, R. 2012 El rostro de los Mayllkus en Socaire: la forma y el contenido en los Andes Atacameños del Norte de Chile. In *América: Tierra de Montañas y Volcanes, I*, edited by M. Loera Chávez y Peniche, S. Iwaniszewski, and R. Cabrera, 103–129. Instituto Nacional de Antropología e Historia, Mexico.

Reinhard, J. 2012 Sacred Mountains and Pre-Inca Cultures of the Andes. In *América: Tierra de Montañas y Volcanes, I*, edited by M. Loera Chávez y Peniche, S. Iwaniszewski, and R. Cabrera, 51–72. Instituto Nacional de Antropología e Historia, Mexico.

Rey Castelao, O. 2006 *Los mitos del Apostol Santiago*. Nigratrea, Santiago de Compostela.

Troncoso, A., D. Pavlovic, F. Acuto, R. Sánchez, and C. González-García 2012 Complejo Arquitectónico Cerro Mercachas: arquitectura y ritualidad incaica en Chile central. *Revista Española de Antropología Americana* 42(2):293–319.

Vitry, C. 2012 Las montañas sagradas y la culturas preincaicas de los Andes. In *América: Tierra de Montañas y Volcanes, I*, edited by M. Loera Chávez y Peniche, S. Iwaniszewski, and R. Cabrera, 73–101. Instituto Nacional de Antropología e Historia, Mexico.

Chapter Three

Toward an Anthropology of Sacred Mountains

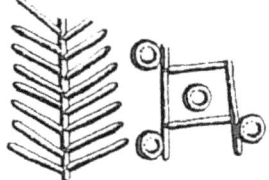

Phillips Stevens Jr.

Abstract *Students of the anthropization of mountain landscapes must look for evidence of ritual activity. Cultural reverence for striking geologic protuberances—mountains, tors, inselbergs, large boulders, replicated in human-made mounds—is probably universal. This chapter applies the author's model of a "vertical dimension" of religious beliefs to understand the universal belief in elevated divinities, and the conceptualization of a sacred mountain. Some representative examples from world ethnology, and some possibly universal symbolic themes, are reviewed. The concept of the "horned mountain," perhaps coined by art and architecture historian Vincent Scully, is examined for the possibility of wider ethnological application. For example, it is suggested that the central Balinese Hindu temple at Besakih was constructed in relation to the sacred volcanic Mount Agung, in a way similar to the positioning of the Minoan palace at Knossos vis-à-vis Mount Juktas.*

"I have been to the mountain top . . . and I have seen the Promised Land."

—Martin Luther King Jr., April 3, 1968

Mountains considered "sacred" are so numerous around the world that a search for ritual sites should be routine in any mountain archaeological investigations. In his lavish 1990 popular work, *Sacred Mountains of the World*, Edwin Bernbaum includes many hundreds of examples from all regions of the world. World ethnology indicates that reverence for striking geologic protuberances is probably culturally universal. Sacred mountains are multivocal—they are mythic, symbolic, metaphoric, economic, political, and more. And mountains generate unique sensory reactions in people.

An "anthropology of" anything must draw from both ethnographic and ethnological perspectives, and should consider biological bases for cultural traits. The cross-cultural patterns revealed through ethnology suggest potentially universal cultural traits, and cultural anthropologists consider universality of cultural traits as suggestive of bases in human neurobiology. Recent advances in that field provide real evidence for what has been unsatisfactorily called a human "ecological unconscious," based on measures of human reactions to natural environments. This has led to a new psychological subfield, ecopsychology, which has generated some important studies (e.g., Kahn and Hasbach 2012) and its own journal.

The phrase "sacred mountain" is widely and loosely used. The terms we use must be defined, and their cross-cultural validity ascertained. My discussion intends to include all elevated geologic protuberances—mountains, tors, hills, inselbergs, large boulders, and such features replicated in human-made mounds and built structures, like pyramids and ziggurats. "Sacred" has various popular meanings, as we will see later. In anthropology and religious studies it is the English term for a culturally universal concept, usually meaning imbued with supernatural power of some sort. "Power" or "energy" or "vitality" or "essence" are variants on a universal concept, one which varies greatly in nature and intensity. It is what distinguishes "holy water." In the form of biblical "glory" displayed by God and his angels it is dangerous, even fatal to people. The concept of the sacred invariably means that access to it is limited by some supernaturally sanctioned restrictions, as expressed in the concept of taboo and therefore, as Durkheim (1915) famously demonstrated, conceptually separate from "profane" or ordinary, mundane, or secular. The profane is always in danger of being damaged by the sacred—but far more seriously, the sacred can be "polluted"—rendered impure or "unclean"—by the intrusive profane. Pollution is contagious and potentially both mystically and physically destructive.

Why a mountain is regarded as sacred may vary widely. It is usually explained in a myth. In the times of "The Beginnings," before history began, important things happened on mountaintops. Mountains are widely regarded as the residences of various spiritual beings, and on their summits divine wisdom, laws, and practical rules for the guidance of society were received by the culture founders, and later, in history, by various mystics and prophets and spiritual healers. It was on Mount Moriah that Abraham prepared to sacrifice his son Isaac (Genesis 22) and on Mount Sinai that Moses received instructions from God (Exodus 19ff.), and so on.

The shape of the mountain might be a factor. Fertility is of central concern to people, and is a common motif in religious and cosmological symbolism; so resemblance to breasts (like the Paps of Anu, near Killarney, Ireland, named for an early Celtic goddess) or phalluses (see, e.g., Mount Shivling, in Indian Himalaya, the "lingam of Shiva") give special quality to mountains. And such features enhance the widespread theme of mountain-as-nurturer. Discussing the history of reverence for Tibet's Mount Kailas, of central importance to Hindus and Buddhists, Alex McKay (2005) describes this theme:

> There were, and are, local variations but the basic model is that these mountains are linked to the origin myths of the tribe dwelling at their base, which worship the mountain as its protective deity. The mountains dominated the landscape and were the source of the rivers that watered their herds, the herbs that cured their illnesses and the weather that shaped their environment.

The deity who dwelled on, or was, the mountain was a protective deity: it protected the tribe and its herds in return for worship. Even today, Tibetans may travel with a little bag of soil from their local mountain, which is seen as protecting them from harm. (92)

Kailas is indeed a great provider; it is the origin of three great rivers of Asia, Indus, Ganges, and Brahmaputra. (And make note of McKay's last sentence; we will refer to it later.) The role of montane ecology in explanation of sacredness has subsequently been raised by Meher-Homji (2013) and others.

Felipe Criado-Boado in his keynote address to this conference also stresses the critical economic role mountains may play in the welfare of societies in their valleys or along the rivers created by their runoff. This fact generates the concept widespread among communities living at the bases of mountains, that the mountain has an important cosmological role as Provider or Nurturer. Similar sentiments are expressed by residents of the Andes (see Castro and Aldunate 2003; Davis 2012; Toohey 2013).

In his chapter Criado-Boado presents what is surely the most common explanation of the sacredness of a mountain: that it is a "stairway to heaven." In my teaching and writing about the anthropology of religion I represent a system of religious beliefs as operating along two dimensions, which I argue characterize all religious systems:

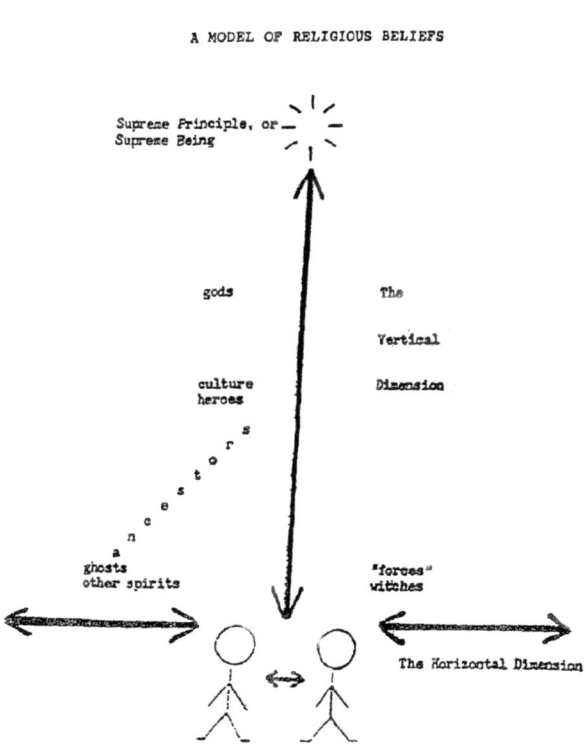

Figure 3.1. Representation of a system of religious beliefs as operating along two dimensions.

Through cultural evolution and anthropomorphism the vertical dimension reflects recognition of sun and rain, warmth and growth, and daylight, and also storm and destruction, and night—all masculine; and the moon, which is feminine. The earth, recipient of the male energy, is invariably feminine. Mountains may be either, or both. So, the top of the vertical dimension is the abode of the Supreme Being or Principle, and at levels below it may be the gods and demigods, culture heroes, and often ancestors. The mountain may also be the collective realm of souls—Heaven, or the steps to it. A culture's religious system reflects the social in structure as well as sentiment, and if the society is ranked and hierarchical, the classic Mount Olympus provides the model for the structure of supernatural agencies. The label "Olympian," I think, was first applied to the religious structures of centralized and hierarchical societies by the late Anthony F. C. Wallace (1966).

The "Horizontal Dimension" consists of beings on the human level of existence. Ghosts, various classes of spiritual beings, natural forces, witches, and variations on fairies and "little people" are the denizens of the horizontal dimension. The stick figures at the bottom represent human society. The double-pointed arrows indicate reciprocal exchange.

All people have religion, and a goal of all religions is to approach the sacred and to benefit from its power. The most powerful of sacred beings are on the vertical dimension, and the closer one can get to them the more likely one's entreaties will reach them; therefore, ritual sites and altars are frequently elevated. The frequent references to "high places" in the Hebrew Bible are to such elevated places of worship.

Mountains are models of and for conceptual hierarchical religious structures; they are also models for religious architecture. Ziggurats and pyramids are clear examples. The famous step pyramid temple of Borobudur in Java is understood to explicitly represent Mount Meru, the home of deities in Hindu and Buddhist mythology (see Nas 2007:29), and the niches in its sides containing statues of deities or culture heroes (e.g., bodhisattvas) are replicas of the cave residences of the gods on the sides of the sacred mountain, as described in the myths.

There are other meanings—and sociopolitical implications—of sacredness in mountains. In a dissertation written for his doctorate in the University at Buffalo Anthropology Department in 2016, Adam Dunstan (2016) studied Diné (Navajo) concepts of the San Francisco Peaks in Arizona, particularly focusing on the conceptual pollution caused by artificial snowmaking by proprietors of a ski area. The San Francisco range has long been recognized as sacred and has been presented as representative both of ecological relationships among American Indians and of the legal and other implications of commercial intrusions into native lands (see, e.g., Hamilton 2015). Dunstan noted that the concept of the "sacred" is culturally relative; that different cultures may conceptualize the same geographic space differently; and, indeed, as Dorothy Lee (1952) had emphasized long ago, a geographic space might not be distinguished as separate, as people and land may be interconnected in a cosmic whole. And Dunstan notes that some Diné traditions regard the San Francisco Peaks as a living, sentient being, and other native American traditions indicate that *all* land was considered "sacred."

Mountains are solid, rooted, permanent; and therefore metaphorical for social, ethnic, or national aspiration and identity. Jared Farmer (2008) observed that Mount Timpanogos, in Utah's Wasatch Range, was not extraordinary to the original inhabitants; it was *made* "sacred" by Mormon immigrants who wanted to establish a homeland and a history, motivated by an image of the biblical Mount Zion. And writing about popular reaction to the proposed development of a ski resort in Saami territory of northern Norway, Svi Ellen Kraft summarizes a process we might call "political sacralization." A report by the Saami parliament

> connected sacredness to Sami traditions in the past and to current laws on the protection of Sami cultural memories. This, then, was a case of sacredness constructed outside the context of organized religions and ongoing religious traditions, as well as a case of using secular laws as the primary basis for definitions of sacredness.
>
> Through this process, love for the mountain appears to have grown deeper and more religious, both for the Sami as well as for other northern Norwegians. Neither more nor less authentic than those of the past, these concepts of sacredness belong to the late modern world of law culture, nature romanticism, and to pan-indigenous spirituality as a "religion" in the making. (Kraft 2010:53)

And this case shows that we must realize that a "mountain landscape" may extend some distance from the mountain itself.

The Mountain as Metaphor

The mountain has been a theme in twentieth-century popular psychology and New Age spiritualism. American writer Frank Waters (1982), proposing an evolutionary development of human consciousness, expressed a representative theme that he considered to be universal:

> Eventually the ego in turn experienced spiritual enlightenment which again related it to the mother of all creation, the unconscious. Hence the function of the sacred mountain was to enable man to surmount his worldly existence at its summit, and achieve transcendental unity with the universe.
>
> A man-made stone pyramid and even the body of man was in effect a sacred mountain. At its apex, either on the summit of a sacred mountain, at the apex of a pyramid, or in the mind-center of a human pyramid, man sought an expansion of his spiritual consciousness. (Waters 1982:64)

Modern people have disregarded the traditional peoples whose land they exploited "for industrial gain," says Waters, and thereby we

> have bought out the physical energy derived from their gold, oil, coal, and uranium at the expense of the psychical energy so equally necessary. Becoming spiritually bankrupt, we are beginning to learn that our relationship to the earth includes a psychical as well as a physical ecology. (64)

Waters pays tribute to the Oglala Lakota shaman Black Elk, who is representative of the collective sentiment of an oppressed people, and whose biography is a classic of Indigenous literature. In his Great Vision, which he claimed to have experienced in about 1872 at the age of nine, he recalls elders promising him that "the thunder beings . . . shall take you to the high and lonely center of the earth that you may see" (Neihardt 2008:21):

> Then I was standing on the highest mountain of them all, and round about me was the whole hoop of the world. And while I stood there I saw more than I can tell and I understood more than I saw. . . . And I saw that it was holy. (33)

Black Elk's vision of the mountaintop experience evokes others, most clearly the prototype experienced by Moses in Exodus, replicated in Martin Luther King's famous speech, made the day before his assassination. The mountain metaphor appears frequently in the Bible; "my holy mountain" is God's own metaphor for his creation (Isaiah 65:25).

The metaphor of the mountain is useful in commerce. Advertisers know that "mountain water" (as in beer) can mean clean and pure; "mountain-grown" (as in coffee) means really special. But countless other features of nature have been used as metaphors—sea, forest, tree, beach, desert, cliff, among others. Of course, because people are creatures of nature. The relationship to nature felt by rural folk is clear, but the romanticization of nature has always been an inevitable feature of urban, industrialized culture. Something fundamentally human is going on.

What Is It About Mountains?

In his great work referred to at the beginning of this essay, Edwin Bernbaum, a Senior Fellow at the Mountain Institute and himself a worldwide mountaineer, uses elaborately descriptive language to describe human emotional response to mountains. Listen to just a couple of many such paragraphs:

> As the highest and most dramatic features of the natural landscape, mountains have an extraordinary power to evoke the sacred. The ethereal rise of a ridge in mist, the glint of moonlight on an icy face, a flare of gold on a distant peak—such glimpses of transcendental beauty can reveal our world as a place of unimaginable mystery and splendor. In the fierce play of natural elements that swirl about their summits—thunder, lightning, winds and clouds—mountains also embody powerful forces beyond our control, physical expressions of an awesome reality that can overwhelm us with feelings of wonder and fear. (1990:xiii)

In Bernbaum's descriptions "the sacred" is an emotional response. In a description of the "experience of the sacred," which he says (many times) that mountains evoke in people, he writes:

> Like the sight of a mountain peak breaking free from the earth to leap toward the open sky, the experience of the sacred can send our spirits soaring to sublime heights of bliss and rapture, uplifting us with visions of beauty and goodness beyond our wildest dreams. The sacred

can also give us a sense of reassuring serenity and fulfillment. The fascination that it inspires leads to feelings of love and devotion so intense that we would give anything, even our lives, to remain in its presence. (xvi)

Note that what Bernbaum is writing about is *awe*, and this human reaction to something wondrous has generated some recent investigation in the field of psychology, to which we will return shortly. He concludes the preceding paragraph with the statement, "Mountains, in particular, have the power to arouse such feelings of overwhelming devotion." He had said earlier, "Mountains have an extraordinary power to evoke the sacred." He is expressing what is in fact a widespread cultural assumption: mountains are actors, they are agents, they contain and project power. I might insert "mountain" as a category on my "Model of Religious Beliefs," probably just above Culture Heroes.

Of the possibly thousands of lines of such testimony by hundreds of writers, I will cite just one more, just for us New Yorkers. The Adirondack Mountains are tiny in comparison to the great mountain ranges of the world, but hikers like them because of their long, steep ascents and spectacular summit views. In 1898 William James, the author of the classic *The Varieties of Religious Experience*, went camping on Mount Marcy, at 5,344 feet the highest peak in New York State. In a letter he wrote about a sense of transcendence he felt that night, which, according to his biographers, was an inspiration for his book (James 1969:2, 76–77). I am a regular hiker of the Adirondacks, and I have summited Marcy many times. I have experienced the awe of standing in the valley looking up—and a different level of awe, tinged with fear, of standing on the summit looking out and down.

But, what's really going on? The anthropological science of cultural ecology developed in the 1950s out of millennia of human speculation about people's relationships to nature. Any studies of anthropization—part of the theme of this conference—should incorporate the principles of cultural ecology. It was long assumed in Western cultures that people with frequent exposure to nature are healthier than shut-ins, and this was finally demonstrated scientifically by landscape architect Roger Ulrich in a still influential study published in *Science* in 1984. In the same year E. O. Wilson (1984) put forth his "biophilia" hypothesis: people have an innate affinity with nature, and this connection generates many psychological and social benefits. There is no doubt today of the existence of what has been called an "ecological unconscious" (Smith 2010; Stevens 2010). The sense that people and their activities are interconnected in nature is surely universal in world ethnology and is a theme of Dorothy Lee's classic 1952 essay, "Religious Perspectives in Anthropology."

Roger Ulrich's early work started a snowball of studies and writings on "healing landscapes," which continues today. He wrote the foreword to a 2014 survey edited by Clare Cooper Marcus and Naomi Sachs, *Therapeutic Landscapes*. Such studies of people and landscapes have mostly involved vegetation, but seascapes are also included. Mountains are landscapes, and presumably people have the same sorts of beneficial relationships with them. But it seems to me that something unique is happening between people and mountains, that it may vary if the view is from below looking up or from top looking out and down, and I think this hasn't been studied.

A sense of scale is certainly evident and might be a factor. We could start with inselbergs, massive and startling outcrops of rock in a generally level wooded, savannah, or desert environment. Important examples are Zuma Rock in Nigeria, sacred to the Gwari and other peoples near Abuja; and Uluru (Ayers Rock) in Australia, powerfully sacred to all Aboriginal peoples. Inselbergs are remarkable, awesome, and frequently considered sacred by people ecologically connected to them. Is it their sheer massiveness? The fact that they are apparently one hunk of solid rock? Many of these massive things are regarded as animated in some way; they are the homes of spirits, or they are sentient beings themselves.

In the kingdom of Bachama, in Nigeria, where I conducted anthropological fieldwork in the 1960s, 1970s, and 1990s, three such features are prominent in the savannah, and the summit of each is considered the residence of a deity, selected by it as a place from which to survey and protect the people. Among the related Bata, adjacent on the east, I collected a tale of a local hero called Makwada. He was a historic character, credited with having saved his people, and some neighboring peoples as well, from the jihadist Muslim Fulani led by Usman dan Fodio in the early eighteenth century. His name is memorialized in various ways in Bachama and Bata culture. But the story of Makwada's life parallels the hero stories of classic mythology, as analyzed by Lord Raglan (1934) and others. All heroes of folklore experience a transforming time away from society, from which they return ready for their next role. This is evident also in the "vison quest" of Siberian and American shamans. Makwada's transformation is effected by a huge rock that trained him and infused him with power (Stevens 1973).

Mountains are unique structures, but they are part of the landscape, and the very land itself with which people are intimately connected. This is explicit in the Andean concept of Pachamama, at once a goddess (popularly known as the "Earth Goddess") and a cosmological system including mountains and valleys and animal and human ecology (see Castro and Aldunate 2003; Davis 2012). And so the bioecological insights of scholars like Roger Ulrich must be considered in our quest to understand the role of mountains in human culture.

At this point I want to return to some of Bernbaum's florid descriptions of the effects of mountains on people. He had said that mountains are "physical expressions of an awesome reality that can overwhelm us with feelings of wonder and fear" (1990:xiii). For some decades psychologists have been interested in awe, defined as "an emotional response to perceptually vast stimuli that defy one's accustomed frame of reference in some domain. People typically experience awe in response to asocial stimuli like natural wonders, panoramic views, and beautiful art" (Piff et al. 2015:883). A number of studies of the generation of and social-psychological implications of awe have been conducted recently and published in journals supported by the American Psychological Association (*Emotion*; *Journal of Personality and Social Psychology*; *Psychology of Aesthetics, Creativity, and the Arts*; *Psychology of Religion and Spirituality*). I will cite just one study here, and one later. Over a series of five studies Paul Piff and colleagues (2015) investigated social implications of the experience of awe as generated by natural and cultural phenomena. Their studies included putting one group of their subjects in a grove of mature, towering eucalyptus trees and asking them to gaze upward for one minute; another group was put at the base of a tall urban building and given the same instruction. Both groups were then given reactive tests, which indicated that both experiences of awe diminished certain negative emotions but that the group that experienced awe in nature had diminished senses of their individual selves and heightened prosociality—altruism, active interest in helping others. They suggest that natural awe "leads to prosocial tendencies by broadening the individual's perspective to include entities vaster and more powerful than oneself and diminishing the salience of the individual self" (Piff et al. 2015:895–896). Piff and others had participated in a contemporary study that summarizes, advances, and updates this field of investigation (Zhang et al. 2014).

None of the awe studies I perused used the term "ecopsychology" or made any reference to the work of Roger Ulrich and his school. One study looked at the nature of awe generated by photos of sky taken from earth, and of deep space taken from the Hubble telescope (Sylvia et al. 2015); results were compared to awe generated by powerful music, but none of these studies mentioned mountains or any type of land- or seascape. But surely we can extrapolate to mountains from the two studies of nature-generated awe. Something important to the structure of society and culture is clearly going on.

The quotation we used by Alex McKay, "Tibetans may travel with a little bag of soil from their local mountain, which is seen as protecting them from harm" (2005:92), describes an instance of magical thinking, but importantly for this discussion it explicitly illustrates the connection people feel with their environments. In the specific case of Tibet, whose native inhabitants feel that much of their cultural legacy has been stolen by China, this is an example of what ecopsychologists call "solastalgia" (Smith 2010), defined as "the pain experienced when there is recognition that the place where one resides and that one loves is under immediate assault . . . a form of homesickness one gets when one is still at 'home'" (Smith 2010:36).

The "Horned Mountain"

One of my most memorable courses during my undergraduate years at Yale was History of Art 12, taught in the fall 1959 semester by Vincent Scully, wherein he advanced his theories of horn symbolism in the Minoan palace of Knossos. Directly aligned with the cleft-peaked Mount Juktas stood Arthur Evans's so-called "horns of consecration," and in the arena below maidens performed—or, at least, were depicted in art as performing—the acrobatics of the bull dance. The famous *labrys*, double-headed axes of the ritual regalia, echoed the horn motif. And he spoke of his concept of the "horned mountain." All were connected; as he said, "The landscape and the temples together form an architectural whole, were intended by the Greeks to do so, and must therefore be seen in relation to each other" (Scully 1962:2). The human ritual both empowers and draws power from the natural environment. His theory is summarized in his 1962 work, *The Earth, the Temple, and the Gods*. In a 1963 *Art Bulletin* review of that work, classical archaeologist Homer Thompson is skeptical, for a number of reasons based in contemporary thinking about Greek architecture. Scully responded with a terse defense of his position in the next issue of that journal (1964).

Inexplicably those lectures of Scully's stayed in my memory. A couple of decades later, as my anthropological career matured, I realized that there is strong evidence from world ethnology that the basis for Scully's theory, separate from its applicability to classical Greek culture and architecture, was sound and really insightful. I don't know whether he had consulted anthropological literature, but he could have: Dorothy Lee's classic 1952 essay, expressly written for college freshmen, was available. And these recognitions had much earlier been expressed by French philosopher Lucien Levy-Bruhl, whose early writings on "primitive mentality" (1923) stressed what he called the "law of participation"—that traditional preindustrial peoples are "mystically" interconnected with things in nature, not intrinsically distinct from them.

In anthropology and other sciences it is today generally assumed and unremarkable that people worldwide consider themselves, their emotions, and their social relations to be integral with the rest of nature; that many of their rituals are essential in the maintenance of natural cycles; and that they align their physical and conceptual structures with features of their environment. The easiest examples are seen in east-west orientation, with explicit east/sunrise/birth and west/sunset/death symbolism in architecture and ritual activity. In their study of Andean ritual sites Castro and Aldunate (2003) publish photographs of tenth-century stone shrines, built to exactly replicate the shapes of mountains and positioned in precise alignment with them. Moreover, they show, modern-day churches and burial grounds are similarly constructed and aligned. The Andes Mountains contain what one title claims are "the world's highest archaeological sites" (Reinhard and Ceruti 2010) and Jason Toohey (2013) reviews three important recent works on many different aspects of Andean sacred geography and cosmology (Bassie-Sweet 2008; Besom 2009; Reinhard and Ceruti 2010).

At the Mesolithic site of Lepenski Vir (nine to seven millennia BC) in Serbia the trapezoidal ground plans of houses seem intended to directly mirror the shape of the prominent Mount Treskavac directly across the Danube River. Dušan Borić (2008:116) says, "The community in the Danube Gorges might have underlined the explicit links between this landmark as the *axis mundi* of its cosmology and the built spaces, which replicated the cosmological order. By mimicking its shape in the construction of buildings, the structures might have been seen to acquire the durability and permanence of the mountain itself."

What all these scholars are discussing is, in fact, one of the commonest forms of magical thinking, based in the principle of similarity cited by J. G. Frazer in his classic theory of sympathetic magic developed in various editions of his great work, *The Golden Bough*, first published in 1890 and expressed in its fullest form in the tenth edition, 1910–1911. This principle, that similar things have causal connections with each other, seems universal in cultural conceptions and I have argued that it is basic to human cognition (Stevens 2006). One magical symbol that seems to have nearly universal representation is horns.

Horns as power symbols, probably basically phallic images, are extremely widespread around the world, even more so than their various female counterparts as represented by the cowrie (esp., *monetaria moneta* in Africa), the *yoni*, and many others. Examples are numerous. Various examples of "horned gods" are recorded in the ancient world; exemplary is Baal/Hadad, in Ugaritic texts the lord of the sky who governed the rain and thus fertility of the earth. His emblems were bulls or rams. Ancient buildings were strengthened by the incorporation of real animal horns in their foundations and walls (Potts 1990); the *bucrania* of Çatal Höyük and other Neolithic archaeological sites are well known and seem representative of what Ian Hodder calls "phallocentric symbolism" (2010:33ff.). The horn motif worked its way into later Islamic architecture. Ancient astronomers described the crescent phases of planets as "horned," and in his writings on planetary phases Galileo resurrected the label "horns of Venus." The horned moon, rather than the full moon, was more commonly represented as generator of power by medieval and early modern artistic renderings of Satanic, witchcraft, and other "occult" activities . . . and there are countless examples of horns as magical objects in the ethnographic literature.

In a contribution to the 2011 IEMA conference on sacrifice I wrote of God's orders to Aaron about the construction of the horned altar, in Exodus 27 and 29 (Stevens 2011). Horns at the four corners of altars serve to concentrate power on the altar itself, where the material substance of the offering transmits its mystical essence to its spiritual target. Several examples of horned altars of varying size and purpose have been excavated in Israel, and recently a horned altar carved out of solid rock was discovered in the hills of Judea (Elitzur and Nir-Zevi 2004).

The shape of an active volcano changes, but its cone can often have a concave profile that resembles horns. This is evident in two sacred volcanoes, Mexico's Popocatepetl and Japan's Fujiyama, or Mount Fuji. For many years I have shown in my classes the film by Larry Gartenstein, with Orson Welles's great narration, *The Eleven Powers*, depicting the great once-in-a-century Eka Dasa Rudra in Bali, the festival celebrating the eleven major manifestations of Shiva. The great sacrifice, the culmination of the five to seven days of ritual activities, takes place at the central temple at Besakih, built on the lower slopes of the active volcano Gunung Agung, regarded as "the navel of the world." The sacred space, including the altar and other ritual areas, are at the top of a long flight of steps. The top of the staircase is framed by two structures called *candi bentar*, "split shrine." *Candi*, "shrine" or Buddhist stupa, is a common motif in Hindu/Buddhist architecture throughout Indonesia, and gates and passageways are frequently framed by *candi bentar*. These at Besakih strikingly resemble horns, and their alignment with the summit of the sacred mountain is stunningly reminiscent of Scully's interpretation of the Knossos horns. Figure 3.2 is a photo from promotional literature issued by the Balinese tourist company CV.Balinicho, found at balinicho.com.

Figure 3.2. Photo from promotional literature issued by the Balinese tourist company CV.Balinicho (balinicho.com).

The eager market for rhinoceros horn throughout eastern Asia indicates belief in the magical power of at least that type of horn; however, through perusal of prominent architectural studies (Beng 1999; Davison and Granquist 1999; Davison 2003; Dawson and Gillow 1994; Nas 2007) and the salient English-language ethnographic and ethnological literature, I have been unable to find any evidence of horn symbolism in Balinese or Indonesian cultural conception or architecture. Nevertheless, this coincidence is striking and worthy of further investigation.

Scholars for a long time have sought explanations for the universality and extraordinary power of religious beliefs, especially as manifested in various altered states of consciousness and sensory reactions such as the "religious thrill" studied by William James and the "mountain experiences" described by Edwin Bernbaum. Recent advances in neurobiology have produced a flurry of publications in recent decades on possible biological bases for religious beliefs—some titles are illustrative: *The God Gene: How Faith Is Hardwired into Our Genes* (Hamer 2004); *The "God" Part of the Brain* (Alper 2006); *Why God Won't Go Away: Brain Science and the Biology of Belief* (Newberg et al. 2001); *Fingerprints of God: What Science Is Learning about the Brain and Spiritual Experience* (Hagerty 2009); and more. So far, none have worked very well. I am ready to fall back on Pascal Boyer's theory of "the naturalness of religious ideas" (1994) and his later *Religion Explained: The Evolutionary Origins of Religious Thought* (2002). He concludes that religious explanations are logical human reactions to natural phenomena. And we must include mountains among them.

Acknowledgments

I thank Peter Biehl and Stephen Dyson for their invitation to participate in the 2017 IEMA conference, and I extend my congratulations to them on the tenth anniversary of this unique institution. Special thanks to Tamara Dixon for technical assistance with illustrations for both the conference presentation and this chapter, and to Jacob Brady for referring me to Dušan Borić's 2008 suggestions on a possible cosmological significance of household structures at Lepenski Vir.

References

Alper, M. 2006 *The "God" Part of the Brain: A Scientific Interpretation of Human Spirituality and God*. Sourcebooks, Naperville, IL.

Bassie-Sweet, K. 2008 *Maya Sacred Geography and the Creator Deities*. University of Oklahoma Press, Norman.

Beng, Tan Hock 1999 *Indonesian Accents: Architecture, Interior Design, Art*. Visual Reference Publications, New York.

Bernbaum, E. 1990 *Sacred Mountains of the World*. Sierra Club, San Francisco.

Bernbaum, E. 2006 Sacred Mountains: Themes and Teachings. *Mountain Research and Development* 26(4):304–309.

Besom, T. 2009 *Of Summits and Sacrifice: An Ethnohistoric Study of Inka Religious Practices*. University of Texas Press, Austin.

Borić, D. 2008 First Households and "House Societies" in European Prehistory. In *Prehistoric Europe: Theory and Practice*, edited by A. Jones, 109–142. Wiley-Blackwell, Malden, MA.

Boyer, P. 1994 *The Naturalness of Religious Ideas: A Cognitive Theory of Religion*. University of California Press, Berkeley.

Boyer, P. 2002 *Religion Explained: The Evolutionary Origins of Religious Thought*. Basic Books, New York.

Castro, V., and C. Aldunate 2003 Sacred Mountains in the Highlands of the South-Central Andes. *Mountain Research and Development* 23(1):73–79.

Davis, W. 2012 Sacred Geography. In *Ecopsychology: Science, Totems, and the Technological Species*, edited by P. H. Kahn Jr. and P. Hasbach, 285–308. MIT Press, Boston.

Davison, J. 2003 *Introduction to Balinese Architecture*. Periplus, Singapore. Distributed by Tuttle, North Clarendon, VT.

Davison, J., and N. Enu 2014 *Balinese Architecture*. Periplus, Hong Kong.

Davison, J., and B. Granquist 1999 *Balinese Architecture*. Periplus, Hong Kong.

Dawson, B., and J. Gillow 1994 *The Traditional Architecture of Indonesia*. Thames & Hudson, New York.

Dunstan, A. 2016 Toxic Desecration: Science and the Sacred in Navajo Environmentalism. PhD dissertation, Department of Anthropology, State University of New York at Buffalo.

Durkheim, E. 1915 *The Elementary Forms of the Religious Life*. Translated by J. W. Swain. George Allen & Unwin, New York.

Elitzur, Y., and D. Nir-Zevi 2004 Four-Horned Altar Discovered in Judean Hills. *Biblical Archaeology Review* (May–June):35–39.

Farmer, J. 2008 *On Zion's Mount: Mormons, Indians, and the American Landscape*. Harvard University Press, Cambridge.

Gartenstein, L., O. Welles, et al. 1979 *The Eleven Powers*. Film. Filmmakers Library, New York.

Hagerty, B. B. 2009 *Fingerprints of God: What Science Is Learning about the Brain and Spiritual Experience*. Riverhead Books, New York.

Hamer, D. 2004 *The God Gene: How Faith Is Hardwired into Our Genes*. Doubleday, New York.

Hamilton, L. S. 2015 When the Sacred Encounters Economic Development in Mountains. *The George Wright Forum* 32(2):132–140.

Hodder, I. (ed.) 2010 *Religion in the Emergence of Civilization: Çatalhöyük as a Case Study*. Cambridge University Press, New York.

James, H., III (ed.) 1969 [ca. 1910] *The Letters of William James*. 2 vols. Kraus, New York.

James, W. 1901–1902 *The Varieties of Religious Experience: A Study in Human Nature—Being the Gifford Lectures on Natural Religion Delivered at Edinburgh in 1901–1902*. Longmans, Green, London.

Kahn, P. H., Jr., and P. Hasbach (eds.) 2012 *Ecopsychology: Science, Totems, and the Technological Species*. MIT Press, Boston.

Kraft, S. E. 2010 The Making of a Sacred Mountain: Meanings of Nature and Sacredness in Sápmi and Northern Norway. *Religion* 40:53–61.

Lee, D. 1952 Religious Perspectives in Anthropology. In *Religious Perspectives in College Teaching*, edited by H. N. Fairchild, 338–359. Ronald Press, New York.

Levy-Bruhl, L. 1923 *Primitive Mentality*. Translated by L. A. Clare. George Allen & Unwin, London.

Marcus, C. C., and N. Sachs 2014 *Therapeutic Landscapes: An Evidence-Based Approach to Designing Healing Gardens and Restorative Outdoor Spaces*. Wiley, New York.

Meher-Homji, V. M. 2013 Sacred Mountains: Their Ecological Importance. *Current Science* 105(12):1655.

McKay, A. 2006 Kailas: The Making of a Sacred Mountain. *The Middle Way* 81(2):91–103.

Nas, P. J. M. 2007 Past in the Present: Architecture in Indonesia. KITLV Press, Leiden.

Neihardt, J. G. (ed.) 2008 [1932] *Black Elk Speaks: Being the Life Story of a Holy Man of the Oglala Sioux*. State University of New York Press, Albany.

Newberg, A., E. D'Aquili, and V. Rause 2001 *Why God Won't Go Away: Brain Science and the Biology of Belief*. Ballantine Books, New York.

Pickett, E. 1971 The Animal Horn in African Art. *African Arts* 4(4):47–53, 80.

Piff, P. K., P. Dietze, M. Feinberg, D. Stancato, and D. Keltner 2015 Awe, the Small Self, and Prosocial Behavior. *Journal of Personality and Social Psychology* 108(6):833–899.

Potts, D. T. 1990 Some Horned Buildings in Iran, Mesopotamia, and Arabia. *Revue d'assyriologie et d'archeologie orientale* 84:33–40.

Raglan, Lord [F. R. Somerset] 1934 The Hero of Tradition. *Folklore* 45:212–231.

Reinhard, J., and M. Costanza Ceruti 2010 *Inca Rituals and Sacred Mountains: A Study of the World's Highest Archaeological Sites*. Cotsen Institute of Archaeology Press, Los Angeles.

Scully, V. 1962 [1969] *The Earth, the Temple, and the Gods: Greek Sacred Architecture*. Rev. ed. Trinity University Press, San Antonio.

Scully, V. 1964 Letter. *Art Bulletin* 46(1):119–120.

Smith, D. B. 2010 Is There an Ecological Unconscious? *New York Times Magazine*, January 31, 36ff.

Stevens, P., Jr. 1973 Makwada: The Deification of a Bata Culture Hero. Paper presented to the Northeastern Anthropological Association, Burlington, VT, April.

Stevens, P., Jr. 2006 Magic. *Encyclopedia of Anthropology*, edited by H. J. Birx, 1512–1518. Sage, Thousand Oaks, CA.

Stevens, P., Jr. 2010 Letter: Is There an Ecological Unconscious? *New York Times Magazine*, February 20, 10.

Stevens, P., Jr. 2011 Anthropology and Sacrifice. In *Diversity of Sacrifice: Form and Function of Sacrificial Practices in the Ancient World and Beyond*, proceedings of 2011 Conference of the Institute for European and Mediterranean Archaeology (IEMA), edited by Carrie Murray, 15–29. State University of New York Press, Albany.

Sylvia, P. J., K. Fayn, E. Nusbaum, and R. E. Beaty 2015 Openness to Experience and Awe in Response to Nature and Music: Personality and Profound Aesthetic Experiences. *Psychology of Aesthetics, Creativity, and the Arts* 9(4):376–384.

Tan, H. B. 1999 *Indonesian Accents: Architecture, Interior Design, Art*. Visual Reference, New York.

Thompson, H. A. 1963 Letter. *Art Bulletin* 45(3):277–280.

Toohey, J. L. 2013 Feeding the Mountains: Sacred Landscapes, Mountain Worship, and Sacrifice in the Maya and Inca Worlds. *Reviews in Anthropology* 42:161–178.

Ulrich, R. S. 1984 View from a Window May Influence Recovery from Surgery. *Science* 224:420–423.

Wallace, A. F. C. 1966 *Religion: An Anthropological View*. Random House, New York.

Waters, F. 1982 Symbols and Sacred Mountains: Comparable Themes in Buddhism and American Indian Religion. *Phoenix Journal of Transpersonal Anthropology* 6(1–2):59–75.

Wilson, E. O. 1984 *Biophilia*. Harvard University Press, Cambridge.

Zhang, J. W., P. K. Piff, R. Iyer, S. Koleva, and D. Keltner 2014 An Occasion for Unselfing: Beautiful Nature Leads to Prosociality. *Journal of Environmental Psychology* 37:61–72.

CHAPTER FOUR

An Integrated Approach to the Archaeology of a Sacred Mountain

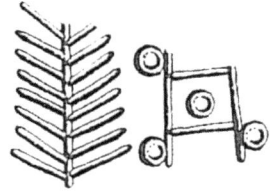

Sacred Geography, Mobile Pastoralism, and Longue Durée in the Mongolian Altai Mountains

Cecilia Dal Zovo

Abstract *This chapter offers an overview of the archaeological landscape of the Gobi-Altai Mountains and the main results of the research project Archaeology of a Sacred Mountain, which focuses on the natural and cultural heritage of the Ikh Bogd Uul (3,957 m), Bayankhongor Aimag, Mongolia. The local pastoral landscape is explored in relation to late prehistoric funerary monuments and layered sacred geographies, from a long-term perspective. In this context, both pastoral cyclicity and rituality appear tightly interwoven. They apparently permeate the social, ritual, and economic space, as they also shape the human relationship with the animals, and the "animated" high-mountain environment. In this frame, the local landscape is thus interpreted as part of a persistent and articulated interaction. The inclusion of traditional cosmologies and local ecology into the archaeological analysis demonstrates the significance of integrated strategies applied to the archaeology of upland regions and mountain landscapes in Eurasia as elsewhere.*

INTRODUCTION

The cultural and physiographic framework of the Archaeology of a Sacred Mountain project, which started in 2009, is the semi-arid and high-mountain landscape of Ikh Bogd Uul Mountain (3,957 m), in the province of Bayankhongor *aimag*, in South Mongolia. The mountain gave the name to the research project, as the local toponym Ikh Bogd Uul could be translated directly from *khalkha* Mongolian as "the great sacred mountain." Ikh Bogd Uul Mountain—alternately, IBU Mountain—forms a clearly identifiable profile in the range of the Eastern Altai Mountains, which then merge into the rocky Gobi Desert and the arid steppes of the Valley of Lakes (Cemark et al., 2005:255). This arid steppe region is interspersed with paleo-lakes and saltpans such as the Orog Lake. The research area thus comprises the entire IBU Mountain and the Orog Lake, covering more than 6,500 sq km (Figures 4.1 and 4.2).

In 2002, an international joint initiative, promoted by the Institute of Applied Geology of the Italian National Research Council (Irpi-CNR Padova) and the Institute of Archaeology of the Mongolian Academy of Sciences (MAS), launched a broad program in the area. Headquarters were established at Bogd *sum* village, in order to develop regular geological and archaeological research, combined with social actions of cooperation with the local communities (Fuggetta, 2006; Günchinsüren et al. 2006; Marcolongo et al., 2002 and 2005). The Archaeology of a Sacred Mountain fieldwork (2006–2011) has been integrated into the frame of this research and cooperation program.

An Integrated Archaeological Research: Sacred Mountains and Local Communities

Mountains at the Center: A Eurasian Perspective

In Mongolia, mountains are central features of the local landscape, as well as of the individual, social, and religious experience (Davaa Ochir 2008; Lindhal 2010; Pedersen 2006;

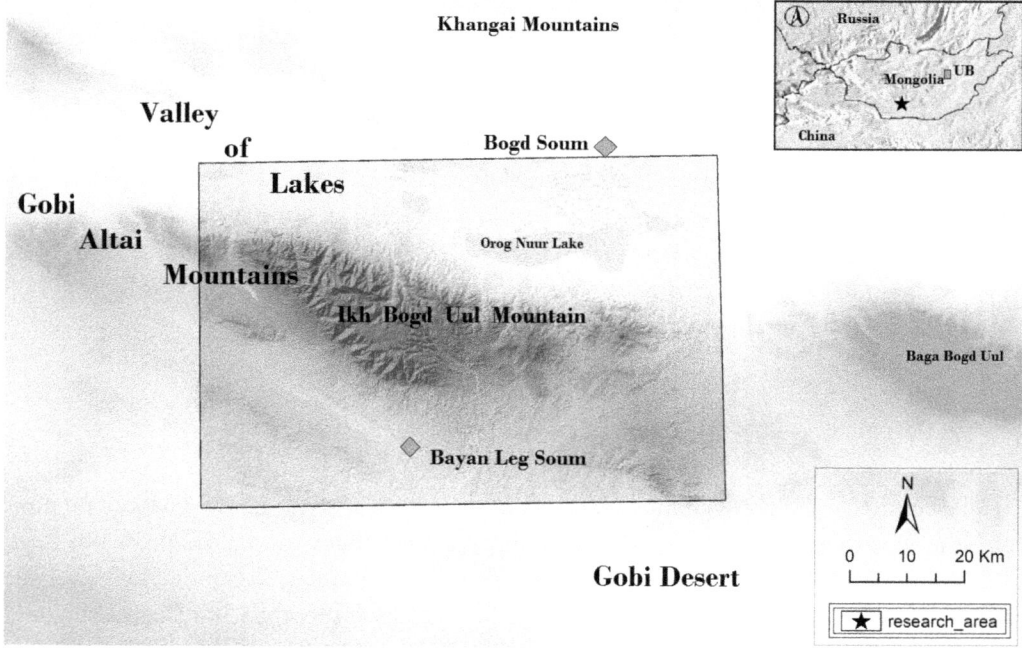

Figure 4.1. Research area, place names, and geographic terms mentioned in the text.

Wallace 2015). Likewise, Ikh Bogd Uul has been identified as the pivoting element of the Archaeology of a Sacred Mountain project (Figure 4.2). Moreover, high-mountain landscapes and uplands belong to the everyday experience of the herders, today as in the past. They attract human agency for economic and pastoral purposes, while shaping, at the same time, the local visual and symbolical perception. In this sense, they equally interweave the multiform evidence of pastoral and sacred geographies, as attested also in neighboring regions of Central Eurasia (Bellezza 2005; Bernbaum 2016; Blondeau and Steinkellner 1996; Bonnefoy and Doniger 1993; Debreczeny 2011; Hori 1966; Huber 1999; Roux 1963). McKay (2015:25) has convincingly argued that the sacred mountains of the Sino-Tibetan-Himalayan region can be understood within a unique, broad Pan-Asian tradition. This phenomenological category can thus be extended to Ikh Bogd Uul and, perhaps, the whole area of the Altai Mountains, currently distributed between the modern borders of Mongolia, Russia, China, and Kazakhstan. The Ikh Bogd Uul and the Altai Mountains, nonetheless, could be also analyzed in the frame of a broad Eurasian horizon that may contribute toward a comparative discussion on sacred mountains, pastoral landscapes, and heritage in a wider geographic and cultural milieu (Kohl 2006; Kuzmina 2008; see also chapters by Criado-Boado, Georgiadis, and Stevens in this volume). By this Eurasian setting, I refer to the dynamic phenomenon of linguistic, genetic, economic, stylistic, symbolical, and technological interconnections, which intensified as early as the second millennium BC, if not before (Anthony 2007; Doumani et al. 2015; Frachetti 2014; Haak et al. 2015; Hanks and

Figure 4.2. The flat summit of IBU Mountain and Orog Nuur Lake viewed from the north, on the paleo-terraces of Tuyn Gol River south of Bogd Village.

Linduff 2009; Kristiansen and Larsson 2005; Pokutta et al. 2019; Lee 2013; O'Sullivan and Hommel 2020; Sánchez-Mázas et al. 2008; Spengler et al. 2014; Tumen 2011; Taylor et al. 2020; Zhou et al. 2020). Here, I explore three aspects of the sacred and pastoral mountain geographies of Mongolia, and, in particular, of IBU Mountain, which can be significant from a comprehensive and comparative Eurasian perspective: sacralization and monumentalization of the mountain landscape, pastoral mobility, and longue durée.

Sacralization, Ecology, Heritage

The sacred mountains of Mongolia are traditionally encompassed within an animated cosmology and a balanced ecology that are the cornerstones of the multifaceted relationship between the local communities, the surrounding landscape, and the ancestral or spiritual forces that are believed to govern or inhabit it (Buyandelger 2013; Dal Zovo 2019; Halemba 2006; Kristensen 2004; Lindskog 2019; Pedersen 2007; Pegg and Yamaeva 2012; Watters 2021). It is worth noting, in this regard, that Mongolia has a long-lasting tradition of granting legal protection to outstanding mountain landscapes, which is historically documented since the thirteenth century AD (Chimedsengee et al. 2009). Mountains, together with certain summits, mountain passes, rivers, springs, and water surfaces, appear actively incorporated also into Lamaist-Buddhist sacred geographies since the sixteenth century, as reflected in the mapping records of the time (Charleux 2021; Pratte 2021; Wallace 2015).

Interestingly, since 2008 IBU Mountain has been safeguarded through the declaration of a regional park that covers most of the mountain area (Figure 4.6). This was possible thanks to a participatory process that revealed the strong bond that the local communities of Bogd, Bayan Leg, and Bayan Gobi maintain with the mountain (Bedunah and Schmidt 2000; Fernandez-Gimenez 2000; Schmidt 2006). The genesis of Ikh Bogd Uul Regional Park is especially relevant in light of the increasing exploitation of Mongolian land and resources, which are currently endangered by mining activities and overgrazing for cashmere production (Batkhishig 2012; Günchinsüren et al. 2011; Rossabi 2005; Upton 2012). Ikh Bogd Uul Regional Park safeguards the local natural and cultural landscape, showing, at the same time, the binomial nature of the local ecology, which intertwines environmental and cultural preservation (Baird 2014; Humphrey et al. 1993; Watters 2021). Harmony with the surrounding world is, or at least used to be, an essential aspect of traditional pastoral ecology. Today, the local communities supervise access and exploitation of pasture reservoirs and water sources, balancing the alternation of seasonal shifts in the context of progressive aridification (Blanc et al. 2013; Murphy 2011).

Similarly, as regards cultural preservation, on IBU Mountain ancient remains and other materialities, such as abandoned pastoral campsites, are notably found undisturbed on the soil surface (Figures 4.3 and 4.5). Besides the low human impact in this high-mountain environment, this is probably the result of the traditional respect that local communities have for stone features, the environment, and the ancestral and spiritual agencies that animate it. In this frame, altering or polluting the land, and digging on it, or contaminating water sources, is considered a serious offense.

Figure 4.3. Abandoned winter pastoral campsite with corral for animals (*left*) next to late prehistoric funerary mound (*right*) and guide B.D.'s car as scale, in the inner mountain valley of Koshuun Ulzii, IBU Mountain.

This is probably why, on several occasions, local herders expressed their appreciation for the fact that the project Archaeology of a Sacred Mountain did not involve further excavations on IBU Mountain. Indeed, the project mainly applied noninvasive archaeological techniques, such as surveying, GPS positioning, photographic documentation, 3D photogrammetry, and archaeoastronomic measurements (Dal Zovo et al. 2014; Dal Zovo 2016; Dal Zovo and González García 2018), thus adapting the field research with ecological values, IBU practices, and worldviews of the present local communities.

Verticality, Sacred Geographies, and Funerary Monumentality in Mongolia

Sacred Mountains and Archaeology

In the Central Eurasian and Mongolian tradition, certain mountains are not only viewed as landmarks (Pedersen 2006) but also, and above all, as powerful entities per se, or, alternatively, sanctified by virtue of the mighty spirits that inhabit them (on this distinction, see for instance Bilegsaikhan 2017). The sacralization of Mongolian mountains is intrinsically connected with their exceptional spatial and physical dimensions, in particular, elevation and verticality. This seems to be equally inferable from other archaic Central Eurasian cosmologies (Baldick 2000; Blondeau and Steinkellner 1996; Debreczeny 2011; Hahn 1988; Heissig 1980; McKay 2015; Tucci 1980; Waida 1973; Wei B. 2014; Wei C. 2018). Nonetheless, analysis of the material and spatial dimension of rituality, such as that embedded in the articulation of sacred geography, can be challenging for archaeological analysis (Bertemes and Biehl 2001; Gosden 2020; Insoll 2004; Ingold 2012; Lyons and Casey 2016; Smith 1987). This is true not only from a theoretical perspective, but also in terms of methodology, when dealing with immaterial heritage and survey in high-altitude areas (Biagetti and Lugli 2016; Ceruti 2018). In this case, one could also wonder how the sacred quality of Mongolian mountains revealed by present ritual practices and other sources could be approached from an archaeological perspective.

Following the theoretical framework proposed by Moser and Feldman (2014), here I consider the sacred dimension of the IBU mountain landscape as the result of a reciprocal and persistent relationship between ritual and place, between the local cosmology and topography, rather than an a priori category. Accordingly, in the research area ancient sacred landscapes have been addressed through the analysis of both the localization of Bronze Age funerary mounds in the pastoral mountain landscape and their long-term influence in the local sacred geography (see Hazod 2016 for a Tibetan comparison).

Moreover, I considered other aspects, namely the local toponymy. It is worth noting that Ikh Bogd Uul can be directly translated as "great sacred mountain," or, alternatively, "mountain of the great saint" (Lessing et al. 1960). Interestingly, *bogd* is often interpreted as a Mongolian-Tibetan version of the name of Buddha, otherwise possibly related to the ancient Mongolian word *burkhan*, which probably designated a pre-Buddhist deity (Laufer 1916; Poppe 1956). Then, it seems safe to assume that the place name could be a first indication of the holiness locally attributed to the mountain and its central role in the sacred geography, which is consistent with the divine qualities persistently tied to Mongolian elevations over time (Davaa Ochir 2008:38).

Late Prehistoric Funerary Mounds and Ancestral Spirits: A Genealogy

The sacredness of Mongolian mountains is entailed within the idea of an animated landscape controlled by *genii loci* or master spirits of the place (*ezed*), who can dwell inside, over, or as identical to mountains, hills, and outstanding elevations (Bilegsaikhan 2017; Humphrey 1995. Similarly, in Old Turkic and early Mongolian sources, mountains often appear as deities themselves (Bawden 1994; Lindhal 2010; Marazzi 2005:6; Tatár 1996).

The ancestral and master spirits of the place are worshipped at *ov* sites (Figure 4.4) that are located in elevated and panoramic areas, or in correspondence with mountain passes, fords, and crossroads representing key features of the local pastoral and nomadic landscape (Davaa Ochir 2008; Huber 1999; Lindskog 2016).

An Integrated Approach to the Archaeology of a Sacred Mountain 57

Figure 4.4. Traditional Mongolian *ovoo* cairns on Zaisan Hill, at the foot of Bogd Khan Uul Mountain, a sacred elevation protected by official decree since 1783, south of Ulaanbaatar city center (Mongolia).

From an archaeological perspective, it is interesting to note that those conceptualizations could be rooted in many ancient pastoral practices and beliefs. In the IBU research area, I investigated the hypothesis that the cosmology relative to holy mountains, sacred places, and *ovoo* cairns could be related to the local late prehistoric funerary and ritual phenomenon of monumental stone mounds (Dal Zovo 2021). This correspondence was seminally introduced by the Mongolian linguist, historian, and anthropologist Rintchen (1959) and echoed in the work of the French historian Paul Roux (1963 and 1966).

One of the most relevant material aspects that could be used to support this reasoning is the architectonic, symbolic, and locational affinity that modern *ovoo*s often display with late prehistoric mounds. The origin and evolution of these cairns have been studied little in archaeology (Evans and Humphrey 2003; but see Coningham 2013 for the Himalayan and Gazizova 2021 for the Caspian area).

However, it seems quite suggestive that in the local folklore the genealogy of master spirits of the place is often associated with a funerary dimension, namely the dead and spirits of the ancestors (Davaa Ochir 2008). In several accounts, master spirits are also linked to ancient funerary mounds located in elevated places and mountain areas (Heissig 1980; Roux 1963).

In local folklore, it is equally possible to trace a recurrent relationship between ancestors, master spirits of the place, funerary areas, and outstanding natural features or critical resources of the local landscape, such as mountain passes, peaks, and high pastures, as well as springs, rivers, and lakes (Roux 1966). All these elements are encompassed in the powerful concept of *nutag*, the community or individual homeland (Baival and Fernández-Giménez 2012; Stolpe 2020), which is regulated according to precise ecological principles (Birtalan, 2012). It may therefore happen that a sunny mountain slope, intersected by a river or a stream, can not only represent a suitable pasture area but also an ideal funerary location, as recorded in present Eastern Mongolia (Ruhlmann 2009).

Late Prehistoric Mounds on IBU Mountain

With regard to ancient funerary places, the monumental late prehistoric mounds that are distributed across Western and Central Mongolia can be located on elevated summits and mountain slopes but also by riverbanks and mountain lakes, along seasonal streams of inner mountain valleys, or at their mouth (Allard and Erdenebaatar 2005; Honeychurch et al. 2007; Johannesson 2017; Ochir-Goryaeva 2017; Seitsonen et al. 2014; Wright 2007). Again, these localizations can be often shared with materialities that belong to later sacred geographies, such as *ovoo* cairns, Buddhist stupa altars, and modern or living pastoral paths and campsites (Figures 4.3 and 4.4).

On IBU Mountain, more than 1,100 late prehistoric mounds have been documented in the research area through fieldwork and analysis of satellite images (Dal Zovo et al. forthcoming). Their localization patterns and architectonic features can be broadly ascribed to the Mongolian Late Bronze and Iron Ages, which is to say the second half of the second millennium and the first millennium BC (Fitzhugh 2009; Littleton et al. 2012; Makarewicz et al. 2018; Taylor et al. 2019). Three radiocarbon datings relative to the large necropolis southwest of Orog Nuur Lake were made available after the excavation of correspondent burial mounds (Marcolongo 2005; Günchinsüren 2006). The time span indicated by the radiocarbon dating (1420–900 cal BC) fits nicely with the results of other recent excavations in the region of Eastern Altai and the Valley of Lakes (Miyamoto et al. 2017), as well as with the chronology of Mongolian late prehistory (Amartuvshiin et al. 2020; Günchinsüren 2017; Honeychurch 2015; Turbat et al. 2021; Wright 2021). The funerary and monumental phenomena of Mongolian mounds certainly diversified in the course of time, both in architectonic and spatial terms. On IBU Mountain, I documented outstanding individual mounds with large stone fences, also known as *khirigsuur*, especially in the high-pasture area of the mountain and on high hilltops, while large clusters of burials are located on lower slopes, at the mouth of large inner valleys, or in the open area between the mountain and Orog Nuur Lake (see Davis-Kimball 2000; Houle and Erdenebaatar 2009; Wright 2007 for comparison).

Localization and Symbolism of Mounds

This localization pattern seems particularly relevant in light of the symbolism of mound architecture. Their tumuli-form structure can symbolically allude to verticality and elevation (Ingold 2010), and, by extension, to the abstraction of mountains as pillars or *axis mundi*, which is particularly significant also in later Central Eurasian cosmologies (Baldick 2000; Coningham 2013; Hori 1966; Marazzi 2009; Windfuhr 2006). Indeed, mounds actively concurred in the development of long-term monumental landscapes of Mongolia (Wright 2017). In this frame, the "Altaic" cosmology that sees mountains and bodies of water as liminal and "connective" features, which can give access to the divine or upper world, or, alternatively, to the world of the dead (Rozwadowski 2001; Tatár 1996; Waida 1973) can be equally meaningful for a comprehensive understanding of the mound phenomenon.

Moreover, ancient mounds share with mountains two fundamental aspects, namely, persistence and massiveness (Ingold 2010). In this sense, they could be understood as durable monumental features attracting the visual perception and conveying a deep symbolism that could be diversely incorporated and reinterpreted in the cosmology, ritual, and material culture associated with the Mongolian landscape over time (Figures 4.5 and 4.6).

Figure 4.5. Mongolian Late Bronze Age *khirigsuur*: a round-fenced mound with deer stone stela on the top of Puntsag Ovoo Hill, overlooking a mountain pass in the high-pastures area of Ikh Bogd Uul.

Figure 4.6. Late prehistoric mound adapted as an *ovoo* at the entrance of Ikh Bogd Uul Regional Park (road sign in the background).

Pastoral Paths and Cyclicity

Pastoral and Ritual Mobility

In analyzing the stratification of cosmologies and funerary geographies in the Mongolian mountains, it is also imperative to consider that the sacred and transitional qualities attributed to mountains are profoundly connected with mobility and particularly ritual movement, such as pilgrimages as attested for several high-mountain regions in Central Eurasia and elsewhere (Bellezza 2005; Ceruti 2019; Charleux 2017; Eck 2012; Huber 1999; Kakalis and Goesch 2018; McKay 2015).

Here, I also explore another type of movement, that is, pastoral mobility, in light of its significant ritual character. In particular, I refer to the cyclical pastoral shifts that presently characterize the social, economic, and ecological experience of the local herders, as they probably did in the second and first millennium BC (Haruda 2018; Houle 2016; Ventresca Miller et al. 2020). In Mongolia, seasonal displacements are traditionally regulated in timing and access rights to allocated resources, such as high pastures or water sources (Erdenebaatar 2003; Devienne 2013; Fernandez-Gimenez and Batbuyant 2004; Finke 2004; Undargaa 2016). As a result, the periodic access to elevated pastures, mountain passes, and mountaintops is profoundly ritualized (Ahearn 2016; Aubin 2002; Shingiray

2016). Indeed, climbing to high-pasture areas for the summertime not only represents a seasonal shift that is necessary for the herders and their herds but also an allegorical change of state that carries complex symbolical and cosmological implications (Davaa Ochir 2008).

The study of pastoral mobility on IBU Mountain aimed at identifying how long-term cyclicity and seasonal shifts could materialize in the local landscape over time. This research question prompted a spatial analysis that innovatively takes IBU into account in terms of the pastoral paths that are presently in use and detectable both in the landscape and satellite images and compares them with the localization of late prehistoric mounds, among other spatial features (Dal Zovo et al. forthcoming).

Although the details cannot be examined here, a few observations that resulted from the spatial analysis can be of some interest to our discussion. In terms of present or modern pastoral mobility, the first aspect worth highlighting is that movement apparently takes place through specific and quite stable routes, which form a highly intertwined network.

The dirt paths connect all pastoral campsites between them and to the high-mountain area, in the lower arid steppe around Orog Nuur Lake, and the main routes crossing the region of the Gobi-Altai and the Valley of Lakes. Modeling on local physiography, they cut the southern and northern middle slope of IBU Mountain, while running parallel to seasonal streams in inner valleys (Figure 4.7).

Figure 4.7 View to the east from Tsagaan Övdög, with Orog Nuur and Valley of Lakes in the background. In the foreground, a late prehistoric mound and a track running along midway the northern slope of Ikh Bogd Uul, in a location also known as a former Chinese post station.

Furthermore, paths display a consistent spatial proximity to modern springs and wells mapped through 1949 historical cartography). This proximity of the mobility network to water sources has been consistently confirmed by anthropological analysis in other arid areas of Mongolia and the Gobi-Altai region (Blanc et al. 2013; Fernandez-Gimenez 1999; Meissner et al. 2004). Moreover, the pastoral network across IBU Mountain might be important not only at a local level but could also have innervated the long-distance routes, later known as Silk Roads, that interconnected Eurasia as early as the third/second millennium BC (Gorbunova 1993; Honeychurch 2014; Kuzmina 2008; Shelach-Lavi 2014; Spengler et al. 2014).

An Ancient Landscapes of Movement

Another significant element of the mobility network across IBU Mountain is its consistent contiguity to late prehistoric mounds and present pastoral paths on IBU Mountain. Truly, due to the extended ramification of the mobility network, ancient mounds could never be farther than 2 km from the present pastoral paths. However, the vast majority of mounds are placed within a distance of 250 m to any modern pastoral path, and never farther than 1 km. This spatial proximity, verified through spatial and statistical analysis, cannot be interpreted in strict causative terms. Nonetheless, it is useful to illuminate the twofold pastoral and sacred character associated with local mobility and embedded in the landscape of IBU Mountain. In this context, two considerations can be further suggested. First, it seems likely that the interaction in the landscape between funerary and ritual geographies and pastoral mobility has an ancient origin, which could be dated to, or connected with, practices and materialities that intensified since the second millennium BC. Secondly, it seems possible to trace long-term stability of the mobility network on and across IBU Mountain, at least until the generalization of motorized transportation in the second half of the twentieth century. This interpretation, far from supporting a view of passive immobility of the local landscape and societies, rather aims at recognizing the persistent aspect of certain spatial choices, on par with reiterative pastoral practices, in the economic, religious, and social spheres that materialize together on IBU Mountain.

Persistence and Longue Durée in the Domestic Pastoral Landscape

Pastoral Campsites on IBU Mountain

As I could verify for the connection between modern paths and ancient funerary places, here I would like to consider the persistence of local spatial choices in relation to pastoral campsites. In the archaeological landscape of IBU Mountain, cyclicity seems indeed to materialize also in the recurrent occupation of domestic places, particularly of winter campsites.

Thanks to the integration of the information obtained from fieldwork, historical cartography, and the analysis of satellite images, more than 1,300 modern pastoral campsites (either in use or abandoned) have been documented in the research area. From the material and architectonic point of view, they can be roughly classified as either winter or summer campsites, although there are also different residence sites for the intermediate seasons.

Winter campsites have stone fences in order to protect the herds from the freezing cold and wild animals during the winter nights and summer camps do not always have durable architectonic features; rather, they have been located by integrating the observation of satellite images with the information provided by local herders (see Figure 4.8).

Long-Term Occupation of Pastoral Campsites

On IBU Mountain, as elsewhere in the Mongolian countryside, winter campsites characteristically display deep layers of dung soil that is carefully maintained in order to provide insulation and protection to the herds during the harsh season (Kazato 2005; Vainshtein 1980). The chronological depth of the stratified deposits of dung in the corrals at winter campsites has not been archaeologically verified for the research area. Nevertheless, a long-

Figure 4.8 Baga Shiree: abandoned winter campsite with rock art carvings on IBU Mountain, with a herd of goats from a neighboring camp. View from the southwest, October 2010.

term occupation of domestic sites on IBU Mountain can be partially inferred from suitable comparisons in Mongolia or neighboring regions where horizontal or vertical accumulation of domestic activities have been confirmed by radiocarbon datings consistently spanning from the second millennium BC to modern times (Frachetti and Mar'yashev 2007; Gardner and Burentogtokh 2018).

In the IBU research area, moreover, I could often document Bronze and Iron Age rock art motifs at modern or present campsites, especially in the high-mountain zone and on the natural stone walls protecting winter campsites that are still in use, or only recently abandoned, as recorded elsewhere in Mongolia (Lugli 2008). It seems safe to assume, then, that the long-term occupation of pastoral winter sites, which entails practical and symbolic aspects that are deeply interconnected, could be often highly conservative.

Mongolian herders, in fact, tend to consider their winter residence the most important of the four seasonal camps in terms of association with the ancestral *nutag*, or homeland (Kazato 2005:243; Vainshtein 1980:83). There, at the end of January or in early February, they celebrate the Mongolian New Year, *Tsagaan Sar*, which is an important occasion to renew family links to the memory of ancestors, while performing traditional rituals (Bekbassar 2005; Lacaze 2006; Pegg and Yamaeva 2012). These ceremonies, together with the cyclical occupation of the campsites, can be interpreted as a process of renovating the ancestral connection with the land, thus contributing toward strengthening their family or social identity in connection with the local landscape (Ahearn 2016).

In this sense, the periodical rituals performed at campsites as well as at specific sacred places on IBU Mountain might have served to mark elements of power, identity, and memory of local communities over time. Likewise, the periodic returns to seasonal camps seem to encompass cosmological principles that are consistent with the long-term appropriation and vivification of the local sacred geography.

Final Remarks on Continuity and Change at Ritual and Pastoral Sites

As we have seen through the archaeological analysis of the IBU landscape, cyclicity appears to be an essential element in both the ritual and domestic spheres at pastoral campsites, as occurs in many other aspects of the Mongolian pastoral tradition (Baumann 2008). This analysis of cyclical pastoral practices and its connection with a calendric rituality can therefore contribute to identifying diverse and concurrent aspects of adaptations, modification, and accumulation of other ritual practices in the pastoral landscape and uplands of Mongolia.

This might be the case for the systematic incorporation, mentioned above, of ancient sacred and funerary geographies in the local Buddhist topography and cosmology in the Mongolian landscape (Heissig 1980; Humphrey 1995; Neumann Fridman 2004). In terms of material culture, this process can be compared with the reshaping of architectonic features of prehistoric mounds as "traditional" *ovoo* cairns (see Figures 4.5 and 4.6), along with the adaptation of ancient ritual practices performed at *ovoo* sites (Dal Zovo 2021; Wright 2007).

In the high pastures of IBU Mountain, the monumental Late Bronze Age *khirigsuur* mound at the top of Puntsag Ovoo Hill has been not only transformed into an *ovoo* cairn (see Figures 4.5 and 4.6), but it has also received a toponym inspired by the Buddhist-Tibetan epics of victorious monks fighting against evil spirits of the place (Bellezza 2005; Davaa Ochir 2008; Lide and Stuart 1992). Likewise, one of the most relevant *ovoo* cairns high on the mountain not only bears a Buddhist name, Gegenii Ovoo, but it also has an architectonic affinity with Buddhist stupa altars (Dal Zovo 2021). Likewise, modern or living pastoral campsites contain or are set right next to late prehistoric rock art engravings, which are often superimposed by later Buddhist motifs, dedications, and recent drawings (see O'Sullivan 2021 for comparison).

On a stone wall richly decorated with late prehistoric rock art at the winter campsite of Altan Shiree, I also documented a series of footprints that could be interpreted as a rare attestation of a Buddhist iconographic theme (Rozwadowski 2018). They are engraved on the northern stone wall of the pastoral campsites where B.D., an expert and respected local herder and my guide on the mountain, usually spends the winter with his family and herds. In other cases, such as at the rock art cluster of Khun Tolgoi, near Altan Shiree, I documented ancient zoomorphic engravings superimposed by Tibetan inscriptions. All these material elements can also be interpreted, in my view, as part of the multiform phenomenon of longue durée that likely shaped the sacred and pastoral landscape of IBU Mountain.

Conclusion

In this chapter, I tentatively define persistent features that characterized and stratified the sacred and pastoral landscape of IBU Mountain over time. Mongolia's archaeological mountain landscapes are not, however, fossil records that reached us intact and unmodified from the distant past. Rather, I suggest that they should be considered as complex palimpsests, which can be profitably analyzed in an interdisciplinary, integrated perspective and in the frame of a comparative Eurasian perspective. This requires taking into account local cosmologies and ecology, focusing on the local ethics associated with landscape and heritage. In this sense, I argue that anthropological and ethnographic sources are indispensable tools for understanding the Mongolian archaeological landscape.

As a result, we can observe how local pastoral mobility seems to interweave multiform interactions with the high-mountain landscape, which can be ascribed to diverse chronological contexts. Such interactions can also reverberate in the long-term making of spatial choices, cosmologies, and sacred geographies (see for comparison Ferguson et al. 2009; Snead et al. 2009). In this frame, mobility can be interpreted as an essential element of human interaction with the mountain. This "mobile" agency, based on cyclicity, proximity, and ecological balance, likely permeated the local landscape—the pastoral and sacred geographies, as well as cosmological projections and ecology—of the local communities over time. The seasonal movements to campsites and high-pasture areas seem to be deeply interwoven with the periodical rituality performed at certain sacred and funerary places of IBU

Mountain. Likewise, persistent spatial decisions, cyclically reiterated, might have diversely materialized and accumulated in the landscape.

In this sense, the shaping and reshaping of pastoral and sacred geographies in the region of Valley of Lakes and the Gobi-Altai Mountains may be, in my view, a fertile ground for looking for comparisons and correspondences in the upland areas of Eurasia and beyond (Ingold 2021; Jackson and Wright 2014). The long-term stratification of human activities, or longue durée, seems indeed to emerge as one of the most relevant features in the palimpsestic landscape of IBU Mountain. In this sense, I believe that a systematic analysis of long-term processes and an expanded focus on longue durée and its materialization in the high-mountain landscapes of Mongolia could contribute toward a holistic reflection on resilient pastoral and sacred geographies in upland regions.

Moreover, by approaching complex landscapes through an integrated and interdisciplinary analysis, it is possible to stimulate a broader and more creative dialogue on sacred mountains and local heritage (Criado-Boado 2014; Olsen 2012; Smith and Wobst 2005). In this frame, intersected narratives can be combined together as part of a physical and intellectual involvement with both the landscape and the people who inhabit it, or did so even in the distant past (Ingold 2012). In this way, the archaeological record and sacred and pastoral geographies of IBU Mountain can be ethically encompassed in the sensitive process that affects the social and collective creation of heritage, memory, and identity, both at a local and global level.

Acknowledgments

This contribution was realized thanks to the postdoctoral program GAIN-Xunta de Galicia 2017–2020 at the Institute of Heritage Sciences (Incipit-CSIC) of Santiago de Compostela, during an eighteen-month visiting period at the Institute of Turkic Studies, Freie Universität Berlin. It is based on research developed in the frame of a JAE-PreDoc fellowship from the Spanish National Research Council (CSIC). The fieldwork for the Archaeology of a Sacred Mountain project was carried out after the agreement between Incipit-CSIC and the Institute of Applied Geology of the Italian National Research Council (Irpi-CNR), with the financial support of the Spanish Institute of Cultural Heritage (IPCE) and the Spanish Ministry of Culture. All field research has been conducted after the agreement between Irpi-CNR and the Institute of Archaeology of the Mongolian Academy of Sciences, within the international program funded by the Italian Ministry of Foreign Affairs and Regione Veneto (Italy).
My gratitude goes to the director of the project, Bruno Marcolongo, and to Giovanna Fuggetta, coordinator of the cooperation activities. Special thanks are due to the Institute of Archaeology of the Mongolian Academy of Sciences, to the local administration of Bogd, as well as to the Fund for Empowerment of Rural Women (Ulaanbaatar), for their essential support in the logistic aspects of my fieldwork. I am also immensely thankful to B.D., local guide, herder, mountain expert, and companion in exploration on the mountain, and to Yolanda Seoane Veiga, who joined the fieldwork in 2011. Many thanks to César Parcero,

Alejandro Güimil, and César A. González-García for their invaluable assistance in spatial and statistical analysis. Finally, I would like to thank the editor of this volume, Arnau Garcia-Molsosa, and the IEMA Conference, for this opportunity to join a valuable discussion on high-mountain landscapes.

References

Ahearn, A. 2016 The Role of Kinship in Negotiating Territorial Rights: Exploring Claims for Winter Pasture Ownership in Mongolia. *Inner Asia* 18:245–264.

Allard F., and D. Erdenebaatar 2005 Khirigsuur, Ritual and Mobility in the Bronze Age of Mongolia. *Antiquity* 79:547–563.

Anthony, D. 2007 *The Horse, the Wheel, and Language: How Bronze Age Riders from the Eurasian Steppes Shaped the Modern World*. Princeton University Press, Princeton.

Amartuvshiin, Ch., and B. Batdalai B. (eds.) 2020 *Archaeologiin Mongoliin-2020 Erdem shinjilgeenii khurlyn emkhetgel* [Archaeology of Mongolia in 2020]. Mongolian Academy of Science and National University of Mongolia, Ulaanbaatar.

Aubin, F. 2002 Le déplacement absolu: le pastoralisme nomade des Mongols. In *Aller et venir: faits et perspectives*, 331–344. Université of Paris-Sorbonne, Paris.

Baird, M. 2014 Heritage, Human Rights, and Social Justice. *Heritage and Society* 7(2):139–155.

Baival, B., and M. Fernández-Giménez 2012 Meaningful Learning for Resilience-Building among Mongolian Pastoralists. *Nomadic People* 16(2):53–77.

Baldick, J. 2000 *Animal and Shaman: Ancient Religions of Central Asia*. I. B. Tauris, London.

Batkhishig, B. 2012 Community-Based Rangeland Management and Social Ecological Resilience of Rural Mongolian Communities. PhD dissertation, Colorado State University, Fort Collins.

Baumann, B. 2008 *Buddhist Mathematics according to the Anonymous Manual of Mongolian Astrology and Divination*. Brill, Leiden.

Bawden, C. 1994 *Confronting the Supernatural: Mongolian Traditional Ways and Means*. Harrassowitz, Wiesbaden.

Bedunah, D., and S. Schmidt 2000 Rangelands of Gobi Gurvan-Saikhan National Conservation Park, Mongolia. *Rangelands* 22(4):18–24.

Bekbassar, N. 2005 Astronomical Practices and Ritual Calendar of Euro-Asian Nomads. *Folklore* 31:101–120.

Bellezza, J. V. 2005 *Spirit-Mediums, Sacred Mountains, and Related Bon Textual Traditions in Upper Tibet: Calling Down the Gods*. Brill, Leiden.

Bernbaum, E. 2016 Sacred Mountains in Asia: Themes and Implications for Protected Areas. In *Asian Sacred Natural Sites*, edited by B. Verschuuren and N. Furuta, 52–62. Routledge, London.

Bertemes, F., and P. Biehl 2001 The Archaeology of Cult and Religion, an Introduction. In *The Archaeology of Cult and Religion*, edited by P. Biehl, F. Bertemes, and H. Meller, 11–24. Archaeolingua, Budapest.

Biagetti, S., and F. Lugli (eds.) 2016 *The Intangible Elements of Culture in Ethnoarchaeological Research*. Springer, New York.

Bilegsaikhan, T. 2017 Some Remarks on *Ovoo* Worship among the Dariganga Mongols. *Rocznick Orientalistyczny* 70(2):261–273.

Birtalan, Á. 2012 Sacral Communication of Darkhad Shamans: Some Aspects of Verbal Communication. *Acta Orientalia* 65(2):235–256.

Blanc, M., C. Oriol, and S. Devienne 2013 Un siècle d'évolution du système pastoral de la steppe désertique de Mongolie: diminution de la mobilité des troupeaux, dérégulation de l'accès aux parcours et crise de surpâturage. *Études Mongoles et Sibériennes, Centrasiatiques et Tibétaines* 43–44:https://doi.org/10.4000/emscat.2154.

Blondeau, A. M., and E. Steinkellner 1996 *Reflections of the Mountain: Essays on the History and Social Meaning of the Mountain Cult in Tibet and the Himalaya*. Österreichische Akademie der Wissenschaften Press, Wien.

Bonnefoy, Y., and W. Doniger 1993 *Asian Mythologies*. University of Chicago Press, Chicago.

Buyandelger, M. 2013 *Tragic Spirits: Shamanism, Memory, and Gender in Contemporary Mongolia*. University of Chicago Press, Chicago.

Cemark, J., L. Opgenoorth, G. Miehe 2005. Isolated Mountain Forests in Central Asian Deserts: A Case Study from the Govi-Altay, Mongolia. In *Mountain Ecosystems: Studies in Treeline Ecology*, edited by G. Broll and B. Keplin, 253–273. Springer, Berlin.

Ceruti, C. 2018 Inca Mountaintop Shrines and Glaciers in the High Andes. *Journal of Glacial Archaeology* 3:59–78, https://doi.org/10.1558/jga.34465.

Ceruti, M. C. 2019 Practical Spirituality and Journey with Sacred Mountains. In *Practical Spirituality and Human Development*, 495–509. Palgrave Macmillan, Singapore.

Charleux, I. 2017 Chinese, Tibetan and Mongol Buddhists on Mount Wutai (China) from the 18th to the 21st Century. In *Pilgrimage and Ambiguity: Sharing the Sacred*, edited by A. Hobart and T. Zarcone, 87–118. Sean Kingston, Herefordshire, UK.

Charleux, I. 2021 *Ovoo*s on Late Qing Dynasty Mongol Banner Maps (Late 19th-early 20th Centuries). *Études Mongoles et Sibériennes, Centrasiatiques et Tibétaines* 52:DOI: https://doi.org/10.4000/emscat.5237.

Chimedsengee, U., A. Cripps, V. Finlay, G. Verboom, V. M. Batchuluun, and V. D. L. Khunkhur 2009 *Mongolian Buddhists Protecting Nature: A Handbook on Faiths, Environment, and Development*. Alliance of Religions and Conservation, Ulaanbaatar.

Coningham, R., K. Acharya, and K. Strickland 2013 The Earliest Buddhist Shrine: Excavating the Birthplace of the Buddha, Lumbini (Nepal). *Antiquity* 87(338):1104–1123.

Criado-Boado, F. 2014 Archaeologies of Spaces: An Inquiry into Modes of Existence of XScapes. In *Paradigm Found: Archaeological Theory, Present Past and Future*, edited by Kristiansen K., L. Smejda, and J. Turek, 61–83. Oxbow Books, Oxford.

Dal Zovo, C. 2016 Archaeology of a Sacred Mountain: Mounds, Water, Mobility, and Cosmologies of Ikh Bogd Uul, Eastern Altai Mountains, Mongolia. PhD dissertation, University of Santiago de Compostela.

Dal Zovo, C. 2019 Sacred Mountains, Ancestors, and Power: Origin and Development of the Veneration of Burkhan Khaldun Mountain in the Mongol Empire. In *Nomadic Empires of Eurasia: Proceedings of the Fourth Congress of Medieval Archaeology of Eurasian Steppes (16–21 September 2019)*, edited by N. Kradin, 132–135. BSC SB RAS, Ulan-Ude.

Dal Zovo, C. 2021 *Ovoo* Cairns and Ancient Funerary Mounds: Piling Up a Monumental Tradition? *Études Mongoles et Sibériennes, Centrasiat et Tibétaines* 52: https://doi.org/10.4000/emscat.4925.

Dal Zovo, C., and A. C. González-García 2018 The "Path of the Spirits": A Preliminary Approach to a North-West/South-East Oriented Rows of Cairns in the Altai Mountains, Mongolia. *Mediterranean Archaeology and Archaeometry* 18(4):399–407.

Dal Zovo, C., A. C. González-García, and Y. Seoane-Veiga 2014 Orientation of Bronze Age Mounds in Mongolian Altai Mountains. *Mediterranean Archaeology and Archaeometry* 14(3):223–232.

Dal Zovo, C., C. Parcero-Oubiña, A. Guimila-Farina, and A. C. Gonzalez-Garcia Forthcoming Mapping Human Mobility and Analysing Spatial Memory: A Palimpsest Landscape in the Gobi-Altai Mountains.

Davaa Ochir, G. 2008 Oboo Worship: The Worship of Earth and Water Divinities in Mongolia. PhD dissertation, University of Oslo.

Davis-Kimball, J. 2000 The Beiram Mound: A Nomadic Cultic Site in the Altai Mountains (Western Mongolia). In *Kurgans, Ritual Sites and Settlements in Eurasian Bronze and Iron Age*, edited by J. Davis-Kimball, E. Murphy, L. Koryakova, and L. Yablonsky, 89–106. BAR International Series. Archaeopress, Oxford.

Debreczeny, K. 2011 Wutai Shan: Pilgrimage to the Five-Peaked Mountain. *Journal of the International Association of Tibetan Studies* 6:1–133.

Devienne, S. 2013 Régulation de l'accès aux parcours et évolution des systèmes pastoraux en Mongolie. *Études Mongoles et Sibériennes, Centrasiatiques et Tibétaines* 43–44: https://doi.org/10.4000/emscat.2104.

Doumani, P., M. Frachetti, R. Beardmore, T. Schmaus, R. Spengler, and A. Mar'yashev 2015 Burial Ritual, Agriculture, and Craft Production among Bronze Age Pastoralists at Tasbas (Kazakhstan). *Archaeological Research in Asia* 1–2:17–32.

Eck, D. 2012 *India: A Sacred Geography*. Harmony Books, New York.

Erdenebaatar, B. 2003 Mongolia Case Study I: Studied on Long-Distance Transhumant Grazing Systems in Uuvs and Khusvsgul *Aimags* of Mongolia. In *Transhumant Grazing Systems in Temperate Asia*, edited by J. Suttle and S. Reynolds, 31–53. FAO, Rome.

Evans, C., and C. Humphrey 2003 History, Timelessness and the Monumental: The Oboos of the Mergen Environs, Inner Mongolia. *Cambridge Archaeological Journal* 13(2):195–211.

Ferguson, T., L. Berlin, and L. Kuwanwisiwma 2009 Kukhepya: Searching for Hopi Trails. In *Landscapes of Movement: Trails, Paths, and Roads in an Anthropological Perspective*, edited by J. Snead, C. L. Erickson, and J. A. Darling, 20–41. University of Pennsylvania Museum of Archaeology and Anthropology, Philadelphia.

Fernandez-Gimenez, M. 1999 Sustaining the Steppes: A Geographical History of Pastoral Land Use in Mongolia. *Geographical Review* 89(3):315–342.

Fernandez-Gimenez, M. 2000 The Role of Mongolian Nomadic Pastoralists' Ecological Knowledge in Rangeland Management. *Ecological Applications* 10(5):1318–1326.

Fernandez-Gimenez, M., and B. Batbuyant 2004 Law and Disorder: Local Implementation of Mongolia's Land Law. *Development and Change* 35(1):141–165.

Finke, P. 2004 Le pastoralisme dans l'ouest de la Mongolie: contraintes, motivations et variations. *Cahiers d'Asie Centrale* 11(12):245–265.

Fitzhugh, W. 2009 The Mongolian Deer Stone–Khirigsuur Complex: Dating and Organization of a Late Bronze Age Menagerie. In *Current Archaeological Research in Mongolia*, edited by J. Bemmann, H. Parzinger, E. Pohl, and D. Tseveendorj, 183–199. Rheinische Friedrich-Wilhelms-Universität, Bonn.

Frachetti, M. 2015 Nomadic Mobility, Migration, and Environmental Pressure in Eurasian Prehistory. In *Mobility and Ancient Society in Asia and the Americas*, edited by M. Frachetti and R. Spengler, 7–16. Springer, New York.

Frachetti, M., and A. Mar'yashev 2007 Long-Term Occupation and Seasonal Settlement of Eastern Eurasian Pastoralists at Begash, Kazakhstan. *Journal of Field Archaeology* 32:221–242.

Fuggetta, G. 2006 *Studio di pre-fattibilità per un progetto di micro-credito per le donne indigenti del somon di Bogd (aimag Bayankhongor)*. CNR-Irpi Italian National Research Council, Institute of Applied Geology, Padova.

Gardner, W., and J. Burentogtokh 2018 Mobile Domiciles of the Eurasian Steppe: Archaeological Evidence of Possible Dwelling Space during the Early Iron Age. *Journal of Field Archaeology* 43(5):345–361, DOI:10.1080/00934690.2018.1475994.

Gazizova, V. 2021 Sacred Heights in the Topography of Flatlands: Ovaa Kurgans in the Kalmyk Buddhist Landscape. *Études mongoles et sibériennes, centrasiatiques et tibétaines* 52.

Gorbunova, N. 1993 Traditional Movements of Nomadic Pastoralists and the Role of Seasonal Migrations in the Formation of Ancient Trade Routes in Central Asia. *Silk Road Art and Archaeology* 3:1–10.

Gosden, C. 2020 *The History of Magic: From Alchemy to Witchcraft, from the Ice Age to the Present*. Penguin, United Kingdom.

Günchinsüren, B. 2017 The Archaeology of Mongolia's Early States. In *Handbook of East and Southeast Asian Archaeology*, edited by J. Habu et al., 707–732. Springer, New York.

Günchinsüren, B., J. Altschul, and J. Olsen (eds.) 2011 *Protecting the Past, Preserving the Present: Report on Phase One Activities of the Oyu Tolgoi Cultural Heritage Program Designed for Ömnögovi Aimag*. Sustainability East Asia LLC Report, Ulaanbaatar.

Günchinsüren, B., B. Marcolongo, D. Bazargur, and J. Gantulga 2006 *A Report of the Fieldwork Conducted by the Joint Italian-Mongolian Expedition "Gobi Geoarchaeology."* La Garangola, Padova-Ulaanbaatar.

Haak, W., I. Lazaridis, and N. Patterson, 2015 Massive Migration from the Steppe Was a Source for Indo-European Languages in Europe. *Nature* 522:207–211.

Hahn, T. 1988 The Standard Taoist Mountain and Related Features of Religious Geography. *Cahiers d'Extrême-Asie* 4:145–156.

Halemba, A. 2006 *The Telengits of Southern Siberia: Landscape, Religion, and Knowledge in Motion*. Routledge, London.

Hanks, B., and K. Linduff (eds.) 2009 *Social Complexity in Prehistoric Eurasia: Monuments, Metals, and Mobility*. Cambridge University Press, Cambridge.

Haruda, A. 2018 Regional Pastoral Practice in Central and Southeastern Kazakhstan in the Final Bronze Age (1300–900 BCE). *Archaeological Research in Asia* 15:146–156.

Hazod, G. 2016 Territory, Kinship and the Grave: On the Identification of the Elite Graves in the Burial Mound Landscape of Imperial Central Tibet. In *Tibetan Genealogies*, edited by G. Hazod and W. Shen, 1–79. Renmin University, Beijing.

Heissig, W. 1980 *The Religions of Mongolia*. Routledge and Kegan Paul, London.

Honeychurch, W. 2014 From Steppe Roads to Silk Roads: Inner Asian Nomads and Early Interregional Exchange. In *Nomads as Agents of Cultural Change: The Mongols and Their Eurasian Predecessors*, edited by R. Amitai, M. Biran, and A. A. Yang, 50–87. University of Hawaii Press, Honolulu.

Honeychurch, W. 2015 *Inner Asia and the Spatial Politics of the Empire: Archaeology, Mobility, and Culture Contact*. Springer, New York.

Honeychurch W., J. Wright, and C. Amartuvshin 2007 A Nested Approach to Survey in the Egiin Gol Valley, Mongolia. *Journal of Field Archaeology* 32(4):369–383.

Hori, I. 1966 Mountains and Their Importance for the Idea of the Other World in Japanese Folk Religion. *History of Religions* 6(1):1–23.

Houle J. L. 2016 Long-Term Occupation and Seasonal Mobility in Mongolia: A Comparative Analysis of Two Mobile Pastoralist Communities. In *Fitful Histories and Unruly Publics: Rethinking Temporality and Community in Eurasian Archaeology*, edited by K. O. Weber, E. Hite Emma, L. Khatchadourian, and A. Smith, 155–174. Brill, Leiden.

Houle, J. L., and D. Erdenebaatar 2009 Investigating Mobility, Territoriality, and Complexity in the Late Bronze Age. In *Current Archaeological Research in Mongolia*, edited by J. Bemmann, H. Parzinger, E. Pohl, and D. Tseveendorj, 117–134. Rheinische Friedrich-W-Universität, Bonn.

Huber, T. 1999 *The Cult of Pure Crystal Mountain: Popular Pilgrimage and Visionary Landscape in Southeast Tibet*. Oxford University Press, Oxford.

Humphrey, C. 1995 Chiefly and Shamanist Landscapes in Mongolia. In *The Anthropology of Landscapes: Perspectives on Place and Space*, edited by H. Hirsch and M. O'Hanlon, 135–162. Clarendon Press, Oxford.

Humphrey, C., M. Mongush, and B. Telengid 1993 Attitudes to Nature in Mongolia and Tuva: A Preliminary Report. *Nomadic Peoples* 33:51–61.

Ingold, T. 2010 The Round Mound Is Not a Monument. In *Round Mounds and Monumentality in the British Neolithic and Beyond*, edited by J. Leary, T. Darvill, and D. Field, 253–260. Oxbow Books, Oxford.

Ingold, T. 2012 No More Ancient, No More Human: The Future Past of Archaeology and Anthropology. In *Archaeology and Anthropology: Past, Present and Future*, edited by D. Shankland, 77–89. Berg, London.

Ingold, T. 2021 *Correspondences*. Polity Press, Cambridge.

Insoll, T. 2004 *Archaeology, Ritual, Religion*. Routledge, London.

Jackson, S. E., and J. Wright 2014. The Work of Monuments: Reflections on Spatial, Temporal and Social Orientations in Mongolia and the Maya Lowlands. *Cambridge Archaeological Journal* 24(1):117–140.

Johannesson, E. 2017 Echoes in Eternity: Social Memory and Mortuary Stone Monuments in Bronze-Iron Age Mongolia. In *Fitful Histories and Unruly Publics: Rethinking Temporality and Community in Eurasian Archaeology*, edited by K. O. Weber, E. Hite Emma, L. Khatchadourian, and A. Smith, 80–108. Brill, Leiden.

Kakalis, C., and E. Goetsch (eds.) 2018 *Mountains, Mobilities, and Movement*. Palgrave Macmillan, London.

Kazato, M. 2005 What Is *O'voljoo* for the Mongolian Herders? The Right to Land in Pastoral Regions in Post-Socialist Mongolia. In *Coexistence with Nature in a "Glocalizing" World*, edited by K. Hiramatsu, 240–246. Proceedings of Seventh Kyoto University International Symposium. Kyoto University.

Kohl, P. 2006 The Early Integration of Eurasian Steppe with the Ancient Near East: Movements and Transformations in the Caucasus and Central Asia. In *Beyond the Steppe and the Sown*, edited by D. Peterson, L. Popova, and A. Smith, 3–39. Brill, Leiden.

Kristensen, B. 2004 The Living Landscape of Knowledge: An Analysis of Shamanism among the Duha Tuvinians of Northern Mongolia. PhD dissertation, Specialerække no. 317, Institut for Antropologi, University of Copenhagen.

Kristiansen, K., and B. Larsson 2005 *The Rise of Bronze Age Society: Travels, Transmissions and Transformations*. Cambridge University Press, Cambridge.

Kuzmina, E. 2008 *The Prehistory of Silk Road*. Edited by V. Mair. University of Pennsylvania Press, Philadelphia.

Lacaze, G. 2006 L'orientation dans les techniques du corps chez les Mongols. *Études Mongoles et Sibériennes, Centrasiatiques et Tibétaines* 36–37:163–205.

Laufer, B. 1916 Burkhan. *Journal of the American Oriental Society* 36:390–395.

Lee, C. 2013 The Population History of China and Mongolia from the Bronze Age to the Medieval Period. In *Bioarchaeology of East Asia: Movement, Contact, Health*, edited by C. Pechenkina and M. Oxenham, 61–84. University Press of Florida, Gainesville.

Lessing, F. (ed.) 1960 *Mongolian-English Dictionary*. University of California Press, Berkeley.

Lide, F., and K. Stuart 1992 Folklore concerning Tsong-kha-pa. *Asian Folklore Studies* 51(2):219–242.

Lindhal, J. 2010 The Ritual Veneration of Mongolia's Mountains. In *Tibetan Ritual*, edited by J. I. Cabezon, 225–248. Oxford University Press, New York.

Lindskog, B. 2016 Ritual Offerings to *Ovoo*s among Nomadic Halh Herders of West-Central Mongolia. *Études Mongoles et Sibériennes, Centrasiatiques et Tibétaines* 47: https://doi.org/10.4000/emscat.2740.

Lindskog, B. 2019 Managing Uncertainty, Beckoning Security: Ritual Offerings to a Local *Ovoo* in Mongolia. *Ethnos*, DOI:10.1080/00141844.2019.1699143.

Littleton, J., B. Floyd, B. Frohlich, M. Dickson, T. Amgalangtogs, S. Karstens, and K. Pearlstein 2012 Taphonomic Analysis of Bronze Age Burials in Mongolian *Khirigsuurs*. *Journal of Archaeological Science* 39:3361–3370.

Lyons, D., and J. Casey 2016 It's a Material World: The Critical and On-Going Value of Ethnoarchaeology in Understanding Variation, Change and Materiality. *World Archaeology* 48(5):609–627, DOI:10.1080/00438243.2016.1214619.

Lugli, F. 2008 Gli accampamenti invernali e primaverili dei nomadi dell'Arkhangai e dell'Ovorkhangai settentrionale. In *Charcoals from the Past: Cultural and Palaeoenvironmental Implications*, edited by G. Fiorentino and D. Magri, 159–166. BAR. Archaeopress, Oxford.

Makarewicz, C., C. Winter-Schuh, H. Byerly, and J. L. Houle 2018 Isotopic Evidence for Ceremonial Provisioning of Late Bronze Age *Khirigsuurs* with Horses from Diverse Geographic Locales. *Quaternary International* 476:10.1016/j.quaint.2018.02.030.

Marazzi, U. 2005 *From the Literary Heritage of Turkic South Siberia: Šor Folkloric and Shamanic Texts*, Annali 65(95). Università L'Orientale, Naples.

Marazzi, U. 2009 [1984] *Testi dello sciamensimo siberiano e centro-asiatico*. UTET, Turin.

Marcolongo, B. 2002. *The Gobi Joint Project 2002 CNR-MAS*. Istituto Ricerca e Protezione Idrogeologica, CNR, Padova. http://www.arch3.eu/siti/mongolia/pages/spedizioni2002.html.

Marcolongo, B. 2005 *General Report of the Fieldwork Conducted by the Joint Italian-Mongolian CNR-MAS Expedition "Gobi Altayn Geoarchaeology."* La Garangola, Padova.

McKay, A. 2015 *Kailas Histories: Renunciate Traditions and the Construction of Himalayan Sacred Geography*. Brill, Leiden.

Meissner, B., D. Wyss, and S. Ohem 2004 GIS-Based Mapping and Evaluation of the Current Socioeconomic Situation of Pastoralism in Bulgan Somon. *Arid Ecosystems* 10:118–112.

Miyamoto, K., T. Adachi, T. Amgalantgus, B. Natsag, L. Delgermaa, K. Funahashi, . . . and S. Yonemoto 2017 Excavations at Bor Ovoo and Khyar Kharaach Sites: The Second Report on Joint Mongolian-Japanese Excavations in Outer Mongolia.

Moser, C., and C. Feldman 2014 *Locating the Sacred: Theoretical Approaches to the Emplacement of Religion*. Oxbow Books, Cambridge.

Murphy, D. 2011 Going on Otor: Disaster, Mobility, and the Political Ecology of Vulnerability in Uguumur, Mongolia. PhD dissertation, University of Kentucky, Lexington.

Neumann Fridman, E. J. 2004 *Sacred Geography: Shamanism among the Buddhist Peoples of Russia*. Akadémiai Kiado, Budapest.

Ochir-Goryaeva, M. 2017 The Peculiarities of the Geographical Distribution of the Pazyryk Kurgans. *Ancient Civilizations from Scythia to Siberia* 23(2):329–354. Brill, https://doi.org/10.1163/15700577-12341320.

Olsen, B. 2012 Symmetrical Archaeology. In *Archaeological Theory Today*, edited by I. Hodder, 208–227. Polity Press, Cambridge.

O'Sullivan, R. 2021 Replication in Rock Art Past and Present: A Case Study of Bronze and Iron Age Rock Art in the Altai, Eastern Eurasia. *Journal of Archaeological Method and Theory* 28:387–412, https://doi.org/10.1007/s10816-020-09460-z.

O'Sullivan, R., and P. Hommel 2020 Fantastic Beasts and Where to Find Them: Composite Animals in the Context of Eurasian Early Iron Age Art. In *Art in the Eurasian Iron Age: Context, Connections and Scale*, edited by Peter Hommel, Courtney Nimura, Helen Chittock, and Chris Gosden, 53–70. Oxbow Books, https://doi.org/10.2307/j.ctv13gvh20.9.

Pedersen, M. 2006 Where Is the Centre? The Spatial Distribution of Power in Post-Social Rural Mongolia. In *Mongols from Country to City: Floating Boundaries, Pastoralism, and City Life in the Mongol Lands*, edited by O. Brunn and L. Narangoa, 82–105. NIAS Press, Copenhagen.

Pedersen, M. 2007 Tame from Within: Landscapes of Religious Imagination among the Darhads of Northern Mongolia. In *The Mongolia-Tibet Interface: Opening New Research Terrains in Inner Asia*, edited by U. Bulag and H. Diemberger, 175–196. Brill, Leiden.

Pegg, C., and E. Yamaeva 2012 Sensing "Place": Performance, Oral Tradition, and Improvisation in the Hidden Temples of Mountain Altai. *Oral Tradition* 27(2):291–398.

Pokutta, D. A., A. P. Borodovskiy, Ł. Oleszczak, P. Tóth, & K. Lidén 2019 Mobility of Nomads in Central Asia: Chronology and 87Sr/86Sr Isotope Evidence from the Pazyryk Barrows of Northern Altai, Russia. *Journal of Archaeological Science: Reports* 27:101897.

Poppe, N. 1956 On Some Geographic Names in the Jāmi' al-Tawārīx. *Harvard Journal of Asiatic Studies* 19(1/2):33–41.

Pratte, A. S. 2021 Mapping the Steppe: The Politics of Cartography in Qing Mongolia, 1780–1911. PhD dissertation, Harvard University Graduate School of Arts and Sciences, Cambridge.

Rintchen, B. 1959 *Les matériaux pour l'étude du chamanisme Mongol: sources littéraires*. Otto Harrassowitz, Wiesbaden.

Rossabi, M. 2005 *Modern Mongolia: From Khans to Commanders to Capitalists*. University of California Press, Berkeley.

Roux, J. P. 1963 *La mort chez les peuples Altaïques anciens et médiévaux d'après les documents écrits*. Librairie d'Amérique et d'Orient Adrien-Maisonneuve, Paris.

Roux, J. P. 1966 *Faune et flore sacrées dans les sociétés altaïques*. Librairie d'Amérique et d'Orient Adrien-Maisonneuve, Paris.

Rozwadowski, A. 2001 The Petroglyphs of Central Asia from the Viewpoint of the Indo-Iranian Hypothesis. *Indo-European Studies Bulletin* 9(2):9–19.

Rozwadowski, A. 2018 Rock Art of Northern, Central, and Western Asia. In *The Oxford Handbook of the Archaeology and Anthropology of Rock Art*, edited by B. David and I. J. McNiven, 151–175. Oxford University Press, New York.

Ruhlmann, S. 2009 L'enterrement chez les Mongols contemporains: le cercueil, la tombe et la yourte miniature du mort. *Études Mongoles et Sibériennes, Centrasiatiques et Tibétaines* 40: https://doi.org/10.4000/emscat.1521.

Sánchez-Mázas, A., R. Blench, M.D. Ross, I. Peiros, and M. Lin (eds.) 2008 *Past Human Migrations in East Asia: Matching Archaeology, Linguistics, and Genetics*. Routledge, London.

Schmidt, S. 2006 Pastoral Community Organization, Livelihoods and Biodiversity Conservation in Mongolia's Southern Gobi Region. *USDA Proceedings, RMRS-P* 39:18–29.

Seitsonen, O., J-L Houle, and L. Broderick 2014 GIS Approaches to Past Mobility and Accessibility: An Example from the Bronze Age Khanuy Valley, Mongolia. In *Past Mobilities: Archaeological Approaches to Movement and Mobility*, edited by J. Leary, 79–111. Ashgate, UK.

Shelach-Lavi, G. 2014 Steppe Land Interactions and Their Effects on Chinese Cultures during the Second and Early First Millennia BCE. In *Nomads as Agents of Cultural Change: The Mongols and Their Eurasian Predecessors*, edited by R. Amitai, M. Biran, and A. Yang, 10–31. University of Hawai'i Press, Honolulu.

Shingiray, I. 2016 Paths, Pathos, and Portables: Nomadic Culture and Materiality of Movement in the Black Lands of Kalmykia. In *Fitful Histories and Unruly Publics: Rethinking Temporality and Community in Eurasian Archaeology*, edited by K. O. Weber, E. Hite Emma, L. Khatchadourian, and A. Smith, 108–152. Brill, Leiden.

Smith, C. and M. Wobst M. (eds.) 2005 *Indigenous Archaeologies: Decolonizing Theory and Practice*. Routledge, London.

Smith, J. 1987 *To Take Place: Towards Theory in Ritual*. University of Chicago Press, Chicago.

Snead, J., C. L. Erickson, and J. A. Darling 2009 Making of Human Space: Archaeology of Trails, Paths and Roads. In *Landscapes of Movement, Trails, Paths and Roads in an Anthropological Perspective*, edited by J. Snead, C. L. Erickson, and J. A. Darling, 1–19. University of Pennsylvania Museum of Archaeology and Anthropology, Philadelphia.

Spengler, R., M. Frachetti, P. Doumani, L. Rouse, B. Cerasetti, E. Bullion, and A. Mar'yashev 2014 Early Agriculture and Crop Transmission among Bronze Age Mobile Pastoralists of Central Eurasia. *Proceedings of the Royal British Society* 281(1783):20133382.

Stolpe, I. 2020 Nutag und mobilität: zur dynamisierung mongolischer heimatkonzepte. In *Heimat revisited: Kulturwissenschaftliche Perspektiven auf einen umstrittenen Begriff*, edited by D. Bönisch, J. Runia, and H. Zehschnetzler, 209–233. De Gruyter, Berlin.

Tatár, M. M. 1976 Two Mongol Texts concerning the Cult of the Mountains *Acta Orientalia Academiae Scientiarum Hungarie* 30(1):1–58.

Tatár, M. M. 1996 Mythology as an Areal Problem in the Altai-Sayan Area. In *Shamanism and Northern Ecology*, edited by J. Pentikainen, 267–278. De Gruyter, Berlin.

Taylor, W., S. Wilkin, J. Wright, M. Dee, M. Erdene, and J. Clark 2019 Radiocarbon Dating and Cultural Dynamics across Mongolia's Early Pastoral Transition. *PLoS ONE* 14(11):https://doi.org/10.1371/journal.pone.0224241.

Taylor, W. T., J. Clark, J. Bayarsaikhan, et al. 2020 Early Pastoral Economies and Herding Transitions in Eastern Eurasia. *Scientific Report* 10(1001): https://doi.org/10.1038/s41598-020-57735.

Tucci, G. 1980 *The Religions of Tibet*. Routledge and Kegan Paul, London.

Tumen, D. 2011 Anthropology of Archaeological Populations from Northeast Asia. *Journal of Archaeology of Dankook University* 11:23–50.

Turbat, Ts., J. Gantulga, N. Bayarkhuu, D. Batsukh, N. Turbayar, N. Erdene-Ochir, N. Batbold, and Ts. Tselkhagarav 2021 *Deer Stone Culture of Mongolia and Neighboring Regions*. Mongolian Academy of Sciences and National University of Mongolia, Ulaanbaatar.

Undargaa, S. 2016 *Pastoralism and Common Pool Resources: Rangeland Co-management, Property Rights, and Access in Mongolia*. Routledge, London.

Upton, C. 2012 Mining, Resistance and Pastoral Livelihoods in Contemporary Mongolia. In *Change in Democratic Mongolia: Social Relations, Health, Mobile Pastoralism, and Mining*, edited by J. Dierkes, 223–248. Brill, Leiden.

Vainshtein, S. 1980 *Nomads of South Siberia: The Pastoral Economies of Tuva*. Cambridge University Press, Cambridge.

Ventresca Miller, A. R., R. Spengler, A. Haruda, B. Miller, S. Wilkin, S. Robinson, . . . and N. Boivin 2020 Ecosystem Engineering among Ancient Pastoralists in Northern Central Asia. *Frontiers in Earth Science* 8:168.

Waida, M. 1973 Symbolism of "Descent" in Tibetan Sacred Kingship and Some East Asian Parallels. *Numen* 20(1):60–78.

Wallace, V. 2015 Buddhist Sacred Mountains, Auspicious Landscapes, and Their Agency. In *Buddhism in Mongolian History, Culture, and Society*, edited by V. Wallace, 221–242. Oxford University Press, Oxford.

Watters, R. 2021 The Middle of the Story: *Ovoo*s and the Ecological Imagination in Mongolian Conservation. *Études Mongoles et Sibériennes, Centrasiatiques et Tibétaines* 52: DOI:https://doi.org/10.4000/emscat.5194.

Wei B. 2018 The Sacred Imagination of Mountains and Its Spatial Influence in Early Medieval China: The Case of Mount Tiantai *Social Sciences in China* 39(1):132–164.

Wei C. 2014 *Building a Sacred Mountain: The Buddhist Architecture of China's Mount Wutai*. University of Washington Press, Seattle.

Windfuhr, G. 2006 The Stags of Filippovka: Mithraic Coding on the Southern Ural Steppe. In *The Golden Deer of Ancient Eurasia: Perspectives on the Steppe Nomads of Ancient World*, edited by J. Aruz, A. Farkas, and E. Valz Fino, 46–81. Metropolitan Museum of Art Symposia, New York.

Wright, J. 2007 Organizational Principles of Khirigsuur Monuments in the Lower Egiin Gol Valley, Mongolia. *Journal of Anthropological Archaeology* 26:350–365.

Wright, J. 2017 The Honest Labour of Stone Mounds: Monuments of Bronze and Iron Age Mongolia as Costly Signals. *World Archaeology* 49(4):547–567, DOI:10.1080/00438243.2017.1360791.

Wright, J. 2021 Prehistoric Mongolian Archaeology in the Early 21st Century: Developments in the Steppe and Beyond. *Journal of Archaeological Research* 29:431–479, https://doi.org/10.1007/s10814-020-09152-y.

Zhou, X., J. Yu, R. Spengler, H. Shen, K. Zhao, J. Ge, et al. 2020 5,200-Year-Old Cereal Grains from the Eastern Altai Mountains Redate the Trans-Eurasian Crop Exchange. *Nature Plants* 6:78–87, DOI:10.1038/s41477-019-0581-y.

CHAPTER FIVE

The Mountainscape of the Peak Sanctuary at Leska on Kythera

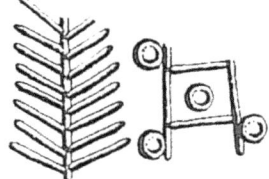

Mercourios Georgiadis

Abstract   *A new methodology regarding the research conducted on peak sanctuaries and more generally of sites within mountainscapes is proposed here. The peak sanctuary of Leska on Kythera is used as a case study, where different archaeological methods are applied and various research questions are addressed. It becomes apparent that the landscape plays a vital role for the understanding of the activities, practices, and beliefs that existed in this region. It is highlighted that the paths, which the pilgrims followed in order to access the extra-settlement sanctuary, had a special significance and that at least at times they played a dynamic role in the cult conducted at Leska. Furthermore, visibility as well as other senses were central for the symbolic importance and rituals performed at this site. The recovered finds and the absence of others provide a better image of the practices and their associated beliefs. The new methodological approach presented here illustrates new dimensions and the better appreciation of a sacred site as part of a complex and highly symbolic mountainscape setting.*

INTRODUCTION

Mountains, as with any other landscape, can have multiple meanings and roles in any society and culture. Sites of various character and a number of uses and resources are available in these contexts. The shapes, sizes, and topographies of mountains vary to a great degree, which affect the way they have been exploited. They can form boundaries as well as corridors of communications according to different cultural, temporal, and spatial variables. Frequently they are considered marginal areas due to the more dispersed, smaller in size, and in some cases seasonal character of habitation patterns. However, more often than not they represent regions of strategic importance, where various forms of interaction take place.

On mountains different taskscapes were performed, often simultaneously, and diverse exploitation strategies were followed. All of them depended on the mountainous landscape and the cultural characteristics of each period. However, they also have a symbolic role with local or super-local significance through associated mythological narratives and/or the presence of sacred sites. This study will focus on a specific sacred site, the peak sanctuary of Leska, which was located in a mountainscape. Peak sanctuaries consisted of a phenomenon that appeared during the second millennium BC on the island of Crete and elsewhere. Leska was part of a complex landscape where sites of various characters coexisted. In order to interpret such a complicated mountainscape a new methodological approach will be proposed. The research conducted in other peak sanctuaries so far can provide some useful analogies that can help in analysis of the landscape. Leska will consist of a specific case study, which will be seen within its contemporary and localized context. This site is a peak sanctuary that belongs to the MB III-LB I period in the Aegean chronology, that is, the eighteenth to the sixteenth centuries BC. It allows an early study of the sacralization process, its meaning, and the form it had in a mountainscape in this part of the world.

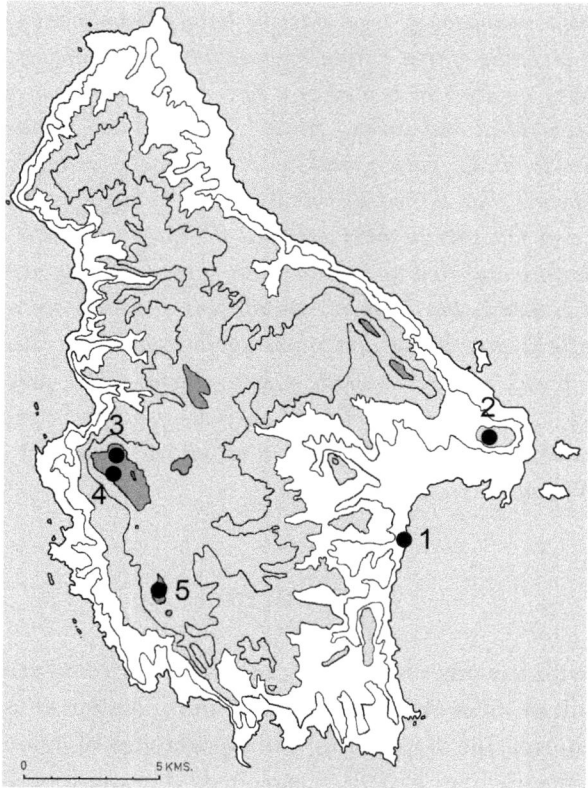

Figure 5.1. Sites discussed in text: 1: Kastri; 2: Ayios Yeoryios sto Vouno; 3: Leska peak; 4: Katafygadi cave; 5: Drymonas top (contours at 100 m). Adapted from Coldstream and Huxley 1972.

Already during the first half of the second millennium BC in the Aegean a formalization of the sacred can be observed. Specialized areas and buildings were reserved as sanctuaries within and outside the settlements, ritual activities can be identified, specialized symbols and objects related only with rituals have been recovered, and iconographic narratives with religious connotations have been recognized (Jones 1999; Kyriakidis 2005; Rutkowski 1971, 1986; Warren 1988). The lack of texts is a drawback, but apart from that a systematization and formalization of rituals can be seen during this period, arguing for the establishment of a religion with similar characteristics and shared rituals and beliefs across the Aegean. However, in these agropastoral communities religion, politics and society were closely integrated and interrelated to a degree that is difficult to separate (Younger and Rehak 2008:165). Close analogies and many similarities in the rituals, sacred expressions, and beliefs from the contemporary Near East and Egypt have also been noted, but still elements such as monumental-sized temples and statues of deities were lacking in the Aegean.

Peak Sanctuaries

Mountains were the earliest places where extra-settlement sanctuaries had been established in the Aegean Bronze Age (Rutkowski 1986). They already appeared on the island of Crete from the late third millennium BC onward (Branigan 1970:103; Peatfield 1987:90, 1992:125; Platon 1951:158; Rutkowski 1986:12, 94). There are mainly two forms of extra-settlement sanctuaries: peak sanctuaries and sacred caves. The origin of the first type may have been earlier (Manning 2008:109; Nowicki 1994:37, 40), but there is not enough evidence to support this. Peak sanctuaries appear to be earlier in date, while some of the sacred caves have been located within mountain areas. The first were founded before the establishment of the palaces on Crete, suggesting that they were not directly associated with them in their initial stages (Marinatos 1993:116; Nowicki 2007a:1–2). Their large numbers in the eastern part of the island contend that they served a population living in a dispersed settlement pattern in a hilly area (Jones 1999:29; Kyriakidis 2005:113–114; Manning 2008:109; Peatfield 1983:273, 1987:92, 1990:126; Rutkowski 1971:16–17, 1986:94). Only when the palaces reached the peak of their influence do they seem to have the extra-settlement sanctuaries under their control. One of the consequences of this was the decrease of the active peak sanctuaries, but the remaining ones had become larger in size, richer in deposited goods, often with buildings constructed in their space (Peatfield 1990:127; Platon 1951:120, 146, 158–159; Rutkowski 1986:79, 87, 1991:16, 20). The fall of the palaces marked the decline of peak sanctuaries on Crete from the LB II (fifteenth century BC) period onward.

An important issue in Aegean prehistory is the standardization that can be identified in these extra-settlement sanctuaries. They seem to have two categories of shared characteristics: their landscape elements and the material remains found in them. Peak sanctuaries were located on top of hills/mountains or alternatively on prominent slopes (Peatfield 1990:119, 1992:62–63, 2009:253; Rutkowski 1991:21). They were overlooking lowland areas, while at the same time they were clearly visible from the settlements (Kyriakidis 2005:51; Peatfield 1990:119, 1992:60, 2007:297, 2009:253; Sakellarakis 2011:10, 113, 123). In almost all cases there was intervisibility between peak sanctuaries, whose symbolic meaning is still unclear (Peatfield 1983:276, 1990:119, 1992:60, 2007:297, 2009:253). Their altitude varied from as low as 200 masl up to 1,500 m (Nowicki 2007a:5, 28; Peatfield 1983:274, 2007:297, 2009:253; Rutkowski 1971:15–16, 1986:73–74, 1991:13; Sakellarakis 2011:123), which means that they were founded on relatively low mountains when considering the topography of Crete, whose highest peaks reached 2,400 m above sea level. The low altitude of their location is also associated with their easy access from the lowland regions (Nowicki 2007a:24; Peatfield 1983:275, 1992:60, 2007:297, 2009:253; Rutkowski 1991:17). The material finds common in peak sanctuaries that have been recovered include figurines, ceramic and stone vessels, as well as other categories of objects.

There are about thirty sites that have been recognized as peak sanctuaries across Crete (Nowicki 2007a; Peatfield 1987). The standardization of the landscape and material elements discussed earlier have led some scholars to propose that peak sanctuaries shared the same cult. However, the study of these sites had been fragmentary and limited in character, while no peak sanctuaries on Crete had been properly published (Sakellarakis 2011:4–6). More thorough and systematic research has shown that there are many common elements, but there were also many differences, emphasizing the variability that existed between them (Jones 1999; Kyriakidis 2005).

The construction of buildings in peak sanctuaries have also been studied in relation to their control by the contemporary palatial centers on Crete (Peatfield 1990:127; Rutkowski 1971:18), and their orientation based on archaeoastronomic observations (Blomberg and Henriksson 2006; Henriksson and Blomberg 1996, 2011). Nevertheless, their results were limited and their meaning remains elusive. Another important research question in recent years has been related to the paths and routes that lead to these sites. A well-paved road connecting the palace of Knossos with the Juktas peak sanctuary has been identified (Karetsou 1981:151; Karetsou and Mathioudaki 2012:100–102). Another has been recognized at Traostalos in eastern Crete (Soar 2009:91–93), and a path in the central-west connected three peak sanctuaries and a sacred cave west of the Knossos area (Rethemiotakis 2009:189; Sakellarakis and Panagiotopoulos 2006:68). These examples underline the symbolic significance of pilgrimage in extra-settlement sanctuaries during the MB III–LB I period (eighteenth to sixteenth centuries BC) on Crete. It is also of particular interest that in specific mountainous landscapes there was a concentration of more than one cultic sites. At Juktas there were possibly three more sacred sites along with the peak sanctuary, while at Kofinas there was one more (Karetsou 1981:137–138; Nowicki 2007b:577). They suggest that, at least in certain examples, mountainscapes were complex sacred sites where various cultic activities were performed in close proximity to each other.

Another source of information has been the contemporary iconographic representation of mountainous landscapes and the sacred sites in them. The latter examples in particular provide an outlook of how they visualized, understood, and associated the specific mountainscapes with the divine. In a seal from Knossos a mountain is depicted within a sacred area on top of which a female holding a staff is shown in a clear reference to a goddess (Evans 1935:608, fig. 597:Ae). At the Zakros rhyton a shrine containing altars is shown on top of a mountain with limited vegetation, demarcated by horns of consecration, which comprise religious symbols (Platon 1968:170, 192–193). The scene is devoid of humans, but birds and wild goats are depicted, heraldically placed around the highest peak of the mountain, shown at the central upper part of the main section. The mountain peak in this scene is believed to be of high symbolic value, and its shape is found in the back of the seat of the throne in the Throne Room at the palace of Knossos (Marinatos 2010:67; Niemeier 1987:163, 165–166). This symbolic association, along with the orientation of the court of the Knossos palace toward the Juktas peak sanctuary, is believed to be of a high cultic significance. The sacredness of the mountain and its deity(ies) is visually connected with rituals and cultic performances taking place at the heart of the palace in a symbolic heterotopia. Thus, all activities were sanctified and protected by this intervisibility that was established between palace and peak sanctuary, and between the deity and the participants in the rituals.

Kythera and the Case Study of Leska

The Landscape Setting of Kythera

Kythera has been the only island in the Aegean, outside Crete, where the peak sanctuaries have been recovered with certainty (Figure 5.1). There have been other reports, but at Kythera Ayios Yeoryios sto Vouno peak sanctuary has been excavated and thoroughly published (Sakellarakis 1996, 2011, 2012, 2013a, 2013b).

Kythera is a medium-small island by Aegean standards (ca. 300 sq km), located 40 km northwest of the west end of Crete. It had already been affected by the Cretan culture from the mid-third millennium BC and followed the material fashion of the larger island in ceramics, stone, architecture, and burials until the mid-second millennium BC (Coldstream and Huxley 1972; Sakellarakis 1996, 2011). Kythera is a hilly island with a few coastal plains and low inland plateaus, and a few water resources in the form of springs and seasonal streams. It is a semi-arid place with low vegetation and some trees across the island. During the MB III-LB I phase (eighteenth to sixteenth centuries BC) it developed a settlement pattern unique to this island. A central port existed at Kastri in the central-east part of Kythera, while a concentration of sites were formed in close proximity around it. Beyond the Kastri region a dispersed settlement pattern of small sites in the size of one or two farmsteads was developed, often in distances of a few hundred meters between them (Bevan 2002; Bevan et al. 2002; Broodbank and Kyriatzi 2007).

The excavation at both the settlement of Kastri (Coldstream and Huxley 1972) and the peak sanctuary at Ayios Yeoryios sto Vouno (Sakellarakis 1996, 2011, 2012, 2013a, 2013b) have provided a good basis for understanding the peak sanctuary phenomenon beyond Crete. Ayios Yeoryios sto Vouno is located on the top of the second highest peak of the hill on a rather prominent position toward Kastri and the plain around it. It also played the role of a landmark for approaching ships and navigation, both in that period as well as in later times. It is within the altitude of the Cretan counterparts, while it allows for easy access from various sides. It also offers clear intervisibility with Kastri and all the settlements in the surrounding plain and a large part of central Kythera. The numerous finds recovered during excavation argues for prolonged use by a large congregation of people and rich finds deposited as offerings to the venerated deity(ies). The construction of terraces has been noted, suggesting that some form of building and space management had taken place at the site, possibly sponsored by the settlement residing at Kastri. The finds include an impressive number of small drinking cups, conical cups, and some cooking vessels. There were some figurines, among which the bronze ones stand out for their impressive numbers when compared with Cretan analogues (Sapouna-Sakellarakis 2012). Some stone vessels and their material signify the luxury character of these objects, while one has a Linear A inscription that is rather rare outside of Crete (Sakellarakis 1996). The bones are relatively limited in number, mainly representing the consumption of caprids at the site, while fired remains have been recovered at the site too (Sakellarakis 2011; Trantalidou 2013). Among the bone finds, the ones from chickens are of particular interest, since they belong almost certainly in MB III-LB I strata (Trantalidou 2013). They are limited in number, but a chicken was a rare animal at this time in the Aegean and it could have been considered a luxurious meat for sacrifice and consumption. The topographic characteristics and the material remains recovered at Ayios Yeoryios sto Vouno are compatible with the ones recognized at the peak sanctuaries on Crete so far, and scholars have agreed with this identification.

Leska is a new peak sanctuary identified more recently on the island (Figure 5.2), which is located in the central-eastern part of Kythera on Mount Mermigkari (Georgiadis

Figure 5.2. Leska top, view from east.

2012). The mountain is the highest and the largest in size on the island with three peaks, Mermigkari (509 masl), Leska (495 masl), and Katafygadi (467 masl). East of this mountain a lowland area with fertile plateaus and low slopes existed, while to the northeast of this area rich water resources were available. Prior to our research on this area two sites were known, a pithos burial in the southwestern slope and a stone vessel, possibly belonging to another burial, in the southeastern slope of the Mermigkari peak, and a cave close to the Katafygadi top (Petrocheilos 1984; Tsaravopoulos 2012). Both sites were within the MB III–LB I period, with the latter providing ceramic remains as well as human bones (Bartsiokas 1998:33, figs. 70–71; Petrocheilos 1984:63–64). There is an open question regarding the character of this cave, whether it was a burial site, perhaps an ossuary, or a cultic site related with the veneration of the dead. In both scenarios there is no direct analogy on Crete or another Aegean island from this period. Despite this uncertainty, it is clear that some kind of ritual activity was happening at this site, and it will be considered here as a ritual site.

The site of Leska was located by chance in the early 2000s, but no systematic study had taken place there. The knowledge of the settlement pattern at Kythera, the presence of the peak sanctuary at Ayios Yeoryios sto Vouno, and the presence of ritual-related sites on Mount Mermigkari formed the context in which Leska and the landscape of Mount Mermigkari were studied. A new methodological approach was designed bearing in mind the research conducted on peak sanctuaries in Crete and the questions that have arisen there. Thus, the research was designed to have three stages and involved three different methodological tools: an extensive survey, an intensive survey, and an excavation.

Extensive Survey

An extensive survey was selected in the broader area of Mount Mermigkari, aiming at understanding its complex landscape with all its characteristics. In that framework, the dramatic local topography would allow the recovery of the pathways that allowed access from the lowland to the upper part of this large and high mountain. This would permit us to trace the routes the pilgrims, pastoralists, and any other people may have followed while visiting the mountain during the MB III–LB I period. Due to the position of Mount Mermigkari at the western end of the island and the local topography, access from the mainland was possible from the eastern and southern lowland areas in relation to the mountain.

The extensive survey has demonstrated that the lower slopes of the mountain were occupied during the period under review. Small habitational remains appear to have existed in the eastern slopes of the Mermigkari peak. These small sites come into accordance with the finds of the dispersed settlement pattern of farmsteads described mainly in the central-eastern part of Kythera. They are also supported by their proximity to the burial sites that had already been known in this part of the mountain. Another similar single site of possible habitation has been located at the lower northern slopes of the Leska peak. Thus, it seems that the mountain was a site that had multiple uses and a diverse character, including habitation areas and a burial ground, and it also had a sacred character. Moreover, it could be expected that due to its size and relatively easy accessibility there was an extensive exploitation of the available land, which would be ideal for pastoral activities, especially during the warmer months of the year. Mount Mermigkari was a complex landscape for the local people of the MB III-LB I period associated with various activities and beliefs.

There have been three paths identified, leading from the lowland area to the upper part of the mountain, with the application of this research method. The first could be called the northern route, which included a path on the northern slopes of Leska peak that provided access to the inner plateau of the mountain formed by the three tops (Figure 5.3:A). In this case Leska was the first site of ritual character that one could visit, followed by the Katafygadi cave, and then to the south the burial sites in the Mermigkari peak could be visited. The second path provided access to the upper part of the mountain through the east side. Here there are two important variations in the route with one providing access from the northeast and another from the southeast. In the first variation the pilgrims would come from the northeastern rich area of the Mylopotamos lowland area, which possesses springs, a perennial stream, and a seasonal stream (Figure 5.3:B1). This path would gain access to the center of the three peaks through the crest formed between the Mermigkari and Leska tops. The second variation would be a route on the lower eastern slopes along the Mermigkari peak providing access to the sites there and meeting the last part of the first variation providing access to the central plateau (Figure 5.3:B2). In both cases Leska would be visible from a distance and closer to visit than Katafygadi cave. In the second variation some burial sites would have been more easily accessible to visit. The third route was possible from the south,

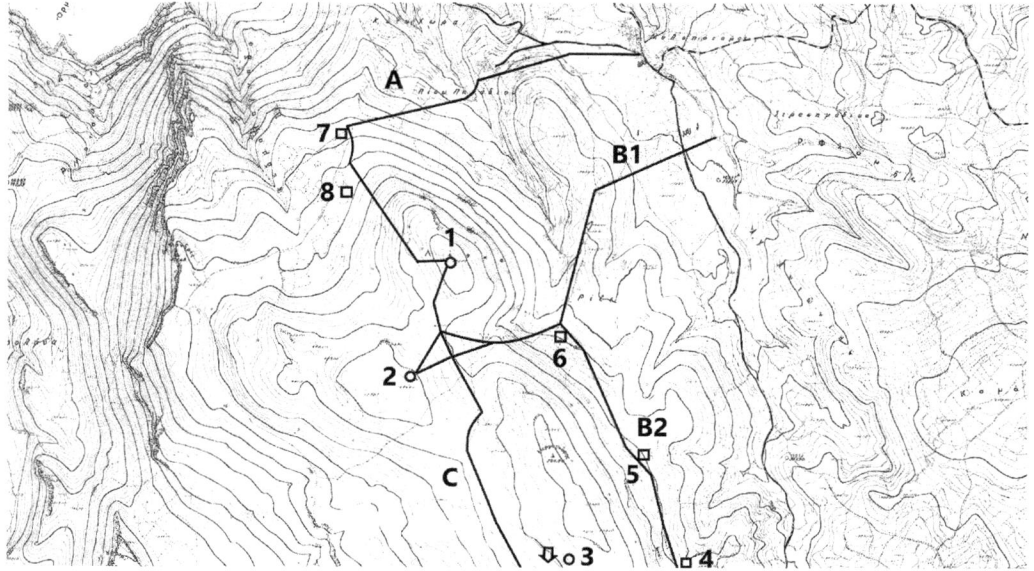

Figure 5.3. A: North Path; B1: Northeastern Path; B2: Southeastern Path; C: Southwestern Path; 1: Leska peak; 2: Katafygadi cave; 3: Lazarianika grave; 4: Merm.1; 5: Merm.2; 6: Merm.3; 7: Merm.4; 8: Merm.5 (HGMS, scale 1:5,000).

allowing access from the southern lowland area through the low slopes that existed in the southwestern part of the Mermigkari top (Figure 5.3:C). In this case the burial sites were the first location that could be visited, while access to the Katafygadi cave could be reached before the peak sanctuary on Leska. However, it is interesting to note that before getting access to the cave, which is visible only when someone is very close to it, this path provided clear visibility to the top of Leska.

People standing on the top could be seen at least 1 km away when approaching this site from the south. This provides an additional significance since pilgrims moving through the various paths could have visual contact with the peak and the performed rituals taking place there by the people that had already reached the specific sacred locale. In that way even the people moving into the landscape could participate in a distant way with the ceremonies of the sanctuary.

In the framework of this it was possible to interpret the small pebbles and unworked pieces of chert that were recovered in the area of the peak sanctuary as offerings. Similar examples have been reported in a few more cases of peak sanctuaries on Crete as well as on Ayios Yeoryios sto Vouno. Unclear or context-specific interpretations have been proposed for their presence at these sites, which in most cases remain unsatisfactory as explanations. At Leska top both items are geologically and topographically alien, which means that they were brought purposefully by human agents from another landscape setting. The pebbles proved to be from stream beds and not the coast, which is found east of Leska top through the pathways providing access from the east of the mountain, especially through the route of the first variation. The pieces of chert are part of the geological consistency exposed on the lower eastern slopes of Mermigkari top and through the second variation of the eastern pathway. Thus, it seems that pilgrims passing from these two distinct routes collected these pieces of stone and brought them to the sanctuary as part of a heterotopic meaning with a highly symbolic character. The interpretation that has been put forward links these objects symbolically with a request for rain (Georgiadis 2016).

Intensive Survey

The presence of pottery remains on top of Leska was known before the beginning of the current research. However, the upper part of the mountain consisted of a relatively large oblong plateau. In order to determine the area of focus for the specific fieldwork an intensive survey was conducted. The plateau was divided into 10 by 10 m tracts within which all surface remains were collected. There were twenty-four tracts overall, which established that there were two sites on the peak area of Leska.

The first was 20 m north/northwest of the highest point of the mountain, where sherds and tiles of the historic period were recovered. They seem to suggest the presence of a small structure, covered by black-glazed tiles, where black-glazed fine wares were deposited. They appear to belong to the Classical period and it may have been used until the Hellenistic period or later. Black-glazed tiles were commonly used in sanctuaries and public buildings rather than ordinary residences. Thus, their presence, along with the quality of the recovered ceramics and the location of this site on the top of the mountain argues more convincingly for the identification of a small shrine rather than a building related to pastoralism.

The second site was immediately south/southwest of the highest point at Leska. The core of this site was in an area 20 by 10 m while a high concentration existed around it in three more tracts (10 by 10 m). In this case, the ceramics represented the MBA and LBA of the island and belonged to an entirely different phase. The preference for the locale directly associated with the top of the mountain was intriguing, since it contained part of this site.

The importance of landscape at this location is emphasized by the audibility and visibility it offered. During the day we worked at the site, shouting and carpentry work were heard on top of the mountain from the lower slope habitation areas, when the air/wind conditions allowed. In days of particularly powerful northeast winds even the sounds of bushes were heard on the top of the mountain. When clear atmospheric conditions existed a very large part of the island was visible, while it would become clear that one was located on an island, surrounded by the sea. To the east Ayios Yeoryios sto Vouno with its peak sanctuary allowed clear intervisibility between them with a possible symbolic association through specific dates when the solar movement linked the two sites (Georgiadis 2016). A view toward the south permits an intervisibility with Mount Drymonas, where another peak sanctuary may have been active during this period (Fragkou and Tsaravopoulos, personal communication). The Maleas and Tainaron capes and peninsulas of the southern Peloponnese could be seen as well as the Mount Taygetos tops, 100 km to the northwest. Toward the south Anitkythera island is visible as well as the White Mountains of western Crete, 150 km to the southeast. However, there are times during the year, including summer months, that clouds reside over Leska and Mermigkari, making visibility rather low to the people visiting this site.

The location of this site and the visibility it provided to the participants of the rituals allowed for an understanding of their position in the world both physically, what surrounded them, and symbolically, their proximity and/or relation to the deity(ies). The sanctuary at Leska provided them with an *axis mundi* in which the physical and sacred were most probably inseparable to the eyes of the people at the time.

Excavation

Excavation was conducted with the help of trenches that were opened in the core area identified during the intensive survey and beyond, where it became possible to determine the approximate size and area within which the sanctuary developed. It is believed to have been about 260 sq m, while the excavated trenches represent close to one-third of its size. Part of the sanctuary was in an area where the bedrock was exposed to a high degree, making the available excavated sample even more significant quantitatively.

There are three categories of finds that were absent during the excavations conducted at the Leska top (Georgiadis 2012). The first absence is that no building, wall, or posthole was identified in the areas studied. It seems that no permanent or seasonal structure was founded while the sanctuary was active. In contemporary examples from Crete there are peak sanctuaries both with structures and without. At Ayios Yeoryios sto Vouno, also on Kythera, walls have been recovered, but they are equally likely to belong to structures or simple terraces. This is not found on Leska, where no enclosed wall or terrace wall appears to have been built within the sanctuary space. The second is the absence of fire remains, arguing that no related activity took place there. Thus, no food preparation, sacrifice, or other use of fire, whether ritual-related or practical, was happening at the sanctuary. The third is the lack of bones observed in all trenches excavated at the Leska top. It seems that no animal sacrifice or consumption was taking place at this sanctuary. This appears to be an oddity when considering the pastoral landscape in which Leska was located as outlined earlier. However, this observation appears not to be random, but deliberate on behalf of the cult participants and indicative of the rituals performed and not allowed to be performed there.

The ceramics represent the largest category of artifacts recovered in the area of the sanctuary. Their fabric suggest that they were locally made from the two main clay sources of the island in the north and the central east, where production centers are believed to have been active (Kyriatzi 2003). The types of vessels represented in this pottery assemblage provide an image of the practices performed while people visited this site. The majority of the vessels belong to drinking cups in a variety of shapes. They are followed by cooking wares, which are found in considerable numbers. This is a very interesting pottery type when considering that no fires or bones have been found in the site. It can be argued that the food was not prepared in situ but was brought ready-made from the habitation areas, while no meat was included in these meals. Serving vessels in the form of jugs and medium and large bowls in different shapes are also common, especially ones related to serving liquids. Storage containers in the form of jars, amphoras, and pithoi appear to be infrequent in this assemblage.

The pottery identified from Leska emphasizes the importance of feasting, the sharing of food and drink by the participants of the cultic activities. The liquid element and the lack of bones could suggest that libations were a dominant aspect of the ritual practices rather than animal sacrifice. The latter trend has already been considered, but when bearing in mind the symbolic importance attributed to communal consumption of food in a pastoral environment it could be proposed that animal consumption was purposefully avoided, perhaps a taboo in the local practices and beliefs. This point is underlined by the presence of fires and animal bones at the contemporary peak sanctuary of Ayios Yeoryios sto Vouno 13.5 km east of Leska (Sakellarakis 2011; Trantalidou 2013).

Other finds include a small number of figurines, one animal and a few representing horns of consecration (Minoan cultic symbols), a handful of stone tools, and a few metal items. In addition, a single feature in the area of the sanctuary stands out for two reasons, for its topography and for the finds associated with it. The highest point of the mountain is a part of the exposed bedrock that stands out from its surroundings due to its size. It is part of the sanctuary, but it also demarcates the northern boundary of the sanctuary space. Furthermore, all the metal objects recovered during excavation were found around it, suggesting a special character within the sanctuary. The symbolic significance of the mountain peak has been well discussed in the Minoan iconography and it is believed that it had a sacred role (Georgiadis 2016). This exposed bedrock could have been used as a baetyl with all the related epiphany rituals (Warren 1988), as depicted in contemporary Minoan art (Georgiadis 2016).

Discussion

The location of the sanctuary at Leska has all the landscape characteristics found in the other peak sanctuaries on Crete as well as Ayios Yeoryios sto Vouno on Kythera. Its presence offers intervisibility with the latter sanctuary, with a possible symbolic importance not attested in the Cretan examples. The material remains recovered at Leska can also be identified as similar in character and use with the ones found and studied in the other peak sanctuaries. Thus, it seems that it was in many respects typical, but smaller and poorer at the same time, possibly serving a small, dispersed agropastoral population in a radius of a few kilometers, while local idiosyncrasies seem to have existed.

The sanctuary at Leska was an integral part of the pastoral environment without any form of artificial separation or alteration, and no human intervention existed, such as lighting a fire. However, at the same time there was a symbolic antithesis between the resources of the surrounding landscape and cultic related practices within the sanctuary. No animals were sacrificed or consumed by the participants, many of which would have been associated with pastoralism to some degree. At the same time animals were free to pass through or stay within the sanctuary space when no gatherings or rituals were performed at this site. Perhaps the welfare of the animals was part of the local beliefs expressed through a taboo for their exploitation at least within the cultic activities of the specific sanctuary.

The emphasis on liquids could be seen as a ritual counterbalance to the lack of animal sacrifices. The presence of rich water resources only east of Leska peak, the practice of heterotopia with symbolic association to rain, and the importance of libations and liquid consumption as part of the rituals in the sanctuary strengthen this hypothesis. It is possible that water and rain were primary concerns for the life of the people and animals, as well as the fertility of the land in the semi-arid environment of Kythera. Thus, it could be proposed that a sky-weather deity was worshiped at Leska that communicated with the pilgrims through the baetyls, accepted liquid nonblood offerings, and required no alterations or exploitation of the animal resources that existed in the surrounding mountainscape.

Its assessment opened a new understanding for the study of pilgrimage on a regional level for Kythera. The example of Leska demonstrated that the research conducted on pilgrimage should not be seen as a passive process of people moving through the landscape. On the contrary it could be an active one, where individuals or groups participated in a number of episodes of cultic or noncultic character. The collection of pebbles or pieces of chert through the pathways they passed by in the case of Leska was part of a ritually related activity, which had a form of symbolic heterotopia. Thus, the movement of the pilgrims through the landscape could have been a dynamic and highly symbolic activity. Research oriented toward a landscape approach could highlight these important aspects of extra-settlement cult.

The way in which this study was designed and proceeded has emphasized the complicated character of the specific mountainous landscape. The application of various research methods has highlighted different aspects and characteristics in the use of this mountainscape within its own temporal and spatial context. It became apparent that the landscape of Mount Mermigkari was complex, including habitational, burial, and cultic aspects. The latter two provide an image of a heavily symbolic area with multiple meanings that were interconnected through the common landscape and probably the rituals that were taking place. The diverse research method proposed here emphasized that the site of Leska was not a single site, but part of a complex and multi-meaning landscape. The mountainscape in which it was located highlighted the significance of the sacred character this peak sanctuary had for the contemporary regional population.

Some Thoughts on Cultural Heritage

It is often the case that archaeological research is seen as an autonomous event that ends with the last day of fieldwork. This is especially true for sites that have not recovered something spectacular in order to act as organized archaeological sites, or which are in remote locations. However, it is believed that the appreciation of mountainscapes could be achieved by modern visitors. This could become possible after a useful discussion that would include other experts, local or national authorities, and others parties.

Thus, in the framework of the current study it could be proposed that the cultural heritage and the knowledge from the proposed research are not incompatible, but that they can be combined to the benefit of the public. Modern trekking routes could be organized in a way that allows the paths used by pilgrims in the Bronze Age past to be followed by present visitors. Through these paths information regarding the local flora and fauna, as well as the diachronic cultural importance and character of the mountain and the way it was used could be provided. Special signs could provide all of this data in specific locations along the paths, making trekking an informative and interesting activity. Reaching the peak of Leska could be seen as a trekking experience with a strong cultural character, where the significance of mountains in different periods of the past could be highlighted. At this point signs with information regarding the sanctuary and its associated rituals and beliefs could be provided to the visitors. At the same time the role of the surrounding landscape and important landmarks that can be viewed should also be demarcated and explained to the trekkers. The current road system, the sites and services of the closest village, Mylopotamos, could promote and sustain such cultural activity including a mountain area. With limited effort and cost by the local authorities in collaboration with archaeologists this could provide a new and alternative trekking experience to the visitors of Kythera with a strong cultural and environmental character.

References

Bartsiokas, A. 1998 Παλαιοντολογία των Κυθήρων, Εταιρεία Κυθηραϊκών Μελετών 9, Athens.
Bevan, A. 2002 The Rural Landscape of Neopalatial Kythera: A GIS Perspective. *Journal of Mediterranean Archaeology* 15(2):217–256.

Bevan, A., E. Kiriatzi, C. Knappett, E. Kappa, and S. Papachristou 2002 Excavation of Neopalatial Deposits at Tholos (Kastri), Kythera. *Annual of the British School at Athens* 97:55–96.

Blomberg, M., and G. Henriksson 2006 Minoan Orientations in Context. Πεπραγμένα του Θ Διεθνούς Κρητολογικού Συνεδρίου Α4, Herakleion:319–331.

Branigan, K. 1970 *The Foundations of Palatial Crete: A Survey of Crete in the Early Bronze Age*. Routledge, London.

Broodbank, C. 1999 Kythera Survey: Preliminary Report on the 1998 Season. *Annual of the British School at Athens* 94:191–214.

Broodbank, C., and E. Kiriatzi 2007 The First "Minoans" of Kythera Revisited: Technology, Demography, and Landscape in the Prepalatial Aegean. *American Journal of Archaeology* 111:241–274.

Coldstream, J. N., and G. L. Huxley 1972 *Kythera: Excavations and Studies*. Faber and Faber, London.

Evans, A. 1935. *The Palace of Minos IV*. Macmillan, London.

Georgiadis, M. 2012 Leska: A New Peak Sanctuary on the Island of Kythera. *Journal of Prehistoric Religion* 23:7–23.

Georgiadis, M. 2014. The Physical Environment and the Beliefs at Leska, a New Peak Sanctuary on Kythera. In *Physis*, edited by G. Touchais, R. Laffineur, and F. Rougemont, 481–484. Aegaeum 37, Liège.

Georgiadis, M. 2016 The Metaphysical Beliefs and Leska. In *Metaphysis: Ritual, Myth and Symbolism in the Aegean Bronze Age*, edited by E. Alram-Stern, F. Blakolmer, S. Deger-Jalkotzy, R. Laffineur, and J. Weilhartner, 295–302. Aegaeum 39, Leuven.

Henriksson, G., and M. Blomberg 1996 Evidence for Minoan Astronomical Observations from the Peak Sanctuaries on Petsophas and Traostalos. *Opuscula Atheniensia* 21(6):99–114.

Henriksson, G., and M. Blomberg 2011 The Evidence from Knossos on the Minoan Calendar. *Mediterranean Archaeology and Archaeometry* 11(1):59–68.

Jones, D. W. 1999 *Peak Sanctuaries and Sacred Caves in Minoan Crete: A Comparison of Artefacts*. Paul Åströms Förlang, Jonsered.

Karetsou, A. 1980 Το ιερό κορυφής Γιούχτα (1979–1980). Πρακτικά της Αρχαιολογικής Εταιρείας: 337–353.

Karetsou, A. 1981 The Peak Sanctuary of Mt. Juktas. In *Sanctuaries and Cults in the Aegean Bronze Age*, edited by R. Hägg and N. Marinatos, 137–153. Svenska institutet i Athen, Stockholm.

Karetsou, A., and I. Mathioudaki 2012 The Middle Minoan III Building Complex at Alonaki, Juktas: Architectural Observations and Pottery Analysis. *Creta Antica* 13:83–107.

Kyriakidis, E. 2005 *Ritual in the Bronze Age Aegean: The Minoan Peak Sanctuaries*. Duckworth, London.

Kyriatzi, E. 2003 Sherds, Fabrics and Clay Sources: Reconstructing the Ceramic Landscapes of Prehistoric Kythera. In *Metron: Measuring the Aegean Bronze Age*, edited by K. P. Foster and R. Laffineur, 123–130. Aegaeum 24, Liège.

Kyriatzi, E. 2010 "Minoanising" Pottery Tradition in the Southwest Aegean during the Middle Bronze Age: Understanding the Social Context of Technological and Consumption Practice. In *Mesohelladika: The Greek Mainland in the Middle Bronze Age*, edited by A. Phillipa-Touchais, G. Touchais, S. Voutsaki, and J. Wright, 683–699. Bulletin de Corrrespondance Hellénique, Paris.

Manning, S. W. 2008 Protopalatial Crete: Formation of the Palaces. In *The Aegean Bronze Age*, edited by C. W. Shelmerdine, 105–120. Cambridge University Press, Cambridge.

Marinatos, N. 1993 *Minoan Religion: Ritual, Image, and Symbol*. University of South Carolina Press, Columbia.

Marinatos, N. 2010 *Minoan Kingship and the Solar Goddess: A Near Eastern Koine*. University of Illinois Press, Urbana.

Niemeier, W.-D. 1987 On the Function of the "Throne Room" in the Palace at Knossos. In *The Function of the Minoan Palaces*, edited by R. Hägg and N. Marinatos, 163–168. Svenska institutet i Athen, Stockholm.

Nowicki, K. 1994 Some Remarks on the Pre- and Protopalatial Peak Sanctuaries in Crete. *Aegean Archaeology* 1:31–48.

Nowicki, K. 2007a Some Remarks on New Peak Sanctuaries in Crete: The Topography of Ritual Areas and Their Relationships with Settlements. *Jahrbuch des Deutschen Archäologisches Instituts* 122:1–31.

Nowicki, K. 2007b Ritual in the Bronze Age Aegean: The Minoan Peak Sanctuaries by Evangelos Kyriakidis. Review by Krzysztof Nowicki. *American Journal of Archaeology* 111(3):576–578.

Peatfield, A. A. D. 1983 The Topography of Minoan Peak Sanctuaries. *Annual of the British School at Athens* 78:273–279.

Peatfield, A. A. D. 1987 Palace and Peak: The Political and Religious Relationship between Palaces and Peak Sanctuaries. In *The Function of the Minoan Palaces*, edited by R. Hägg and N. Marinatos, 89–93. Svenska institutet i Athen, Stockholm.

Peatfield, A. A. D. 1990 Minoan Peak Sanctuaries: History and Society. *Opuscula Atheniensia* 18:117–131.

Peatfield, A. A. D. 1992 Rural Ritual in Bronze Age Crete: The Peak Sanctuary at Atsipadhes. *Cambridge Archaeological Journal* 2(1):59–87.

Peatfield, A. 2007 The Dynamics of Ritual on Minoan Peak Sanctuaries. In *Cult in Context: Reconsidering Ritual in Archaeology*, edited by D. A. Barrowclough and C. Malone, 297–300. Oxford University Press, Oxford.

Peatfield, A. 2009 The Topography of Minoan Peak Sanctuaries Revisited. In *Archaeologies of Cult: Essays on Ritual and Cult in Crete in Honor of Geraldine C. Gesell*, edited by A. L. D'Agata and A. van de Moortel, 251–259. Princeton University Press, Princeton.

Petrocheilos, I. E. 1984 *Τα Κύθηρα, από την Προϊστορική Εποχή ως τη Ρωμαιοκρατία*. University of Ioannina, Ioannina.

Platon, N. 1951 Το ιερό Μαζά (Καλού Χωρίου Πεδιάδος) και τα Μινωικά ιερά κορυφής. *Κρητικά Χρονικά* 5:96–160.

Platon, N. 1968 The Palace of Kato Zakro. In *Ancient Crete*, edited by S. Alexiou, N. Platon, and H. Guanelli, 163–232. Thames and Hudson, London.

Rethemiotakis, Y. 2009 A Neopalatial Shrine Model from the Minoan Peak Sanctuary at Gournos Krousonas. In *Archaeologies of Cult: Essays on Ritual and Cult in Crete in Honor of Geraldine C. Gesell*, edited by A. L. D'Agata and A. Van de Moortel, 189–199. Princeton University Press, Princeton.

Rutkowski, B. 1971 Minoan Cults and History: Remarks on Professor B. C. Dietrich's Paper. *Historia: Zeitschrift für Alte Geschichte* 20(1):1–19.

Rutkowski, B. 1986 *The Cult Places of the Aegean*. Yale University Press, New Haven.

Rutkowski, B. 1991 *Petsophas: A Cretan Peak Sanctuary*. Art and Archeology, Warsaw.
Sakellarakis, Y. 1996 Minoan Religious Influence in the Aegean: The Case of Kythera. *Annual of the British School at Athens* 91:81–99.
Sakellarakis, Y. 2011 *Κύθηρα: Το Μινωικό Ιερό Κορυφής στον Άγιο Γεώργιο στο Βουνό 1: τα Προανασκαφικά και η Ανασκαφή*. Βιβλιοθήκη της εν Αθήναις Αρχαιολογικής Εταιρείας, Athens.
Sakellarakis, Y. 2012 Μινωικά χάλκινα μικροαντικείμενα. In *Κύθηρα: Το Μινωικό Ιερό Κορυφής στον Άγιο Γεώργιο στο Βουνό 2: Τα Ευρήματα*, edited by Y. Sakellarakis, 213–238. Βιβλιοθήκη της εν Αθήναις Αρχαιολογικής Εταιρείας, Athens.
Sakellarakis, Y. 2013a *Κύθηρα: Το Μινωικό Ιερό Κορυφής στον Άγιο Γεώργιο στο Βουνό 3: Τα Ευρήματα*. Βιβλιοθήκη της εν Αθήναις Αρχαιολογικής Εταιρείας, Athens.
Sakellarakis, Y. 2013b *Κύθηρα: Ο Άγιος Γεώργιος στο Βουνό: Μινωική Λατρεία-Νεότεροι Χρόνοι*. Βιβλιοθήκη της εν Αθήναις Αρχαιολογικής Εταιρείας, Athens.
Sakellarakis, Y., and D. Panagiotopoulos 2006 Minoan Zominthos. In *Mylopotamos from Antiquity to the Present: Environment, Archaeology, History, Folklore, Sociology*, edited by I. Gavrilaki and Y. Tzifopoulos, 47–75. Historical and Society of Rethymnon, Rethymnon.
Sapouna-Sakellarakis, E. 2012 Χάλκινα ειδώλια. In *Κύθηρα: Το Μινωικό Ιερό Κορυφής στον Άγιο Γεώργιο στο Βουνό 2: Τα Ευρήματα*, edited by Y. Sakellarakis, 1–212. Βιβλιοθήκη της εν Αθήναις Αρχαιολογικής Εταιρείας, Athens.
Soar, K. 2009 The Archaeology of Minoan Performance. Unpublished PhD thesis, University of Nottingham.
Trantalidou, K. 2013 Αρχαιοζωολογικά κατάλοιπα και ζητήματα της ορνιθοπανίδας. In *Κύθηρα: Το Μινωικό Ιερό Κορυφής στον Άγιο Γεώργιο στο Βουνό 3: Τα Ευρήματα*, edited by Y. Sakellarakis, 463–563. Βιβλιοθήκη της εν Αθήναις Αρχαιολογικής Εταιρείας, Athens.
Tsaravopoulos, A. 2012 Χρονικό της αρχαιολογικής έρευνας στα Κύθηρα στις τέσσερις δεκαετίες που ακολούθησαν τη δημοσίευση του έργου των G. L. Huxley και J. N. Coldstream για τα Κύθηρα. In *George Leonard Huxley, Επιστροφή στα Κύθηρα*, 19–26. Εκδόσεις Φίλων Μουσείων Κυθήρω, Kythera.
Warren, P. 1988 *Minoan Religion as Ritual Action*. Gothenburg University, Gothenburg.
Younger, J. G., and P. Rehak 2008 Minoan Culture: Religion, Burial Customs, and Administration. In *The Aegean Bronze Age*, edited by C. W. Shelmerdine, 165–185. Cambridge University Press, Cambridge.

CHAPTER SIX

Exploring Seasonal Transhumance of Hunter-Gatherers and Neolithic Pastoralists in Poland's High Tatras and Foothill Lowlands

Applying Landscape Archaeology Methodologies from the Colorado Rockies to the Western Carpathians

Robert H. Brunswig and Pawel Valde-Nowak

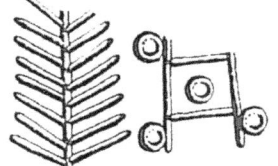

Abstract *This chapter's authors have individually conducted archaeological research programs in different world regions: Robert Brunswig in the Southern Rocky Mountains (USA) and Pawel Valde-Nowak in the Harz and Schwarzwald Mountains (Germany) and Western Carpathians of Poland and Slovakia. Rocky Mountain landscape studies modeled eleven thousand years of seasonal transhumance by Native American hunter-gatherers from lower elevation mountain valleys to high-elevation forest and tundra, following seasonal migrations of game animals. The Rocky Mountain modeling was based on more than two decades of high- and mid-elevation mountain archaeology surveys and supporting paleoclimate studies. Western Carpathian research has, among many other cultural periods, been successful in reconstructing Neolithic pastoralist and farming community life in mid- and low-mountain landscapes. Both scholars draw on their experience and past mountain landscape studies to describe an emerging collaborative research project designed to conduct advanced field studies and generate (and test) archaeological landscape models of past hunter-gatherer populations as well as pastoralist and early farming community seasonal transhumance migrations between lowland river valleys of Poland's Podhale Basin and high-altitude forests and meadows in its adjacent High Tatra Mountains.*

The Tatra National Park–Poland (TPN) Cultural Landscapes Project is an international collaboration of the University of Northern Colorado (Greeley, Colorado, USA) and Jagiellonian University's Institute of Archaeology (Krakow, Poland). The project's lead investigators, and this chapter's authors, are Robert Brunswig, University of Northern Colorado, USA, and Pawel Valde-Nowak, Jagiellonian University, Poland. The University of Northern Colorado has conducted mountain research in the US Southern Rocky Mountains since 1996 (cf. Brunswig 2004a, 2004b, 2005, 2012, 2014a, 2014b, 2015; Brunswig, Doerner and Diggs 2014; Brunswig, McBeth, and Elinoff 2009; Diggs and Brunswig 2013) while Jagiellonian University's Dunajec Project in Poland's Tatra and Beskidy Mountains (western Carpathians) and Foothills began in 1985 (cf. Kienlin and Valde-Nowak 2008, Kienlin et al. 2014; Nadachowski and Valde-Nowak 2015; Valde-Nowak 1991, 2008, 2009a, 2009b, 2010, 2013a, 2013b, 2014, 2015; Valde-Nowak and Nadachowski 2014; Valde-Nowak et al. 2003). The collaborative Tatra Park project integrates alternative but highly complementary interdisciplinary methods, technologies, and research designs of two research projects that have long explored cultural (archaeological) landscapes in two similar mountain regions on different continents (Figure 6.1).

The American mountain research program integrates large-area field surveys and selected open site excavations with comprehensive geological, lithic tool material source, and paleoclimate studies while using advanced spatial analysis and mapping methods based

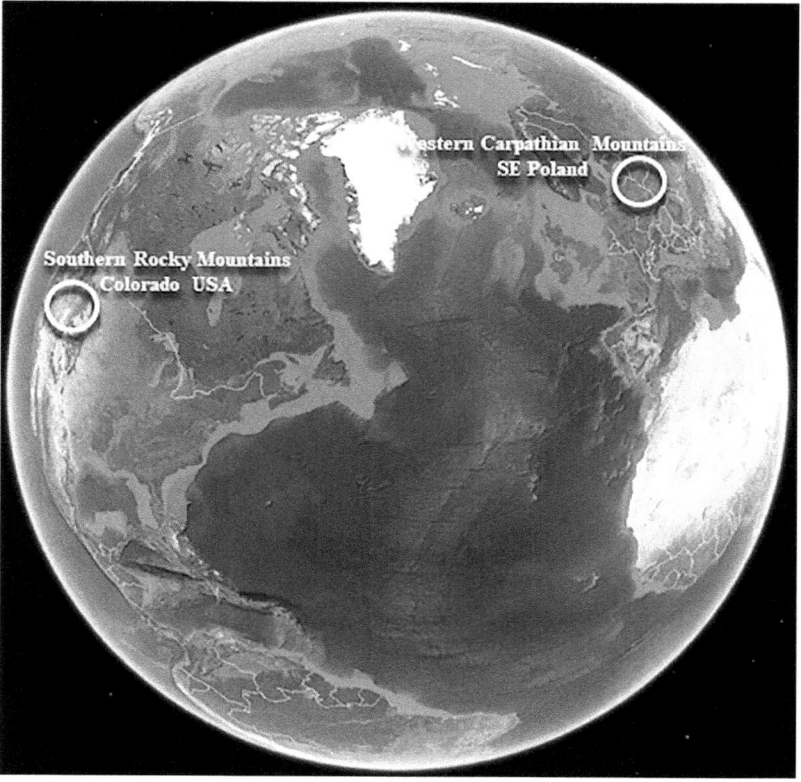

Figure 6.1. Earth image showing relative locations of the authors' mountain research regions (baseline planet image from GoogleEarth™ Pro).

on field use of survey-grade Global Positioning System (GPS) instruments and lab-based application of ArcGIS™ (Geographic Information System) software (cf. Brunswig 2015; Brunswig and Diggs 2014; Brunswig et al. 2014; Diggs and Brunswig 2013; Doerner 2014). Poland's Dunajec Project, in contrast, has focused on smaller targeted ground surveys with high-resolution excavations of complex, often deeply stratified, cave and open-air sites with long occupation histories extending over millennia or even tens of millennia (cf. Kienlin and Valde-Nowak 2008, 2014; Nadachowski and Valde-Nowak 2015; Valde-Nowak 1991, 2009a, 2009b, 2010, 2013a, 2014; Valde-Nowak and Nadachowski 2014; Valde-Nowak et al. 2003). Interdisciplinary support studies for the Polish project have included lithic tool sourcing, archaeological fauna, prehistoric human remains, site geology, and paleo-climate modeling (cf. Nadachowski and Valde-Nowak 2015; Valde-Nowak 2013b, 2015; Valde-Nowak and Nadachowski 2014).

Concepts of Montane Transhumance in European Prehistory

A central Tatra Park Project goal is to document seasonal migratory transhumance between the park's high montane, subalpine, and alpine environmental zones and lower mid mountains and foothills to the north. Transhumance refers to the economically (e.g., natural resource-based) driven, seasonal migration of animals and humans between ecologically and topographically varied landscapes within geographic regions. For transhumance to be advantageous for a species (animal or human), a region should present a seasonally defined deficit of one or more important natural resources in one subregion and possess relatively greater resource abundance in another (usually adjacent) region or subregion in an alternate season. Both human and animal seasonal migrations associated with transhumance can be classified as either horizontal, moving between geographic areas and eco-zones having limited rises or falls in elevation or vertical, involving more pronounced vertical ascents and descents (e.g., traveling between lower elevation valleys or plains and higher hills or mountains) (cf. Arnold and Greenfield 2006; Brunswig 2015:46–52; Carrer 2012, 2015; Geddes 1983; Hafner and Schwöer 2018). Seasonal movements between differing, adjacent eco-zones, as an example, migration into seacoast regions with summer season abundance of fish and sea mammals from inland winter camp areas or involving movement of hunting parties following migratory game herds from low-elevation mountain fall-winter-spring camps to high-tundra grazing land, reflect both the annual rhythm of human, animal, and plant cycles and their intimate economic codependency. Other types of natural resources, the presence of tool raw material (high-quality lithic stone or metal ores), seasonal concentrations of food and medicinal plants, mineral deposits (e.g., salt), and wild or domestic animal forage plants, can also contribute to the benefits of transhumant economic systems.

Methods for inferring human transhumance from archaeological and paleo-environmental records are diverse and frequently dependent on local and regional circumstances of geological and archaeological preservation. More common methods include chemical isotope ratios of carbon and nitrogen in human and animal bone and teeth, analysis of radiocarbon-dated bog and archaeological sediments for organic content, magnetic susceptibility, pollen, and charcoal content (associated with climate-related [e.g., natural] and anthropogenic [forest-clearing] fires), and transhumant migratory transfer of geographically sourced tool materials and mollusk shells outside their geologic origin locations (cf. Brunswig 2015:84–91; Dietre et al. 2014, 2016; Galop et al. 2013; Kienlin and Valde-Nowak 2002–2004; Leigh et al. 2016; Martin 2015; Nehlich et al. 2009; Rey et al. 2013; Riehl 2006).

Documentation of mountain (vertical) transhumance by prehistoric humans is increasingly common in Eurasian archaeological research programs. Evidence of seasonal migrations into higher mountain zones from lower valleys and foothills is frequently linked to diachronically defined positive or negative paleoclimate conditions while their complete or relative absence may be due to colder glacial episodes when plant growth, persistent cold climate, and active mountain glaciers discouraged human and animal transhumance. Table 6.1 provides data for a small sample of archaeological site and site landscape studies in Eurasian mountain ranges that have produced evidence interpreted as representing seasonal transhumance. The oldest sites cited in the table are later period Neanderthal (Late Mousterian) hunting camps, lithic tool-manufacturing and quarry sites, and mountain passes, the latter having served as conduits (choke-points) important for game ambushes and transit through mountains territories. The table's three Mousterian examples range from ca. 65,000 to 40,000 cal ^{14}C BP and cover a deep (north-south) area of latitude, from Northern Greece's Pindus Mountains and the French Pyrenees to the Russian Caucasus. The next lower (younger) sequence of sites and cultural periods shown in Table 6.1 are from the Swiss Alps. They represent four successive cultural traditions from the Late Pleistocene (ca. 18,000 cal ^{14}C BP) through the Mid Holocene (ca. 4,300 cal ^{14}C BP): the Magdalenian, the Pleistocene-Holocene transitional Terminal Magdalenian-Azilian, the Mesolithic, and ending with the Neolithic. Swiss Alp highland adaptations by Middle and Late Magdalenian hunters appear to have occurred several millennia after the height of Late Glacial Maximum (LGM) cooling when substantial valley glacier retreat and alpine, subalpine, and upper montane ecosystems recovery were well underway. Magdalenian through Mesolithic sites were hunter-gatherer based and represented by open and sheltered hunting camps, lithic tool material quarries, and stone tool manufacturing localities. At ca. 7,700 cal ^{14}C BP, both archaeological and paleoenvironmental records document establishment of small farming and stock-raising communities in foothill areas and initiation of summer pasturing of domestic animals in mountain zones as high as 2,800 m. Bog pollen throughout the Swiss Neolithic suggests progressive anthropogenic high-altitude deforestation and increases in grass meadows and open pastureland between 7,700 and 4,300 cal ^{14}C BP. Paleoclimate records that parallel the Swiss Alp tradition's chronologies show that mid- and high-mountain colonization occurred in generally warmer (often moister) climate cycles, the exception being a millennium-long hiatus of cool and dry conditions during Terminal Pleistocene (Younger Dryas) neoglaciation between 13 and 12 ka (BP) (^{10}Be chronology) (Moran et al. 2016).

Although examples illustrating early mountain-associated transhumance in Table 6.1 are intentionally limited in number due to space requirements, they represent a sample of a much larger body of literature that demonstrates existence of transhumance economic patterns in Continental Europe since late Neanderthal times.

TABLE 6.1. EXAMPLES OF INFERRED TRANSHUMANT CULTURAL TRADITIONS
IN THE EURASIAN MID-LATE PLEISTOCENE AND EARLY-MID HOLOCENE

Site Type(s)	Cultural Tradition	Chronology (cal ¹⁴C BP)	Geography/ Environment	Elevation(s)	Subsistence System	Climate Notes
Open Camps, Open Lithic Quarries[1]	Late Mousterian (Neanderthal)	~55,000–45,000	High Pindus Mountains Northern Greece	1200–2100m	Hunting, Lithic Procurement/ Manufacturing	Interstadial Generally Warm Period/Cold Intervals
Cave Grotte du Noisetier[2]	Late Mousterian (Neanderthal)	47,802–46,339	Central Pyrenees France	825m	Hunting, Crossing Mountains (France-Spain)	Interstadial Generally Warm Period/Cold Intervals
Caves, Open Camps, Open Lithic Quarries[3]	Late Mousterian (Neanderthal)	~65,000–40,000	Northwest Caucasus Mountains Russia	900–1310m	Hunting, Lithic Material Procurement, Tool Manufacturing	Interstadial Generally Warm Period/Cold Intervals
Caves, Rockshelters, Open Camps[4]	Middle Magdalenian	18,000–16,450	Swiss Alps Lower Mountains Subalpine–Alpine	400–500m	Hunting, Lithic Material Procurement, Tool Manufacturing	Post-LGM Initial Deglaciation Warming
Caves, Rockshelters, Open Camps[4]	Late Magdalenian	14,950–13,950	Swiss Alps Mid Upper Mountains Alpine Zone	400–600m	Hunting, Lithic Material Procurement, Tool Manufacturing	Accelerated Deglaciation Rise in Treeline Continued Warming
Caves, Rockshelters, Open Camps[4]	Terminal Magdalenian-Azilian	12,600–12,000	Swiss Alps Mid-Upper Mountains Alpine Tundra	400–1000m	Hunting, Lithic Material Procurement, Tool Manufacturing	Substantial Deglaciation Warming

continued on next page

TABLE 6.1. CONTINUED.

Site Type(s)	Cultural Tradition	Chronology (cal ¹⁴C BP)	Geography/Environment	Elevation(s)	Subsistence System	Climate Notes
Open Camps[5]	Mesolithic	10,350–7,700	Swiss Alps Upper Mountains Alpine–Above Treeline	Above 1000m (max 2500m)	Hunting-Fishing, Lithic Material Procurement	Post Younger Dryas–Rapid Holocene Warming[3]
Rockshelters, Open Camps[6]	Neolithic	7,700–4,300	Swiss Alps Upper Mountains Alpine–Above Treeline	~2800m	Pastoralism, Hunting-Fishing, Cross-Mtn Trade, High Mountain Anthropogenic Deforestation in Late Neolithic	Early-Mid Holocene Warm-Cool Cycles Generally Positive Climatic Conditions

[1] Efstratiou et al. 2006, 2014
[2] Mourre et al. 2004, 2008
[3] Hoffecker and Cleghorn 2000; Pinhasi et al. 2011
[4] Leesch et al. 2012; Mevel 2013
[5] Bullinger and Huber 2010; Cornelissen and Reitmaier 2016
[6] Dietre et al. 2014, 2016; Hafner and Schworer 2017; Martin 2015; Rey et al. 2013

Note: Mesolithic high-altitude use appears to have been variable over time and space, subject to periodic Early Holocene warm-cool climate fluctuations.

Tatra National Park–Poland Archaeological Planning and Research Strategies

The Tatra Park region and southeastern Poland's cultural history has extreme time-depth, extending a half million years into the past. Figure 6.2 provides a broad summary of known or proposed archaeological cultural traditions with their associated chronologies and provides a generalized inference of archaeological/historical site/human site (population) densities based on current literature.

Hypothetically, based on contemporary archaeological evidence in the Tatra Mountains and Foothills, subject of the Tatra Park Cultural Landscapes (high mountains) and ongoing Dunajec (mid-low mountains and foothills) projects, potentially includes any or all the cultural traditions listed in figure 6.2. Cave and open-air site occupations belonging to all those traditions occur in lesser to greater frequency in southeastern Poland. Most notably, Late Mousterian, Gravettian/Epigravettian, Magdalenian, and Mesolithic through His-

Southeastern Poland Cultural/Archaeological Occupation Sequence	Approximate Chronologies (BP=Before Present)	Population/Site Density in Tatra Mountains, Foothills, and Foreland Region
1. Acheulian-*Homo ergaster* to *Homo heidelbergensis*	500,000-300,000 BP	Low to Non-Existent
2. Mousterian-*Homo sapiens neanderthalensis* Mousterian of Acheulian Tradition (MTA)/Micoquian/Mousterian	300,000/230,000-35,000 BP	Low to Moderate, Late Phase Occupations More Abundant
3. Aurignacian-*Homo sapiens sapiens*	38,000-35,000 BP	Low to Non-Existent
4. Cultural Hiatus? No occupations or still missing evidence	35,000-27,000 BP	Non-Existent at Present
5. Gravettian I-Interstadial Warm Phase-Regional In-migration of Hunter-Gatherers from South of Carpathians	27,000-24,000 BP	Low and Periodic
6. Gravettian IIa-Northern Ice Sheet-Seasonally Migrating Tundra Hunters from South of Mountains-Late Glacial Maximum	24,000-22,000 BP	Low
7. Gravettian IIb-Northern Ice Sheet Seasonally Migrating Tundra Hunters-Slow Warming from Late Glacial Maximum	22,000-17,000 BP	Moderately to Relatively Abundant
8. Magdalenian-Continued Late Glacial Warming, Permanent Tundra-Cold Forest Hunters North of Carpathians	18,600-17,500 BP (Early) 16,500-11,000 BP (Late)	Low (Early Magdalenian) Moderate (Late & Epi Magdalenian)
9. Mesolithic-Younger Dryas Cold to Early Holocene Warming Neolithic (early pottery-farming-pastoralism, Baden, Linear Band Complexes)-Mid Holocene	Transitional-Mesolithic-11,000-7,500 BP Neolithic-7,500-4,200 BP	Low (Mesolithic) Moderately to Relatively Abundant (Neolithic)
10. Copper-Bronze Age-Foothill Farming Villages, Summer Transhumance Herds-Foothills to Mountains and Return	4,200-2,800 BP	Moderately to Relatively Abundant
11. Iron Age-Warriors, Farming-Livestock, Scythian Invasions	2,800-2,400 BP	Moderately to Relatively Abundant
12. "Roman"-Medieval-Trade with Rome, Migrations to South, Christianity, Early Slavic In-Migrations, Later Slavic Pastoralists (including the Vlach & Goral)-Sheep-Goat-Cattle Transhumance	"Roman"-2,100-14,00 BP Medieval-1,400-400 BP	Abundant, Then Depopulation (Late Roman-Post-Roman) Medieval Population Increase (Slavs 1400-1500 BP, later Vlach & Goral, 400-500 BP)
13. Recent Historic-Foreign Invasions, Wars	400 years ago to Present	Abundant

Figure 6.2. Chart of the cultural/archaeological timeline for Northeastern Europe and Poland based on a review of current literature. Column 3 (*far right*) provides a very broad estimate of human site (and by inference population) density in the Tatra Mountain region (high and mid mountains, foothills, and Upper Vistula River "foreland").

toric cultures are represented in north slope Western Carpathian mid-mountain, foothill, and river valley upland regions, including Tatra mid- and low-mountain and foothills subregions. Tatra National Park, constituting the High Tatras with the Western Carpathians' only alpine and alpine-subalpine ecotone environmental zones, aside from inventory surveys of historic mines and ore processing facilities, has never been archaeologically surveyed. To date, only two sites, a Late Magdalenian camp (immediately outside the park's northern boundary) and a Neolithic blade core (in an upper montane tributary valley) (Rydlewski 2006; Tunia 1977; see below), make up its formal archaeological inventory. Evidence of earlier Mid- and Late Pleistocene archaeology in the park, with the possible exception of its numerous limestone caves and valley-margin ridgelines, is likely obscured or destroyed by valley glaciation and long-term erosion and sediment burial. Some periods may be also absent due to severe cold climate and limited plant and animal resources, such as during the most recent Late Glacial Maximum (LGM), locally designated the Late Weichselian Stadial. Other impediments to identifying archaeological sites within Tatra Park and nearby mid-mountain and river corridors to the north (downslope) are frequent heavy ground cover, which obscures discovery of surface artifacts and features, and the relative lack of agricultural plowing, which often provides some degree of surface archaeology visibility in the region.

Hypothesizing the Presence of Higher Probability Visibility Transhumance Cultural Traditions in the High Mountains of Tatra National Park and Its Adjacent Lowland Foothills and River Valleys

Although there is good probability of discovering archaeological evidence for any (or most) of the cultural traditions listed in Figure 6.2 within and adjacent to Tatra National Park, a review of local and regional publications and site records, and results of a short 2017 field reconnaissance of a proposed park survey area by one of the authors (Brunswig), suggest substantial evidence exists for three cultural and chronological periods believed to include seasonal transhumance patterns, the latest Pleistocene Late Magdalenian Tradition and the Neolithic and Bronze Ages.

Late Pleistocene Magdalenian Hunters in the Tatra Mountains and Southeastern Poland

By 18,000 BP, the Magdalenian Tradition, with its Western European roots, emerged in Poland and northeastern Europe. Early advancement of Magdalenian populations into modern-day Polish territory, technologically a variant of western Europe's Middle Magdalenian Period, spread west to east through southern and south-central Poland (Kozłowski 1987; Połtowicz 2005; Połtowicz-Bobak 2006, 2009, 2012, 2013; Weniger 1987). In Poland, one of the earliest Magdalenian occupations occurs at Maszycka Cave where Middle Magdalenian levels are radiocarbon-dated (cal ^{14}C) at ca. 18,558–17,908 BP (Bobak and Połtowicz-Bobak 2013–2014:57–58, Table 1). Between a thousand and fifteen hundred years later, cave and open-air Late Magdalenian sites substantially increased in south-central and southeastern Poland, including on the Kraków-Częstochowa Upland and, to the south, into the Tatra Mountains and Foothills (e.g., in the Podhale Basin) and the lower-elevation Sandomierz Basin to the east (Bobak and Połtowicz-Bobak 2013–2014; Bobak et al. 2013, 2017; Fiedorczuk et al. 2007; Komar et al. 2010; Łanczont et al. 2002; Schild 2014; Valde-Nowak and Muzyczuk 2000). Late Magdalenian site occupations date from ca. 16,500 to 12,500 cal ^{14}C BP. Stratified Late Magdalenian deposits at several cave or open hunting camp sites in central and southeastern Poland are radiocarbon-dated between 16,053 and 12,760 cal ^{14}C (cf. Bobak and Połtowicz-Bobak 2013–2014:58–61, Table 1; Bobak et al. 2013; Lorenc 2006, 2013). Open camp sites appear mainly situated near rivers and hill passes where game animals could be observed and hunted. Magdalenian occupation assemblages typically reflect hunting and processing (meat, hide, bone . . .) artifacts, largely consisting of tools modified from long narrow blades. Carved bone and ivory portable art (human and animal forms) are relatively common along with bone tools (awls, needles . . .) (Fiedorczuk et al. 2007; Kozłowski 1987; Kufel-Diakowska and Wilczyński 2014). Magdalenian hunting for large herbivores, such as reindeer, woolly rhinoceros, horses, and to a lesser extent woolly mammoth, provided primary food sources and materials for shelter and nonlithic tools (hides, bone, and ivory). Some camps have evidence of hide shelters (conical tents) along with open stone-slab floors and work areas and it is believed some sites, situated in sheltered areas with local water and trees, were associated with winter residences. Other, more common, short-term camp sites served as migratory hunting bases used in seasonal rounds, following game species such as reindeer on seasonal migrations between summer and winter territories. Emerging Late Magdalenian archaeology, including detailed lithic raw material studies at southwest Poland's Sowin 7 site, led to the hypothesis that some Magdalenian hunting populations were engaged in logistically organized hunting-collecting behavior (cf. Wiśnewski et al. 2012:392–399). Although Late Magdalenian populations in modern-day Polish territory lived a few thousand years after Late Glacial Maximum (LGM) extreme cold when Ice Age climate was slowly warming, environmental studies show climate remained significantly colder and drier than at present and Magdalenian hunting bands occupied largely treeless park-tundra landscapes (cf. Komar et al. 2010).

Climate and environmental conditions in Tatra Park, its associated Tatra Mountain ranges, and lower foothills and river valley areas to the north were, in the mid-late Magdalenian periods, conducive to Pleistocene game herds of bison, reindeer, elk, and even a late presence of mammoth. Maximum LGM glacier expansion in the High Tatra peaks and valleys of Tatra National Park occurred between 28,000 and 21,000 BP (Kłapyta et al. 2016; Zasadni and Kłapyta 2014). After 21,000 BP, Tatra Park glaciers retreated with onset of Bølling/Allerød Interstadial (Late Glacial) warming. Tatra Park glacial cirque lake pollen profiles show they were largely ice-free between 16,000 and 13,600 cal BP (cf. Kłapyta et al. 2016:133). Latest Pleistocene (Bølling/Allerød) interstadial warming, which ended with the Younger Dryas cold episode at ca. 12,000–11,000 cal BP, "was characterized by a continental climate with relatively warm summer months, which enhanced forest expansion via the species *Pinus sylvestris* and *Pinus Cembra*. An improvement in climate conditions led to a substantial (400–500 m) rise in the upper timberline to at least 1250 m in the northern Tatra slopes" (Kłapyta et al. 2016:133)

Three decades of limited archaeological surveys in the Spisko-Gubałowskie Foothills and Orawa-Nowy Targ (Podhale) Basin by Jagiellonian University have so far identified thirteen Late Upper Paleolithic-era Late Magdalenian and descendent culture (Federmesser and Świderian) open camp and cave sites within 40 km (1–2 days foot-travel) of Tatra Park's lower (northern) boundary (see Figure 6.3; Valde-Nowak et al. 2014, 2016, 2018). All are in mid-mountain foothills and river basin valleys downslope of the lower (southern) boundary of Tatra National Park where the closest, Witow I, is immediately adjacent (within 50 m) to a narrow valley entrance into the park. Witow I is a Late Magdalenian lithic scatter (three tools), which likely represents a seasonal hunting (or hunt staging) camp (cf. Rydlewski 2006) (see Figure 6.3 for its location). Witow I sits on a raised remnant terrace overlooking *three* closely spaced Tatra Park valley entrances with interior access to the park's mountain ridgelines and peaks, numerous limestone caves, meadows, and upland forests, and only 9 km south, providing easy access to Tatra Divide passes between Polish and Slovakian sides of the Western Carpathians. A brief exploratory survey by one of the authors (Brunswig) in 2017 documented a 4 m diameter boulder ring deeply embedded on a side-valley stream bank, a feature type consistent with known Magdalenian hide-tent foundations elsewhere in Europe (Brunswig 2018:22–26; Brunswig and Valde-Nowak 2018). Pending future-planned excavation and dating of the feature by potentially associated diagnostic artifacts or radiocarbon-dated hearth charcoal, it is not presently possible to know the feature's chronology or cultural affiliation. However, the feature, believed to represent foundations of a prehistoric temporary camp structure, a hide tent, does have an analogue in the region's Upper Paleolithic archaeology. On the Białka River in the Orawa-Nowy Targ (Podhale) Basin, 11 km north of the park, a Late Ice Age open camp, Nowa Biała I, was excavated by coauthor Pawel Valde-Nowak in 1985–1986, 2012, and 2014 (Valde-Nowak 1987, 2003:7; Valde-Nowak and Kraszewska 2014:10–11). The camp, used by Epi-Magdalenian Federmesser (partly contemporary with and culturally descendant from the region's Late Magdalenian culture) hunters, included a tent-feature with internal hearth, visible as a circular stained soil-outline, similar in shape and size to the Tatra Park stone ring but lacking its foundation rocks. Charcoal from the feature's internal hearth was radiocarbon-dated to ca. 13 157 cal ^{14}C BP, two millennia prior to the end of the region's Late Pleistocene. Further downslope (north) of Witow I, 13–15 km from the Tatra Park boundary at Podczerwone and Koniówa, Late Magdalenian camp deposits were excavated from a Czarny Dunajec (Black Dunajec) Pleistocene terrace scarp in the 1980s (Rydlewski and Valde-Nowak 1981a, 1981b). Nine other Upper Paleolithic camp sites, as shown in Figure 6.3, have been found on terraces and adjacent floodplains of the Biały Dunajec and Białka Rivers, both which head-water upslope in Tatra National Park and served as natural seasonal migratory routes into and from the park's forests and valley meadows.

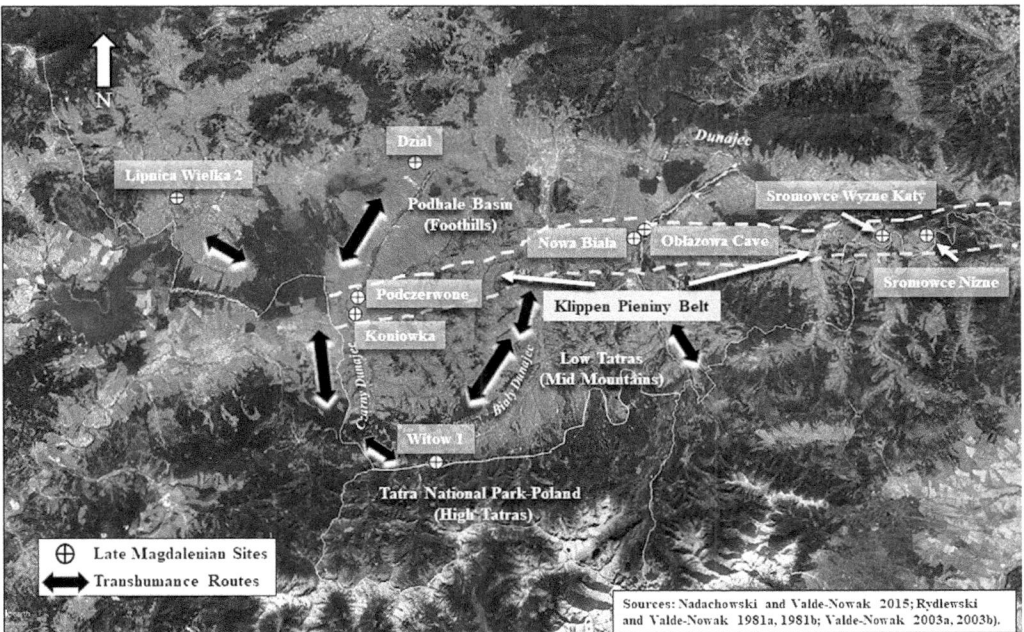

Figure 6.3. Locations of Late Upper Paleolithic Late Magdalenian and descendent culture (Federmesser and Świderian) sites and proposed river corridor transhumance routes from Tatra Park through the Spisko-Gubalowskie Foothills and Orawa-Nowy Targ (Podhale) Basin. Later Early Holocene Mesolithic sites are also shown. Upper Paleolithic culture sites within 30 km (a 1–2 day walk) of Tatra Park's lower (north) boundary are captioned with a white background. (The figure's base map is composed over a GoogleEarth™ Pro Satellite Image.)

One of those sites, Obłazowa Cave, in the lower elevation Orawa-Nowy Targ (Podhale) Basin (Figure 6.3), has produced occupation deposits (layer III) with Late Magdalenian blade tools and faunal remains of reindeer and horse, which produced bone radiocarbon dates ranging from 14,815–14,055 cal ^{14}C BP (Nadachowski and Valde-Nowak 2015). A stone figurine of Lalinde-Gönnersdorf style was also found here (Valde-Nowak et al. 2018). Immediately adjacent to Obłazowa Cave, on an adjacent Pleistocene terrace, is Nowa Biała I, the aforementioned Epi-Magdalenian (Federmesser) open-air camp with its circular tent feature (Valde-Nowak 1987, 2003:7; Valde-Nowak et al. 2013–2014:71, 73).

East of the Tatras and Podhale Basin, in the Sandomierz Basin, river valley and foothill surveys and excavations produced evidence of short-term Magdalenian open camps, most situated in valley settings conducive to observing and hunting migratory game herds of reindeer, horses, and bison (cf. Bobak et al. 2017; Hołub et al. 2016). Given the relative abundance of Late Magdalenian sites in the Tatra mid-mountains and Podhale low mountains and foothills, and existence of a hunting camp on the park's northern boundary, with two other camps less than 15 km north and downslope of the park (see Figure 6.3), it is certain the park's valleys and ridgetop slopes once attracted summer migratory herds of Late Pleistocene game, notably reindeer and red deer (elk), herds which, in turn, brought Magdalenian hunting bands into the area on their own annual summer season transhumant rounds. At the same time, Tatra, Podhale, and Orawa-Nowy Targ Magdalenian (and descendant Federmesser and Świderian culture) hunting camps, like those in the Sandomierz Basin, would have been well positioned to systematically track and ambush game herds migrating in late spring and early summer to higher elevation grazing ranges. Although longer-term winter camps in the Tatra region may have existed in protective caves, rock shelters, well-sheltered open wintering sites with hide-covered tents, Magdalenian winter camps also may have been concentrated further south and east, such as at Wilczyce in the Sandomierz Basin Uplands east of the Tatras (cf. Schild 2014).

Neolithic and Bronze Age Archaeology in the Western Carpathians

By 7,500 BP, southeastern Poland was home to Neolithic populations practicing early phase agriculture involving domestic livestock (sheep, goats, cattle) and cereal grain production (wheat and barley) along with continued supplemental hunting and wild plant food gathering (cf. Bogucki 2014; Bogucki and Grygiel 1993; Czekaj-Zastawny 2008; Dolukhanov et al. 2005; Lityńska-Zając et al. 2014). Heavily influenced by Neolithic cultural traditions in western areas of Northern Europe, southeastern Poland's Neolithic populations were characterized by use of microlithic stone tools, ground stone axes, early plainware, often design-incised pottery, and small permanent to semi-permanent villages with small to large rectangular post-walled, thatched "long houses" (Bogucki 2014; Valde-Nowak 2013a). In the Wiśnicz Foothills, northwest of Tatra Park (downstream of the Podhale Basin Foothills), early (Linear Band Keramik [LBK]), middle (Malice Culture), and late (Baden Complex) Neolithic phase sites, while practicing cereal (wheat and barley) farming (Lityńska-Zając et al. 2014:210–211), are believed to have been engaged in animal pastoralism (Valde-Nowak 2013a). Closely spaced clusters of longer-term, and at least semi-permanent, settlements are located on the subregion's high river valley hill ridges, locations less subject to cool-air drainage and more conducive to crop raising than valley bottoms (Valde-Nowak 2013a, 2014:41–42). However, short-term occupation sites, often situated in higher mid-mountain and high mountain locations considered to have been associated with summer pastoral migrations to upland mountain meadows and stream corridor grasslands, are also known (Valde-Nowak 2014:42–46). Concentrations of Neolithic sites in the Wiśnicz Foothills and adjacent Beskidy Mountains and in the Kraków-Częstochowa Upland (Upper Vistula) are considered to have practiced seasonal pastoral transhumance between lowland and highland zones (Bogucki 2014:8–10; Valde-Nowak 2013a, 2014:222–223; Valde-Nowak and Tarasiński 2007).

The case of the Early-Middle-Late Neolithic and Early Bronze Age Łoniowa 18 site in the Wiśnicz Foothills, with its large Early Neolithic 42.5 m long house with internal floor burials, illustrates the richness and complexity of Neolithic cultural adaptations in the broader Tatra region (cf. Valde-Nowak 1998, 2009a, 2013a:95–101, 2014). Łoniowa 18's radiocarbon-dated Neolithic occupation subperiods are the Early Neolithic (Linear Band Keramik Culture/LBK), dated at ca. 7,200 cal ^{14}C BP (three dates) and the Middle Neolithic (Malice Culture), dated at ca. 6,700 cal ^{14}C BP (one date) (Valde-Nowak 2009a). The presence of LBK ceramics shows the site was occupied throughout *all* regional Neolithic phases, including the latest, represented by a single Funnel Beaker potsherd (Valde-Nowak 2013a:97, 100). Finally, evidence of Early Neolithic contact of Łoniowa 18 residents with Bükk Culture populations in Slovakia south of the Carpathians is documented by the presence of Bükk pottery (Valde-Nowak 2009a:20, 2013a:99, 2014:31). Evidence for cross-Carpathian contact with Early Neolithic Slovakia is further shown by the presence of Slovakian obsidian at Łoniowa 18 (Valde-Nowak 2013a:98,100). Evidence of mountain routes taken for transporting Early to Middle Neolithic Slovakian pottery and obsidian across the western Carpathians through High Tatra passes (within Tatra Park) remains undocumented, but their transport could also have occurred over lower passes through the Beskidy and Bieszczady mountain ranges to the east or through lower passes into modern Slovakia a few kilometers west of the narrow width (~19 km) of High Tatra peaks and Tatra Park. In addition to Łoniowa 18, Early Neolithic Bükk ceramics, belonging to an eastern Slovak variant (Eastern Linear Pottery Culture) of southeast Poland's LBK Culture, are recorded from several other Polish sites in the upper Vistula Basin, showing direct north-south cross-Carpathian cultural (and likely trade) contacts (cf. Kabaciński et al. 2015; Kozłowski et al. 2014). In some cases, the Polish sites also produced eastern Slovakian obsidian (e.g., lithic material trade) in close association with Bükk pottery.

Łoniowa 18 and four other Wiśnicz Foothills sites, Gwoździec, Żerków, Biesiadki, and Tworkowa, are situated on river-margin ridgelines with rich loess soils (cf. Valde-Nowak 2014). The "villages" are described (Valde-Nowak 2009a:28, 2014:46) as a closely spaced, collectively organized concentration of very small settlements (hamlets) thought to have composed a single dispersed farming-pastoralist community. Excavations at Łoniowa and Gwoździec revealed Neolithic-era cultivation of emmer wheat (*Triticum dioccon*), while remains of barley (*Hordeum vulgare*) were identified at Gwoździec (Lityńska-Zając et al. 2014). Neolithic pollen and macro-botanical evidence for slash-and-burn forest clearance for farming and livestock grazing in low mountain and foothills areas on the northern margins of the Podhale Foothills occurs in Kamiennik bog deposits, which produced a Late Neolithic–dated (5,380–5,630 cal yr ^{14}C BP) yew bow fragment (Margielewski et al. 2010: 145–148, Table 1; see Figure 6.4 for its location). Kamiennik's radiocarbon-dated deposits document "the first traces of human activity" at ca. 6,500 cal ^{14}C BP believed associated with area forest clearance for farming and livestock grazing and a "very distinct stage of deforestation" at ca. 5,300 cal ^{14}C (Margielewski et al. 2010:148, Figure 3, Table 1).

Immediately east of the Podhale Basin and Tatra mountain range, in Poland's eastern Małopolskie and western Podkarpackie provinces, are the neighboring Beskidy and Bieszczady mountain ranges. Those ranges, although averaging 1,200–1,300 m lower than the park's High Tatras, are still among the Western Carpathians' highest ranges, with the Beskidys ranked second highest. The Beskidys' lower mountains and foothills, equivalent to those of the Tatra's Podhale Basin, occupy its Jasło-Krosno Basin. Over the past few decades, large areas of the eastern Małopolskie and western Podkarpackie provinces have been subjected to extensive archaeological ground surveys whose results are integrated into computer-based, digitized site maps as part of the AZP (Archeologiczne Zdjęcie Polski–Archaeological Picture of Poland Project) database, provincial-level subsets of the national AZP (Archaeological Monuments of Poland) site database program established in 1978 (cf. Dulęba et al. 2015; Pelisiak 2014:143–144, 2016a:212; Przybyła and Blajer 2008; Rączkowski 2011). Long-term Beskidy surveys, as of 2013, had covered ~14,500 sq km and recorded more than ten thousand Neolithic through Early Bronze Age sites, including village settlements, short-term camps, and small artifact scatters. Pelisiak (2014:150–153), based on Late Neolithic site distributions in the Beskidy Mountains and Foothills, proposed two interrelated land-use patterns in adjacent lower elevation and higher elevation "landscape zones": 1) foothills and lower mountains and 2) mid- and higher mountain forest areas. In the lower landscape zone, its Late Neolithic settlement pattern consists of what are interpreted as substantially permanent settlements supported by crop farming and animal husbandry with evidence of forest clearance for cropland, and small villages with four to seven wood-framed houses. Higher-elevation Beskidy Mountain (mid-upper mountain) areas have, to date, provided no evidence of *permanent settlements* but do contain short-term camp occupations believed to represent short-term warm-season sites designed to support transhumant-driven, warm-season domestic animal grazing (pastoralist) and upland hunting (Pelisiak 2016c:215–216). Successive Late Neolithic cultural traditions represented in the Beskidy and Jasło-Krosno region are the Funnel Beaker (FBC) and Corded Ware (CWC) cultures (Pelisiak 2016c:213–215). The distinction between Late Neolithic lowland and upland site patterns is viewed as reflecting a seasonal migratory (transhumance) economic system where

> animals might have been kept in the villages during the late autumn, winter and early spring, and driven to the pastures located further away from the villages in the deeper [higher mountains] parts of the Carpathians (late spring, summer and early autumn. (Pelisiak 2014:151)

Bordering the Beskidy Mountains to the east are the Bieszczady Mountains with their lower (northern) foothills-river valley and piedmont zones. AZP database-recorded sites in the Bieszczady region include thousands of early through late Neolithic and Bronze Age farming-pastoralist settlements in its piedmont and foothills zones and short-term activity and temporary camp sites in mid- and high-mountain areas (Pelisiak 2012, 2014, 2016a, 2016c; Pelisiak and Kruk 2014; Pelisiak and Maj 2013). Archaeological surveys in the Bieszczady mid- and high-mountain zones, while having significantly less area coverage than in more populated lowland areas, have documented Late Neolithic (and generalized Neolithic) through Bronze Age lithic scatters and isolated artifacts, hypothesized as representing transhumant pastoralist herding camps (Pelisiak 2016a:250, 2016c:215–216; Pelisiak and Kruk 2014). Higher altitude bog sediment coring programs have produced pollen evidence of anthropogenic forest disturbance, interpreted as representing tree and shrub clearance to facilitate grass meadow expansion for more productive summer grazing pastures, further supporting mid- and high-mountain Neolithic and Bronze Age transhumance (cf. Pelisiak

2016c:239, 250–251; Pelisiak and Maj 2013: 265; Ralska-Jasiewczowa 1969, 1972, 1980; Wacnik et al. 2016). Another attraction for summer highland grazing areas during the Neolithic and Bronze Ages (and other periods as well) would have been salt (thermal) springs, which provided valuable minerals and saline-rich vegetation for migratory livestock herds (Pelisiak 2008; Pelisiak and Kruk 2014). Salt springs also exist near Tatra National Park and its mid-mountains to the north, presenting a similar attractant for wild herd animals and pastoralist livestock in times past.

Given the high density of Late Neolithic and Early Bronze Age sites in adjacent Beskidy-Jasło-Krosno and Bieszczady Mountain-Foothills subregions immediately east of the Tatra-Podhale region, it is probable that, as archaeological survey coverage of the Tatra-Podhale Basin increases and the Tatra Park Project proceeds, we may find similar Neolithic–Bronze Age settlement patterns, including direct evidence of early pastoral transhumance into the mid and high Tatra Mountains (cf. Figure 6.4). At present, evidence for Neolithic (and later Bronze Age) occupation in Tatra National Park remains documented only by a single Neolithic blade core recovered from the park's Kondratowa Valley (elevation 1,350 m) (Tunia 1977) as well as many inventories of Orawa-Type in the form of small surface collections of stone artifacts characteristic for so-called terminal flint industry associated with Bronze Age *sensu largo* (Kopacz and Valde-Nowak 1987; Valde-Nowak 1986).

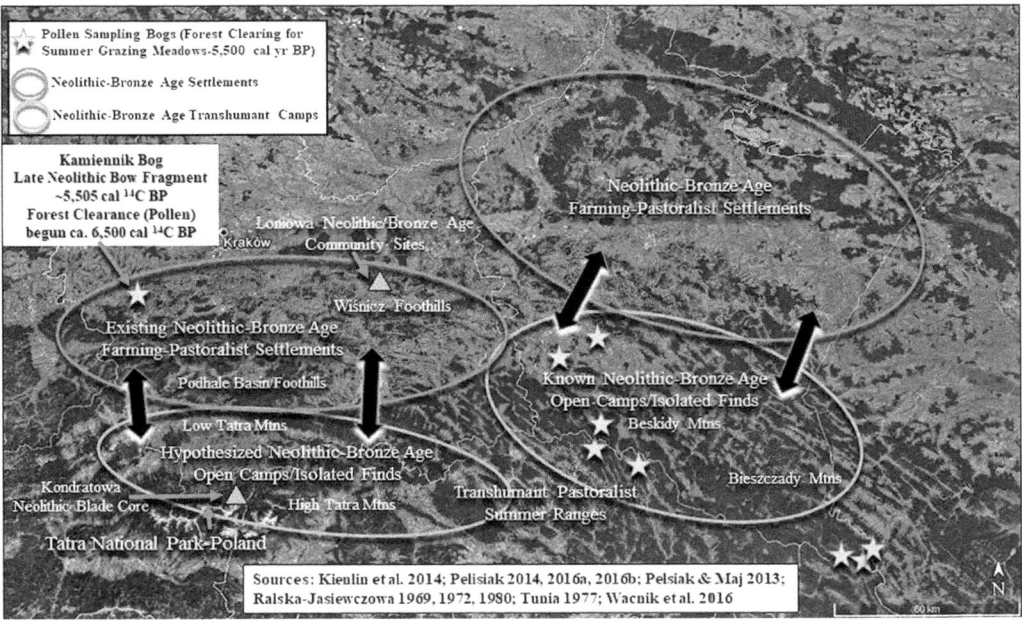

Figure 6.4. Map showing Beskidy and Bieszczady mountain range areas with concentrations of lower river valley and foothills located Neolithic through Bronze Age farming settlements and related open camps and isolated artifacts in higher mountains thought to represent pastoral transhumance. Stars indicate locations of bog sites that have produced prehistoric Neolithic-era botanic (including pollen) evidence of mountain ecosystem changes interpreted as reflecting transhumant domestic animal grazing effects.

Implementing Cultural Landscape Research for Documenting Long-Term Seasonal Transhumance in SE Poland's Tatra Mountains and Foothills

Southeast Poland's Tatra Mountains are a geographic landscape highly suited for investigation and modeling past human settlement populations once engaged in seasonal transhumance between low-altitude piedmont, foothills, and low-mountain environmental zones and higher-elevation mountains. Examination of the region's current archaeological and paleoclimatic records suggests, minimally, that human transhumance systems were in practice during the latest Pleistocene (Magdalenian Tradition) and early millennia of the region's agricultural-pastoralist cultural periods (Neolithic and Bronze Ages). The Tatra Cultural Landscapes Project, which focuses on Tatra National Park–Poland, home to the Western Carpathians' primary expanse of high-tundra, tundra-subalpine ecotone, and Pleistocene glaciation, as well as neighboring lower-elevation mountains, foothills, and river drainages, is particularly appropriate landscape to pose questions about the roles and forms of ancient transhumance systems. Utilizing advanced methods in archaeology, artifact analysis, paleoclimate and ecological reconstruction, Geographic Information Systems (GIS), high-resolution Global Positioning Systems (GPS), and accumulated decades of mountain research experience by this chapter's authors, we believe there is a good probability that significant progress can be made in future years in conducting meaningful field investigations and modeling prehistoric and historic settlement and vertical transhumance patterns in Poland's Tatra Mountain, Foothills, and Piedmont.

References

Arnold, E. R., and H. J. Greenfield 2006 The Origins of Transhumant Pastoralism in Temperate Southeastern Europe: A Zooarchaeological Perspective from the Central Balkans. *BAR International Series*. Oxford University Press, Oxford.

Bobak, D., and M. Połtowicz-Bobak 2013–2014 Bayesian-Age Modelling of the Magdalenian Settlement in the Territory of Present-Day Poland. *Recherches Archéologiques* 5–6:51–67.

Bobak, D., M. Łanczont, P., M. Połtowicz-Bobak, A. Nowak, B. Kufel-Diakowska, J. Kusiak, and K. Standzikowski 2017 Magdalenian Settlement on the Edge of the Loess Island: A Case Study from the Northern Foreland of the Carpathians (SE Poland). *Quaternary International* 438:158–173.

Bobak, D., T. Płonka, M. Połtowicz-Bobak, and A. Wiśniewski 2013 New Chronological Data for Weichselian Sites from Poland and Their Implications for Paleolithic. *Quaternary International* 296:23–36.

Bogucki, P. 2014 The Western Carpathian Highlands during the Neolithic. In *Settlement, Communication and Exchange around the Western Carpathians*, edited by T. L. Kienlin et al., 3–11. Archaeopress Archaeology, London.

Bogucki, P., and R. Grygiel 1993 The First Farmers of Central Europe: A Survey Article. *Journal of Field Archaeology* 20(4):399–426.

Brunswig, R. H. 2004a Hunting Systems and Seasonal Migratory Patterns through Time in Rocky Mountain National Park. In *Ancient and Historic Lifeways of North America's Rocky*

Mountains: Proceedings of the 2003 Rocky Mountain Anthropological Conference, edited by R. H. Brunswig and W. B. Butler, 392–409. Department of Anthropology, University of Northern Colorado, Greeley.

Brunswig, R. H. 2004b Paleoindian Colonization of Colorado's Southern Rockies: New Evidence from Rocky Mountain National Park and Adjacent Areas. In *Ancient and Historic Lifeways of North America's Rocky Mountains: Proceedings of the 2003 Rocky Mountain Anthropological Conference*, edited by R. H. Brunswig and W. B. Butler, 264–281. Department of Anthropology, University of Northern Colorado, Greeley.

Brunswig, R. H. 2005 *Prehistoric, Protohistoric, and Early Historic Native American Archeology of Rocky Mountain National Park: Final Report of Systemwide Archeological Inventory Program Investigations by the University of Northern Colorado (1998–2002).* Department of Anthropology, University of Northern Colorado, Greeley.

Brunswig, R. H. 2012 Apachean Archaeology of Rocky Mountain National Park, Colorado, and the Colorado Front Range. In *From the Land of Ever Winter to the American Southwest: Athapaskan Migrations, Mobility, and Ethnogenesis*, edited by D. Seymour, 20–36. University of Utah Press, Salt Lake City.

Brunswig, R. H. 2014a Paleoindian Cultural Landscapes and Archaeology of North Central Colorado's Southern Rockies. In *Frontiers in Colorado Paleoindian Archaeology: From the Dent Site to the Rocky Mountains*, 2nd ed., edited by R. H. Brunswig and B. L. Pitblado, 261–310. University Press of Colorado, Boulder.

Brunswig, R. H. 2014b Risks and Benefits of Global Warming and the Loss of Mountain Glaciers and Ice Patches to Archeological, Paleoclimate, and Paleoecology Resources. *Ecological Questions* 20:99–108.

Brunswig, R. H. 2015 Modeling Eleven Millennia of Seasonal Transhumance and Subsistence in Colorado's Prehistoric Rockies, USA. *Contributions in New World Archaeology* 8:43–102.

Brunswig, R. H. 2018 *Report of an Archaeological Reconnaissance Pre-Survey of the Lejowa and Kościeliska Valleys, Tatra National Park Poland: Report to the Tatra National Park-Poland (TPN) Office of Research*. Department of Anthropology, University of Northern Colorado, Greeley.

Brunswig, R. H., and D. Diggs 2014 GIS Modeling of Intermediate Scale Lithic Landscapes in the Colorado Rockies: The Case of Ballinger Draw. In *Lithics in the West: Using Lithic Analysis to Solve Archaeological Problems in Western North America*, edited by D. H. MacDonald, W. Andrefsky Jr., and P-L. Yu, 75–96. University of Montana Press, Missoula.

Brunswig, R. H., J. Doerner, and D. Diggs 2014 Eleven Millennia of Human Adaptation in Colorado's High Country: Modeling Cultural and Climatic Change in the Southern Rocky Mountains. In *Climates of Change: The Shifting Environments of Archaeology*, edited by S. Kulyk, C. G. Tremain, and M. Sawyer, 273–286. University of Calgary, Chacmool Archaeological Association, Calgary.

Brunswig, R. H., S. McBeth, and L. Ellinoff 2009 Re-enfranchising Native Peoples in the Southern Rocky Mountains: Integrated Contributions of Archaeological and Ethnographic Studies on Federal Lands. First co-author with Dr. S. McBeth (UNC) and L. Elinoff (Stanford University). In *Post-Colonial Perspectives in Archaeology*, edited by P. Bikoulis, D. Lacroix, and M. Pueramaki-Brown, 55–69. Chacmool Archaeological Association, Calgary.

Brunswig, R. H., and P. Valde-Nowak 2018 Archaeological Reconnaissance Pre-Survey of the Lejowa and Kościeliska Valleys, Tatra National Park, Poland. *Acta Archaeologica Carpathica* 53:49–55.

Bullinger, J., and R. Huber 2010. Au Temps des Chasseurs-Cueilleurs. *Archéologie Suisse* 33:15–21.

Carrer, F. 2012 Upland Sites and Pastoral Landscapes: New Perspectives into the Archaeology of Pastoralism in the Alps. In *Apsat 1: Teoria e Metodi Della Ricerca sui Paesaggi d'Altura*, edited by G. P. Brogiolo, D. E. Angelucci, A. Colecchia, and F. Remondino, 101–116. SAP Società Archeologica, Mantova.

Carrer, F. 2015 Herding Strategies, Dairy Economy and Seasonal Sites in the Southern Alps: Ethnoarchaeological Inferences and Archaeological Implications. *Journal of Mediterranean Archaeology* 28(1):3–22.

Cornelissen, M., and T. Reitmaier 2016 Filling the Gap: Recent Mesolithic Discoveries in the Central and Southeastern Swiss Alps. *Quaternary International* 423:9–22.

Czekaj-Zastawny, A. 2008 Linear Band Pottery Culture in the Upper Vistula River Basin. *Sprawozdania Archeologiczne* 60:31–72.

Dietre, B., C. Walser, K. Lambers, T. Reitmaier, I. Hajdas, and J. N. Haas 2014 Palaeoecological Evidence for Mesolithic to Medieval Climatic Change and Anthropogenic Impact on the Alpine Flora and Vegetation of the Silvretta Massif (Switzerland/Austria). *Quaternary International* 353:3–16.

Dietre, B., C. Walser, W. Kofler, K. Kothieringer, I. Hajdas, K. Lambers, T. Reitmaier, and J. N. Haas 2016 Neolithic to Bronze Age (4850–3450 cal. BP) Fire Management of the Alpine Lower Engadine Landscape (Switzerland) to Establish Pastures and Cereal Fields. *The Holocene* 27(2):181–196.

Diggs, D., and R. Brunswig 2013 The Use of GIS and Weights-of-Evidence Modeling in the Reconstruction of a Native American Sacred Landscape in Rocky Mountain National Park, Colorado. In *Continuity and Change in Cultural Mountain Adaptations: From Prehistory to Contemporary Threats*, edited by L. R. Lozny and D. Bates, 207–228. Springer-Verlag Studies in Human Ecology and Adaptation Series. Springer-Verlag, New York.

Doerner, J. 2014 Late Quaternary Prehistoric Environments of the Colorado Front Range Rocky Mountains. In *Emerging Frontiers in Colorado Paleoindian Archaeology*, 2nd ed., edited by R. H. Brunswig and B. L. Pitblado, 51–85. University Press of Colorado, Boulder.

Dolukhanov, P., A. Shukurov, D. Gronenborn, D. Sokoloff, V. Timofeev, and G. Zaitseva 2005 The Chronology of Neolithic Dispersal in Central and Eastern Europe. *Journal of Archaeological Science* 32:1441–1458.

Dulęba, P., P. Wroniecki, and R. Brejcha 2015 Non-destructive Survey of a Prehistoric Fortified Hill Settlement in Marchocice, Little Poland. *Sprawozdania Archeologiczne* 67:245–258.

Efstratiou, N., P. Biagi, P. Elefanti, P. Karkanas, and M. Ntinou 2006 Prehistoric Exploitation of Grevena Highland Zones: Hunters and Herders along the Pindus Chain of Western Macedonia (Greece). *World Archaeology* 38(3):415–435.

Efstratiou, N., P. Biagi, D. E. Angelucci, and R. Nisbet 2014 Highland Zone Exploitation in Northwestern Greece: The Middle Paleolithic Levallois Sites of the Pindus Range of Western Macedonia. *SAA Archaeological Record* (March):38–42.

Fiedorczuk, J., B. Bratlund, E. Kolstrup, and R. Schild 2007 Late Magdalenian Feminine Flint Plaquettes from Poland. *Antiquity* 81:97–105.

Galop, D., D. Rius, C. Cugny, and F. Mazier 2013 A History of Long-Term Human-Environment Interactions in the French Pyrenees Inferred from the Pollen Data. In *Continuity and Change in Cultural Adaptation to Mountain Environments*, edited by L. R. Lozny, 19–30. Springer-Verlag Studies in Human Ecology and Adaptation Series. Springer-Verlag, New York.

Geddes, D. S. 1983 Neolithic Transhumance in the Mediterranean Pyrenees. *World Archaeology* 15:52–66.

Hafner, A., and C. Schwörer 2018 Vertical Mobility around the High-Alpine Schnidejoch Pass: Indications of Neolithic and Bronze Age Pastoralism in the Swiss Alps from Paleoecological and Archaeological Sources. *Quaternary International* 484:3–18.

Hoffecker, J. F., and N. Cleghorn 2000 Mousterian Hunting Patterns in the Northwestern Caucasus and the Ecology of the Neanderthals. *International Journal of Osteoarchaeology* 10:368–378.

Hołub, B., M. Łanczont, and T. Madeyska 2016 Examples of Landscape Reconstructions Near the Eastern Range of the Magdalenian Occupation (SE Poland) based on GIS Analysis. *Anthropologie* 54(3):205–230.

Kabaciński, J., I. Sobkowiak-Tabaka, Z. Kasztovszky, S. Pietrzak, J. J. Langer, K. T. Biró, and B. Maróti 2015 Transcarpathian Influences in the Early Neolithic of Poland: A Case Study of Kowalewko and Rudna Wielka Sites. *Acta Archaeologica Carpathica* 50:5–32.

Kienlin, T. L., and P. Valde-Nowak 2008 Studies on the Bronze Age Settlement in the Area of Dunajectals (Wiśnicz-Hills, Lesser Poland). *History* 83(2):189–221.

Kienlin, T. L., M. Korczyńska, and K. Cappenberg 2014 Alternative Trajectories in Bronze Age Landscapes and the "Failure" to Enclose: A Case Study from the Middle Dunajec Valley. In *Settlement, Communication and Exchange around the Western Carpathians*, edited by T. L. Kienlin et al., 159–200. Archaeopress Archaeology, London.

Kienlin, T. L., and P. Valde-Nowak 2002–2004 Neolithic Transhumance in the Black Forest Mountains, SW Germany. *Journal of Field Archaeology* 29(1/2):29–44.

Kienlin, T. L., and P. Valde-Nowak 2008 Studies on the Bronze Age Settlement in the Area of Dunajectals (Wiśnicz-Hills, Lesser Poland). *History* 83(2):189–221.

Kienlin T. L., P. Valde-Nowak, M. Korczyńska, K. Cappenberg, J. Ociepka (eds.) 2014 *Settlement, Communication and Exchange around the Western Carpathians*. International workshop held at the Institute of Archaeology, Jagiellonian University, Kraków, October 27–28, 2012. Archaeopress, Oxford.

Kłapyta, P., J. Zasadni, J. Pociask-Karteczka, A. Gajda, and P. Franczak 2016 Late Glacial and Holocene Paleoenvironmental Records in the Tatra Mountains, East-Central Europe, Based on Lake, Peat Bog and Colluvial Sedimentary Data: A Summary Review. *Quaternary International* 415:126–144.

Komar, M., M. Łanczont, P. Valde-Nowak, K. Bałaga, B. Hołub, J. Kusiak, P. Mroczek, and P. Zielinski 2010 Paleoenvironmental Background and Age of the Late Paleolithic Settlement in SE Poland (A Case Study from the Sandomierz Upland and Carpathians). *Open Geography Journal* 3:55–66.

Kopacz, J., and P. Valde-Nowak 1987 From Studies of Flint Industries of the Circum Carpathian Epi-Corded Ware Cultural Circle (C.E.C.C.). In *Archaeologia interregionalis: New in the Stone Age Archaeology*, edited by J. K. Kozłowski and S. K. Kozłowski, 183–210. Wydawnictwo Uniwersytetu Warszawskiego, Warsaw.

Kozłowski, J. K. 1987 Le Magdalénien en Pologne. In *Le Magdalénien en Europe: E.R.A.U.L.* 38:31–49.

Kozłowski, J. K., M. Kaczanowska, A. Czekaj-Zastawny, A. Rauba-Bukowska, and K. Bukowski 2014 Early/Middle Neolithic Western (LBK) vs. Eastern (ALPC) Linear Pottery Cultures: Ceramics and Lithic Raw Materials Circulation. *Acta Archaeologica Carpathica* 46:37–76.

Kufel-Diakowska, B., and J. Wilczyński 2014 The Camp of Upper Paleolithic Hunters in Targowisko 10 (S Poland). In *International Conference on Use-Wear Analysis*, edited by J. Marreiros, N. Bicho, and J. Gibaja Bao, 73–182. Cambridge Scholars, Cambridge.

Łanczont, M., T. A. Madeyska, A. Muzyczuk, and P. Valde-Nowak, P. 2002 Hłomcza-Magdalenian Settlement Site in the Polish Carpathians. In *Starsza i Srodkowa Epoka Kamienia w Karpatach Polskich*, edited by J. Gancarski, 147–188. Muzeum Podkarpackie w Krośnie, Krosno.

Leesch, D., W. Müller, E. Nielsen, and J. Bullinger 2012 The Magdalenian in Switzerland: Recolonization of a Newly Accessible Landscape. *Quaternary International* 272–273:191–208.

Leigh, D. S., T. L. Gragson, and M. R. Coughlan 2016 Colluvial Legacies of Millennial Landscape Change on Individual Hillsides: Place-Based Investigation in the Western Pyrenees Mountains. *Quaternary International* 402:61–71.

Lityńska-Zając, M., M. Hoyo, and K. Cywa 2014 Plant Remains Found in Archaeological Sites in the Carpathian Foothills: Preliminary Report. In *Settlement, Communication and Exchange around the Western Carpathians*, edited by T. L. Kienlin et al., 207–221. Archaeopress Archaeology, London.

Lorenc, M. 2006 Radiocarbon Dating of Some Late Pleistocene Faunal Assemblages in Caves in Poland. *Acta Zoologica Cracoviensia* 49A(1–2):41–61.

Lorenc, M. 2013 Radiocarbon Ages of Bones from Vistulian (Weichselian) Cave Deposits in Poland and Their Stratigraphy. *Acta Geologica Polonica* 63(3):399–424.

Margielewski, W., M. Krąpiec, P. Valde-Nowak, and V. Zernitskaya 2010 A Neolithic Yew Bow in the Polish Carpathians: Evidence of the Impact of Human Activity on Mountainous Paleoenvironment from the Kamiennik Landslide Peat Bog. *Catena* 80(3):141–153.

Martin, L. 2015 Plant Economy and Territory Exploitation in the Alps during the Neolithic (5000–4200 cal BC): First Results of Archaeobotanical Studies in the Valais (Switzerland). *Vegetation History Archaeobotany* 24:63–73.

Mevel, L. 2013 Magdalenian Pioneers in the Northern French Alps, 17 000 cal BP. *Antiquity* 87:384–404.

Moran, A. P., S. Ivy-Ochs, M. Schuh, M. Christl, and H. Kerschner 2016 Evidence of Central Alpine Glacier Advances During the Younger Dryas–Early Holocene Transition Period. *Boreas* 45(3):398–410.

Mourre, V., L. Bruxelles, D. Colonge, S. Costamagno, V. Laroulandie, D. Rambaud, C. Thiébaut, and J. Viguier 2004 *Le Site Moustérien de la Grotte du Noisetier à Fréchet-Aure (Hautes-Pyrénées): Rapport de Fouille programmée annuelle*. SRA Midi-Pyrénées.

Nadachowski, A., and P. Valde-Nowak 2015 New Late Pleistocene Faunal Assemblages from Podhale Basin, Western Carpathians, Poland: Preliminary Results. *Acta Zoologica Cracoviensia* 58(2):181–194.

Nehlich, O., J. Montgomery, J. Evans, S. Schade-Lindig, S. L. Pichler, M. P. Richards, and K. W. Alt 2009 Mobility or Migration: A Case Study from the Neolithic Settlement of Nieder-Mörlen (Hessen, Germany). *Journal of Archaeological Science* 36:1791–1799.

Pelisiak, A. 2008 Late Neolithic Settlements and the Salt in the Carpathians. In *Man and Mountains: Palaeogeographical and Archaeological Perspectives*, edited by T. Kalicki and B. Szmoniewski, 51–63. Studies of the Institute of Geography UJK, Kielce.

Pelisiak, A. 2012 The Corded Ware Culture Barrows in the Cultural Landscape of the Eastern Polish Carpathians during III and II Millennium BC and the Monumental Structures between the Carpathians and the Baltic Sea in the Neolithic and the Early Bronze Age. In *"As Time Goes By": Monumentality, Landscapes and the Temporal Perspective—Proceedings of the International Workshop "Socio-Environmental Dynamics over the Last 12,000 Years: The*

Creation of Landscapes II," edited by M. Furholt, M. Hinz, and D. Mischka, 215–230. R. Habelt, Kiel.

Pelisiak, A. 2014 Settlement, Economy and Climate between 3200 and 2500 BC: Late Neolithic Transformations in South-Eastern Poland. In *Settlement, Communication and Exchange around the Western Carpathians*, edited by T. L. Kienlin, 143–158. Archaeopress Archaeology, London.

Pelisiak, A. 2016a Economic and Social Changes and Climate between 3200 and 2500 B.C.: Late Neolithic Transformations in Southeastern Poland. In *Climate and Cultural Change in Prehistoric Europe and the Near East*, edited by P. F. Biehl and O. P. Nieuwenhuyse, 237–256. State University of New York Press, Albany.

Pelisiak, A. 2016b Siliceous Raw Material from Bieszczady Mountains: Sources and Use. *Archaeologia Polana* 54:21–31.

Pelisiak, A. 2016c The Beginnings of Mobile Husbandry in the Mountain Periphery of Southeastern Poland. In *Transitional Landscapes? The 3rd Millennium BC in Europe, 2016 Proceedings of the International Workshop "Socio-Environmental Dynamics over the Last 12,000 Years: The Creation of Landscapes III (15th–18th April 2013),"* edited by M. Furholt, R. Grossman, and M. Szmyt, 209–227. Bonn.

Pelisiak, A., and J. Kruk 2014 Saltwater Springs and the Exploitation of the Eastern Carpathians in the Late Neolithic Period. In *Szkice Neolityczne*, edited by K. Czyarniak, J. Kolenda, and M. Markiewicz, 285–300. Wydawnictwo Instytutu Archeologii i Etnologii Polskiej Akademii Nauk, Wrocław.

Pelisiak, A., and Z. Maj 2013 New Neolithic and Early Bronze Age Finds from the Bieszczady Mountains (Wetlina River Valley and Its Surroundings). *Acta Archaeologica Carpathica* 48:265–272.

Pinhasi, R., T. F. G. Higham, L. V. Golovanova, and V. B. Doronichev 2011 Revised Age of Late Neanderthal Occupation and the End of the Middle Paleolithic in the Northern Caucasus. *Proceedings of the National Academy of Sciences* 108(21):8611–8616.

Połtowicz, M. 2005 The Magdalenian Period in Poland and Neighbouring Areas. *Archaeologia Baltica* 7:21–28.

Połtowicz-Bobak, M. 2006 The Eastern Borders of the Magdalenian Culture Range. *Analecta Archaeologica Ressoviensa* 1:11–26.

Połtowicz-Bobak, M. 2009 Magdalenian Settlement in Poland in the Light of Recent Research. In *Humans, Environment and Chronology of the Late Glacial of the North European Plain*, edited by M. Street, N. Barton, and T. Terberger, 55–66. Proceedings of the 15th U.I.S.P.P. Congress, September 2006, Lisbon.

Połtowicz-Bobak, M. 2012 Observations on the Late Magdalenian in Poland. *Quaternary International* 272–273:297–307.

Połtowicz-Bobak, M. 2013 *Wschodnia Prowincja Magdalenienu*. Wydawnictwo Uniwersytetu Rzeszowskiego, Rzeszów.

Przybyła, M. S., and W. Blajer 2008 *Struktury Osadnicze w Epoce Brązu i Wczesnej Epoce Zelaza na Obszarze Podkarpackiej Wysoczyzny Lessowej Między Wisłokiem i Sanem*. Jagiellonian University, Kraków.

Rączkowski, W. 2011 Integrating Survey Data: The Polish AZP and Beyond. In *Remote Sensing for Archaeological Heritage Management*, edited by D. C. Cowley. EAC Occasional Paper No. 5:153–150. Europae Archaeologia Consilium (EAC), Brussels.

Ralska-Jasiewczowa, M. 1969 Ślady Kultury Człowieka w Diagramach Pyłkowych z Bieszczadów Zachodnich. *Acta Archaeologica Carpathica* 11(1):105–108.

Ralska-Jasiewczowa, M. 1972 Remarks on the Late-Glacial and Holocene History of Vegetation in the Eastern Part of Polish Carpathians. *Berichte der Deutschen Botanischen Gesellschaft* 85:101–112.

Ralska-Jasiewczowa, M. 1980 Late-Glacial and Holocene Vegetation of the Bieszczady Mts. (Polish Eastern Carpathians). Naukowe, Państwowe Wydawn.

Rey, F., C. Schwörer, E. Gobet, D. Colombaroli, J. F. N. van Leeuwen, S. Schleiss, and W. Tinner 2013 Climatic and Human Impacts on Mountain Vegetation at Lauenensee (Bernese Alps, Switzerland) during the Last 14,000 Years. *The Holocene* 23(10):1415–1427.

Riehl, S. 2006 Nomadism, Pastoralism and Transhumance in the Archaeobotanical Record: Examples and Methodological Problems. In *Die Sichtbarkeit von Nomaden und Saisonaler Besiedlung in der Archäologie: Multidisziplinäre Annäherungen an ein Methodisches Problem*, edited by S. R. Hauser, 105–125. Orientwissenschaftliche Hefte 21, Mitteilungen des SFB, Halle.

Rydlewski, J. 2006 The Earliest Paleolithic Site in the Polish Tatras. *Acta Archaeologica Carpathica* 41:5–9.

Rydlewski, J., and P. Valde-Nowak 1981a Koniówka. Badania 1980. *Informator Archaeologiczny*:12–13. Ośrodek Dokumentacji Zabytków Wydawnictwo, Warszawa.

Rydlewski, Jacek, and P. Valde-Nowak 1981b Podczerwone: Badania 1980. *Informator Archaeologiczny*:19. Osrodek Dokumentacji Zabytków Wydawnictwo, Warszawa.

Schild, R. (ed.) 2014 *Wilczyce: A Late Magdalenian Winter Hunting Camp in Southern Poland*. Institute of Archaeology and Ethnology Polish Academy of Sciences, Warsaw.

Tunia, K. 1977 Découverte d'un Nucleus en Silex dans la Vallée de Kondratowa (à 1350 m d'altitude) dans les Monts Tatra. *Acta Archaeologica Carpathica* 17:145–148.

Valde-Nowak, P. 1986 Inventare des Orawa-Typus und ihre Bedeutung in der Bezeichnung der Besiedlung aus der Frühbronzezeit in der Karpaten. In *Urzeitliche und Frühhistorische Besiedlung der Ostslowakei in Bezug zu den Nachbargebieten*, edited B. Chropovsky, 115–123. Archeologický ústav SAV, Nitra.

Valde-Nowak, P. 1987 Entdeckung der Paläolithischen Fundstellen im Tal deer Białka Tatrzańska-Flusses. *Acta Archaeologica Carpathica* 27:5–35.

Valde-Nowak, P. 1991 Studies in Pleistocene Settlement in the Polish Carpathians. *Antiquity* 65:593–606.

Valde-Nowak, P. 1998 Badania Osady Neolitycznej w Łoniowej (Pogórze Wiśnickie). *Acta Archaeologica Carpathica* 34:195–206.

Valde-Nowak, P. 2003 Upper Paleolithic Sequence. In *Oblazowa Cave, Human Activity, Stratigraphy and Paleoenvironment*, edited by P. Valde-Nowak, A. Nadachowski, and T. Madeyska, 44–80. Institute of Archaeology and Ethnology PAS, Krakow.

Valde-Nowak, P. 2008 Isolated Grave of the Baden Culture from the Polish Beskidy Mts. In *The Baden Complex and the Outside World*, edited by M. Furholt, M. Szmyt, and A. Zastawny, 139–140. Studien zum Archäologie in Ostmitteleuropa, 4, Bonn.

Valde-Nowak, P. 2009a Early Farming Adaptation in the Wiśnicz Foothills in the Carpathians: Settlements at Łoniowa and Żerków. *Recherches Archéologiques* SN 1:15–35.

Valde-Nowak, P. 2009b Obłazowa and Hłomcza: Two Paleolithic Sites in the North Carpathian Province of Southern Poland. In *Lithic Materials and Paleolithic Societies,* edited by B. Adams and B. S. Blades, 196–207. Wiley-Blackwell, Oxford.

Valde-Nowak, P. 2010 Mousterian Sequences of the Obłazowa Cave (Polish Carpathians). *Studia Archeologiczne* 41:1–11.

Valde-Nowak, P. 2013a New Light on Bandkeramik Longhouses. In *Environment and Subsistence-Forty Years after Janusz Kruk's Settlement Studies*, edited by S. Kadrow and and P. Włodarczak, 93–103. Rzeszów, Institute of Archaeology UR and Verlag Dr. Rudolf Habelt GmbH, Bonn.

Valde-Nowak, P. 2013b The North-Carpathians Province of Silica Rocks during Stone Age. In *The Lithic Raw Material Sources and Interregional Human Contacts in the Northern Carpathian Regions*, edited by Z. Mester, 87–98. Polska Akademia Umiejętności, Kraków.

Valde-Nowak, P. 2014 Long Houses on Hilltop Camps in the Mountains: Some Aspects of the Neolithic in the Dunajec Project. In *Settlement, Communication and Exchange around the Western Carpathians*, edited by T. L. Kienlin et al., 27–49. Archaeopress Archaeology, London.

Valde-Nowak, P. 2015 Worked *Conus* shells as Pavlovian Fingerprint: Obłazowa Cave, Southern Poland. *Quaternary International* 359–360:153–156.

Valde-Nowak, P., M. Cieśla, A. Kraszewska, K. Kerneder-Gubała, K. Rak, and M. Wawrzcak 2016 Sites from the Stone Age in Dunajec River Upper Catchment Basin: New Perspective. *Acta Archaeologica Carpathica* 51:293–306.

Valde-Nowak, P., and A. Kraszewska 2014 Nowa Biała and Sromowce Niżne-Late Paleolithic Central Carpathian Sites with Arched-Backed Points. *Acta Archaeologica Carpathica* 49:5–35.

Valde-Nowak, P., A. Kraszewska, and C. Magda 2017 Magdalenian Figurine from Obłazowa Cave. *Acta Archaeologica Carpathica* 52:299–304.

Valde-Nowak, P., A. Kraszewska, M. Cieśla, and A. Nadachowski 2018 Late Magdalenian Camp-site in a Rockshelter at the Obłazowa Rock. In *Multas per Gentes et Multa per Saecula*, edited by P. Valde-Nowak, K. Sobczyk, M. Nowak, and J. Źrałka, 175–183. Institute of Archaeology, Jagiellonian University, Krakow.

Valde-Nowak, P., A. Kraszewska, and D. Stefański 2013–2014 Arch-Backed and Tanged Point Technocomplexes in the North Carpathian Zone. *Recherches Archéologiques* 5–6:69–85.

Valde-Nowak, P., and A. Muzyczuk 2000 Magdalenian Settlement at Hłomcza (Polisch Carpathians). *Acta Archaeologica Carpathica* 35:5–32.

Valde-Nowak, P., and A. Nadachowski 2014 Micoquian Assemblage and Environmental Conditions for the Neanderthals in Oblazowa Cave, Western Carpathians, Poland. *Quaternary International* 326–327:146–156.

Valde-Nowak, P., A. Nadachowski, and T. Madeyska (eds.) 2003 *Obłazowa Cave, Human Activity, Stratigraphy and Paleoenvironment*. Institute of Archaeology and Ethnology PAS, Krakow.

Valde-Nowak, P., and A. Tarasiński 2007 A Site of the Baden Culture in the Middle Beskid Mountains. *Acta Archaeologica Carpathica* 41:69–83.

Wacnik, A., D. Nalepka, W. Granoszewski, Adam Walanus, E. Madeyska, K. Cywa, K. Szczepanek, and E. Cieslak 2016 Development of Modern Forest Zones in the Beskid Niski Mts. and Adjacent Area (Western Carpathians) in the Late Holocene: A Palaeobotanical Perspective. *Quaternary International* 415:303–324.

Weniger, G. C. 1987 Magdalenian Settlement Pattern and Subsistence in Central Europe. In *The Pleistocene Old World*, edited by O. Soffer, 201–215. Springer Science & Business Media, New York.

Wiśniewski, A., M. Furmanek, M. Borowski, K. Kądziołka, A. Rapiński, and K. Winnicka 2012 Lithic Raw Material and Late Paleolithic Strategies of Mobility: A Case Study from Sowin 7, SW Poland. *Anthropologie* 50(4):391–409.

Zasadni, J., and P. Kłapyta 2014 The Tatra Mountains during the Last Glacial Maximum. *Journal of Maps* 10(3):440–456.

CHAPTER SEVEN

The Onset of Alpine Pastoral Systems in the Eastern Alps

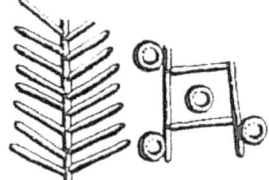

Klaus D. Oeggl, Daniela Festi, and Andreas Putzer

Abstract *The onset of alpine pasture is a matter of highly controversial debate both in archaeology and in paleoecology of Central Europe. Regrettably any archaeological evidence for the existence of a Neolithic alpine pastoral system is missing up to now and the assumption is based on palynological data only. However, the palynological record is also ambiguous because pasture indicators in alpine regions react positive on grazing as well as on fertilization induced by a higher runoff of precipitation. Thus, classical alpine pasture indicators reflect both grazing pressure and climatic change in the high altitudes of the Alps.*

Anyhow, alpine pastoral systems are a common practice in Alpine animal husbandry. There are three main reasons for its practice: 1) climatic, 2) economic, and 3) cultural ideology. In this study we tested the aforementioned reasons in an interdisciplinary study on the beginning of pastoral activities in high altitudes in the Eastern Alps. This is conducted by palynological analyses of peat deposits aligned on an altitudinal transect through the central part of the Eastern Alps situated at the timberline (1,600–2,400 masl) and combined with archaeological surveys. Our studies reveal that grazing pressure is reflected at the earliest since the Bronze Age, which is corroborated by archaeological findings near the palynologically investigated sites.

INTRODUCTION

Since the discovery of the Neolithic glacier mummy "Ötzi" in the nival belt of the main alpine ridge, the onset of alpine pasture is a matter of a highly controversial debate both in archaeology and in paleoecology of the Eastern Alps. The implication is that his sojourn in the high altitudes of the Alps is connected with pastoral nomadism. Regrettably, any archaeological evidence for the existence of such Neolithic alpine pastoral systems is absent up to now. The assumption is based on palynological studies of several peat deposits near the Iceman's discovery site only. These pollen diagrams reveal a vegetation change about one thousand years before the lifetime of the Iceman. Distinct rises in the percentage values of pollen indicative for human interference suggest that this vegetation change is caused by grazing livestock on high-altitudinal grasslands (Bortenschlager 2000). However, this is a striking early indication for grazing in the alpine regions and requires independent confirmation.

Numerous caprine dung pellets have been recovered at the Iceman's discovery site that date from 5400 to 2000 BC (Kutschera et al. 2014). Plant macro remains and pollen analyses were conducted on about 120 of these dung pellets to evaluate if these droppings derive from livestock or from game by reconstructing their diet and the vegetation they fed on (Oeggl et al. 2009). The approach was to create a calibration data set of pollen spectra of modern sheep/goat feces and to test if the pollen data enable a discrimination of droppings deriving from grazing in high or low altitudes. After this assumption was verified the pollen data of the subfossil dung pellets were numerically compared with the modern calibration data set. Amazingly, all dung pellets from the discovery site grouped with the high-altitudinal modern droppings. Furthermore, findings of plant remains growing only in the alpine and nival zone (>2,400 masl)—like alpine rock-cress (*Arabis alpina*), alpine moon daisy (*Leucanthemopsis alpina*), glacier buttercup (*Ranunculus glacialis*), snowbed willow (*Salix herbacea*), and purple saxifrage (*Saxifraga oppositifolia*)—corroborate a browsing of these animals in the alpine belt and confirm the results from pollen analyses: it is dung from game.

Moreover, palynological analysis from a peat bog adjacent to the Rofenhöfe hamlet, which is the highest permanent settlement in the Eastern Alps and about 10 km linear distance north from the Iceman's discovery site, shows a decline of the timberline at the time of the Iceman, but no evidence for grazing until the Late Bronze Age (Tschisner 1996).

These aforementioned results raised serious questions about such an early pasture activity in the high-alpine regions observed by Bortenschlager (2000). This is much more striking, because the increase of pasture indicators in his study coincides with well-known climatic variations in the Eastern Alps (Bortenschlager 1992): the so-called Rotmoos 1 (5500–5000 BC) and Rotmoos 2 (4000–4500 BC) fluctuations. Considering this, the justified question arises: What do we observe through pollen analysis?

Methodological Questions

The basic assumption is that the grazing of ungulates has influence on energy flow and nutrient cycling in ecosystems and causes a change in the relative abundance of species in the vegetation cover (Hobbs 1996). Usually foraging selectivity of herbivores leads to an increase of unpalatable and of chemically or morphologically defended plants on pastures.

This is also observable in pollen analyses and Behre (1981) provided a distinguished compilation of the pollen rain in different pastures and grazed forests, which was groundbreaking for the tracing of anthropogenic impact on the vegetation of European lowlands since the Neolithic. However, plant–herbivore relations are complex and such vegetation changes depend on different factors. In addition to plant tolerance and herbivore forage selectivity, foraging frequency and ungulate density play a decisive role (Augustine and McNaughton 1998). Another decisive factor is the added input of nitrogen in the upper soil levels by urine and feces of the ungulates, which may destabilize the plant composition (Hobbs 1996) and result in a plant diversity change.

Anyhow, it should be borne in mind that Behre (1981) defined the "classical" anthropogenic indicators for the lowlands and the application of his anthropogenic indicators to areas marginal to Central and Northern Europe has to be conducted with utmost caution. The consideration of the ecological demands of these taxa and their pollen dispersal is crucial, as Brun (2011) has pointed out in her critical review of human indicators in pollen diagrams. Moreover, most of the anthropogenic indicators (e.g., *Plantago lanceolata*, *P. major*, *P. media*, *Rumex acetosa*) reach their altitudinal limit at about 1,900 m in the Eastern Alps (Polatschek 2000) and are improper for the detection of local grazing impact in alpine grasslands. Much more a compilation of grazing indicators *sensu* Bortenschlager (2000) in respect to their pollination mechanism, pollen source area, representation, and indicative values (Table 7.1) shows the complexity of the problem. Diverse pollen types vary in their pollination and pollen behavior. Indicators suitable for grazing in high altitudes depend strongly on their local pollen source area and underrepresentation in the natural pollen rain. All these pollen types (e.g., *Aconitum*, *Anemone nemorosa*-type, *Bartsia*-type, *Euphrasia*, Fabaceae, *Gentianella campestris*-type, Gentianaceae, *Oxytropis*-type, *Pedicularis*, *Rhinanthus*) are insect pollinated of local origin. This means that their regular observation in pollen slides requires a high number of total grains counted resulting in a necessary pollen sum count of about ten thousand grains or more (Mosimann 1962, 1963). Such demands for statistical control are time-consuming and hardly satisfied.

In fact, several pollen types are indicative for both pasture and irrigation, that only a few pollen types are appropriate as true pasture indicators (cf. Table 7.1). Indeed, if classical pasture indicators *sensu* Bortenschlager (2000) are applied in the high-alpine regions of the Central Alps, we observe an increase in these pollen types depending on altitude of the investigated site in between 3,100–3,600 yrs cal BC or 3,800–4,400 yrs cal BC. Both periods mark cold spells in the Eastern Alps (Bortenschlager 1992; Magny et al. 2004) with increased precipitation, resulting in a higher runoff and higher loading with mineral particles, which may cause a natural manuring of the grass mats and consequently induce a diversity change.

In consideration of this complexity, indicators are required that enable evidence for pastoral activities in high-altitudinal regions without ambiguity. A vegetation change is often linked with plant diversity changes and thus the drivers for plant diversity are decisive. Pierce et al. (2007) discovered that disturbance determines niche differentiation, coexistence, and biodiversity in alpine communities. Grazing means biomass destruction, which selects for regenerative traits, fecundity, and rapid completion of life cycle. This opportunistic strategy corresponds to ruderalism *sensu* Grime (2001). Contrary to lowlands, where competition usually controls plant interactions, abiotic stress is high in alpine habitats resulting in positive interactions among plants (Callaway et al. 2002). The different effect of stress to plants subject to altitude is also the reason why the application of "classical" pasture indicators (*sensu* Behre 1981; Bortenschlager 2000) in high-altitudinal sites results in ambiguous findings. Therefore distinct evidence for the onset of grazing in high-alpine regions requires the design of a specific calibration data set representative for a distinct investigation area (cf. Mazier et al. 2006, 2009). Here we show a case study for the southern Ötztal Mountains, the living space of the Neolithic Iceman (Bortenschlager and Oeggl 2000). The objective is to detect the onset of pastoral activities by pollen analysis in the high-altitudes of the Ötztal Mountains. We used a modern analogue technique to define specific grazing indicators for the subalpine and alpine regions of the investigation area. Then we applied these grazing indicators on pollen studies from the subalpine and alpine regions. In addition, we completed archaeological surveys near the studied sites to validate the palynological findings.

The Investigation Area

The investigation area is located in the Ötztal Mountains south of the main alpine ridge and comprises the high-montane and subalpine regions between the Schnals Valley in the east and the Schlandraun in the west (Figure 7.1). This area was selected because the Neolithic Iceman spent his entire life in the territory south of the discovery site (Müller et al. 2003) and there exists some Neolithic findings in the valley bottoms of the Vinschgau (Steiner 2007). Moreover, a historic transhumance route runs along the Schlandraun, divides the nearby Lagaun mire (site 3 in Figure 7.1) with one branch to the village Kurzras and the other to Vernagt Lake (site 1 in Figure 7.1). Both routes cross the main alpine ridge and end north in Vent (see Figure 7.1), where the grazing grounds of the South Tyrolean farmers are still located today (Werner 1969). Furthermore, it is reasonable that the first grazing impact becomes visible in the alpine and subalpine regions located in the immediate vicinity of the Iceman's place of residence.

An archaeological survey of the Schlandraun Valley provided the first findings concerning high-altitudinal pasture, although definitely younger than the Iceman's lifetime (Mahlknecht 2005). There stone structures associated with alpine pasture are unearthed and have been dated to the Late Bronze Age, besides one ^{14}C-date of a charcoal layer within a stone enclosure predating it, to the very early Copper Ages, which needs further investigation. Based on these studies we selected five mires arrayed in an altitudinal transect along the traditional transhumance route in the Schlandraun and Schnals Valleys. The first and lowermost site is Lake Vernagt situated in the high-montane region about 1,689 masl (site 1 in Figure 7.1). Today the site is submerged at the bottom of a power plant. Meadows and pastures characterize the surrounding vegetation, as well as a larch-arolla pine forest (*Larici-Pinetum cembrae*) in the south and a grazed larch forest to the north. The second is the Schwarzboden mire (site 2 in Figure 7.1) located in the subalpine regions about 2,150 masl.

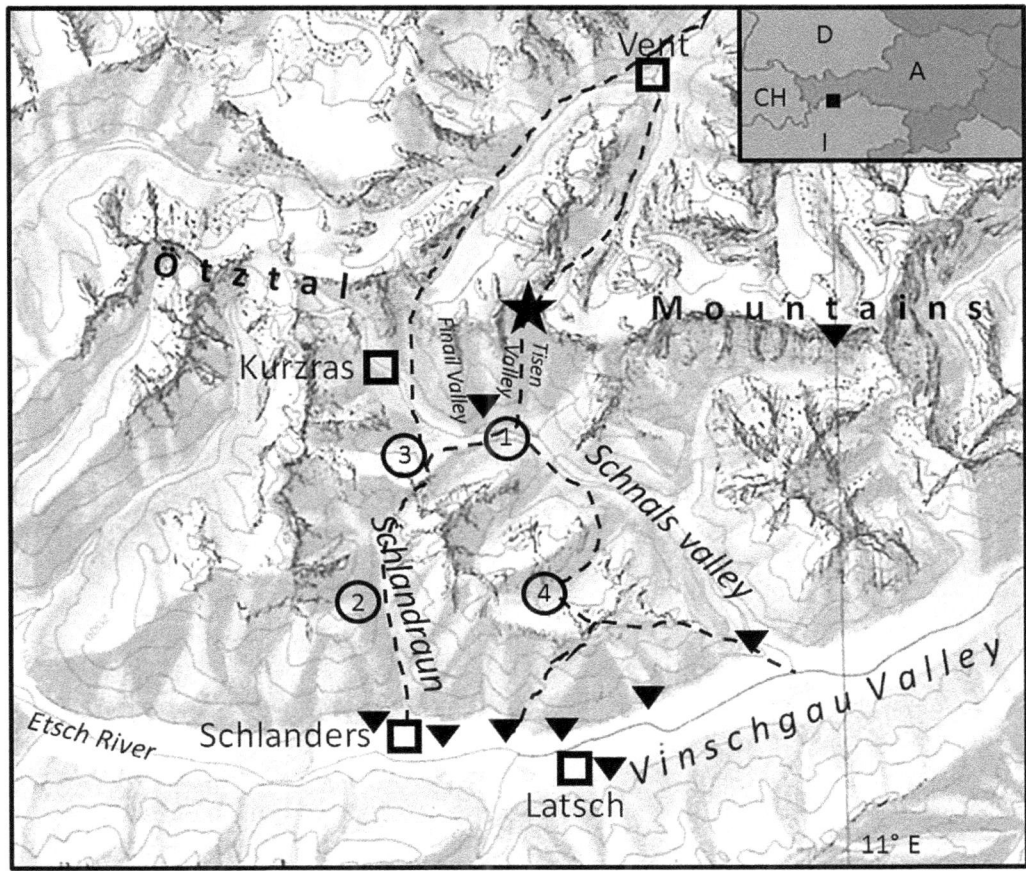

Figure 7.1. Topographic map of the investigation area: the small black square of the inserted rectangle in the right corner shows the location of the study area at the Austrian/Italian border; dotted line = ancient track; asterisk = discovery site of the Neolithic glacier mummy Ötzi; ○ = investigated sites; □ = settlements, ▼ = Neolithic findings; A = Austria; CH = Switzerland; D = Germany; I = Italy; 1 = Lake Vernagt; 2 = Schwarzboden mire; 3 = Lagaun mire; 4 = Penaud mire.

Subalpine grasslands and a sparse grazed larch-arolla pine forest (*Larici-Pinetum cembrae*) dominate the recent vegetation. The Lagaun mire lies at 2,180 masl (site 3 in Figure 7.1), also covered in a sparse grazed larch-arolla pine forest (*Larici-Pinetum cembrae*). The highest and last site is the Penaud mire, located at the timberline at 2,330 masl (site 4 in Figure 7.1) surrounded by alpine grasslands, single larch (*Larix decidua*), and arolla pine (*Pinus cembra*) trees. For a more detailed description of the sites, we refer to Festi et al. (2014). All the selected mires show a sufficient thickness of deposits and are located near stone structures believed to be connected with prehistoric pasture activities (cf. Mahlknecht 2005; Putzer 2009; Putzer et al. 2016b). Their analysis will provide new evidence about the beginning and practice of local seasonal transhumance in the area.

Methods

Fieldwork

The sediment core of Lake Vernagt derives from a technical coring and has been provided by Enel Energia Spa hosted in Bozen. The sediment lithology of the core is diverse, where organic and inorganic layers alternate. Only the organic layers (detritus gyttja and peat) covering the periods from the Neolithic to the Iron Ages have been analyzed in this study. The peat deposits of all three mires have been extracted by lowering a plastic tube (10 cm diameter) to the bedrock.

Laboratory Work

Pollen analyses. Subsamples of standard volume were collected in standard intervals. The samples have been chemically digested according to the standard method (Faegri and Iversen 1989) and afterward treated with HF 20 percent if needed. Pollen has been identified under a light microscope at a maximum magnification of 600x, using the modern pollen reference collection of the Botanical Institute of Innsbruck University, as well as standard identification keys (Beug 2004; Faegri and Iversen 1989; Moore et al. 1991; Punt 1976–2009). Pollen grains, micro-charcoal, and NPPs (non-pollen palynomorphs) were quantified and the results are displayed graphically in the form of percentage diagrams calculated and plotted with the FAGUS software, developed at the Botanical Institute of Innsbruck University. Pollen, charcoal, and NPP percentage values were calculated using terrestrial pollen as 100 percent. For Vernagt Lake, a minimum of one thousand terrestrial pollen grains (AP and NAP) per sample were counted whenever possible. For Schwarzboden, Lagaun, and Penaud, eight hundred pollen grains per sample were counted, when possible, whereby Cyperaceae are excluded from the pollen sum. In this study, we display simplified pollen diagrams and for further details, we refer to Festi et al. (2014).

The Evaluation of Specific Grazing Indicators. The palynological reconstruction of the grazing activity demands the creation of specific pasture indicators for the investigation area as mentioned earlier. Here we used a modern pollen analogue technique described by Mazier et al. (2009) to establish pasture indicator calibration data sets for the altitudinal regions according to where the study sites are located (Festi et al. 2014). Pasture indicator pollen types were selected according to their affinity to the variable "grazing" pressure by performing statistical analyses such as Canonical Analyses and Canonical Correspondence Analyses (ter Braak and Smilauer, 1998), as well as calculation of the weighted average optimum (WA_{opt}) of pollen in relation to grazing. The applicability of taxa takes into account the Davis indices of association (Davis 1984) and the ecological behavior of the plant species producing the pollen type. This strict selection resulted in two calibration data sets, one for the montane belt (up to 1,600 masl) and one for the subalpine regions (1,800–2,500 masl). In the next steps hereby described, a proper calibration data set has been used for each site according to the site's altitude. For the Lagaun, Schwarzboden, and Penaud mires located at or above the timberline the subalpine calibration data set has been applied, which encompasses *Campanula/Phyteuma*-type, *Rumex acetosella*-type, Gentianaceae, *Plantago alpina*-type, *Rhinanthus*-type, while for the Lake Vernagt fossil record (located on the valley bottom) the montane calibration data set, composed by *Artemisia*-type, *Plantago lanceolata*-type, Chenopodiaceae, Brassicaceae, Cichorioideae pollen, has been applied. Table 7.2 lists the WA_{opt} scores of the selected pasture indicators since their values are used in the following steps of the reconstruction. The WA_{opt} score has a value between 0 and 1, expressing the preference for grazing calculated for a pollen type. The higher the value, the higher the preference for pasture activity and hence its validity as a pasture indicator. The reconstruction of pasture activities in the study area has been obtained by calibrating the percentage values of the pasture indicators occurring in the fossil pollen diagrams as follows: the WA_{opt} value of each indicator (Table 7.2) has been multiplied by the corresponding pollen percentage value observed in the fossil pollen diagrams (Figures 7.2–7.5), obtaining a calibrated pasture indicator value. For each sample a cumulative value of pasture indicators has been calculated summing up the values of the calibrated indicators. This results in a value representative for pasture for each sample. For every site, the pasture values have been transformed into z-scores. Only scores >0 were generally considered to be indicative for pasture activities, assuming that scores <0 represent the natural occurrence of the evaluated pasture indicators.

TABLE 7.1. POLLEN TYPES USED AS GRAZING INDICATORS BY BORTENSCHLAGER (2000); THEIR POLLEN TRANSFER, DISPERSAL, AND INDICATOR VALUES ACCORDING TO OEGGL (1994): L = LOCAL, R = REGIONAL, O = OVERREPRESENTED, U = UNDERREPRESENTED, X = INDIFFERENT, + = INDICATIVE, − = NOT INDICATIVE

pollen type	pollen transfer by	pollen source	pollen representation	pasture	irrigation fertilization
Chenopodiaceae	wind	(L), R	O	+	+
Plantago, P. lanceolata-type	wind	(L), R	X	+	+
Rumex-, Rumex acetosa-type	wind	(L), R	O	+	+
Urtica, Urticaceae	wind	R	O	+	+
Alchemilla-type, Rosaceae	insects	L	U	+	+
Aconitum, Anemone nemorosa-type, Ranunculaceae	insects	L, (R)	U	+	−
Bartsia-type, *Euphrasia, Pedicularis, Rhinanthus*, Scrophulariaceae	insects	L, (R)	U	+	−
Gentianella campestris-type, Gentianaceae	insects	L	U	+	−
Chaerophyllum-type, *Heracleum*-type, *Ligusticum mutellina*-type, *Pimpinella major*-type, Apiaceae	insects	(L), R	U	+	+
Oxytropis-type, Fabaceae	insects	L	U	+	−
Lotus, Trifolium, Fabaceae	insects	L	U	+	+
Plantago major-type	insects	L, (R)	U	+	+

Radiocarbon Dating. Samples have been selected after initial, orienting pollen analyses and were measured at the Vienna Environmental Research Accelerator (VERA) of the Faculty of Physics, Isotope Research, University of Vienna (Austria), at Beta Analytic of Miami (USA), and at Curt-Engelhorn-Zentrum Archäometrie gGmbH (MAMS) Mannheim (Germany). Data were calibrated using Oxcal 4.1 (Bronk Ramsey 2009) with atmospheric data from Intcal 0.9 (Reimer et al., 2009).

Results

First, we view the vegetation history of the area under consideration of the "classical" pasture indicators *sensu* Bortenschlager (2000) mentioned earlier (cf. Table 7.1). We restrict it to the prehistoric sequences because we want to demonstrate the discrepancies between the two methods described. It is expected that the first grazing pressure becomes visible in the alpine grass mats; therefore, we start our compilation at the highest located site.

Grazing Reconstruction with Classical Pasture Indicators

At the beginning of the Neolithic the Penaud mire—located at 2,330 m—was surrounded by a larch-arolla pine forest (*Pinus cembra* and *Larix*; Figure 7.2) and located at the timberline. Single specimens of spruce (*Picea*) might have reached this altitude. However, these trees characterize the forest vegetation during the Neolithic. Around 4500 cal BC spruce (*Picea*) and pine (*Pinus*) show expanding tendencies, and pasture indicators occur in higher frequencies. At about 3500 cal BC arolla pine (*Pinus cembra*) and spruce (*Picea*) decline, which displays a timberline depression or an opening of the subalpine forest. The values of grasses (Gramineae) and pasture indicators remain more or less stable. The first obvious vegetation change at Penaud happens around 2200 cal BC, when grasses (Gramineae), some herbs, and pasture indicators start to expand at the expense of dwarf pine (*Pinus mugo*) and larch (*Larix*). Arolla pine (*Pinus cembra*) and spruce (*Picea*) were affected by this event too. This depression of the forest favored further local expansion of green alder (*Alnus*), which had begun already around 2500 cal BC, indicating wetter and cooler climatic conditions. At the transition to the Late Bronze Age a decline in pine (*Pinus*) combined with an expansion of grasses (Gramineae) indicates a further vegetation change connected with pasture activities. The human interference is corroborated by the occurrence of coprophilous fungi, and higher micro-charcoal values indicate increased fire events. This opening of the vegetation also persisted in the Early Iron Age.

About 100 m in altitude lower in the Lagaun mire we find a similar situation at the beginning of the Neolithic. Around the mire thrives a larch-arolla pine forest (Figure 7.3). At about 4500 cal BC larch (*Larix*) and spruce (*Picea*) decline, whereby some herbs expand, and the pasture indicators show increasing tendencies. In about 3000 cal BC a hiatus—probably caused by the Holocene event 3 (Bond et al. 1997)—interrupts the sequence for about eight hundred years. Then a larch-arolla pine forest still thrives around the mire, but the forest is open as the high amount of grasses (Gramineae) show. In addition, herbs

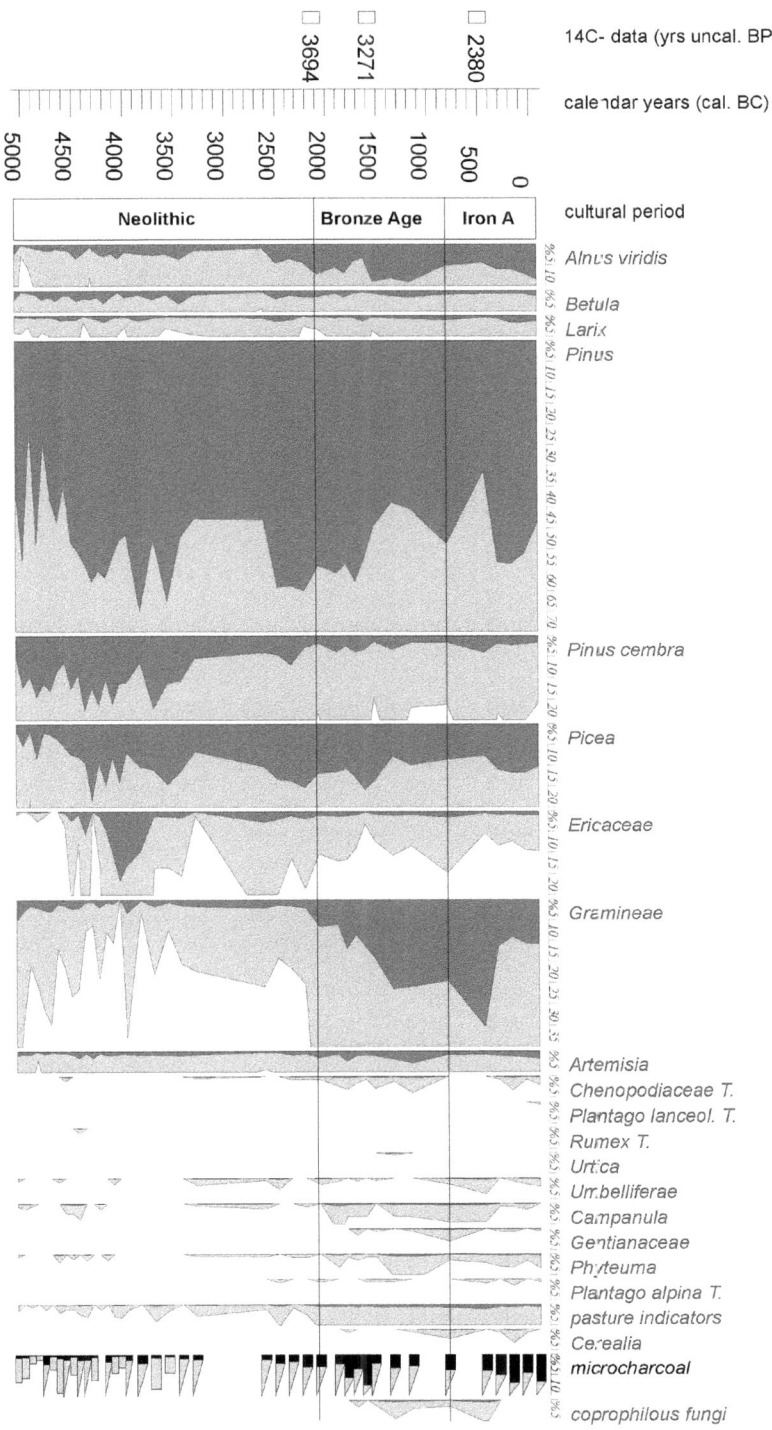

Figure 7.2. Relative pollen diagram of the Penaud mire. The prehistoric sequences are displayed and only taxa of significance are given. A = Age, T = type.

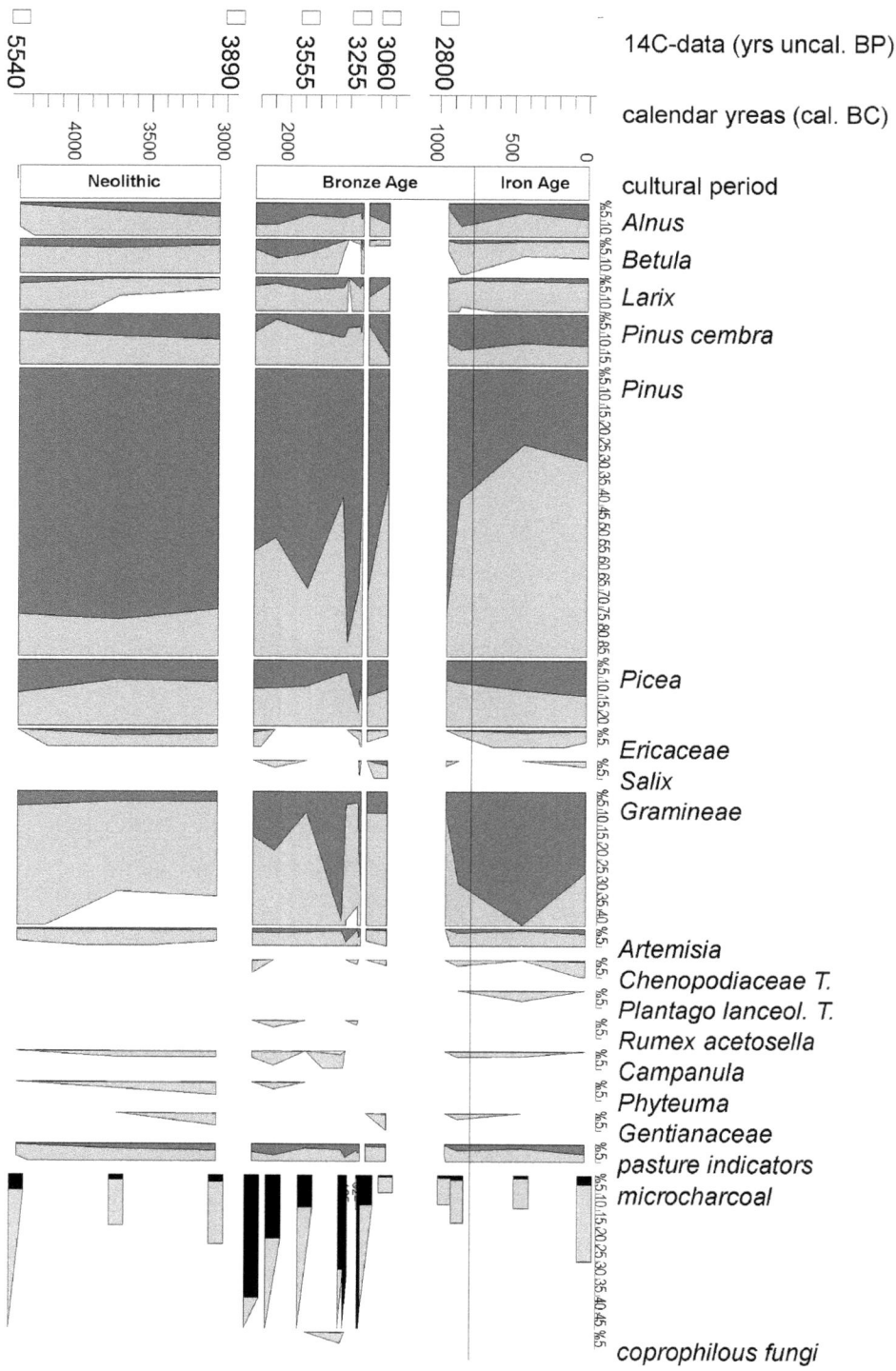

Figure 7.3. Relative pollen diagram of the Lagaun mire. The prehistoric sequences are displayed and only taxa of significance are given.

are more frequent, the pasture indicators occur in percentage values, and higher values of micro-charcoals indicate a higher fire activity. At about 1400 cal BC another hiatus ends the observability of this development. However, the hiatus is short; only a few decades afterward the pollen deposition starts again. Now pine (*Pinus*) declines, whereas arolla pine (*Pinus cembra*) expands and the grasses (Gramineae) are diminished as well as the pasture indicators. At about 1200 cal BC a further hiatus envelopes the vegetation development for about two hundred years. Then in the Late Bronze Age, the mire is still surrounded by a larch-arolla pine forest with dwarf pine (*Pinus mugo*). At the transition to the Iron Age pine (*Pinus*) declines, grasses (Gramineae) expand and pasture indicators increase again, indicating grazing activities until Roman times.

At almost the same altitude of the Lagaun mire, the Schwarzboden mire is located (2,150 m; Figure 7.4) about 150 m below the recent timberline in a small side valley of the Schlandraun. Pollen deposition in this mire starts around 5000 cal BC and reflects a larch-arolla pine forest (*Larix*, *Pinus cembra*) intermingled with spruce (*Picea*). The larch-arolla pine forest is disturbed, indicated by the occurrence of birch (*Betula*), green alder (*Alnus*), and dwarf pine (*Pinus*). Avalanches most probably caused the disturbance in repeated intervals like the alternating maxima and minima of the climax trees (*Pinus cembra*, *Pinus*) and the pioneer trees (*Betula*) suggest. Grasses (Gramineae) expand during the clearing phases and pasture indicators occur in increased high values between 5000 and 2500 cal BC. Then, at the transition to the Bronze Age, follows a more stable vegetation situation, reflected by constant values and smooth curves of larch (*Larix*) and spruce (*Picea*). Only arolla pine (*Pinus cembra*) shows a decline at 2000 cal BC, but the grasses (Gramineae) do not react and the pasture indicators diminish around the Late Bronze Age. A significant vegetation change in the Schwarzboden pollen record is the clearing of the forests during the Iron Age, at 850 cal BC. An increase in fire activity and the presence of chenopods (Chenopodiaceae), *Plantago lanceolata*-type, and cereal pollen grains indicate that the reduction of the pine-spruce and larch forests and the extension of the alpine grassland are connected to human activity.

The pollen record from Lake Vernagt (Figure 7.5) starts at about 3600 cal BC, when the lake is surrounded by a spruce (*Picea*) forest with pine (probably *P. sylvestris*, according to the altitude of the site) and larch (*Larix*). At about 3500 cal BC green alder (*Alnus*), pine (*Pinus*), and grasses expand and spruce (*Picea*) becomes subdominant in the forests. Pasture indicators display increased values. Then, about 2600 cal BC, spruce (*Picea*) becomes the dominant tree again, whereas green alder (*Alnus*), arolla pine (*Pinus cembra*), and grasses decline, and as a consequence the pasture indicators do as well. Contrarily, larch (*Larix*) starts to expand in the montane forests. Unfortunately, a hiatus of about one thousand years interrupts this sequence as well. During the Late Bronze Age, spruce (*Picea*) and pine (*Pinus*) are codominant in the forests. Larch (*Larix*) constitutes a considerable portion of the forests, which are open as the high values of grasses (Gramineae) reflect. Pasture indicators are recorded in remarkable proportions. At the end of the Bronze Age, the expansion of spruce (*Picea*) and pine (*Pinus*) reflects a recovery of the forests and the grasses vanish. Again, the vegetation development of about two hundred years is missing due to a hiatus. Between 600 and 350 cal BC for the first time a marked opening of the forest is observed, together

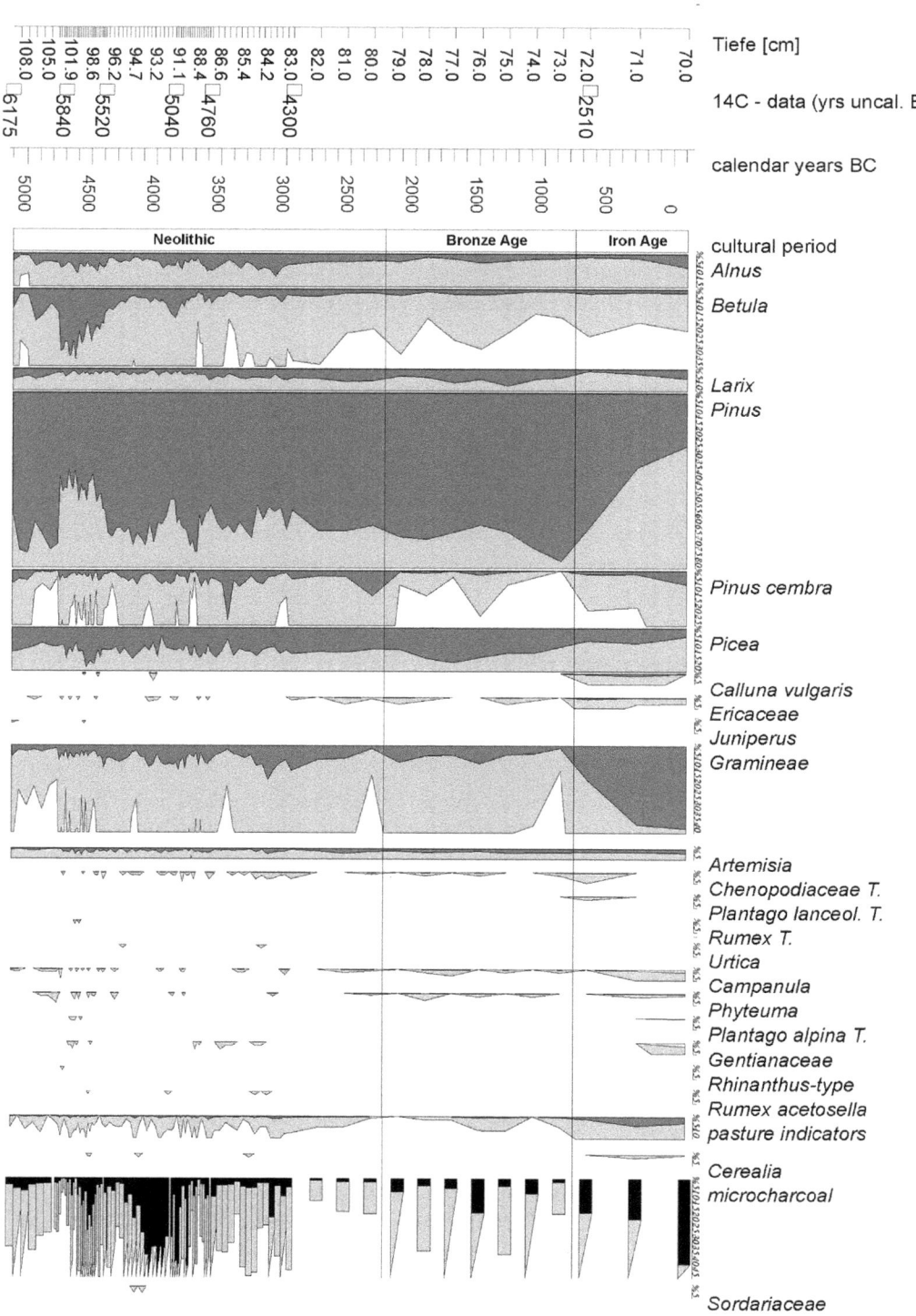

Figure 7.4. Relative pollen diagram of the Schwarzboden mire. The prehistoric sequences are displayed and only taxa of significance are given.

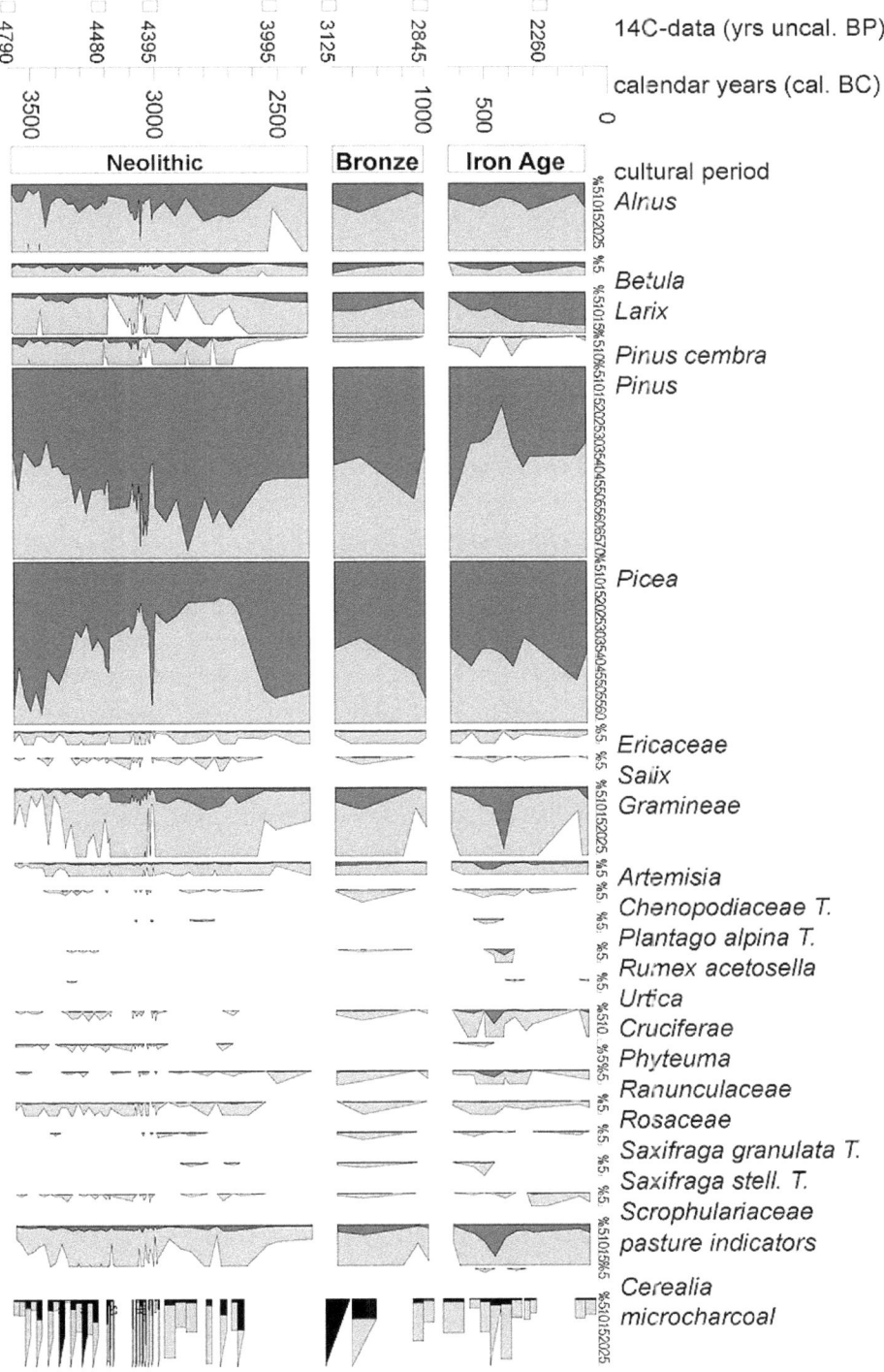

Figure 7.5. Relative pollen diagram of Lake Vernagt. The prehistoric sequences are displayed and only taxa of significance are given. Bronze = Bronze Age.

with the first occurrence of cereal (Cerealia), plantain (*Plantago alpina*-type), sheep's sorrel (*Rumex acetosella*), and chenopod (Chenopodiaceae) pollen, indicating human activity near the study site. During this phase larch (*Larix*) expands considerably in the forests, reaching values of 10 percent and becoming one of the dominant tree taxa present in the area around Lake Vernagt.

Detecting the Onset of Grazing Activities

As we have shown, the classical pasture indicators disclose grazing activities in the area already in the Neolithic period. In the Penaud mire the first increase in these indicators is around 4500 cal BC, which vanishes around 4000 cal BC and starts again at 3000 cal BC (Figure 7.2). The most prominent increase is recorded at about 1500 cal BC. In the Lagaun mire we observe the first increase of pasture indicators about 3500 cal BC and a high grazing impact at the beginning of the Bronze Age (Figure 7.3). In the Schwarzboden mire pasture indicators are observed from the very beginning of pollen sedimentation, but the first distinct increase of pasture indicators is recognized about 3500–3000 cal BC (figure 7.4). Then follows a decline until the Bronze Age. During the Middle Bronze Age higher values of pasture indicators are recorded again, which fade away in the Late Bronze Age. At the beginning of the Iron Age, pasture indicators rise again with the expansion of grasses and clearing of pine (*Pinus*) and spruce (*Picea*). Finally, we observe increased pasture indicators in the Lake Vernagt deposits from 3500 to 2500 cal BC (Figure 7.5). After an interruption of about one thousand years pasture indicators occur in remarkable values in the Middle Bronze Age as well as in the Iron Ages.

Generally, the pattern of the classical pasture indicators with its earliest occurrences in the uppermost site confirms the studies by Bortenschlager (2000) and suggest that already in the Neolithic livestock grazed in the high altitudes of the Ötztal Mountains. However, early grazing impact in the highest altitudes seems plausible, not least for energetic purposes because no forest clearing is required to create pastures. Furthermore, grazing pressure increases with progressing time. To test this assumption, we applied the specific grazing indicators for the investigation area as described in the methodological section. For more details we refer to Festi et al. (2014). The results are compiled for all four sites in Figure 7.6. This summary discloses that in all sites the specific pasture indicators suggest grazing since the Bronze Age. It is relevant that the Lagaun and Schwarzboden mire show the earliest effects of grazing at both sites. Both sites are located along the traditional transhumance route from the Vinschgau across the main alpine ridge (Werner 1969).

Discussion

The comparison of the two approaches to detect grazing pressure in high altitudes reveals that the classical pasture indicators applied in high-altitudinal regions seem to overestimate human interference (Figure 7.6.). Finally, all pollen diagrams of this study show increased classical pasture indicators between 3000 and 3500 cal BC, and thus about one thousand

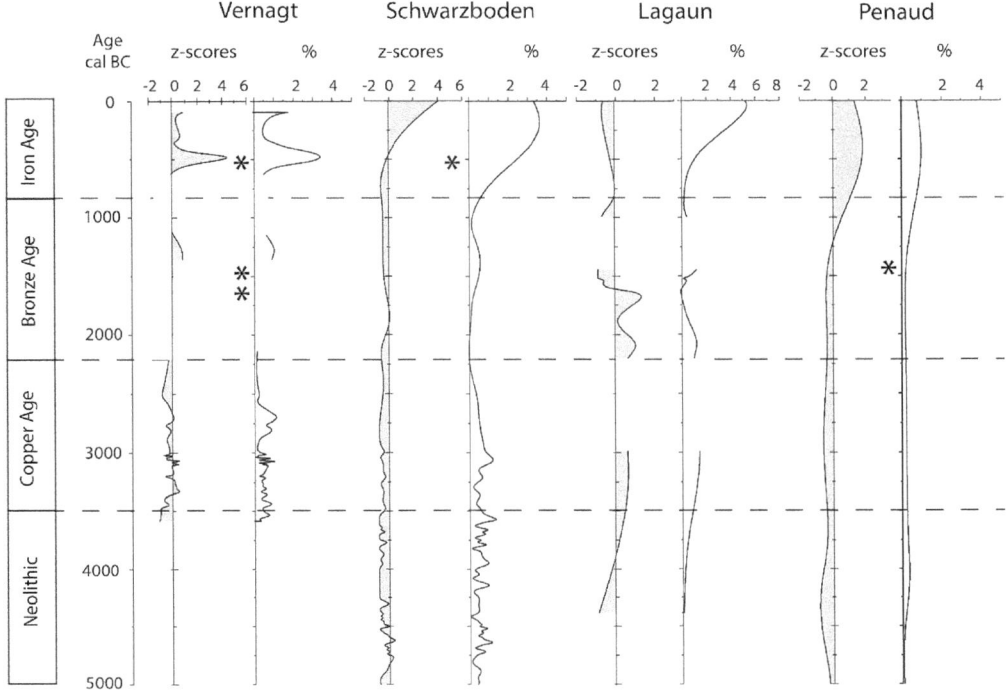

Figure 7.6. Compilation of the grazing indicators: for each investigated site the direct comparison of the z-scores of our specific grazing indicators (in gray) and the percentage values of the classical pasture indicators are given. The asterisk indicates the evidence of archaeological structures related to pasture activities.

years before our approach. The taxa involved are *Campanula*, Chenopodiaceae, *Phyteuma*, Ranunculaceae, and Urticaceae. They all occur in minor quantities and do not exceed the 1 percent limit, which means that predominantly single pollen grains are recorded in the counts. The few Neolithic findings in the Vinschgau (Steiner 2007) let us assume that the population pressure of both humans and livestock was low at that time. Therefore, it is expected that early grazing provokes a weak or moderate pollen signal. Either way, the observed pattern of the herb pollen mentioned earlier corresponds to the natural occurrence of these taxa in the pollen rain. Hence, it may suggest grazing but also might be indicative of a climatic induced vegetation change, as mentioned before, in particular because the period in question is well known in the Alps for a climatic deterioration with higher precipitation and runoff (Magny et al. 2004). This also applies to former studies by Bortenschlager (2000) but also to similar studies in the neighboring regions like in the eastern (Dietre et al. 2014) and northwestern Swiss Alps (Schwörer et al. 2015).

Results that are much more accurate provides the approach with the evaluation of specific grazing indicators for the investigation area by Mazier et al. (2009) used in this study. However, the compilation in Figure 7.6 shows that even the specific grazing indicators provide a positive result around 3500 and 3000 cal BC for some sites studied. Particularly Vernagt Lake in high-montane and Lagaun mire in subalpine regions are affected. A closer look at these grazing indicators revealed that in the case of Lake Vernagt only *Artemisia* and Chenopodiaceae could be perceived as potential significant indicators for grazing in the montane belt (cf. Table 7.2). Both pollen types occur regularly in the sporomorph content of the air and travel long distances. They can manifest themselves in the pollen rain at sites with low pollen production (Jochimsen 1986). The latter applies to mountain regions, where pollen production decreases with elevation (Markgraf 1980). Given that this phenomenon is temperature sensitive, the same pattern is obtained during cold spells and thus both pollen types are inapplicable for grazing indication in high-altitudinal sites. However, more doubts arise if the complete pollen spectrum is considered. The pollen types are recorded in a phase of the pollen diagram, where more than 90 percent arboreal pollen and about 5 percent grass pollen (Gramineae) reflect a closed forest in the surroundings. Furthermore, the involvement of alpine *Artemisia* species (like *A. genipi* and *mutellina*, which are indicative of pioneer and scree plant communities in the alpine and nival belts), in the pollen content seems plausible, in particular since the lake is situated in the hydrological catchment of glacial streams. The latter is also the reason for the occurrence of pasture indicators significant for the subalpine and alpine regions, which have no meaning for montane regions (cf. Table 7.2).

TABLE 7.2. WEIGHTING AVERAGE VALUES (WA_{opt}) OF PASTURE INDICATORS IN ORDER OF IMPORTANCE: THE HIGHER THE VALUE THE HIGHER THE PREFERENCE FOR PASTURE ACCORDING TO FESTI ET AL. (2014)

Pollen type	WA_{opt}
montane zone	
Artemisia-type	0.990
Plantago lanceolata-type	0.925
Chenopodiaceae	0.896
Brassicaceae	0.687
Cichorioideae	0.528
subalpine zone	
Rhinantus-type	0.928
Geum-type	0.922
Campanula/Phyteuma-type	0.842
Urticaceae	0.841
Rumex acetosella-type	0.794
Plantago alpina-type	0.769
Gentianaceae	0.724

Similar conditions prevail in the case of the Lagaun mire, which is located in the same hydrological catchment area as Lake Vernagt. Therefore, the Lagaun pollen diagram shows related patterns like Lake Vernagt. Also between 3500 and 3000 cal BC pasture indicators occur, when the pollen diagram of the Lagaun mire is characterized by high amounts of arboreal (>93%) and poor grass pollen (>5%) indicative of a closed forest in the surroundings. Within this period single pollen of *Campanula*, *Phyteuma*, and Gentianaceae occur. Given that the mire is situated in the inundation area of a glacial stream, a hydrological transport from alpine regions also seems plausible.

Regardless, later periods provide conclusive results, as Figure 7.6 shows. Since the Bronze Age the pollen sequences of all investigated sites show distinct values of pasture indicators, which are all validated by archaeological findings with the exception of the Lagaun mire, where only Mesolithic and Late Iron Age finds have been proven so far (Putzer et al. 2016a). In the Penaud mire and on the margins of the Schwarzboden mire stone structures of an alpine cabin have been unearthed concurrent with the rise of pasture indicators. Near Lake Vernagt, a concentration of findings covering the complete Bronze and Iron Ages has been identified. There, at the mouth of the Finail Valley, a seasonal occupation layer dated from the Early to Late Bronze Age is evidenced. Much more, two sanctuary sites maintained from the Middle Bronze Age until the Early Iron Age substantiate the lively human activity in this area (Putzer et al. 2016b). For sure, the finding of a loom weight in one of the sanctuaries is noteworthy, documenting a pastoralist economy based on secondary products at that time (Putzer et al. 2016a).

These results coincide with findings from adjacent regions in the Alps. Studies by Mandl (2003) in the Dachstein region further east of our investigation area reveal that there the onset of alpine pasture begins in the Middle Bronze Age. West of our study area in the northeastern Swiss Alps Reitmaier et al. (2018) conducted stable isotope studies on cattle molars from the Bronze Age village Ramosch-Mottata in Grisons. There, variations in the Sr-isotope values suggest a change in animal husbandry at the beginning of the Late Bronze Age, which is construed as the onset of vertical transhumance in this region of the Alps. Furthermore, fatty acid analyses of incrustations on pottery sherds from the same area attest to dairying since the Iron Age (Carrer 2016). Recent studies on an alpine lake further west in the French Alps is devoted to the detection of early alpine pasture by sediment DNA (Giguet-Covex et al. 2014). In the Neolithic sediments some sequences (between 50 and 100) of cattle DNA were detected. The next evidence of cattle follows in the Late Iron Age, but now in company with ovicaprids and horses. However, even the authors view this isolated Neolithic evidence critically and further confirmation is needed. Nevertheless, this novel and promising study concludes that there in the French Alps alpine pasture was practiced since the Late Iron Age, which is validated by archaeological findings. Moreover, in the Southern Limestone Alps Pini et al. (2016) examined the question of early alpine pasture in the Oglio River catchment, which focused on the Valcamonica famous for its prehistoric rock carvings. They analyzed several peat and lake deposits from the montane to the alpine regions and observed the first impact of alpine pasture in the Early Bronze Age.

Conclusions

In this study, we tested the hypothesis of Neolithic alpine pasture in the Ötztal Mountains by creating a modern calibration data set for grazing indicators specific for the investigation area. Then we applied these specific grazing indicators on four peat and lake sediment sequences located along the traditional transhumance route in the Schnals Valley. We could verify that alpine plant communities are susceptible to grazing, but it is a matter of scale. Furthermore, pasture indicators may differ in regions due to different environmental behavior of the involved taxa and the different pollen dispersal mechanisms in mountains. A comparison of the two approaches with classical pasture indicators and our specific grazing indicators revealed a difference of several thousand years between the onset of grazing in the high altitudes of the Ötztal Mountains. Our studies reveal that grazing pressure is reflected in pollen diagrams in the high altitudes at the earliest since the Bronze Age, which is validated by archaeological findings near the palynologically investigated sites. Moreover, small-scale vegetation changes might not be detectable by pollen analysis alone. Only if a threshold of disturbance is passed, an impact on the vegetation cover is expected and observed. That is why the evidence of seasonal/vertical transhumance needs a multidisciplinary approach involving archaeology, paleoecology, and stable isotopes.

Acknowledgments

This study is the result of two research projects supported by the FWF Austrian Science Foundation (grant no. 21129-G19) and the Autonomen Provinz Bozen—Südtirol, Abteilung Bildungsförderung, Universität und Forschung (grant no. B35E12000330003). We are grateful to Enel S.p.A., Bozen/Südtirol for providing access to Lake Vernagt sediment cores and we also would like to thank Werner Kofler and Stefan Schwarz, University of Innsbruck, and Torstein Sjovold, University of Stockholm, for their help and fruitful discussions during the fieldwork.

References

Augustine D. J., and S. T. McNaughton 1998 Ungulate Effects on the Functional Species Composition of Plant Communities: Herbivore Selectivity and Plant Tolerance. *Journal of Wildlife Management* 62:1165–1183.

Behre K.-E. 1981 The Interpretation of Anthropogenic Indicators in Pollen Diagrams. *Pollen et Spores* 23:225–245.

Beug, H. J. 2004 *Leitfaden der Pollenbestimmung für Mitteleuropa und angrenzende Gebiete*. Pfeil Verlag, Munich.

Bond, G., W. Showers, M. Cheseby, R. Lotti, P. Almasi, P. deMednocal, P. Priore, H. Cullen, I. Hajdas, and G. Bonani 1997 A Pervasive Millennial-Scale Cycle in the North Atlantic Holocene and Glacial Climates. *Science* 278:1257–1266.

Bortenschlager, S. 1992 Die Waldgrenze im Postglazial. In *Paleovegetational Development in Europe and Regions Relevant to Its Paleofloristic Evolution: Proceedings of the Pan-European Paleobo-*

tanical Conference Vienna, 19–23 September 1991, edited by J. Eder-Kovar, 9–13. Museum for Natural History Vienna, Styria, Graz.

Bortenschlager, S. 2000 The Iceman's Environment. In *The Iceman and His Natural Environment: Paleobotanical Results—The Man in the Ice, Volume 4*, edited by S. Bortenschlager and K. Oeggl, 11–27. Springer, Vienna.

Bortenschlager, S., and K. Oeggl (eds.) 2000 *The Iceman and His Natural Environment: Paleobotanical Results—The Man in the Ice, Volume 4*. Springer, Vienna.

Bronk Ramsey, C. 2009 Bayesian Analysis of Radiocarbon Dates. *Radiocarbon* 51(1):337–360.

Brun, C. 2011 Anthropogenic Indicators in Pollen Diagrams in Eastern France: A Critical Review. *Vegetation History and Archaeobotany* 20:135–142.

Callaway, R. M., R. W. Brooker, P. Choler, Z. Kikvidze, C. J. Lortie, R. Michalet, L. Paolini, F. I. Pugnaire, B. Newingham, E. T. Aschehoug, C. Armas, D. Kikodze, and B. J. Cook 2002 Positive Interactions among Alpine Plants Increase with Stress. *Nature* 417:844–848.

Carrer, F., A. C. Colonese, A. Lucquin, E. Petersen Guedes, A. Thompson, K. Walsh, T. Reitmaier, and O. E. Craig 2016 Chemical Analysis of Pottery Demonstrates Prehistoric Origin for High-Altitude Alpine Dairying. *PLoS One* 11(4):e0151442. doi:10.1371/journal. pone.0151442.

Davis, O. K. 1984 Pollen Frequencies Reflect Vegetation Patterns in a Great Basin (USA) Mountain Range. *Review of Paleobotany and Palynology* 40:295–315.

Dietre, B., C. Walser, K. Lambers, T. Reitmair, I. Hajdas, and J. N. Haas 2014 Paleo-ecological Evidence for Mesolithic to Medieval Climatic Change and Anthropogenic Impact on the Alpine Flora and Vegetation of the Silvretta Massif (Switzerland/Austria). *Quaternary International* 353:3–16.

Faegri, K., and J. Iversen 1989 *Textbook of Pollen Analysis*. Alden Press, London.

Festi, D., A. Putzer, and K. Oeggl 2014 Mid and Late Holocene Land-Use Changes in the Ötztal Alps, Territory of the Neolithic Iceman "Ötzi." *Quaternary International* 353:17–33.

Giguet-Covex, C., J. Pansu, F. Arnad, P.-J. Rey, C. Griggo, L. Gielly, I. Domaizon, E. Coissac, F. David, P. Choler, J. Poulenard, and P. Taberlet 2014 Long Livestock Farming History and Human Landscape Shaping Revealed by Lake Sediment DNA. *Nature Communications*. DOI:10.1038/ncomms4211.

Grime, J. P. 2001 *Plant Strategies, Vegetation Processes and Ecosystem Properties*, 2nd ed. Wiley, New York.

Hobbs, T. N. 1996 Modification of Ecosystems by Ungulates. *Journal of Wildlife Management* 60:695–713.

Jochimsen, M. 1986 Zum Problem des Pollenflugs in den Hochalpen. *Dissertationes Botanicae* 90:1–249.

Kutschera, W., G. Patzelt, E. Wild, B. Haas-Jettmar, W. Kofler, A. Lippert, K. Oeggl, E. Pak, A. Priller, P. Steier, N. Wahlmüller-Oeggl, and A. Zanesco 2014 Evidence for Early Human Presence at High Altitudes in the Ötztal Alps (Austria/Italy). *Radiocarbon* 56:923–947.

Magny, M., U. Leuzinger, S. Bortenschlager, and J. N. Haas 2004 Tripartite Climate Reversal in Central Europe 5600–5300 Years Ago. *Quaternary Research* 65:3–19.

Mahlknecht, M. 2005 Der alpine Brandopferpatz am Grubensee im Maneid-Tal. *Der Schlern* 79:7.

Mandl, F. 2003 *Almen im Herzen Österreichs: Dachsteingebirge—Niedere Tauern—Salzkammergut—Totes Gebirge*. ANISA, Haus i. E., Austria.

Markgraf, V. 1980 Pollen Dispersal in a Mountain Area. *Grana* 19:127–146.

Mazier, F., D. Galop, C. Brun, and A. Buttler 2006 Modern Pollen Assemblages from Grazed Vegetation in Western Pyrenees, France: A Numerical Tool for More Precise Reconstruction of Past Cultural Landscapes. *The Holocene* 16:91–103.

Mazier, F., D. Galop, M. J. Gaillard, C. Rendu, C. Cugny, A. Legaz, O. Peyron, and A. Buttler 2009 Multidisciplinary Approach to Reconstructing Local Pastoral Activities: An Example from the Pyrenean Mountains (Pays Basque). *The Holocene* 19(2):171–188.

Moore, P. D., J. A. Webb, and M. E. Collinson 1991 *Pollen Analysis*, 2nd ed. Blackwell Science, Oxford.

Mosimann, J. E. 1962 On the Compound Multinomial Distribution, the Multivariate β-Distribution and Correlation among Proportions. *Biometrica* 49:65–82.

Mosimann, J. E. 1963 On the Compound Negative Multinomial Distribution and Correlations among Inversely Sampled Pollen Counts. *Biometrica* 50:47–54.

Müller, W., H. Fricke, A. N. Halliday, M. T. McCulloch, and J.-A. Wartho 2003 Origin and Migration of the Alpine Iceman. *Science* 302:862–866.

Oeggl, K. 1994 Palynological Record of Human Impact on Alpine Ecosystems. In *Highland Zone Exploitation in Southern Europe: Monografie di "Natura Bresciana," 20*, edited by P. Biagi and J. Nandris, 107–122. Museo civico di scienze naturali di Brescia, Brescia.

Oeggl, K., A. Schmidl, and W. Kolfer 2009 Origin and Seasonality of Subfossil Dung from the Iceman's Discovery Site (Eastern Alps). *Vegetation History and Archaeobotany* 18:37–46. DOI:10.1007/s00334-008-0188-0.

Pierce, S., A. Luzzaro, M. Caccianiga, R. M. Ceriani, and B. Cerabolini 2007 Disturbance Is the Principal α-scale Filter Determining Niche Differentiation, Coexistence and Biodiversity in an Alpine Community. *Journal of Ecology* 95:698–706.

Pini R., C. Ravazzi, A. Aceti, L. Castellano, R. Perego, T. Quirino, and F. Vallè 2016 Ecological Changes and Human Interaction in Valcamonica, the Rock Art Valley, since the Last Deglaciation. *Alpine and Mediterranean Quaternary* 29(1):19–34.

Pini, R., C. Ravazzi, L. Raiteri, A. Guerreschi, L. Castellano, and R. Comolli 2017 From Pristine Forests to High-Altitude Pastures: An Ecological Approach to Prehistoric Human Impact on Vegetation and Landscapes in the Western Italian Alps. *Journal of Ecology* 105:1580–1597. DOI:10.1111/1365-2745.12767.

Polatschek, A. 2000 *Flora von Nordtirol, Osttirol und Vorarlberg*. Band 3. Tiroler Landesmuseum Ferdinandeum Innsbruck.

Punt, W. 1976–2009 *The Northwest European Pollen Flora, vol. 1-2-3-4-5-6*. Elsevier, Amsterdam.

Putzer, A. 2009 Eine prähistorische Almhütte auf dem Schwarzboden im Maneidtal, Südtirol/Vinschgau. *Archaeologia Austriaca* 93:33–43.

Putzer, A., D. Festi, and K. Oeggl 2016a Was the Iceman Really a Herdsman? The Development of a Prehistoric Pastoral Economy in the Schnals Valley. *Antiquity* 90:319–336.

Putzer, A., D. Festi, S. Edlmair, and K. Oeggl 2016b The Development of Human Activity in the High Altitudes of the Schnals Valley (South Tyrol/Italy) from the Mesolithic to Modern Periods. *Journal of Archaeological Science: Reports* 6:136–147.

Reitmaier, T., T. Doppler, A. W. G. Pike, S. Deschler-Erb, I. Hajdas, C. Walser, and C. Gerling 2018 Alpine Cattle Management during the Bronze Age at Ramosch-Mottata, Switzerland. *Quaternary International* 484:19–31.

Reimer, P. J., M. G. L. Baillie, E. Bard, A. Bayliss, J. W. Beck, P. G. Blackwell, C. Bronk Ramsey, C. E. Buck, G. S. Burr, R. L. Edwards, M. Friedrich, P. M. Grootes, T. P. Guilderson,

I. Hajdas, T. J. Heaton, A. G. Hogg, K. A. Hughen, K. F. Kaiser, B. Kromer, F. G. McCormac, S. W. Manning, R. W. Reimer, D. A. Richards, J. R. Southon, S. Talamo, C. S. M. Turney, J. van der Plicht, and C. E. Weyhenmeyer 2009 IntCal09 and Marine09 Radiocarbon Age Calibration Curves, 0–50,000 years cal. BP. *Radiocarbon* 51(4):1111–1150.

Schwörer, C., D. Colombaroli, P. Kaltenrieder, F. Rey, and W. Tinner 2015 Early Human Impact (5000–3000 BC) Affects Mountain Forest Dynamics in the Alps. *Journal of Ecology* 103:281–295.

Steiner, H. 2007 Die bronze- und urnenfelderzeitliche Siedlung. In *Die befestigte Höhensiedlung am Ganglegg im Vinschgau—Südtirol: Ergebnisse der Ausgrabungen 1997–2001 (Bronze/Urnenfelderzeit) und naturwissenschaftliche Beiträge*, edited by H. Steiner, 17–393. *Forschungen zur Denkmalpflege in Südtirol Band 3*. TEMI Editrice, Trent.

ter Braak, C. J. F., and P. Smilauer 1998 CANOCO *Reference Manual: User's Guide to Canoco for Windows Software for Canonical Ordination (Version 4)*. Centre of Biometry, Wageningen.

Tschisner, C. 1998 Palynologische Untersuchungen zur holozänen Waldgrenz- und Klimaentwicklung im Ötztal anhand der Profile "Rofenmoos" und "Moor am Rofenberg." *Diplomarbeit der Universität Innsbruck*. 109 + 5 Diagramme, Innsbruck.

Werner, K. H. 1969 Die Almwirtschaft des Schnalstales. *Veröffentlichungen der Universität Innsbruck 20*. University of Innsbruck, Innsbruck.

Chapter Eight

Central Alpine Environments as Mountain Cultural Landscapes from Prehistory to Contemporary Past

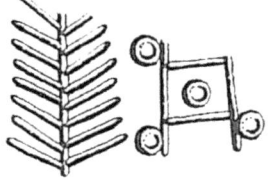

Franco Nicolis

Abstract *The current framework of knowledge as it regards human occupation of the alpine environment in ancient times is no longer conditioned by the traditional image of poor, inhospitable areas inhabited by coarse, warlike peoples. The prevailing picture today is of regions with considerable economic potential. A case study site will be presented where a series of clues have been found suggesting pioneering colonization of the high mountains between the end of the Early Bronze Age and the beginning of the Middle Bronze Age.*

During the Late and Final Bronze Age (fourteenth century to eleventh century BC) the metal production and diffusion in Europe develops into a continental-size organized system. Within this frame a substantial copper metal production is observed in the highlands of the Trentino area, undoubtedly related to diffusion of the products within a larger area.

Today global warming is changing the alpine landscape. The melting of ice is bringing to light evidence of the human presence at high altitudes from prehistory to contemporary times. The icon of this phenomenon is Ötzi the Iceman. But a lot of other evidence is coming to light from the Alps, first of all the remains of the battlefields fought during the First World War.

Cultural Landscapes

On the twenty-fifth of September, twelve hundred and sixty-four, at break of day, the Duke of Auge appeared at the summit of the keep of his castle, there to consider, be it ever so little, the historical situation. It was somewhat confused. A few odd remnants of the past were still lying around here and there, rather messily. On the banks of a nearby gully two Huns were camping; quite near them a Gaul, a Haeduan, perhaps, was boldly immersing his feet in the fresh, running water. On the horizon were outlined the flabby silhouettes of tired Romans, nether Norsemen, old Francs and Christmas Carolingians. A few Normans were drinking calvados.

The Duke of Auge sighed, but nevertheless continued his careful examination of these antiquated phenomena.

The Huns were preparing some steak tartare, the Gauloise smoking a gitane, the Romans were drawing the Greeks, the Norsemen were snoring, the Francs were looking for their sooterkins, and the Carolingians were waiting to see whether anyone was concealing any Ossetians. The Normans were drinking calvados.

"So much history," said the Duke of Auge to the Duke of Auge, "so much history, just for a few puns and a few anachronisms. I think it's pathetic. Shan't we ever get away from it?" (Queneau 2018:7; Barbara Wright translation)

What Raymond Queneau represents at the beginning of *Les fleurs bleues* (*The Blue Flowers*) is a funny atlas in which the depth of time and the discontinuity of historical events are flattened on the surface of a metahistoric landscape. It is the exact description of a cultural landscape through a thought that is constructed as a poetic invention, presents itself with a literary language, and takes the form of a metaphor. What, in fact, are "A few odd remnants of the past . . . still lying around here and there, rather messily" if not the scattered elements that mark the history of our real territory in different eras; what are "the flabby silhouettes" if not the "relics" of prehistoric castellieri, Roman roads, medieval towers?

The "nature" of the "cultural" landscape (the oxymoron is desired) is the cast shadow, the little defined, the nuanced, the fuzzy, the transparency, the trace. It is the nature of the palimpsest: "A palimpsest is, literally, a parchment whose first inscription has been scratched to substitute another for it, but where this operation has not irreparably erased the original text so that one can read the old under the new, as by transparency" (Genette 1982:4; my translation).

But, as happens with the palimpsests, even for reading, understanding, interpreting, and describing cultural landscapes, poetic imagination or literary narration are not enough, but adequate discipline, technique, and tools are needed.

The discipline that is dedicated to the discovery of the hidden traces under the visible surface of the landscape, to their unveiling, and to their knowledge more than any other is archaeology. Our discipline, through the interpretation of material testimonies, tries to reconstruct the history of man, the dynamics of its development and the processes of its change along the flow of time and in relation to the evolution of the environment as a result of natural phenomena (climate change, catastrophic events, etc.).

The image we have of the territory and the landscape, both from a global perspective and from a perspective closer to us, is that of a static, stable element that does not change in the time of human life. In particular, the natural evolution of mountain environments usually takes place on a fairly long time scale, and therefore the immediate perception we have of the landscape is similar: indistinct and without historical significance.

The variety of mountain environmental contexts often corresponds to the richness and temporal depth of cultural landscapes, the result of the sum of human actions and natural events that have occurred over long periods of time. These testify to the complexity of the relationship that man has always had with the environment, its strategies to adapt or to transform it, the difficulties of finding the right balance between compatible use and senseless exploitation.

But why do we need to know the history of cultural landscapes in the third millennium AD? The most convincing answer is found in the European Landscape Convention signed in Florence on October 20, 2000: we must be "aware that the landscape contributes to the formation of local cultures and that it is a basic component of the European natural and cultural heritage, contributing to human well-being and consolidation of the European identity" (Council of Europe 2020:preamble).

The safeguarding of this heritage, which "means an area, as perceived by people, whose character is the result of the action and interaction of natural and/or human factors" (Article 1—Definitions) is an action of the highest social value. To be able to protect it, however, you must first know it. Only through knowledge can one think of implementing valid and virtuous actions for the protection of an asset.

The Alps

The mountain environment is often perceived as a natural barrier. In reality, the alpine environment is certainly a physical and geographical border but also represents an area of cultural encounter permeable to influences from the north and south, and the network of connections between the two alpine sides contributed to connecting the Mediterranean world and that of central and northern Europe. The existence of relations between the two alpine slopes testifies to the presence, even in the mountain environment, of social and economic structures able to manage flows, exchanges, trade, cultural interaction.

Since the Mesolithic, trade in raw materials and goods does not represent isolated phenomena. Mobility through the Alps is symbolically represented by Ötzi—the Iceman. In addition to being near one of the passes that allow the crossing of the mountain range (still used today by transhumant shepherds of Val Venosta in Italy to reach the Vent Valley in Austria) he brought with him raw materials and tools of southern origin, such as a small flint dagger from the Lessini Mountains in the province of Verona.

However, even the idea that the Alps were only transit routes for goods, ideas, and people is misleading. In part, this is due to the fact that archaeological research in the alpine environment has often been conducted along large infrastructural works, especially railways and highways. This led to a picture of the ancient alpine population along the main valleys, along which highways and railways still run today. In fact, more extensive research conducted in recent decades, not only in Trentino but throughout the Alps, have allowed us to move from the traditional idea of poor or inhospitable territories, still linked to the stereotype proposed by Roman sources, to the image of territories with great economic potential, where human groups settled permanently to exploit their resources and often established a relationship of stability and balance with the environment.

Unfortunately, our knowledge of the ancient population of the alpine territories does not yet seem adequate to represent the actual nature and the real consistency of human settlement during the different periods, the decisive taking of possession and the capillary action of control of most of the territories by the ancient populations. The fact that vast mountain territories have not yielded great evidence of prehistoric human occupation can be explained not so much with their real absence but with the lack of archaeological research. This chapter presents three cases of approach to the mountain environment by human groups driven by very different motivations, in a very wide space of time that spans from the Bronze Age to the First World War.

Going Up the Mountain: The Pioneers of the New Frontier of the Bronze Age

In the central part of the southern alpine territories human presence at high altitudes aimed at hunting trips for large mammals (deer, ibex, etc.) is documented from the Middle Paleolithic to the Mesolithic. During the Neolithic period, however, evidence is very scarce: the productive economy model finds its own sphere of interest in the territories of the great river valleys. Available archaeological data seem to indicate a new approach to the mountain during the final phases of the Early Bronze Age (twenty-second to seventeenth century BC). The most significant data in understanding the beginnings of this new phase of interest come from the Storo Dosso Rotondo site in Trentino (Nicolis et al. 2016) (Figure 8.1).

Storo Dosso Rotondo is located in the central sector of the Southern Alps, at 1,857 masl. The archaeological excavations, which began in 1998 and are still ongoing, have investigated only a small part of the site. The interdisciplinary investigation of the stratigraphic context has allowed the documentation of four construction phases, evidenced by at least seventy-six postholes (Figure 8.2). In the first three phases, four dwelling structures have been identified with vertical bearing piles placed in the ground, while in the fourth phase a fifth housing structure has been recognized with a new construction technique that provides an insulating foundation of stone blocks laid at right angles on which a wooden structure must have rested.

Comparative analysis of archaeological and naturalistic data allows us to propose a reconstruction of ancient vegetation and some dynamics related to the organization of this high-altitude site. Archaeological materials (pottery and flint tools) frame the site's attendance at the beginning of the Middle Bronze Age, while a 14C dating of a charcoal sample provided the following measure: KIA12453 3387 ± 31 BP corresponding to 1751–1616 BC cal (95.4% probability), which is placed in a phase of transition between the Early Bronze Age and the Middle Bronze Age. The collected elements suggest that the structures were immersed in a compact spruce. The limit of the arboreal vegetation seems to have been placed at about 2,200–2,400 masl in this period. The absence of the larch, a pioneer species that spontaneously establishes itself on open areas and more degraded soils at high altitudes, also in relation to the opening of the pastures, would be an indication that the practices of deforestation were at an early stage. Probably only the area affected by the settlement had been cleared.

For environmental reasons (altitude, soil, and forest cover) it seems possible that any agricultural activity could be practiced in Dosso Rotondo: cereals and fruit had to be trans-

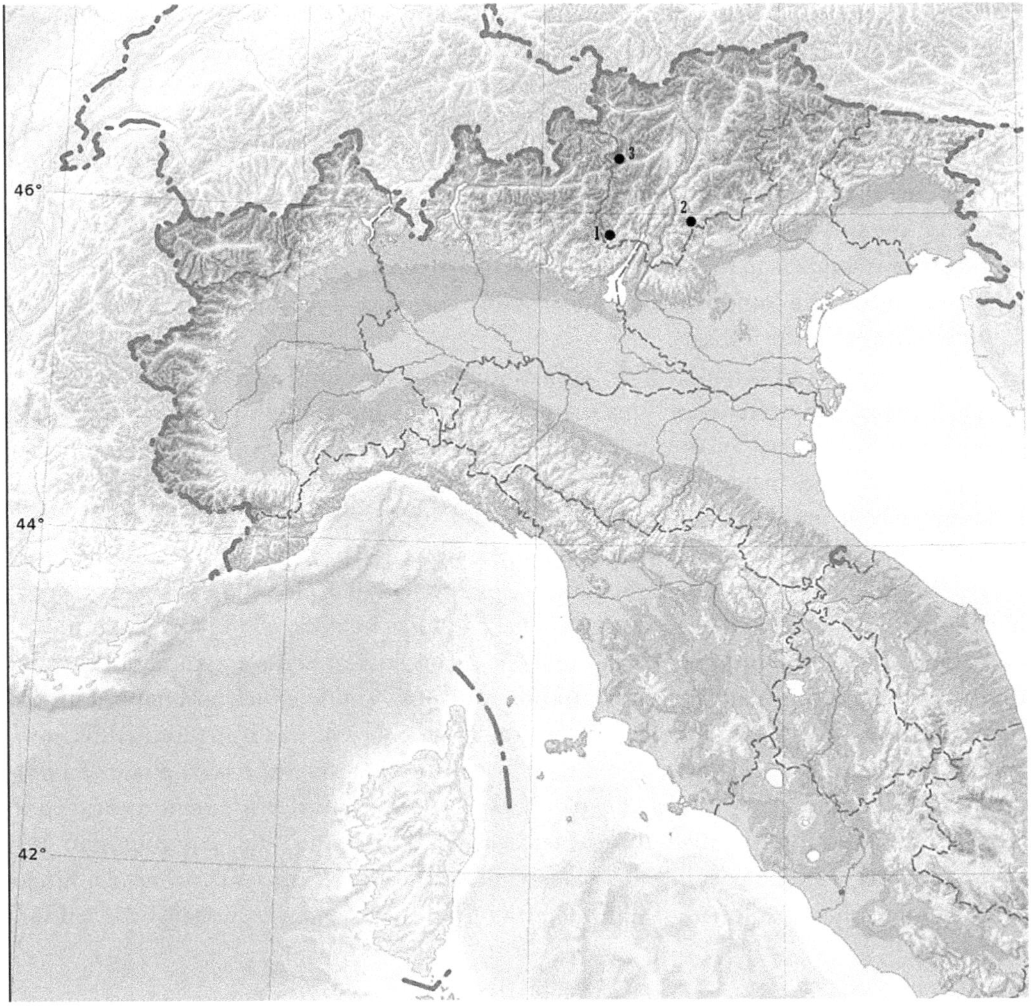

Figure 8.1. The Trentino region in the context of the Italian Peninsula. 1. Storo Dosso Rotondo site; 2. Luserna Pletz von Mozze site; 3. Punta Linke site.

Figure 8.2. Storo Dosso Rotondo: general view of the area (arrow indicates the archaeological site) and excavation area with postholes.

ported from the settlements located in the valley bottom or collected at lower altitudes. The wear-use observed on the flint sickle blades (treatment of domestic cereals) are likely to refer to activities carried out further downstream. Unfortunately, due to the acidity of the soil, no data regarding animal breeding has been kept, while the practice of hunting is very probable. A reliable interpretation of the real meaning and nature of the activities that took place on the site of Storo Dosso Rotondo in the current state of research is only conceivable. However, the site was a seasonal settlement most likely linked to mountain pasture activity. Some observations made from archaeobotanical analyses suggest that the stay in the settlement was about one hundred days and therefore corresponds to the classic attendance of summer farms of historical age.

The presence of ceramic finds with multiple perforations referring to at least two strainers (sieves), interpreted as "cheese strainers" in the most recent phase of occupation, allows us to hypothesize in situ processing of milk and its products (Figure 8.3). Specific analyses are planned on any organic residues present on the strainer fragments, which hopefully can provide more precise information in this regard.

The impression obtained from the comparison of the data available for the Storo Dosso Rotondo site is that it is in the presence of a system of exploitation of the territory at high altitude still at an initial stage. It was likely a pioneer colonization of the high mountain ranges, by a community with a cultural and technological heritage typical of the valley or lowland areas. This involves a small number of people and livestock and has not yet led to profound modifications of the natural environment, characterized by a forest rather compact, with limited grazing areas. We are therefore witnessing the embryonic phase of a process that will lead to a new model of exploitation and economic development connected to a different approach to the high-altitude territories by the alpine valley communities. This is a model that will remain valid for a long time, excluding recent years, when the model of mountain tourist exploitation did not bring dramatic changes to most of the cultural landscapes.

The "Copper Rush"

During the Late and Final Bronze Age (mid-fourteenth to eleventh century BC), a vast and complex network was developed in Europe for the production and diffusion of metal objects and tools, the so-called "metallurgical koine." This implies not only the circulation of standardized typologies but also the organization of the exchange of finished products and the high mobility of the metallurgists. This phenomenon presupposes the existence of a complex economic system that favors the procurement and production of raw materials, copper, manages long-distance cultural relations, and controls the international commercial traffic circuits. The protohistoric metallurgical production system in Trentino is clearly connected with this vast network of relationships that characterizes the *world system* of the Bronze Age, certainly playing a primary role (Silvestri et al., 2014; Silvestri et al., 2015; Pearce et al., 2019; Bellintani, Sivestri 2021).

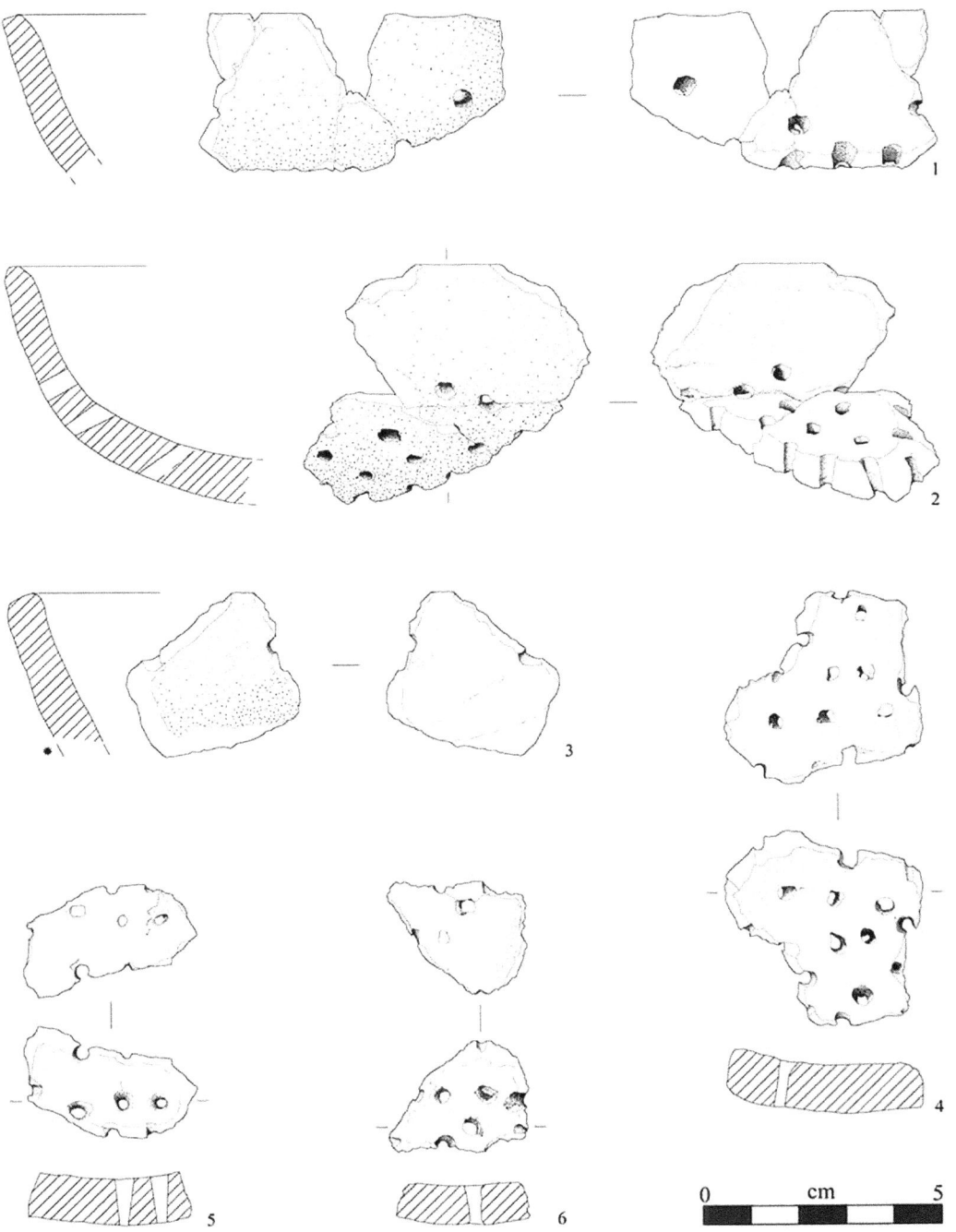

Figure 8.3. Storo Dosso Rotondo: fragments of strainers. Drawings by Livia Stefan.

In fact, in the territory of the province of Trento, in particular on the Lavarone Luserna and Vezzena plateaus, in the Val dei Mocheni and in Val di Cembra, it is testified, during the Late and Final Bronze Age, a metallurgical production activity of almost "industrial" size, which evidently responded to a demand for raw materials that could not come only from local markets. The impressive metallurgical production of the plateaus, witnessed by dozens of sites with immense waste dumps, probably did not supply only the local markets but had to be used to supply metal for other traffic circuits, first of all that of the Po Valley sites, like Frattesina, central places where in addition to the production and distribution of raw materials and exotic and precious objects, transactions with the Mycenaean post-palatial communities also took place (Pearce 2020).

The knowledge of this important component of cultural development in the south alpine territory is due first to the pioneering research by Ernst Preuschen in the 1960s, and then to a research project conducted in the eighties and nineties by the Office of Archaeological Heritage of the Autonomous Province of Trento and the Bergbau Museum of Bochum (D) (Cierny 2008). This, in particular, demonstrated the vastness of the archeometallurgical phenomenon carried out through the extensive exploitation of the local sources of supply of copper ore (chalcopyrite) and led to the identification of numerous sites of copper production.

One of the largest sites is located in Luserna Pletz von Mozze at about 1,300 masl (see Figure 8.1.2). Extensive stratigraphical research, even if not exhaustive, conducted from 2005 to 2010, led to the identification of a large area destined for casting activity between the Late Bronze Age and the Final Bronze Age. The research has allowed for the recognition of an extension of the site, identification of different fire structures, roasting beds (Figure 8.4), accessory structures, and large areas of accumulation of processing waste (coarse slag and flat slag). The materials relating to prehistoric attendance are well represented by pottery, faunal remains, and a fragmented bronze pin.

While leaving aside the important information that archaeological investigations have provided at the level of knowledge about technological processes (Addis et al., 2016), the site of Luserna Pletz von Mozze is an important case study for understanding the dynamics

Figure 8.4. Luserna Pletz von Mozze: general view of the excavation area and detail of a fire structure, probably a roasting bed.

and processes related to archeometallurgical protohistoric production on the southern slope of the Alps. The wide extension of the site, its internal structure, and the enormous mass of waste accumulated near the areas where the work was carried out are clear indications of a production of copper of industrial dimensions. This implies not only a careful management of production activities but also the coordination of the entire economic and social system involved in the production of metal: in a context of specialized work, it was necessary to manage the supply of food resources (agriculture, livestock) for the sustenance of persons specialized in metallurgical processing. In this context the practice of mountain pasture could constitute a part of the economic system designed to provide the necessary elements of subsistence to specialized groups. It was also essential to manage relations with the other elements of society and with groups outside the production area.

The experimental archaeology activities highlighted the complexity of the operating chains that led to the production of raw materials. These needed highly developed and specialized knowledge and technical skills. The fact that the activity of metallurgical production arises in a sudden way leads us to believe that it is probable that the workers employed in these activities came from other regions and specifically from geographical areas in which mining and copper production activities had developed, in particular from the northern side of the Alps.

Unlike the case of the mountain pioneer approach documented in Dosso Rotondo, in the case of the protohistoric metallurgical production of the highlands of Trentino, we are facing, in our opinion, the arrival of external populations who had at their disposal the metallurgical know-how and the sole purpose of exploiting the mineral resources of the highlands to the point of exhaustion. The exploitation continued for only a few generations and caused a disastrous environmental impact. Above all this impact was due to the use of an enormous amount of wood, which most likely led to a drastic reduction of the forests, and to the accumulation of waste that still today marks the landscape of these territories. This dynamic of development was repeated many centuries later, during the Middle Ages, when peoples still linked to mining activity and metal production arrived in these same territories from Bavaria, bringing with them, in addition to technological skill, a dialect which remains a direct testimony in the present German-speaking Cimbrian minorities.

THE GREAT WAR:
POWER, TECHNOLOGY, AND THE "URBANIZATION" OF THE HIGH MOUNTAINS

The Great War was the most important and devastating historical event of the contemporary age. In addition to exterminating millions of soldiers and civilians, it also brought war to territories that had never seen it before. If we exclude the historical crossing of the Alps by Hannibal, the high mountains had always remained unscathed by war. The development of a technology specially developed for the war brought small groups of soldiers, structures, and infrastructures to the highest altitudes, up to the top of Ortles to almost 4,000 masl. This is what is called the "White War," fought in the central-eastern alpine area between the armies of the Austro-Hungarian Empire and the Kingdom of Italy.

At the end of the war most of the testimonies of these events remained embedded in the ice. For some years, however, the effects of global warming with the consequent reduction of glacial coverage have led to the emergence of the evidence related to the war: remains of structures, barracks, scattered materials, weapons, ammunition, and often also remains of fallen soldiers' bodies. As part of the contemporary archaeology experience, after some activities conducted in collaboration with the "Pejo 1914–1918 La Guerra sulla porta" museum on the Piz Giumela at 3,593 masl and on Punta Cadini at 3,524 masl. in the Ortles Cevedale massif, the Trento Archaeological Heritage Office decided to tackle a much more complex site, that of Punta Linke (Nicolis 2017) (see Figure 8.1.3).

Punta Linke (3,629 masl) was one of the most important Austro-Hungarian stations of the entire alpine front during the First World War, a front that ran along the border line between the Kingdom of Italy and the Empire of Austria and Hungary in that area. The Punta Linke project has led to exhaustive research, documentation, and recovery of the entire context. This was characterized by the presence of a double cableway system (Figure 8.5). The structures consisted of a hut that housed a mechanical workshop and where the traction motor was located. Then there was a tunnel, about 30 m long, partly dug in permafrost and partly in rock, which allowed crossing the top safely and bringing the carts to the exit to face the last stretch of the cableway line (Figure 8.6).

The archaeological investigation has led to the complete recovery of the hut. The German-made diesel engine, found unassembled in various parts inside the tunnel, was also reassembled and positioned in its original place inside the hut (Figure 8.7).

Outside the structures, most of the objects were found, probably in transit from one cableway station to another. Of great interest was the discovery of about a hundred rye straw overshoes, manufactured with a traditional technique, which were worn by soldiers during their watch activities (Figure 8.8). Inside the hut a postcard with a representation of a sleeping girl addressed to a certain Georg Kristoff, whose text in Czech ends with the greeting "your love abandoned," a sheet that reported handwritten the rules for the proper operation of the cableway and the central page of the magazine *Wiener Bilder* with the representation of people queuing for bread in the capital of the Empire were found.

Figure 8.5. Punta Linke: view of the site from east and exterior view of the transit station.

Figure 8.6. Punta Linke: the final part of the tunnel.

Figure 8.7. Punta Linke: interior view of the transit station today with the engine on its original base.

Today Punta Linke is a place of memory of the Great War, the highest in Europe, and inside it all the materials found during the research have been repositioned. The memory, also the collective memory, has its own space and its own materiality. Those who visit Punta Linke enter the space of memory and touch its materiality. But at Punta Linke the most profound experience is that of smell, which is the same smell that objects emanated a hundred

Figure 8.8. Punta Linke: the overshoes made of rye straw found during excavation and a pair of overshoes after restoration.

years ago. The smell thus becomes a material object, a find. In that space the smell of those objects is the smell of war, it is war itself (Nicolis 2017). At Punta Linke, there is no museum showcase between the visitor and the materiality of memory, the smell of engine oil, gear grease, tar paper. There is no filtering membrane. There is no didactic apparatus at Punta Linke, the war must not be understood; in Punta Linke war is perceived—you breathe it, you live it. Apparently, we enter a time machine, but in reality the visitor is not brought back in time: at Punta Linke, it is the past that comes upon us.

The archaeology of the Great War does not intend to rewrite history. What archaeologists can do is open a window in the memory space and document the materiality of small contexts that can provide important information on the life and death of soldiers, and sometimes bring to light their remains. The recovery of the soldiers' bodies is a distinct chapter of the archaeological research on the Great War, which operates according to particular perspectives and methods, due to the very nature of the remains. The commitment of the Archaeological Heritage Office has for years been to collaborate with other institutions for the recovery of the remains of soldiers to allow the proper gathering of all the information needed to search for the identity of the fallen (Gaudio et al., 2020).

The uncontrolled collection of human remains related to the Great War, not conducted with all the attention of an archaeological excavation, can cause not only the loss of important historical information but, even more serious, the definitive loss of identity of the people who will increase the army of Unknown Soldiers.

These soldiers, those of whom today we recover their poor remains, looked at the snowcapped mountains from their positions. What did they see? Wonderful landscapes where you can make beautiful excursions on the snow? Probably not. What they saw were war-scapes in which many of their comrades had died in battle or were overwhelmed by avalanches or killed by cold and disease. Nowadays, close to the installations that skiers take to the slopes, it is possible to see a few rags emerge that turn out to be the material memory of lives of which no memory is preserved (Figures 8.9 and 8.10). What we, as archaeologists, can do is tell the "story without History of their being" (Satta 1979:103).

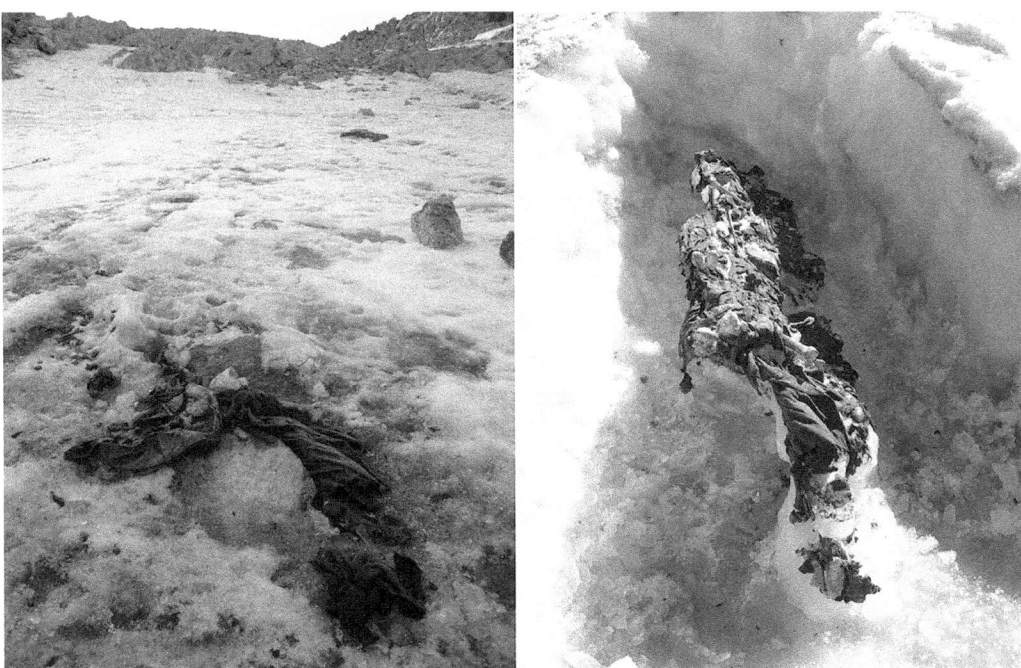

Figure 8.9. Presena glacier: remains of uniforms of Austro-Hungarian soldiers emerging from the ice and remains of two Austro-Hungarian soldiers during the excavation.

Figure 8.10. Presena glacier: part of the uniform of one of the two Austro-Hungarian soldiers.

References

Addis A., I. Angelini, P. Nimis, G. Artioli 2016 Late Bronze Age copper smelting slags from Luserna (Trentino, Italy): interpretation of the metallurgical process. Archaeometry, 58, 1, 96–114.

Bellintani P., E. Silvestri (eds.) 2021 FARE RAME. *La metallurgia primaria della tarda età del Bronzo in Trentino: nuovi scavi e stato dell'arte della ricerca sul campo*. Provincia autonoma di Trento, Trento

Cierny, J. 2008 *Prähistorische Kupferproduktion in den südlichen Alpen*. Der Anschnitt, Beiheft 22.

Council of Europe 2020 European Landscape Convention. https://rm.coe.int/16807b6bc7.

Gaudio D., C. Cattaneo, A. Galassi, F. Nicolis 2020 Men at war, recovery and analysis of soldiers' remains from the WWI and WWII Italian Front. In *WWI and WWII: Legislation, Recovery, Identification and Burial of Human Remains*, edited by Nick Marquez Grant and David Errickson, Forensic Science International, Special Issue.

Genette, G. 1982 *Palimpsestes: La littérature au second degré*. Seuil, Paris.

Nicolis, F., E. Mottes, M. Bassetti, E. Castiglioni, M. Rottoli, and S. Ziggiotti 2016 Going Up the Mountain! Exploitation of the Trentino Highlands as Summer Farms during the Bronze Age: The Dosso Rotondo Site at Storo (Northern Italy). In *Summer Farms: Seasonal Exploitation of the Uplands from Prehistory to the Present*, edited by J. Collis, M. Pearce, and F. Nicolis, 109–138. J. R. Collis, Sheffield.

Nicolis, F. 2017 The Scent of Snow at Punta Linke: First World War Sites as Sense-Scapes, Trentino, Italy. In *Modern Conflict and the Senses*, edited by N. J. Saunders and P. Cornish, 61–75. Routledge, London.

Pearce, M. 2020 The Historical Significance of Frattesina. *Padusa* 56:163–172.

Pearce, M., P. Bellintani, and F. Nicolis 2019 Frattesina and the Later Bronze Age–Early Iron Age Metals Trade: The Absolute Chronology of Smelting Sites in the Trentino-Alto Adige/Südtirol. *Padusa* 55:67–86.

Queneau, R. 2018 *The Blue Flowers*. Translated by B. Wright. New Directions, New York.

Satta, S. 1979 *Il giorno del giudizio*. Adelphi, Milan.

Silvestri, E., P. Bellintani, E. Mottes, and F. Nicolis 2014 Evidence of Mining without Mines: Smelting Activity during the Bronze Age in Trentino. In *Research and Preservation of Ancient Mining Areas*, edited by J. Silvertant, 88–103. 9th International Symposium on Archaeological Mining History, Trento, Valkenburg aan de Geul.

Silvestri, E., P. Bellintani, F. Nicolis, M. Bassetti, S. Biagioni, N. Cappellozza, Degasperi, M. Marchesini, N. Martinelli, S. Marvelli, and O. Pignatelli 2015 New Excavations at Smelting Sites in Trentino, Italy: Archaeological and Archaeobotanical Data. In *Archaeometallurgy in Europe III: Proceedings of the Third International Conference, Deutsches-Bergbau-Museum Bochum, 29 June–1 July 2011*, edited by A. Hauptmann and D. Modarressi-Tehrani, 369–376. Deutsches-Bergbau-Museum, Bochum, Der Anschnitt, Beiheft 26.

CHAPTER NINE

Mountain Archaeology of the Bronze Age Caucasus

From Vertical Pastoralism to Combined Mountain Economy and Mountain Farming

Sabine Reinhold, Andrey B. Belinskiy, and Dmitrij S. Korobov

Abstract *The second half of the second millennium BC sees a fundamental shift from mobile herding economies toward more sedentary forms of pastoralism, and in many parts of Eurasia high-mountain environments played a crucial role in this process. A newly discovered mountain landscape in the North Caucasus with a high density of settlements dating to the second millennium BC offered new information about this process. Due to an excellent visibility of thousands of Late Bronze Age stone-built houses and enclosures, as well as excavation, we were able to target the spatial, economic, and social cross-linkage of one of the earliest documented combined mountain economic systems in Eurasia.*

Up-scaling, we studied singular houses and settlements, micro-regions, as well as the spatial organization of the entire landscape. The architecture revealed communities that adapted gradually to the demands of a sedentary lifestyle, resulting in the development of highly specialized spatial configurations with multifunctional houses that allowed accommodating large herds in winter. Activity area research using microbiological soil studies allowed precise assessments on the location and the quantities of animals in and outside the sites, and GIS analysis allowed predicting seasonal movement of herds within and outside the micro-regions.

INTRODUCTION

Among the most spectacular early sites in European prehistory are the Early Iron Age cemeteries from Hallstatt in the Austrian Alps and the necropolis of Koban in the North Caucasus. Discovered and explored in the mid-nineteenth century, these sites became eponymous for important prehistoric cultures (Reinhold 2007:2–4, 13–21). The mountainous cultural landscapes backing these communities for a long time were not the focus of research interest. New research at Hallstatt and other alpine mining sites (Kern et al. 2008; Stöllner and Oeggl 2016), however, fostered a new awareness of the socioeconomic determinants and the complexity of mountain habitats in which mining and metalworking took place. The new research approaches are part of a conceptual turn in alpine archaeology and a similar turn was initiated in the Caucasus (Korobov and Borisov 2013; Reinhold and Korobov 2007; Reinhold et al. 2017; Reitmeier 2017: 8–10).

The growing awareness of the long history of human occupation in mountains and the complex nature of mountainous cultural landscapes with specific economic and social adaptations has initiated new perspectives in research beyond the typo-chronological study of finds (for the Alps, Collis et al. 2016; Tzortzis and Delestre 2010). Actual research in alpine archaeology focuses on the peculiarities of the vertical economy in mountains, such as studies into prehistoric alpine pastoral economy (Bringemeier et al. 2015; Ebersbach 2002; Mandl 2016; Reitmaier 2017) or on long-term diachronic research in micro-regions (Della Casa 2002; Della Casa et al. 2013; Nicolis et al. 2016; Walsh et al. 2007; among others). A series of new methods such as soil micromorphology, soil microbiology, coprolite and isotope analysis offer new research tools to investigate human activities in high-altitude environments (e.g., Chernysheva et al. 2016; Grupe et al. 2017; Nicolis et al. 2016; Oeggl et al. 2009; Peters et al. 2014).

Landscape-oriented archaeology in other mountain massifs of Europe and Eurasia, however, is still a nascent research theme (Frachetti 2008; Gheyle 2009; Korobov and Borisov 2013; Reinhold et al. 2017; Rendu 2003; among others), although it has the potential to broaden the alpine perspective. Implemented in comparative studies on particular cultural practices in mountainous terrains such as vertical, transhumant animal husbandry, agricultural architectures like field terraces and irrigation systems, or ritual practices in mountains offer a comparative perspective and permit testing models that are established on the basis of ethnoarchaeological research or comparative mountain geography (e.g., Carrer 2015; Carrer 2016; Ebersbach 2002; Ehlers and Kreutzmann 2000; Grötzbach 1976). Studying the correlations of different modern, premodern, and prehistoric economies will increase our understanding of how and when the specific adaptations that characterize mountain economies today worldwide were developed (Ebersbach 2002; Lozny 2013).

Mountain Archaeology in the Caucasus: The Setting

Most high-altitude systems of the Eurasian continent are part of the west-east Alpide or Alpine-Himalayan orogenic belt. They have a similar geology, including substantial and diversified ore deposits (Krismer and Tropper 2016; Twaltschrelidze 2001). The Alps and the Caucasus are the most northern mountain massifs in this belt, situated within the Atlantic climate regime. The climate in the Greater Caucasus is, therefore, temperate. A forest steppe and alpine meadow vegetation are graduated in vertical zones, yet more continental climatic conditions render the eastern areas largely treeless. The high-mountain zone lies above 1,500 masl in most parts of the Caucasus. The seasons are characterized by a maximum of precipitation in early summer (Meckelein 1998). The South or Lesser Caucasus, divided from the northern range by the lowlands of rivers Rioni, Kura, and Araxes, are part of a larger mountain system including the Pontic Mountains and the Taurus as well as the Iranian Zagros massif. Climate conditions here are more continental.

The Greater Caucasus mountain range (Figure 9.1) today forms the political border between Russia in the north and Georgia in the south, while Georgia, Armenia, and Azerbaijan share the South Caucasus. The Greater Caucasus borders the Eurasian steppe belt in the north and is situated between the Black and Caspian Seas. The highest peak of the main range rises to 5,205 masl, while the highest peak in general, the volcano Mount Elbrus that pushes through the basement rock, towers up to 5,642 masl. The mountain valleys usually combine a lower part, bordered by gorges cut into ascending limestone plateaus, a considerable step with up to 1,000 m difference in altitude where the limestone plateaus bordering the crystalline rock and glacier-shaped high valleys connected to the passes crossing the main range (Meckelein 1998).

Despite this, the mountain range is comparatively easy to cross. It usually extends less than 80 km north to south, and most major rivers run south-north or north-south leading to numerous passes (Merzbacher 1901). For subsistence, the Greater Caucasus offers a wide

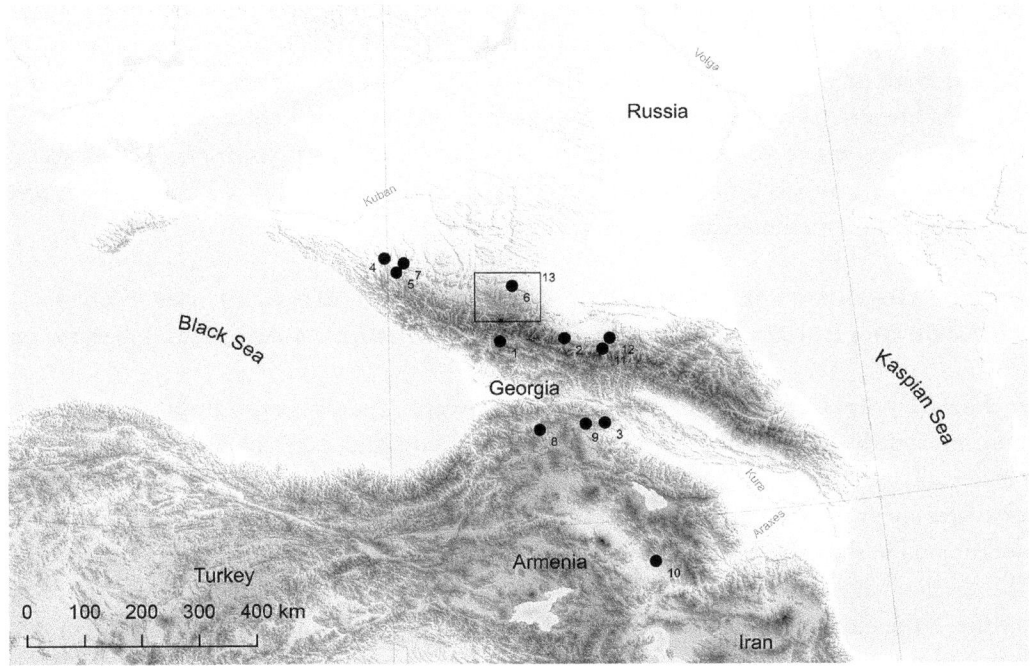

Figure 9.1. The Caucasus mountain system and sites mentioned in the text. 1 Dzudzuna, Kotis, Tsona Klde, 2 Cmi, 3 Arukhlo, 4 Unakozovskaya, 5 Meshoko, 6 Zamok, Novosvobodnaya-Klady, 8 Chobareti, 9 Sakdrisi, 10 Dzdaghi salt mines, 11 Zagli Barzond, 12 Koban, 13 LBA case study area.

range of different ecological niches accessible with comparatively minimal exertion. Ecological intermediary zones, a characteristic of mountain-steppe borderlands, offer diverse and fodder-rich landscapes ideal for mobile and semi-mobile pastoral economies (Spengler et al. 2013). The Caucasian high mountains add alpine and high-alpine meadow pastures rich in *leguminosae* and herbage (Donitia et al. 2003). In the valleys valuable timber grows, including fodder and fruit trees, and after fields are cleared, cereals can be cultivated well up to 1,800–1,900 masl in the central mountains and up to 2,400 masl in Dagestan (Radde 1900).

As in the Alps, the Caucasus are rich in mineral resources, particularly metal, salt, and precious stones. These resources have been exploited from the fourth millennium BC onward (copper: Chernykh 1992; Maisuradze and Gobedishvili 2001; Tschartolani 2001; gold: Gambashidze and Stöllner 2016; salt: Marro et al. 2010). Mining and metal production played a major role in the economy of the Caucasus, which was a hub for metal technology in the fourth millennium BC (Hansen 2011). Metal was exported not only to the south to serve Mesopotamian markets but likewise to the north to the populations living in the steppe zone.

From this arises the question of what role the mid- and high altitudes played in the cultural development of the Caucasian population. When and why did these populations first move into the mountain valleys and into the highland pastures? Was their motivation the exploitation of metals, as is still discussed for the advance into the high valleys of the Alps, or rather (for a critical overview, see Stöllner 2016) the quest for new pastures? What regions were preferred for settlement during the Holocene expansion of humans in this region? How intensive was the presence of humans in the various zones of the mountains? Is it possible to prove seasonal exploitations of resources and pastures prior to a permanent settlement, or complex economic cycles of mountain farmers, as they are known from premodern mountain ethnography of the region (Stadelbauer 1984)?

The Holocene Settlement in the Mountain Zones of the North and South Caucasus: The Emergence of Mountain-Adapted Lifestyles

A short overview of the human presence in the Greater Caucasus exposes surprisingly few, non-noteworthy disruptions between late Quaternary and early Holocene occupations (Bader and Tsereteli 1989; Gabunia and Tsereteli 2003; Meshveliani et al. 2007). Mountain cave sites are proof of continued visits. These sites, such as Kotis or Dzdzuna Klde (Georgia), are situated in the river valleys at considerably high altitudes, up to 2,150 masl (Tsona Klde) (Meshveliani et al. 2007:49). Their faunal assemblages consist of hunted species. An open-air site in the North Caucasian Alagir gorge at 1,700 masl in 2007 revealed likewise repeated occupation from the mid-seventh to the mid-sixth millennium BC (Rostunov et al. 2009). From the Neolithic Layer 3 at the site of Cmi (Russia) originates the oldest directly dated ceramic vessel in Caucasia with a date of 7010±10 BP (5981–5843 cal BC 1σ). The faunal assemblages nevertheless prove an exclusively hunter-gatherer economy with cervids, wild sheep, and bears.[1]

Only in the flood plains of the South Caucasian Kura and the Araxes river valleys can Neolithic sites be associated with a real Near Eastern type of Neolithic lifestyle (Helwing et al. 2017; Hovsepyan and Willcox 2008). These early settlers had, to some degree, explored the mountainous landscape in their immediate vicinity, yet both wild flora and fauna are rarely found (Benecke 2017; Neef et al. 2017). The kill-off pattern of domesticated cattle, however, indicates pastoral herding practices (Benecke 2017:367–369). The site is surrounded by mid-altitude mountain ranges, and it is most likely that some kind of exploitation of summer pastures in the South Caucasus came along with the initial neolithization in the sixth millennium BC.

No indications of an agropastoral Neolithic are known from the northern side of the Greater Caucasus in the sixth and early fifth millennium BC, but from some Neolithic[2] sites at the Lower Don, some hotly disputed domesticated animal species have been reported (e.g., Gorelik and Cybrii 2007; for profound critique Motuzaite-Matuzeviciute 2012). The role of the Caucasus Mountains in the transfer of these domesticates is highly debated and still unsolved (Gorelik et al. 2014:248–249). The indicators for domesticated animals in the mountains themselves do not predate the mid-fifth millennium BC (Stolyar and Formozov 2009). This is the epoch when the first habitation sites appeared at the northern flank of the Caucasus (Korenevskiy 1998; Korenevskiy 2009; Trifonov 2015). Their layers include domesticated animals and plant species (Kasparov and Sablin 2009; Lebedeva 2011). The Near Eastern Neolithic lifestyle had obviously been introduced with a population advancing through the mountain passes from the southern to the northern side of the mountains (Wang et al. 2019). Evidence for sedentary and agropastoral communities, then, comes from a number of settlement sites in the piedmonts of the North Caucasus, such as Meshoko (Russia) in the Northwest Caucasus, or Zamok (Russia) near the mineral spa of Kislovodsk (Korenevskiy 1998). Several cave sites and rock-shelters in the Northwest and Central Caucasus mountain valleys, however, revealed the presence of Eneolithic groups in considerable altitudes (Korenevskiy 2009; Rostunov 2007:58–63). The locations of the Eneolithic settlements in the lower parts of the North Caucasian mountain valleys and in their piedmonts, respectively, are a noteworthy adaptation of the South Caucasus lowland Neolithic communities to a mountain environment. Meshoko (720 masl) as well as Zamok (900 masl) are situated atop promontories with vertical rock faces, both ca. 20 km south of the actual border between the foothills and mountains themselves (Figure 9.2). A warmer climatic regime than the modern one with more open, steppe-like landscapes can be projected from on-site pollen records at Zamok (Korenevskiy 1998); the setting of both sites, however, is mountainous. Only the Agunbek settlement in Nalchik (Russia) is situated on flat terrain, yet likewise directly in front of the piedmonts. Agriculture in the vicinity of the habitation sites can be reconstructed from the lithic assemblage as well as from a large number of grinding stones, and initial paleobotanic evidence confirms farming (Lebedeva 2011). The location of fields is uncertain, as the direct vicinity of these sites is not suitable for farming (Figure 9.2). Meshoko moreover is a fortified site of about 42 ha, with some parts having been suggested as enclosures for animals, chiefly cattle and sheep/goats. An interesting aspect of the Eneolithic faunal assemblages here is the high frequency of pig bones (Kasparov and Sablin 2009). Pigs compose up to 48 per-

Figure 9.2. Meshoko, view from the settlement on the nearby gorge.

cent of the complete collection at the Meshoko settlement and 36 percent at the slightly later Meshoko cave site (Hambleton and Maltby 2016). This could indicate an economy where the forested mountain river valleys and slopes were exploited to fatten pigs, pasture goats, and collect wild plants, while cattle and sheep were probably herded from the settlements (Hambleton and Maltby 2016:21–23).

The Eneolithic on the northern slope of the Greater Caucasus is the first sedentary agropastoral Neolithic adaptation to a low- to mid-mountain environment (Figure 9.3.A). It involves different processes of appropriation of the mountain terrain for habitation and subsistence, such as increasing the shares of pigs or goats more fit for mountainous terrain (Hambleton and Maltby 2016). While large shares of the northern cultural assemblage reveal typological and ideological links, choice of settlement location and fortification differ from the southern ancestors of the Eneolithic population, as the topographies of both Neolithic and Eneolithic in the South Caucasus do not reveal similar defense tactics. Possibly the fortification of some places implies the existence of a neighboring, "nonvisible" local population hostile to the new settlers or some kind of felt precariousness in a pristine landscape. It is remarkable that on the southern mountain flank and in the South Caucasus, the local Sioni-Tsopi groups did not adapt equally. Sioni-Tsopi sites are few, usually small-scale and short-term, still keeping to the flood plains of the major rivers (Marro 2007).

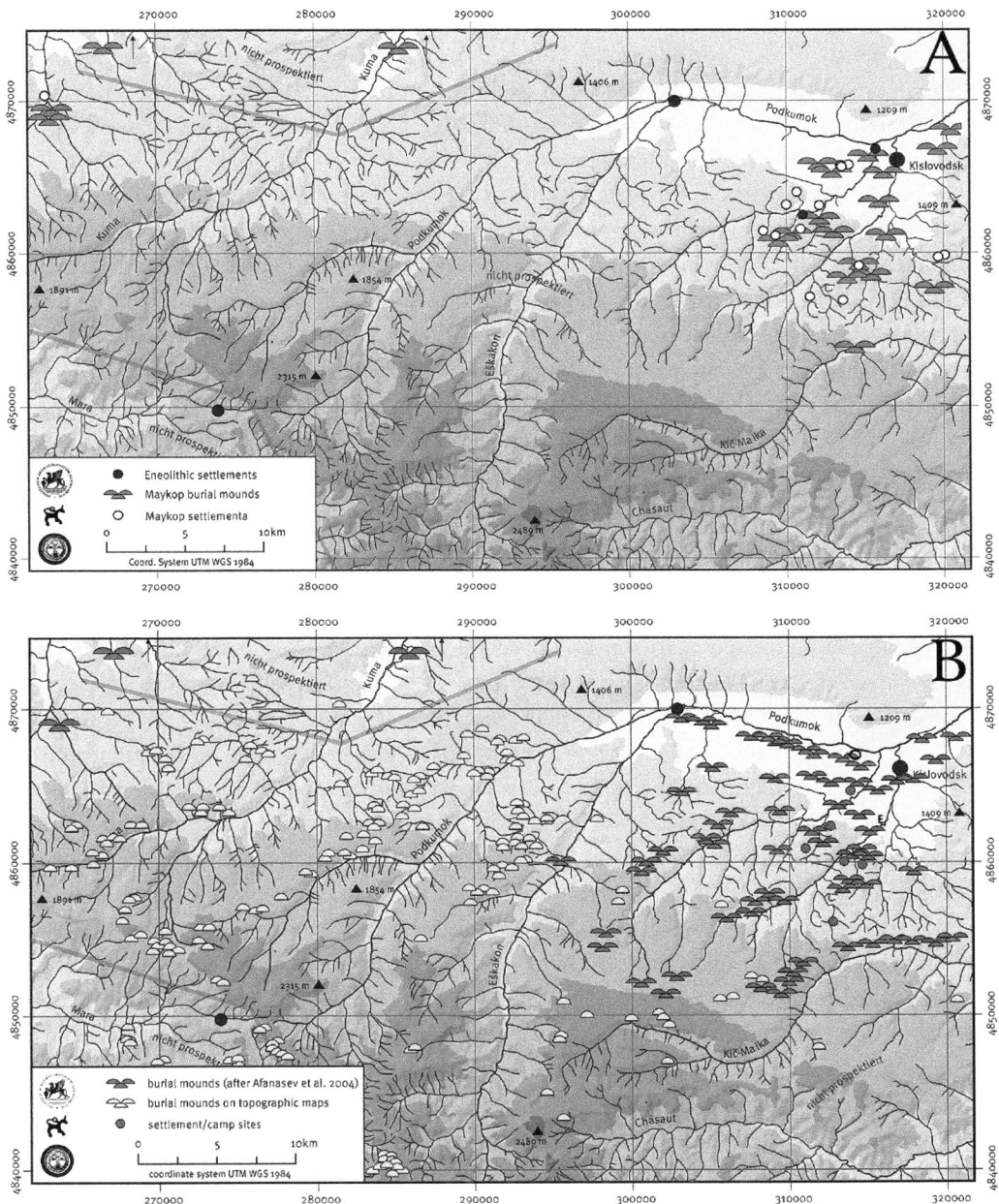

Figure 9.3. Archaeological sites in the Kislovodsk area from the fifth to the third millennium BC. A. Eneolithic and Maykop sites, late fifth/fourth millennium BC. B. Middle Bronze Age burial mounds.

The Neolithic way of life that was started in the late fifth millennium BC continued into the fourth millennium BC. In the north, Maykop communities inhabited the foothills and lower mountain valleys as did the Eneolithic population before (Figure 9.3.A). Maykop economies, however, seem to have shifted toward a more pastoral-like economy (Hambleton and Maltby 2016). Cattle was now the dominant species, and Maykop sites are found more frequently in the foothills of the North Caucasian steppe zone than in the mountain valleys (Korenevskiy 2004). Maykop sites burst out in numbers, and Maykop is the epoch when the North Caucasus piedmonts, foothill, and steppe zones were established for the first time as densely populated landscapes.

There are only a few indicators of Maykop finds in the higher parts of the mountain valleys, but the flourishing metallurgy of this time required the exploitation of mountain-based mineral resources (Chernykh 1992). Until now, however, the ore deposits of Maykop metals remain undiscovered. In the West, sites like the Novosvobodnaya settlement, dating to the first half of the fourth millennium BC, or the neighboring but later Klady necropolis, prove there was permanent occupation of the piedmonts (Rezepkin 2012). Similarly, Maykop settlement sites are still found in the Kislovodsk basin (Korenevskiy 1998; Reinhold and Korobov 2007). Remarkably, they have changed to open locations optimal for mountain farming. Agricultural tools and a few paleobotanic findings from other sites suggest a mixed agropastoral economy including low-altitude farming (Lebedeva 2011).

We witness in the south a first expansion into the Lesser Caucasus with the emerging Kura-Araxes culture in the second half of the fourth millennium BC. Permanent settlements and the full spectrum of domesticated animal and plant species are well documented in mountainous landscapes (Hovsepyan 2015; Palumbi 2016). A case study from Chobareti at 1,615 masl (Georgia) demonstrates the degree of adaptation of Kura-Araxes mountain communities to the particularities of their landscapes (Kakhiani et al. 2013; Messager et al. 2015). The growing familiarity with the mountainous landscapes and their resources possibly acted as a major driving force to explore accessible minerals. Gold was mined and processed by Kura-Araxes groups at the Sakrsisi site (Georgia) (Gambashidze and Stöllner 2016). Salt mines exploited by Kura-Araxes communities have been discovered in Nakhichevan (Marro et al. 2010). Both reveal well-organized, work-sharing communities as part of an overall economic system integrated into supra-regional exchange.

During the third millennium BC, the sedentary lifestyle, however, disappears from the archaeological record. First in the North Caucasus, and somewhat later in the South Caucasus, habitation sites vanish. Instead of settlements, burial mounds are now the predominant archaeological sources. Mounds were built in the north as early as the Late Eneolithic and witnessed a first peak of popularity during the Maykop period (Korenevskiy 2012). By the Middle Bronze Age (MBA), they became the sole indicator for human presence, but mounds are now found in every ecological niche, including the entire high-altitude zone of the Greater Caucasus. In the greater vicinity of the Kislovodsk study area, thousands of MBA burial mounds occupy the lowlands and the piedmonts (Figure 9.3.B), but likewise the highland plateaus up to heights of 2,350 masl (Reinhold et al. 2017:215–218, Fig. 151–152). A charcoal sample from a looted MBA tomb near the Gumbashi pass at 2,100 masl was dated to 4185±24 BP (2878–2705 cal BC 1σ), that is, the early third millennium BC. This date corresponds to the traditional datings of high-altitude mound necropolises in Georgia (Chartolani 1989). The Central Caucasus high-altitude zone likewise revealed a growing number of cemeteries, but here some habitation sites are known as well (Rostunov 2007:64–82). Short-term settlements and cemeteries have been documented in the Koban gorge at Zagli Barzond (Russia) at 1,550 masl and in the upper Alagir gorge at Cmi (Russia), both dating to the second half of the third millennium BC (Albegova and Tsvetkova 2015; Rostunov 2007:75–77). The nature of this high-altitude occupation is still uncertain, as no specific economic studies have targeted these sites; even economic studies have revealed a focus on cattle breeding and have documented the cultivation of cereals for the third and second millennium BC (Antipina 2015; Lebedeva 2015). They are probably related to an increasing exploitation of metal resources, but no prehistoric mining activities have been investigated in these areas so far.

The sheer number of burial mounds, as well as the presence of the settlements, indicates a much more intensive exploitation of the high-altitude zone than before. We must consider a mobile vertical pastoral system that shifted from the piedmont areas into the high mountains on a regular basis. At least temporarily, large populations were transferred into the high altitude landscapes in the North Caucasus. The presence of such a large number of burial monuments at high altitudes forces one to consider a sacral or ritual connotation of these landscapes (Stark 2009). From an ideological viewpoint, the high-mountain zone was increasingly and effectively included into the human *oicumene*, with the sites in the central high-mountain valleys indicating a first occupation for longer periods.

From Mountain Nomadism to Combined Alpine Economy: The Late Bronze and Early Iron Age in the Kislovodsk–Mount Elbrus Plateau Zone

The discovery of a large number of archaeological sites in the high-mountain plateaus south of the spa at Kislovodsk in 2004 (Figure 9.4) opened up investigations into a next level of adaptation to mountain environments in the North Caucasus that transformed the high-mountain landscapes in the second millennium BC from an area of temporary pastoral and ritual occupation into a permanently inhabited cultural landscape (Reinhold and Korobov 2007; Reinhold et al. 2017).

The sites not only revealed an unexpected presence of large Late Bronze Age populations in the mountainous zone above 1,400 masl, but also demonstrated a high degree of internal structuration and a considerable chronological dynamic. By dividing these sites into typo-chronological phases, we can follow up the appropriation of the high-mountain landscape both as an economic and social sphere. This process was associated with the introduction of enduring architecture with stone foundations and a wooden upper structure, that is, a visual occupation of the landscapes with permanent dwellings (Reinhold 2016).

The settlement process described here was studied between 2006 and 2015 by an international team from Germany and Russia (Belinskiy et al. 2009; Reinhold et al. 2007; Reinhold et al. 2017). The excellent visibility of the sites allowed the systematic use of remote sensing techniques (Reinhold et al. 2016). Using a combination of aerial image mapping and ground GPS survey, we were able to thoroughly document and map nearly all visible features (Reinhold et al. 2016). Geophysical, archaeological, and geoarchaeolog-

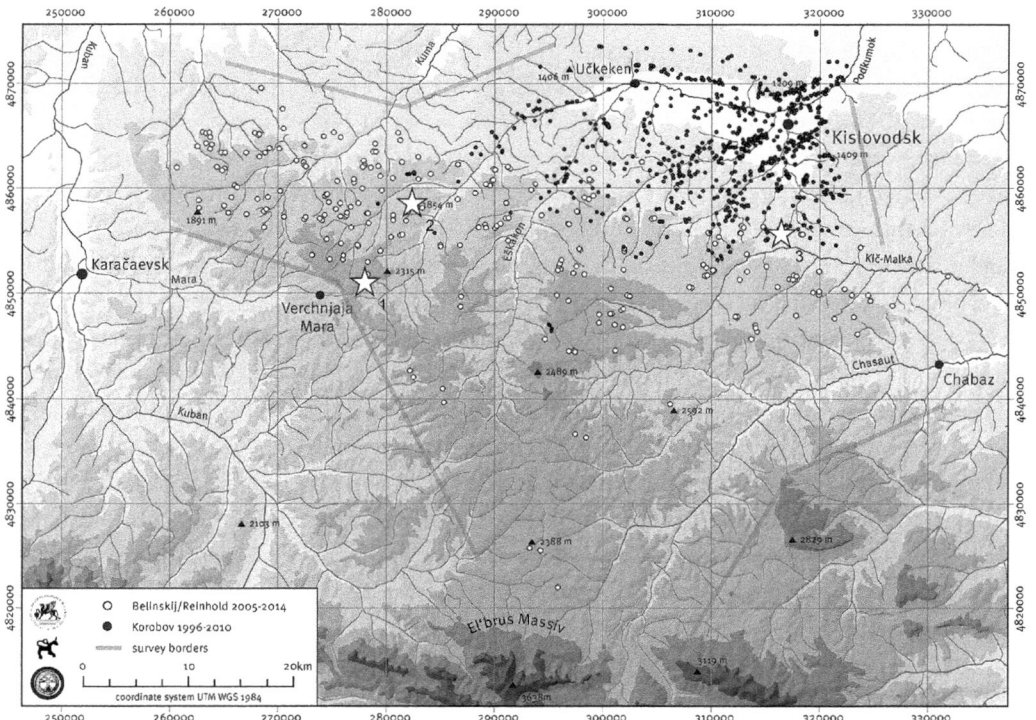

Figure 9.4. Late Bronze Age sites at high altitudes. 1 Gumbashi pass, 2 Ransyrt 1, 3 Kabardinka 2.

ical surveys in combination with targeted excavations and GIS analyses are at the basis of the reconstruction of an entire cultural landscape. A new method of soil studies targeting microorganisms allowed the localization of animal presence in the settlements and in the houses (Peters et al. 2014). This method gave unparalleled insight into the economic activities within our mountain settlements. The analysis of faunal and paleobotanical data as well as isotopic studies finally gave access to herding strategies and, in correlation with the GIS analyses, made it possible to model the economic systems of the Late Bronze Age mountain dwellers on the whole (Antipina 2013; Knipper et al. 2017).

The earliest permanent settlements that we discovered are small, camp-like structures with a linear arrangement of houses (Figure 9.5.A). Excavations in a house at the site of Kabardinka 2 (house 23) (Figure 9.6) date this first phase with permanent domestic architecture to the sixteenth and fifteenth century BC (Reinhold 2016; Reinhold 2017). Kabardinka 2 is one of few settlement sites where first linear, and later symmetrical oval settlement layouts were found side by side and thus became central to our research. The linear configurations of small, single-roomed houses with stone sockets are not the first instances of stone architecture found on the plateaus. The earliest site, Ransyrt 1, dating to the late eighteenth/seventeenth century BC, is a ritual site with an exceptional layout and activity,

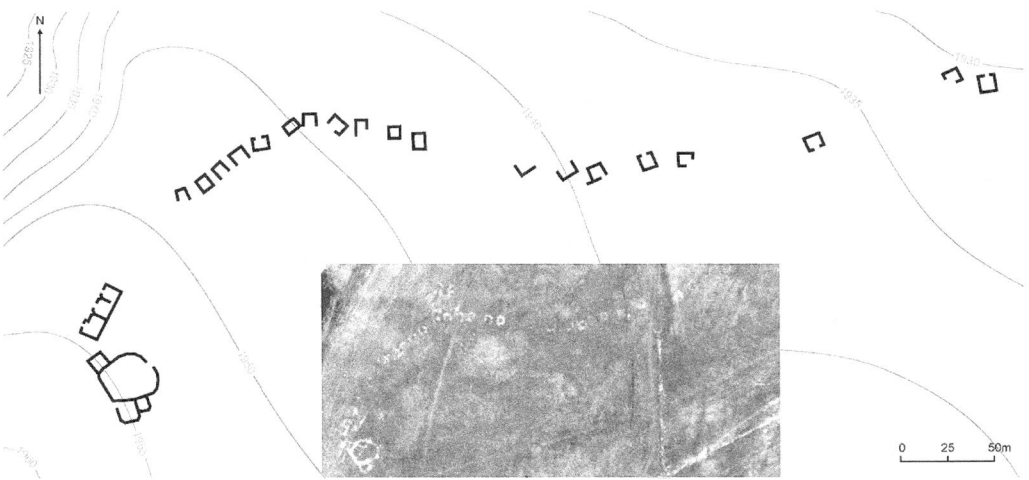

Figure 9.5. Aerial image and sketches of settlement layouts: A. Linear settlement Pokunsyrt 38. B. Linear and symmetric sites Pokunsyrt 10 and 11. C. Symmetric-oval settlement Pokunsyrt 23.

yet it implies a still portable domestic architecture, that is, mobile groups that have not yet started to establish themselves with permanent houses in the area they occupy (Reinhold 2017:183–184).

Soil analysis around the house excavated at Kabardinka 2 did not reveal indications of animals in or around the dwelling, but some of the sites with a linear layout have a central enclosure that may have accommodated communal herds. The linear settlement layout still resembles mobile camp structures. It allows easy access and a high degree of social flexibility, even more when the houses were not used as permanent dwellings but as temporal abodes in a seasonal cycle, exploring lowland and alpine pastures (Reinhold et al. 2017:218–228, figure 153, tables 20–22).

The reconstruction of potential herd sizes in our study is based on the size of enclosures or stables, a supposed chronological synchrony of sites and the calculation of maximal and minimal numbers of animals that can be wintered there according to space allowances per animal (Antipina 2013; Reinhold 2016; for methods Reinhold et al. 2017:152–157). For the initial stage of permanent occupation of the high plateaus, we unfortunately only have limited information. However, we measured enough potential stable areas in enclosures to predict floor space for part of the herds kept by the first settlers. From the mapping of the sites we can presume there were 444 houses, with the number of inhabitants ranging between ca. 2,000 and 2,200, assuming 5 to 7 persons per household (Reinhold et al. 2017:152–160) (Figure 9.9). The communities could keep at least 3,200–6,000 head of cattle in their enclosures. How many of them had been contemporaneous is difficult to predict from the limited number of radiocarbon dating so far. The epoch of the linear settlements, however, did not last more than 150–200 years.

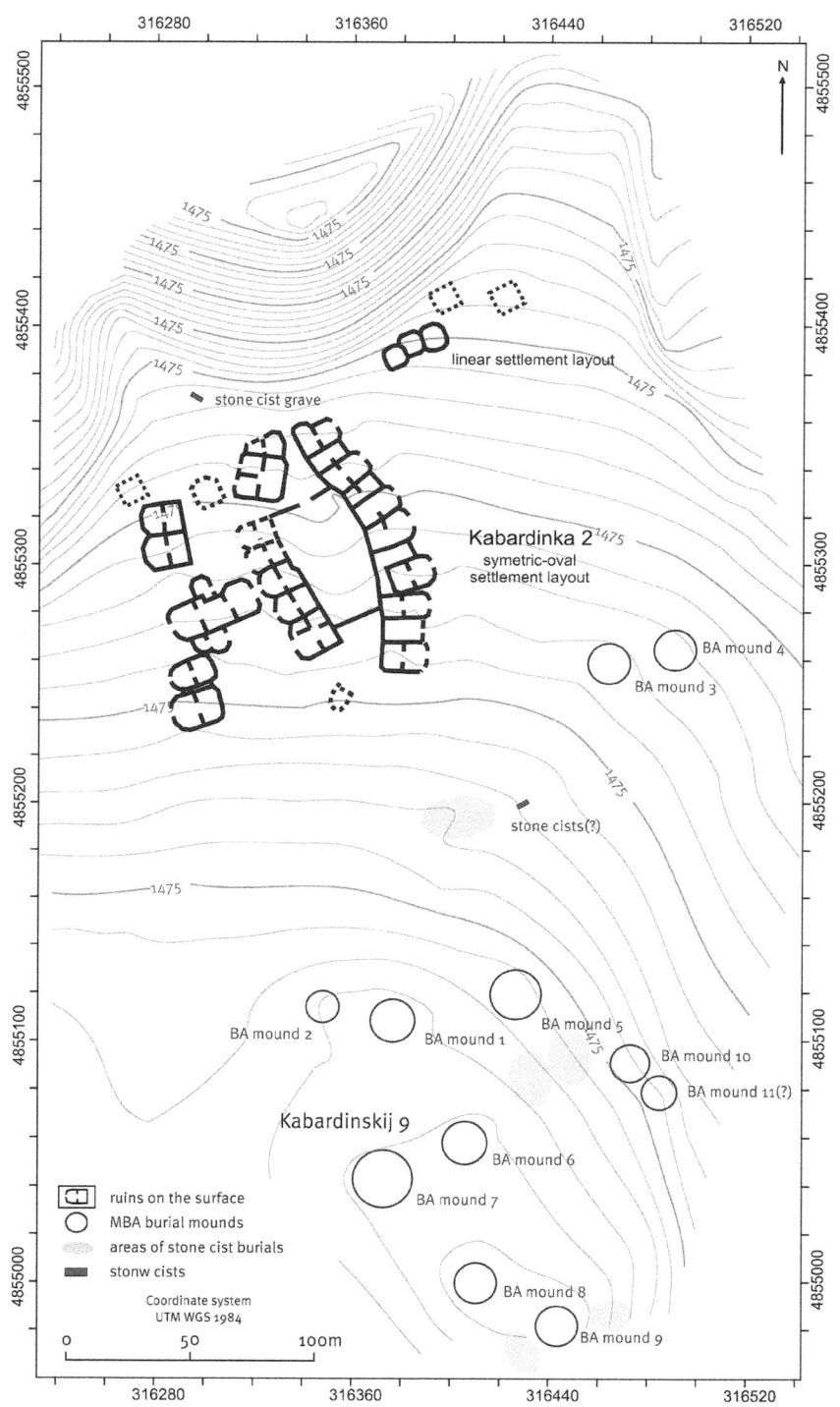

Figure 9.6. Kabardinka 2, MBA mounds, and LBA settlements.

We do not have detailed analysis of herd compositions at that time because the Kabardinka 2 house 23 was nearly empty of bones. Later herd compositions from settlement layers at Kabardinka 2 (house 14) indicate a frequency of 51 percent sheep/goat, 40 percent cattle, 5 percent horse, and 4 percent various species. Pasture requirements for cattle amount to 1.5 ha, including areas for cutting winter fodder, and a ratio of 1:8 for cattle and sheep is suggested for grazing territory, that is, eight sheep need the same share of pasture as one cow (Ebersbach 2002:156–158). If we calculate using these numbers, we can estimate that a minimum of 5,100–9,000 ha of pasture would be necessary to feed the predicted number of animals.[3] Cost-weighted buffer zones of the terrain around the sites calculated in GIS prove more than 15,000 ha available within a 5 km buffer around the sites. Local pasturing thus would have been an option for these early permanent settlers. A more detailed look at some micro-areas, however, demonstrates that this is not true for all communities. Identical stone tools from the Kabardinka 2 excavations and from a small campsite at over two thousand masl near a modern pastoral trail indeed indicate a seasonal upward shift of herds during this initial stage of permanent high-altitude exploitation. Similarly, a radiocarbon date from a Kislovodsk valley site dating to 3240±50 BP (1535–1440 cal BC 1σ) confirms activities in the lower river basin. We can reconstruct from that a seasonal shift of herds between valleys and high-mountain pastures with permanent bases in the linear settlements in the upper parts of this system.

All linear sites are situated above 1,700 masl; the most elevated site is 2,100 masl and the cited small pastoral camp is situated even higher. Despite the high elevations of the sites, grain imprints have been found on sherds from the initial phase. Agriculture already played a certain role during the final MBA. In the North Caucasus it is documented only at the lowland site of Ekashevsk, but in the South Caucasus a settlement with considerable grain storage and grinding facilities was found recently on the Trialei plateau at 1,560 masl (Lopan and Maslov 1999; Narimanishvili and Amiranashvili 2010).

What motivated the first communities to place themselves permanently, or at least semi-permanently, with their base camps at such altitudes? On the one hand, a shift toward increasing sedentarism and a settled form of pastoralism is a general trend in large parts of Eurasia in the early second millennium BC (Anthony et al. 2016; Reinhold 2017; van Hoof et al. 2012). On the other hand, the centuries prior to the settlement of the plateaus count as some of the most arid phases ever documented in the steppe zone of southern Russia. An extremely dry climate with hot summers and cold winters brought an end to the steppe communities by at least the seventeenth century BC (Borisov et al. 2011; Shishlina 2008). Simultaneously the forests in the lower mountain zone started to expand. A population that lived predominantly on livestock products would find new pastures only above the tree line. We should not forget that, at this point, the high-altitude pastures had been part of the human *oicumene* for at least one thousand years. If the burial mounds represent a sacred ancestral landscape to at least some of the new mountain settlers, for which we have evidence from the material culture, we should not be surprised. A landscape that was likewise cold but lush with water and good pastures would have been a welcome alternative to a dried-out steppe or to animal husbandry within dense forests (for nomads and forests, see de Planhol 1965). The familiarity with the high-altitude landscapes and potential territorial claims might have been other pull-factors for the mountains.

From neighboring regions at the south side of the Great Caucasus we know that an intensive exploitation of metal started in the mid-second millennium BC (Maisuradze and Gobedishvili 2001; Tschartolani 2001). The central Caucasian high-mountain valleys likewise hosted communities that must have exploited metal at a large scale. No mines are known due to a lack of targeted research, but cemeteries with thousands of bronze artifacts appear during the early second millennium BC (Motzenbäcker 1996). Our study area is located outside the Caucasian ore mineralization zone; thus metal exploitation and processing should not be considered as a major driving force to settle this mountain area. Yet, the passes to the south lead directly into the mining areas of Racha and Svanetia.

After an intermediate episode in the fifteenth century BC, where the linear settlements start to form more closed, circular configurations and an internal differentiation of household units begins to take place (Reinhold 2016), we witness the emergence of an extremely efficient system of combined mountain economy practices from the fourteenth to the tenth century BC. This phase in the development of mountain settlements is characterized by a highly adapted settlement layout constituted by a new type of multifunctional dwelling (Figure 9.5.B–C; Figure 9.6). The vast majority of the more than 130 settlements of that period known by now have a symmetrically structured oval layout formed by large houses that stand side by side, forming a protective wall around a large central plaza. This plaza is sometimes divided by walls and accessible only via small gates. The form of the settlements is ideal for keeping livestock as well as for effective herd management, that is, to separate male and female or young and old animals, respectively (Ebersbach 2002:141–145). The ground floors of the large houses cover an average of 100–160 sq m divided into two rooms. Houses are built with high-quality stone sockets (Reinhold 2016; Reinhold 2017). Microbacterial soil studies, combined with arguments from geophysics as well as preserved bone and ceramic distribution, made it possible to designate the rooms bordering the central plaza as human habitation areas, while the rooms bordering the settlements outside proved a repeated or permanent animal presence (Antipina 2013; Peters et al. 2014). The presence of animals not only in the site but also inside the houses was enormously consequential for reconstructing life and economy of this epoch. First, we had to divide the number of potential inhabitants in the houses between humans and animals. Second, we could calculate the number of inhabitants from floor space in the houses, and from the stable areas the size of the flocks that could be wintered per household. Space allowances for cattle rate from 6 to 9 sq m floor space in a stable, horses require more than 15 sq m, while sheep theoretically can be squeezed into 1 sq m per individual (Antipina 2013). Usually, however, sheep are wintered outside, since they do not like enclosed rooms. From this it was possible to calculate, for example, the symmetrical settlement at Kabardinka 2 a total number of 147 to 270 livestock units and 110 to 154 human inhabitants (Reinhold et al. 2017:52–61, figure 45, tables 1 and 2). The shares of each household are not similar but are relatively equally distributed at about 10–13 livestock units. On the plateaus, 117 symmetric and 19 irregularly shaped settlements have been mapped. At least for the symmetrical sites, a serial of twenty-three radiocarbon dates from seven stratified sites prove that they existed contemporaneously and that their occupation lasted 250–350 radiocarbon years each. Surface finds at most sites revealed close typological relations, thus it cannot be excluded that most sites existed at one point or another simultaneously. For the calculation of the economic system, this would lead us to a potential of 1,512 houses (i.e., households), inhabited by ca. 7,400—and up to 10,500—persons that could winter between 29,500 and 44,400 units of livestock (Table 9.1). The total area encompassing these sites is 850 sq km. It would have held a potential population of 8.7–12.4 persons/sq km. This number equals population densities of the nineteenth century in the same area (Shamanov 1972).

The economy acting as a base for this astonishingly high population and huge number of settlements was obviously centered on very efficient herding management. However, paleobotanical finds of cereals and a large number of grinding tools prove the existence of some kind of mountain agriculture as well. Fields have not been localized yet, but we would expect them to lie in the vicinity of the sites.

If we have a look at the high livestock numbers it is questionable whether the herds were maintained locally from the settlements. At Kabardinka 2, a site that is situated in a micro-region together with nine other contemporaneous settlements, the area or pasture and mowing of winter fodder would require a total of ca. 1,500–3,200 ha (Figure 9.7). In order to feed the population with agricultural products we could expect additionally 80–160 ha of fields (based on calculations from Ebersbach 2002; Reinhold et al. 2017:152–160). The land available in a 5 km buffer around all sites is ca. 2,800 ha. It is implausible that these

TABLE 9.1 HYPOTHETICAL ECONOMIC RANGE OF THE BRONZE AGE MOUNTAIN ECONOMIES AT THE MOUNTAIN PLATEAUS

	Epoch of the linear settlement layouts (16th–14th centuries BC)	Epoch of the linear settlement layouts (13th–10th centuries BC)	rate of increase
potential households (mapped house units)	444	1,512	3.4
potential inhabitants (5–7 persons/household)	2165–2.031	7385–10.546	3.4
local population density	2,5–3,5 P / sqkm	8,7–12,4 P / sqkm	3.5
potential herd sizes that can be wintered at plazas or stables	min. 3.232–5.938	29.539–44.368	9
herd density	min. 6,6–10,5 livestock unit / sqkm	47,6–73,5 livestock unit / sqkm	7.3
potential fields	423–1.185 ha	1.511–4.241 ha	2.8
demand in fields	5.112–8975 ha	40.496–62.531 ha	8
maximal available terrain in 5 km buffer zone	15.226 ha	40.218 ha	

communities could have maintained their livestock in the vicinity of the sites year-round. At least some of the meadows near the settlements must have been spared from regular grazing to cut winter fodder by shifting herds onto summer pastures. This consideration from spatial analysis is supported by the archaeozoological results. The faunal spectrum indicates an exploitation of cattle for meat, while sheep and goats were exploited for dairy products (Antipina 2013). The statistical basis for interpretation is not large, but kill-off pattern and age structure suggest that most animals were probably not kept locally. Some remained in the settlements and were slaughtered all-year-round. The Kabardinka 2 animal population and its exploitation patterns mirrored nearly one-to-one the mountain farming economy of a herdsmen neighbor near one of our excavation sites. A house with gardens and small fields was run by his wife, who kept four to five cows in summer from the village at 1,500 masl. He, himself, was pasturing five hundred sheep, forty cows, and two horses together with two aids on pastures at a distance of ca. 10 km and at 2,100 masl from June to September.

The end of the highly efficient Late Bronze Age combined mountain agriculture and permanent settlement, flourishing on the mountain plateaus for at least three hundred years starting in the eleventh century BC, when the first groups of settlers left for the mountain valleys (Figure 9.8). A radiocarbon date from a settlement below a later agricultural terrace dates to 2850±50 BP (1085–930 cal BC 1σ). It revealed ceramics typical for the

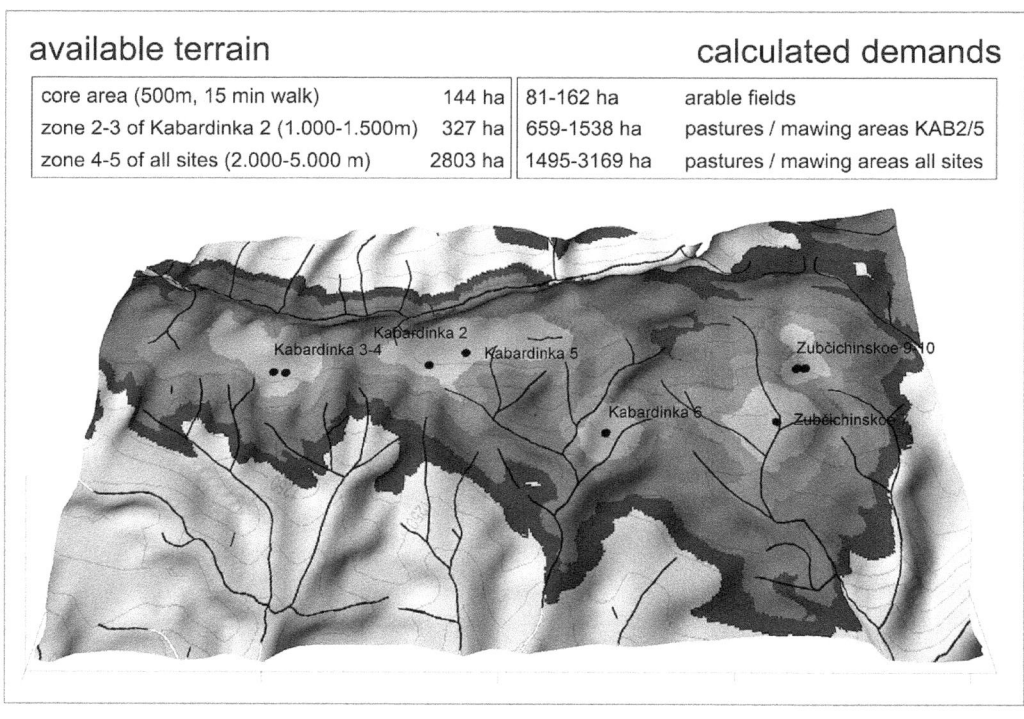

Figure 9.7. Cost-weighted buffer zones around the Kabardinka micro-region sites: demands versus available terrains.

early Koban culture, that is, the valley-based LBA/EIA archaeological culture. Koban sites, including settlements and cemeteries, pop up in the Kislovodsk valley during the tenth century BC in each part of this mountain basin. By the late tenth century BC, all mountain settlements had been abandoned (Reinhold et al. 2017:240–244). The latest date of 2685±50 BP (895–800 cal BC 1σ) was provided by the debris of house 14 at Kabardinka 2, which was dismantled deliberately, and marks the end of the mountain episode. The shifted communities continued their lives in the Kislovodsk basin, without much indication of a crisis.

The shift might have been triggered by a warm and dry climatic period starting after 900 BC, which favored agriculture in the valleys and probably exhausted the intensively exploited pastures. Typological links in the material culture prove the Early Iron Age (EIA) inhabitants of the valleys to be the descendants of the LBA mountain-dwellers (Reinhold et al. 2012). They shifted to an intensive agriculture, represented by huge agricultural terraces and paleobotanical proof of cereal and millet cultivation. How many and where they kept animals is the topic of an ongoing study of our project partners who have explored the history of the Kislovodsk basin agricultural landscape for the last ten years (Korobov and Borisov 2013). The shift toward an agropastoral mountain farming economy is also mirrored in the isotopic pattern of Bronze and Iron Age diets that confirm a share of meat or dairy

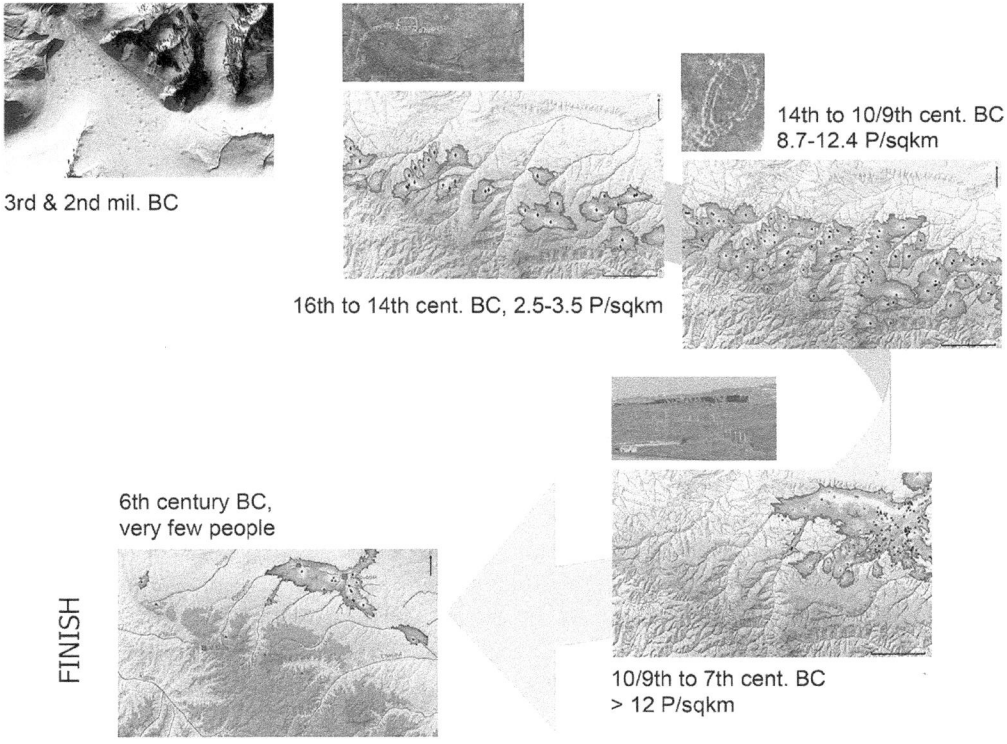

Figure 9.8. Settlement dynamics in the central North Caucasus from the third millennium BC to the sixth century BC.

products as high as before, but that now reveal a significant indication of millet consumption (Knipper et al. 2017). The intensive and unsustainable economy was severely hit by an ecological catastrophe probably in the mid-eighth century BC, when heavy rains washed down barren alluvial soil onto the terraces and fields (Korobov and Borisov 2013:1100). The number of archaeological sites and their sizes reduced considerably and during the sixth century BC the Kislovodsk basin fell to waste for the next six hundred years at least.

Conclusion

The Caucasus mountain system in north as in the south reveals a rather untypical occupation of mountainous terrains from the fifth millennium BC onward if we compare site density and the intensity of cultural activities in the high mountain zone with other mountain systems (see, e.g., Della Casa et al. 1999; Frachetti 2008; Gheyle 2009). Mountain economies in the Caucasus oscillated between more sedentary agropastoral and more mobile pastoral lifeways over the millennia. After an initial advance into the mountain massifs during the late fourth millennium BC in the south and in the third millennium in the north, however, site (i.e., population) densities remained considerably high. Metallurgy, salt exploitation, and regional trade certainly played an important role in Caucasian economies, but basic subsistence of all mountain populations had been pastoralism with shares of agriculture, and in a more or less settled form.

The LBA settlement explosion at high altitudes outlined for the North Caucasian micro-region near Kislovodsk is symptomatic of practically all Caucasia and the neighboring mountain zones. The landscapes of the Lesser Caucasus are similarly intensively inhabited and reveal comparable oscillations (Smith et al. 2009). This epoch sees the first stable and dense mountain dwelling communities in Eurasia living permanently in the high mountain zone. These communities developed essential technologies and social strategies for a flourishing life in a harsh environment. Thus they are a kind of template for later combined mountain farming communities, possibly not only in the Caucasus.

Notes

1. I thank Prof. Dr. Norbert Benecke, Department of Natural Sciences DAI, Berlin, for the information on the unpublished animal species identification.
2. The term "Neolithic" is used here for archaeological sites dating to the seventh and sixth millennium BC that are characterized either by a Near Eastern type of early farming economy (Shulaveri-Shomutepe Neolithic) or the presence of ceramics (eastern European and forest-type Neolithic). Most of the eastern European Neolithic cultural groups used ceramics and polished stone tools but continued employing a hunter-gatherer economy. For the terminology, see Piezonka 2012, and Mazurkevich and Dolbunova 2012 with a wider debate on the early Neolithic in Eastern Europe.
3. In the following we will not calculate sheep/goat and cattle separately but use an average livestock unit representing a ratio of 1.5:1:5 of horse:cattle:sheep (for details, see Ebersbach

2002:137). For species equivalent numbers, see Reinhold et al. 2017:155, Table 15; among others.

REFERENCES

Albegova (Tsarikayeva), Z. Kh., and N. A. Tsvetkova 2015 Poseleniye Chidgom—novyy pamyatnik ranney—sredney bronzy v Severnoy Osetii: predvaritel'nyye itogi issledovaniy. In *Materialy okhrannykh arkheologicheskikh issledovaniy: goroda, poseleniya, mogil'niki*, vol. 17, edited by Z. Kh. Albegova (Tsarikayeva) and A. V. Engovatova, 4–49. Perfektum, Cheboksary.

Anthony, D., D. Brown, P. Kuznetsov, O. Mochalov, and A. Khokhlov (eds.) 2016 *Bronze Age Landscape in the Russian Steppes*. Cotsen Institute, Los Angeles.

Antipina, E. E. 2013 Modeli drevnego skotovodstva na Kavkaze: arkheozoologicheskie isledovaniya na poselenii Kabardinka 2. *Analiticheskie issledovaniya laboratorii estestvennohauchnykh metodov* 3:126–141.

Antipina, E. E. 2015 Chidgom—epokha bronzy: osteologicheskaya kollektsiya. In *Materialy okhrannykh arkheologicheskikh issledovaniy: goroda, poseleniya, mogil'niki*, vol. 17, edited by Z. Kh. Albegova (Tsarikayeva) and A. V. Engovatova, 50–56. Perfektum, Cheboksary.

Bader, O. N., and L. Tsereteli 1989 Mesolit Kavkaza. In *Mesolit SSSR*, edited by L. V. Klochov, 93–105. Arkheologiya SSSR, Nauka, Moscow.

Belinskiy, A. B., S. N. Korenevskiy, and S. Reinhold 2009 Landshaftnaya arkheologiya na Severnom Kavkaze: pervyye rezultaty issledovaniya predgornogo landshafta Kislovodska epokhi pozdnego bronzogo—rannego zheleznogo beka. *Materialy po izucheniyu istoriko-kulturnogo naslediya Severnogo Kavkaza* 9:177–220.

Benecke, N. 2017 Exploitation of Animal Resources in Neolithic Settlements of the Kura Region (South Caucasia). In *The Kura Projects*, edited by B. Helwing, T. Aliyev, B. Lyonnet, G. Farhad, S. Hansen, and G. Mirtskhulava, 357–369. Archäologie in Iran und Turan 16. Dietrich Reimer Verlag, Berlin.

Borisov, A. V., R. A. Mimokhod, and V. A. Demkin 2011 Paleopochvy i prirodnye ucloviya yuzhnorosskikh stepey v postkatakombnoe vremya. *Kratkie Soobshcheniya Instituta Arkheologii* 225:144–154.

Bringemeier, L., R. Krause, A. Stobbe, and L. Röpke 2015 Expansions of Bronze Age Pasture Farming and Environmental Changes in the Northern Alps (Montafon, Austria and Prättigau, Switzerland): An Intergrated Palaeoenvironmental and Archaeological Approach. In *The Third Food Revolution? Setting the Bronze Age Table—Common Trends in Economic and Subsistence Strategies in Bronze Age Europe*, edited by J. Kneisel, M. Del Corso, W. Kierleis, H. Scholz, N. Taylor, and V. Tiedtke, 181–200. Verlag Dr. Rudolf Habelt, Bonn.

Carrer, F. 2015 Herding Strategies, Dairy Economy and Seasonal Sites in the Southern Alps: Ethnoarchaeological Inferences and Archaeological Implications. *Journal of Mediterranean Archaeology* 28:3–22.

Carrer, F. 2016 The "Invisible" Shepherd and the "Visible" Dairyman: Ethnoarchaeology of Alpine Pastoral Sites in the Val di Fiemme (Eastern Italian Alps). In *Summer Farms: Seasonal Exploitation of the Uplands from Prehistory to the Present*, edited by J. Collis, M. Pearce, and F. Nicolis, 97–107. Sheffield Archaeological Monographs 16. R. Collis, Sheffield.

Chartolani, Sh. G. 1989 *Kistorii nagor'ya zapadnoy Gruzii doklassovoy epokhi*. Metsniyereba, Tbilisi.

Chernykh, E. N. 1992 *Ancient Metallurgy in the USSR: The Early Metal Age*. Cambridge University Press, Cambridge.

Chernysheva, E., D. S. Korobov, and A. V. Borisov 2017 Thermophilic Microorganisms in Arable Land around Medieval Archaeological Sites in Northern Caucasus, Russia: Novel Evidence of Past Manuring Practices. *Geoarchaeology*:1–8.

Collis, J., M. Pearce, and F. Nicolis (eds.) 2016 *Summer Farms: Seasonal Exploitation of the Uplands from Prehistory to the Present*. Sheffield Archaeological Monographs 16. R. Collis, Sheffield.

Della Casa, P. 2002 *Landschaften, Siedlungen, Ressourcen: Langzeitszenarien menschlicher Aktivität in ausgewählten alpinen Gebieten der Schweiz, Italiens und Frankreichs*. Éd. Mergoil, Montagnac.

Della Casa, P., B. Bass, and F. Fedele 1999 The Grisons Alpine Survey 1995–1997: Methods, Results and Prospects of an Interdisciplinary Research Program. In *Prehistoric Alpine Environment, Society, and Economy*, edited by P. Della Casa, 151–172. Universitätsforschungen zur prähistorischen Archäologie. Habelt, Bonn.

Della Casa, P., L. Naef, and T. Reitmaier 2013 Valleys, Pastures and Passes: New Research Issues from the Swiss Central Alps. *Preistoria Alpina* 47:39–47.

Donitia, N., Z. V. Karamsheva, A. Borhidi, and U. Bohn 2003 Sub-Mediterranean-Subcontinental Herb-Grass Steppes, Locally Meadow Steppes (*Festuca valesiaca*, *Stipa spp.*, *Bothriochloa ischaemum*, *Chrysopogon gryllus*), Alternating with Oak Forests (*Quercus pubescens*, *Q. robur*, *Q. pedunculiflora*) with *Acer tataricum* (L8). Electronic document, http://www.floraweb.de.

Ebersbach, R. 2002 *Von Bauern und Rindern*. Basler Beiträge zur Archäologie vol. 15. Schwabe, Basel.

Ehlers, E., and H. Kreutzmann (eds.) 2000 *High Mountain Pastoralism in Northern Pakistan*. Erdkundliches Wissen vol. 132. Steiner, Stuttgart.

Frachetti, M. D. 2008 *Pastoralist Landscapes and Social Interaction in Bronze Age Eurasia*. University of California Press, Berkeley.

Gabunia, M., and L. Tsereteli 2003 Mezoliti kavkasshi [The Mesolithic in the Caucasus]. *Dziebani* 12:5–30.

Gambashidze, I., A. Hauptmann, R. Slotty, and Ü. Yalçin (eds.) 2001 *Georgien: Veröffentlichungen aus dem Deutschen Bergbau-Museum Bochum* vol. 100. Dt. Bergbau-Museum, Bochum.

Gambashidze, I., and T. Stöllner 2016 *The Gold of Sakdrisi: Man's First Gold Mining Enterprise*. Marie Leidorf, Rahden/Westphalia.

Gheyle, W. 2009 Highlands and Steppes: An Analysis of the Changing Archaeological Landscape of the Altay Mountains from the Eneolithic to the Ethnographic Period. Unpublished PhD dissertation, University of Ghent.

Gorelik, A. F., and A. V. Cybrii 2007 Die spätneolithische Siedlung Kemennaja II am Unteren Don. *Eurasia Antiqua* 13:21–42.

Gorelik, A. F., A. V. Cybrii, and V. V. Cybrii 2014 O chem povedali cherep tura, topor i zhenskie statuetki? K voprosu nachalnoy neolitizacii Nizhnego Podonya. *Stratum Plus* (2):247–282.

Grötzbach, E. 1982 *Das Hochgebirge als menschlicher Lebensraum*. Eichstätter Hochschulreden vol. 33. Minerva, Munich.

Grupe, G., A. Grigat, and G. C. McGlynn (eds.) 2017 *Across the Alps in Prehistory: Isotopic Mapping of the Brenner Passage by Bioarchaeology*. Springer, Berlin.

Hambleton, E., and M. Maltby 2016 The Animal Bones from Excavations in Meshoko Cave in the Northern Caucasus. Electronic document, http://eprints.bournemouth.ac.uk/24860/1/MeshokoCaveReportJuly2016.pdf.

Hansen, S. 2011 Technische und soziale Innovationen in der zweiten Hälfte des 4: Jahrtausends v. Chr. In *Sozialarchäologische Perspektiven: gesellschaftlicher Wandel 5000–1500 v. Chr. zwischen Atlantik und Kaukasus*, edited by S. Hansen and J. Müller, 153–191. Archäologie in Eurasien. von Zabern, Mainz.

Helwing, B., T. Aliyev, B. Lyonnet, G. Farhad, S. Hansen, and G. Mirtskhulava (eds.) 2017 *The Kura Projects: Archäologie in Iran und Turan 16*. Dietrich Reimer Verlag, Berlin.

Hovsepyan, R. 2015 On the Agriculture and Vegetal Food Economy of Kura-Araxes Culture in the South Caucasus. *Paléorient* 41(1):69–82.

Hovsepyan, R., and G. Willcox 2008 The Earliest Finds of Cultivated Plants in Armenia: Evidence from Charred Remains and Crop Processing Residues in Pisé from the Neolithic Settlements of Aratashen and Aknashen. *Vegetation History and Archaeobotany* 17(Suppl. 1):S63–S71.

Kakhiani, K., A. Sagona, C. Sagona, E. Kvavadze, G. Bedianishvili, E. Massager, L. Martin, E. Herrscher, I. Martkopishvili, J. Birkett-Rees, and C. Longford 2013 Archaeological Investigations at Chobareti in Southern Georgia, the Caucasus. *ANES* 50:1–138.

Kasparov, A. P., and M. V. Sablin 2009 Faunicheskie ostatki poseleniya Meshoko na Severnom Kavkaze. In *Meshoko: drevneyshaya krepost Predkavkazya*, edited by A. D. Stolyar and A. A. Formozov, 215–223. Gosudarstvenny Ermitazh, Saint Petersburg.

Kern, A., K. Kowarik, A. W. Rausch, and H. Reschreiter (eds.) 2008 *Salz-Reich*. Verlag des Naturhistorischen Museums Wien, Vienna.

Knipper, C., S. Reinhold, J. Gresky, A. B. Belinskiy, and K. W. Alt 2017 Economic Strategies at Bronze Age and Early Iron Age Upland Sites in the North Caucasus: Archaeological and Stable Isotope Investigations. In *Isotopic Investigations of Pastoralism in Prehistory*, edited by A. R. Ventresca Miller and C. A. Makarewicz, 123–140. Themes in Contemporary Archaeology. Routledge, Abingdon.

Korenevskiy, S. N. 1998 Poselenie Zamok u gorodka Kislovodska (nizhniy sloy). *Materialy po izucheniyu istoriko-kulturnogo naslediya Severnogo Kavkaza* 1:96–147.

Korenevskiy, S. N. 2004 *Drevneishie Zemledeltsy i Skotovody Predkavkazya: Maikopsko-Novosvobodnenskaya obschnost*. Nauka, Moscow.

Korenevskiy, S. N. 2009 Poselenie eneoliticheskoy epokhi Predkavkazya Yazeneva Polyana: Nasledie P. A. Ditlera. *Stratum Plus* (2):393–418.

Korenevskiy, S. N. 2012 *Rozhdenie Kurgana: pogrebalnye pamjatniki eneoliticheskogo vremeni Predkavkazja i Volgo-Donskogo mezhdurechia*. Taus, Moscow.

Korobov, D. S., and A. V. Borisov 2013 The Origins of Terraced Field Agriculture in the Caucasus: New Discoveries in the Kislovodsk Basin. *Antiquity* 87(338):1086–1103.

Krismer, M., and P. Tropper 2016 Die Entstehung der Gesteine und Erzlagerstätten der Ostalpen. In *Bergauf Bergab: Eine Zeitreise durch 10.000 Jahre Bergbau in den Ostalpen*, edited by T. Stöllner and K. Oeggl, 13–17. Veröffentlichung aus dem Deutschen Bergbau-Museum Bochum. Leidorf, Rahden/Westphalia.

Lebedeva, E. Y. 2011 Pervye rezultaty arkheobotanicheskikh issledovanii na arkheologicheskikh pamyatnikakh Adygei. *Analiticheskie issledovaniya laboratorii estestvennohauchnykh metodov* 2:244–257.

Lebedeva, E. Y. 2015 O gornom zemledelii v Osetii v epokhu bronzy (arkheobotanicheskiye issledovaniya na poselenii Chidgom). In *Materialy okhrannykh arkheologicheskikh issledovaniy: goroda, poseleniya, mogil'niki*, vol. 17, edited by Z. Kh. Albegova (Tsarikayeva) and A. V. Engovatova, 68–77. Perfektum, Cheboksary.

Lopan, O. V., and V. E. Maslov 1999 Ekashevskoe poselenie: pamyatnik epokhi bronzy v Ingushetii. In *Drevnosti Severogo Kavkaza*, edited by V. I. Markovin, 61–88. Nauka, Moscow.

Lozny, L. R. (ed.) 2013 *Continuity and Change in Cultural Adaptation to Mountain Environments: From Prehistory to Contemporary Threats*. Springer, New York.

Maisuradze, B., and Gobedishvili G. 2001 Alter Bergbau in Ratscha. In *Georgien*, edited by I. Gambashidze, A. Hauptmann, R. Slotty, and Ü. Yalçin, 130–135. Veröffentlichungen aus dem Deutschen Bergbau-Museum Bochum. Dt. Bergbau-Museum, Bochum.

Mandl, F. 2016 Die Geschichte der Almwirtschaft auf dem Dachsteingebirge. In *Bergauf Bergab: Eine Zeitreise durch 10.000 Jahre Bergbau in den Ostalpen*, edited by T. Stöllner and K. Oeggl, 34–43. Veröffentlichung aus dem Deutschen Bergbau-Museum Bochum. Leidorf, Rahden/Westphalia.

Marro, C. 2007 Upper-Mesopotamia and Transaucasia in the Late Chalcolithic Period (4000–3500 BC). In *Les cultures du Caucase*, edited by B. Lyonnet, 77–94. CNRS Éditions. Éditions Recherche sur les Civilisations, Paris.

Marro, C., V. Bakhshaliyev, and S. Sanz 2010 Archaeological Investigations on the Salt Mine of Dzudagi (Nakhichevan, Azerbaidjan). *TÜBA-AR* 13:229–244.

Mazurkevich, A., and E. Dolbunova 2012 The Most Ancient Pottery and Neolithisation of Eastern Europe. *Fontes Archaeologici Posnanienses* 48:143–159.

Meckelein, W., and J. Stadelbauer 1998 *Nordkaukasien: Stuttgarter Geographische Studien* vol. 127. Geographisches Institut der Universität, Stuttgart.

Merzbacher, G. 1901 *Aus den Hochregionen des Kaukasus*. Duncker & Humblot, Leipzig.

Meshveliani, T., G. Bar-Oz, O. Bar-Yosef, A. Belfer-Cohen, E. Boaretto, N. Jakeli, I. Koridze, and Z. Matskevich 2007 Mesolithic Hunters at Kotias Klde, Western Georgia: Preliminary Results. *Paléorient* 33:47–58.

Messager, E., E. Herrscher, L. Martin, E. Kvavadze, I. Martkopishvili, C. Delhon, K. Kakhiani, G. Bedianishvili, A. Sagona, L. Bitadze, M. Polumac'h, A. Guy, and D. Lordkipanidze 2015 Archaeobotanical and Isotopic Evidence of Early Bronze Age Farming Activities and Diet in the Mountainous Environment of the South Caucasus: A Pilot Study of Chobareti Site (Samtskhe-Javakheti Region). *Journal of Archaeological Science* 53:214–226.

Motuzaite-Matuzeviciute, G. 2012 The Earliest Appearance of Domesticated Plant Species and Their Origins on the Western Fringes of the Eurasian Steppe. *Documenta Praehistorica* 39:1–21.

Motzenbäcker, I. 1996 *Sammlung Kossnierska: Museum für Vor- und Frühgeschichte* vol. 3. Museum für Vor- und Frühgeschichte, Berlin.

Narimanishvili, G., and J. Amiranashvili 2010 Jenisi Settlement. In *Bak'o-T'bilisi-Džeikani Samchret' Kavkasiis milsadeni da ark'eologia Sak'art veloši*, edited by G. A. Gamkrelidze, 224–253. Sak'art'velos Erovnuli Muzeumi, Tbilissi.

Neef, R., A. Decaix, and M. Tengberg 2017 Agricultural Practices and Paleoenvironment of the Southern Caucasus during the Neolithic: A Transect along the Kura River. In *The Kura Projects*, edited by B. Helwing, T. Aliyev, B. Lyonnet, G. Farhad, S. Hansen, and G. Mirtskhulava, 371–377. Archäologie in Iran und Turan 16. Dietrich Reimer Verlag, Berlin.

Nicolis, F., E. Mottes, M. Bassetti, E. Castiglioni, M. Rottoli, and S. Ziggiotti 2016 Going Up the Mountain! Exploitation of the Trentino Highlands as Summer Farms during the Bronze Age: The Dosso Rotondo Site at Storo (Northern Italy). In *Summer Farms: Seasonal Exploitation of the Uplands from Prehistory to the Present*, edited by J. Collis, M. Pearce, and F. Nicolis, 109–138. Sheffield Archaeological Monographs 16. R. Collis, Sheffield.

Oeggl, K., A. Schmidl, and W. Kofler 2009 Origin and Seasonality of Subfossil Caprine Dung from the Discovery Site of the Iceman (Eastern Alps). *Vegetation History and Archaeobotany* 18(1):37–46.

Palumbi, G. 2016 The Early Bronze Age of the Southern Caucasus. Electronic document, http://www.oxfordhandbooks.com/view/10.1093/oxfordhb/9780199935413.001.0001/oxfordhb-9780199935413-e-14.

Peters, S., A. V. Borisov, S. Reinhold, D. S. Korobov, and H. Thiemeyer 2014 Microbial Characteristics of Soils Depending on the Human Impact on Archaeological Sites in the Northern Caucasus. *Quaternary International* 324:162–171.

Piezonka, H. 2012 Stone Age Hunter-Gatherer Ceramics of Northeastern Europe: New Insights into the Dispersal of an Essential Innovation. *Documenta Praehistorica* 39:23–51.

Planhol, X. de 1965 Les Nomades, la Steppe et la Forêt en Anatolie. *Geographische Zeitschrift* 53(2/3):101–116.

Radde, G. 1899 *Grundzüge der Pflanzenverbreitung in den Kaukasusländern von der unteren Wolga über den Manytsch-Scheider bis zur Scheitelfläche Hocharmeniens*. Die Vegetation der Erde vol. 3. Engelmann, Leipzig.

Reinhold, S. 2007 *Die Spätbronze- und frühe Eisenzeit im Kaukasus*. Universitätsforschungen zur prähistorischen Archäologie vol. 144. Habelt, Bonn.

Reinhold, S. 2016 Late Bronze Age Architecture in Caucasia and Beyond: Building a New Lifestyle for a New Epoch. In *At the Northern Frontier of Near Eastern Archaeology*, edited by E. Rova and M. Tonussi, 337–366. Publications of the Georgian-Italian Shida Kartli Archaeological Project. Brepols, Turnhout.

Reinhold, S. 2017 Sedentism as Innovation Process: Technological and Social Perspectives on the Development of Architecture of a Bronze Age. In *The Interplay of People and Technologies*, edited by S. Burmeister and R. Bernbeck, 161–203. Topoi—Berlin Studies of the Ancient World. Edition Topoi, Berlin.

Reinhold, S., A. B. Belinskiy, and D. S. Korobov 2016 Caucasia Top-Down: Remote Sensing Data for Survey in a High Altitude Mountain Landscape. *Quaternary International* 402:46–60.

Reinhold, S., A. B. Belinskiy, D. S. Korobov, J. W. E. Fassbinder, A. V. Borisov, and S. Peters 2007 Landschaftsarchäologie im Nordkaukasus: Erste Ergebnisse der Untersuchung der Vorgebirgslandschaft bei Kislovodsk während der Spätbronze- und frühen Eisenzeit. *Eurasia Antiqua* 13:139–180.

Reinhold, S., and D. S. Korobov 2007 The Kislovodsk Basin in the North Caucasian Piedmonts: Archaeology and GIS Studies in a Mountain Cultural Landscape. *Preistoria Alpina* 42:183–207.

Reinhold, S., D. S. Korobov, and A. B. Belinskiy 2012 Formation und Transformation einer bronzezeitlichen Gebirgslandschaft im Nordkaukasus. In *Austausch und Kulturkontakt im Südkaukasus und seinen angrenzenden Regionen in der Spätbronze-/Früheisenzeit (Ende 2./Anfang 1. Jt. v.Chr.)*, edited by A. Mehnert, G. Mehnert, and S. Reinhold, 9–25. Schriften des Zentrums für Archäologie und Kulturgeschichte des Schwarzmeerraumes. Beier & Beran, Langenweißbach.

Reinhold, S., D. S. Korobov, and A. B. Belinskiy 2017 *Landschaftsarchäologie im Nordkaukasus*. Archäologie in Eurasien vol. 38. Habelt, Bonn.

Reitmaier, T. 2017 Prähistorische Alpwirtschaft: Eine archäologische Spurensuche in der Silvretta (CH/A), 2007–2016. *Jahrbuch Archäologie Schweiz* 11:7–53.

Rendu, C. 2003 *La montagne d'Enveig: Història*. Trabucaire, Canet.
Rezepkin, A. D. 2012 *Novosvobodnenskaja kul'tura: na osnove materialov mogil'nika "Klady."* Nestor-Istorija, Saint Petersburg.
Rostunov, V. 2007 *Epokha eneolita: srednej bronzy Centralnogo Kavkaza*. Severo-Osetinskiy institut gumanitarnych i socialnykh issledovaniy, Vladikavkaz.
Rostunov, V., S. Lyakhov, and S. Reinhold 2009 Cmi: Eine Freilandfundstelle des Spätmesolithikums und Frühneolithikums in Nordossetien (Nordkaukasus). *Archäologische Mitteilungen aus Iran und Turan* 41:47–74.
Shishlina, N. I. 2008 *Reconstruction of the Bronze Age of the Caspian Steppes: Life Styles and Life Ways of Pastoral Nomads*. Archaeopress, Oxford.
Shamanov, I. M. 1972 Skotovodstvo i khozyaystvennyy byt karachayevtsev v 19.—nachale 20 v. *Kavkazskiy Etnograficheskiy Sbornik* 5:67–97.
Smith, A. T., R. S. Badalyan, and P. Avetisyan 2009 *The Archaeology and Geography of Ancient Transcaucasian Societies*. Oriental Institute Publications vol. 134. Oriental Institute of the University of Chicago, Chicago.
Spengler, R. N., III, M. D. Frachetti, and G. J. Fritz 2013 Ecotopes and Herd Foraging Practices: In the Steppe/Mountain Ecotone of Central Asia during the Bronze and Iron Ages. *Journal of Ethnobiology* 33(1):125–147.
Stadelbauer, J. 1984 Bergnomaden und Yaylabauern in Kaukasien: Zur demographischen Entwicklung und zum sozioökonomischen Wandel bei ethnischen Gruppen mit nicht-stationärer Tierhaltung. *Paideuma* 30:201–225.
Stark, S. 2009 Materielle Raumaneignung und kognitive Konstruktion von landscape: Perspektiven des archäologischen Zugangs am Beispiel einer Feldstudie in Tadžikistan. In *Raum, Landschaft, Territorium*, edited by R. Kath and A.-K. Rieger, 103–148. Reichert, Wiesbaden.
Stöllner, T. 2016 Die Besiedlungsgeschichte der Ostalpen in der Früh- bis Mittelbronzezeit: Kolonisation und wirtschaftlicher Neuanfang. Teil 1. In *Bergauf Bergab: Eine Zeitreise durch 10.000 Jahre Bergbau in den Ostalpen*, edited by T. Stöllner and K. Oeggl, 117–124. Veröffentlichung aus dem Deutschen Bergbau-Museum Bochum. Leidorf, Rahden/Westphalia.
Stöllner, T., and K. Oeggl (eds.) 2016 *Bergauf Bergab: Eine Zeitreise durch 10.000 Jahre Bergbau in den Ostalpen*. Veröffentlichung aus dem Deutschen Bergbau-Museum Bochum vol. 207. Leidorf, Rahden/Westphalia.
Stolyar, A. D., and A. A. Formozov (eds.) 2009 *Meshoko: drevneyshaya krepost Predkavkazya*. Gosudarstvenny Ermitazh, Saint Petersburg.
Trifonov, V. A. 2015 Berge und die Ebenen: ein Modell der kulturellen Entwicklung im westlichen Kaukasus im 5. und 3. Jt. v. Chr. Горы и равнины: модель культурного развития Западного Кавказа в V–III тыс. до н.э. In *Der Kaukasus im Spannungsfeld zwischen Osteuropa und Vorderem Orient: Dialog der Kulturen, Kultur des Dialoges*, edited by M. T. Kashuba, S. Reinhold, and V. A. Alekshin, 113–117. IIMK RAN, Saint Petersburg.
Tschartolani, S. 1989 *K istorii nogorya zapadnoy Gruzii doklassovoy epokhi*. Mecniereba, Tbilisi.
Tschartolani, S. 2001 Alter Bergbau in Swanetien. In *Georgien: Schätze aus dem Land des Goldenen Vlies*, edited by I. Gambashidze, A. Hauptmann, and R. Slotta, 120–129. Deutsches Bergbau-Museum, Bochum.
Twaltshrelidze, A. 2001. Erzlagerstätten in Georgien. In *Georgien*, edited by I. Gambashidze, A. Hauptmann, R. Slotty, and Ü. Yalçin, 78–89. Veröffentlichungen aus dem Deutschen Bergbau-Museum Bochum. Dt. Bergbau-Museum, Bochum.

Tzortzis, S., and X. Delestre (eds.) 2010 *Archéologie de la montagne européenne*. Edition Errance, Paris.

van Hoof, L., O. Dally, and M. Schlöffel 2012 Staying Home or Staying with Your Cattle? Different Reactions to Environmental Changes in the Late Bronze Age of the Lower Don Area (Southern Russia). In *Landscape Archaeology Conference (LAC 2012)*, edited by W. Bebermeier, R. Hebenstreit, E. Kaiser, and J. Krause, 71–75. Exzellenzcluster 264 Topoi. Edition Topoi, Berlin.

Ventresca Miller, A. R., and C. A. Makarewicz (eds.) *Isotopic Investigations of Pastoralism in Prehistory*. Themes in Contemporary Archaeology vol. 4. Routledge, Abingdon.

Walsh, K., F. Mocci, and J. Palet-Martinez 2007 Nine Thousand Years of Human/Landscape Dynamics in a High Altitude Zone in the Southern French Alps (Parc National des Ecrins, Hautes-Alpes). *Preistoria Alpina* 42:5–18.

Wang, Chuan-Chao, Sabine Reinhold, Alexey A. Kalmykov, Antje Wissgott, Guido Brandt, Choongwon Jeong, Olivia Cheronet, et al. 2019 Ancient Human Genome-Wide Data from a 3000-Year Interval in the Caucasus Corresponds with Eco-Geographic Regions. *Nature Communications* 10(1):590, https://doi.org/10.1038/s41467-018-08220-8.

Wilkinson, T. C. 2014 *Tying the Threads of Eurasia*. Sidestone Press, Leiden.

Chapter Ten

Landscape Archaeology in Eastern Pyrenees High Mountain Areas (Segre and Ter Valleys, Northeast Iberian Peninsula)

Human Activities in the Shaping of Mountain Cultural Landscapes

Josep M. Palet, Hèctor A. Orengo, Arnau Garcia-Molsosa, Tania Polonio, Ana Ejarque, Yannick Miras, and Santiago Riera

Abstract *Since 2004, an integrated archaeological and paleoenvironmental research program has been developed in the Eastern Pyrenees (Andorra and Catalonia), with the aim of studying the long-term landscape shaping of Mediterranean high-mountain environments. This program involved extensive surveying, GIS, excavation, and radiocarbon dating of archaeological structures and the integration of multiproxy paleoenvironmental data. The results underline the existence in these areas of diverse land use and resource management strategies during the past millennia, which included fire-driven forest openings, grazing, woodland, mining, and melting activities. This diversity of activities has led to complex cultural landscapes in the high Pyrenean areas. During the Early Neolithic, human clearance was diversified in its spatial distribution and short-lived, allowing the recovery of subalpine forests after impacts. A major landscape change occurred in the valleys since the Middle Neolithic–Late Neolithic transition (~3600 cal BC) until the Early Bronze Age (~1600 cal BC) when the alpine grassland belt expanded and human settlements were documented at ca. 2,500 masl. Roman times report a diversification of practices. An important period in livestock expansion is documented from the second to third centuries and during late antiquity. In medieval times (ninth to tenth century), a largely grazed landscape resulted in a wide deforestation. Later on, during the modern and contemporary periods, an intensive transhumant grazing exploitation characterized these valleys' land use. The history of this landscape furnishes new data for the development of management tools for the sustainability of Mediterranean highlands.*

Introduction

Research into the occupation and exploitation of mountain areas has been conditioned for a long time by the marginality in which these environments were traditionally perceived by historiography. In addition, factors such as the intensity of erosion processes, topography, poor conservation of the archaeological record, or dense forest cover have restricted field research. This lack, at the same time, has encouraged a marginal perception of the mountain areas. Thus, the mountain and, above all, the high mountain, had traditionally been perceived as a natural environment, characterized by the marginality of human activities.

Certainly, this situation has been changing in the last decades, thanks to a growing interest in the occupation and exploitation of European mountain spaces over time. The pioneering works developed by C. Rendu in the Cerdanya valley in the 1990s (Rendu 2003), by E. Gassiot in the Catalan Western Pyrenees (Gassiot and Jiménez 2006), and that coordinated by P. Leveau in the western Alps (Palet et al. 2003; Segard 2009; Walsh et al. 2007; Walsh et al. 2005; Walsh and Mocci 2003) constitute the starting point of a research line in Europe that has developed new projects enriched with the methods and techniques of landscape archaeology (Gassiot et al. 2014; Gassiot 2016; Orengo et al. 2014a, 2014b; Palet et al. 2013, 2014; Putzer et al. 2016; Walsh et al. 2014). Paleoenvironmental studies have also had a growing impact with multidisciplinary and diachronic approaches (Ejarque 2013; Ejarque et al. 2009, 2010; Galop 1998; Miras et al. 2007, 2010; Pèlachs et al. 2009).

The results obtained in different European mountain areas have questioned the traditional image, showing that human impact on these spaces has been intense and that these areas constitute real cultural landscapes, shaped over time.

In this context, "new archaeologies" such as "mountain archaeology" or "archaeology of pastoralism" have been defined, with approaches closely linked to landscape archaeology. These studies are multidisciplinary, based on the correlation of archaeological, historical, paleoenvironmental, and ethnographic data. In addition, high-mountain areas are ideal environments for the analysis of socioenvironmental interactions over time, that is, to study human resilience to natural variability, and landscape dynamics (Gassiot 2016; Palet et al. 2012).

Cultural landscape values are also a sustainable resource for society. In this sense, the possibilities of knowledge transfer are significant as these areas are often protected with natural and cultural heritage regulations. The results can be, for example, incorporated into social and environmental plans and contribute to the development of future management and territorial heritagization policies (Criado-Boado et al. 2015).

In this framework, since 2004, the Landscape Archaeology Research Group (GIAP-ICAC) has developed a program on settlement and land use on high-mountain areas. In the Pyrenees, this research has been done in three areas located in the Andorran valleys of the Madriu, Perafita, and Claror (MPCV); in La Vansa valley in the Cadí Range; and in the Ripollès, in the upper river Ter valleys (Núria, Coma de Vaca, and Coma del Freser valleys) (Ejarque 2013; Ejarque et al. 2009; Ejarque et al. 2010; Euba 2009; Orengo et al. 2013, 2014a, 2014b; Palet et al. 2013, 2014, 2016) (Figure 10.1). The main aim of these projects is to characterize settlement dynamics, land use, and the shaping of high-mountain cultural

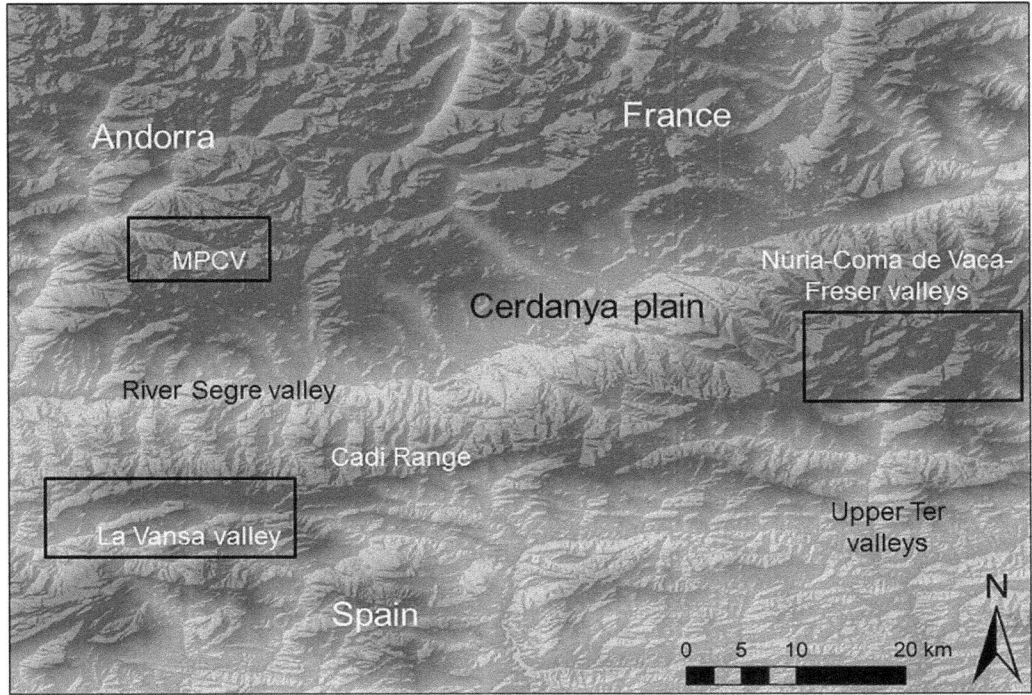

Figure 10.1. Map with indication of the studied areas in the Eastern Pyrenees.

landscapes. The research is focused on an interdisciplinary perspective, based on the integration of landscape archaeology data.

In Andorra, the studied area benefited from inscription by UNESCO on the list of World Heritage in the category of Cultural Landscape of MPCV. The studied sector was extended between the subalpine stadium (1,700–2,200 m), with the presence of black pine forests and firs, and the Alpine stadium (2,200–2,900 m), dominated by pastures and screes. A second area of research was placed in the western sector of the Cadí Range, between subalpine and alpine areas, from the height of 1,700 m to the main ridge line (2,400 m). This area has a special interest in mining, pastoral, and forest resources. These projects ended in 2010. Finally, a third area of study, still in progress, is situated in the Eastern Pyrenees in the upper Ter valley, above the 2,000 masl.

Methodology

The landscape archaeology approach included researchers from a diverse array of historical and paleoenvironmental sciences in order to unravel the long-term human–landscape relation that resulted in these cultural landscapes. These disciplines include palynology, sedimentology, geochemistry, anthracology, and archaeology. The methodology was designed in order to obtain a high degree of correspondence between the archaeological and the paleoenvironmental records based on the premise that local scale case studies are the most suitable approach to analyzing human–environment interactions, particularly in upland environments (Ejarque 2013). The comparability of these will be guaranteed by the use of high-resolution temporal and spatial frameworks.

In this regard, the study cases offer a perfect setting. The presence of multiple peatbogs and lakes from which paleoenvironmental sequences were obtained is matched by numerous closely located multiperiod archaeological sites. In this sense, archaeology has been integrated to data offered by paleoenvironmental sciences. It contributes a very useful information type since it can provide data specifically related to the use humans made of the landscape. This data is chronologically and spatially referenced. The characterization of archaeological data allows the documentation of specific human activities on the landscape, which can be linked to human-related disturbances in the paleoenvironmental record by means of radiocarbon dating.

In order to retrieve a significant amount of archaeological data the studied areas were surveyed and, later, the most representative structures were subjected to test pit digging. They intended to record the structure typology but they also were designed to recover information related to landscape human use and to obtain adequate samples for radiocarbon dating. Recording methodology included, besides the standard recording of all materials, the sieving of all sediment from the occupation levels. Also, from each excavated unit a minimum of four liters of sediment was conserved for environmental sampling. Some natural soils located close to archaeological structures were also excavated in order to correlate natural sedimentation to that documented inside human occupied structures. This is especially important since stone-made habitation structures tend to present occupation levels in the inner part of the structures, which have been previously removed with respect to the circulation level outside them. The excavation of test pits outside the structures can confirm that occupation levels are limited to the space covered by the habitation structure and that are related to it. In this way, the dating of circulation levels preserved under the structures can be avoided, previous to their construction, with no relation to human habitation (Orengo 2013).

A total number of twelve wetlands from these valleys were studied for paleoenvironmental analyses: two lakes and ten peatbogs (Ejarque 2013; Ejarque et al. 2009; Miras et al. 2007, 2010, 2015; Riera et al. 2017). These sequences have been studied following a high temporal resolution for the main phases of human occupation in the valleys, which allows the optimal comparison with archaeological data. These multiproxy sequences include the study of pollen, non-pollen palynomorphs (NPPs)—that is, dung-related fungal spores, parasite eggs, and macrocharcoal particles that can be indicative of local highland human activities such as grazing or anthropogenic fires. The inclusion of these proxies provides a local counterpart to the mainly regional character of the highland pollen record, which can be analyzed in relationship with the local presence of archaeological structures. Also, the distribution of multiple sequences in different sectors within the valleys offers a high spatial resolution that allows the documentation of differences in local land uses and their resulting impact in local landscapes and vegetation, which can be compared with the archaeological sites distribution (Ejarque et al. 2010).

Landscape and Heritage in High-Mountain Environments

A total of 430 structures were attested in Núria and Coma de Vaca valleys (upper Ter), from which 45 were subjected to test pit digging and 38 AMS radiocarbon dates were obtained in archaeological sequences. They are associated entirely with livestock activities (huts, enclosures, milking structures) (Palet et al. 2016). In the Cadí Range, a total of 139 structures associated with livestock, farming field systems, mining, smelting kilns, and charcoal mounds were documented. Archaeological excavations were carried out in five sites and a total of twenty-nine AMS radiocarbon dates were available (Palet et al. 2013, 2014). In Madriu-Perafita-Claror valleys (MPCV), a total of 421 structures of different chronologies and typologies (huts, enclosures, kilns, charcoal mounds) were recorded related to livestock activities and the exploitation of forest resources. In these valleys, a total sixty-one radiocarbon dates were obtained from fifty-five structures excavated. While the structures located in the Perafita-Claror valley are related to livestock activities, in the Madriu valley, the exploitation strategies developed a wider spectrum (grazing, forest exploitation) (Palet et al. 2013, 2016; Palet and Orengo 2015) (Figure 10.2).

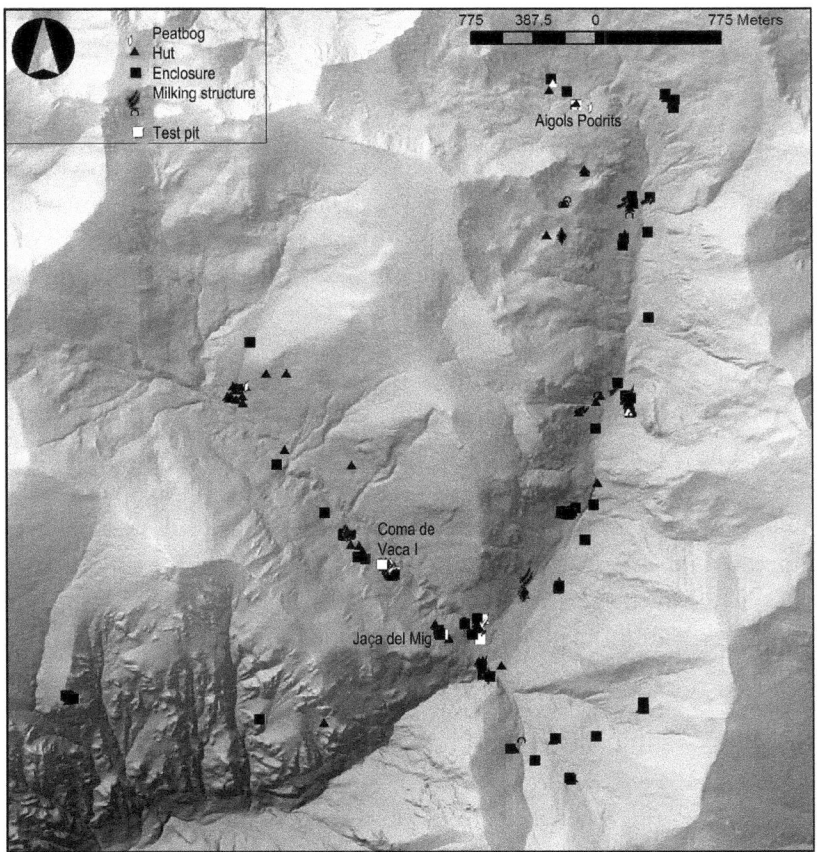

Figure 10.2. Archaeological map of Coma de Vaca and Coma del Freser valleys (upper Ter), with indication of the structures subjected to test pit digging.

The chronological model obtained from radiocarbon dates indicates the first evidences of grazing activities from the Early Neolithic (in the Andorran valleys), and from the end of the Middle Neolithic (in the upper Ter and Cadí Range). Settlement evolution can be followed to modern times, with the presence of a discontinuity related to a hiatus in landscape dynamics in the Bronze and Iron Ages. The results have allowed developing a history of human activities carried out in these valleys over time. They allow drawing a densely exploited landscape, showing the deep and ancient human occupation of these high-mountain spaces.

The First Evidence of Grazing Activities: From the Early Neolithic to the Bronze Age

GIAP's research in MPCV documented the first evidence of grazing activities in the Early Neolithic, in the mid-fifth millennium BC, related to the existence of a small-scale human and livestock frequentation (Orengo et al. 2014a).

The archaeological survey attested evidence of occupation in two dry-stone huts, one situated at 2,518 masl at Pleta de les Bacives I site, in Madriu valley; the other, roughly circular, located at Orris de la Torbera de Perafita I site, in Perafita valley. In this area, livestock activities intensify during the Middle Neolithic and the transition with the Late Neolithic, as it is documented in several shepherd huts and livestock enclosures with occupation levels dated at the end of the fourth and in the third millennium BC (Torbera de Perafita I, Planells de Perafita) (Orengo 2010; Orengo et al. 2014a).

It should be noted that these archaeological remains present a correlation with the paleoenvironmental data obtained in MPCV, which show during the Neolithic (5650–3050 cal BC) the occurrence of woodland clearances coeval with increases of anthropic indicators (nitrophilous-ruderal taxa and coprophilous fungal spores) pointing to the existence of local pastoral practices in different sectors of the valley. During the Early Neolithic (5650–4350 cal BC), human frequentation in the MPCV was related to itinerant and seasonal pastoral practices that entailed small-scale and short-lived forest openings for livestock grazing followed by forest recovery (Ejarque 2013; Orengo et al. 2014a). Such early human impacts became more intense during the Middle Neolithic and the transition with the Late Neolithic when the stronger human frequentation attested archaeologically in the valleys resulted in more intense and permanent landscape openings. Indeed, since 4350 cal BC longer-lasting pastoral fire-related pine clearings are documented in the subalpine areas of the Madriu valley, while in the Perafita valley since 3600 cal BC increased human occupation above 2,500 m resulted in the long-lived expansion of alpine grasslands and the intensification of grazing activities (Ejarque et al. 2010; Miras et al. 2010; Orengo et al. 2014a.).

In Núria and Coma de Vaca valleys, the earliest livestock activities also date from the mid-fourth and the third millennium BC (Palet et al. 2016, 2019). It is worth mentioning a cave occupation in the Cova del Catau de l'Ós site (cave 338) in the valley of Núria in the Forat de l'Embut area, dated at the mid-fourth millennium BC. The cave is located on the edge of an itinerary that leads to Finestrelles pass and to Cerdanya plain, in a limestone substrate area. Excavations at the cave entrance provided abundant charcoal, pottery, very fragmented fauna, and numerous fragments of malachite in various cuvette hearths related to the exploitation of this mineral. The charcoal analysis indicated the almost exclusive presence of *Pinus uncinata*, which suggests a nearby pine forest (Euba 2016). In this same sector, an occupation level related to livestock activities dated at the Late Neolithic was documented (cal 2205 BC–2019 BC). This level also provided abundant charcoal with the presence of *Pinus uncinata*, reinforcing the idea of a forest environment close to the site (Euba 2016).

Neolithic livestock occupation has also been attested in the nearby valleys surveyed in this sector (Coma de Vaca and Coma del Freser), where preliminary paleoenvironmental data reinforce the lowering of the forest limit due to fire.

Different livestock structures are associated to grazing activities in the upper Freser valley, an area rich in water resources and pastures, well connected through an east-west corridor under the main ridge line (at around 2,500 masl). Two archaeological sites have been identified in the pastures surrounding Aigols Podrits peatbog at 2,468 masl. Aigols Podrits I is characterized by a Late Neolithic livestock enclosure (cal 2876 BC–2627 BC), which closes an area of about 100 sq m. Aigols Podrits II attested a cuvette hearth arranged with stone blocks, associated to an occupation level dated at the end of the Middle Neolithic (3300–2900 BC). The anthracological analysis of these levels also indicates the exclusive presence of *Pinus uncinata*, associated to a forested landscape in this higher part of the valley (Euba 2016) (Figure 10.3).

Figure 10.3. General view of Aigols Podrits I and II sites in the upper Freser valley. Photo by J. M. Palet.

The presence of livestock activities in the Late Neolithic is also documented at Coma de Vaca I site (2,110 m). Paleo-soils related to occupation remains from this period and the beginning of the Bronze Age have been attested (cal 2029 BC–1779 BC), with abundant cooking pottery (containers, bowls, and pots), related to a settlement destroyed by later constructions.

These data are coherent with the archaeological evidence documented in the MPCV, in which several sites recorded different structures related to important pastoral activities since the end of the fourth millennium BC and during the Late Neolithic (Orengo et al. 2014a). Els Estanys site (2,530 m) in the Madriu valley should be noted in particular. This settlement is composed by a group of four habitation structures and two enclosure areas. All elements show an integrated construction, which suggests the synchrony of all structures. Radiocarbon dates obtained present a continuous occupation from 2356 ± 113 cal BC to 2,080 ± 114 cal BC, corresponding to the last stages of the Late Neolithic and the beginning of the Bronze Age.

During this period anthropic action becomes, for the first time, intense enough to result in a perdurable landscape change in the uppermost areas of the Madriu valley. Indeed, paleoenvironmental analyses performed near els Estanys site attest to the local clearance of pine woodlands and the expansion of alpine grasslands coeval to the expansion of grazing activities. From this moment onward the upper areas of the valley will remain deforested until today due to continuous human pressure (Ejarque 2013; Orengo et al. 2014a). These deforestations answer the need to create grazing areas in the upper high-mountain valleys; however, prehistoric landscape change was not systematic or generalized, as only specific areas within the highland valleys were transformed into grasslands, notably, those around human settlements such as Els Estanys site.

Roman Period and Late Antiquity

As in other areas in the Pyrenees, the period that comprises the Bronze and Iron Ages is not attested in the archaeological evidence (Gassiot 2016:125–145). Probably this hiatus does not mean the abandonment of human activities, but rather a change in settlement patterns and in the typology of domestic structures, as the paleoenvironmental records in MPCV suggest the continuity of anthropic activities.

The anthropization of Pyrenean high-mountain landscapes is thus part of a long-term dynamic. In this sense, antiquity means a new important phase in settlement intensification and land use. In general terms, in Roman times, there is an increase in activities, with a more diversified and specialized landscape exploitation in the upper Segre (livestock, pitch and charcoal production, and iron metallurgy), and a more intense livestock activity in the upper Ter (Orengo et al. 2013; Palet et al. 2014; Palet et al. 2016).

The first evidence is situated in the upper Freser at the site of Aigols Podrits II. A quadrangular shepherd hut characterized by a dry-stone basement and a posthole in the interior to support the roof have been excavated in this site. The occupation levels provided a long iron nail related to the structure, cooking ware, and Iberian pottery, consequent with their radiocarbon dating in the second to first centuries BC (Palet et al. 2017, 2019).

Coma de Vaca valley shows an intense livestock occupation from the first century AD to Late Roman and Visigoth times (seventh century AD). Especially noteworthy is a drystone shepherd hut situated at Coma de Vaca I site, dated by Roman pottery between the end of the first century AD and the second century AD (terra sigillata, African cookware). The structure, located in a livestock site at 2,150 masl, defines a rectangular area of about 20 sq m and is slightly overexcavated (Figure 10.4). The hut was probably used for pastoral and forest exploitation. Its situation on the edge of a path that crosses this sector of the Pyrenees from east to west suggests that it could have also served as a stop or control point (Palet et al. 2014, 2016, 2019).

In the Puigmal massif, at Fontalba site (2,100 masl), a shepherd hut and a livestock enclosure also provided abundant Roman pottery (terra sigillata, African cookware), which

Figure 10.4. Ortophotography of the Roman hut 114 in Coma de Vaca I site, with detail of Roman occupation levels 214–215 and the early medieval reoccupation. Photo by A. Garcia and H. A. Orengo.

suggests trade activity in these high-mountain environments, well connected with Roman trade networks (Palet et al. 2016, 2019).

In MPCV, the research also attested the importance and the intensity of pastoral activities reflected in the presence of several livestock structures. A group of three simultaneously small-sized oval livestock enclosures was found in the upper Madriu valley dated in the first century AD. It was located at 2,313 masl in a moraine ridge overlooking an area of small ponds and peatlands. In this same valley, a shepherd hut at Pleta de les Bacives I site was located in a glacial basin forming an enclosed area at 2,517 masl. The structure was small-sized and oblong-shaped, the occupation layer was excavated on the ground, and the abandonment level was radiocarbon dated at the fifth century. In the Perafita valley, a milking corridor was dated by radiocarbon in the fourth century AD. In this valley, a shepherd hut on Planells de Perafita I site, dated in the middle of the third century AD, reinforce the presence of structures related to livestock exploitation in Roman times (Orengo 2010:263–279; Palet et al. 2013; Palet and Orengo 2015). Livestock activities are also attested in the west side of the Cadí Range at around 2,030 m in the Goleró and Pradell sites, in two enclosures dated between the fourth and the fifth centuries AD (Palet et al. 2009).

The paleoenvironmental data in MPCV corroborate this situation, documenting a general increase in landscape openness and pastoral activities between 300 cal BC and 800 cal AD, with the expansion of alpine grasslands as well as of nitrophilous and ruderal taxa and dung-related fungal spores (Ejarque et al. 2010; Ejarque 2013; Miras et al. 2007).

On the other hand, a total of seven pitch kilns were located in MPCV dated from the second to the seventh century AD (Orengo et al. 2013). Some pitch kilns were cut by paths and fragments of kiln wall and charcoal were scattered along it. Others were located through surface concentrations of charcoal and fragments of kiln wall. M157 (Figure 10.5), the only kiln fully excavated, was lying close to the surface. This structure has a circular plan of around 1.8 m in diameter, with baked clay walls of about 10 cm wide, preserved to a variable height of around 30 cm. The structure base presents a thermo-altered clay soil over which a pavement of flat stones was built. This pavement is covered with baked clay creating a smooth surface sloped toward a 20 cm orifice on the lower part of the wall. This hole would lead through a baked clay channel toward a reservoir. Pine logs (*Pinus uncinata*) in the evacuation hole were in the first stages of the carbonization process (Euba 2009). They correspond to trees with main boughs of around 10 cm in diameter, which carry high quantities of resin that could still be seen in their surface both macro- and microscopically. In the excavation of kiln M052 it has been possible to find a group of logs piled beside the kiln related with the distillation process. Their diameters were similar to those of the branches from the M157 evacuation hole and their length varied from 40 to 50 cm. Axe cut marks were still visible in their extremes (Euba 2009) (Figure 10.6).

Paleoenvironmental evidence obtained from peatlands located at close proximity to the kilns provides further insights into this type of Roman forest exploitation. The sequences studied indicate intensified local opening of the subalpine pine forest and the extension of grasslands in the area since the first century AD until the seventh century AD, coinciding with the use of the pitch kilns (Ejarque 2013; Orengo et al. 2013). Woodlands were most

Figure 10.5. Pitch kiln M157 at the Riu dels Orris III site in the Madriu valley (Andorra). Photo by J. M. Palet.

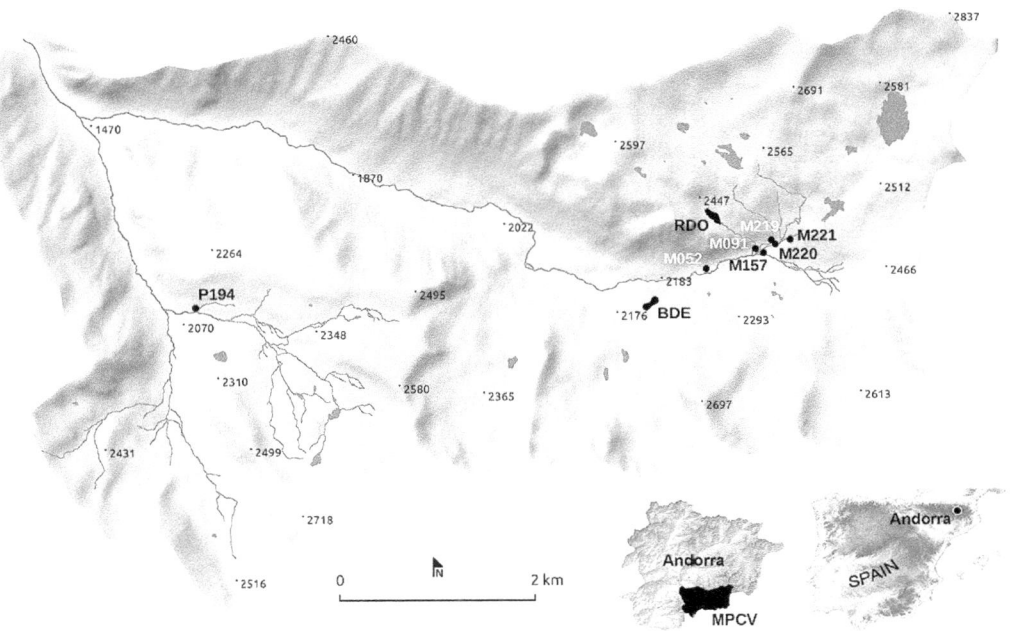

Figure 10.6. Archaeological map with the situation of the seven pitch kilns attested in MPCV (Andorra). Map by H. A. Orengo.

likely cleared through tree-felling, as the low frequency of local fires low concentration of macrocharcoal particles documented in the peat profiles during this period indicates low local burning (Ejarque 2013; Miras et al. 2007). The axe marks found in the logs from the M052 kiln further support that local pines were cut off to feed the kilns (Orengo et al. 2013). The correlation between the pine opening phases recorded at the Riu dels Orris fen and the dated use activity of the kilns indicates the existence of three different pitch production episodes interbedded by short-lived forest recoveries following the end of the production phases. When both initial and final dates have been obtained for the kilns, they indicate the structure to be in use during a period of slightly over two hundred years. In each of these episodes, at least two resin kilns were active at the same time (Orengo et al. 2013).

Pliny specifies that pitch is extracted from the torch-tree or *Pinus mugo*, a high-altitude European pine of which the *Pinus mugo uncinata*, the one identified in the study area, is a subspecies (*Nat. Hist.* XVI.52). Both archaeological and written sources agree in characterizing pitch production as typical of mountain areas where resin-rich *Pinus mugo*, in the case of the Pyrenees, can be exploited. This type of high-mountain intensive forest exploitation could only be economically feasible in market-oriented economies with a well-developed distribution network (Orengo 2010:274–275; Orengo et al. 2013).

The research in the Cadí Range allows documenting another activity in Roman times, typical of high-mountain areas: the extraction and first treatment of iron (Palet et al. 2013, 2014). This activity was attested in two sites situated in the west side of the range at around 2,030 masl: the Goleró and Pradell sites. A total of three iron reduction kilns were excavated and dated in Roman times at the Goleró site (Figure 10.7). They served for a first treatment

Figure 10.7. Iron kilns at the El Goleró site in the Cadí Range (upper Segre valley). Photo by J. M. Palet.

of iron and provided abundant archaeological material: Iberian pottery and terra sigillata, African cookware. This material together with the radiocarbon dates obtained suggests an occupation from the first century BC to the second century AD (Palet et al. 2013, 2014). In the Pradell site, several trenches for mineral extraction were also attested. Unfortunately, paleoenvironmental data obtained at the Pradell fen (1,915 masl) are only available from the early sixth century AD. Immediately preceding late Roman grazing activities, documented in the area between the third and fifth centuries AD may however have contributed to the relatively open woodland documented at the beginning of the record (~525 cal AD), which happened in a context of moderate grazing and mining activities (Ejarque et al. 2009).

The intensity of pastoral activities in late antiquity is very remarkable in the upper Ter valley. Several remains have been attested in two relevant sites from this period, Fontalba (2,100 masl), on the south side of the Puigmal massif, and Jaça del Mig (2,080 masl), in Coma de Vaca valley. Both sites documented a set of huts and livestock enclosures occupied in different phases from the fourth to the seventh centuries AD. There is a continuity in the occupation of both livestock areas in early medieval times, related to long-distance transhumance (ninth and eleventh centuries).

The abundant archaeological material recovered in these structures (cookware, glass, metal objects) suggests that these pastoral sites were of a certain entity in relation with the importance and the intensity of livestock activities in these valleys from late antiquity. Paleoenvironmental sequences in the upper Ter valley record several phases of deforestation between the sixth and the eighth centuries, related to the exploitation of pastures and the extension of livestock activities (Palet et al. 2012; Palet et al. 2014).

The Roman period evidences, therefore, a diversification, specialization, and spatialization of economic activities. Data obtained suggest a contrast between nearby study areas where human activities show a greater complementarity: the intensification of livestock activities in the upper Ter valley, a more diversified exploitation in MPCV (livestock, pitch, and charcoal production) and iron metallurgy in Cadí Range (Palet et al. 2013; Palet et al. 2014).

Therefore, in Roman times, the Pyrenees in general and high mountains in particular, constituted complementary spaces that offered specific resources of great importance. The intensity of these human activities defines them as accessible, well-connected areas, fully integrated into an economy and a society that, in part, depended on these resources (Leveau and Palet 2010; Orengo et al. 2013).

Rome and Mountain Territories

Landscape archaeology results reinforce the image of Pyrenean mountain areas highly occupied in Roman times. This fact has also been attested in other Pyrenean valleys in relation with iron metallurgy (Gassiot 2016; Gassiot and Jiménez 2006). During the Roman period, the studied areas were a part of the Ceretania, which according to Strabo (*Geog.* III.4.11) covered the central area of the Pyrenees. Pliny the Elder (*Nat. Hist.* III.3.22–23) confirms this when he describes the Ceretan territory as limiting with that of the Vascons. *Iulia Libica*, modern Llívia (Girona), was the city of the Ceretans as stated by Ptolomeus (*Geog.* II.6.68–69) and acted as the main urban and administrative center of the region.

The research carried out in nearby areas, in the north of the Cerdanya in the Enveig mountain, had proposed, on the contrary, a retreat during the Roman period of seasonal livestock activities, a situation that was interpreted as a reflection of a certain marginality of mountain activities in favor of farming activities in lower plains (Rendu 2003:520). In this sense, landscape studies in Atlantic Pyrenean sectors (Ossau Valley) (Rendu et al. 2013) or in the western Alps (Segard 2009; Walsh 2005) concur that the Roman period did not correspond to a phase of increase of livestock activity.

This contrast is probably related not with a decline of economic activities in mountain areas but with the specialization and diversification of human activities at regional, as well as at the microregional level (Leveau and Palet 2010; Palet et al. 2014). In fact, the studied valleys were well connected through an old Pyrenean road network linking Gallia Narbonense to Hispania Tarraconense. In the center of these valleys, the Cerdanya plain stands out, where the Roman city of Iulia Libica (Llívia) is located, founded in the last quarter of the first century BC (Olesti 2014:357–359). This Roman town was therefore the center of an important road network that connected with the surrounding mountains.

It is important to note that archaeological data coincide in pointing out that from the late empire and especially in late antiquity, the anthropization of these mountain areas is intensified due to the increase of livestock activities. In the studied areas, this is especially visible in the Cadí Range and in the upper Ter valley. Human impact in this period was important enough to create a new landscape configuration that will have continuity in medieval and modern times, with a greater landscape homogenization, characterized by the expansion of extensive transhumant activities.

Conclusions

European high-mountain areas cannot be considered as isolated and marginal spaces as mountain anthropogenic deforestation episodes related to the creation and maintenance of pastoral grasslands have been documented from the Early Neolithic onward. Pastoralism has therefore played a decisive role in the human shaping of mountain cultural landscapes.

Methodologically, the use of high spatial and temporal resolution analysis in landscape archaeology has proved to be a priceless tool for relating historical, archaeological, and paleoenvironmental results and for assessing local human occupation and the distinctive nature of highland land use practices on a microregional scale.

During the Early Neolithic, human clearances were diversified in their spatial distribution, allowing the recovery of alpine forests after impacts. A major landscape change occurred in the studied valleys since the Middle Neolithic–Late Neolithic until the Early Bronze Age when the alpine grassland belt expanded. Roman times report a diversification of practices including mining, metallurgy, pine resin exploitation, charcoal production, grazing activities, and livestock that are related to significant deforestation processes.

The archaeological and paleoenvironmental studies emphasize the intense human activity in Roman times. In antiquity, the development of microregional research suggests a heterogeneous landscape shaping, characterized by variability in land use strategies. A diversification of economic activities has been documented, especially in MPCV, with forest exploitation and livestock activities. In Roman times, the exploitation of pine for pitch production and charcoal stands out. The expansion of livestock activities is well attested from the second to third centuries and during late antiquity, especially in the upper Ter valleys and in the Cadí Range. This process could probably be in the origin of long vertical historical transhumance in Northeast Catalonia.

It has been suggested, in this sense, that high Pyrenean mountains in Roman times constituted accessible and well-communicated territories, fully integrated into the Roman sociocultural complex and extra-regional trade networks. Thus, in this period, the Pyrenees and the high mountains in particular should be considered as a complementary area that offered resources of great importance (Leveau and Palet 2010; Orengo et al. 2013).

Landscape dynamics attest a clear expansion of pastoralism from early medieval times (ninth to tenth centuries) in the studied valleys, with a reuse of Roman structures and the use of new spaces, now clearly specialized in specific livestock activities (milking structures for cheese production). In this period, a largely grazed landscape resulted in wide deforestation.

The results show that important historical processes of social change, such as that of Romanization or the formation of feudal societies, have had a deep impact in mountain landscapes, proving that these were intimately linked to the historical processes documented at lower altitudes.

Finally, the potential of archaeological and environmental research in mountain areas has been pointed out in order to define them as cultural landscapes. This is important in order to underline the archaeological heritage as a management tool and a cultural resource in areas protected for their landscape value. In this sense, the history of these landscapes furnishes new data for the sustainable development of Mediterranean highlands.

REFERENCES

Criado-Boado, F., D. Barreiro, and R. Varela-Pousa 2015 Sustainable Archaeology in Post-crisis Scenarios. In *Fernweh: Crossing Borders and Connecting People in Archaeological Heritage Management: Essays in Honour of Prof. Willem J. H. Willems*, edited by M. van den Dries, J. van der Linde, and A. Strecker, 56–60. Sidestone Press, Leiden.

Ejarque, A. 2013 *La alta montaña pirenaica: génesis y configuración holocena de un paisaje cultural. Estudio paleoambiental en el valle del Madriu-Perafita-Claror (Andorra)*. British Archaeological Reports I.S. 2507, Oxford.

Ejarque, A., R. Julià, S.Riera, et al. 2009 Tracing the History of Highland Human Management in the Eastern Pre-Pyrenees (Spain): An Interdisciplinary Palaeoenvironmental Approach. *The Holocene* 19(8):1241–1255.

Ejarque, A., Y. Miras, S. Riera, et al. 2010 Testing Microregional Variability in the Holocene Shaping of High Mountain Cultural Landscapes: A Palaeoenvironmental Case Study in the Eastern Pyrenees. *Journal of Archaeological Science* 37(7):1468–1479.

Euba, I. 2009 *Análisis antracológico de estructuras altimontanas en el valle de la Vansa-Sierra del Cadí (Alt Urgell) y en el valle del Madriu (Andorra): explotación de recursos forestales del Neolítico a época moderna*. Documenta 9, ICAC, Tarragona.

Euba, I. 2016 *Resultats de les análisis antracològiques de la vall de Núria i Coma de Vaca: campanyes 2011, 2012, 2013, i 2015*. Final report, ICAC, Tarragona.

Galop, D. 1998 *La forêt, l'homme et le troupeau dans les Pyrénées: 6000 ans d'histoire de l'environnement entre Garonne et méditerranée—Contribution palynologique*. Université de Toulouse-Le Mirail, Toulouse.

Gassiot, E. (ed.) 2016 *Arqueología del pastoralismo en el Parque Nacional d'Aigüestortes i Estany de sant maurici: Montañas humanizadas*. CSIC, Madrid.

Gassiot, E., and J. Jiménez 2006 El poblament prefeudal de l'alta muntanya dels Pirineus occidentals catalans (Pallars Sobirà i Alta Ribagorça). *Tribuna d' Arqueologia* 2004–2005:89–122.

Gassiot, E., D. Rodríguez, A. Pèlachs, R. Pérez, R. Julià, M.-C. Bal, and N. Mazzucco 2014 La alta montaña durante la Prehistoria: 10 años de investigación en el Pirineo catalán occidental. *Trabajos de prehistoria* 71(2):261–281.

Leveau, P., and J. M. Palet 2010 Les Pyrénées romaines, la frontière, la ville et la montagne: L'apport de l'archéologie du paysage. *Pallas* 82:171–198.

Miras, Y., A. Ejarque, S. Riera, H. A. Orengo, and J. M. Palet 2015 Andorran high Pyrenees (Perafita Valley, Andorra): SerraMijtana fen. *Grana* 54 (4): 313–316.

Miras, Y., A. Ejarque, H. A. Orengo, S. Riera, J. M. Palet, and A. Poiraud 2010 Prehistoric Impact on Landscape and Vegetation at High Altitudes: An Integrated Palaeoecological and Archaeological Approach in the Eastern Pyrenees (Perafita valley, Andorra). *Plant Biosystems* 144(4):946–961.

Miras, Y., A. Ejarque, S. Riera, J. M. Palet, H. A. Orengo, and I. Euba 2007 Dynamique holocène de la végétation et occupation des Pyrénées andorranes depuis le Néolithique ancien, d'après l'analyse pollinique de la tourbière de Bosc dels Estanyons (2180 m, Vall del Madriu, Andorre). *C. R. Palevol: Paléontologie humaine et préhistoire* 6:291–300.

Olesti, O. 2014 *Paisajes de la Hispania romana: La explotación de los territorios del Imperio*. DSTORIA EDICIONS, Sabadell.

Orengo, H. A. 2010 Arqueología de un paisaje cultural pirenaico de alta montaña: Dinámicas de ocupación del valle del Madriu-Perafita-Claror (Andorra). PhD dissertation, Universitat Rovira i Virgili-ICAC, Tarragona.

Orengo, H. A. 2013 Combining Terrestrial Stereophotogrammetry, DGPS and GIS-Based 3D Voxel Modelling in the Volumetric Recording of Archaeological Features. *ISPRS Journal of Photogrammetry and Remote Sensing* 76:49–55.

Orengo, H. A., J. M. Palet, A. Ejarque, et al. 2013 Pitch Production during the Roman Period: An Intensive Mountain Industry Directed towards Long Distance Trade? *Antiquity* 87(337):802–814.

Orengo, H. A., J. M. Palet, A. Ejarque, et al. 2014a Shifting Occupation Dynamics in the Madriu-Perafita-Claror Valleys (Andorra) from the Early Neolithic to the Chalcolithic: The Onset of High Mountain Cultural Landscapes. *Quaternary International* 353:140–152.

Orengo, H. A., J. M. Palet, A. Ejarque, et al. 2014b The Historical Configuration of a UNESCO World Heritage Site: The Cultural Landscape of the Madriu-Perafita-Claror Valley. *Archeologia Postmedievale* 17:333–343.

Palet, J. M., A. Garcia, H. A. Orengo, et al. 2014 Ocupación y explotación de espacios altimontanos pirenaicos en la antigüedad: visiones desde la arqueología del paisaje. In *Atti del*

IV Convegno Internazionale di Studi Veleiati, edited by P. L. Dall'Aglio, C. Franceschelli, and L. Maganzani, 455–470. Ante Quem, Bologna.

Palet, J. M., A. Garcia, H. A. Orengo, and T. Polonio 2016 Ocupacions ramaderes altimontanes a les capçaleres del Ter (Vall de Núria i Coma de Vaca, Queralbs): resultats de les intervencions arqueològiques 2010–2015. In *XIII Tretzenes Jornades d'Arqueologia de les Comarques de Girona*, 67–75. Dpt. Cultura, Generalitat de Catalunya, Banyoles.

Palet, J. M., A. Garcia, and T. Polonio 2017 *Informe de les intervencions arqueològiques a Coma de Vaca i Coma del Freser (Queralbs, Ripollès) 2016*. ICAC, Tarragona.

Palet, J. M., R. Julià, S. Riera, et al. 2012 Landscape Systems and Human Land-Use Interactions in Mediterranean Highlands and Littoral Plains during the Late Holocene: Integrated Analysis from the InterAmbAr Project (North-Eastern Catalonia). *eTopoi: Journal of Ancient Studies*, edited by W. Bebermeier, R. Hebenstreit, E. Kaiser, and J. Krause 3:305–310.

Palet, J. M., P. Olmos, A. Garcia-Molsosa, T. Polonio, T., and H. A. Orengo. 2019 Occupation et anthropisation des espaces de haute montagne dans les vallées de Nuria et Coma de Vaca (Gerona, Espagne): résultats des recherches archéologiques et patrimoniales. In *La conquête de la montagne: des premières occupation humaines à l'anthropisation du milieu. Actes des congrès nationaux des sociétés historiques et scientifiques*, edited by A. Deschamps, S. Costamagno, P. Y. Milcent, J. M. Pétillon, C. Renard, N. Valdeyron, 1–25. Éditions du Comité des Travaux Historiques et Scientifiques, Open Edition books, Paris.

Palet, J. M., and H. A. Orengo 2015 La configuració d'un paisatge cultural patrimoni de la humanitat a la vall del Madriu-Perafita-Claror: visions des de l'arqueologia del paisatge. In *Recull de conferències 2012–2013/Debats de recerca 6–7*, 178–192. Andorra la Vella.

Palet, J. M., H. Orengo, A. Ejarque, et al. 2011 Formas de paisaje de montaña y ocupación del territorio en los Pirineos orientales en época romana: estudios pluridisciplinares en el valle del Madriu-Perafita-Claror (Andorra) y en la Sierra del Cadí (Cataluña). *Bolletino di Archeologia on line: Proceedings of the 17th International Congress of Classical Archaeology* (Rome):67–79.

Palet, J. M., H. A. Orengo, A. Ejarque, Y. Miras, I. Euba, and S. Riera 2013 Arqueología de paisajes altimontanos pirenaicos: formas de explotación y usos del medio en época romana en valle del Madriu-Perafita-Claror (Andorra) y en la Sierra del Cadí (Alt Urgell). In *Paysages ruraux et territoires dans les cités de l'Occident romain: Actes du colloque AGER IX*, edited by J.-L. Fiches, R. Plana, and V. Revilla, 329–340. Presses universitaires de la Méditerranée, Montpellier.

Palet, J. M., F. Ricou, and M. Segard 2003 Prospections et sondages sur les sites d'altitude en Champsaur (Alpes du Sud). *Archéologie du Midi Médiéval* 21:199–210.

Pèlachs, A., J. Nadal, J. M. Soriano, D. Molina, and R. Cunill 2009 Changes in Pyrenean Woodlands as a Result of the Intensity of Human Exploitation: 2,000 Years of Metallurgy in Vallferrrera, Northeast Iberian Peninsula. *Vegetation History and Archaeobotany* 18(5):403–416.

Putzer A., D. Festi, S. Edlmair, and K. Oeggl 2016 The Development of Human Activity in the High Altitudes of the Schnals Valley (South Tyrol/Italy) from the Mesolithic to Modern Periods. *Journal of Archaeological Science Reports* 6:136–147.

Rendu, C. 2003 *La montagne d'Enveig: Une stive pyrénéenne dans la longue durée*. Trabucaire, Perpignan.

Rendu, C., C. Calastrenc, M. Le Couédic, D. Galop, D. Rius, C. Cugny, and M. C. Bal. 2013 Montagnes et campagnes d'Oloron dans la longue durée: Premiers résultats d'un programme interdisciplinaire. In *D'Iluro à Oloron Sainte-Marie, un millénaire d'histoire (Colloque d'Oloron, 2006): Aquitania* (Suppl. 29):37–68.

Riera, S., R. Julià, Y. Miras, et al. 2017 Climate Variability, Human Use and Landscape Change of High Mountain Environments: Coma de Vaca and Ter Valleys, Eastern Pyrenees. In *Past Global Changes, Pages, 5th Open Science Meeting, Global Challenges for Our Common Future: A Paleoscience Perspective*, 355–356. Pages, Zaragoza.

Segard, M. 2009 *Les Alpes occidentales romaines: Développement urbain et exploitation des ressources des régions de montagne (Gaule Narbonnaise, Italie, provinces alpines)*. Université de Provence, Aix-en-Provence.

Walsh, K. 2005 Risk and Marginality at High Altitudes: New Interpretations from Fieldwork on the Faravel Plateau, Hautes-Alpes. *Antiquity* 79(304):289–305.

Walsh, K., M. Court-Picon, J.-L. de Beaulieu, et al. 2014 A Historical Ecology of the Ecrins (Southern French Alps): Archaeology and Palaeoecology of the Mesolithic to the Medieval Period. *Quaternary International* 353:52–73.

Walsh, K., and F. Mocci 2003 9000 ans d'occupation du sol en moyenne et haute montagne: la vallée de Freissinières dans le Parc national des Ecrins (Freissinières, Hautes-Alpes). *Archéologie du Midi Médiéval* 21:185–198.

Walsh, K., F. Mocci, M. Court-Picon, S. Tzortzis, and J. M. Palet 2005 Dynamique du peuplement et activités agro-pastorales durant l'âge du Bronze dans les massifs du HautChampsaur et de l'Argentierois (Hautes-Alpes). *Documents d'Archéologie méridionale* 28:25–44.

Walsh, K., F. Mocci, and J. M. Palet 2007 Nine Thousand Years of Human/Landscape Dynamics in a High Altitude Zone in the Southern French Alps (Parc Nacional des Ecrins Hautes-Alpes [05]). *Preistoria Alpina* 42:9–22.

Chapter Eleven

Southern Norway's Mountain Landscapes

Between National Romantic Legends and the Political Economy of Agropastoralism

Christopher Prescott and Lene Melheim

Abstract *Archaeological investigations of the southern Norwegian mountains have a 170-year-long history. Interpreting the growing body of data has understandably been in light of political context and reigning theoretical premises. Key elements here are projects of recreating a nation-state, perceptions of ethnicity, ecological frameworks, and reigning concepts of local evolution. Hydroelectric development from the late 1950s led to a large body of archaeological and environmental data, multidisciplinary projects, and a modern management regime. The projects are numerous, and two upland project areas are particularly used to discuss later developments, Hardangervidda (the central Norwegian mountain plateau) and projects in the uplands of the inner tracts of the Sognefjord. These projects not only transformed perceptions of the history of the uplands, but also were a major force in modernizing Norwegian archaeology and cultural heritage management. In recent years, the melting of high-altitude ice patches promises to bring new data to the fore but also generate new developments in upland management practices and remind us of the threat of global warming.*

In Scandinavia, Mountains Are Prominent

A quick glance at a topographic map demonstrates that mountains take up a lot of the Scandinavian Peninsula and most of its western part, Norway. About 3 percent of contemporary Norway is cultivated, 37 percent is forest, including the subalpine belt of mountain birch. About 30 percent of Norway is above the tree line (varying from 200 to 1,200 masl depending how far north). The Scandinavia Mountains are an old mountain chain, worn down by glaciations, and therefore not spectacularly high altitude. Since Scandinavia lies far north, a quarter of the peninsula is north of the Arctic Circle, and alpine conditions like treeless landscapes, extreme weather conditions, glaciers, and permanent snow patches start at altitudes lower than more southerly parts of Eurasia and the Americas.

In the early Holocene, after deglaciation made the upland regions of Norway accessible to humans, the mountains were quickly drawn into seasonal patterns of exploitation. Here, large herbivores (primarily reindeer, but also European elk/moose) were the attractive resource, though other species were exploited, as were lithic resources. Later, in the Neolithic, enigmatic patterns in the Early and Middle Neolithic (3950 BC to 2400 BC), primarily weak pollen readouts (e.g., Indrelid and Moe 1983; Kvamme et al. 1992), have been interpreted as indications of seasonal pasturing. Though such claims are dubious, humans might have intensified use in some periods or even actively manipulated the vegetation to create clearings in the Mesolithic and Neolithic (Selsing 2016). With the transition to the Late Neolithic (ca. 2400–2350 BC), lowland farms were established and western Scandinavia was integrated into an evolving Nordic region of interaction. At this time, the central southern uplands were drawn into the agropastoral economic cycles of resource exploitation focused on transhumant pastoralism. However, upland exploitation of wild game, mineral resources, and travel continued, if in a more complex economic context. This pattern has virtually lasted until the present.

After the First World War, the development of hydroelectric power escalated, accelerating again after the Second World War. Hydroelectric projects entailed dams, reservoirs, quarries, power stations, and infrastructure. Hydroelectricity was a central part of industrialization and modernization, providing cheap, dependable power for a not very wealthy country. Hydroelectric construction was also important from a cultural historical perspective, as the destruction and flooding of many mountain valleys severely affected archaeological and historical sites. An expanded infrastructure into the mountains promoted recreational use and other developments, while marking an end to age-old summer farming practices. The latter entailed a change in the anthropogenic impact that had created and maintained upland landscapes for centuries.

On the other hand, hydroelectric development spurred a reenergized archaeological research thrust. Two prominent archaeologists, Anders Hagen and Irmelin Martens, argued the need for rescue excavations in advance of hydroelectric developments (Hagen 1959, 1997; Martens 1988; Martens and Hagen 1961). Their initial efforts in the late 1950s were successful in terms of securing financing and making significant archaeological discoveries. These early endeavors sparked legislative and administrative processes that ensued in a series of well-funded projects from 1960 to 1990. After the era of hydroelectric power development, there have been small-scale rescue projects and reexploration of dammed valleys. Numerous individual finds, like the Kjølskarvet "quartzite" quarry (Johansen 1978), the steatite quarry at Kvikne (Skjølsvold 1969), the early settlements at Fløyrlivatn (Bang-Andersen 1990), were not an initial archaeological response to hydroelectric developments, but were inspired by mountain archaeology in its wake. An empirical and methodological development of the last decade is ice patch archaeology, mapping and collecting well-preserved artifacts that come forth as high-altitude ice patches melt in response to global warming.

The rescue projects and "mountain perspectives" provided inspiration in archaeology extending beyond those interested in high altitudes, and drove debates and developments in method, theory, interdisciplinary collaboration, and historical-anthropological approaches (e.g., Bjørgo 1986; Hofseth 1980; Indrelid 1973; Johansen 1970, 1978). In retrospect, upland archaeology not only changed our knowledge and perception of the uplands but significantly altered approaches in archaeology and knowledge of the past resource exploitation of the Scandinavian Peninsula (e.g., Indrelid et al. 2015; Stene 2014; Stene and Wangen 2017). With its ambiguous ties with hydroelectric development, mountain archaeology still became associated with critical heritage studies and politics, contributing to debates about issues like Saami rights, heritage preservation, and management. Environmentalism as well as regional agendas used the past in the politics of the present (Hagen 2002). In northern Norway, the Alta-Kautokeino dam and power plant construction, and archaeology's role during the conflicts and their aftermath deserves explicit mention. The events in the late 1970s have historical dimensions that have formed Saami policy and practices since.

In southern Norway, three suites of multidisciplinary projects (Figure 11.1) are used in the following discussion to outline the evolving premises and results of upland archaeology. First, there are projects centered on the mountain plateau in southern Norway, Hardangervidda (Indrelid 1994, 2014). Second, attention is on work in Sogn centered on the development of

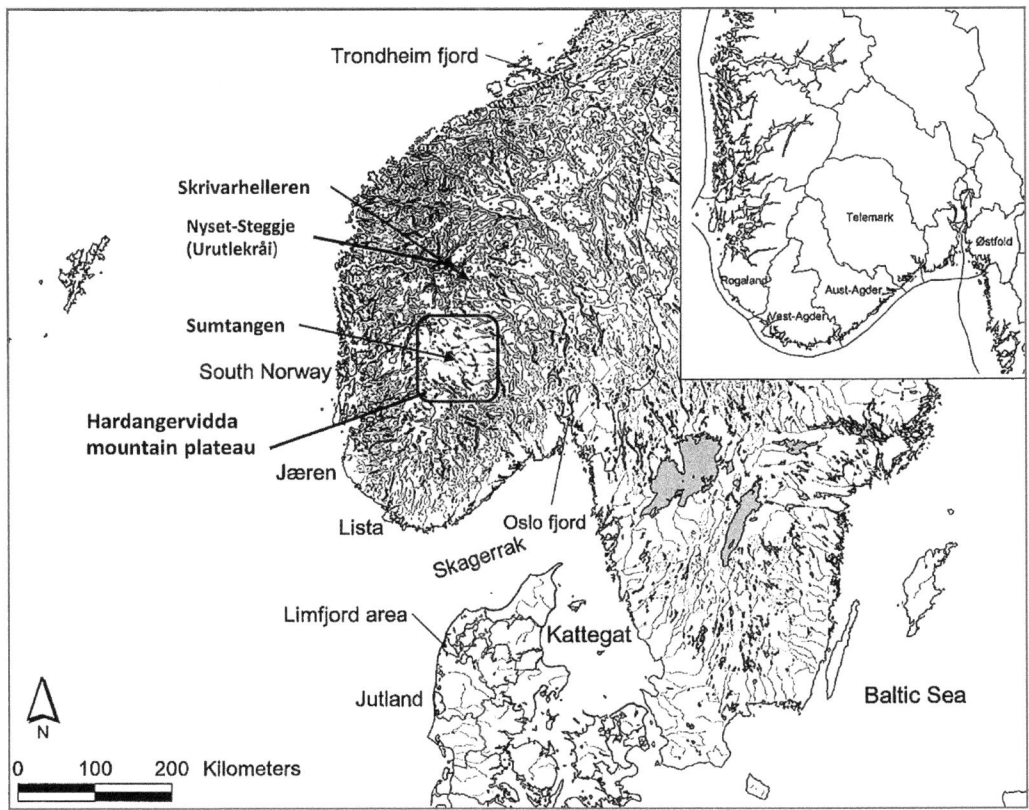

Figure 11.1. Map of southern Scandinavia indicating topographical features. The Sumtangen, Nyset-Steggje, and Skrivarhelleren site complexes are indicated. Map by Håkon Glørstad and Christopher Prescott.

the Tyin-Steggje-Nyset river systems (spilling over into neighboring valleys Lærdal, Aurland, and Leikanger; cf. Bjørgo et al. 1992; Johansen 1970; Prescott 1991, 1995). Third, the contemporary thrust toward ice patch archaeology particularly in the higher central Norwegian mountains centered on Jotunheimen (Callanan 2014a, 2015; Finstad & Pilø 2010, 2011).

Conceptual Histories

"Nature" is a referential category throughout modern and contemporary Scandinavia—carrying connotations of primordial authenticity and referential moral values of ruggedness, simplicity, and purity that transcend time. In our contemporary urban world, the mountains, *fjellet*, incarnate nature at its purest. Of course, this is a myth. The modern mountain landscape is strongly shaped by humans; summer farming, fauna management, industrial development, roads, and recreational facilities. The perception of pure mountain nature is tied to activities central to national and, to an extent, romantic identity narratives (cf. Steinsland 2014; Svensen 2012). The huntsman and trapper are historical archetypes—embodying the rugged mountain man. The summer farms, or shielings, and the dairymaids and shepherds associated with them carry a host of romantic connotations (see the yearbooks of the hiking association, *Den norske turistforening*, published since 1865).

The romantic myths of primordial nature, seasonal hunting, and summer farming feed into resilient ideas of the mountains as something apart and wild, sometimes inhabited by outcasts, generating perceptions of prehistoric uplands as a liminal space beyond the control of lowland farming societies and inhabited by primordial groups. These ideas are found in folk myths that often explained old structures and telltale signs of settlement, for example, the traces of fires found in rock-shelters attributed to outlaws driven from the villages and forced to etch out a sorry existence outside of society. Not only projecting recent historical perceptions onto the landscapes of the past, but the primordial nature of the environment was projected onto the assumed ancient inhabitants, which was again ascribed to the Saami minority (Christie 1842; Hansen 1904) or other indigenous hunter groups (Johansen 1973, 1978). Thus, premises of deep culture and separate histories of upland groups were integrated with narratives of national and ethnic identities that existed and exist in symbiosis with political agendas.

The historical transhumant summer farms and shielings of the uplands were seasonal (Reinton 1955; Stene et al. 2009; Svensson 2015). Shepherds moved from station to station into higher altitudes with the ripening of the vegetation in the spring and early summer, arriving at the high-altitude farm building for the summer. This agropastoral institution historically known from the 1700s to around the 1950s is described in detail in a few comprehensive studies (especially Reinton 1955, 1961), and many local studies and accounts. The seasonal exploitation of the uplands was a fine-tuned system of production that maximized pastoral production. Shielings also served as a staging base for fishing and hunting, offered travelers simple accommodations, and as such were vital to communications across the mountains. The seasonally exploited uplands were an important economic institution, producing a surplus to not only help the farm households through the winters but also to allow participation in market exchanges with wool, brown cheese, and butter. More than any other preindustrial practice, summer farms with their grazing of animals and use of wood as fuel created important elements of what is today's "mountain nature": a depressed tree line, open landscape, upland meadows, bogs, and many of the paths and roads that serve hikers and flocks today (Austrheim et al. 2015).

Antiquarian and Archaeological Histories

The history of research of the mountain plateau Hardangervidda is diverse (Indrelid 1994; Martens 1988). Though intermittently mentioned in older texts, the mountains as a subject of historical research began in 1842 with a short article by W. F. K. Christie (1842). Christie, a lawyer, was secretary to the constitutional assembly at Eidsvoll in 1814 and later involved in programs for Norwegian national sovereignty. He recognized the need for national institutions, as well as the development of educational programs, science, and history. He created the Bergen Museum in 1825 and published two volumes of *URDA* (1837, 1842), an eclectic antiquarian-historical journal. His article "Spoer af finske eller lappiske folks ophold i oldtiden paa høifjeldene i Bergens Stift" describes how he had heard rumors of farmers who had found mounds of bone and reindeer antlers at Lake Finsevatn, later renamed Finsbergsvatn (Sumtangen, Figure 11.2). He sent someone to confirm these

Figure 11.2. Photograph of the Sumtangen Peninsula (Lake Finsbergsvatn, Hardangervidda). The Sumtangen site has been central to mountain archaeology since the 1830s, and remains so today. The peninsula is to the left in the small sound in the middle of the picture. To the right is the Hardangerjøkulen glacier (1,876 masl). Reindeer were chased or herded down from the glacier and into the water. Hunters rowed out to kill them, pull them onto land at Sumtangen, and butcher them. The ruins of two large stone-built huts (that could accommodate ten to fifteen people) from around AD 1200 are visible on the surface, though deposits extending back to the Neolithic are found here, too. Middens from the Middle Ages with the remains of several thousand reindeer are found outside the huts (Indrelid and Hufthammer 2011). Photo by Svein Indrelid, University of Bergen.

reports, and two house ruins were identified. Publishing descriptions of these structures and deposits, and comparing them with similar observations from Finnmark to the far north, he concluded they could be evidence of a primordial population. He then refers to some place names and arrives (mistakenly) at the conclusion "that it proves that Finnish or Lappish people have lived and stayed here in the high mountains" (Christie 1842:408–409).

Apart from being a "commonsense" narrative supported and supporting contemporary perceptions, there is probably an underlying narrative agenda bound up with Norwegian nationalism also found in work contemporary to that of Christie, for example, of one of the founding fathers of Norwegian history, Peter A. Munch (1852:v). He held that history's task was to serve the nation-building project and advocated a historical settlement narrative in support of the refounding of the Norwegian nation-state. Munch's sources were meagre: archaeology was poorly developed (this is sixteen years after Thomsen's publication of the Danish version of *Guide to Northern Archaeology* in 1836) and ancient texts were sparse. Therefore, Munch used a little comparative Indo-European linguistics, some folk myths, some classical texts, and a lot of imagination to construct an ethnic history. Though mainly preoccupied with assumed postglacial migration of various Germanic groups associated with modern states, Munch mentions the "Turanics" (Mongols, Finnish-Ugrians, and Turkish groups) and uses them as an opposition to the Indo-Europeans. Though subscribing to a theory of an inland indigenous group, the narrative remains chronologically (both relative and calendrical) obscure. As archaeology developed, and theories like Munch's were abandoned on empirical and conceptual grounds, alternatives were put forward, usually subscribing to a counternarrative of lowland farmers exploiting upland resources on a seasonal basis. Though more material became available in the following decade, and both archaeological and multidisciplinary arguments grew in sophistication, there was still a lack of upland data, a weak referential archaeological framework, and limited interpretative discourse outside of fundamental national and ethnic agendas.

The foundations for an empirically responsive cultural history of the mountains improved with Johannes Bøe's investigations at Sumtangen and other sites on Hardangervidda during the Second World War. Bøe's work indicated the chronological depth of human use of the mountains, extending back to the Stone Age, tied the materials to the Nordic chronotypological systems (Bøe 1942), and in retrospect provided grounds to refute theories of an ethnically separate inland population (Hagen 1997). For whatever reason, Bøe's work did not put an end to theories of indigenous isolation, and separate and confused cultural histories—which have been proposed virtually up to the present (if within different agendas). Perhaps the most sophisticated interpretative history from this time was Bjørn Hougen's book *Fra seter til gård*—"From shieling to farm" (1947). Here, Hougen turned arguments a bit on their head, advocating a pivotal role for the upland peripheries in the evolution of central institutions like the farm and iron production.

Bøe's work did not have the impact it perhaps could have had, partly because the archaeology of the mountains simply did not attract much attention. In the late 1950s, things were on the cusp of changing, driven by, for archaeology, fortuitous events: the advent of radiocarbon, the initiation of well-funded rescue excavations, interdisciplinary ambitions, and theoretical and methodological revitalization associated with New Archaeology—and extensive hydroelectric development projects. Martens (1988) described investigations from the 1950s into the 1980s of high-altitude drainage systems as a vitamin injection in Norwegian archaeology. This is probably an understatement: mountain archaeology was a driving force in the modernization of Norwegian (and northern Swedish) archaeology.

HYDROELECTRIC DEVELOPMENT: A CURSE AND A BLESSING?

Though hydroelectric power provided Norway with cheap and moderately clean energy, hydroelectric development is destructive. It destroys the original plant and fauna ecology in river systems and the surrounding valleys, and it disturbs hydrological, sedimentological, and biological systems in the receptor bodies—whether fjords or lakes. Dry riverbeds, fluctuating water levels, roads, quarries, reservoirs, dams, power stations, power lines, tunnels, and landfills permanently alter the landscape. Archaeological sites are removed, disturbed, or flooded—though the recent revisitation of previously flooded valleys indicates that there is still a significant potential for research in drainage systems dammed fifty years ago (e.g., Amundsen and Finstad 2007; Bjørkli et al. 2016; Mjærum and Wammer 2016; Reitan 2006).

Still, hydroelectric development has been beneficial for archaeology. In the late 1950s Martens and Hagen tentatively won approval and modest funding for investigating a suite of upland river systems on the southern and eastern perimeters of Hardangervidda in advance of hydroelectric development. Though outcomes at that stage could not be predicted, these initial investigations were successes in terms of archaeological knowledge and method, as well as heritage management (Martens and Hagen 1961). Their initiative led to a succession of upland projects financed as part of hydroelectric developments (Indrelid 2009), for example, Tyin, Røldal-Suldal (Odner 1969), Lærdal (Johansen 1970, 1978), Alta (Simonsen 1987), Hardangervidda (Indrelid 1994; Johansen 1973), Breheimen (Randers 1986), Fløyrlivatn (Bang-Andersen 1990), and the last of the large-scale predevelopment projects Nyset-Steggje (Bjørgo et al. 1992). Since Nyset-Steggje there have been numerous, if restricted, surveys and excavations tied to renewal of fifty-year concessions (Indrelid 2009; see, e.g., Mjærum and Wammer 2016), and programs have been established for the management of heritage along regulated watercourses (Skogstrand 2020).

Some of these projects primarily produced material and data, and some of these are now mostly forgotten. In some cases, though original gray reports or publications had little impact, the results have been incorporated in later studies of broader themes (e.g., Mikkelsen 1989; Solheim 2012). Some projects led to studies with strong theoretical agendas that created much debate at the time, either representing a lasting referential point (Odner 1969) or having a contemporary influence (Johansen 1969, 1978). Two projects (and ensuing follow-ups), Hardangervidda (with later work related to the Sumtangen site [Indrelid and Hufthammer 2011]) and Nyset-Steggje (using older excavations from Tyin, with a follow-up at Skrivarhelleren [Prescott 1991]) can be held forth in terms of impact. These projects, and the ensuing studies, embody a comprehensive set of characteristics that to a certain degree are taken for granted today: research questions, theoretical premises, methodological experimentation, interdisciplinary approaches (especially toward ecological disciplines), robust empirical data, and multiperiod investigations. These projects therefore engendered research discussions and interpretative assertions far beyond "mountain research," particularly in relation to commonly accepted wisdom, the interpretation of interdisciplinary data, and heritage issues. A third case, not immediately dependent on hydroelectric development but improbable without the preceding decades of mountain archaeology, is ice patch archaeology and the recovery of frozen organic materials (Callanan 2012, 2014a). Although not matured to its scientific potential in terms of problems and interpretation, these finds can potentially add new archaeological information, raise issues about heritage and preservation, and contribute to public discussions about climate warming (Åstveit 2007; Callanan 2016; Finstad and Pilø 2010; Nesje et al. 2012). Hardangervidda, Nyset-Steggje, and ice patch archaeology are case studies explored in the following.

Hardangervidda Mountain Plateau: To Boldly Go Where No Archaeologist Has Gone Before

Hardangervidda is Europe's largest mountain plateau, 1,100 to 1,400 masl with glaciated peaks up to 1,860 masl. Short steep valleys lead to the fjords of the west, while long forested valleys meander to lower-lying regions of the east and south. Reindeer and summer pastures were important resources in preindustrial times, as were mineral resources (quartz, quartzite, fine-grained stone, and iron). Filling the center of southern Norway, Hardangervidda has also been crisscrossed by seasonally used paths and tracks serving regional (e.g., west-east cattle drives) and local transportation (to and from shielings), and gathering people at seasonal markets, already in the Viking period (Loftsgarden 2017; Loftsgarden et al. 2017). Later, since the advent of the age of urbanism, the plateau was exploited for recreation and hydroelectricity.

As indicated earlier, Hardangervidda was of archaeological interest from the mid-1800s. Systematic research developed from the late 1950s along the southern and eastern margins. In the late 1960s, plans to develop the central parts of the plateau spurred Anders Hagen and Arne B. Johansen to examine previous and contemporaneous investigations in Norway and Sweden (especially inspired by *Norrland's Early Settlement* 1968–1974; Baudou and Biörnstad 1972). They ramped up focus on knowledge production (instead of purely rescue-oriented excavations), they initiated investigations guided by research questions, instead of strictly adhering to areas directly affected by dams, reservoirs, and roads. For this purpose they managed to procure additional funding that opened the whole plateau up for investigation, and—importantly—permitted experimentation with methods and tests of research strategies. The Hardangervidda Project for Interdisciplinary Culture Research ran from 1970 to 1974. The goal was authentic interdisciplinary integration, involving archaeology, toponymy, ethnology, botany, zoo-osteology, and quaternary geology (Hagen 2002; Indrelid 1994). The result, as summed up by participants (Indrelid 2009; Johansen 1993), was more multidisciplinary than cross- or interdisciplinary and is an expressive case study of how ideals of interdisciplinary research are difficult to put into practice (Prescott 2013).

Important results are concerned with climate, early settlement, reindeer hunting, and traces of iron production (Indrelid 2009). Here, two areas of study are important, the exploration of the Late Iron Age and medieval settlement and the Neolithic. Recent studies, sparked by the older investigations, have reexplored mass reindeer hunting. These studies started with material from the Sumtangen house sites and middens, as well as other similar nearby house remain sites from central Hardangervidda (Indrelid et al. 2007; Indrelid and Hufthammer 2011). Research has expanded to comparatively study Roman Iron Age and medieval (possibly including Viking Age) bone assemblages from this and other nearby Hardangervidda sites, as well as two in the Dovre mountains, 400 km to the north (Hufthammer et al. 2011). The archaeological and zoological materials demonstrate variability between periods and geography—the Roman Iron Age data suggest a focus on meat, which is also the case for the Dovrefjell materials from the medieval period. The medieval data from Hardangervidda indicate a focus on the collection of antlers. The archaeological materials here—especially runic inscriptions—demonstrate affiliations with the wider Nordic world. This is supported by analysis of material from the medieval city of Bergen that points to comb production and trade based on reindeer antler (Hansen 2017). The link between coastal Bergen and mountain Sumtangen is also indicated through DNA comparisons (Indrelid and Hufthammer 2011:52–53). The materials that in many ways center on Sumtangen demonstrate that hunting is integrated in and responsive to the surrounding society's social organization and economies—and part of a northern European system of trade and production.

Moving back in time to the Stone Age, the context and processes concerned with the introduction of agriculture have been subject to extensive, but inconclusive, debate also in Norway. The Norwegian context, with marginal climate for agriculture, circumstantial and insubstantial bodies of positive data, and partially conflicting evidence (especially when disciplinary boundaries between biology and archaeology are crossed) render the region an interesting case study. The general discussion of neolithization was reinvigorated in the 1970s through pollen analysis, radiocarbon, and spatial analyses (Bakka and Kaland 1971). The Hardangervidda project provided a case that still raises questions about the interpretation of the archaeological and palynological materials. Apart from lithic debitage, projectile points (ground slate, tanged blade points, single-edged points) dominate the archaeological materials from the Early and Middle Neolithic periods (4000–2400 BC) (Indrelid 1994:202). Only four Neolithic axes (battle-axes and flint axes from before 2400 BC) and eighty-three flakes or projectile points produced from ground flint axes are found on twenty-seven sites, while thirty-three sherds of Neolithic ceramics, from two sites, were recovered (Indrelid 1994:182, 254). Though the archaeology is rich, the quantity of "Neolithic" finds is low, and it is, for example, reasonable to interpret flint axes primarily as cores, that is, lithic raw material and not used as axes. The late Early and Middle Neolithic sherds and axe fragments were not from the oldest Neolithic phases. Preservation of faunal material is poor, and of the fifty-five Early and Middle Neolithic bone fragments, no bone of domesticated species are identified. In terms of practice and networks, there are several interpretative avenues suggested by the archaeological material, but agropastoral production does not seem to be one of them.

However, in the pollen material there is pollen from species often interpreted as indicative of grazing: ribwort plantain (*Plantago lanceoláta*), nettles (*Urtíca*), and wormwood (*Artemísia*). These were found in six (of eleven) radiocarbon-dated diagrams. In each case, there is usually one or two pollen grains, and these can be the result of transport from other areas, that is, not reflect vegetation or activities in the area. The oldest dates for ribwort plantain potentially predate 5200 BC, that is, are Late Mesolithic. Though Svein Indrelid and Dagfinn Moe (1983) point out some general source critical problems with the dates, suggesting that the values might be too old, the initial readouts substantially predate the ceramics and axe fragments. The pollen of grazing indicators thus have no corresponding archaeological Neolithic materials. Comparing the Stone Age period with historical periods of heavy pastoral activity, Indrelid and Moe point out that the "[pollen] spectra from the modern era do not diverge substantially from the oldest cultural readouts from the Neolithic, even though we know summer farming has been present through the last 2–400 years." The authors hesitantly conclude that though there is "no proof of pastured domesticated species," still, they believe "there is a basis to assert that Hardangervidda in the Neolithic . . . was visited by groups with a background in the SE-Norwegian agricultural population" (Indrelid and Moe 1983:65, translated by CP).

At the time, these results and their interpretation were generally accepted, but as with many paleobotanical reports of feeble agropastoralism in marginal environments, there was a sense of uncertainty as to how to deal with the observations. On an empirical level there are the usual issues concerning the limited pollen readouts and correlating dates. Indrelid attempted to resolve this by placing the evidence in a larger geographical context, distinguishing between what is found on an individual specialized site, as opposed to the general content within cultural horizons and broad patterns. Interpretatively, there are problems in identifying how the negligible quantities of relevant pollen grains actually came to be deposited here, how to contextualize the upland pollen by reference to lowland Neolithic cultures in Norway (particularly the Funnel Beaker Culture)—cultures that also lack direct indications of agropastoralism. Further questions arise if the radiocarbon dates are taken at face value, and the proposed pastoral activities start in the Mesolithic (as in lowland diagrams, cf. Prøsch-Danielsen and Simonsen 2000). Theoretically, it is difficult to understand why hunters (even if based in an agropastoral Neolithic culture context) would bring cattle, sheep, or goats on a seasonal hunting expedition, and how a very marginal, nearly nonexistent activity could be socially, culturally, and biologically reproduced, without noticeable developments, for 1,600 years, and without leaving robust traces. Methodologically, the diagrams raise questions about what is actually reflected in a pollen diagram, and how discrepancies between archaeology and palynology should be approached.

The indisputable establishment of the farm in southern Norway, and thus agriculture, happened around the transition to the Late Neolithic around 2400–2350 BC and developed through the Bronze Age. Indrelid (2009:39) mentions small huts, use of rock-shelters, and pollen data as indications of the impact the transition to a farming society had in the uplands. The data from Hardangervidda are inconclusive before the formal Nordic Bronze Age (1700–500 BC). This is partly because research focus was on the Neolithic, Iron, and Middle Ages, as well as methodological choice of adopting a morphological approach to "Stone Age" artifacts and a slightly undifferentiated culture concept. This arguably left sites undiscovered and the Late Neolithic period (2350–1700 BC) indistinct. Importantly, there was no adequate assemblage of faunal material, and the pollen evidence was not coherent except for in diagrams based on samples taken close to a few archaeological sites of an Early and Late Bronze/Pre-Roman Iron Age date (Indrelid 1994:234).

Valleys in Sogn: The Nyset-Steggje Project and Its Aftermath

The Nordic Late Neolithic, Bronze, and Iron Ages would be a focus of two later projects: Nyset-Steggje and the following excavations in the Skrivarhelleren rock-shelter. Archaeological surveys were instigated in the mountain areas of Årdal in 1981 in response to hydroelectric development of two mountain drainage systems: Nyset and Steggje. While Hardangervidda is best understood in relation to a mountain plain where there are few constricting features beyond bodies of water, the Nyset-Steggje project was conducted in clearly narrower valleys. As the drainage systems were to be developed, all impacted areas were systematically surveyed by surface walking and test pitting, and a number of sites were excavated (Bjørgo et al. 1992). Apart from field methods (systematic surveys, integration of archaeology and pollen botany, and an intensive radiocarbon program), within a broad chronological scope (from deglaciation to the Reformation), the Nyset-Steggje project focused on two main themes: the final phase of struck lithics (i.e., bifaces) and the Iron Age summer farms.

Sixteen house sites exhibit major investment and production in the upland areas from the end of the Roman Iron Age to the Middle Ages. Though this could be viewed in terms of local subsistence, the scale of production is indicative of surplus production for trade, and the artifact material—especially beads made out of exotic materials—demonstrates a far-reaching network. In sum, the upland settlements are best interpreted as an expression of intensive seasonal summer farming activity—with dairy activities, metalworking, and textile working, as well as hunting and fishing (based on Bjørgo et al. 1992). The relatively large and solid house sites, and the finds associated with them, were clearly integrated in well-established farm societies that were part of the broader Nordic world. As such, the material echoes the overarching understanding of the Hardangervidda data. The investigations also underscored cross-disciplinary and methodological issues concerning palynological and archaeological data discussed earlier in conjunction with Hardangervidda.

Urutlekråi: An Example of Methodological Issues

At Nyset-Steggje an extensive palynology program (more than twenty-five sampling sites and diagrams) aimed at investigating land use practices was instigated (Kvamme et al. 1992), and issues similar to those relevant to Hardangervidda were also discussed here (Prescott

1995). For example at the site complex of Urutlekråi–Vikastølen (Figure 11.3), two large Viking Age summer farmhouses and a medieval house site were located 190 m from each other (Bjørgo et al. 1992). The landscape of more recent times is shaped through summer pasturing and characterized by localized meadows, juniper patches, mountain birch, and suppressed tree lines. Two pollen cores taken 0.5 m apart at a pollen-sampling site in a bog at Urutlekråi (Bjørgo et al. 1992; Kvamme et al. 1992) should be ideally situated to explore the sites and the general activities in the vicinity. Still, the pollen diagrams did not demonstrate significant impact on the vegetation, even in periods when other sources demonstrated substantial human activity. Recalling the tentative conclusion from the discussion of the Hardangervidda diagrams, where there were weak readouts from the Neolithic, the Urutlekråi diagram could be comparatively interpreted in light of similar weak readouts from the historical epoch. The hypothesis and palynological conclusion from Nyset-Steggje was that the diagrams only illuminated a small area around the individual sampling site; though patterns in several diagrams demonstrated broader trends, the restricted number

Figure 11.3. The Urutlekråi site (970 masl, Vikadalen, Årdal). The standing hut is a shieling built in the 1870s and was in use for nearly one hundred years. Before being flooded in connection with hydroelectric development, sites associated with summer shielings from the Late Bronze Age to the Middle Ages were excavated here as part of the Nyset-Steggje project (1981–1987). The upland meadows exhibit a vegetation pattern typical of upland landscapes subjected to long-term intensive grazing. Photo by Christopher Prescott.

of species in the upland vegetation seems to mask developments (Kvamme et al. 1992). To reflect specific archaeological sites and historical landscape developments, palynological sites must be close to archaeological sites. Though experience showed this strategy to give readouts, it does raise questions about what activities were actually registered (or not) in the diagrams: broader use of the landscape or very localized impact at the settlement itself (e.g., trampling, clearing, and waste deposition)?

Inadvertently, the Urutlekråi pollen-sampling site was in a bog on the outskirt of a large Late Bronze Age/Early Pre-Roman Age site found later: Urutlekråi 47. Though not initially recognized, the deposits from the site's refuse area continued into the pollen-sampling site. This settlement site was characterized by lithics (e.g., 748 points) and lithic production (206,500 struck pieces). Furthermore, important aspects are the remains of a small hut, asbestos-tempered ceramics, a single piece of bronze, and a fragment of a soapstone vessel (Bjørgo et al. 1992). A nearby, archaeologically contemporaneous site (Kalvebeitet 27) yielded a fragmentary crucible. Of 1,225 burnt bone fragments 2 were from birds and 1,223 mammals, including a single bone of sheep/goat (Lie 1992). Urutlekråi 47 is one of a group of Late Neolithic to Pre-Roman Iron Age sites characterized by bifacial lithics in these valleys. These sites were used in a discussion concerning the cultural, economic, social, and technological nature of the assumed peripheral Nordic regions. The fundamental (and, in retrospect, simplistic) question was to what extent there were domesticated animals. To this end, understanding the economic context of this seasonal settlement was deemed instrumental. Apart from the archaeology (that demonstrated hunting), the pollen diagrams (that demonstrated opening of the vegetation on the site) were explored. However, in methodological terms, with the aim of understanding production and landscape, the strategy of pollen analysis from the intra-site deposits was misguided, as interpreting readouts in the site's midden as an expression of broader landscape developments (Kvamme et al. 1992) was theoretically, methodologically, and interpretatively precarious (Prescott 1995). The core problem is appreciating that human practices in the landscape have significantly different parameters and effects than other ecological factors.

The palynology in combination with the archaeology and the geographical context generated a renewed discussion about what the pollen diagrams said about Bronze Age activities. From an archaeological vantage point, the palynological methodology led to a circular result: a marked readout in the Urutlekråi diagrams was because the sampling site was located within the site. However, given that sampling was from archaeological sediments within an activity area, the question was raised whether the diagrams reflected site activities like trampling, waste deposition, wood collecting, or general stockholding in the area—and whether the Urutlekråi diagrams could be used to differentiate between them (Bjørgo et al. 1992; Kvamme et al. 1992; Prescott 1995). The debate was thus a methodological issue about procedures and interpretative parameters in upland archaeopalynology, spilling over to palynology in archaeology in general (Prescott 1995), with ramifications for the choice of paleobotanical methods. Urutlekråi was a focus for this discussion because of the excellent archaeological and stratigraphic context and data. The problem was thus less whether the diagrams indicate pastoral practices, and more what the diagram can say about the landscape and the human practices that shaped it. Other pollen diagrams were interpreted as showing surprising and unlikely results comparable to those from Hardangervidda: Early Neolithic pasturing or cereal cultivation in the Early Iron Age, 970 masl, above the tree line (Kvamme et al. 1992).

Skrivarhelleren: Beyond the "Neolithication Paradigm"

The basic questions concerning people using the uplands before the Iron Age were initially whether they had domesticated animals, and whether they were part of the Nordic Late Neolithic and Bronze Age world or another northern hunter-gatherer society. Organic preservation on the Nyset-Steggje sites was poor, no serious attempt at collecting macro-fossils was implemented, and it remained unclear what palynology could say. To address issues, research excavations in a rock-shelter, Skrivarhelleren (Figure 11.4), were conducted in 1987–1989 (Prescott 1991), and again in 2013–2015 (Prescott and Melheim 2018).

Figure 11.4. The Skrivarhelleren rock-shelter site (790 masl, Moadalen, Årdal). The rock-shelter is under the lenticular-shaped rock face in the middle of the picture. Excavations were conducted in 1987–1989, 2013–2015. Cultural deposits up to 2 m in depth span much of the period from the Nordic Late Neolithic (2350 BCE) to the modern era. Photo by Christopher Prescott.

The rock-shelter is in an upland valley over a ridge from one of the Nyset-Steggje valleys, Moadalen valley 790 masl. The valley itself had previously yielded few archaeological finds, though surveys around Lake Tyin (1,070 masl), which drains into the Moadalen valley, had produced numerous Stone Age sites.

The area underneath the rock lip is cool year round and relatively protected from the elements. There are stratified deposits over an area of several hundred square meters, and deposits are up to 2 m in depth and chronologically spanning from ca. 2400–2350 BC to AD 1700 (Prescott 1991, 1995). The excavations and water-sieving and flotation program produced large amounts of bone and some seed material. The zoological materials contained sheep, goat, and cattle, wild species from environments spanning from high-alpine mountains to the fjords and sea: seashells, marine mammals, freshwater and marine fish, deer, fowl, mustelids, bear, among others. The plant material contained some cereals (barley and wheat), marine bladder weed, and other wild plants. The archaeological materials—bone, antler, lithic materials, metal, ceramics, refractory materials, amber, among others—demonstrate affiliations and interaction locally, regionally, and with other regions in Northern and Central Europe.

The initial questions of whether there was an agropastoral component and cultural affiliations were framed in a "Neolithication perspective." That is, was there some degree of agropastoralism or were the inhabitants hunter-gatherers? Was there a relict hunter-gatherer culture? Were influences northern or southern Scandinavian? Combining spatial patterns, archaeological finds, and biological materials, the initial questions readily seemed naïve and biased. The data were interpreted as remains of a moderately complex agropastoral farm economy that exploited a range of resources in various niches on a seasonal basis. Production activities included metal casting; working shell, bone, and antler; hunting for furs and hides; production and use of pitch; textile working; and perhaps specialized wool production (Prescott and Melheim 2017). Moving beyond early metallurgy (Prescott 1991), the potential for early experimentation with copper ore exploitation is explored in recent studies (Melheim 2012a, 2012b, 2015; Melheim and Prescott 2016; Prescott 2006). Instead of "influence," the data indicated integration into the Nordic world. Elements of the Bell Beaker Culture, Nordic Late Neolithic, and Bronze Age were apparent (Prescott 1995). The rapid transformation from previous hunter-gatherer cultures to a full-fledged agropastoral society happened under Bell Beaker stimulus (Melheim and Prescott 2016; Prescott and Glørstad 2015). Thus, far from isolated relict groups on the fringes of the politically and economically developed Nordic world, the mountain regions were integrated into Nordic politics, networks, and economic systems (Melheim 2012b; Prescott 1995; Prescott and Melheim 2017).

Ice Patches: A Race against Time and a Climate Warning

As hydroelectric development has slowed, so have large-scale archaeological mountain projects. As a consequence of semi-centennial renewals of hydroelectric concessions, renewed investigations around old reservoirs have generated some new materials (e.g., Mjærum and

Wammer 2016; Reitan 2006). However, a new thrust is to recover organic finds from the high-altitude ice patch assemblages (Åstveit 2007; Callanan 2014a, 2015; Finstad and Pilø 2011; Pilø et al. 2018; Pilø et al. 2020b). As opposed to glaciers, ice patches do not have internal movement, and they accumulate and melt vertically and the contained materials are not transported and ground to pieces. Ice patches therefore can contain frozen organic material as old as the origin of the ice (Figure 11.5). The most famous example is not Norwegian, but the Iceman from the Italian Alps. This find demonstrates the potential and, as organic material will quickly decompose after thawing, the narrow window of opportunity for recovering these materials.

Global warming is melting the ice patches, and as this happens organic materials from the Neolithic to the present (Callanan 2015), like textiles (e.g., Vedeler and Jørgensen 2013) and leather (e.g., Finstad and Vedeler 2008), various bows and arrows (Callanan 2013, 2014b), and other equipment like sledges, skis, and "scaring sticks" come forth. The rare finds excite the public and archaeologists alike. Though exciting, and demonstrating use of the high-altitude areas, whether for hunting or transportation, the ice patch finds are to an extent stand-alone discoveries, partially unanalyzed, and without a broader historical contextualization. Thus, as with upland finds of previous eras, it is important to integrate these finds into the broader cultural discourse of other altitudes, as well as analyze the finds and contexts and biases in the find material (see, e.g., Callanan 2015; Martinsen 2015; Pilø et al. 2020a; Solli 2018).

Figure 11.5. A Bronze Age shoe from the melting ice patch at Kvitingkjølen, Lom, Oppland. Numerous organic objects preserved in the ice for centuries and millennia are recovered as ice patches melt in response to a warmer climate. Photo by Ann Christine Eek, Museum of Cultural History. © 2018 Kulturhistorisk museum, UiO / CC BY-SA 4.0.

The pressing issue of management has matured into annual campaigns. This entails being at the right place at the right time to document and collect finds as they emerge from the snow and ice. Today, a main goal is the implementation of a management strategy to secure these finds for future study before most of the conserving context of ice melts away (Callanan 2016). The finds have already forcefully communicated a lesson of importance, also experienced in other cold environments. Warming is extending beyond variations of the climate regime of the last four thousand years; global warming is real. Of course, the threat to humanity and other life forms is the principal issue; however, undiscovered archives for human knowledge concerning culture and environment will also be destroyed in the near future.

In a way, this echoes the challenges of the 1950s hydroelectric development. It was a threat to archaeology and historical landscapes, but it was also an opportunity. Anders Hagen and Irmelin Martens grasped the opportunity and initiated a management program. Sixty years later, we can conclude that the resulting production of knowledge was a catalyst for archaeology that has contributed with tremendous knowledge.

Concluding Remarks

Mountain archaeology was initiated within a recognizable national and ethnic narrative. It might seem that this narrative's strength was drawn from a lack of robust material and data. However, even after coherent data emerged, for example, with Bøe's Hardangervidda expedition during the Second World War, these narratives remained resilient. Indeed, though no longer dominant, they live on today, often supplanted by popular perceptions of nature and the uplands as primeval. Hydroelectric development led to generous funding, large multidisciplinary projects, and a flood of data. These projects experimented with methods and were involved in broader theoretical and interpretative trends. Upland archaeology was important for the processual streams of thought in the 1970s, as well as some of the dismantling of processual archaeology in favor of neodiffusionism and agent approaches from the late 1990s. As such, mountain archaeology and the culture history of the uplands has evolved from an interpretative field and archaeological practice separated from the cultural history of the lowlands, to archaeological narratives integrated in northern European trajectories and practices.

Substantial issues in interdisciplinary work, for example, in conjunction with the Hardangervidda project or the use of palynology, stood out in the wake of large projects. This was partly because these projects experimented with methods and research fieldwork, but also because the environmentally and geographically marginal uplands—as seen from a lowland, agricultural perspective—seem to bring added contrasts and clarity to the questions at stake.

The transformation of mountain archaeology has strong methodological and theoretical elements. However, there also seem to be strong empirical drivers—opinions have changed and questions have been formulated in confrontation with new data. If not a defense for an empiricist approach to archaeology, this does indicate that the process of creating data and generating interpretations from materials rescued under the onslaught of hydroelectric development or out of the melting high-altitude ice patches will provide new insights in the years to come.

There is perhaps a perception that the mountains are vast, virginal landscapes. A quick glance at a map of hydroelectric development (Mjærum and Friis 2016) shows that nondeveloped drainage systems are rare. Add roads, construction of recreational facilities, power lines, tourism, and industrial development and it is clear that the postwar impact on the Norwegian uplands is massive. In terms of contemporary relevance, the antiquity and context of the ice patch finds serve as a stark reminder of global warming.

Though providing archaeology with resources, there is an inherent paradox to mountain archaeology. It has produced significant and genuinely original insights into Scandinavia's past—and will continue to do so. At the same time the generous funding, the large-scale projects, and innovative methodology are in response to large-scale, fundamentally destructive activities, whether we are dealing with the construction of reservoirs, building of roads, or ice patches that are melting. Sites are destroyed, flooded, or buried. Contexts are disturbed, ice is melting away, and the objects they contain are displaced or rapidly decompose, while landscapes and ecosystems are permanently altered. To date there has been a race to recover the objects and knowledge they embody before destruction. Perhaps archaeologists have an obligation to participate in discussions about human use of the planet more strongly, drawing not only on the long historical experiences archaeology provides but also on our own experiences of contemporary destruction.

References

Amundsen, H. R., and E. Finstad 2007 Aursjøenprosjektet 2006. Sluttrapporten. *Kulturhistorisk rapport 2007-4*. Oppland Fylkeskommune, Lillehammer.

Åstveit, L. I. 2007 Høyfjellsarkeologi under snø og is: Global oppvarming, fonnjakt og funn fra snøfonner datert til steinalder. *Viking* 70:7–22.

Austrheim, G., K. L. Hjelle, P. J. E. Sjøgren, K. Stene, and A. M. Tretvik (eds.) 2015 *Fjellets kulturlandskap: Arealbruk og landskap gjennom flere tusen år*. DKNVS Skrifter 3. Museumsforlaget AS.

Bakka, E., and P. E. Kaland 1971 Early Farming in Hordaland, Western Norway: Problems and Approaches in Archaeology and Pollen Analysis. *Norwegian Archaeological Review* 4(2):1–35.

Bang-Andersen, S. 1990 The Myrvatn Group, a Preboreal Find-Complex in Southwest Norway. In *Contributions to the Mesolithic in Europe*, edited by P. M. Vermeersch and P. Van Peer, 215–226. Leuven University Press, Leuven.

Baudou, E., and I. Biörnstad 1972 The Early Norrland Research Project. In *Early Norrland 1: Paleo-ecological Investigations in Northern Sweden*, edited by P. Huttunen, I. U. Olsson, K. Tolonen, and M. Tolonen, 7–8. Kungl. Vit. Historie och Antikvitets Akademien, Stockholm.

Bjørgo, T. 1986 Mountain Archaeology: Preliminary Results from Nyset-Steggje. *Norwegian Archaeological Review* 19(2):122–127.

Bjørgo, T., S. Kristoffersen, and C. Prescott 1992 *Arkeologiske undersøkelser i Nyset-Steggjevassdragene 1981–87*. Arkeologiske Rapporter 16, Historisk Museum, Universitetet i Bergen 17, Bergen.

Bjørkli, B., E. K. Friis, and A. Mjærum 2016 Tesse et arkeologisk eldorado og en innfallsport til fjellfisket. In *Fjellfisket i fortiden: Årtusener med svømmende rikdom*, edited by A. Mjærum and E. U. Wammer, 15–36. Portal forlag, Kristiansand.

Bøe, J. 1942 *Til Høgfjellets historie: Boplassen på Sumtangen ved Finsevatn på Hardangervidda*. Bergens Museums Skrifter 21. Bergens Museum, Bergen.

Callanan, M. 2012 Central Norwegian Snow Patch Archaeology: Patterns Past and Present. *Arctic* 65(1):178–188.

Callanan, M. 2013 Melting Snow Patches Reveal Neolithic Archery. *Antiquity* 87(337):728–745.

Callanan, M. 2014a Out of the Ice: Glacial Archaeology in Central Norway. PhD thesis, NTNU Trondheim. Available at: https://brage.bibsys.no/xmlui/handle/11250/229726.

Callanan, M. 2014b Bronze Age Arrows from Norwegian Alpine Snow Patches. *Journal of Glacial Archaeology* 1:25–49.

Callanan, M. 2015 Chronological Patterns among Archaeological Finds from Snow Patches in Central Norway, 1914–2011. In *Exploitation of Outfield Resources: Joint Research at the University Museums of Norway*, edited by S. Indrelid, K. L. Hjelle, K. Stene, B. Berglund, M. Callanan, S. H. H. Kaland, and L. Stenvik. University Museum of Bergen, Bergen.

Callanan, M. 2016 Managing Frozen Heritage: Some Challenges and Responses. *Quaternary International* 402:72–79.

Christie, W. F. K. 1842 Spoer af Finske eller Lappiske Folks ophold i Oldtiden paa Høifjeldene i Bergens Stift. *Urda, et norsk-antiqvarisk-historisk tidsskrift* 2(4):408–409.

Finstad, E., and L. Pilø 2010 *Kulturminner og løsfunn ved isbreer og snøfonner i høyfjellet: Økt sårbarhet som følgje av nedsmelting—global oppvarming*. Kulturhistoriske skrifter 2010–1. Oppland fylkeskommune, Lillehammer.

Finstad, E., and L. Pilø 2011 Historien. In *Jotunheimen: Historien, maten, turene*, edited by E. Finstad, R. Marstein, L. Pilø, J. Stokstad, and A. Brimi, 10–63. Gyldendal, Oslo.

Finstad, E., and M. Vedeler 2008 En bronsealdersko fra Jotunheimen. *Viking* 71:61–70.

Hagen, A. 1959 Vassdragsreguleringer og høyfjellsarkeologi: Synspunkter og resultater i forbindelse med undersøkelsene i 1958 i Vest-Telemark. *Universitetets Oldsaksamling Årbok 1956–57*, 98–150. Universitetets Oldsaksamling, Oslo.

Hagen, A. 1997 *Gåten om Kong Raknes Grav*. Cappelen, Oslo.

Hagen, A. 2002 *Et arkeologisk liv*. Primitive Tider, Oslo.

Hansen, A. 1904 *Landnåm i Norge: En utsigt over bosætningens historie*. W. C. Fabritius, Kristiania.

Hansen, G. 2017 Domestic and Exotic Materials in Early Medieval Norwegian Towns: An Archaeological Perspective on Production, Procurement and Consumption. In *Viking-Age Transformations: Trade, Craft and Resources in Western Scandinavia*, edited by Z. T. Glørstad and K. Loftsgarden, 59–94. Routledge, London.

Hofseth, E. H. 1980 *Fjellressursenes betydning i yngre jernalders økonomi: Sammenlignende studie av bygdene øst og vest for vannskillet i Nord-Gudbrandsdal*. AmS-Skrifter 5, Arkeologisk Museum i Stavanger, Stavanger.

Hougen, B. 1947 *Fra seter til gård*. Norsk Arkeologisk Selskap, Oslo.

Hufthammer, A. K., O. F. Bratbak, and S. Indrelid 2011 A Study of Remains and Butchery Patterns from Medieval Mass-Hunting of Reindeer in the South Norwegian Mountain Districts. *Quaternary International* 238:55–62.

Indrelid, S. 1973 *Hein 33—En steinalderboplass på Hardangervidda: Forsøk på kulturell og kronologisk analyse*. Årbok for Universitetet i Bergen. Humanistiske serie 1972, 1. Universitetet i Bergen, Bergen.

Indrelid, S. 1994 *Fangstfolk og bønder i fjellet: Bidrag til Hardangerviddas førhistorie 8500–2500 år før nåtid*. Universitetets Oldsaksamling Skrifter. Ny rekke 17. Universitetets Oldsaksamling, Oslo.

Indrelid, S. 2009 *Arkeologiske undersøkelser i vassdrag: Faglig program for Sør-Norge*. Riksantikvaren, Oslo.

Indrelid, S. 2014 *Oppdagelser på Hardangervidda*. Nord 4 forlag, Kvinherad.

Indrelid, S., and A. K. Hufthammer 2011 Medieval Mass Trapping of Reindeer at the Hardangervidda Mountain Plateau, South Norway. *Quaternary International* 238:44–54.

Indrelid, S., A. K. Hufthammer, and K. Røed 2007 Fangstanlegget på Sumtangen, Hardangervidda—utforskningen gjennom 165 år. *Viking* 70:125–154.

Indrelid, S., K. L. Hjelle, K. Stene, B. Berglund, M. Callanan, S. H. H. Kaland, and L. F. Stenvik (eds.) 2015 *Exploitation of Outfield Resources: Joint Research at the University Museums of Norway*. University Museum of Bergen, Bergen.

Indrelid, S., and D. Moe 1983 Februk på Hardangervidda i yngre steinalder. *Viking* 46:36–71.

Johansen, A. B. 1970 *Høyfjellsfunn ved Lærdalsvassdraget*. Den teoretiske bakgrunn og det første analyseforsøk. Universitetetsforlaget, Bergen.

Johansen, A. B. 1973 Iron Production as a Factor in the Settlement History of the Mountain Valleys Surrounding Hardangervidda. *Norwegian Archaeological Review* 6(2):84–101.

Johansen, A. B. 1978 *Høyfjellsfunn ved Lærdalsvassdraget II: Naturbruk og tradisjonssammenhenger i et sør-norsk villreinområde i steinalder*. Universitetetsforlaget, Bergen.

Johansen, A. B. 1993 Hardangerviddaprosjeketet: Hensikt og resultater. *Heimen: lokalhistorisk tidsskrift* 30:21–29.

Kvamme, M., J. Berge, and P. E. Kaland 1992 *Vegetasjonshistoriske undersøkelser i Nyset-Steggjevassdragene*. Arkeologiske Rapporter 17, Historisk Museum, Universitetet i Bergen 17. Bergen.

Lie, R. W. 1992 Osteologisk materiale. In *Arkeologiske undersøkelser i Nyset-Steggjevassdragene 1981–87*, edited by T. Bjørgo, S. Kristoffersen, and C. Prescott, 320–327. Arkeologiske Rapporter 16. Historisk Museum, Universitetet i Bergen, Bergen.

Loftsgarden, K. 2017 Marknadsplassar omkring Hardangervidda: ein arkeologisk og historisk analyse av innlandets økonomi og nettverk i vikingtid og mellomalder. Unpublished PhD thesis, University of Bergen.

Loftsgarden, K., M. Ramstad, and F.-A. Stylegar 2017 The Skeid and Other Assemlies in the Norwegian "Mountain Land." In *Viking-Age Transformations: Trade, Craft and Resources in Western Scandinavia*, edited by Z. T. Glørstad and K. Loftsgarden, 232–249. Routledge, London.

Martens, I. 1988 Vassdragsundersøkelsen: en vitamininnsprøytning for norsk arkeologi? In *Festskrift til Anders Hagen*, edited by S. Indrelid, S.H.H. Kaland, and B. Solberg, 40–49. Arkeologiske Skrifter Historisk Museum 4. Historisk Museum, Universitetet i Bergen. Bergen.

Martens, I., and A. Hagen 1961 *Arkeologiske undersøkelser langs elv og vann*. Norske Oldfunn 10. Universitetets Oldsaksamling, Oslo.

Martinsen, J. 2015 Unmoving Ice Patches and Instances of Biased Recovery Patterns. *Journal of Glacial Archaeology* 2:51–72.

Melheim, L. 2012a Reconsidering a Periphery: Scenarios of Copper Production in Southern Norway. In *Local Societies, Identities and Responses: The Bronze Age in Northern Europe*, edited by N. Anfinset and M. Wrigglesworth, 89–107. Equinox, London.

Melheim, L. 2012b Towards a New Understanding of Late Neolithic Norway: The Role of Metal and Metalworking. In *Becoming European: The Transformation of Third Millennium Northern and Western Europe*, edited by C. Prescott and H. Glørstad, 70–81. Oxbow Books, Oxford.

Melheim, L. 2015 *Recycling Ideas: Bronze Age Metal Production in Southern Norway*. BAR International Series 2715. Archaeopress, Oxford.

Melheim, L., and C. Prescott 2016 Exploring New Territories—Expanding Frontiers: Bowmen and Prospectors on the Scandinavia Peninsula in the 3rd–2nd Millennia BC. In *Comparative Perspectives on Past Colonisation, Maritime Interaction and Cultural Integration*, edited by L. Melheim, H. Glørstad, and Z. T. Glørstad. New Directions in Anthropological Archaeology, Equinox Books, Sheffield.

Mikkelsen, E. 1989 *Fra jeger til bonde: Utviklingen av jordbrukssamfunn i Telemark i steinalder og bronsealder*. Universitetets Oldsaksamling Skrifter. Ny rekke 11. Universitetets Oldsaksamling, Oslo.

Mjærum, A., and E. K. Friis 2016 Epilog: Noen pessimistiske tanker om tilstanden til kulturminnene ved våre fjellvann. In *Fjellfisket i fortiden: Årtusener med svømmende rikdom*, edited by A. Mjærum and E. U. Wammer, 229–237. Portal forlag, Kristiansand.

Mjærum, A., and E. U. Wammer (eds.) 2016 *Fjellfiske i fortiden: Årtusener med svømmende rikdom*. Portal forlag, Kristiansand.

Munch, P. A. 1852 *Det norske Folks Historie: Første Deel. 1ste Bind*. Chr. Tønsbergs Forlag, Christiania.

Nesje, A., L. H. Pilø, E. Finstad, B. Solli, V. Wangen, R. S. Ødegård, K. Isaksen, E. N. Støren, D. I. Bakke, and L. Andreassen 2012 The Climatic Significance of Artefacts Related to Prehistoric Reindeer Hunting Exposed at Melting Ice Patches in Southern Norway. *The Holocene* 22(4):485–496.

Odner, K. 1969 *Ullshelleren i Valldalen, Røldal: En studie i økologiske tilpasninger på grunnlag av et forhistorisk arkeologisk materiale*. Årbok for Universitetet i Bergen. Humanistiske serie 1969, 1. Universitetet i Bergen, Bergen.

Pilø, L. H., E. Finstad, C. Bronk Ramsey, J. R. P. Martinsen, B. Solli, A. Nesje, V. Wangen, M. Callanan, and J. H. Barrett 2018 The Chronology of Reindeer Hunting on Norway's Highest Ice Patches. *Royal Society Open Science*:1–10.

Pilø, L. H., J. H. Barrett, T. Eiken, E. Finstad, S. Grønning, J. R. Post-Melbye, A. Nesje, J. Rosvold, B. Solli, and R. S. Ødegård 2020a Interpreting Archaeological Site-Formation Processes at a Mountain Ice Patch: A Case Study from Langfonne, Norway. *The Holocene* 3(3):469–482.

Pilø, L. H., E. Finstad, and J. H. Barrett 2020b Crossing the Ice: An Iron Age to Medieval Mountain Pass at Lendbreen, Norway. *Antiquity* 94:437–454.

Prescott, C. 1991 *Kulturhistoriske undersøkelser i Skrivarhelleren*. Med et bidrag av Eli-Christine Soltvedt. Arkeologiske rapporter 14, Historisk Museum, Universitet i Bergen.

Prescott, C. 1995 *From Stone Age to Iron Age: A Study from Sogn, Western Norway*. British Archaeological Reports, international series, 603. Oxford.

Prescott, C. 2006 Copper Production in Bronze Age Norway? In *Historien i Forhistorien: Festskrift til Einar Østmo på 60-årsdagen*, edited by H. Glørstad, B. Skar, and D. Skre, 183–190. Kulturhistorisk Museum, Universitet i Oslo, skrifter nr. 4. Oslo.

Prescott, C. 2013 Archaeology vs. Science: Or Taking Knowledge-Based Communication Seriously? *Current Swedish Archaeology* 21:39–44.

Prescott, C., and H. Glørstad 2015 Expanding 3rd Millennium Transformations: Norway. In *The Bell Beaker Transition in Europe: Mobility and Local Evolution during the 3rd Millennium BC*, edited by M. P. P. Martinéz and L. Salanova, 77–87. Oxbow Books, Oxford.

Prescott, C., and L. Melheim 2017 Textiles from the Peripheries? Upland Evidence from Norway. In *New Perspectives on the Bronze Age: Proceedings of the 13th Nordic Bronze Age Symposium Held in Gothenburg 9th to 13th June 2015*, edited by S. Bergerbrant and A. Wessman, 313–326. Archaeopress, Oxford.

Prescott, C., and L. Melheim 2018 Arkeologiske undersøkelser i Skrivarhelleren (gnr 9 /bnr 1) 2013 og 2015. Unpublished report. Bergen Museum, Universitetet i Bergen.

Prøsch-Danielsen, L., and A. Simonsen 2000 Palaeoecological Investigations towards the Reconstruction of the History of Forest Clearance and Coastal Heathlands in Southwestern Norway. *Vegetation History and Archaeobotany* 9:189–204.

Randers, K. 1986 *Breheimenundersøkelsene 1982–1984. I: Høyfjellet*. Arkeologiske Rapporter 17, Historisk Museum, Universitetet i Bergen 10. Bergen.

Reinton, L. 1955 *Sæterbruket i Noreg I*. Inst. For saml. Kulturforskning. Oslo.

Reinton, L. 1961 *Sæterbruket i Noreg III*. Inst. For saml. Kulturforskning. Oslo.

Reitan, G. 2006 Rapport fra arkeologisk utgravning. Aursjøprosjektet. Boplassfunn: samiske ildsteder fra vikingtid/middelalder og boplasser fra bronsealder. KHM, Fornminneseksjonen, Universitetet i Oslo, Oslo.

Selsing, L. 2016 *Intentional Fire Management in the Holocene with Emphasis on Hunter-Gatherers in the Mesolithic in South Norway*. AmS-Skrifter 25. Arkeologisk Museum i Stavanger, Stavanger.

Simonsen, P. 1987 *Altakraftverkene: Kulturhistoriske registreringer og utgravinger 1982*. Tromura, kulturhistorie 8. Tromsø Museum, Tromsø.

Skjølsvold, A. 1969 Et keltertids klebersteinsbrudd fra Kvikne. *Viking* 33:139–199.

Skogstrand, L. 2020 *Arkeologiske undersøkelser i vassdrag. Faglig program for Midt- og Nord-Norge*. Riksantikvaren, Oslo.

Solheim, S. 2012 Lokal praksis og fremmed opphav: Arbeidsdeling, sosiale relasjoner og differensiering i østnorsk steinalder. Unpublished PhD thesis, Faculty of Humanities. University of Oslo, Norway.

Solli, B. 2018 Reindeer Hunting, Materiality, Entanglement and Society in Norway. *Journal of Glacial Archaeology*, 1–26.

Steinsland, G. 2014 *Dovrefjell i tusen år: Mytene, historien og diktningen*. Vigmostad & Bjørke, Oslo.

Stene, K. 2014 *I randen av taigaen: bosetning og ressursutnyttelse i jernalder og middelalder i Østerdalen*. Gråfjellprosjektet 4. Portal forlag, Kristiansand.

Stene, K., I. Holm, and E. Svensson (eds.) 2009 *Liminal Landscapes: Beyond the Concepts of "Marginality" and "Periphery."* Unipub forlag, Oslo.

Stene, K., and V. Wangen 2017 The Uplands: The Deepest of Forests and the Highest of Mountains: Resource Exploitation and Landscape Management in the Viking Age and Early Middle Ages in Southern Norway. In *Viking-Age Transformations: Trade, Craft and Resources in Western Scandinavia*, edited by Z. T. Glørstad and K. Loftsgarden, 160–187. Routledge, London.

Svensen, H. 2012 *Bergtatt: Fjellenes historie og fascinasjonen for det opphøyde*. Aschehoug, Oslo.

Svensson, E. 2015 Upland Living: The Scandinavian Shielings and Their European Sisters. In *Nordic Middle Ages—Artefacts, Landscape and Society: Essays in Honour of Ingvild Øye on Her 70th birthday*, edited by I. Baug, J. Larsen, and S. S. Mygland, 289–300. University of Bergen Archaeological Series 8, University of Bergen, Bergen.

Thomsen, C. J. 1836 *Ledetraad til Nordisk Oldkundskab*. Möllers bogtrykkeri, Copenhagen.

Vedeler, M., and L. B. Jørgensen 2013 Out of the Norwegian Glaciers: Lendbreen—A Tunic from the Early First Millennium AD. *Antiquity* 87(337):788–801.

CHAPTER TWELVE

Comparison between Medieval and Modern Landscape

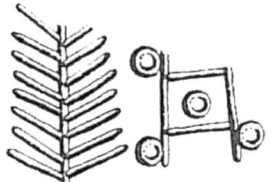

The Impact of Pastoral Activities in South Greenland

Emilie Gauthier

Abstract *Agriculture in southern Greenland has a two-phases history: with the Norse, who first settled and farmed the region between 985 AD and ca. 1450 AD, and with the recent reintroduction of sheep farming (1920 AD to the present). The agricultural sector in Greenland is expected to grow over the next century as anticipated climate warming extends the length of the growing season and increases productivity. This chapter tries to demonstrate the relative impacts of modern and Norse agricultural activities. Pollen, non-pollen palynomorphs (NPPs), sediment mass accumulation rates, diatoms and chironomids analyses, and stable isotopes of nitrogen provide a comprehensive history of both phases of agriculture and their associated impacts on the landscape. Our findings question the veracity of the catastrophic scenario of overgrazing and land degradation considered to have been the major factor responsible for Norse settlement demise. They also shed light on the sustainability of modern practices and their consequences for the future of agriculture in Greenland.*

With a surface area of 2,166,086 sq km, Greenland is the largest island in the world. The polar cap covers most of the country and only 410,449 sq km of land are free of ice. This Arctic territory has long attracted researchers: ethnologists, paleoclimatologists, geologists and biologists are numerous among them. However, very few have considered vegetation history of this icy zone. Furthermore, what is the value of studying human impact on the environment when it is known that Greenland was belatedly populated (around 2500 BC) by hunter-gatherers originating in North America? Surprisingly, Norse farmers have ventured into these regions, which were a priori unwelcoming for them, during the centuries of the medieval climatic optimum (Figure 12.1). Beyond the romantic aspect of

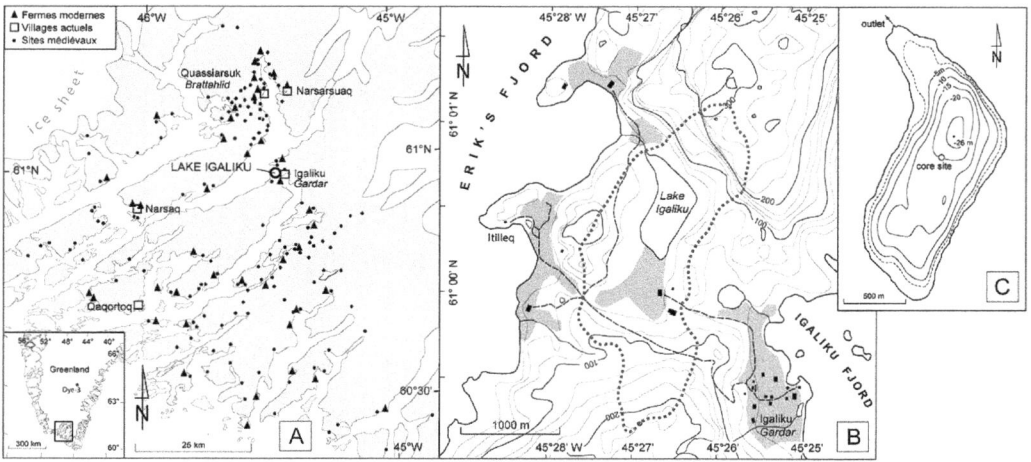

Figure 12.1. Localization of Lake Igaliku. A. Map of the Eastern settlement in South Greenland. Black dots represent Norse archaeological sites and black triangles, recent farms. B. Map of the catchment of Lake Igaliku (drawn in dotted line). C. Bathymetry of Lake Igaliku and localization of the coring.

the Norse adventure in southern Greenland (which begins with Erik the Red in 985 and ends around 1450), this epic is a reference model particularly adapted to the study of the relations between human communities and environment, from conquest to abandonment. At the dawn of the twentieth century, agriculture, now practiced by Inuit people, was reintroduced in the form of sheep breeding. This development of agropastoral practices in two chronologically distinct phases then appears as original in comparison with what happened in Europe. In the old world, paleoenvironmental analyses showed that the impact of man on the environment began as early as the Neolithic period. The process was continuous, or almost, and today's landscapes are the result of several millennia of successive land uses. The Greenlandic pattern of colonization by farmers is much less complex and, as is the case in European mountainous areas, farming activities constrained by climate are limited to herbivorous breeding. In this case, the Greenlandic scenario appears to be particularly well adapted to a comparison, to a round trip between these two phases of activities. It is this "retro-observation," particularly well documented, which makes it of interest to study agriculture history in Greenland.

Since 2006, the chrono-environment laboratory in Besançon has been interested in the development of agriculture on the southern coast of Greenland (Igaliku region, 61° 00'N, 45° 26'W, 15 masl). Three main objectives have guided the study:

- Understand the mechanisms of interaction between climatic and anthropogenic forcing on the sedimentary dynamics of lake systems whose catchment had been exploited by Norse farmers and/or contemporary farmers;

- study the relations between man and the environment from conquest to abandonment, especially during the medieval period;
- using the results of the twentieth century, based on paleoenvironmental analyses and precise data (temperature, livestock, etc.), measure the environmental changes linked to the influence of medieval agriculture.

Unlike researchers who have already addressed environmental aspects of these former Greenlandic farming activities (Edwards et al. 2008; Schofield et al. 2007, 2008, 2010; Schofield and Edwards 2011; Ledger et al. 2013; Ledger et al. 2017), we have chosen to study lake sediments instead of sequences from peatlands. Although more accessible, they are often disturbed by changes in water level, effects of frost, and where these sites are very close to habitats, as is often the case, by human and herbivores' impact.

Land Use under Constraint

At a lower latitude than Icelandic agricultural areas (between 64 and 66° N), southern Greenland does not benefit from a milder climate. On the contrary, Iceland takes advantage of the direct thermal input of the North Atlantic marine current, whereas Greenland temperatures are influenced by the descent of cold and iceberg polar waters from the East Greenland Current (Masson-Delmotte et al., 2012). However, Southern Greenland, where the Norse Eastern settlement was established in 985, has a much more favorable climate than the rest of the island thanks to the temperate supply of the Irminger current flowing from the North Atlantic. The meteorological data (Cappelen et al. 2001) of the Narsarsuaq station (17 km north of Igaliku) shows average temperatures of 0.9 °C, nearly 195 days of frost per year, and annual precipitation of 615 mm. With this cold and relatively dry climate, southern Greenland remains a very difficult region to practice agriculture. However, climatic conditions are even more unfavorable in the so-called Norse Western settlement, which is located near the Arctic Circle. The winter period is more severe, with seven to nine months of the year under cover of snow and ice. On the other hand, summer days are longer than in low latitudes, which nevertheless allows mild temperatures, especially at the end of fjords where summer temperatures can sometimes exceed 20 °C.

These difficult climatic conditions have conditioned not only the type of agriculture practiced but also its evolution during the five centuries of Norse settlement (Berglund 1986). Early settlers developed an economy based almost exclusively on pastoralism (Gad 1970; Jones 1986; Schofield et al. 2007), despite a few cereal-growing experiments revealed by paleoenvironmental analyses (Buckland et al. 2009; Edwards et al. 2008; Schofield et al. 2007; Ledger et al. 2013). They have imported domestic animals usually bred in Iceland: cattle, sheep, goats, horses, dogs, and pigs (chicken are not represented in the archaeozoological fauna). In South Greenland, where grasslands can only be grazed four to five months a year, during winter survival of herbivores depends on a supply of forage. This is particularly true for cattle that have to be kept at the barn for at least six to seven months during the winter and require about 2.5 tons of fodder per head, that is, about 1 ha of grassland. Goats and sheep, more resistant to the Greenlandic climate and especially less greedy, were quickly favored (Dugmore et al. 2005). Due to the short growing season, the production and harvesting of sufficient forage for wintering herbivores was at the center of the settlers' concerns. To spread pastures and cultivated land, they cleared the "Greenlandic forest" composed mainly of tree birch (*Betula pubescens*, only found in sheltered areas of southern Greenland), dwarf birches (*Betula glandulosa*), and arctic willows (*Salix glauca*).

This region is also subject to foehn wind. These warm, dry winds of gravity origin can flow from the ice sheet for several days and cause catastrophic droughts for agricultural production. Some authors consider summer drought, rather than the shortness of the vegetative season, to be the major constraint faced by the Scandinavian colonies (Nørlund and Roussell 1929). The lack of water, coupled with the draining nature of the soil, made irrigation a necessity (Adderley and Simpson 2006), as evidenced by the remains of canals discovered at numerous sites, such as Garðar Igaliku (Arneborg 2005). In order to optimize the productive potential of the colonized areas, the Norse settlers also practiced fertilization (Buckland et al. 2009) and developed the practice of transhumance. Structures of simple construction, related to Icelandic and Norwegian sæters, were thus discovered. The Norwegian term "sæter" refers to groups of pens and shelters used during summer transhumance (*sæterbruk*). The herds were then grazed for pasture, while the land near the farms, fertilized and irrigated, was preserved for the production of fodder for the winter. Some sæters were to be used as a unit of milk production, and enclosures permitted the collection of manure while some others were only used to produce forage (Albrethsen and Keller 1986). However, survival couldn't rely solely on farming activities: hunting and fishing were an important part of the resources (Arneborg et al. 1999; Barlow et al. 1997; Dugmore et al. 2005; Massa et al. 2011).

Despite these constraints, settlements rapidly developed to ca. two thousand inhabitants (Lynnerup 1998; Madsen 2014). The eastern settlement quickly became important and included a cathedral, a dozen churches, and from 190 to 220 farms of various dimensions concentrated mainly around the fjords of Igaliku and Tunulliarfik (Eiriksfjord in medieval times). The size of the farms can be very spectacular, like that of the Garðar site (medieval name of Igaliku). This farm, founded by Erik the Red's daughter and her husband, is by far the most imposing of medieval Greenland. At least fifty-two archaeological structures, including numerous animal pens (Nørlund and Roussell 1929), have been surveyed. The count of the barns shows that the site could accommodate more than one hundred head of cattle, not to mention goats and sheep. The site is strategically located in the center of the eastern settlement, upstream of the Igaliku Fjord and only separated from the Tunulliarfik Fjords by a small pass easily accessible by boat. This location probably explains why the Norwegian clergy established the Greenlandic diocese (Arneborg 2007). These rich historical and archaeological data have motivated our choice to concentrate our research on this region in the first place.

The Norse Abandonment

The chronology of the Norse Eastern settlement demise is less precise than the settlement history and still subject to debate (Arneborg 2015; Diamond 2005; Dugmore et al. 2007).

An episcopal emissary mentions the abandonment of the Western settlement as early as the year 1350 (Schofield et al. 2019). The last written testimony of the presence of the Scandinavians in the Eastern settlement is a letter from 1409 announcing a wedding celebrated in the church of Hvalsey (Qaqortoq region) the previous year.

Among the explanations given for the depopulation of the medieval Greenland population are climate change (Barlow et al. 1997; Dansgaard et al. 1975; Stuiver et al. 1995), decline in trade links with Iceland and Europe, European piracy raids, conflicts with Inuit, and congenital infertility and epidemics (Diamond 2005; McGovern 2000). Authors often agree on the primordial role of the climatic deterioration during the Little Glacial Age. The cold and increasing occurrence of storms caused a fall in agricultural yields, isolated the colonies of Europe, and cut off the Labrador woodland route.

For a long time, little was known about the evolution of land use and its adaptation to the first impact of the Little Ice Age. On this subject, two schools with apparently paradoxical theories clashed. The first have argued for the destruction of resources caused by the excessive development of sheep flocks, which would have led to a very significant degradation of the vegetation cover leading to catastrophic soil erosion (e.g., Fredskild 1992; Diamond 2005; Orlove 2005). This end, based more on speculation than on physical evidence, seemed unlikely and many studies have shown evidence of an adaptation of agropastoral practices and food supply to environmental conditions (e.g., Arneborg 2015; Jackson et al. 2018). However, it still finds an echo in the context of the current media coverage of environmental problems.

Many researchers now refer to the reorganization of the Norse economy from agropastoralism to hunting and fishing. The analysis of the archeozoological collections accumulated during the excavations is rich in teachings and shows, on several sites, an evolution of the meat supply between the beginning and the end of the colonization (Arneborg et al. 1999, 2012). It appears that pig, poorly adapted to climatic conditions, disappeared rapidly from Greenland. For the same reasons, herds of cows gradually decreased in favor of sheep and goats. These changes in husbandry practices were accompanied by an increasing use of wild resources, as evidenced by the increase in seal, caribou, and bird remains in archaeological sites. These findings are corroborated by ^{13}C isotopic analysis of human bones, which indicates that Greenlanders were increasing their consumption of marine food resources during the thirteenth and fourteenth centuries. These results indicate that the share of the marine food of the populations increased from 20 percent at the beginning of the occupation to almost 80 percent toward 1450, showing the increasing importance of sealing and fishing.

Despite cooling, the Norse succeeded in adapting to their environment by changing their diet. However, the evolution of the climate led to the weakening of a socioenvironmental system close to its limits. As evocated by Arneborg (2015:269), Norse demise was probably more complex than the result of a simple climate forcing.

> Ultimately, the Norse Greenlanders fell victim to both major environmental and global economic changes, and the most obvious answer to the declining years would have been to emigrate. From the middle of the fourteenth century both Iceland and Norway had suffered greatly from several diseases that had diminished the population substantially and left farms deserted (e.g., Orrman 1997). New inhabitants would have been welcomed.

The Contribution of Sedimentary Archives

In order to perceive the real impact of these Norse farmers on their environment, our approach is resolutely multidisciplinary and integrates biotic (pollen, spores, diatoms, chironomids . . .) as well as abiotic proxies (sedimentology, geochemistry . . .). Our recent studies on Lake Igaliku, located at the very center of the Eastern settlement, highlight human impact in different ways, depending on the proxy discussed (Bichet et al. 2013; Gauthier et al. 2010; Guillemot et al. 2015; Massa et al. 2012a and b; Millet et al. 2014; Perren et al. 2012). A robust chronology, based on 18 ^{14}C dates, ^{210}Pb, and ^{137}Cs measurements, provides a very accurate assessment of changes in vegetation and detrital fluxes in lake sediments. Palynology (pollen and spores) shows the first human impact on vegetation just before 1000 AD, with a decrease in pollen values of white birch, the only tree in Greenland (other trees are considered shrubs). At the same time, coprophilous fungal spores increase, indicating grazing pressure (Davis and Shafer 2006; Van Geel and Aptroot 2006; Gauthier et al. 2010). From the middle of the twelfth century, the percentages of *Rumex acetosa* type increased. Sorrel is quite common in grazed environments and is traditionally considered an anthropogenic indicator (e.g., Behre 1981). In Greenland, this nonindigenous taxa was unintentionally introduced by Norse (Fredskild 1973). At Igaliku, this plant took nearly one hundred years to establish and grow (Gauthier et al. 2010). Sediment analysis has been used to quantitatively reconstruct the erosion generated by farmers and/or climate change. The introduction of livestock and the creation of hay meadows were the cause of an acceleration of erosion that reached up to 10 mm per century, which is twice as high as natural erosion. A large number of biogeochemical parameters (Ti, diatom concentration, C / N ratio, δ13C and δ15N . . .) confirms the anthropogenic origin of this erosion. However, by ca. 1300, the spores of coprophilous fungi and erosion decreased. Climatic reconstruction curves based on ^{18}O analysis in ice cores (Kaufman et al. 2009) and the study of chinomids spectra of the lake (Millet et al. 2014) perfectly show a cooling phase. These results cast doubt on the scenario of medieval overgrazing, which, leading to permanent land degradation, would have been the major factor in the abandonment of the colonies (Diamond 2005). Diatom analysis also suggests that land use development in the catchment has not affected the lake ecosystem (Millet et al. 2014; Perren et al. 2012); the lake remained oligotrophic throughout the Norse period. Although the tree cover regenerated, sorrel remained in the environment after the disappearance of Norse activities, showing incomplete plant resilience.

Agriculture Today and Tomorrow

The upper part of the Lake Igaliku sequence has perfectly recorded the recent events of the twentieth century and the beginning of the twenty-first century. Thus, the reintroduction of sheep at the beginning of the twentieth century had effects quite similar to those observed during the Norse period: the percentages of birch (*Betula*), willow (*Salix*), and juniper (*Juniperus*) decreased, while *Rumex acetosa* type increased. Coprophilous fungi spores reappeared and erosion slowly increased; however, the lake remained oligotrophic until the end of the 1970s. The intensification of agricultural practices in the 1980s (Egede 1982) was first recorded by sedimentological analysis: Intensive mechanization results in an unprecedented erosion rate of up to 23 mm per century, five times higher than natural conditions. Approximately 500 kg of nitrogen fertilizer per ha are currently used each year to foster forage production around Lake Igaliku (Miki Egede, personal communication). At the same time, the effluents of increasingly large sheepfolds go directly into the lake. The diatoms clearly show an unprecedented upheaval of the lake ecosystem: the lake is now mesotrophic for the first time in its existence for nearly ten thousand years (date of the beginning of the sedimentary sequence in Lake Igaliku; Massa et al. 2012b).

All biotic and abiotic proxies studied show that Norse land use had little effect on the environment. The agriculture developed from the 1920s to the 1980s resulted in an impact quite similar to that of the Norse period. Fortunately, data of prime importance are available for the modern period: meteorological records and the evolution of the sheep population. During this period, despite global warming, some very cold winters caused a spectacular mortality of sheep (for example, in 1967, 60 percent of the sheep died due to a very long winter). In order to mitigate these annual variations in climate, Greenland authorities have decided to set up modern agriculture using winter stabling. Fodder requirements have increased. New plots were created and seeded; the growth of forage has been greatly accelerated.

Retro-Observation of Farming Activities and Climatic Conditions

From the medieval period to now, climate forcing has greatly encouraged or constrained the life of Greenlandic farming societies (Figure 12.2). The first three centuries of medieval set-

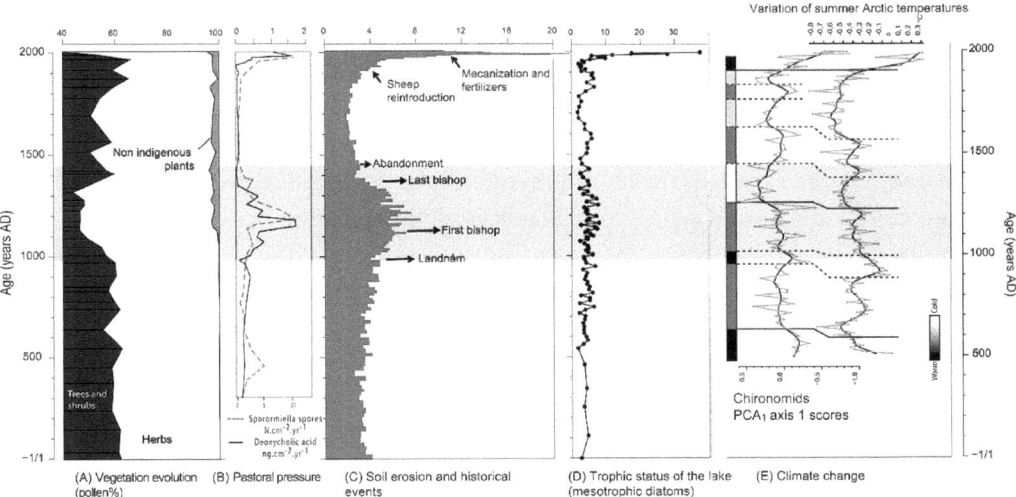

Figure 12.2. Synthetic figure of the different proxies analyzed over the last two millennia: A. Simplified pollen diagram (in percentage) of the period of the last two millennia. B. Evolution of pastoral pressure markers with the desoxycholic acid and *Sporormiella* influx (Guillemot et al. 2015). C. Soil erosion and the main historical events of the Norse period (Massa et al. 2012a and b). D. The trophic status of the lake with the curve (in percentage) of mesotrophic diatoms (Perren et al. 2012). E. Climate change with PCA axis 1 of chironomids and changes in summer Arctic temperatures (Millet et al. 2014).

tlement, before the beginnings of the Little Ice Age, and the agricultural development of the 1920s to 1980s, are quite similar from an anthropic and climatic point of view. Although the historical data are numerous, the contemporary period is even better documented, especially with regard to brutal climatic events. Long and very cold winters (like that of 1967) certainly existed during the medieval period (Madsen 2014). The very high-resolution analysis of the period 1920–1980 should therefore make it possible to define markers (biotic or abiotic) of these climatic accidents and their consequences on agropastoral activities.

During the summers of 2011 and 2013, fieldwork allowed us to carry out a coring campaign in various lakes, to check the different types of impact: lakes outside the archaeological context and outside pastoral areas, lakes with Norse ruins and without a recent farm, lakes comprising both Norse ruins and recent farms in their catchment area. Chironomids analysis (Millet et al. 2014) has highlighted the local climatic fluctuations of the last millennium. The climatic transition of the beginning of the fourteenth century, which is concomitant with the end of the medieval farming expansion, is particularly evident. The assemblages of chironomids vary according to climatic conditions, at least until 1980, with the recent period being subject to anthropogenic and climatic forcing accentuated by the association of a mechanized agriculture with global warming. A transfer function would enable the comparison of the temperatures of the twentieth century and those of the medieval period. Other parameters have been tested, for example, molecular biomarkers (Guillemot et al. 2015, 2016). The bile acid markers of sheep offer a good means of monitoring pastoral pressure evolution, already demonstrated by coprophilous fungi spores. Unfortunately we only have a global evolution of Greenlandic sheep number; the variation of livestock at a local scale (e.g., farms catchment) is not currently accessible for the twentieth century. So it is currently impossible to approximate the number of livestock that have grazed in these catchment basins during the medieval period. However research on the topic is still ongoing.

The recent farming development in South Greenland offers a unique model allowing an original "retro-observation" of practices. The story is discontinuous: for nearly five centuries, the environment had the opportunity to regenerate. Farmers of the twentieth century have faced an ecological situation almost comparable (with the exception of nonnative plants) with the pristine landscape that greeted Norse arrival a millennia ago. The Greenlandic model has the particularity that it not only allows us to compare a current state with an original state in order to understand the evolution of an ecosystem submitted to human impact; it offers the rare opportunity to compare two states, their respective evolution, and human impact on the environment. Even better, the period from 1920 to 1980 can be used to improve our perception of the medieval period. If all these data allow us to better understand the complex interactions between climate, pastoralism, and landscape shaping during the medieval period, they should also inform us about the sustainability of current farming activities and their consequences for the future of agriculture and the environment in Greenland.

Contribution of Retro-Observation to Cultural Heritage

Greenland has two kinds of cultural heritage, the Norse and the Paleoeskimo/Inuit heritages. If southern Greenland landscape has been recently shaped by human activities, it would be an error to think that this country remains entirely untamed. Human activities such as mining and industrial fishing have changed the ecosystems, and global warming has put in danger a great number of archaeological sites. Among the six thousand sites surveyed in Greenland, a great number are threatened by erosion, thawing permafrost, shrub expansion, and, in south Greenland, by the extension of hay fields (Harmsen et al. 2018).

In 1955, Claude Lévi-Strauss remarkably wrote about the multimillennial interactions between man and the environment, underlining the lack of discernment and lucidity of men in the landscapes they had created. His travels had enabled him to become aware of the difference that existed, for instance, between American and European landscapes:

> We know nothing of untamed Nature, our own landscape is entirely subject to our needs and desires. If it sometimes strikes us as untamed, it is either because—in our forest for instance—its change operates to a slower rhythm; or because—as in the mountains—the problems were of such complexity that Man has tackled them in detail rather than in one systematic assault. Such coherence as has resulted from these innumerable individual initiatives now seems to share the original primitive character of the mountain world, whereas in fact it is due to an interlocking chain of decision and enterprises, each of which seemed at the time to be independent of others. . . . this sublime harmony, far from being the spontaneous expression of Nature herself, is the result of agreement long sought for between mankind and the site in question. What causes us to gape, in all simplicity, are the traces of our bygone enterprise.

This passage of *Tristes tropiques* (Lévi-Strauss 1961:98) admirably describes the progressive nature of these modifications and their near illegibility for man, who, through lack of comparative elements, is incapable of perceiving these environmental transformations. Palynologists, paleolimnologists, sedimentologists, and other paleoenvironmental scientists have long been studying the evolution of human–environment interactions through the study of multiyear sedimentary sequences. Are they retro-observing without knowing it? They probably are, with the difference that the notion of retro-observation places the current period at the center of concerns. It is not a matter of understanding these interactions over a specific period of our history, but rather of determining how these interactions ultimately led to the formation of the landscapes and living conditions. In rare cases, such as in Greenland, in a context of strong environmental forcing and when practices have changed little, the current period (in fact the subcurrent one) can be used as a reference to clarify or even quantify past activities. This should also be true in areas without major diversification in agriculture over time or with a specialization of agricultural activities (e.g., from subsistence poly-agriculture to exclusive pastoralism in mountainous area). As for more classical retro-observations, different temporalities can be envisaged: the decade, the century, or the millennia, everything depends on what researchers wish to show. It therefore seems more than necessary to define the spatial scale and the approach adopted, the means used and the aim to be achieved.

Acknowledgments

The 2006 and 2007 fieldwork and first analyses were funded by the University of Franche-Comté, the CNRS, the Burgundy region, and external contracts; the 2009 fieldwork was funded by the French Polar Institute; and the 2011, 2013, and ongoing analyses were funded by the Green Greenland ANR project, led by V. Masson-Delmotte, which brings together French and international partners (LSCE, Chrono-environnement, LGGE, LGP, UVSQ, Nîmes University, CNRM . . .). A special thanks to all my colleagues from Besançon and elsewhere working in Greenland, Vincent Bichet, Andrès Curras, Typhaine Guillemot, Charly Massa, Bianca Perren, Christophe Petit, and Hervé Richard.

References

Adderley, W. P., I. A. Simpson 2006 Soils and Palaeo-Climate Based Evidence for Irrigation Requirements in Norse Greenland. *Journal of Archaeological Science* 33:1666–1679.

Albrethsen, S. E., and C. Keller 1986 The Use of the "Saeter" in Medieval Norse Farming in Greenland. *Arctic Anthropology* 23:91–107.

Arneborg, J. 2005 Greenland Irrigation Systems on a West Nordic Background: An Overview of the Evidence of Irrigation Systems in Norse Greenland c. 980 and 1450 AD. In *Water Management in Medieval Rural Economy*, edited by J. Klápste, 137–145. Institute of Archaeology, Academy of Sciences of the Czech Republic, Ruralia V, Památky Archeologicke—Supplementum, Prague.

Arneborg, J. 2007 *Saga Trails—Brattahlid, Gardar, Hvalsey Fjord's Church and Herjolfnesnes: Four Chieftains' Farmsteads in the North Settlements of Greenland—A Visitor's Guidebook.* The National Museum of Denmark, Copenhagen.

Arneborg, J. 2015 Norse Greenland: Research into Abandonment. *Medieval Archaeology in Scandinavia and Beyond: History, Trends and Tomorrow*, 257–271.

Arneborg, J., J. Heinemeier, N. Lynnerup, H. L. Nielsen, N. Rud, and A. E. Sveinbjörnsdóttir 1999 Change of Diet of the Greenland Vikings Determined from Stable Carbon Isotope Analysis and 14C Dating of Their Bones. *Radiocarbon* 41:157–168.

Arneborg, J., N. Lynnerup, and J. Heinemeier 2012 Human Diet and Subsistence Patterns in Norse Greenland AD c. 980–AD c. 1450: Archaeological Interpretations. *Journal of the North Atlantic* 3:119–133.

Barlow, L. K., J. P. Sadler, A. E. J. Ogilvie, P. C. Buckland, T. Amorosi, J. H. Ingimundarson, P. Skidmore, A. J. Dugmore, and T. H. McGovern 1997 Interdisciplinary Investigations of the End of the Norse Western Settlement in Greenland. *The Holocene* 7:489–499.

Behre, K. E. 1981 The Interpretation of Anthropogenic Indicators in Pollen Diagrams. *Pollen and Spores* 23:225–245.

Berglund, J. 1986 The Decline of the Norse Settlements in Greenland. *Arctic Anthropology* 23:109–135.

Bichet, V., E. Gauthier, C. Massa, B. Perren, C. Petit, O. Matthieu, and H. Richard 2013 History and Impacts of South Greenland Farming Activities: An Insight from Lake Deposits. *Polar Record* 49(03):210–220.

Buckland, P. C., K. J. Edwards, E. Panagiotakopulu, and J. E. Schofield 2009 Palaeoecological and Historical Evidence for Manuring and Irrigation at Garðar (Igaliku), Norse Eastern Settlement, Greenland. *The Holocene* 19:105–116.

Cappelen, J., B. V. Jørgensen, E. V. Laursen, L. S. Stannius, and R. S. Thomsen 2001 The Observed Climate of Greenland, 1958–99: With Climatological Standard Normals, 1961–90. *DMI Technical Report* No. 00-18. Danish Meteorological Institute, Copenhagen.

Davis, O. K., and D. S. Shafer 2006 *Sporormiella* Fungal Spores, a Palynological Means of Detecting Herbivore Density. *Palaeogeography, Palaeoclimatology, Palaeoecology* 237:40–50.

Dansgaard, W., S. J. Johnsen, N. Reeh, N. Gundestrup, H. B. Clausen, and C. U. Hammer 1975 Climatic Changes, Norsemen and Modern Man. *Nature* 255:24–28.

Diamond, J. 2005 *Collapse: How Societies Choose to Fail or Survive*. Penguin Books, London.

Dugmore, A. J., M. J. Church, P. C. Buckland, K. J. Edwards, I. Lawson, T. H. McGovern, E. Panagiotakopulu, I. A. Simpson, P. Skidmore, and G. Sveinbjarnardóttir 2005 The Norse *Landnám* on the North Atlantic Islands: An Environmental Impact Assessment. *Polar Record* 41:21–37.

Dugmore, A. J., C. Keller, and T. H. McGovern 2007 Norse Greenland Settlement: Reflections on Climate Change, Trade, and the Contrasting Fates of Human Settlements in the North Atlantic Islands. *Arctic Anthropology* 44:12–36.

Edwards, K. J., J. E. Schofield, and D. Mauquoy 2008 High Resolution Paleoenvironmental and Chronological Investigations of Norse Landnám at Tasiusaq, Eastern Settlement, Greenland. *Quaternary Research* 69:1–15.

Egede, K. 1982 Detail Plan for fåreavlen i Sydgrønland. Printed report, Fåreavlskonsulenttjenesten, Upernaviarssuk.

Fredskild, B. 1973 Studies in the Vegetational History of Greenland. *Meddelelser om Grønland* 198(4):1–245.

Fredskild, B. 1992 Erosion and Vegetational Changes in South Greenland Caused by Agriculture. *Geografisk Tidsskrift-Danish Journal of Geography* 92:14–21.

Gad, F. 1970 *History of Greenland Vol. 1 Earliest Times to 1700*. Hurst, London.

Gauthier, E., V. Bichet, C. Massa, C. Petit, B. Vannière, and H. Richard 2010 Pollen and Non-pollen Palynomorph Evidence of Medieval Farming Activities in Southwestern Greenland. *Vegetation History and Archaeobotany* 19:427–438.

Guillemot, T., V. Bichet, E. Gauthier, R. Zocatelli, C. Massa, and H. Richard 2016 Environmental Responses of Past and Recent Agropastoral Activities on South Greenlandic Ecosystems through Molecular Biomarkers. *The Holocene*: 0959683616675811.

Guillemot, T., R. Zocatelli, V. Bichet, J. Jacob, C. Massa, C. Le Milbeau, H. Richard, and E. Gauthier 2015 Evolution of Pastoralism in Southern Greenland during the Last Two Millennia Reconstructed from Bile Acids and Coprophilous Fungal Spores in Lacustrine Sediments. *Organic Geochemistry* 81:40–44.

Harmsen, H., J. Hollesen, C. K. Madsen, B. Albrechtsen, M. Myrup, and H. Matthiesen 2018 A Ticking Clock? Preservation and Management of Greenland's Archaeological Heritage in the Twenty-First Century. *Conservation and Management of Archaeological Sites* 20:175–198.

Jackson, R., J. Arneborg, A. Dugmore, C. Madsen, T. McGovern, K. Smiarowski, and R. Streeter 2018 Disequilibrium, Adaptation, and the Norse Settlement of Greenland. *Human Ecology* 46:665–684.

Jones, G. 1986 *The Norse Atlantic Saga: Being the Norse Voyages of Discovery and Settlement to Iceland, Greenland, and North America*. Oxford University Press, New York.

Kaufman, D. S., D. P. Schneider, N. P. McKay, C. M. Ammann, R. S. Bradley, K. Briffa, G. H. Miller, B. L. Otto-Bliesner, J. T. Overpeck, B. M. Vinther, Arctic Lakes 2k Project Members, M. Abbott, Y. Axford, B. Bird, H. J. B. Birks, A. E. Bjune, J. Briner, T. Cook, M. Chipman, P. Francus, K. Gajewski, A. Geirsdottir, F. S. Hu, B. Kutchko, S. Lamoureux, M. Loso, G. MacDonald, M. Peros, D. Porinchu, C. Schiff, H. Seppa, and E. Thomas 2009 Recent Warming Reverses Long-Term Arctic Cooling. *Science* 325:1236–1239.

Ledger, P. M., K. J. Edwards, and E. J. Schofield 2013 Shieling Activity in the Norse Eastern Settlement: Palaeoenvironment of the "Mountain Farm," Vatnahverfi, Greenland. *The Holocene* 23:810822.

Ledger, P. M., K. J. Edwards, and E. J. Schofield 2017 Competing Hypotheses, Ordination and Pollen Preservation: Landscape Impacts of Norse Landnám in Southern Greenland. *Review of Palaeobotany and Palynology* 236:1–11.

Lévi-Strauss, C. 1961 *Tristes tropiques*. Translated by John Russel. Criterion Books, New York.

Lynnerup, N. 1998 *The Greenland Norse*. Museum Tusculanum Press, Copenhagen.

Madsen, Christian Koch 2014 Pastoral Settlement, Farming, and Hierarchy in Norse Vatnahverfi, South Greenland. University of Copenhagen, unpublished PhD thesis.

McGovern, T. H. 2000 The Demise of Norse Greenland. In *Vikings: The North Atlantic Sagas*, edited by W. W. Fitzburg and E. I. Ward, 327–339. Smithsonian Institution Press, Washington.

Massa, C., V. Bichet, E. Gauthier, P. Perren, O. Mathieu, C. Petit, F. Monna, J. Giraudeau, R. Losno, and H. Richard 2012a A 2,500-Year Record of Natural and Anthropogenic Soil Erosion in South Greenland. *Quaternary Sciences Reviews* 32:119–130.

Massa, C., B. Perren, E. Gauthier, V. Bichet, C. Petit, and H. Richard 2012b A 10 ka Record of Environmental Change from Lake Igaliku, South Greenland. *Journal of Palaeolimnology* 48(1):241–258.

Masson-Delmotte, V., M.-S. Seidenkrantz, E. Gauthier, V. Jomelli, G. Adalgeirsdottir, J. Arneborg, U. Bhatt, V. Bichet, B. Elberling, F. Gillet-Chaulet, M. van den Broeke, Hesselbjerg, J. Christensen, X. Fettweis, H. Gallee, C. Massa, B. Perren, C. Ritz, D. Swingedouw, A. de Vernal, B. Vinther, and D. A. Walker 2012 Greenland Climate Change: From the Past to the Future. *WIREs Climate Change 2012*, doi:10.1002/wcc.186.

Millet, L., C. Massa, V. Bichet, V. Frossard, S. Belle, and E. Gauthier, E. 2014 Anthropogenic versus Climatic Control in a High-Resolution 1,500-Year Chironomid Stratigraphy from a Southwestern Greenland Lake. *Quaternary Research* 81:193–202.

Nørlund, P., and A. Roussell 1929 Norse Ruins at Gardar: The Episcopal Seat of Medieval Greenland. *Meddelelser om Grønland* 76:1–171.

Perren, B., C. Massa, V. Bichet, E. Gauthier, O. Mathieu, C. Petit, and H. Richard 2012 A Paleoecological Perspective on 1,450 Years of Human and Climate Impacts in South Greenland. *The Holocene* 22(9):1025–1034.

Schofield, J. E., and K. J. Edwards 2011 Grazing Impacts and Woodland Management in Eriksfjord: Betula, Coprophilous Fungi and the Norse Settlement of Greenland. *Vegetation History and Archaeobotany* 20:181–197, DOI 10.1007/s00334-011-0281-7.

Schofield, J. E., K. J. Edwards, and C. Christensen 2008 Environmental Impacts around the Time of Norse Landnám in the Qorlortoq Valley, Eastern Settlement, Greenland. *Journal of Archaeological Science* 35:1643–1657.

Schofield, J. E., K. J. Edwards, and J. A. McMullen 2007 Modern Pollen–Vegetation Relationships in Subarctic Southern Greenland and the Interpretation of Fossil Pollen Data from the Norse Landnám. *Journal of Biogeography* 34:473–488.

Schofield, J. E., K. J. Edwards, T. M. Mighall, A. Martínez Cortizas, J. Rodríguez-Racedo, and G. Cook 2010 An Integrated Geochemical and Palynological Study of Human Impacts, Soil Erosion and Storminess from Southern Greenland since c. AD 1000. *Palaeogeography, Palaeoclimatology, Palaeoecology* 295:19–30.

Schofield, J. E., D. M. Pearce, D. W. Mair, B. R. Rea, J. M Lea, N. A. Kamenos, A. Nicholas, M. A. Schoenrock, D. I. Barr, and K. J. Edwards 2019 Pushing the Limits: Palynological Investigations at the Margin of the Greenland Ice Sheet in the Norse Western Settlement. *Environmental Archaeology*, 1–15.

Stuiver, M., M. Grootes, and T. F. Braziunas 1995 The GISP2 Delta 18O Climate Record of the Past 16,500 Years and the Role of the Sun, Ocean, and Volcanoes. *Quaternary Research* 44:341–354.

Van Geel, B., and A. Aptroot 2006 Fossil Ascomycetes in Quaternary Deposits. *Nova Hedwigia* 82:313–329.

Chapter Thirteen

Neolithic Penetration of the European Mid-Mountains

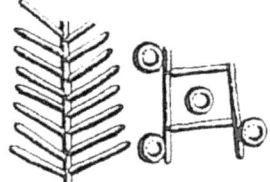

Pawel Valde-Nowak

Abstract *A survey of main views on the significance of European Mid-Mountains for early agrarian groups will be presented. Former proposals of exclusion of these terrains from the Neolithic ecumene will also be addressed. It will confront special characteristics of archaeological sources, settlement-geographical observation, ethnographic, and paleobotanical evidence. The chapter will also stress a bid of recognition of these terrains as a domain of seasonal moving of groups, most probably pastoral in character.*

One can easily show the entirely different face of archaeology of those terrains, if compared to the classic centers recognized explicitly by the casus of the chunks of fertile soils arisen out of the loess. The mentioned lugging can be explained with the ultimate form of the Neolithic settlement trails in the mountains.

In the last years the interest of Neolithic relics in the mountains has increased. More accurate results of palynological analysis played a large role in this. Archaeologists still better understand the utmost form of archaeological remnants from the Neolithic in the mountains. There is more evidence for penetration of such regions already in the Early Neolithic. Such findings, as well as in the Late Neolithic, are not connected with transitional passing through the mountains, as it thought before.

Introduction

The Neolithic period in the development of human society is characterized by the introduction of cereal crops, the raising of animals, the emergence and spread of sedentism, and technological advances such as the firing of pottery and the building of dwelling structures. It contrasts sharply with the previous hundreds of thousands of years during which hunting and gathering was the basis of subsistence. Our current image of the European Neolithic is dominated by discoveries made in places where Neolithic settlers established their villages, which persisted from generation to generation. These places are areas with fertile arable soils that permitted stable settlement.

The broader geographical context of European Neolithic settlement, however, is still poorly understood, particularly in the areas surrounding these fertile areas with black earths and brown earths formed from loess. These intervening areas are known as the European Mid-Mountains, and archaeological and paleoenvironmental evidence indicates that they were also of interest to Neolithic people.

Archaeology of Mid-Mountains: General Remarks

In Central Europe, the name "Mid-Mountains" is applied to mountain ranges with absolute altitudes up to about 1,500 m and significant relative heights. They are characterized by deeper and narrower valleys than the low mountains and the similar heights of their peaks. In Poland, the best example of such mountains are the Beskidy Mountains. In Germany there are many mountain groups included in the Deutsche Mittelgebirge, such as the Bavarian Forest, the Black Forest, the Harz, the Taunus, and the Thuringian Forest. Sometimes these mountains are identified as "forests" because they are covered by dense tree cover, mixed deciduous forest in their lower parts, and coniferous forest in higher elevations.

Archaeological research on the Mid-Mountains of Central Europe is not in an advanced state. There were many factors involved. The German archaeologist Harwig Löhr, speaking about the German Highlands, wrote:

> Grossräumig wären hier Mittelgebirge zu nennen, für die Thesen von einer „späten" Aufsiedlung, z. B. seit der Urnenfelderzeit, aufgestellt wurden . . . , die einmal akzeptiert und wiederholt . . . sich möglicherweise als Drehpunkt einer Teufelsspirale auswirken: da keine frühere Besiedlung erwartet wird, wird nicht danach gesucht, da nicht gesucht wird, wird nicht gefunden, die Fundleere bestätigt die These usw.

> Generally it can be pointed out for the Mid-Mountains, for which the thesis of the "late" inhabitation was put . . . , which once accepted and repeated . . . , started to operate as an axis of a vicious circle. Since earlier settlement has not been anticipated, it is not being sought, and since it has been not sought, it is not being found; the lack of findings proves this thesis. (Löhr 1985:103)

Recreating the history of mountain settlement is difficult. Archaeologists have conducted a long and deep discussion on this subject for years. Based on the lack of fertile soils and the predominance of rocky soils, archaeologists and historians have simply excluded the possibility of Neolithic settlement in the Mid-Mountains. Their skepticism is compounded by various factors. For example, systematic prospection for archaeological sites (e.g., Parczewski 1974, 1976) yielded negative results: finds were almost completely absent on the surfaces of today's arable fields. Thus, historical researchers—historians and archaeologists—have jointly created a set of negative assumptions, emphasizing the lack of arable soils, unfavorable climate, and shorter growing season in the mountains. Although they are correct in paying attention to the impact of such factors, they are wrong to build a myth of mountainous areas being neglected by Neolithic settlement a priori.

Still another negative assumption led to the creation of another myth, namely, the postulated existence of a "raw material desert" in the mountains due to the dominant presence of primarily sedimentary rocks in geological formations, for example, those in the Polish Carpathians. Under this assumption, the lack of local siliceous rocks with good flaking qualities seriously impeded the establishment of Paleolithic, Mesolithic, and Neolithic settlements. This is well illustrated by the first remarks about the possibilities for the exploitation of radiolarite in the Pieniny and Tatra Mountains (Kowalski and Kozłowski 1959). Based on the opinion of the geologist K. Birkenmajer (see Kowalski and Kozłowski 1959, footnote), tectonic fracturing of the Pieniny radiolarites precluded use of the Polish deposits of this rock as a raw material for artifacts during the Stone Age. Today we know that this was a misconception since many local stone raw materials were used for the production of tools and weapons in mountainous areas during the Stone Age.

This negative attitude of scholars was not merely based on the meager archaeological and geoarchaeological premises. In addition, they overestimated the destructive force of slope erosion, which was believed to have destroyed what scant prehistoric traces existed, including those of the Neolithic period. In reality, paradoxically, archaeological sites are very well protected in mountainous areas, the result of the delay of several thousand years in the introduction of large-scale land cultivation. Were we to compare the conditions of archaeology in the mountains with those in the loess basins or on the black earths of the European lowlands (for example, in Lower Silesia and Kuyavia), we would find that many mountain sites were naturally protected by vegetation cover like forests and grasslands, which the enclaves of fertile soils have been continuously cultivated for over seven thousand years. The consequences of this for the condition of archaeological data are easy to guess.

The persistence of skepticism among archaeologists was supported by the uncritical acceptance of the view of the geomorphologist Leszek Starkel on the amount of mineral deposits that were removed from the Polish Carpathians during the Late Glacial and Holocene periods. Starkel stated:

> Notwithstanding several episodes of increased denudation due to human activity, the removal of mineral deposits from the Carpathians lasted throughout the entire Holocene and the Late Glacial. Assuming an average volume of 500,000 m³ of material displaced per km², it can be calculated that from the entire 22,000 km² of the Polish Flysch Carpathians, a volume of about 10 billion m³ of material was removed, thus lowering the surface of the entire Polish Flysch Carpathians by an average of 0.5 meters. (Starkel 1960:186)

It is difficult to contradict Starkel's statement, but it should be noted that, although his calculations may be accurate, they do not explain erosion at any one place in any particular mountain group. Probably where erosion undercut the sides of river valleys, an enormous amount of material was removed, whereas on gentle, wooded slopes, it was probably negligible. It is difficult under these circumstances to presume the widespread destruction of montane archaeological sites by erosion.

Starkel's analysis was subsequently tested through experimental geomorphological research carried out at the Scientific Station of the Institute of Geography and Spatial Organization of the Polish Academy of Sciences in Szymbark, near Gorlice. It was found that erosion of wooded and grass-covered Carpathian slopes is small but dramatically increases in cultivated fields (Gil 1976). Thus, the hypothesis of the protection of archaeological sites by the natural plant cover in these areas until disturbance by the introduction of field crops is supported. Across the vast areas of highland Central Europe, especially the Mid-Mountains, this only occurred in modern times. In montane areas, plant cover protects archaeological remains from erosion.

After years of research and discussion, we can now present positive responses to the aforementioned negative assumptions and draw attention to such elements of the mountain environment that may encourage settlement in prehistoric areas such as:

- Different forest composition creates attractive and novel habitats (?)
- Special features of montane biotopes, such as anadromous fish runs (e.g., salmon)
- Access to montane sources of raw materials, including silicious rocks and copper

Evidence of Neolithic Activity from the European Mid-Mountains

Stray Finds

Until recently, the role of mountain areas for Neolithic people was viewed simply as territory to be passively transited, probably through river valleys, while the possibility of penetration into highlands was discounted. The basis for this view was the strong cultural convergence of Neolithic groups known from either side of mountain ranges such as the Western Carpathians or the Sudetens. It was thus logical to hypothesize crossings of these massifs by communities of a particular culture. This was presumed to take place without any long-term stopping points, which thus made the archaeological visibility of such activity zero.

Changed methods of archaeological prospection and the changing views of the possibility of prehistoric settlements in mountain areas that began in the late 1970s showed that this skepticism was erroneous. The discovery of many macrolithic stone tools, primarily axes and adzes for which the context had not been known for decades, clearly indicated a peripheral zone of Neolithic settlement deep in the mountains. Although the range of mountain finds was unusual (exclusively axes and adzes), it was no longer possible to ignore them.

Surveys Provide Context

Subsequently, surface surveys were undertaken in selected areas of the Mid-Mountains, including the Black Forest and Bavarian Forest in Germany and the Polish Carpathians

(Kienlin and Valde-Nowak 2004). These resulted in the discovery of many Stone Age sites represented by small flint artifacts. Some of these could be attributed to the Paleolithic and Mesolithic, but some, however, have Neolithic characteristics, for example of the Cham Group in the Bavarian Forest and the Funnel Beaker (Figure 13.1) and Corded Ware (Figure 13.2) cultures in the Beskidy range of the Polish Carpathians.

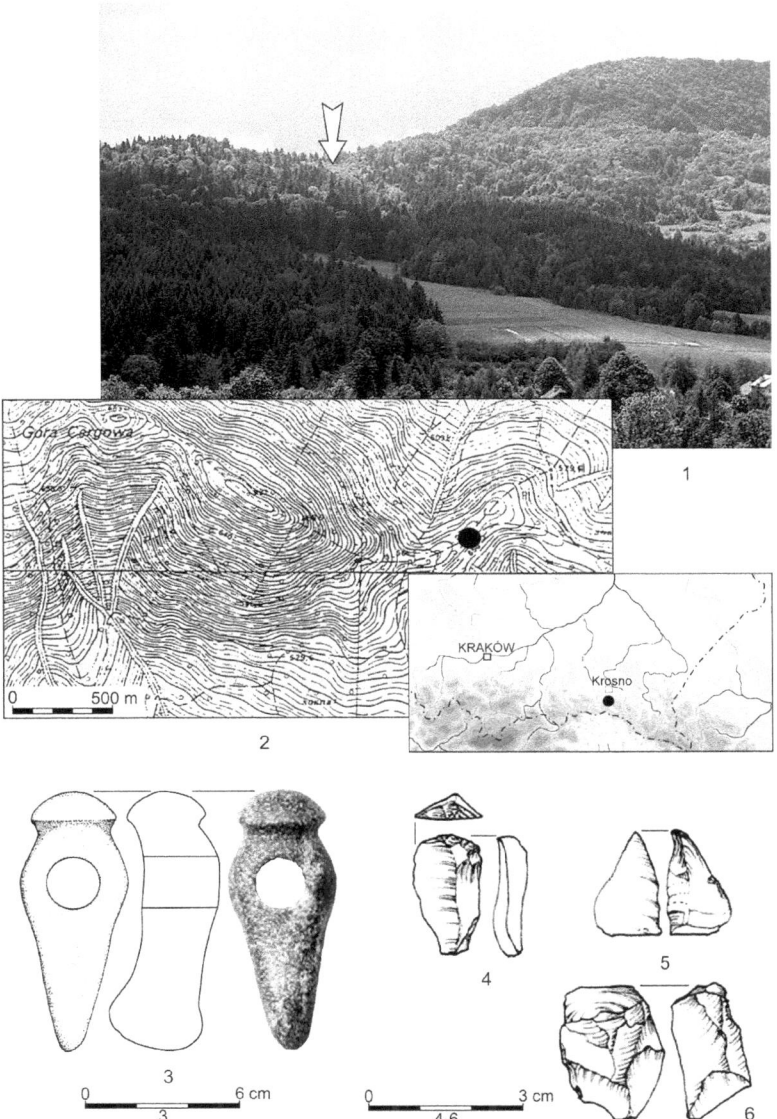

Figure 13.1. Nieznajowa, distr. Krosno, Lower Beskidy Mountains. General view of the Cergowa Mount, 716 masl (1) with the topography (2) and localization (arrow) of stray finds of hammer axes (3) of Funnel Beaker Culture and small stone artifacts (4–6) found close to the axe.

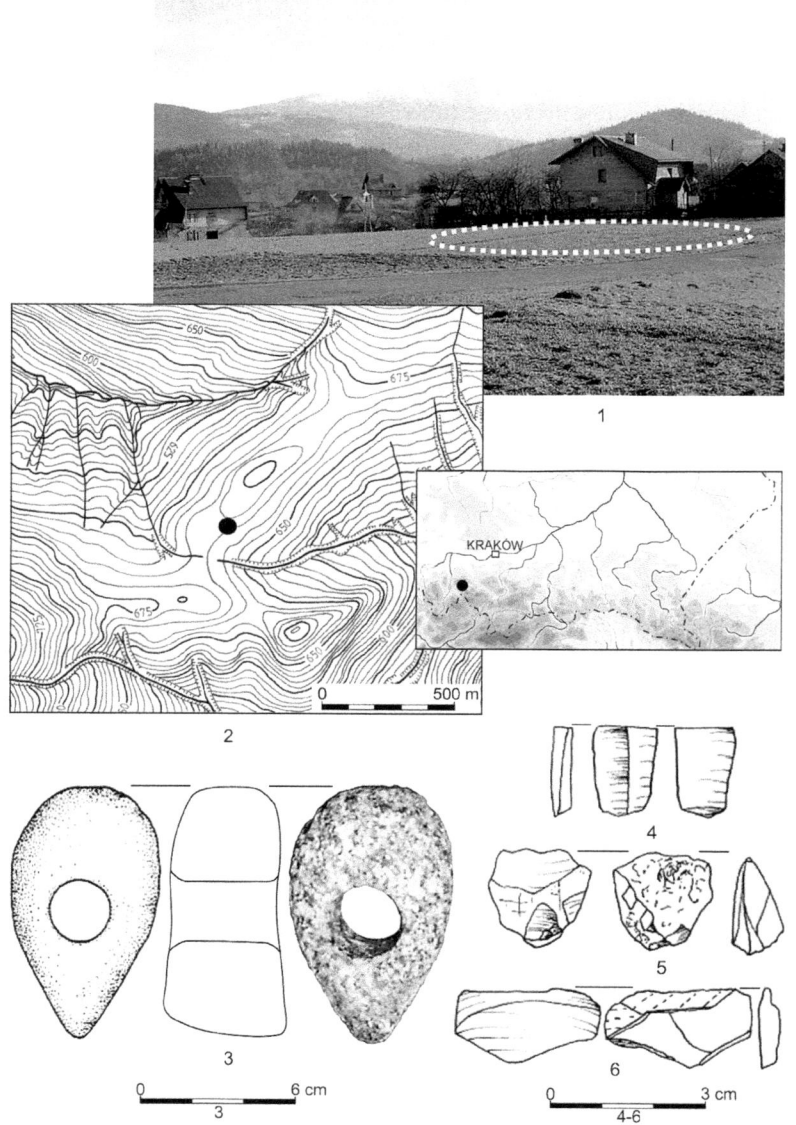

Figure 13.2. Zawoja-Przysłop, distr. Sucha Beskidzka, High Beskidy Mountains. General view of the Babia Góra massif, 1,725 masl (1) with the topography (2) and localization (dotted ellipse) of stray finds of hammer axes (3) of Corded Ware Culture and small stone artifacts (4–6) found close to the axe.

Verification through excavation showed that these finds are not accompanied by ceramics or subsurface features. For this reason, the conclusion was drawn that these represented mobile forms of Neolithic settlement in these regions (Valde-Nowak 2002:89–105). The difference between Neolithic mountain settlements and those found in the basins with fertile soils lay in the limited use of ceramics and the marked reduction of artifact inventories to a few flint types, which nonetheless provided context for the discoveries of axes and adzes. The forces of erosion were not responsible for this reduction in the range of artifact types, but rather the very nature of Neolithic settlement and its range of activities are reflected in the "strange" character of the archaeological record of the mountains.

Paleobotany: Pastoralism versus Cultivation

Another line of evidence that influenced the skeptical attitude of archaeologists toward the existence of abundant, chronologically differentiated traces of prehistoric activity in montane areas was the results of paleobotanical research and reactions to them. The overall lack of traces of cereals in pollen diagrams supported the hypothesis of settlement gaps. Isolated grains of cereal pollen were considered to have been the result of long-distance transport. Other indicators of human presence that appeared in pollen diagrams were ignored. These included evidence of forest destruction, probably resulting from the gathering of deciduous winter fodder and the release of small herds of cattle into the forests in the late spring, summer, and early autumn. This type of grazing activity is recorded by the appearance of various herbaceous plants, such as *Plantago lanceolata*, which correlates with anomalous fluctuations in the curves of deciduous trees like ash, elm, lime, and willow. It is highly significant that such indicators are not accompanied by traces of fires, so it is necessary to exclude the use of burning for forest clearance and the preparation of fields for cultivation.

The palynologists who conducted research in the mid-mountains interpreted the changes they observed in levels corresponding to the Younger and Late Neolithic in various ways. To a lesser or greater degree, however, they associated them with forest grazing and seasonal settlement (Knipping 1989; Lang 1973; Rösch 2012; Wacnik et al. 2001). In this context, it is appropriate to cite Peter Rasmussen's study (1990), which superbly examined variants of forest management, and which has influenced the work of many paleogeographers like Austad (1988).

The findings of both archaeologists and ethnologists who study pastoral settlements must be taken into consideration in this discussion. Pastoral sites are ephemeral, different from the more visible Neolithic settlements in the fertile basins. The artifact inventories found in places inhabited by pastoralists are very modest, reduced to only the most essential elements, with almost no clay vessels (e.g., Bradley 1992; Chang 2009; Cribb 1990).

Key Questions

Previous experience in the archaeological study of mountain areas has provided information about many Neolithic traces, but they are equivocal. It is difficult to decide whether the mountain finds, which are certainly Neolithic, are an expression of broader and more significant cultural processes or whether they represent insignificant episodes.

If we accept the authenticity of these traces as Neolithic, then the question arises as to why Neolithic people wanted, or needed, to leave the fertile enclaves. The most parsimonious answer lies in the fact that they were interested in areas suitable for the maintenance of livestock herds during the warmer months, thus conserving pastures and fodder resources closer to the permanent settlements lying outside the highland zone on fertile soils. Such a system of seasonal pastoralism represents a form of transhumance (Bentley 2007; Doppler et al. 2017; Gerling et al. 2017).

This leads to the next question, namely: Did these Neolithic communities alter their culture or household behavior in the upland areas? Leaving the enclaves of fertile soils and entering the mountains could have caused major changes in artifact assemblages due to new tasks and perhaps a seasonal change in lifestyle. There is evidence to this effect from the younger period, that is, the Late Neolithic, when the mountains were penetrated as a result of seasonal grazing, as reflected in the results of palynological research.

In the case of the Early Neolithic, it is still difficult to speak of such a tendency. If the Linearbandkeramik colonists entered the mountain landscapes, which can be seen in exceptional circumstances, then their cultural inventory did not undergo significant changes. A group of Linearbandkeramik settlements is found at the foot of the Slovakian Tatras at Poprad-Matejovce and Strane pod Tatrami (Soják 2002). These are typical Linearbandkeramik settlements with many types of pits, long houses, and large assemblages of flint artifacts and ceramics, located at a high altitude, about 600 masl in the Low Tatras and High Tatras of today's Slovak Republic. There is nothing to indicate that the cultural inventory of the inhabitants of these highland settlements differs significantly from the materials found at Linearbandkeramik settlements located outside the mountainous areas in the fertile enclaves. Isolated macrolithic polished stone tools with Early Neolithic features are occasionally found outside the village sites, but their topographic position is relatively connected with the lower part of a gradual slope in the valley.

A series of large Linearbandkeramik settlements in the Carpathian Foothills on the central Dunajec indicate the selection of the highest parts of the landscape, the crests of hills.

In the course of field work it turned out that at Łoniowa there exists a multicultural and vast settlement (ca. 3 ha) and nearly 800 sq m were explored. Apart from Malice features (so far not detected in the Carpathians), the remains of a long (41.5 m) Early Neolithic house were discovered (Valde-Nowak 2014). One of the achievements of field work was a complete recording of traces of the house, and the acquisition of proofs of synchronization of all of its structural elements. In many aspects the house in question is an exceptional feature (Figure 13.3).

The long house from Łoniowa differs in several respects from known European houses of the LBK population. The first difference is a surprising presence of "apses" in the outline of both clay pits that accompany such houses at the western and eastern sides. Other original elements are traces of an arc-like enclosure at the southern side of the house. However, an entirely new element in Early Neolithic architecture (meaning the Linear Band Pottery Culture) are two pits, located within outlines of the house, next to the western wall. They were interpreted as "cellars," although in none of the hundreds of European sites with houses of that type were such cellars discovered. After the exploration of the features

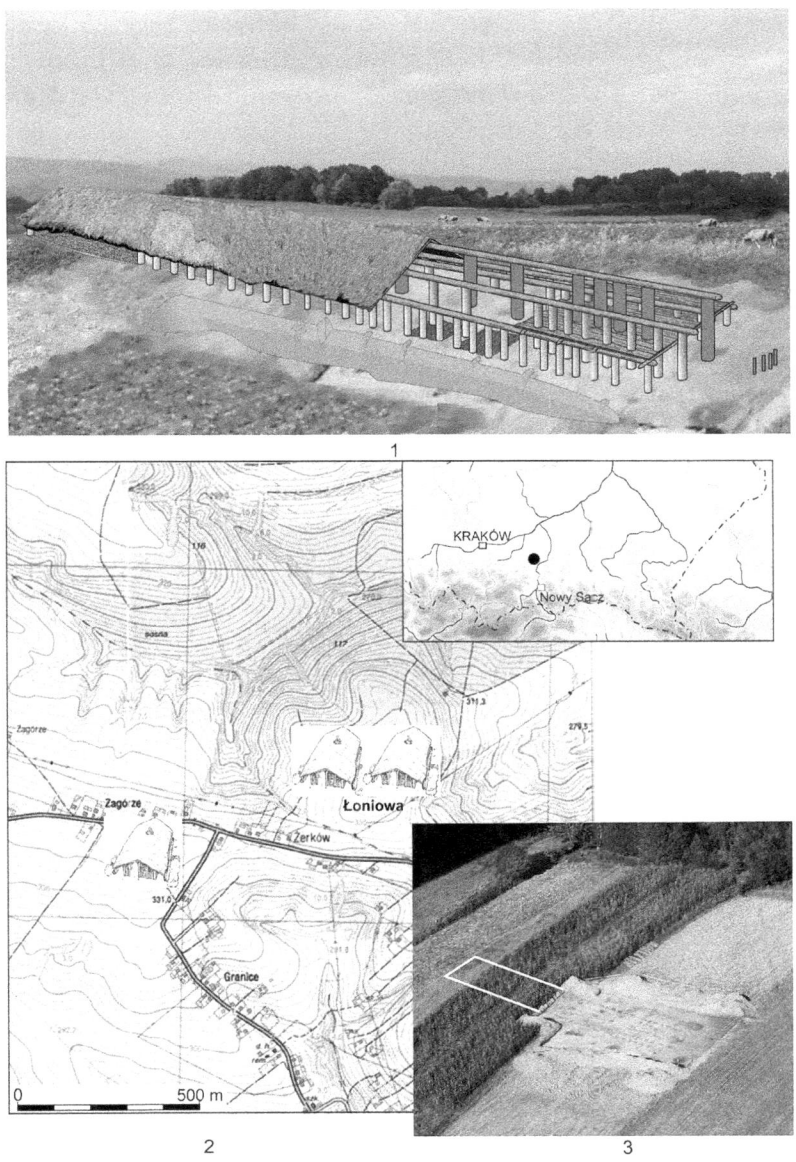

Figure 13.3. Łoniowa, distr. Brzesko, site 18—West Carpathians Wiśnicz Foothill. Model (1), topographic position, (2) and aerial view of Linearbandkeramik long house no. 2 during excavations.

in question, a totally different interpretation can be assumed. At least one of these features should be considered a grave due to its regular outline (rectangular with rounded corners), flat bottom, and a set of portable objects found in it (a fine-ware cup, twelve-pieces of flint deposit, and two microlith trapezoids made of Jurassic flint) well established in the standard of the Linear Pottery Culture.

The works encompassed also site Żerków and Biesiadki. They are located no more than 700 m to the west-southwest from the site at Łoniowa. Over thirty features were investigated in the course of field work. Some of them turned out to be clay pits related to a long house of the Linear Band Pottery Culture. The rest were postholes, also connected with a house.

Unlike other LBK sites, both settlements are located exactly on the Wiśnicz Foothills culmination, on the Dunajec and Uszwica watershed (Valde-Nowak 2013). Hundreds of the LBK sites that have been discovered so far were located in low landscape zones, close to rivers and streams. Such locations are exceptional at the scale of the European range of Early and Middle Neolithic settlement (Bogucki 2003; Bogucki et al. 2012; Grygiel 2004, 136–138, fig. 75; Kruk 1980; Lüning and Stehli 1989, 115, 118, fig. 6, fig. 9; Zimmermann et al. 2004, 69, fig. 10).

It is not easy to explain this phenomenon. The explanation might refer to a transit role of the whole settlement. On the other hand, one should remember that in the Carpathians it is a common phenomenon that cold air sinks to the valleys and stays there for a long time, while the upper parts of foothills and mountain tops are warmed by the sun for much longer. Therefore, a zone of occupation located at a higher altitude could be, in Early Neolithic conditions, optimal for settlement and economy.

During the Late Neolithic, the situation changes. Relatively abundant macrolithic polished stone tools comprise the sole category of finds. They are not accompanied by ceramics or features, such as pits. During the investigation of the areas around axe and adze finds, very detailed searches revealed assemblages with several kinds of small flint artifacts.

Based on the research up to this point, including the spatial analysis of individual finds, the geographic preferences of Neolithic people in the highlands can be confirmed. During the Late Neolithic, sites are frequently located in the higher topographic zones, in areas of flattened hilltops, saddles, and local passes, while the relatively few Early Neolithic finds do not show such a tendency and are located in lower parts of the landscape (Figures 13.4 and 13.5), with the exception of the Carpathian Foothills at the settlements of Łoniowa, Żerkow, and Biesiadki, which are discussed earlier.

An affirmative answer can be given to the question: Can Neolithic settlement really be studied in the highlands?

In all of the mountain groups that have been studied, a similar tendency to penetrate these areas during the Late Neolithic, at the latest, can be observed. The opening of the road to further targeted research on the montane Neolithic was made possible by a critical analysis of the evidence: on one hand, the hundreds of stone axes and adzes and, on the other, the results of palynological research on mountain peat bogs (Valde-Nowak 2002). All previous interpretive proposals, such as calling the axes and adzes "thunderbolts" (*Donnerkeile*) or hoards in uninhabited places, are not sustained in the face of such critical review.

Recent Extraordinary Finds from the Beskidy Range and the Divergence of the Mid-Mountain Neolithic from the Lowland Neolithic

Figure 13.4. Jaroszowice, distr. Wadowice, Lower Beskidy Mountains. General view of the Skawa River valley (1) with the localization (arrow) and topography (2) of stray finds of shoe-last celts (3) of Late Linearbandkeramik; small stone artifact series have been found in the vicinity during verification.

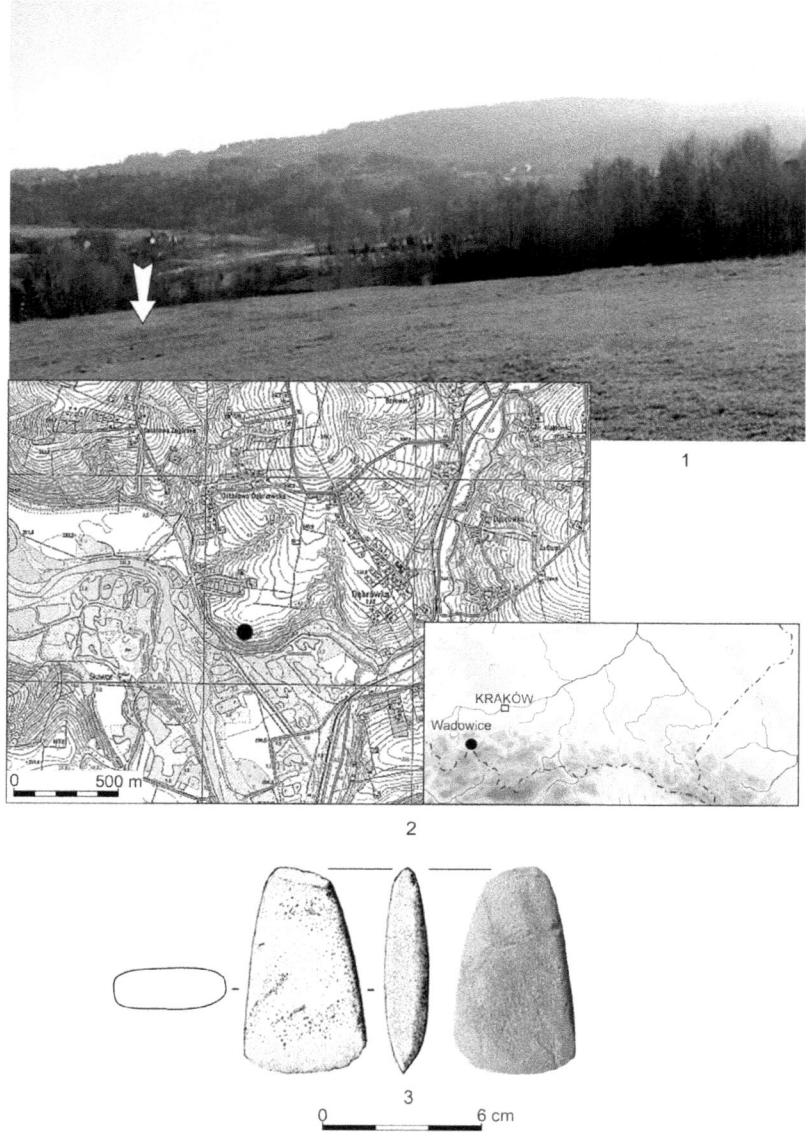

Figure 13.5. Dąbrówka, distr. Wadowice, Lower Beskidy Mountains. General view of the Skawa River valley (1) with the localization (arrow) and topography (2) of stray finds of shoe-last celts (3) of Linearbandkeramik; small stone artifact series have been found in the vicinity during verification.

The first discovery of an unusual nature concerns a fragment of a bow made of yew wood, indicating prehistoric hunting activity, found in the sediments of a landslide peat bog (at a depth of 330 cm) on the northern slopes of Mount Kamiennik in the Polish Flysch Carpathians (Margielewski et al. 2010). Radiocarbon dating (Poz-21566: 4830±30 BP;

3670–3620 cal BC) of this unique artifact suggests its connection with the activity of Neolithic people linked to the Funnel Beaker Culture. This is one of the very few Neolithic bows found in Europe. The sequence of peat bog deposits that have formed since the Atlantic period offer a record of the paleoclimatic changes of the Middle and Late Holocene, as well as traces of the human impact in these and subsequent periods. Paleoenvironmental changes identified in the peat horizon bearing the artifact are marked by the delivery of minerogenic, "high energy" deposits (with charcoal) to the peat bog, as well as distinct changes in plant communities. These phenomena confirm the significant human impact on landslide areas. The study also confirms that landslide peat bog deposits are very sensitive indicators of paleoenvironmental changes.

The second example concerns two isolated burials of the Baden Culture that were found in the mountainous landscape of the Middle Beskidy Mountains, far from Baden settlement concentrations in Lesser Poland and northern Slovakia (Valde-Nowak 2008), which are also significant in this context. In terms of the interpretation of the isolated graves, it must be taken into consideration that the nearest sites of the Baden Culture in Poland are located about 50 km from these locations as the crow flies (Godłowska 1979; Zastawny 1999), and they are over 80 km in the direction of the Slovak Republic in the other direction (Soják 2001).

These two burials were situated at a distance of approximately 350 m from each other. The space between them was carefully examined and, interestingly, no marks contemporary with these features were found. The finds date back to the period from the mid-fourth millennium BC cal until the early third millennium. One of the pots represents the Baden Culture in its developed form (Zagórze 1), whereas the other (Zagórze 2) belongs to the Early Boleráz environment from the Drahanovice or even Proto-Boleráz phase, as well as to TRB from the BR III phase (Valde-Nowak et al. 2015). The last one represents a single pot placed bottom-up with no other artifacts inside the feature, which implies that it may have been a grave. The form of the pot and its technological characteristics correspond to this interpretation. One vertical, massive pebble situated close to the pot, as well as some other stones in the vicinity, could be associated with the feature. It may have been an element of surrounding stones damaged by time or even a part of a tomb stele.

What can these explicitly isolated Baden burials deep in the Polish Carpathians mean? One possible explanation is that this was a burial of a roving shepherd. This would also explain the aforementioned stray finds of axes and hammer axes. Another possibility is the death of a member of a Baden group moving along the river valley and his subsequent burial, far from his settlement. In any case, this discovery indicates that sedentary Neolithic communities often, or at least occasionally, penetrated the mountain zone.

In addition, there is a lot of evidence for strong differences between the archaeology in the mountains and the lowlands. It turns out that, for example, the Neolithic pit fillings, blackish in the loess area, are bright gray or "silverish" in some soil types predominantly found in the Central European highlands. If this is unknown to the excavator, the chances of discovering such structures are small due to pedological factors, for example, strong acidity.

Settlement Geography

The Neolithic traces in mountains create an entirely different complex of data when compared to the classic settlement centers. It also turned out over the last decade that Neolithic artifacts were frequently found situated high in the area of saddles and local passes. The aforementioned specific traits of archaeological sources in the mountains, their dissimilarities to materials from lowlands, give a different picture of prehistoric settlement.

In current low mountain range studies, the settlement geography of the Neolithic remains a key topic. Above all, it is important to note that many of the finds occur outside the valleys that earlier researchers considered the paths of Neolithic passage through the mountains. So the old concept of the mountains simply as areas that were transited by Neolithic communities must be discarded.

A relatively large series of macrolithic polished tools, a few hundred overall, have been analyzed under topographic criteria. It showed that Young and Late Neolithic finds are significantly situated in local saddles and passes. However, Early Neolithic sites are mostly located at a much lower zone of the landscape. Here, a high concentration of Linearbandkeramik villages situated in the Dunajec River basin in the West Carpathians can be once again mentioned. The specific settlement geography allows comparisons between the mountainous sites, for example, using the procedure proposed by Bailey and Davidson (1983) (see Figure 13.6).

Because of the environmental features, such as the sedimentary dynamics and the inversion of temperature, the topography of villages of early farmers shows characteristics very different from those in lowlands. For the assessment of mountainous conditions, it should be taken into consideration whether river valleys channeled communication. If so, settlements in the valleys might have had a special role in communication networks. While the Late Neolithic axes and hammer axes had been found in elevated positions, the Early Neolithic shoe-last celts were found in a far lower zone. Despite such differences, both are traces of deep penetration and are probably linked to camp sites connected with executive economic tasks: pastoralism is one possible explanation. The range, impact, and the intercultural character of the phenomena mentioned earlier point to the conclusion that these issues were economically based.

Conclusion

Intentional human activity in the European Mid-Mountains during the Neolithic, largely in the form of pastoralism and mobile settlement form, seems very likely (Walsh and Mocci 2011). This is demonstrated by the results of paleobotanical research as well as by analogy with pastoral societies in their marked reduction in the equipment of everyday life (Bradley 1992) and the topography of settlement locations.

In the Polish Carpathians, various lines of evidence confirm the presence of stray finds and relatively stable settlements dated from the Early (Linearbandkeramik) to the Late (Baden) Neolithic. Deep into the foothill zone, closer to the Beskidy Mountains, a group of

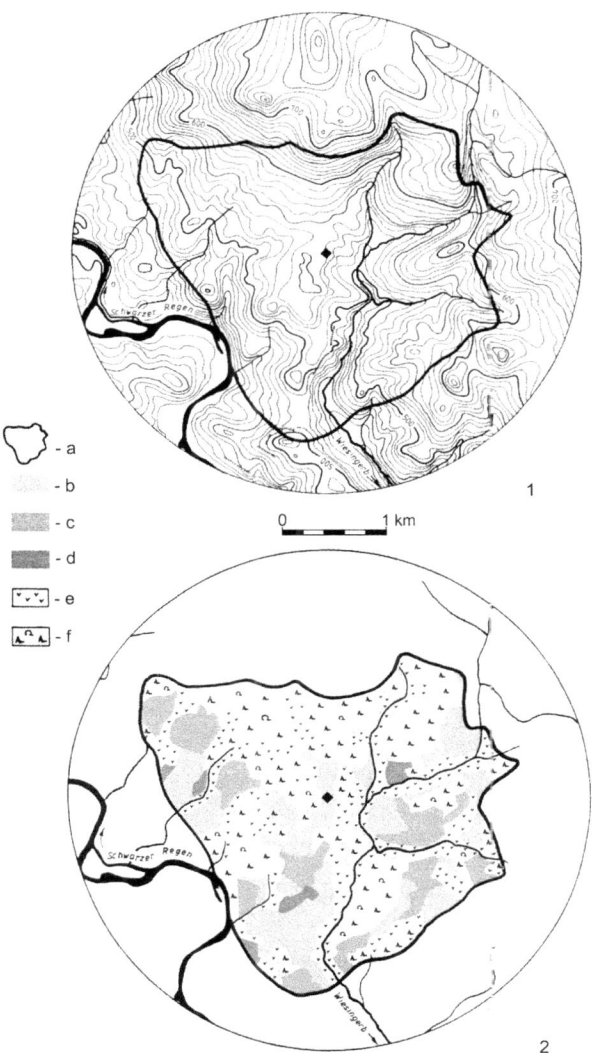

Figure 13.6. Durfeld, distr. Viechtach, Bavarian Forest. Topography in the range of a half-hour walk (1) and agricultural evaluation of soil (2) in the localization (black diamond) of a Late Neolithic axe found during survey. A. Half-hour actualized range (Bailey and Davidson 1983). B–D. Agricultural soil categories (B = best, D = worst), E–F. Green land (E = meadow, F = forest).

early agricultural settlements with long houses was discovered. All these settlements are at elevated locations and may indicate a greater role for cattle breeding and dairy production than elsewhere in the Early European Neolithic (Price et al. 2006).

The Neolithic stray finds of polished stone tools originate from each mountain group. Previously, they were considered to be of little importance. However, the analysis of these tools suggests that the complex of finds from each mountain group represents similar characteristics (chronology, etc.), and that forests and meadows, nowadays dominant in all Central European Mid-Mountains, inhibit the visibility of a great number of Neolithic archaeological remains. On the basis of settlement-geographical analysis, a topographic model of stray finds was constructed. This type of find tends to be located between springs and at the edge of the upland in the vicinity of local saddles, mid-mountain range passages, and generally in elevated watershed zones.

In this context, the discovery of the settlement of Neolithic cattle herders at Thayngen-Weier in the southern foothills of the Black Forest is very important (Guyan 1990; Riehl 2006). Here, evidence of the use of leaves and young twigs as feed for cattle has been found. Seasonal woodland pasture in the mountains is very likely in the light of this discovery, which is also what the palynological diagrams suggests.

At the same time, the ultimate proof of the existence of a pastoral Neolithic in the European highlands is still elusive, for we continue to rely on proxy data. Direct data in the form of storage pits and cultural layers containing the bones of domestic animals are still lacking. Due to the specific lifestyle of pastoral groups, however, we should not wait for the discovery of such traces. The Neolithic footprints recorded so far in the mountain areas, combined with the results of palynological analyses, support the recognition of the European Mid-Mountains as the domain of Neolithic shepherds who practiced seasonal grazing of small herds of livestock and who were based in settlements located on the margins of the mountainous zones.

Acknowledgments

The author is greatly indebted to Dr. Peter Bogucki for every comment greatly improving this manuscript and all the help in its editing.

References

Agirre-García, J., J. M. Edeso-Fito, A. Lopetegi-Galarraga, A. Moraza-Barea, M. Ruiz-Alonso, S. Pérez-Díaz, T. Fernández-Crespo, I. Goikoetxea, M. A. Martínez de Pancorbo, L. Palencia, M. Baeta, C. Núñez, S. Cardoso, and J. A. Mujika-Alustiza 2017 Seasonal Shepherds' Settlements in Mountain Areas from Neolithic to Present: Aralar–Gipuzkoa (Basque country, Spain). *Quaternary International*, https://doi.org/10.1016/j.quaint.2017.03.061

Austad, I. 1988 Tree Pollarding in Western Norway. In *The Cultural Landscape, Past, Present and Future*, edited by H. H. Birks, H. J. B. Birks, P. E. Kaland, and D. Moe, 11–29. Cambridge University Press, Cambridge.

Bailey, G. M., and I. Davidson 1983 Site Exploitation Territories and Topography: Two Case Studies from Palaeolithic Spain. *Journal of Archaeological Science* 10:87–115.

Bentley, A. 2007 Mobility, Specialization and Community: Diversity in the Linearbandkeramik— Isotopic Evidence from the Skeletons. *Proceedings of the British Academy* 144:117–140.

Bogucki, P. 2003 Neolithic Dispersals in Riverine Interior Central Europe. In *The Widening Harvest: The Neolithic Transition in Europe—Looking Back, Looking Forward*, edited by A. Ammerman and P. Biaggi, 249–272. Archaeological Institute of America, Boston.

Bogucki P., D. Nalepka, R. Grygiel, and B. Nowaczyk 2012 Multiproxy Environmental Archaeology of Neolithic Settlements at Osłonki, Poland, 5500–4000 BC. *Environmental Archaeology* 17(1):45–65.

Bradley, R. 1992 *Nomads in the Archaeological Record: Case Studies in the Northern Provinces of the Sudan*. Akademie Verlag, Berlin.

Chang, C. 1993 Pastoral Transhumance in the Southern Balkans as a Social Ideology: Ethnoarcheological Research in Northern Greece. *American Anthropologist* 95(3):687–703.

Cribb, R. 1990 *Nomads in Archaeology*. Cambridge University Press, Cambridge.

Doppler, T., C. Gerling, V. Heyd, C. Knipper, T. Kuhn, M. F. Lehmann, A. W. G. Pikee, and J. Schibler 2017 Landscape Opening and Herding Strategies: Carbon Isotope Analyses of Herbivore Bone Collagen from the Neolithic and Bronze Age Lakeshore Site of Zurich-Mozartstrasse, Switzerland. *Quaternary International* 436(Part B):18–28.

Gerling, C., T. Doppler, V. Heyd, C. Knipper, T. Kuhn, M. F. Lehmann, A.W. G. Pike, and J. Schibler 2017 High-Resolution Isotopic Evidence of Specialised Cattle Herding in the European Neolithic. *PLoS ONE* 12(7):e0180164. https://doi.org/10.1371/journal.pone.0180164

Gil, E. 1976 *Slopewash on Flysch in the Region of Szymbark*. Dokumentacja fizjograficzna 2, Polish Academy of Sciences, Institute of Geography and Spatial Organization, Wrocław.

Godłowska, M. 1979 Plemiona kultury ceramiki promienistej. In *Prahistoria ziem polskich II: Neolit*, edited by W. Hensel and T. Wiślański, 301–317. Ossolineum, Wrocław.

Grygiel, R. 2004 *The Neolithic and Early Bronze Age in the Brześć Kujawski and Osłonki Region (vol. 1) Early Neolithic Linear Pottery Culture*. Konrad Jażdżewski Foundation for Archaeological Research/Museum of Archaeology and Ethnography, Łódź.

Guyan W. U. 1990 Die Moorsiedlungen am "Weier" bei Thayngen. In *Die ersten Bauern*, edited by M. Höneisen, 213–220. Schweizer Landesmuseum, Zurich.

Kienlin, T. L., and P. Valde-Nowak 2004 Neolithic Transhumance in the European Mid-Mountains: The Evidence of Freiamt in the Black Forest Mountains, SW Germany. *Journal of Field Archaeology* 29:29–44.

Knipping, M. 1989 *Zur spat- und postglazialen Vegetationsgeschichte des Oberpfälzer Waldes*. Dissertationes Botanicae 140, J. Cramer, Berlin.

Kowalski, S., and J. K. Kozłowski 1959 O użytkowaniu jaspisu w epipaleolicie Polski południowej. *Materiały Archeologiczne* 1:7–12.

Kruk, J. 1980 *Economy in Southeastern Poland in the 5th–3rd Centuries B.C.* Ossolineum, Wrocław.

Lang, G. 1973 Neue Untersuchungen über die spät- und nacheiszeitliche Vegetationsgeschichte des Schwarzwaldes IV: Das Baldenwegermoor und das einstige Waldbild am Feldberg. *Beiträge zur naturkundlichen Forschungen in Südwestdeutschland* 32:31–51.

Löhr, H. 1985 Sammeln oder suchen? Anmerkung zur archäologischen Feldbegehung. *Archäologische Informationen* 8(2):102–110.

Lüning, J., and P. Stehli 1989 Die Bandkeramik in Mitteleuropa: von der Natur-zur Kulturlandschaft. In *Siedlungen der Steinzeit. Haus, Festung und Kult—Spektrum der Wissenschaft: Verständliche Forschung*, edited by J. Lüning, 110–120. Spektrum der Wissenschaft Verlagsgesselschaft mgH, Heidelberg.

Margielewski, W., M. Krąpiec, P. Valde-Nowak, and V. Zernitskaja 2010 A Neolithic Yew Bow in the Polish Carpathians: Evidence of the Impact of Human Activity on Mountainous Palaeoenvironment from the Kamiennik Landslide Peat Bog. *Catena* 8:141–153.

Parczewski, M. 1974 Przyczynki do dziejów najstarszego osadnictwa w Karpatach polskich. *Acta Archaeologica Carpathica* 14:69–78.

Parczewski, M. 1976 Drobne prace poszukiwawcze w Beskidzie Niskim i Sądeckim. *Acta Archaeologica Carpathica* 16:113–115.

Price, T. D., J. Wahl, and R. A. Bentley 2006 Isotopic Evidence for Mobility and Group Organization among Neolithic Farmers at Talheim, Germany, 5000 BC. *European Journal of Archaeology* 9:259–284.

Rasmussen, P. 1990 Leaf Foddering in the Earliest Neolithic Agriculture: Evidence from Switzerland and Denmark. *Acta Archaeologica (Kobenhavn)* 60:71–86.

Riehl, S. 2006 Nomadism, Pastoralism and Transhumance in the Archaeobotanical Record-Examples and Methodological Problems. In *Die Sichtbarkeit von Nomaden und Saisonaler Besiedlung in der Archäologie: Multidisziplinäre Annäherungen an ein Methodisches Problem*, edited by S. R. Hauser, 105–125. Orientwissenschaftliche Hefte 21, Mitteilungen des SFB, Orientwissenschaftlichen Zentrum der Martin-Luther-Universität Halle-Wittenberg, Halle.

Rösch, M. 2012 Vegetation und Waldnutzung im Nordschwarzwald während sechs Jahrtausenden anhand von Profundalkernen aus dem Herrenwieser See. *Standort.wald* 47:43–64.

Soják, M. 2001 Sidliská ľudu badenskej kultúry na Spiši. In *Otázky neolitu a eneolitu našich zemí*, edited by M. Metlička, 161–190. Západočeské muzeum v Plzni, Plzeň.

Soják, M. 2002 Neolitické sidlisko v Stráňach pod Tatrami, okr. Kežmarok. In *Otazky neolitu a eneolitu našich krajin*, edited by I. Cheben and I. Kuzma, 313–341. Archeologicky Ustav Slovenskej Akademie Vied, Nitra.

Starkel, L. 1960 *Rozwój rzeźby Karpat fliszowych w holocenie*. Wydawnictwa Geologiczne, Warsaw.

Valamoti, S. M. 2015 Detecting Seasonal Movement from Animal Dung: An Investigation in Neolithic Northern Greece. *Antiquity* 81(314):1053–1064.

Valde-Nowak, P. 2002 *Siedlungsarchäologische Untersuchungen zur neolithischen Nutzung der mitteleuropäischen Gebirgslandschaften. Internationale Archäologie 69*. Verlag Maria Leidorf VML, Rahden.

Valde-Nowak, P. 2008 Isolated Grave of the Baden Culture from the Polish Beskidy Mts. In *The Baden Complex and the Outside World*, edited by M. Furholt, M. Szmyt, and A. Zastawny, 139–145. Studien zum Archäologie in Ostmitteleuropa 4. Dr. Rudolf Habelt GmbH, Bonn.

Valde-Nowak, P. 2013 Neolithic Settlement in the Central-European Mountains. In *Comparative Archaeology and Paleoclimatology: Sociocultural Responses to a Changing World*, edited by M. O. Baldia, T. K. Perttula, and D. S. Frink, 261–272. BAR International Series 2456. Archaeopress, Oxford

Valde-Nowak, P. 2014 Long Houses on Hilltop-Camps in the Mountains: Some Aspects of the Neolithic in the Dunajec Project. In *Settlement, Communication and Exchange around the Western Carpathians: International Workshop Held at the Institute of Archaeology, Jagiellonian University, Kraków, October 27–28, 2012*, edited by T. L. Kienlin, P. Valde-Nowak, M. Korczyńska, K. Cappenberg, and J. Ociepka, 27–49. Archaeopress, Oxford.

Valde-Nowak, P., A. Gil-Drozd, A. Kraszewska, and M. Paternoga 2015 The Proto-Boleráz Grave in the Western Beskidy Mts., Lesser Poland. In *The Baden Culture around the Western Carpathians*, edited by M. Nowak and A. Zastawny, 371–380. Krakowski Zespół do Badań Autostrad, Kraków.

Wacnik, A., K. Szczepanek, and K. Harmata 2001 Ślady działalności człowieka neolitu i brązu obserwowane w diagramach pyłkowych z okolic Przełęczy Dukielskiej i terenów przyległych.

In *Neolit i początki epoki brązu w Karpatach Polskich*, edited by J. Gancarski, 207–221. Muzeum Podkarpackie w Krośnie, Krosno.

Walsh, K., and F. Mocci 2011 Mobility in the Mountains: Late Third and Second Millennia Alpine Societies' Engagements with the High-Altitude Zones in the Southern French Alps. *European Journal of Archaeology* 14(1–2):88–115.

Zastawny, A. 1999 Uwagi na temat chronologii osadnictwa kultury badeńskiej w zachodniej części Małopolski. *Sprawozdania Archeologiczne* 5:9–57.

CHAPTER FOURTEEN

Addressing the Complexity of the Paleoenvironmental Impact of Prehistoric Settlement and Protohistoric Urbanism in the Auvergne Mountains (Massif Central, France)

Yannick Miras, Michela Mariani, Florian Couderc, Marlène Lavrieux, and Paul M. Ledger

Abstract *Recent multiproxy paleoenvironmental studies performed in the lower Auvergne mountains in central France have focused on unraveling the localized environmental impact associated with human settlements. They clearly demonstrate that as early as the Neolithic, past human societies have developed complex land use patterns that are patchily distributed in time and space. This results in the long-term configuration of mosaic-like anthropogenic cultural landscapes characterized by a high variability both at micro-local and regional scales. The diachronic research presented in this chapter was performed at a high spatial resolution integrating two case studies situated in the upstream and in the downstream of the catchment of the Veyre River (the mountainous Chaîne des Puys and the intra-mountainous Limagne plain, respectively). This comparison of "upland versus lowland" and the focus on prehistory we proposed in this chapter allow a discussion of: (1) the complexity of paleoenvironmental impacts associated with prehistoric and proto-historic human settlement in terms of woodland clearance, landscape openness, evidence for agriculture, and spatiotemporal variabilities at micro-local and regional scales; (2) the complex interplay between human adaptability, climate oscillations, and environmental evolution; (3) how these two complementary areas operated together through time; and (4) the paleoenvironmental features of the development of proto-urban areas during the Late Bronze and Iron Ages.*

Introduction

To date, the majority of paleoecological research pursued in the mountainous environments of Central and Western Europe has sought to trace long-term Holocene vegetation dynamics and discern if climate or human activity is the main driver of landscape change (Reille et al. 1992). More recently, integrated and multiproxy paleoenvironmental studies have instead focused on unraveling the localized environmental impact associated with human settlements (Davies and Tipping 2004). This is a much-needed approach in the study of mountainous areas that are spatially heterogeneous with a diversified resource distribution. Past human societies have long taken advantage of such landscape diversity by developing complex land use patterns that are irregularly distributed through time and space (Ejarque et al. 2010; Miras 2016). Such land use strategies result in mosaic-like cultural landscapes characterized by high variability both at micro-local and regional scales (Mariani et al. 2017).

Recent integrated archaeological and paleoecological studies from a variety of western European mountains (e.g., Kothieringer et al. 2015; Palet et al. 2007; Surmely et al. 2009; Walsh and Richer 2006) have demonstrated that mountain areas cannot be considered pristine and marginal areas. Rather, they are characterized by long-term human occupation and the development of complex and diverse land uses. Since the Neolithic, the spread of agriculture and the establishment of sedentary communities have had disruptive and cumulative effects on a wide range of natural process. Examples include widespread woodland clearance (Fyfe et al. 2015), eutrophication of water bodies (Hillbrand et al. 2012; Miras et al., 2015), and the alteration of hydrogeomorphological regimes (Lavrieux et al. 2013). The intensity of human impacts on the environment from the Neolithic has even led some authors to suggest that the Neolithic revolution constitutes the true beginning of the Anthropocene (Ruddiman 2003; Smith and Zeder 2013). Thus, the prehistoric period is key to understanding the long-term formation of upland cultural landscapes. Indeed, Orengo et al. (2014) posit that "the formation of cultural landscapes follows a cumulative process in which earlier landscape modifications determine future human uses of the landscapes. Therefore, understanding the origins of cultural landscapes . . . is essential for the correct analysis of their long-term evolution" (141). Examining prehistoric environmental transformations obtained from a "pristine ecological state" is therefore essential as they mark the beginning of a cumulative chain of disturbances that shape the development of cultural landscapes. By scrutinizing the particular features of these early environmental changes—in terms of first responses and/or recoveries of an ecological system—it may be possible to obtain fresh insights into the long-term trajectories of landscape evolution that arise from the complex interplay between human adaptability, climate oscillations, and environmental evolution. However, a reductive approach must be avoided. Prehistoric paleoenvironmental impacts need to be considered in their totality to account for both spatial and temporal variability, in the intensity and modality of land use.

The multiproxy paleoenvironmental research presented in this chapter was conducted with this in mind. Using the mountains of Auvergne in central France as a study region,

Addressing the Complexity of the Paleoenvironmental Impact   255

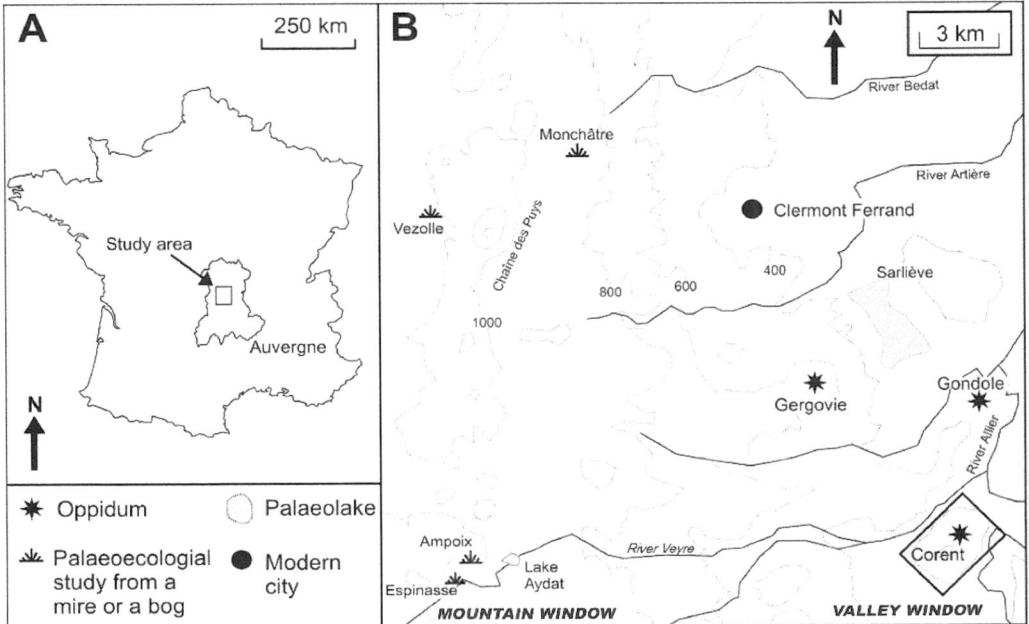

Figure 14.1. A. Location of Auvergne and the study region within France. B. Paleoecological sites and oppida in the drainage basin of the River Veyre.

this diachronic research presents two case studies from the catchment of the Veyre River. The first drains the upstream reaches of the mountainous Chaîne des Puys, while the second drains the intra-mountainous Limagne plain (Figure 14.1). The focus on prehistory and comparison of "upland versus lowland" allow a discussion of: (1) the complexity of paleoenvironmental impacts associated with prehistoric and proto-historic human settlement in terms of woodland clearance, landscape openness, evidence for agriculture, and spatio-temporal variabilities at micro-local and regional scales; (2) the complex interplay between human adaptability, climate oscillations, and environmental evolution; (3) how these two complementary areas operated together through time; and (4) the paleoenvironmental features of the development of proto-urban areas during the Late Bronze and Iron Ages.

The Lower Auvergne Mountains

The tectono-volcanic ensemble of the Chaîne des Puys/Faille de Limagne, located in the French Massif Central, constitutes an emblematic geological landscape with the Limagne geological fault and graben at the east and the mountainous Chaîne des Puys at the west (Boivin et al. 2004) (Figure 14.2). The "Chaîne des Puys" is an elongate quaternary alignment of eighty volcanoes, measuring ca. 32 km north to south and 4 km west to east. The mean altitude is ca. 1,030 masl with a maximum of 1,465 masl reached at the Puy de

Figure 14.2. Current landscapes in the lower Auvergne mountains and the studied sequences. Photo by B. Dousteyssier and Y. Miras.

Dôme. The region constitutes a large part of the Parc Naturel Régional des Volcans d'Auvergne (http://www.parcdesvolcans.fr/). Currently, the dominant land uses are agropastoralism and recreational activities. The mean altitude of the Limagne plain, where the capital city of Clermont-Ferrand is situated, is between 300 and 500 masl and arable agriculture focused on cereals, corn, sugar beet, and rapeseed, is widespread.

Climatically the region is continental with oceanic influences. Precipitation is limited in the Limagne plain (ca. 585 mm yr^{-1}) in comparison to the upland (ca. 800 mm yr^{-1}). Mean annual temperatures are around 11 °C in the valley while they oscillate between 7 and 9 °C in the upland (Bouchet 1987).

The lower Auvergne mountains are situated in the vegetation belt, mainly characterized by neutrophilous beech forests (essentially *Asperulo–Fagion* and *Fageto–Scilletum lilio-hyacinthi* communities) interspersed with fir (*Abies alba* Mill.) (Freydier and Dubreuil 2004). As a consequence of the long-term land use history (Ballut et al. 2012; Miras et al. 2004a, 2015), the current landscape is highly variable at both micro-local and regional scales, and it is dominated by grazed grasslands, meadows, heathlands, and extensive reforestations (mainly conifers such as spruce). This results in the configuration of a complex mosaic-like cultural landscape.

These outstanding geological, environmental, and cultural landscapes are the key factors determining the future registration of the Chaîne des Puys/Faille de Limagne on UNESCO's World heritage list (http://www.chainedespuys-failledelimagne.com/). As a consequence, the region now pays particular attention to environmental legacy, promoting new methods that aim to guarantee the integrity of ecosystems and land use development in these rural territories (Miras et al. 2013). In this sense, a consensus exists today within the scientific community for underlining the relevance of the paleoenvironmental studies in the development of accurate and sustainable environmental policies of the mountain landscapes management, conservation, and legacy (Dearing et al. 2015). Our research was undertaken in this context and permits a detailed reconstruction of the genesis and the long-term shaping of this complex cultural landscape.

Materials and Methods

Three Study Sites Distributed in Two Connected Micro-Local Windows

The upland case study focuses on two nearby sites, both located at the south of the Chaîne des Puys, ca. 25 km southwest of Clermont-Ferrand (Figures 14.1 and 14.2). Lake Aydat (mean depth: 7.4 m; area: 6.105 sq m; maximum depth: 15 m; N 45°39.809'/E 2°59.106'/837 masl) originated from the damming of the Veyre River by a basaltic flow issued from the Puy de la Vache and Puy Lassolas volcanoes and is dated to 8551 ± 400 cal yr BP. The lake lies on a plutonic and metamorphic substratum (granodiorites), partially covered by Late Glacial to Holocene volcanic deposits (Boivin et al. 2004). Coring was carried out in the central and deepest part of the basin, close to the Veyre River delta. The age–depth model was constructed from seventeen AMS radiocarbon dates on leaf and wood fragments distributed throughout the core (Lavrieux et al. 2013). Espinasse fen (500 m wide; surface area of 21 ha, N 45°38'/ E 2°53/ 1,160 masl) is a circular depression surrounded to the north by a volcanic structure, the Puy de l'Enfer. The fen occupies an ca. 70 m deep basaltic maar, formed around 12,400 cal yr BP (Camus 1975). The chronology was constructed from five AMS radiocarbon dates, on bulk organic fraction analyses, distributed throughout the core, details of which are presented in Miras et al. (2004a).

In the lowland window, the study site "Lac du Puy" is situated on the Corent plateau at 550 masl, within the relict volcanic landscape of Limagne, ca. 15 km southeast of Clermont-Ferrand (Figures 14.1 and 14.2). The Lac du Puy is a spring-fed pool located in the northern quarter of the Corent plateau ca. 170 m north of the ongoing excavation of a multiperiod archaeological site (Poux 2012) centered on N 45°40'0.66"/E 3° 11'21.30". The age-depth model for the site (Ledger et al. 2015) was constructed from six AMS radiocarbon dates, on charcoal, pollen, and the bulk organic fraction of sediment sample analyses.

A Multiproxy, Integrated, and High-Resolution Approach

Each of the paleoenvironmental studies presented here were undertaken at high temporal resolution and are based on a regional coordination of micro-local study windows (upland window versus lowland window). In addition, paleoecological data are integrated with archaeological data when available. Complementary bioindicators (pollen and spores, non-pollen palynomorphs or NPP [mainly fungal spores and stomata], and micro-charcoals) were used to better assess: (1) the complexity of the localized paleoenvironmental impact, and (2) the human practices involved (Figure 14.3).

Samples for pollen and non-pollen palynomorphs (NPP) analyses were prepared using standard procedures (Faegri and Iversen 1989). In all instances efforts were made to achieve counts of five hundred land pollen grains per sample; however, poor pollen preservation prevented this for sections of the Lac du Puy/Corent and Espinasse fen cores. Pollen and NPP values were calculated as the percentage of total pollen excluding Cyperaceae, fern spores, and aquatic plants. For the study of Espinasse fen, low pollen counts of 350 pollen grains (hygrophitic plants excluded) were obtained due to the low pollen preservation of this fen. Summary curves adopt an "indicator species" approach (sensu Behre 1981), summing pollen and NPP taxa relative to their ecological affinity in Auvergne (Antonetti et al. 2006) and indicative value of anthropogenic impact (Behre 1981; Cugny et al. 2010; Ejarque et al., 2011; van Geel et al. 1989). Details are presented in Miras et al. (2015).

In addition to pursuing the qualitative "indicator species" approach (cf. Behre 1981), we also undertook the quantitative vegetation reconstructions (sensu Sugita 2007) to convert pollen percentages into past regional vegetation cover data. Myriad factors, such as taphonomy, pollen productivity, and dispersal capabilities influence the representation of vegetation in pollen spectra to the extent that plant taxa may be over- or underrepresented in pollen rain (i.e., the composition of pollen in the atmosphere at a particular point in time [Faegri 1966; Tauber 1965]). Consequently, the relationship between pollen percentages

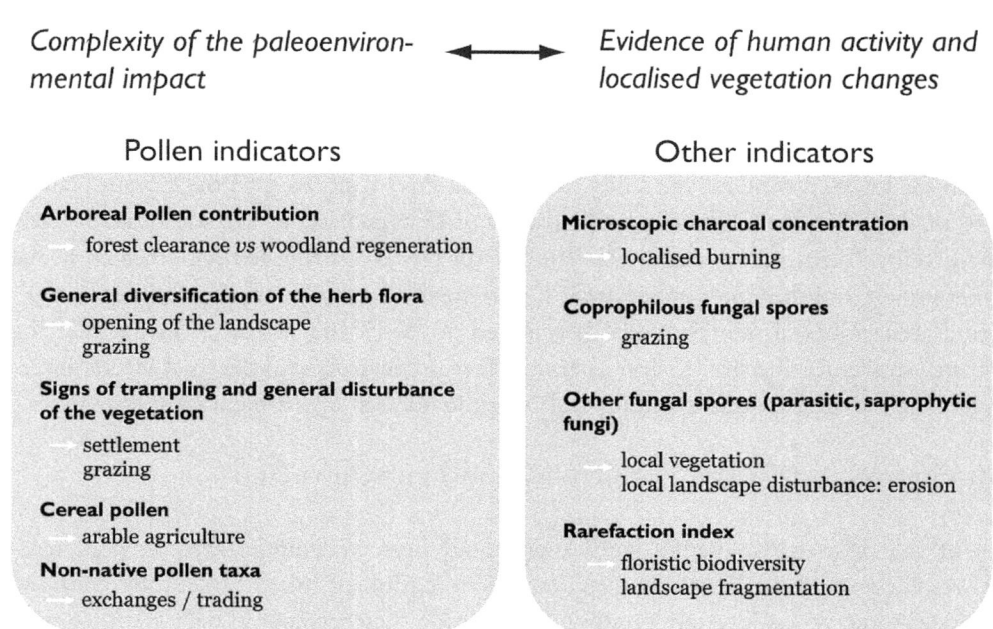

Figure 14.3. Complementarity of the paleoecological bioindicators.

and vegetation cover is often nonlinear. Estimating past vegetation cover from sedimentary pollen composition therefore requires empirical-based modeling of this relationship across different vegetation types. Recent advances in palynology have enabled effective modeling of pollen productivity and dispersal (Gaillard et al. 2010; Sugita 2007). The Landscape Reconstruction Algorithm (LRA), proposed by Sugita (2007), aims to obtain estimates of vegetation abundance on local (<1 sq km up to 5 sq km—which employs the LOVE model) and regional (10^4–10^5 sq km—which employs the REVEALS model) scales. These mechanistic models benefit from including both Pollen Productivity Estimates (PPEs), to adjust for differential pollen productivity, and particulate dispersal and deposition models, to correct for the differential dispersal of pollen types. To account for pollen dispersal differences in our case studies, REVEALS is underpinned by the widely deployed Gaussian Plume Model (GPM) (Prentice 1985; Sugita 1994). The GPM is based on Sutton's air pollutant plume dispersion equation (Sutton 1953). This model was calibrated using the concentration of particles (e.g., pollen) several hundred meters downwind from a point source as spreading outward from the centerline of the plume following a normal probability distribution. REVEALS requires large sites (ideally > 0.5 sq km) (Sugita 2007), thus we ran the model on the combined Aydat and Espinasse datasets in order to reconstruct the regional vegetation cover changes from the upland region. The REVEALS model was run using the DISQOVER package (Theuerkauf et al. 2016) for R employing the Gaussian Plume Model with a wind speed of 3 m.s^{-1}. PPEs and pollen fall speeds for the chosen taxa were derived from the work of Mazier et al. (2012) (Table 14.1).

Finally, rarefaction analysis was undertaken to assess temporal changes in palynological richness, which can be interpreted as an approximate measure of floristic diversity and landscape configuration (Berglund et al. 2008; Birks and Line 1992).

TABLE 14.1. PPEs (WITH THEIR STANDARD ERRORS) AND FALLSPEED OF 13 TAXA ACCORDING TO MAZIER ET AL. (2012)

Species	fallspeed	PPEs	PPE.errors
Abies (fir)	0.12	6.88	1.44
Alnus (Alder)	0.021	9.07	0.1
Betula (birch)	0.024	3.09	0.27
Cereal	0.06	1.85	0.38
Corylus (hazelnut)	0.025	1.99	0.2
Fagus (beech)	0.057	2.35	0.11
Pinus (pine)	0.031	6.38	0.45
Plantago (plantain)	0.029	1.04	0.09
Poaceae (grassland)	0.035	1	0
Quercus (oak)	0.035	5.83	0.15
Secale (rye)	0.06	3.02	0.05
Tilia (lime)	0.032	0.8	0.03
Ulmus (elm)	0.032	1.27	0.05

Prehistoric Environmental Baselines and Attractiveness of the Mid-Mountain Areas

The first step in these studies was to define the mid-Holocene ecological baselines for the study region, which constituted the prehistoric natural environmental context prevailing during the Neolithic. Qualitative and quantitative pollen data and NPP data indicate that at both micro-local and regional scales a forested landscape was well developed in the Auvergne mountains (Figures 14.4 and 14.5). Nevertheless, at Lake Aydat a reorganization of the forest cover is evident from ca. 6550 cal BP (pollen zone Ay–$1_{a/b}$, Figure 14.4, Miras et al. 2015). This corresponds to a progressive substitution of diversified oak woodlands by beech forests that are gradually infilled by fir. The spread of mountain woodland (comprising beech and fir) reached a maximal extension at ca. 5500 cal BP and may be related to the wetter and cooler climate of the Mid-Holocene (Magny and Haas 2004). These high-resolution pollen data also suggest that patches vacated by oak forest were not immediately colonized by mountain woodlands. The substantial rise of the Poaceae values (i.e., grasslands) indicates the expansion of open herbaceous areas and the development of a more heterogeneous landscape. This conclusion is also supported by the high floristic diversity index (pollen zone Ay–1_b, Figure 14.4) which subsequently declined around 5500 cal BP when densely forested landscape reemerged (Miras et al. 2018).

This fragmented and open forest landscape between ca. 6000 and 5750 cal BP (pollen zone Ay–1_b, Figure 14.4) may have been attractive for Middle Neolithic societies. Indicators of local grazing and agriculture (e.g., coprophilous fungi, and ruderal and cereal pollen types) are observed and it is possible that agropastoral activities reinforced these vegetation dynamics (Figure 14.5). Moreover, a subsequent expansion of pioneering trees, mainly pine (*Pinus*), toward the end of the pollen zone Ay–1_b (Figure 14.4), indicates that woodlands were potentially cleared for temporary farming and agriculture. A similar and contempo-

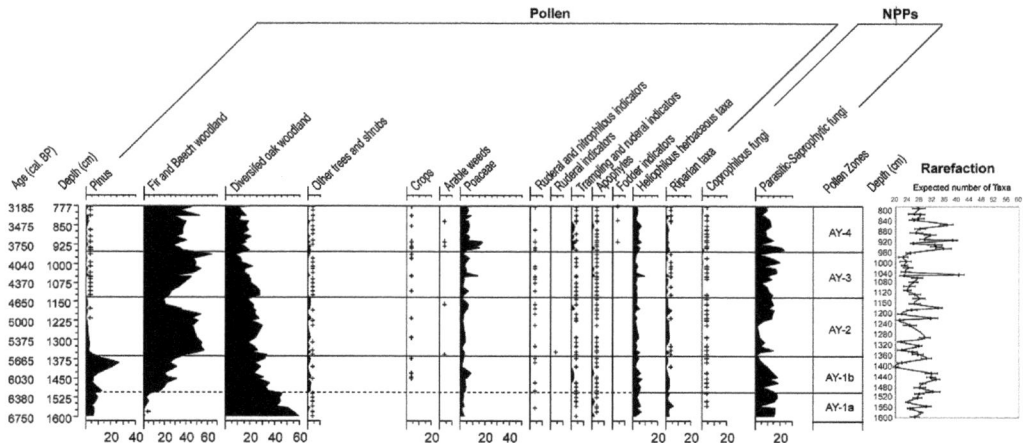

Figure 14.4. Summary percentage pollen and non-pollen palynomorphs diagram of Lake Aydat (837 masl, analysis by Y. Miras), and rarefaction index. + indicates ≤ 1% of the total pollen sum.

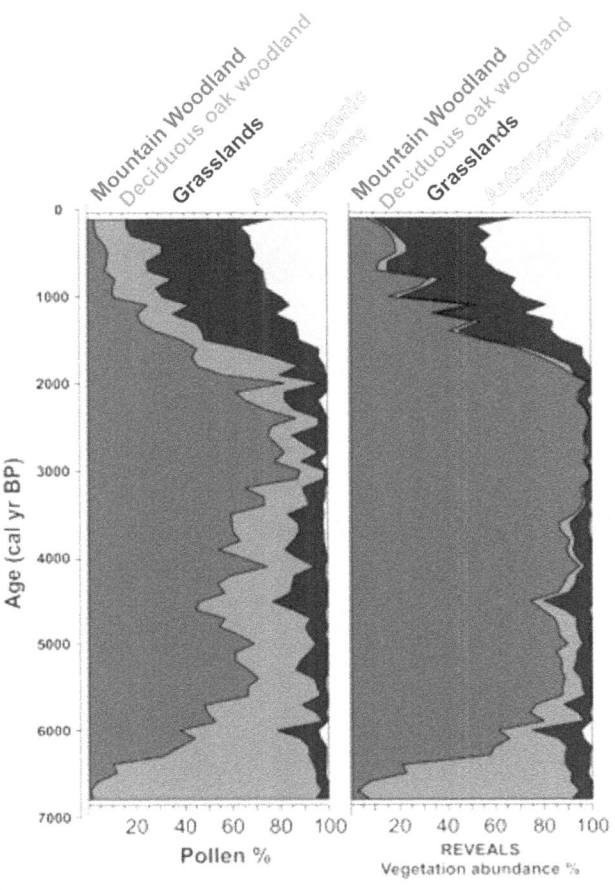

Figure 14.5. Comparison between pollen and vegetation cover percentages (data processing by M. Mariani): summary of Aydat and Espinasse pollen data.

raneous event is also recorded at Espinasse fen (pollen zone E-a/b, Figure 14.6) and at Vézolle, in the north of the Chaîne des Puys (Michelin et al. 2001). Archaeological data from this period is scarce in the upland, but monuments such as "menhir" and "dolmen" indicate human groups were active throughout the Chaîne des Puys during the Neolithic (Surmely and Liabeuf 1998). In the lowland the Middle Neolithic was also an important phase of human occupation. In contrast to the Early and Final Neolithic, funerary remains are abundant (between ca. 4200–3500 cal BC) and point to dense occupation across the Limagne plain. Queyriaux (Cournon-d'Auvergne), situated near Clermont-Ferrand, is a good example of settlement in the lowland areas. At this site, hundreds of structures were excavated and many domestic artifacts were found (Muller-Pelletier and Georjon, 2013). Hilltops in the Limagne valley were also occupied. For example, excavations at sites such as Gergovie point to occupation during the Middle Neolithic and to a lesser extent during the Final Neolithic (Pasty 2016). Indeed, the concentration of Middle Neolithic settlements revealed in recent archaeological research is coherent with the noticeable increase of

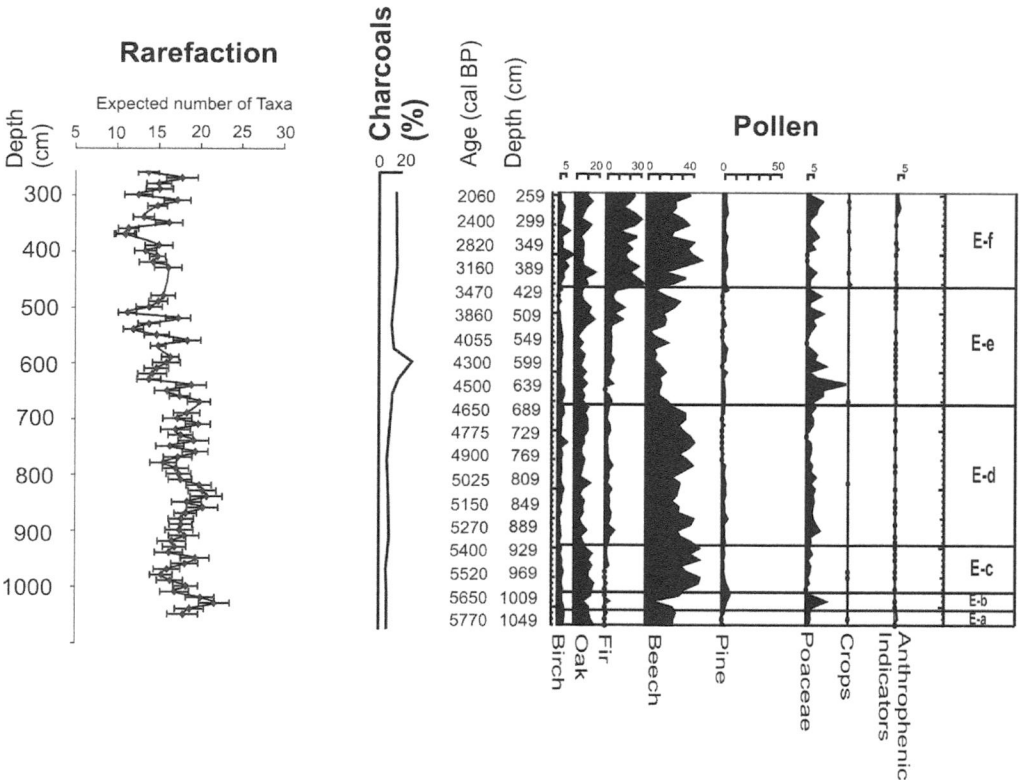

Figure 14.6. Summary percentage pollen diagram of Espinasse fen (1,160 masl, analysis by Y. Miras), charcoal proportions, and rarefaction index. • indicates ≤ 1 percent of the total pollen sum.

the human pressure noted in pollen data from the lowland window (Lac du Puy/Corent sequence, Figure 14.7). The good parallel nature of these activities suggest that the shaping of the Auvergne mountain landscape is contemporary with activity in the lowland valley. In any case, the mountain landscape of Auvergne was undoubtedly subject to early impacts from human societies. Pollen data illustrate slight human impacts in the southern reaches of Auvergne during the Early Neolithic (Surmely et al. 2009). Moreover, these are contemporary with other western European mountain chains (e.g., Pyrenees: Ejarque 2013; Jura: Gauthier 2001; Alps: Court-Picon 2007). Thus, if the beginning of the sixth millennia BC marks the onset of the landscape shaping process, these data imply that the first real threshold period—in terms of the shaping of the cultural landscapes of western European mountains—dates to the Middle Neolithic. For example, similar events are observed in the Andorran Pyrenees where woodland clearings, a lowering of the timberline, and the spread of alpine meadows and grazing date from ca. 6360–5500 cal BP (Ejarque et al. 2010).

It is notable that the first significant human impact observed in the lower Auvergne mountains was initiated during a climatic downturn. This suggests a nondirect relationship between climate fluctuations and human occupation of mountainous areas from as early

ADDRESSING THE COMPLEXITY OF THE PALEOENVIRONMENTAL IMPACT 263

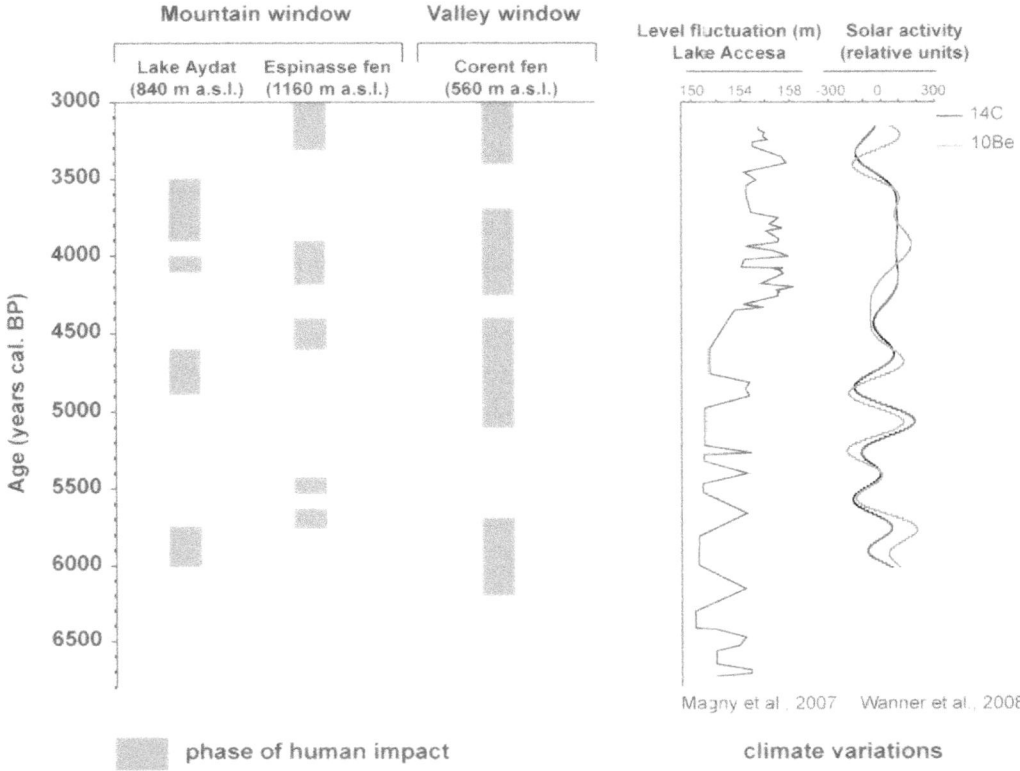

Figure 14.7. Phases of human impact revealed by pollen data in the lower Auvergne mountains compared to climatic oscillations.

as the Middle Neolithic. Similar observations have also been made in the high Pyrenean mountains. Archaeological and pollen data indicate a period of occupation between ca. 5600–5060 cal BP (Miras et al. 2010; Orengo et al. 2014) coincident with marked climatic oscillations and pronounced degradation at ca. 5850 cal BP (Pla and Catalan 2005). Taken together these data suggest that prehistoric societies were highly adaptable and reactive to environmental (mainly climatic) changes.

The Complexity of Paleoenvironmental Impacts

Different Temporal Patterns

Figure 14.7 provides an overview of the main phases of the prehistoric human impacts present in the pollen data from our two study windows. The clearest conclusion is that different rhythms of human impact are evident. Nevertheless, a number of phases, concurrent with those in other western European mountains (Miras et al. 2004b), are notable both upland and in the lowland valley in Auvergne. Particularly noteworthy is the period between 4200 and 3900 cal BP: a key period that has also been identified in the Alps (Jacob et al. 2009) and the Pyrenees (Ejarque 2013; Orengo et al. 2014). In the latter case, both pollen and archaeological data imply that an intensification of pastoral activity was driving the development of a complex landscape organization of high-altitudinal spaces. This suggests that threshold periods exist in the environmental history of the west European mountain areas. However, the micro-local approach we present here demonstrates a more complex reality. Pollen data from Auvergne indicate alternating periods of activity that imply more or less continuous activity in these upland areas. These results would seem to confirm that the development of cultural landscapes is a long-term process that began as early as the Neolithic.

The timing of phases of human impact and climatic fluctuations does not suggest a straightforward relationship between climate and human activity. The majority of the phases of human activities spanned periods characterized by an oscillating climate (e.g., 4900–4600 cal BP), or rapid climatic variations, such as between 4100 and 3800 cal BP. Indeed, this period has recently been divided into a drier episode centered on ca. 4100–3950 cal BP bracketed by two wetter phases dated to ca. 4300–4100 and 3950–3850 cal BP, respectively (Magny et al. 2012).

Different Spatial Patterns

The multiscale approach followed here and the reconstruction of reliable age-depth models reveal spatial variability in the anthropization of the lower Auvergne mountains (Figure 14.7). In the mountain case study, it may be the case that a phase of human impact finished around 4600 cal BP at Lake Aydat (Figure 14.4) as a new one began in the nearby site of Espinasse (Figure 14.6). The mobility of prehistoric societies and their adaptability to environmental changes must therefore be analyzed in terms of spatial reorganizations of human occupations and activities both at micro-local and regional scales. Mountainous cultural landscapes can thus be considered as mosaic-like shifting manipulated landscapes at these two spatial scales.

In the lowland (Lac du Puy/Corent sequence), phases of human impact in the palynological data are concurrent with those revealed by archaeological data (Ledger et al. 2015; Poux 2012). When we compare the lowland and upland sites, some common phases of human impact are evident. In particular, from 4200 cal BP onward, activities in the upland and lowland regions appear synchronous. Therefore, the pollen and archaeological data perhaps indicate the development of an interconnected territory, which may, in part, explain the increased anthropogenic pressure on the environment in the Auvergne mountains. Concomitant increases in human activity are also evidenced by pollen data in different west mountain areas such as the Mediterranean Pyrenees (Galop et al. 2013). In this latter case, Carozza et al. (2015) postulate that the period between 2500 and 2300 BC was an important period of segmentation of space. In turn, this led to the formation of connections between uplands and lowlands and the development of a diverse exploitation of natural resources and economic specializations (such as metallurgy). According to these authors, the establishment of complex land uses and strong territorial connections—where

Addressing the Complexity of the Paleoenvironmental Impact   265

mountainous areas play an important role—may have enabled the societies of the Final Neolithic and Early Bronze Age to buffer against the impacts of climatic oscillations.

Archaeological data are relatively scarce for the Late Neolithic in the Lower Auvergne. However, the Early Bronze Age is a key period of the human occupation in the Limagne plain, which agrees with pollen data. In particular, four archaeological sites attest to a remarkable increase in nucleated domestic settlements. Layat, in Riom (Figure 14.8), was

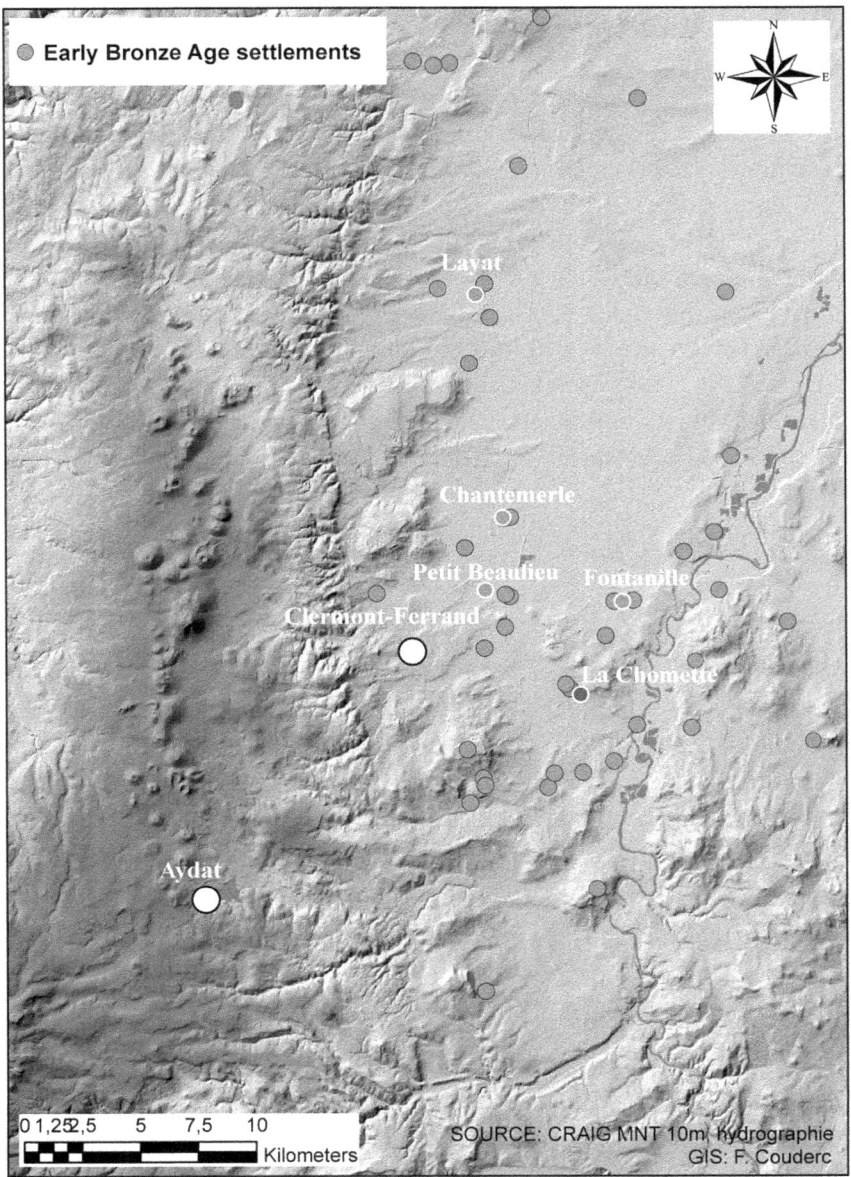

Figure 14.8. Locations of Early Bronze Age settlements in the lower Auvergne. GIS by F. Couderc.

a modest domestic agglomeration and a necropolis occupied between the Early to Middle Bronze Age, ca. 1900 and 1500 BC (Sévin-Allouet 2010). A similar site is Chantemerle, in Gerzat, where an important necropolis was discovered (Vermeulen 2001) (Figure 14.8). Fontanille, in Lempdes, also reveals an important domestic settlement occupied for five centuries, with the most important phase between ca. 1900 and 1700 BC (Hénon 2016) (Figure 14.8). Finally, Petit Beaulieu, in Clermont-Ferrand (Figure 14.8), was a large Early Bronze Age settlement comprising 2,460 structures associated with 35 funerary structures dated to ca. 1900 and 1700 BC (Thirault 2013). Alongside pollen data, the abundance of archaeological sites from this period confirm this phase as a threshold period in the occupation of the both the upland and lowland of the lower Auvergne. Archaeological evidence from the beginning of the Middle Bronze Age is less evident and may indicate a shift in the habitat and socioeconomic structures rather than an abandonment of the Limagne. For example the domestic site of La Chomette, in Cournon d'Auvergne (Figure 14.8), dated to between ca. 1700 and 1600 BC suggests that settlement became more dispersed and less enduring (Carozza and Bouby 2006). Pollen data obtained from both the upland and lowland between ca. 3500 and 3300 cal BP present a slight decline in the anthropogenic pressure, particularly in arable agriculture (end of the pollen zone Ay-4, Figure 14.4) and a general revival of the mountain woodlands at a regional level (Figure 14.5). This data was previously associated with the climatic degradation of the Middle Bronze Age (Miras et al. 2015) but could also be connected to shifting land management suggested by the archaeological data.

Different Intensities and Types of Land Uses

The reconstruction of past regional vegetation cover shows widespread mountain woodland from the Mid- to Late Holocene in the Auvergne mountains (Figure 14.5). In the upland case study, two periods of local landscape management involve a noticeable retreat of this dense mountain forest. In the first of these, the opening of woodland is accompanied by the development of grazing activities with erratic evidence of arable agriculture between ca. 4900 and 4600 cal BP (Lake Aydat, pollen zone Ay-2, Figure 14.4) concurrent with the Late Neolithic/Chalcolithic transition. The second event is characterized by an Early Bronze Age development of small-scale agriculture, between ca. 3900 and 3500 cal BP (transition of the pollen zones Ay-3/4). In both cases, human clearances appear to have induced rapid vegetation change from dense local woodland toward more open and patchy landscapes. This increase in the diversity of vegetation communities is underlined by a rising palynological richness index. The estimate of the forest surfaces cleared suggests that from the Late Neolithic the intensity of the woodland clearance, and the expansion of grasslands, reached a level never reached before (Figure 14.5). Thus, this period appears to represent the second major threshold in the development of the cultural landscape of Auvergne. Pollen data obtained in Lake Aydat, following the Early Bronze Age, indicate that mountain woodlands did not recover to their previous extent, unlike the period following Early Neolithic impacts. This may suggest a progressive loss of resilience in the landscape dynamics in the surroundings of the lake. These data seem to be more local than regional, as mountain woodland abundance (reconstructed by the REVEAL model) tends to increase after this Early Bronze Age impact (Figure 14.5). This suggests that this key period of human impact also induced a first important micro-local variability in the landscape shaping history. Despite this, from the Early Bronze Age onward increasingly intense land use likely converted the "pristine" forested landscape into a more open "semi-natural," grass-rich and patchy landscape (Miras et al. 2018).

Nevertheless, it is uncertain if these differing outcomes were induced by similar land management practices. In the Late Neolithic, the upland pollen sequences reveal two sequential phases of human impact that occurred ca. 4900–4600 cal BP at Lake Aydat and ca. 4600–4400 cal BP at Espinasse fen. This suggests that human activity in this part of the Auvergne mountains was probably sporadic, rather than systematic or permanent. This mode of occupation, marked by spatial variability, is consistent with the highly mobile nature of third and second millennia societies in mountainous areas (Walsh and Mocci 2011). Moreover, there are only rare occurrences of pollen from cereal and arable weeds that would indicate local cultivation. Similarly, the increase in secondary woodland vegetation with high proportions of birch, concurrent with declines in beech and increases in micro-charcoals (pollen zone E-e, Figure 14.6) may reflect slash-and-burn type agriculture (Baum et al. 2016). Indeed, this land use system has also been proposed as dominating the Late and Final Neolithic in the pre-alpine lowlands of southwest Germany (Rösch et al. 2014).

At the beginning of the Early Bronze Age (ca. 3900–3500 cal BP, pollen zones Ay-3/4, [Figure 14.4]), the apparent intensification of anthropogenic pressure may translate to a shift in land management practices related to more intensive cultivation of crops. Pollen data show an increased presence of cereal pollen grains and of the pollen of rye, which is traditionally considered as an arable weed during this period (Behre 1992). This could suggest larger, more intensively, and possibly more permanent cultivated fields (Miras et al., 2021). Similar findings have been evidenced in the northwestern pre-alpine forelands. Permanent cultivation of cereals has been evoked as early as the Late Neolithic, ca. 4300–2400 cal BC (Jacomet et al. 2016). Similarly, carpological data tend to suggest practiced agriculture in permanent fields in the Eastern Iberian Pyrenees, between 900 and 1,500 masl, where environmental conditions were favorable enough, at least in the fifth millennium BC (and probably already in the sixth millennium cal BC, Antolín et al. 2018). The synchronous observation of pollen of alfalfa and peas may also suggest fodder cultivation or possibly crop rotation with N-fixing legumes with the development of permanent cultivation (Baum et al. 2016). Nevertheless, more archaeological and archaeobotanical data (both on-site and off-site) are needed in Auvergne for an accurate assessment of arable agriculture strategies. Moreover, there is a rise in ruderals, trampling and grazing indicators, nitrophilous and fodder plants, and dung-related fungi. Taken together these developments indicate increased pastoral activities developing in more extended meadows. The Early Bronze Age therefore likely constitutes the third threshold period in the long-term development of the cultural landscape in Auvergne.

The comparison of the upland and lowland windows demonstrates that the key indicators of human impact for the period between the Neolithic to the Middle Bronze Age are those of woodland clearance, landscape openness, and evidence of arable agriculture and pastoralism (Figures 14.4, 14.6, and 14.7). Palynological data from the end of the Late Bronze Age to the end of the second Iron Age, however, show significant differences between these two connected areas (Figure 14.9, Ledger et al. 2015). In upland areas, key paleoecological indicators of human settlements are similar to those observed for the previous periods (Figure 14.10). A trend is observed toward an intensification of the opening of the landscape, which culminates at a regional level around ca. 2000–1900 cal BP, and toward a gradual increase in the intensity of agriculture. In the lowland, the key paleoenvironmental features for the end of the Late Bronze Age (ca. 2965–2815 cal BP) and the late second Iron Age (second to first centuries BC) are markedly different. The floristic index for this period is high and suggestive of a compartmentalized landscape with a high diversity of vegetation units. Similarly, this increased biodiversity includes nonnative trees such as fig, plane, chestnut, and walnut (Flottes 2015; Ledger et al. 2015). In particular, chestnut and walnut present concurrently high percentages that may suggest trade and cultural exchange, probably with the Mediterranean world rather than a long-distance pollen transport. Moreover, there is limited evidence of localized agriculture suggesting a spatial specialization of the land uses. Finally, a strong representation of plants indicative of ruderal communities and fungi indicative of an important erosion may be evidence of an important environmental disturbance of the site (Figure 14.9).

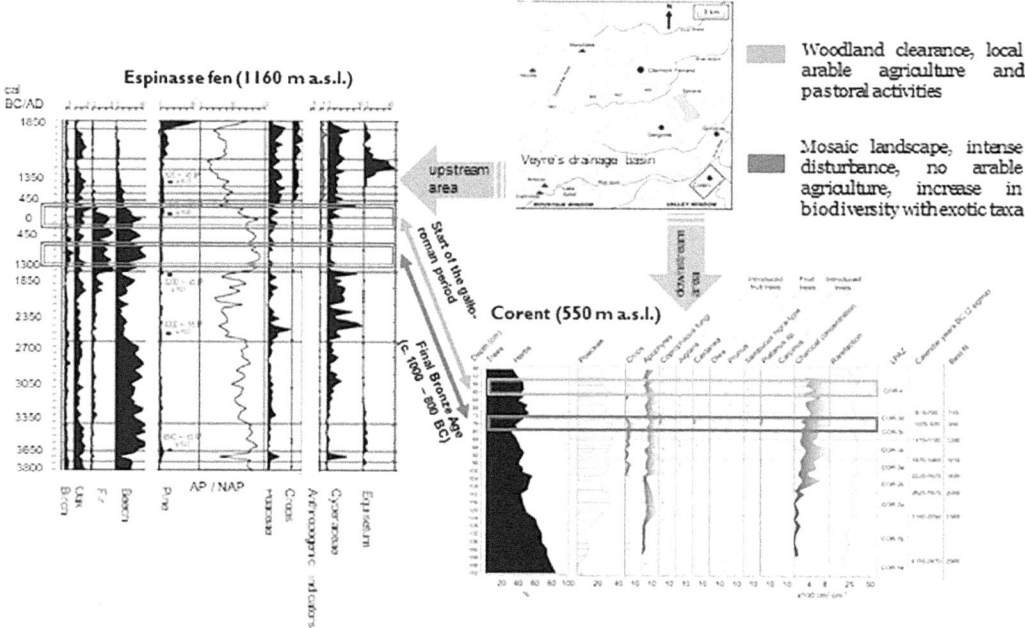

Figure 14.9. Summary percentage pollen diagram of Espinasse fen (1,160 masl) and Lac du Puy/Corent pond (550 masl, analysis by P. M. Ledger): different landscape patterns revealed by pollen data in mountain and lowland areas in Auvergne.

Studies of the development of medieval and industrial era urban environments have shown that plant communities associated with disturbance are well represented (Peglar 1993; Seppä 1997). In addition, increased species diversity is associated with the initial phase of development when intense disturbance generates a diverse array of habitats for species to invade (Seppä 1997). The peculiar features of the landscape changes noted in the lowland area (Figures 14.9 and 14.10) through late protohistory may therefore reflect an increasingly dense settlement, or perhaps a nascent urban environment (Ledger et al. 2015). The consequent decline in the floristic biodiversity index is also significant, as it resembles observations from urban areas. After peaking, diversity has been shown to fall as the initial phase of disturbance is followed by a reduction in the number of available habitats (Seppä 1997). The association of this landscape pattern with the process of proto-urbanization is consistent with archaeological excavations that have revealed two phases of important and nucleated settlement. The material evidence suggests the development of an unusually large and dense settlement ca. 950–800 cal BC, with some proto-urban features (Milcent et al. 2014). This is later followed by the Oppidum of Corent from ca. 125 BC, which persists until the Roman conquest (Poux 2012). This settlement was urban in character with administrative, commercial, and religious buildings, which may explain the paucity of pollen evidence for agriculture. Arable fields probably did not extend inside the oppidum and farming activity likely took place in peri-urban areas. Pollen data also points to increased erosion and a general environmental disturbance associated with this intense urban settlement. Finally, for both periods, the material culture indicates trading links with a number of Mediterranean regions (Poux 2012) and suggests plausible mechanisms for the introduction

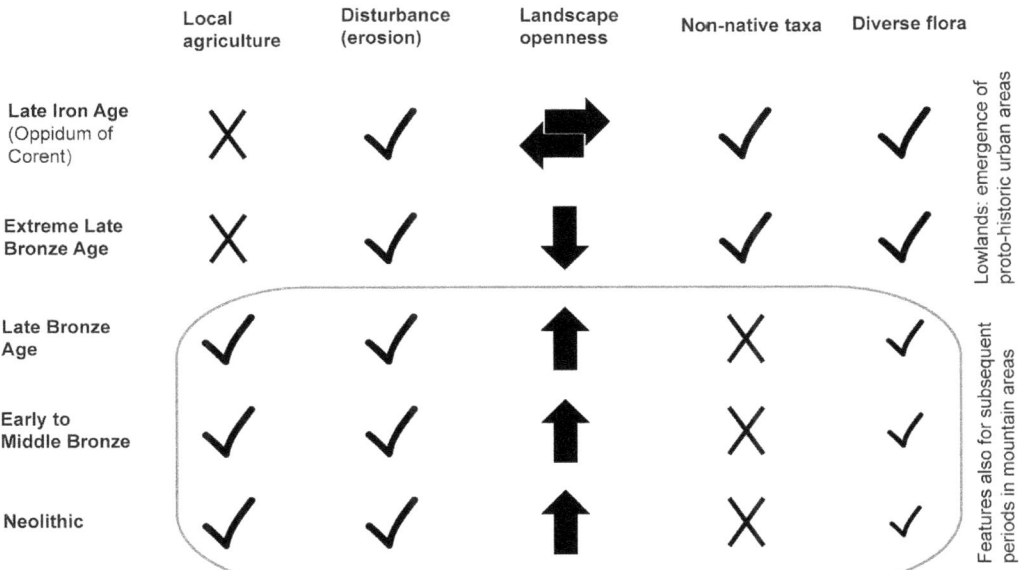

Figure 14.10. Overview of the paleoenvironmental impact in the lower Auvergne during prehistory and protohistory.

and spread of the exotic plant taxa. These early occurrences of nonnative plant taxa may thus be considered palynological fingerprints of long-distance trade and contact, especially with the Mediterranean world. The characterization of this particular landscape pattern possibly linked to proto-urban areas clearly indicates the value of local-scale paleoecological studies and their potential for reconstructing the long-term and nonlinear process of proto-urbanization during protohistory whose process does not only concern the Mediterranean world but also the West and Central Europe (Fernández-Götz and Krausse 2013).

Conclusions

The integration of archaeological and paleoenvironmental data has long been promoted as a means to understand the complex relationship between human societies, climate, and the shaping of their environment. To achieve a meaningful integration of such data, high resolution (both temporal and spatial), multiproxy paleoenvironmental datasets, such as those presented here, are required. The data presented here do not dispute the influence of climatic oscillations on human occupation; rather they indicate the relationship is more complex than is traditionally suggested. Climate warming probably encouraged human activities in the Auvergne mountains, particularly at the beginning of the sixth millennium BC (Surmely et al. 2009), yet the influence is complex and nonlinear, including for prehistory. The adaptability and rapid reactivity of prehistoric societies to environmental changes must therefore be taken into account. This approach follows an appreciation of the complex and long-term configuration—both at micro-regional and macro-regional scales—of mosaic-like anthropogenic cultural landscapes.

The particular focus on prehistory presented here clearly shows that as early as the Neolithic, human activities substantially and diversely impact vegetation dynamics in the mountains of Auvergne. Different threshold periods, whereby human impacts instigate and reinforce subsequent changes, have been identified from the Middle Neolithic until the Early Bronze Age. In subsequent periods, humans play an increasingly important role in the organization, structuration, and evolution of mountain landscapes in Auvergne (Miras et al. 2015, 2018). From the beginning of the Roman period human activities can be considered the sole driver behind the long-term shaping of the fully agricultural landscape that exists today. Mountainous landscapes must therefore be considered as complex and dynamic clusters of cultural ecosystems. The historical and cultural values of mountainous landscapes—besides their ecological value—are also important to take into account for the promotion of the landscape heritage. To achieve this, the integrated approach proposed has to be supplemented with further archaeological research, which is still lacking in Auvergne, especially in the mountain areas. This data is essential in order to properly evaluate and map long-term human occupation of the mountains, the different land management practices involved, and the connections of the uplands with the lowlands. Moreover, recent advances in palynology provide fresh insights as they allow an improved understanding of past vegetation dynamics and provide land-cover data to make a quantitative contribution to landscape management and past cultural dynamics (e.g., Mariani et al. 2017; Trondman et al. 2015).

Finally, the existence of these early prehistoric paleoenvironmental impacts underlines the high vulnerability of mountainous landscapes forming socioecosystems, which are shaped over millennia. It is therefore crucial to consider this long-term heritage when devising future management plans for such ecosystems in the face of modern global changes.

Acknowledgments

This research was supported by the ERODE Project funded by the INSU/CNRS (AP EC2CO 2009) and by the AYPONA project funded by the Regional Council of Auvergne (AAP SHS structurant 2013). M. Mariani was supported by the Australian Institute for Nuclear Science and Engineer (AINSE) Postgraduate Research Award #12039 and the John and Allan Gilmour Research Award 2016 (Faculty of Science, University of Melbourne). We would like to thank Professor Peter Biehl, Professor Stephen Dyson, and Dr. Arnau Garcia-Molsosa of the University of Buffalo for their invitation to participate in the tenth IEMA Visiting Scholar Conference (April 8–9, 2017, Buffalo). We would like to give our warmest thanks to F. Mazier and L. Marquer for the organization of the Summer School CNRS POLQUANT (August 28–September 2, 2016), where the attempts to do land-cover estimates for the Auvergne region were initiated. Many thanks also to A. Blaus, M. Caspers, and A. Hansson for their help during the summer school. Finally, we would like to thank B. Dousteyssier (Maison des Sciences de l'Homme de Clermont-Ferrand, USR3550, CNRS) who took the aerial photographs.

References

Antolín, F., V. Navarrete, M. Saña, Viñeta A., and E. Gassiot 2018 Herders in the Mountains and Farmers in the Plains? A Comparative Evaluation of the Archaeobiological Record from Neolithic Sites in the Eastern Iberian Pyrenees and the Southern Lower Lands. *Quaternary International* 484:75–93.

Antonetti, P., E. Brugel, F. Kessler, J. P. Barbe, and M. Tort 2006 *Atlas de la flore d'Auvergne*. Conservatoire botanique national du Massif Central, Chavaniac-Lafayette.

Ballut, C., Y. Michelin, and Y. Miras 2012 Landscape Human Shaping and Spatial Mobility of Agropastoral Practices in the Chaîne des Puys during Historical Times (Massif Central, France). *Quaternary International* 251:97–106.

Baum, T., C. Nendel, S. Jacomet, M. Colobran, and R. Ebersbach 2016 "Slash and Burn" or "Weed and Manure"? A Modelling Approach to Explore Hypotheses of Late Neolithic Crop Cultivation in Prealpine Wetland Sites. *Vegetation History and Archaeobotany* 25:611–627.

Behre, K.-E. 1981 The Interpretation of Anthropogenic Indicators in Pollen Diagrams. *Pollen and Spores* 23:225–245.

Behre, K.-E. 1992 The History of Rye Cultivation in Europe. *Vegetation History and Archaeobotany* 1:141–156.

Berglund, B. E., M. J. Gaillard, L. Björkman, and T. Persson 2008. Long-Term Changes in Floristic Diversity in Southern Sweden: Palynological Richness, Vegetation Dynamics and Land Use. *Vegetation History and Archaeobotany* 17:573–583.

Birks, H. J. B., and J. M. Line 1992 The Use of Rarefaction Analysis for Estimating Palynological Richness from Quaternary Pollenanalytical Data. *The Holocene* 2:1–10.

Boivin, P., J. C. Besson, D. Briot, and A. Gourgaud 2004 Volcanologie de la Chaîne des Puys. Aydat. Editions du Parc Naturel Régional des Volcans d'Auvergne, Clermont-Ferrand.

Bouchet, C. 1987 Hydrogéologie en milieu volcanique: Le Bassin de la Veyre. PhD thesis, University of Avignon.

Camus, G. 1975 La Chaîne des Puys (Massif central, France): Etude structurale et volcanologique. PhD thesis, Annales des Sciences de l'Université de Clermont, Clermont-Ferrand.

Carozza, L., J. F. Berger, A. Burens, and C. Marcigny 2015 Society and Environment in Southern France from the 3rd Millennium to the Beginning of the 2nd Millennium BC: 2200 BC a Tipping Point? In *A Climatic Breakdown as a Cause for the Collapse of the Old World*, 333–362. Tagungen des Landesmuseums für Vorgeschichte Halle, 23–26 October 2014, Germany.

Carozza, L., and L. Bouby 2006 Un habitat du Bronze moyen à Cournon-d'Auvergne (Puy-de-Dôme): Nouvelles données sur la dynamique du Bronze moyen sur la bordure méridionale du Massif central. *Bulletin de la Société préhistorique française* 103(3):535–584.

Court-Picon, M. 2007 Mise en place du paysage dans un milieu de moyenne et haute montagne du Tardiglaciaire à l'Epoque actuelle: analyse du signal palynologique en Champsaur (Hautes-Alpes, France) à l'interface des dynamiques naturelles et des dynamiques sociales. PhD thesis, University of Franche-Comté, Besançon, France.

Cugny, C., F. Mazier, and D. Galop 2010 Modern and Fossil Non-pollen Palynomorphs from the Basque Mountains (Western Pyrenees, France): The Use of Coprophilous Fungi to Reconstruct Pastoral Activity. *Vegetation History and Archaeobotany* 19:391–408.

Davies, A. L., and R. Tipping 2004 Sensing Small-Scale Human Activity in the Paleoecological Record: Fine Spatial Resolution Pollen Analyses from West Glen Affric, Northern Scotland. *The Holocene* 14:233–245.

Dearing, J., B. Acma, S. Bub, F. M. Chambers, X. Chen, J. Cooper, D. Crook, X. H. Dong, M. Dotterweich, M. E. Edwards, T. H. Foster, M. J. Gaillard, D. Galop, P. Gell, A. Gil, E. Jeffers, R. T. Jones, A. Krishnamurthy, P. J. Langdon, R. Marchant, F. Mazier, C. E. McLean, L. H. Nunes, S. Raman, I. Suryaprakash, M. Umer, X. D. Yang, R. Wang, and K. Zhang 2015 Social-Ecological Systems in the Anthropocene: The Need for Integrating Social and Biophysical Records at Regional Scales. *Anthropocene Review* 2(3–12):220–246.

Ejarque, A. 2013 *La alta montaña pirenaica: génesis y configuración holocena de un paisaje cultural: Estudio paleoambiental en el valle del Madriu-Perafita-Claror (Andorra)*. BAR International Series 2507. Archaeopress, Oxford.

Ejarque, A., Y. Miras, and S. Riera 2011 Modern Pollen and Non-pollen Palynomorph Analogues of Vegetation and Highland Grazing Activities Obtained from Surface and Dung Datasets from the Eastern Pyrenees. *Review of Palaeobotany and Palynology* 167:123–139.

Ejarque, A., Y. Miras, S. Riera, J. M. Palet, and H. Orengo 2010 Testing Microregional Variability in the Holocene Shaping of High Mountain Cultural Landscape: A Palaeoenvironmental Case Study in the Eastern Pyrenees. *Journal of Archaeological Science* 37:1468–1479.

Faegri, K. 1966 Some Problems of Representivity in Pollen Analysis. *Palaeobotanist* 15:135–140.

Faegri, K., and J. Iversen 1989 *Textbook of Pollen Analysis*. John Wiley and Sons, New York.

Fernández-Götz, M., and D. Krausse 2013 Rethinking Early Iron Age Urbanisation in Central Europe: The Heunburg Site and Its Archaeological Environment. *Antiquity* 87:473–487.

Flottes, L. 2015 *Étude carpologique des occupations de l'âge du Bronze final à l'Époque romaine sur le site de Corent (Puy-de-Dôme)*. Mémoire de master, Master Evolution, Patrimoine National et Sociétés, Spécialité Quaternaire et Préhistoire, MNHN.

Freydier P., and P. Dubreuil 2004 *Projet d'animation territoriale agro-environnementale OTAE de la vallée de l'Auzon: Evaluation environnementale*. Conservatoire des Espaces et Paysages d'Auvergne.

Fyfe, R. M., J. Woodbridge, and N. Roberts 2015 From Forest to Farmland: Pollen-Inferred Land Cover Change across Europe Using the Pseudobiomization Approach. *Global Change Biology* 21:1197–1212.

Gaillard, M.-J., S. Sugita, F. Mazier, A.-K. Trondman, A. Brostrom, T. Hickler, J. O. Kaplan, E. Kjellström, U. Kokfelt, and P. Kunes 2010 Holocene Land-Cover Reconstructions for Studies on Land Cover–Climate Feedbacks. *Climate of the Past* 6:483–499.

Galop, D., D. Rius, C. Cugny, and F. Mazier 2013 A History of Long-Term Human–Environment Interactions in the French Pyrenees Inferred from the Pollen Data. In *Continuity and Change in Cultural Adaptation to Mountain Environments from Prehistory to Contemporary Threats*, edited by L. Lozny, 19–30. Series Studies in Human Ecology and Adaptation, Springer-Verlag, Berlin.

Gauthier, E. 2001 Evolution de l'impact de l'homme sur la végétation du massif jurassien au cours des 4 derniers millénaires. Nouvelles données palynologiques. PhD thesis, University of Franche-Comté, Besançon, France.

Hénon, P. 2016 *ZAC de la Fontanille II, Lempdes, Puy-de-Dôme*. Rapport final d'opération, SRA Auvergne.

Hillbrand, M., B. van Geel, A. Hasenfratz, P. Hadorn, and J. N. Haas 2012 Non-pollen Palynomorphs Show Human- and Livestock-Induced Eutrophication of Lake Nussbaumersee (Thurgau, Switzerland) since Neolithic Times (3840 BC). *The Holocene* 24(5):559–568.

Jacob, J., J. R. Disnar, F. Arnaud, E. Gauthier, Y. Billaud, E. Chapron, and G. Bardoux 2009 Impacts of New Agricultural Practices on Soil Erosion during the Bronze Age in French Prealps. *The Holocene* 19:241–249.

Jacomet, S., R. Ebersbach, Ö. Akeret, F. Antolín, T. Baum, A. Bogaard, C. Brombacher, N. K. Bleicher, A. Heitz-Weniger, H. Hüster-Plogmann, E. Gross, M. Kühn, P. Rentzel, B. L. Steiner, L. Wick, and J. M. Schibler 2016 On-Site Data Casts Doubts on the Hypothesis of Shifting Cultivation in the Late Neolithic (c. 4300–2400 cal. BC): Landscape Management as an Alternative Paradigm. *The Holocene* 26(11):1858–1874.

Kothieringer, K., C. Walser, B. Dietre, and L. Karsten Lambers 2015 High Impact: Early Pastoralism and Environmental Change during the Neolithic and Bronze Age in the Silvretta Alps (Switzerland, Austria) as Evidenced by Archaeological, Palaeoecological and Pedological Proxies. *Zeitschrift für geomorphologie supplementary issues* 59(2):177–198.

Lavrieux, M., J. R. Disnar, E. Chapron, J. G. Bréheret, J. Jacob, Y. Miras, J. L. Reyss, V. Andrieu-Ponel, and F. Arnaud 2013 6,700-Year Sedimentary Record of Climatic and Anthropic Signals in Lake Aydat (French Massif Central). *The Holocene* 23:1317–1328.

Ledger, P. M., Y. Miras, M. Poux, and P. Y. Milcent 2015 The Palaeoenvironmental Impact of Prehistoric Settlement and Proto-historic Urbanism: Tracing the Emergence of the Oppidum of Corent, Auvergne, France. *PLoS ONE* 10(4):e0121517.

Magny, M., F. Arnaud, Y. Billaud, and A. Marguet 2012 Lake-Level Fluctuations at Lake Bourget (Eastern France) around 4500–3500 cal BP and Their Palaeoclimatic and Archaeological Implications. *Journal of Quaternary Science* 27:494–502.

Magny, M, J. L. de Beaulieu, R. Drescher-Schneider, B. Vannière, A. V. Walter-Simonnet, Y. Miras, L. Millet, G. Bossuet, O. Peyron, E. Brugiapaglia, and A. Leroux 2007 Holocene Climate Changes in the Central Mediterranean as Recorded by Lake-Level Fluctuations at Lake Accesa (Tuscany, Italy). *Quaternary Science Reviews* 26:1736–1758.

Magny, M., and J. N. Haas 2004 A Major Widespread Climatic Change around 5300 cal yr BP at the Time of the Alpine Iceman. *Journal of Quaternary Science* 19(5):423–430.

Mariani, M., S. E. Connor, M. S. Fletcher, M. Theuerkauf, P. Kuneš, G. Jacobsen, K. M. Saunders, and A. Zawadzki 2017 How Old Is the Tasmanian Cultural Landscape? A Test of Landscape Openness Using Quantitative Land-Cover Reconstructions. *Journal of Biogeography*:1–11.

Mazier, F., M.-J. Gaillard, P. Kuneš, S. Sugita, A.-K. Trondman, and A. Broström 2012 Testing the Effect of Site Selection and Parameter Setting on REVEALS-model Estimates of Plant Abundance Using the Czech Quaternary Palynological Database. *Review of Palaeobotany and Palynology* 187:38–49.

Michelin, Y., V. Vergne, C. Cougoul, and S. Cournut 2001 Variations des teneurs en éléments minéraux dans un bas-marais holocène: la Vézolle (Chaîne des Puys), première recherche des manifestations anthropiques. *Quaternaire* 12(1–2):31–41.

Milcent, P.-Y., M. Poux, S. Mader, M. Torres, and A. Tramon 2014. Une agglomération de hauteur autour de 600 a.c. en Gaule centrale: Corent (Auvergne). In *Transalpinare, Mélanges offerts à A.-M. Adam*, edited by G. Alberti, C. Feliu, and G. Pierrevelcin, 181–204. Ausonius, Bordeaux.

Miras, Y., 2016. *Hétérogénéité des paysages de montagne, variabilités des systèmes d'exploitation et transformations environnementales depuis le Néolithique: approches intégratives, pluri-échelles et multi-proxies*. Habilitation à Diriger des Recherches, Université Blaise Pascal, Clermont-Ferrand, France.

Miras, Y., A. Beauger, M. Lavrieux, V. Berthon, K. Serieyssol, V. Andrieu-Ponel, and P. M. Ledger 2015 Tracking Long-Term Human Impacts on Landscape, Vegetal Biodiversity and Water Quality in the Lake Aydat (Auvergne, France) Using Pollen, Non-pollen Palynomorphs and Diatom Assemblages. *Palaeogeography, Palaeoclimatology, Palaeoecology* 424:76–90.

Miras, Y., G. Galop, E. Gauthier, M. Court-Picon, I. Jouffroy-Bapicot, and H. Richard 2004b Chronology, Dynamics and Impact on Vegetation of Human Activities in French Mountain Areas: A Synthesis for the Alps, Pyrenees, Massif Central and Jura Mountains. Eleventh International Palynological Congress. *POLEN* 14:225–226.

Miras, Y., F. Laggoun-Défarge, P. Guenet, and H. Richard 2004a Multi-disciplinary Approach to Changes in Agro-pastoral Activities since the Subboreal in the Surroundings of the "Narse d'Espinasse" (Puy de Dôme, French Massif Central). *Vegetation History and Archaeobotany* 13:91–103.

Miras, Y., M. Lavrieux, and M. Florez 2013 Holocene Ecological Trajectories in Lake and Wetland Systems (Auvergne, France): A Palaeoenvironmental Contribution for a Better Assessment of Ecosystem and Land Use's Viability in Management Strategies. *Annali di Botanica* 3:127–133.

Miras, Y., J. Lonlac Konlac, A. Beauger, B. Legrand, D. Latour, K. Serieyssol, M. Lavrieux, P. M. Ledge, V. Mazenod, J. L. Peiry, E. Mephu-Nguifo 2021 Tracking Plant, Fungal and Algal Diversity through a Data Mining Approach: Towards Improved Analysis of Holocene Lake Aydat (Puy-de-Dôme, France) Dynamics and Ecological Legacies. *Revues des Sciences naturelles d'Auvergne* 85:83–104.

Miras, Y., M. Mariani, P. M. Ledger, A. Mayoral, L. Chassiot, and M. Lavrieux 2018 Holocene Vegetation Dynamics and First Land-Cover Estimates in the Auvergne Mountains (Massif

Central, France): Key Tools to Landscape Management. *IANSA: Interdisciplinaria Archaeologica Natural Sciences in Archaeology* 9(2):online first.

Miras, Y., H. Orengo, A. Ejarque, S. Riera, J. M. Palet, and A. Poiraud 2010 Prehistoric Impact and Vegetation at High Altitudes: An Integrated Palaeoecological and Archaeological Approach in the Eastern Pyrenees (Perafita Valley, Andorra). *Plant Biosystems* 144(4):924–939.

Muller-Pelletier, C., and C. Georjon 2013 Un vaste établissement chasséen aux Queyriaux (Cournon-d'Auvergne, Puy-de-Dôme). *Bulletin de la Société préhistorique française* 110(2):360–363.

Orengo, H. A, J. M. Palet, A. Ejarque, Y. Miras, and S. Riera 2014 Shifting Occupation Dynamics in the Madriu-Perafita-Claror Valleys (Andorra) from the Early Neolithic to the Chalcolithic: The Onset of High Mountain Cultural Landscapes. *Quaternary International* 353:140–152.

Palet, J. M., A. Ejarque, Y. Miras, S. Riera, I. Euba, and H. A. Orengo 2007 Formes d'ocupació d'alta muntanya a la vall de la Vansa (Serra del Cadí-alt Urgell) i a la vall del Madriu-Perafita-Claror (Andorra): estudi diacrònic de paisatges culturals pirinencs. *Tribuna d'Arqueologia* 2006–2007:229–253.

Pasty, J.-F. 2016 L'occupation préhistorique du plateau de Gergovie (Puy-de-Dôme). Caractérisation des industries lithiques néolithiques. *Revue Archéologique du Centre de la France* 55:1–29.

Peglar, S. M. 1993 The Development of the Cultural Landscape around Diss Mere, Norfolk, UK during the Last 7,000 Years. *Review of Palaeobotany and Palynology* 76:1–47.

Pla, S., and J. Catalan 2005 Chrysophyte Cysts from Lake Sediments Reveal the Submillennial Winter/Spring Climate Variability in the Northwestern Mediterranean Region throughout the Holocene. *Climate Dynamics* 24:263–278.

Poux, M. 2012 *Corent: voyage au cœur d'une ville gauloise*. Editions Errance Paris.

Prentice, I. C. 1985 Pollen Representation, Source Area, and Basin Size: Toward a Unified Theory of Pollen Analysis. *Quaternary Research* 23:76–86.

Reille, M., A. Pons, and J. L. de Beaulieu 1992 Late and Postglacial Vegetation, Climate and Human Action in the French Massif Central. *Cahiers de Micropaléontologie* 7(1–2):93–106.

Rösch, M., A. Kleinmann, J. Lechterbeck, and L. Wick 2014 Botanical Off-Site and On-Site Data as Indicators of Different Land Use Systems: A Discussion with Examples from Southwest Germany. *Vegetation History and Archaeobotany* 23(1):121–133.

Ruddiman, W. F. 2003 The Anthropogenic Greenhouse Era Began Thousands of Years Ago. *Climatic Change* 61:261–293.

Seppä, H. 1997 The Long-Term Development of Urban Vegetation in Helsinki, Finland: A Pollen Diagram from Töölönlahti. *Vegetation History and Archaeobotany* 6:91–103.

Sévin-Allouet, C. (dir.) 2010 *ZA de Layat, Riom, Puy-de-Dôme*. Rapport final d'opération d'archéologie préventive, SRA Auvergne.

Smith, B. D., and M. A. Zeder 2013 The Onset of the Anthropocene. *Anthropocene* 4:8–13.

Sugita, S. 1994 Pollen Representation of Vegetation in Quaternary Sediments: Theory and Method in Patchy Vegetation. *Journal of Ecology* 82:881–897.

Sugita, S. 2007 Theory of Quantitative Reconstruction of Vegetation: Parts I and II. *The Holocene* 17:229–241 and 243–257.

Surmely, F., and R. Liabeuf 1998 Les sépultures mégalithiques en Auvergne: bilan des connaissances. In *La France des dolmens et des sépultures collectives: 4500–2000 avant J.-C.: bilans documentaires régionaux*, edited by P. Soulier, 39–44. Errance, Paris.

Surmely, F., Y. Miras, P. Guenet, S. Tzortzis, A. Savignat, V. Nicolas, B. Vannière, and A. V. Walter-Simonnet 2009 Occupation and Land Use History of a Medium Mountain from the

Mid-Holocene: A Pluridisciplinary Study Performed in the South Cantal (French Central Massif). *Comptes Rendus Palevol* 8:737–748.

Sutton, O. G. 1953 *Micrometeorology*. Quarterly Journal of the Royal Meteorological Society, New York.

Tauber, H. 1965 Differential Pollen Dispersion and the Interpretation of Pollen Diagrams. *Danmarks geologiske undersøgelse* 2(89):1–69.

Theuerkauf, M., J. Couwenberg, A. Kuparinen, and V. Liebscher 2016 A Matter of Dispersal: REVEALSinR Introduces State-of-the-Art Dispersal Models to Quantitative Vegetation Reconstruction. *Vegetation History and Archaeobotany* 25(6):541–553.

Thirault, E., 2013 Petit Beaulieu à Clermont-Ferrand (Puy-de-Dôme): du Campaniforme au Bronze ancien, habitat et nécropole: présentation préliminaire. *Bulletin de l'Association pour la Promotion des Recherches sur l'Âge du Bronze* (11):89–93.

Trondman, A. K., M. J. Gaillard, F. Mazier, S. Sugita, R. Fyfe, A. B. Nielsen, C. Twiddle, P. Barratt, H. J. B. Birks, and A. E. Bjune 2015 Pollen-Based Quantitative Reconstructions of Holocene Regional Vegetation Cover (Plant-Functional Types and Land-Cover Types) in Europe Suitable for Climate Modelling. *Global Change Biology* 21:676–697.

van Geel, B., G. R. Coope, and T. van der Hammen 1989 Palaeoecology and Stratigraphy of the Lateglacial Type Section at Usselo (The Netherlands). *Review of Palaeobotany and Palynology* 60:25–129.

Vermeulen, C. 2001 *Chantemerle, Gerzat, Puy-de-Dôme*. Rapport final d'opération d'archéologie préventive, SRA Auvergne.

Walsh, K., and F. Mocci 2011 Mobility in the Mountains: Late Third and Second Millennia Alpine Societies' Engagements with the High Altitude Zones in the Southern French Alps. *European Journal of Archaeology* 14(1–2):88–115.

Walsh, K., and S. Richer 2006 Attitudes to Altitude: Changing Meanings and Perceptions within a "Marginal" Alpine Landscape—The Integration of Palaeoecological and Archaeological Data in a High Altitude Landscape in the French Alps. *World Archaeology* 38:436–454.

Wanner, H., J. Beer, J. Bütikofer, T. J. Crowley, U. Cubasch, J. Flückiger, H. Goosse, M. Grosjean, F. Joos, J. O. Kaplan, M. Küttel, S. A. Müller, I. C. Prentice, O. Solomina, T. F. Stocker, P. Tarasov, M. Wagner, and M. Widmann 2008 Mid- to Late Holocene Climate Change: An Overview. *Quaternary Science Reviews* 27:1791–1828.

CHAPTER FIFTEEN

Holocene Anthropization of Mid-elevation Landscapes around Pic d'Orhy, Western Pyrenees

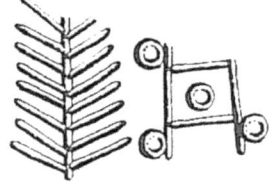

Michael R. Coughlan, David S. Leigh, Ted L. Gragson, and Mélanie Le Couédic

Abstract *We use archaeologically derived chronologies of agropastoral occupation and archives of sedimentary charcoal (a proxy for fire) to examine processes of anthropogenic landscape domestication ("anthropization") for upland landscapes around Pic d'Orhy, French Western Pyrenees. Prevailing accounts establish Middle Holocene agropastoral land use activities as the onset of anthropization in the Pyrenean uplands through regional-level syntheses of paleoecological and archaeological evidence. However, little is known about the timing and spatial patterning of anthropization at the landscape level and even less consideration has been given to the specific socioecological processes responsible for landscape change. In this chapter, we test two alternative hypotheses for the anthropization of landscapes around Pic d'Orhy: (1) Anthropization was an intentional, relatively rapid, and uniform collection of "pulse" deforestation events initiated by phases of land use intensification, and (2) anthropization was a long-term, dynamic, and spatially heterogenous "press" process leading to coevolutionary phases of land use intensification and land conversion. Our results support the hypothesis that anthropization was a spatially and temporally heterogeneous "press" type of disturbance. In conclusion, we suggest that while regional interdisciplinary syntheses are broadly informative, understanding the human behaviors responsible for anthropization may require a finer-grained, landscape-level approach.*

INTRODUCTION

Anthropization is the process of "domesticating" or converting a landscape from a state dominated by "natural" biogeophysical dynamics to a state strongly influenced, if not dominated, by human activities. Scholars have long implicated the Neolithic land use regime, that is, the cultivation of *Cerealia* grass species, directed browsing and grazing by domesticated livestock, and the use of landscape fire as the primary mechanisms driving land conversion from forest to pasture in the upland landscapes of the Pyrenees (Galop 1998; Galop and Jalut 1994; Mazier et al. 2009; Rius et al. 2009). Yet little thought has been given to the character and pace of such processes at spatial and temporal scales of human land use and decision-making, particularly for uplands at more than 500 masl.

In this chapter, we synthesize archaeologically derived chronologies of agropastoral land use and occupation with local archives of sedimentary charcoal, a proxy for anthropization of mid-elevation (900–2000 masl) landscapes around Pic d'Orhy, Western Pyrenees. Mid-elevation landscapes in the Western Pyrenees represent examples of upland tree-line forests converted to grassland pastures. They offer an interesting context for investigating processes of anthropization because these grasslands were evidently never occupied year-round, nor were they terraced or cultivated. With climatic conditions predominantly inhospitable to the cultivation of *Cerealia* genera, mid-elevation landscapes were used logistically as summer pastures (e.g., ca. May–October). Further, these are ancient landscape conversions initiated following the onset of Neolithic lifeways over eight thousand years ago (Galop et al. 2013).

Prevailing accounts establish Middle Holocene agropastoral land use activities as the onset of anthropization in the Pyrenean uplands through regional-level syntheses of paleoecological and archaeological evidence (Carozza et al. 2005; Hernández-Beloqui et al. 2015; Iriarte 2009; Monna et al. 2004; Rius et al. 2012). These accounts characterize anthropization as an orthogenetic (if arrhythmic) sequence of phases of agropastoral land use that intensify through time, reaching a crescendo in the nineteenth century. Human activity is explained vaguely as progressively "impacting" and "penetrating" the landscape through deforestation presumably accomplished by pulses of cutting, burning, and pasturing animals or some combination thereof. However, extrapolating causal explanations concerning human behavior on particular landscapes from course resolution correlations can and has led to simplistic and deterministic accounts about human–environment interactions in general (Berger and Wang 2017; Calaway 2015; Contreras 2017).

Our interdisciplinary, place-based investigation of the timing and spatial patterning of the conversion of mid-elevation forests to grassland pasture increases the resolution of such studies to the landscape level, that is, the level of human decision-making concerning land use and management (Gragson et al. 2015). Here, we report on newly obtained radiocarbon dating of seasonal pastoral occupations, combining our results with previously published radiocarbon dates for archaeological sites located within our project area along the Pyrenean divide. We synthesize these archaeological dates with two newly resolved and one previously published down-core sedimentary charcoal records obtained from zero-order colluvial hollows (4–12 ha in size) in close proximity to dated archaeological sites. Our research design and our discussion of observed environmental and archaeological change builds on theory in socioecological systems (Collins et al. 2010), nonlinear ecological dynamics represented by the alternative stable-states hypothesis (Bowman et al. 2015; McWethy et al. 2013; Wood and Bowman 2012), as well as empirically informed models of human organization and behavior that account for social and ecological incentives and constraints on human agency (Bird et al. 2016; Coughlan 2014; Coughlan and Gragson 2016; Gragson 1998). We test two alternative hypotheses for the mid-elevation landscapes around Pic d'Orhy, each representing opposite ends of the human–environment interaction spectrum: (1) Anthropization was an intentional, relatively rapid, and uniform collection of "pulse" deforestation events initiated by phases of land use intensification, and (2) anthropization was a long-term, dynamic, and spatially heterogeneous "press" process leading to coevolutionary phases of land use intensification and land conversion.

Hypotheses and Theoretical Background

Anthropization as Impact-Pulse Hypothesis

In socioecological systems theory a discrete and rapid disturbance event is referred to as a "pulse" (Collins et al. 2010). The anthropization of mountain landscapes by agropastoral land use has been represented as a progressive "conquest" against primeval forest (Galop et al. 2013), where pulses of intentional forest clearing—at the small catchment level—collectively led to landscape level conversion to grassland. In terms of the actual human behaviors responsible for anthropization, a clearance pulse occurs when farmers, in need of new pasture, intentionally clear the catchment by "slash and burn" methods. A clearance "pulse" can be a onetime event or it can be repeated rotationally until landscape degradation precludes forest regeneration (Roos et al. 2016). In either case, the cause of anthropization is land use intensification linked to either population growth or resource exhaustion (e.g., soil degradation), or some combination of these two factors.

A simplistic model of this hypothesis (Figure 15.1) suggests that the expansion of grassland pasture takes place through a spatially contiguous wave of conversion pulses where, patch by adjacent patch, the landscape is converted. The process is relatively independent of natural controls such as climate and topography (Rius et al. 2009). Indeed, once anthropization is set in motion, linkages to natural controls are irreparably "broken" (Whitlock et al. 2017). At a minimum, given the appropriate depositional contexts, patch-sized catchments (our zero-order hollows) should display evidence of the conversion pulse coincident with archaeological evidence for occupation. For example, the onset of anthropization (the initial conversion pulse) should show a discrete, steep-sloped peak in the sedimentary charcoal accumulation. The charcoal peak should be coincident with nearby archaeological evidence for the intensification of agropastoral occupation, since the responsible agropastoralists would want to efficiently make use of and defend their labor investments.

Resource degradation should also be evidenced post-conversion since new clearings are driven by intensification and presumably overgrazing is occurring on previously cleared pastures. Archaeological evidence might also point to site abandonment in degraded areas or at least a decrease in site density.

Anthropization as Press-Coevolution Hypothesis

Chronic and long-term forcing in socioecological systems is referred to as a "press" (Collins et al. 2010). Presses caused by human activities induce slow, cumulative change while the

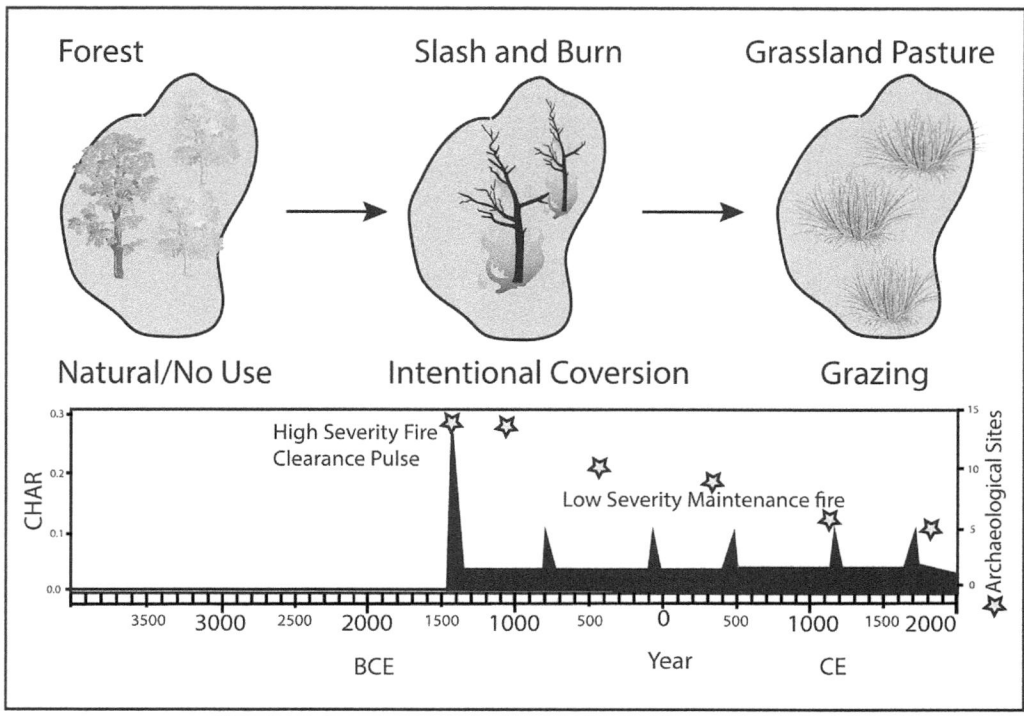

Figure 15.1. Impact-pulse hypothesis at catchment level showing hypothesized charcoal accumulation (CHAR) and archaeological site patterns. Symbols courtesy of the Integration and Application Network, University of Maryland Center for Environmental Science (ian.umces.edu/symbols/).

immediate objectives of the human behaviors responsible for presses entail short-term goals. For example, provisioning of human populations through the extraction of food, fiber, and fuel occurs on a daily basis, but its ecological effects are cumulative over multiple generations (Collins et al. 2010). Long-term changes between landscape and society are viewed as coevolutionary and are not the result of intentional human action (Blondel 2006).

Alternative stable-state theory suggests that webs of stabilizing negative feedbacks between vegetation and disturbance factors such as herbivory (e.g., grazing and browsing) and fire help to maintain particular ecosystem states. Changes in the type, rate, or intensity of fire and herbivore disturbance can initiate positive feedback loops that push systems into novel states, again maintained by new stabilizing feedbacks (Bowman et al. 2015; McWethy et al. 2013; Scheffer et al. 2001; Whitlock et al. 2014). This theory emphasizes that at the landscape level, the transition from closed canopy forest-dominated landscape with negative, stabilizing feedbacks to a grassland-dominated landscape with its own stabilizing feedbacks could entail long time periods (Bowman et al. 2015). Indeed, the theory suggests the occurrence of an intermediate condition involving open woodland and shrub-dominated landscape characterized by positive, destabilizing feedbacks (McWethy et al. 2013; Wood and Bowman 2012).

Persistent, low severity disturbances such as herbivory and low intensity surface fire could trigger coevolutionary, positive feedbacks between land use and landscape. For example, under a land use regime characterized by woodland grazing and occasional burning of undergrowth, mature trees might persist but reproduction would be stymied. After decades and centuries of such a regime, an increasingly open canopy would develop. An open canopy could support more livestock for a longer period. With increased exposure to sun and wind, snow cover would melt faster in spring, providing earlier access to understory grazing. People might allow their animals to spend more time in these forage-rich openings, thus intensifying the land use regime. Positive feedback in open canopy forests between grazing, vegetation, and fire would eventually trigger a regime shift to grasslands and human–landscape dynamics would transition to stabilizing feedback that maintains open grasslands. Feedback should be additionally amplified or dampened by natural controls such as climate and topography, since landscape conversion is not intentionally directed by human decision-making, that is, fire is permitted to run uncontrolled.

Under this hypothesis, anthropization is driven by coevolutionary, positive feedback dynamics between land use, topography, and vegetation (Figure 15.2). At the catchment

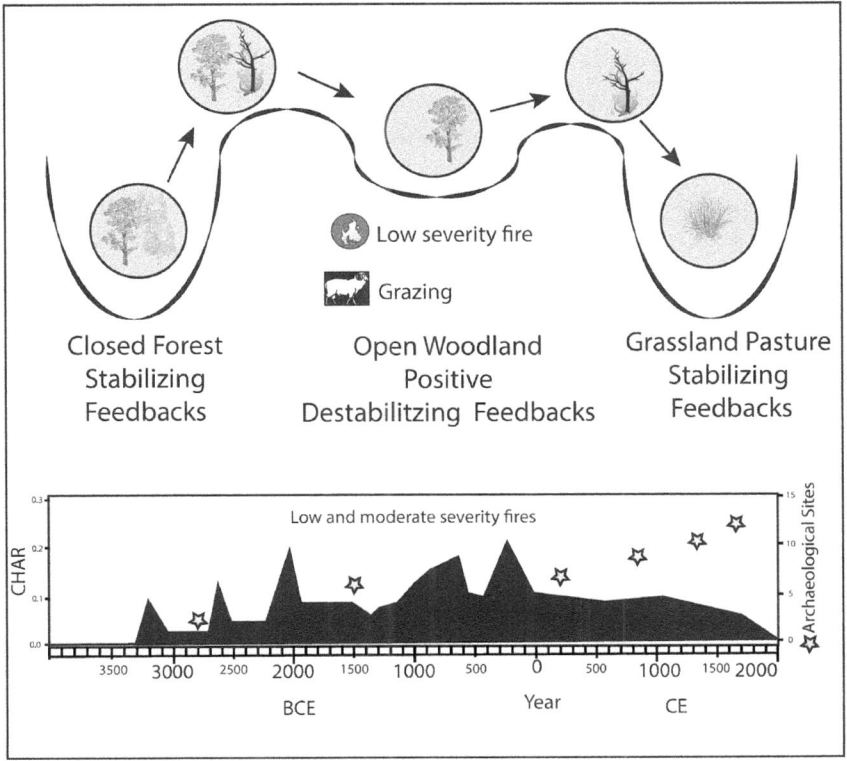

Figure 15.2. Press-coevolution hypothesis with catchment-level alternative stable states (circles), basins of attraction, and feedbacks aligned with hypothesized charcoal accumulation (CHAR) and archaeological site patterns. Symbols courtesy of the Integration and Application Network, University of Maryland Center for Environmental Science (ian.umces.edu/symbols/). Adapted from McWethy et al. 2013.

level, with fire use targeting woody detritus and understory shrubs in a cycle of positive feedback, sedimentary charcoal might register onset of land use as a relatively persistent elevated level of accumulation prior to any large peaks. Multiple peaks in charcoal accumulation could indicate drier periods where climate modulates fire severity. As an overall trend, the distribution charcoal accumulation should show a peak and then decline, leveling off to moderate levels. This is because as the system transitions from forest to grassland, coarse woody fuels decline and fine grassy fuels increase. As a consequence, the peak marks a "tipping point" as the landscape transitions to a new state. Following transition, human–fire–landscape dynamics are characterized by stabilizing feedback indicated by sustained moderate charcoal levels. Catchments with topographic microclimates conducive to fire (i.e., drier, exposed terrain) would favor earliest increase and earliest peak in charcoal accumulation because they are more vulnerable to the effects of fire. Both local and landscape-level archaeological evidence should be sparse in the beginning and intensify well after the transition to grassland pasture as the grazing capacity of the landscape increases.

Materials and Methods

Project and Site Description

Data presented here are derived from interdisciplinary field work conducted over the last decade in the commune of Larrau, France (Lat. 42.962880, Long. –0.950112) (Figure 15.3). Over this time period, we have conducted ethnographic, archaeological, sedimentological, pedological, geospatial, and geophysical analyses on long-term human–environmental interactions (Gragson et al. 2015). Larrau is an ethnically Basque commune that continues to maintain a rural, traditional agropastoral character, despite recent demographic and economic headwinds. Elevations range from about 300 masl to 2,017 masl, with a patchwork of forests and farms dominating up to about 800 masl. From about 800 to 2,000 masl patches of beech (*Fagus sylvatica*) and fir (*Abis alba*) forests gradually give way to subalpine grassland pasture (*Festuca* spp., *Nardus Structa*, *Trifolium aplinum*), which dominates above 1,200 masl. The climate is humid Atlantic with relatively high precipitation (>1,600 mm/yr), and average temperatures are mild (ranging 7–20 °C). Typically upper elevations remain under snow into May with south-facing, exposed slopes opening earlier.

Coupled Archaeological-Biogeophysical Sampling Strategy

Numerous archaeological sites scattered across the upland landscape of Larrau present ample opportunity for investigation. However, viable sedimentary archives are few as bogs are rare and lakes are nonexistent (Leigh et al. 2015a). Initial auger testing at 10 cm contiguous increments of several colluvial stratigraphic profiles beneath zero-order catchments yielded remarkable chronostratigraphic integrity and sedimentary charcoal records indicative of past

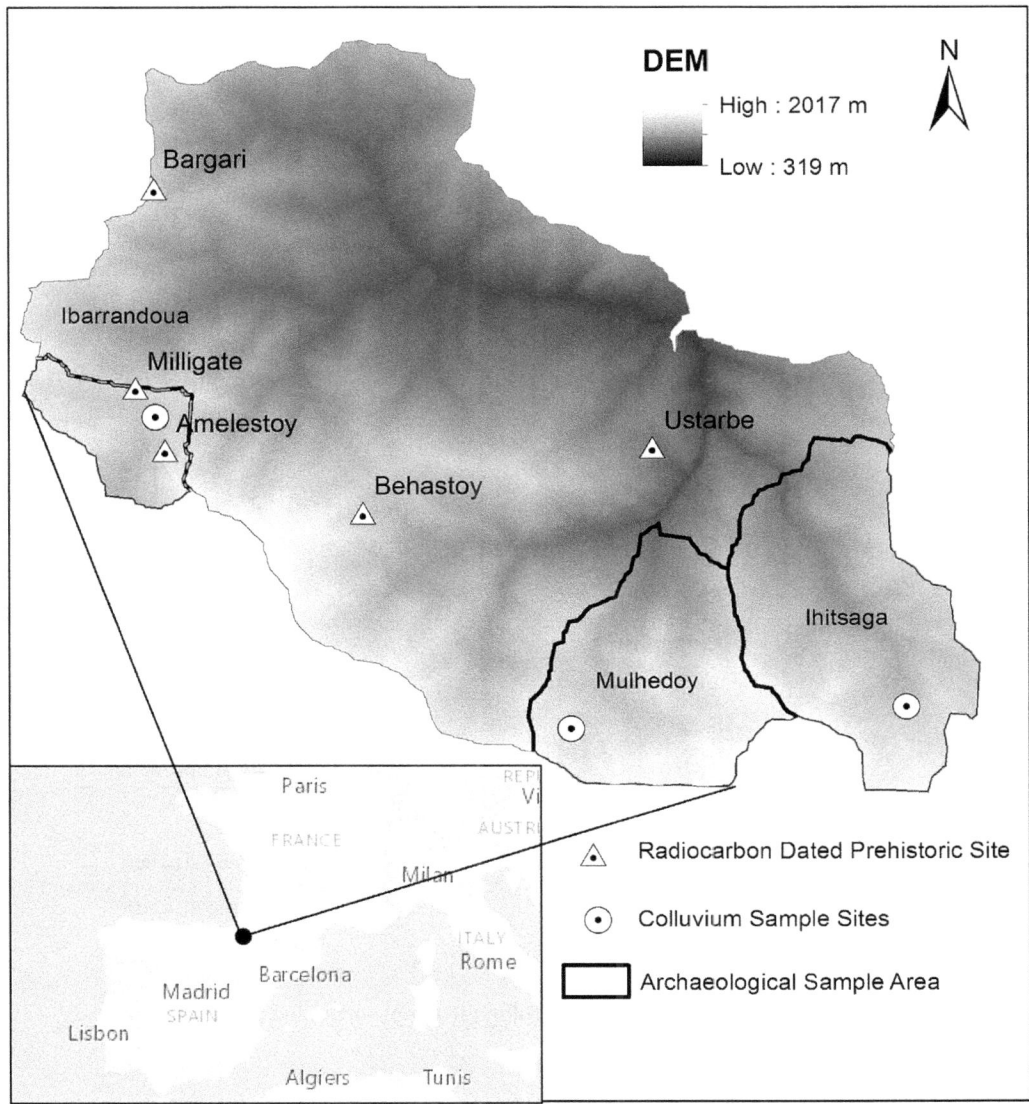

Figure 15.3. Location of project area, colluvium sample sites, archaeological sample areas, and prehistoric sites located in the literature review.

fires (Leigh et al. 2015a; Leigh et al. 2015b). We selected seven archaeological sites for testing and excavation in close proximity (within 200–2,500 m) to these colluvial catchments (Figure 15.4). Two colluvial profiles beneath catchments with the closest archaeological sites (Ibarrandoua and Ihitsaga) were resampled at 5 cm contiguous increments.

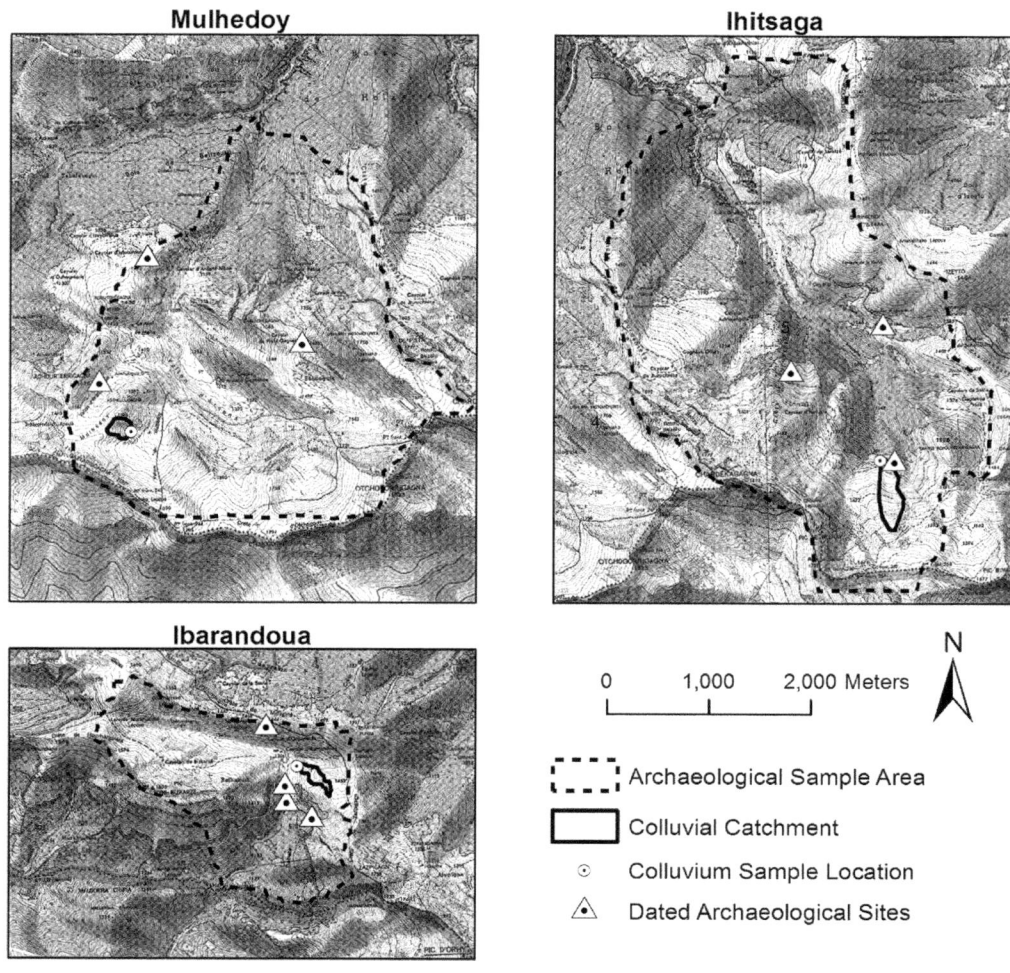

Figure 15.4. Colluvial catchments, archaeological sample area, and radiocarbon-dated archaeological sites.

Archaeological Radiocarbon Sampling

All radiocarbon samples were analyzed by the University of Georgia Center for Applied Isotope Studies. We dated twenty-four samples of archaeological charcoal from the seven archaeological sites (Table 15.A1), including seventeen samples from auger holes (10 cm diameter) within and adjacent to probable pastoral cabin features, and seven samples were collected by Le Couédic and her crew from excavation units within probable cabin features (for additional methods and results details, see Le Couédic et al. 2014).

Auger holes were located at points beside impenetrable structural elements (i.e., rock walls, bedrock) in order to maximize depth and recovery of datable material. Auger holes were bored to a minimum depth of 40 cm unless refused by rock. Where charcoal was present at 40 cm, we continued boring to 10 cm below the last occurrence of charcoal. Sediments were screened using 4.5 mm and 2 mm sieves. Wherever present, charcoal was collected for radiocarbon dating from each vertical increment. Following auger testing, 10–2 sq m excavation units were placed around the augured features, in part to assess the validity of the auger testing method for obtaining accurate site dates, but also to confirm form and function of the features.

Previously Published Dates

We searched the literature for previously published archaeological radiocarbon dates from within 10 km of the project area boundaries. We located references and data for six radiocarbon dates from five sites (Table 15.1, Figure 15.3).

Radiocarbon Date Correction

We used Oxcal 4.3 and the IntCal13 correction curve to calibrate all archaeological radiocarbon dates. The calibration of radiocarbon dates produces complex nonnormal probability distributions that are frequently multimodal. Although conventional methods typically report a median date, where distributions are multimodal, such medians can fall outside of ranges of highest probability density. This source of error is especially problematic when constructing chronologies from multiple radiocarbon dates where dates must be compared to one another (Ramsey 2009). Here we report the confidence intervals (CI) of probability density functions for archaeological radiocarbon dates in order to compare these dates to each other and to colluvial charcoal chronologies.

Off-Site Colluvial Sampling and Charcoal Tabulation

Colluvial slopewash sediments that were eroded from zero-order watersheds (headwater catchments without channels) were preferentially selected for stratigraphic sections, and

TABLE 15.1. Previously Published Archaeological Chronologies for the Project Area

Site Name	Sample Area	C^{14} yr BP	+/–1-sigma	Citation
Bagargi	NA	3490	30	(Ebrard 2013a)
Amelestoy	Ibarrandoua	3340	30	(Courtaud and Dumontier 2012)
Uztarbe	Mulhedoy	3545	30	(Ebrard 2013b)
Millagate 5	Ibarrandoua	2730	60	(Blot 1991)
Millagate 4	Ibarrandoua	2120	60	(Blot and Raballand 1995)
Behastoy	Mulhedoy	2170	60	(Nacfer 1995)

continuous profiles were sampled in 5 cm (Ihitsaga and Ibarrandoua) or 10 cm (Mulhedoy) contiguous intervals with a bucket auger. The Ihitsaga and Mulhedoy sections were previously reported with 10 cm interval samples (Leigh et al. 2015b), but Ihitsaga was reaugured and reanalyzed in 5 cm increments for this study, and Ibarrandoua is a new section reported by Leigh et al. (2016). Age-depth models were based on at least seven calibrated radiocarbon samples from each profile (Leigh et al. 2016; Leigh et al. 2015b) that were fit to depths in the profile with a smoothed spline curve using the Classical Age Model (CLAM) of Blaauw (Blaauw 2010).

Samples were oven-dried at 105 °C, and gently crushed to pass an 8 mm sieve to remove medium and larger gravel. Subsamples of 10–15 g of the <8 mm fraction were soaked in a 100 g/L solution of sodium hexametasphosphate for at least seventy-two hours and then wet-sieved to pass 125 μm mesh. Charcoal >125 μm ensures local sources, as opposed to windblown charcoal from distant sources (Clark and Royall 1995). Also, Higuera et al. (2005) indicate that >125 μm charcoal from small hollow colluvium produces a reliable fire chronology. The >125 μm residue (sand plus organic matter) was oxidized with 5% H_2O_2 to whiten any noncharcoal organic fragments, oven-dried, and then placed into a plastic vial containing liquid sodium polytungstate with a density of 1.75 g cm^{-3} to float the charcoal. The floating fraction was removed by freezing the entire liquid and then rinsing the floated material on to Whatman #1 filter paper using warm water with vacuum filtration. The residue on the filter paper was photographed at 10 μm pixel resolution, and the area of uniquely black charcoal fragments were tabulated with the image analysis program Sigma Scan Pro 5. The area of charcoal is normalized to a cubic centimeter based on an average dry bulk density of 1.5 g cm^{-3}.

Geospatial Analysis of Flammability

For at least the last several hundred years, upland grassland pastures in Larrau have been maintained with low severity fire and managed grazing characterized by daily movement (*parcours*) and seasonal rotation (transhumance) of livestock (Coughlan 2013; Fernández-Giménez and Estaque 2012; Garcia-Ruiz and Lasanta-Martinez 1990; Palu 1992; Rius et al. 2009) (Figure 15.5). Pastoralists control low severity maintenance fires by timing them during periods conducive to igniting targeted vegetation. Burn patterns and resulting vegetation cover iteratively reinforce each other through topographic mediation of landscape flammability (Coughlan 2013, 2014). For example, highly exposed, convex, and south-facing slopes provide conditions of highest flammability since these are the quickest to provide warm and dry areas (xeric sites). Shaded, concave, and north-facing slopes are least flammable (mesic sites). If anthropization of our selected catchments resulted from the long-term press of the pastoral grazing and burning regime, more flammable catchments should convert to grassland before less flammable catchments.

In order to assess the relative topographic flammability of each colluvial catchment, we used a 50 m DEM to extract site exposure, soil moisture (hydrologic convergence), and aspect. For site exposure we constructed an index (Balice et al. 2000; Johnson and Miller

Figure 15.5. Pastoral fire at tree line with Pic d'Orhy in the background. Photo by M. Coughlan, 2011.

2006) ranging from −100 to 100. For site exposure we constructed an index (Balice et al. 2000; Johnson and Miller 2006) ranging from −100 to 100 with positive integers indicating higher exposure to elements and negative numbers indicating more sheltered areas. To estimate soil moisture potential, we used a compound topographic index (or steady state wetness index) where higher values equate to higher wetness (Gessler et al. 1995). For aspect, we converted degrees to radians and took the cosine of the radian to create an index of "northness" where 1 indicates north and −1 indicates south.

Results

Landscape Level

At the landscape level, our combined results (Figure 15.6) show the differential onset of anthropogenic burning for each catchment, ranging from 7000 to 4000 BCE. Log distributions of CHAR illustrate that fire was uncommon until the Early Neolithic when fires were nevertheless very low severity or quite small. All three colluvial records extend back to at least 11500 BCE, but CHAR values are not graphically visible (<0.0001) in both Ihitsaga and Mulhedoy until the Middle Holocene. Sporadic burning is distinctly evident prior to 7500 BCE at Ibarrandoua, but it drops off until about 6000 BCE. It appears likely that a human-directed grazing-fire regime was established in all catchments by about 4000 BCE. Burning activity progressively increased with some brief recessions, sharply peaking only after several millennia of low severity burning at Mulhedoy and Ibarrandoua, and peaking more subtly at Ihitsaga, which is the largest and most topographically complex catchment. Mulhedoy registers the earliest sharp peak during the Middle Bronze Age (ca. 1880 BCE), followed by the peak at Ibarrandoua over 1,500 years later during the Late Iron Age (ca. 333 BCE), and the subtle peak at Ihitsaga during antiquity (ca. 46 CE). As these peaks are pronounced and all peaks are followed by decline and stability of CHAR levels, we suggest that they indicate the transitional tipping points between forest and grassland landscape states.

CHAR peaks at Ibarrandoua and Mulhedoy fell inside of the confidence intervals for two early composite archaeological radiocarbon distributions (Figure 15.6) indicating associ-

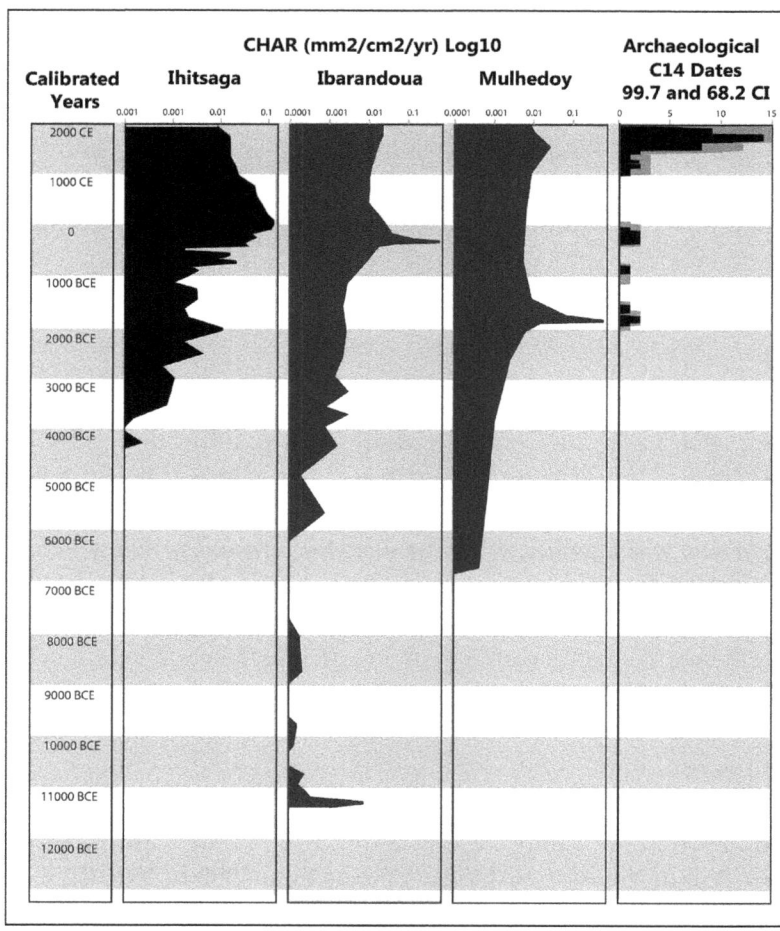

Figure 15.6. Charcoal accumulation (Log scale) with the number of radiocarbon dates from archaeological contexts by probability distribution.

ations between use or occupation of upland areas and burning activities. However, the highest density of archaeological radiocarbon dates register in the last millennia, following at least one thousand years of declining (though still relatively high) CHAR values. It is tempting to interpret the entire confidence interval of an archaeological radiocarbon date as indicative of an occupational phase. However, this is obviously not case. Each confidence interval represents the possibility that a single date corresponds to a specific year. There are only six dates earlier than 1000 CE corresponding to five sites, all from investigations previous to ours. Four of these sites are mortuary sites and the dated material was either human remains (Bagargi, Amelestoy, and Uztarbe) or cremation-associated charcoal (Millagate, features 4 and 5. Unprovenanced charcoal from the fifth site (Behastoy, a pastoral habitation site) also provided a prehistoric result. Although these sites may have been contemporaneous with peak fire activity in our catchments, they hardly resemble evidence for land use intensification. Following, we discuss this issue further along with the catchment-specific results.

Mulhedoy

The Bronze Age peak in CHAR at Mulhedoy likely marks a transition to grassland-dominant landscape. There are no prehistoric sites identified within 2,500 m of the zero-order catchment. However, Figure 15.7 includes the confidence intervals for dates for the two closest

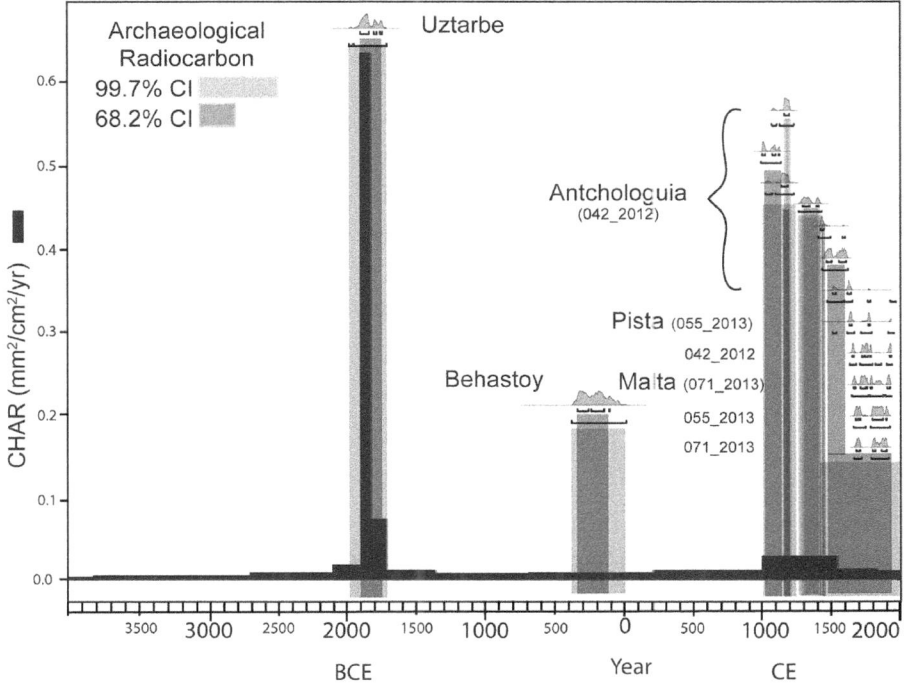

Figure 15.7. Mulhedoy charcoal accumulation (CHAR) black bar graph, showing the probability distributions (99.7% CI, dark gray and 68.2% CI, light gray) for archaeological radiocarbon from nearby sites.

sites (each about 6 km away), Behastoy to the northwest and Uztarbe to the northeast (see Figure 15.3). Peak CHAR at Mulhedoy falls within the 68.2 percent CI for the Uztarbe date. Although Uztarbe is a mortuary site, it is a small cave that could have provided shelter for livestock and herders alike. Behastoy has been identified as a pastoral occupation site and is at a similar elevation to Mulhedoy (1,359 masl), but its date (ca. 400 BCE to 2 CE) falls much later than the peak in CHAR. However, several fragments of ceramic vessels recovered during excavation of the site are indicative of an Early to Middle Bronze Age occupation (Nacfer 1995). If the relative dating is correct, the site could also be coincident with the activities responsible for the Mulhedoy CHAR peak.

A smaller peak beginning around 1000 CE is associated temporally with four archaeological dates possibly indicating the establishment of a nearby (~500 m northwest) pastoral occupation site, "Antchologuia." However, eight additional dates, four from Antchologuia and four from two other sites place the density of occupation and use after 1450 CE, a period of declining CHAR values. In the Basque language, the word "Antchologuia" means shelter of the "dry" ewes, which suggests an association with the transhumant dairying activity known from historic documents to be a dominant land use in the uplands from the Middle Ages onward.

Ibarrandoua

Ibarrandoua (Figure 15.8) presents an interesting case because four of the project area's major prehistoric mortuary sites are nearby, and two of these (Amelestoy and Millagate) are situated within ca. 750 m of the colluvial catchment. Amelestoy is a recently prospected mortuary cave that sits on a steep slope to the south of the colluvial catchment (Courtaud and Dumontier 2012). Human bone from Amelestoy returned a radiocarbon date of ca. 1682–1564 BCE (99.7% CI). CHAR for this period registers around 0.014 sq mm/sq cm/ yr, a level still well below the Holocene average, but nonetheless suggestive of anthropogenic burning. Bagargi, a small mortuary tumulus site sits ca. 4.8 km north of the catchment. The 99.7% CI from Bagargi overlaps with that of Amelestoy and is also not associated with significant change in CHAR.

Millagate, a large cromlech-tumulus site, is perched northwest of the Ibarrandoua colluvial sample site along an exposed east-west running ridge. Jacques Blot (1991, 1995) excavated two cromlech-tumulus features from this site and obtained one radiocarbon date from each. The Millagate 5 date coincides with an uptick in CHAR during the Late Bronze or Early Iron Age: archaeological date ca. 922–814 BCE, CHAR increment mid-point date ca. 927 BCE. The Late Iron Age steep peak in CHAR (mid-point ca. 333 BCE) falls within the 99.7 percent CI for the radiocarbon date from the second feature from Millagate (Millagate 4, ca. 342–51 BCE) and 5.3 percent of the 68.2 percent CI (ca. 343–325 BCE). However, 62.9 percent of the 68.2 percent CI for Millagate 4 is associated with a much lower CHAR value during a period of decline in burning. The confidence intervals for the radiocarbon date from Behastoy, on the opposite side of Pic d'Orhy, ca. 4.6 km to the east, covers a similar time period with 32.3 percent of the 68.2 percent CI ca. 358–277 BCE and the 99.7 percent probability ca. 400 BCE to 2 CE.

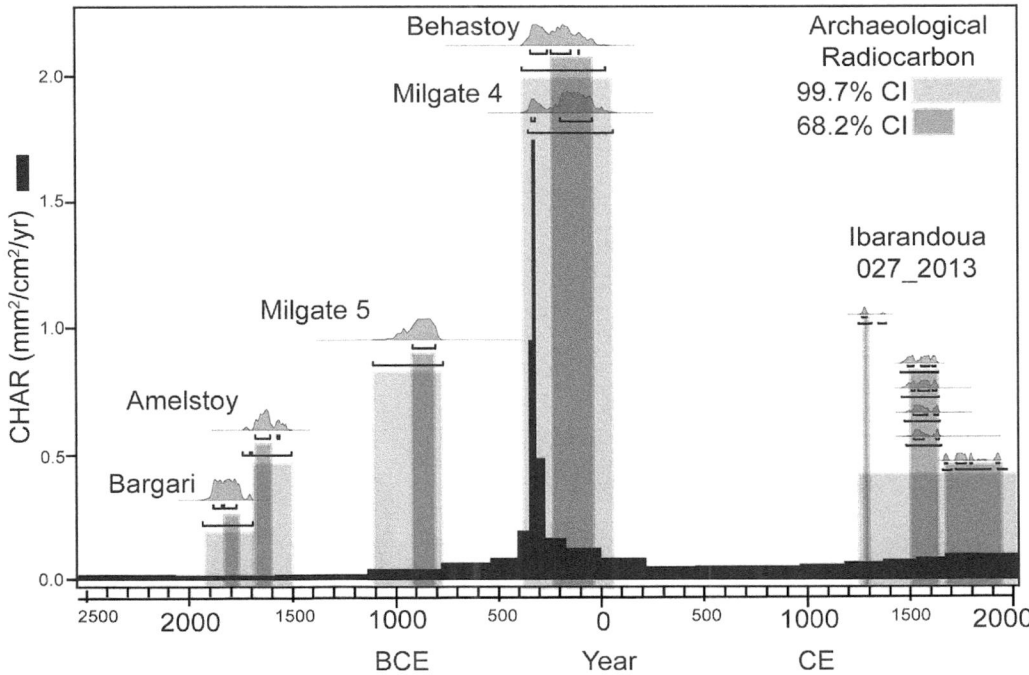

Figure 15.8. Ibarrandoua charcoal accumulation (CHAR) showing the probability distributions (99.7% and 68.2% CI) for archaeological radiocarbon from nearby sites.

Following more than one thousand years of decline, CHAR values begin to slowly increase just after 1000 CE. This increase is sustained into the contemporary period and coincides with the establishment and use of three dated archaeological features directly downslope from the colluvial sample site. These features are probably season pastoral shelters associated with historical ovine dairying actives (99.7% CI ranges 1045 to post-1950 CE).

IHITSAGA

We did not locate any radiocarbon dated prehistoric sites within 10 km of the Ihitsaga colluvial catchment (Figure 15.9). Ihitsaga is a larger catchment and yielded more charcoal than either Ibarrandoua or Mulhedoy. Sustained elevation in CHAR commenced around 6000 BCE with small peaks around 738, 409, and 254 BCE. The major peak occurred around 46 CE followed by a sustained gradual decline in CHAR. We dated features from three historical sites near the colluvial catchment. One of these sites (Ihitsaga 037-2013) was immediately adjacent to the colluvial sample site. Our results indicate an episode of

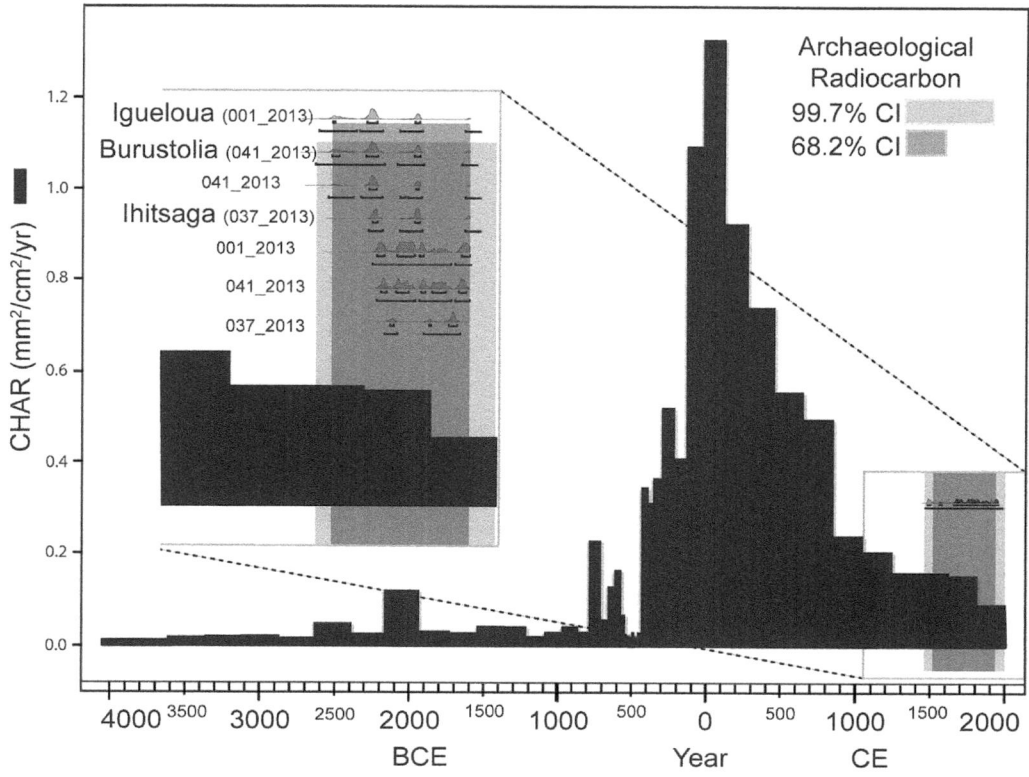

Figure 15.9. Ihitsaga charcoal accumulation (CHAR) showing the probability distributions (99.7% and 68.2% CI) for archaeological radiocarbon from nearby sites.

transhumant dairying activity commencing in the Late Middle Ages (ca. 1265 to 1289 CE) and continued into the contemporary period.

GEOSPATIAL FLAMMABILITY ANALYSIS

Colluvial catchments aligned along a gradient of flammability (Figure 15.10), ranging from Mulhedoy (most flammable) to Ihitsaga (least flammable). Mulhedoy was driest, most exposed, and faced toward the southwest while Ihitsaga was the wettest, least exposed, and faced mostly north.

DISCUSSION AND CONCLUSION

Our results are more consistent with the press-coevolution than the pulse-impact hypothesis. Steep peaks in CHAR at Mulhedoy and Ibarrandoua do leave room for the possibility

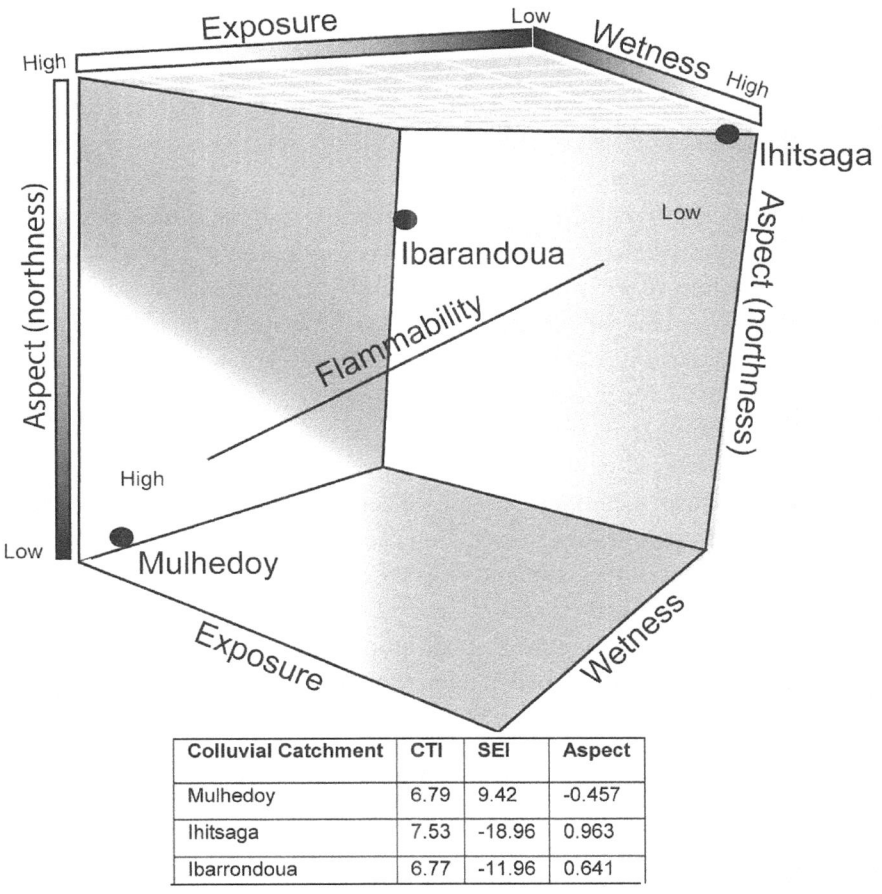

Figure 15.10. Three-way plot of colluvial catchment "climate space" and relative topographic flammability.

Colluvial Catchment	CTI	SEI	Aspect
Mulhedoy	6.79	9.42	-0.457
Ihitsaga	7.53	-18.96	0.963
Ibarrondoua	6.77	-11.96	0.641

of an intentional conversion pulse interpretation. Nonetheless, if Bronze Age and Iron Age farmers did intentionally clear those areas, it was only after millennia of lower severity fire use. In any case, there is no archaeological evidence for land use intensification prior to the Middle Ages with the establishment of the ovine-focused dairying activities. By this time, grassland pasture had probably been the dominant vegetation cover in the uplands for at least a millennium.

Given our expectations of the relative flammability of each catchment, it seems likely that topography and climate were important factors controlling fire behavior and thus the timing of forest to pasture conversion. Mulhedoy is by far the most flammable of the catchments and appears to convert to grassland a full one thousand years ahead of the others. Ibarrandoua, dryer and more exposed than Ihitsaga, was next to transition. These conversion patterns suggest that humans were not simply "impacting" landscape or "breaking" links between vegetation and climate. The process of anthropization of this landscape is one of coevolutionary coupling between humans and the landscape as mediated by microclimate. Just as topographic and climatic controls are important for the maintenance of the current landscape mosaic (Coughlan 2013, 2014), such factors played an important role in the anthropization process itself.

Given our results we hypothesize that upland landscape of the Bronze Age consisted of grassland pasture mostly on the convex, south-facing, exposed slopes. Even at Ihitsaga, the most flammable portions of the catchment were likely characterized by patchy grassland. By the Iron Age, the tree line had receded to moderately sheltered, north-facing areas. The process of forest attrition culminated around two thousand years ago, paving the way for the intensification of upland pasture use in the Middle Ages.

The conventional usage of the anthropization concept implies the intentional, relatively rapid transformation of land (including land cover, soils, or geophysical features) in anticipation of a particular socioeconomic use. When combined with management activities such as human fire use, or land use such as grazing, this use of the term brings to mind practices of "slash and burn," long maligned by foresters, or the relatively rapid conversion of "pristine" forests into degraded rangelands by careless and mobile pastoralists. The association of anthropization (and cognates such as anthropogenic, anthropocene, and anthrome) with the degradation of "nature" is ancient and strongly embedded in scholarship on long-term effects of human–environment interactions (Sayre et al. 2017). Indeed a major focus of the international environmental movement over the last century and a half has been the ongoing degradation of the Earth's "natural" ecosystems through their conversion to meet human economic demand (Marsh 1965; Muir 2011), yet anthropization need not lead inevitably to degradation.

The grassland pastures surrounding Pic d'Orhy show few signs of degradation in spite of their use across the millennia (Leigh et al. 2015a; Leigh et al. 2015b). From the standpoint of long-term viability of ecosystems, goods and services coevolved socioecological systems can exhibit relative sustainability in the face of dynamic interactions (Blondel 2006; Costanza et al. 2007; Redman 2005). In coevolved systems, land conversion is unintentional and occurs gradually, over long time periods. Long-term human–environment interactions have also led to landscape degradation and resource depletion (Redman 1999, 2005). Yet, such degradation is understood as the result of dynamic and complex interactions, rather than simple impacts, and human activities are understood as responding to environmental changes. The conflation of anthropization with degradation obscures the role of human agency and the relative role of human and environment forces in shaping landscapes. We suggest that place-based, local-scale investigations guided by theory in socioecological systems can help refine our understanding of the anthropization processes. Further, without such case studies, the utility of regional-scale approaches for investigating dynamics that lead to sustainable resource use is limited.

Table 15.A.1. Uncorrected Radiocarbon Age for Archaeological Sites

SiteNo	UnitNo & Level	Uncorrected Age_BP	Error	Lab	UGAMS.	SiteName	Colluvial Catchment
042_2012	42AG1, 40–50 cm	270	25	CAIS_UGA	19014	Antchologuia	Mulhedoy
042_2012	42AG1, 30–40cm	350	20	CAIS_UGA	19015	Antchologuia	Mulhedoy
042_2012	42AG2 20–30	870	20	CAIS_UGA	19016	Antchologuia	Mulhedoy
042_2012	42AF4 20–30	970	20	CAIS_UGA	19017	Antchologuia	Mulhedoy
027_2013	27AG3 30–40	310	20	CAIS_UGA	19018	Ibarandoua	Ibarandoua
027_2013	27AG4 20–30	300	20	CAIS_UGA	19019	Ibarandoua	Ibarandoua
027_2013	27AG6 30–40	340	20	CAIS_UGA	19020	Ibarandoua	Ibarandoua
027_2013	27AG6 50–60	700	25	CAIS_UGA	19021	Ibarandoua	Ibarandoua
071_ITEM_2013	71AG2 10–20	90	20	CAIS_UGA	23470	Malta	Mulhedoy
071_ITEM_2013	71AG2 40–50	150	20	CAIS_UGA	23471	Malta	Mulhedoy
055_2014	55AG4 10–20	230	25	CAIS_UGA	23472	Pista	Mulhedoy

continued on next page

Table 15.A.1. Continued.

SiteNo	UnitNo & Level	Uncorrected Age_BP	Error	Lab	UGAMS.	SiteName	Colluvial Catchment
041_2013	41AG3 10–20	250	35	CAIS_UGA	23473	Burustolia Upper	Ihitsaga
041_2013	41AG2 40–50	250	25	CAIS_UGA	23474	Burustolia Upper	Ihitsaga
041_2013	41AG1 10–20	140	20	CAIS_UGA	23475	Burustolia Upper	Ihitsaga
037_2013	37AG2 10–20	60	20	CAIS_UGA	23477	Ihitsaga	Ihitsaga
055_2014	55AG4 40–50	110	20	CAIS_UGA	23478	Pista	Mulhedoy
037_2013	37AG2 30–35	220	20	CAIS_UGA	23479	Ihitsaga	Ihitsaga
042_2012	42A.47 11	180	20	CAIS_UGA	21150	Antchologuia	Mulhedoy
042_2012	42B.47 33	420	20	CAIS_UGA	21151	Antchologuia	Mulhedoy
027_2013	27C.123 3	160	20	CAIS_UGA	21152	Ibarandoa	Ibarandoua
027_2013	27D.124 11	330	20	CAIS_UGA	21153	Ibarandoa	Ibarandoua
027_2013	27E.125 15	0	0	CAIS_UGA	21154	Ibarandoa	Ibarandoua
027_2013	27F.126 38	870	20	CAIS_UGA	21155	Ibarandoa	Ibarandoua
027_2013	27G.126 7	590	20	CAIS_UGA	21156	Ibarandoa	Ibarandoua

TABLE 15.A.2. CORRECTED RADIOCARBON DATES FOR ARCHAEOLOGICAL SITES.
YEARS CE ARE POSITIVE AND YEARS BCE ARE NEGATIVE

Name	Feature	Feature Type	Depth	Material	Unmodelled (BC/AD)		68.20%		99.70%	
Site Designation					from	to	from	to	from	to
Ibarrandoua	027-125	Structure	30–40	Charcoal	1522	1642			1477	1651
Ibarrandoua	027-125	Structure	20–30	Charcoal	1523	1645			1485	1657
Ibarrandoua	027-124	Structure	30–40	Charcoal	1494	1631			1460	1643
Ibarrandoua	027-124	Structure	50–60	Charcoal	1273	1295			1255	1390
Ibarrandoua	027-123	Structure	3	Charcoal	1674	1942			1663	...
Ibarrandoua	027-124	Structure	11	Charcoal	1512	1634			1464	1645
Malta	071-71	Structure	10–20	Charcoal	1698	1917			1681	1930
Malta	071-71	Structure	40–50	Charcoal	1678	1940			1665	...
Pista	055-45	Structure	10–20	Charcoal	1650	1796			1526	1940
Pista	055-45	Structure	40–50	Charcoal	1694	1917			1679	1251
Antchologuia	042-126	Structure	38	Charcoal	1162	1208			1045	1251
Antchologuia	042-126	Structure	7	Charcoal	1317	1400			1296	1415
Antchologuia	042-47	Structure	11	Charcoal	1668	1950			1652	...
Antchologuia	042-47	Structure	33	Charcoal	1442	1466			1427	1618
Antchologuia	042-47	Structure	40–50	Charcoal	1528	1661			1489	...
Antchologuia	042-47	Structure	30–40	Charcoal	1485	1626			1453	1639
Antchologuia	042-126	Structure	20–30	Charcoal	1162	1208			1045	1251
Antchologuia	042-NA	Structure	20–30	Charcoal	1022	1147			1014	1158
Burustolia	041-103	Structure	10–20	Charcoal	1528	1799			1479	...
Burustolia	041-F08	Structure	40–50	Charcoal	1643	1793			1518	...
Burustolia	041-F08	Structure	10–20	Charcoal	1680	1939			1666	1949
Ihitsaga	037-83	Structure	10–20	Charcoal	1708	1912			1691	1921
Ihitsaga	037-83	Structure	30–35	Charcoal	1653	1798			1641	...
Bargari	—	Dolmen-Tumulus	—	Human Bone	–1878	–1769			–1930	–1691
Uztarbe	—	Mortuary-Cave	—	Human Bone	–1940	–1782			–2022	–1747
Behastoy	—	Structure	—	Charcoal	–358	–124			–400	2
Millagate	Millagate5	Cromlec-Tumulus	—	Charcoal	–923	–815			–1115	–779
Millagate	Millagate4	Cromlec-Tumulus	—	Charcoal	–343	–52			–385	54
Amelestoy	—	Mortuary-Cave	—	Human Bone	–1683	–1565			–1743	–1508

Acknowledgments

We gratefully acknowledge officials and residents of the commune of Larrau, France. Logistical support was provided by Dr. Pascal Palu and members of the Laboratoire ITEM, Université de Pau et du Pays de l'Adour. Partial support was provided by the National Geographic Society (grant #9573-14), Coweeta Long Term Ecological Research program funded by the National Science Foundation (award DEB-0823293), and by a Partner University Fund award to the University of Georgia and the Universite de Pau.

References

Balice, R. G., J. D. Miller, B. P. Oswald, C. Edminster, and S. R. Yool 2000 *Forest Surveys and Wildlife Assessment in the Los Alamos Region: 1998–1999*. Los Alamos National Laboratory. Los Alamos, New Mexico.

Berger, E., and H. Wang 2017 Bioarchaeology of Adaptation to a Marginal Environment in Bronze Age Western China. *American Journal of Human Biology* 29(4):1–10.

Bird, D. W., R. Bliege Bird, B. F. Codding, and N. Taylor 2016 A Landscape Architecture of Fire: Cultural Emergence and Ecological Pyrodiversity in Australia's Western Desert. *Current Anthropology* 57(S13):S65-S79.

Blaauw, M. 2010 Methods and Code for "Classical" Age–Modelling of Radiocarbon Sequences. *Quaternary Geochronology* 5(5):512–518.

Blondel, J. 2006 The "Design" of Mediterranean Landscapes: A Millennial Story of Humans and Ecological Systems during the Historic Period. *Human Ecology* 34(5):713–729.

Blot, J. 1991 Le tumulus-cromlech de Millagate V. (Compte rendu de fouilles 1987). *Munibe* (43):181–189.

Blot, J., and C. Raballand 1995 Contribution à l'étude des cercles de pierres en Pays Basque de France. *Bulletin de la Société préhistorique française* 92(4):525–548.

Bowman, D. M. J. S., G. L. W. Perry, and J. B. Marston 2015 Feedbacks and Landscape-Level Vegetation Dynamics. *Trends in Ecology and Evolution* 30(5):255–260.

Calaway, M. J. 2015 Ice-Cores, Sediments and Civilisation Collapse: A Cautionary Tale from Lake Titicaca. *Antiquity* 79(306):778–790.

Carozza, L., D. Galop, F. Marembert, and F. Monna 2005 Quel statut pour les espaces de montagne durant l'âge du Bronze? Regards croisés sur les approches société-environnement dans les Pyrénées occidentales. *Documents d'archéologie méridionale* 28:7–23.

Clark, J. S., and P. D. Royall 1995 Transformation of a Northern Hardwood Forest by Aboriginal (Iroquois) Fire: Charcoal Evidence from Crawford Lake, Ontario, Canada. *The Holocene* 5(1):1–9.

Collins, S. L., S. R. Carpenter, S. M. Swinton, D. E. Orenstein, D. L. Childers, T. L. Gragson, N. B. Grimm, J. M. Grove, S. L. Harlan, and J. P. Kaye 2010 An Integrated Conceptual Framework for Long-Term Social-Ecological Research. *Frontiers in Ecology and the Environment* 9(6):351–357.

Contreras, D. A. 2017 Correlation Is Not Enough: Building Better Arguments in the Archaeology of Human–Environment Interactions. In *The Archaeology of Human–Environment Interactions: Strategies for Investigating Anthropogenic Landscapes, Dynamic Environments, and Climate Change in the Human Past*, edited by D. A. Contreras, 3–22. Taylor & Francis, New York.

Costanza, R., L. Graumlich, W. Steffen, C. Crumley, J. Dearing, K. Hibbard, R. Leemans, Charles Redman, and D. Schimel 2007 Sustainability or Collapse: What Can We Learn from Integrating the History of Humans and the Rest of Nature? *AMBIO: A Journal of the Human Environment* 36(7):522–527.

Coughlan, M. R. 2013 Errakina: Pastoral Fire Use and Landscape Memory in the Basque Region of the French Western Pyrenees. *Journal of Ethnobiology* 33(1):86–104.

Coughlan, M. R. 2014 Farmers, Flames and Forests: Historical Ecology of Pastoral Fire Use and Landscape Change in the French Western Pyrenees, 1830–2011. *Forest Ecology and Management* 312:55–66.

Coughlan, M. R., and T. L. Gragson 2016 An Event History Analysis of Parcel Extensification and Household Abandonment in Pays Basque, French Pyrenees, 1830–1958 AD. *Human Ecology* 44(1):65–80.

Courtaud, P., and P. Dumontier 2012 Larrau, grotte d'Amelestoy. *Bilan scientifique Aquitaine*:183–184.

Ebrard, Dominique 2013a La ciste sous tumulus de Bagargi à Larrau (Pyrénées-Atlantiques) Fouilles P. Boucher, 1968–1872. In *50 ans d'archéologie en Soule: Hommage à Pierre Boucher (1909–1997)*, edited by D. Ebrard, 204–211. Imprimerie Pierrou, Mauléon-Licharre, France.

Ebrard, Dominique 2013b Historique des recherches archéologiques en Soule et débats ouverts. In *50 ans d'archéologie en Soule: Hommage à Pierre Boucher (1909–1997)*, edited by D. Ebrard, 32–37. Imprimerie Pierrou, Mauléon-Licharre, France.

Fernández-Giménez, M. E., and F. F. Estaque 2012 Pyrenean Pastoralists' Ecological Knowledge: Documentation and Application to Natural Resource Management and Adaptation. *Human Ecology* 40(2):287–300.

Galop, D. 1998 La forêt, l'homme et le troupeau six millénaires d'anthropisation du massif pyrénéen de la Garonne à la Méditerranée: contribution palynologique à l'histoire de l'environnnement et du paysage pyrénéens. Thesis, Université de Toulouse-Le Mirail.

Galop, D., and G. Jalut 1994 Differential Human Impact and Vegetation History in Two Adjacent Pyrenean Valleys in the Ariège Basin, Southern France, from 3000 BP to the Present. *Vegetation History and Archaeobotany* 3(4):225–244.

Galop, D., D. Rius, C. Cugny, and F. Mazier 2013 A History of Long-Term Human–Environment Interactions in the French Pyrenees Inferred from the Pollen Data. In *Continuity and Change in Cultural Adaptation to Mountain Environments*, edited by L.R. Lozny, 19–30. Springer. New York.

Garcia-Ruiz, J. M., and T. Lasanta-Martinez 1990 Land-Use Changes in the Spanish Pyrenees. *Mountain Research and Development* 10(3):267–279.

Gessler, P. E., I. D. Moore, N. J. McKenzie, and P. J. Ryan 1995 Soil-Landscape Modelling and Spatial Prediction of Soil Attributes. *International Journal of Geographical Information Systems* 9(4):421–432.

Gragson, T. L. 1998 Potential versus Actual Vegetation: Human Behavior in a Landscape Medium. In *Advances in Historical Ecology*, edited by W. Balee, 213–231. Columbia University Press, New York.

Gragson, T. L, D. S. Leigh, and M. R. Coughlan 2015 Basque Cultural Landscapes of the Western French Pyrenees. *Il Capitale Culturale: Studies on the Value of Cultural Heritage* (12):565–596.

Hernández-Beloqui, B., M. Iriarte-Chiapusso, A. Echazarreta-Gallego, and M. Ayerdi 2015 The Late Holocene in the Western Pyrenees: A Critical Review of the Current Situation of Palaeopalynological Research. *Quaternary International* 364:78–85.

Higuera, P. E., D. G. Sprugel, and L. B. Brubaker 2005 Reconstructing Fire Regimes with Charcoal from Small-Hollow Sediments: A Calibration with Tree-Ring Records of Fire. *The Holocene* 15(2):238–251.

Iriarte, M. J. 2009 Vegetation Landscape and the Anthropization of the Environment in the Central Sector of the Northern Iberian Peninsula: Current Status. *Quaternary International* 200(1):66–76.

Johnson, D. D., and R. F. Miller 2006 Structure and Development of Expanding Western Juniper Woodlands as Influenced by Two Topographic Variables. *Forest Ecology and Management* 229(1):7–15.

Le Couédic, M., A. Champagne, T. Contamine, M. R. Coughlan, T. L. Gragson, and B. S. Haley 2014 Rapport de prospection et sondages, Larrau, Pyrénées-Atlantiques. Campagne 2014, ITEM, EA 3002, Université de Pau et des Pays de l'Adour.

Leigh, D. S., T. L. Gragson, and M. R. Coughlan 2016 Multi-Proxy Record of Land Use Change Derived from Colluvial Soils of the Western Pyrenees Mountains, France. *Proceedings of the EGU General Assembly Conference* Abstracts:16–24.

Leigh, D. S, T. L. Gragson, and M. R. Coughlan 2015a Chronology and Pedogenic Effects of Mid- to Late-Holocene Conversion of Forests to Pastures in the French Western Pyrenees. *Zeitschrift für Geomorphologie* 59(2):225–245.

Leigh, D. S, T. L. Gragson, and M. R. Coughlan 2015b Colluvial Legacies of Millennial Landscape Change on Individual Hillsides: Place-Based Investigation in the Western Pyrenees Mountains. *Quaternary International* 402:61–71.

Marsh, G. P. 1965 *Man and Nature; or Physical Geography as Modified by Human Action*. University of Washington Press, Seattle, Washington.

Mazier, F., D. Galop, M. J. Gaillard, C. Rendu, C. Cugny, A. Legaz, O. Peyron, and A. Buttler 2009 Multidisciplinary Approach to Reconstructing Local Pastoral Activities: An Example from the Pyrenean Mountains (Pays Basque). *Holocene* 19(2):171–188.

McWethy, D. B., P. E. Higuera, C. Whitlock, T. T. Veblen, D. M. J. S. Bowman, G. J. Cary, S. G. Haberle, R. E. Keane, B. D. Maxwell, M. S. McGlone, G. L. W. Perry, J. M. Wilmshurst, A. Holz, and A. J. Tepley 2013 A Conceptual Framework for Predicting Temperate Ecosystem Sensitivity to Human Impacts on Fire Regimes. *Global Ecology and Biogeography* 22(8):900–912.

Monna, F., D. Galop, L. Carozza, M. Tual, A. Beyrie, F. Marembert, C. Chateau, J. Dominik, and F. E. Grousset 2004 Environmental Impact of Early Basque Mining and Smelting Recorded in a High Ash Minerogenic Peat Deposit. *Science of the Total Environment* 327(1–3):197–214.

Muir, J. 2011 *My First Summer in the Sierra*. Houghton Mifflin Harcourt, New York.

Nacfer, M. N. 1995 Behastoy (Larrau-Pyrénées-Atlantiques). *Archéologie des Pyrénées occidentales et des Landes* 14:84–94.

Palu, P. 1992 Rapports entre organisation sociale et écosystème dans la société pastorale souletine. *Sociétés contemporaines*:239–264.

Ramsey, C. B. 2009 Bayesian Analysis of Radiocarbon Dates. *Radiocarbon* 51(1):337–360.

Redman, C. L. 1999 *Human Impact on Ancient Environments*. University of Arizona Press, Tucson, Arizona.

Redman, C. L. 2005 Resilience Theory in Archaeology. *American Anthropologist* 107(1):70–77.

Rius, D., B. Vanniere, and D. Galop 2009 Fire Frequency and Landscape Management in the Northwestern Pyrenean Piedmont, France, since the Early Neolithic (8000 cal BP). *The Holocene* 19(6):847–859.

Rius, D., B. Vanniere, and D. Galop 2012 Holocene History of Fire, Vegetation and Land Use from the Central Pyrenees (France). *Quaternary Research* 77(1):54–64.

Roos, C. I, J. S. Field, and J. V. Dudgeon 2016 Anthropogenic Burning, Agricultural Intensification, and Landscape Transformation in Post-Lapita Fiji. *Journal of Ethnobiology* 36(3):535–553.

Sayre, N. F., D. K. Davis, B. Bestelmeyer, and J. C. Williamson 2017 Rangelands: Where Anthromes Meet Their Limits. *Land* 6(2):31.

Scheffer, M., S. Carpenter, J. A. Foley, C. Folke, and B. Walker 2001 Catastrophic Shifts in Ecosystems. *Nature* 413(6856):591–596.

Whitlock, C., D. Colombaroli, M. Conedera, and W. Tinner 2017 Land-Use History as a Guide for Forest Conservation and Management. *Conservation Biology* 32(1):84–97.

Whitlock, C., D. B. McWethy, A. J. Tepley, T. T. Veblen, A. Holz, M. S. McGlone, G. L. W. Perry, J. M. Wilmshurst, and S. W. Wood 2014 Past and Present Vulnerability of Closed-Canopy Temperate Forests to Altered Fire Regimes: A Comparison of the Pacific Northwest, New Zealand, and Patagonia. *BioScience* 65(2):151–163.

Wood, S. W., and D. M. J. S. Bowman 2012 Alternative Stable States and the Role of Fire–Vegetation–Soil Feedbacks in the Temperate Wilderness of Southwest Tasmania. *Landscape Ecology* 27(1):13–28.

CHAPTER SIXTEEN

Highlands and Lowlands—Different Landscapes, Different Archaeologies?

A Diachronic Micro-regional Case Study from the Western Taurus Mountains (Southwest Turkey)

Ralf Vandam, Eva Kaptijn, Patrick T. Willett, and Jeroen Poblome

Abstract *Mountain ranges comprise a high variety of landscapes and ecologies. This chapter presents a detailed case study from the Western Taurus Mountains (Southwest Turkey) where many of these variabilities occur on a microscale. Here, we investigate to what extent this landscape diversity is reflected in the local archaeology. By comparing the archaeological outcomes from two similar intensive surveys within the Western Taurus Mountains, one focusing on a lowland component (Burdur Plain) and the other on the highlands (Dereköy Highlands), we want to investigate how different landscapes can produce different archaeologies. This research illustrates a complex relationship between the local archaeologies in which a range of factors contributed to these outcomes. Ultimately, the study wants to demonstrate the significance of contextualization of both high- and lowlands.*

INTRODUCTION

Turkey, geographically located between the continent of Europe and Asia, is dominated by mountains, plateaus, and hills. Complex tectonism with volcanic activity and many (still active) fault zones have distinctively shaped the country. East-west oriented folded mountain belts border the littoral areas—in the north the Pontus Mountains and in the south the Taurus Mountains (Figure 16.1.A). Both mountain ranges enclose the Anatolian or Central Plateau, a semi-arid highland in the middle of the country, which transforms toward the western end into the river valley landscapes of the Aegean region. The east of Turkey, on the other hand, is one large mountainous zone where several mountain ranges

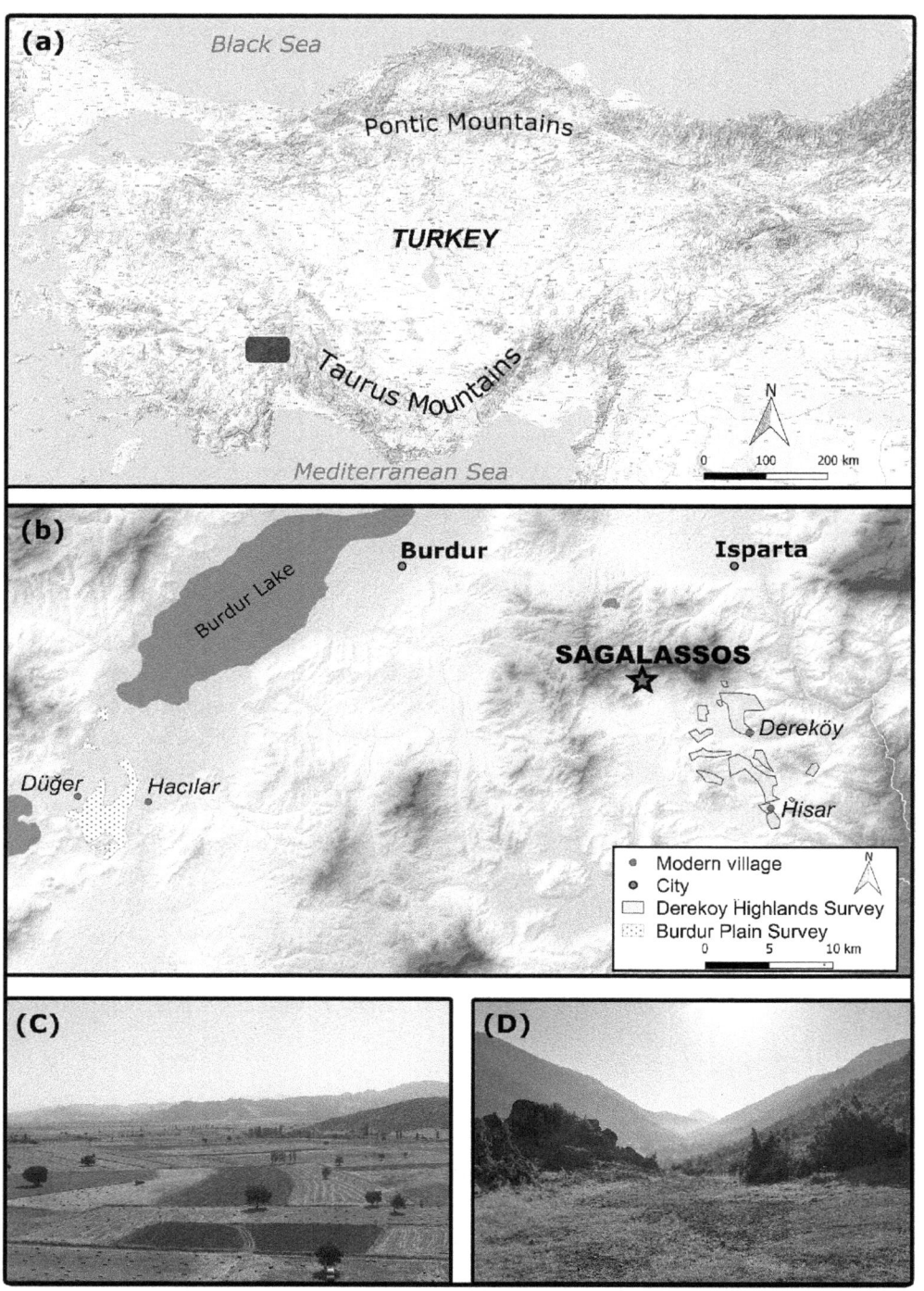

Figure 16.1. A. Overview of Turkey including the Taurus and Pontus Mountains. B. Locations of the two survey research areas in relation to the ancient city of Sagalassos. C. Burdur Plain landscape. D. Dereköy Highlands landscape.

unite, creating one of the most rugged topographies in the country. This mountainous character of Turkey has clear implications on the climate, ecology, resource availability, connectivity, among others, of the different regions, and consequently on their human occupants as well.

This chapter will focus especially on the western extent of the Taurus Mountains in Burdur Province of Southwest Turkey (Figure 16.1.B). The area is rich in archaeology where ancient cities like Sagalassos thrived and used the topography and natural resources to a great extent (Mitchell 1993:70–71). The mountains themselves in Burdur Province are not extremely high compared to other parts of the Taurus Mountains, with peaks up to 2,300 m. And although we are set within a highland region, it is by no means a uniform landscape but rather fragmented and diverse. Large open intermountain fertile plains, small narrow river valleys, badlands, moderate hills, plateaus, and steep mountains all occur in the area. Elevation within the region varies drastically with a range of ca. 2,000 m between its highest and lowest points. The highland areas are in general well watered with permanent and seasonal water sources, which in combination with relatively poor natural drainage due to thick clay subsoils in parts resulted in the formation of marshlands in several of the valley bottoms prior to modern irrigation and agricultural practices. Meanwhile, the relatively thin soil cover on the hillslopes and better drainage in the plains have created zones of semi-aridity. The variety in hydrology combined with the local climatic and geomorphological conditions created a patchwork of vegetative cover—from semi-arid steppic and badlands, to marshes, riparian and deciduous woodlands in the highland valleys, and oro-Mediterranean zones at higher elevations (Paulissen et al. 1993). The differences in average annual temperatures alone between lowland areas (e.g., 13.2 °C in Burdur) and the highlands (e.g., 8.2 °C at Sagalassos) are a significant driving factor in the ecological variety in Burdur Province. In this chapter we deal with this mosaic of landscapes within the mountainous regions. We will present and contrast recent archaeological survey outcomes from the Sagalassos Archaeological Research Project in two different landscapes within the Western Taurus Mountains: a highland area, that is, the Dereköy Highlands, and a lowland area, that is, the Burdur Plain (Figure 16.1.B–D). Both case studies, located 45 km from one another, have been surveyed in a similar way, which makes a comparison possible and allows us to assess how different/similar the attested archaeological patterns are. We will explore whether we have evidence that different landscapes within a micro-region can produce different archaeologies, and if so which factors may contribute to this outcome, or if, on the other hand, we see great archaeological continuity throughout these different landscapes. Ultimately, this chapter aims to put highland archaeology in perspective.

Research Areas

Burdur Plain

The Burdur Plain is set within a large intermountainous basin that is occupied by Lake Burdur, one of the largest lakes in Turkey. The basin itself is defined as a graben structure running between two active faults (Price and Scott 1991). The Burdur Plain, directly south of the lake, is the result of the retreat of this lake, which began in the Late Pleistocene: 25000–20000 BP when it reached its maximum extent (Kıs et al. 1989). Geologically, the plain area is a succession of lacustrine, fluvial, and alluvial deposits (Degryse et al. 2008). The altitude of the basin (950 masl at the edge) rises in accordance with its distance from Lake Burdur (846 masl). The surrounding mountains are not as prominent as in other parts of our research area and can be considered as moderate (ca. 1,000–1,300 masl). Most of the modern villages can be found in the contact zone between the plain and the mountains, close to the many fresh water sources that the basin is rich in. The Burdur Plain is drained by several permanent rivers such as Boz Çayı, Düğer Çayı, and Büğdüz Çayı, and seasonal streams that, along with rainfall and underground water sources, feed Lake Burdur. However, intensive agriculture and the recent construction of water reservoirs have reduced the inflow considerably and resulted in further decreases in the level of the lake (Yıldırım and Uysal 2011). The Burdur Plain can be considered as one of the most fertile areas of Burdur Province and is still intensively cultivated (Figure 16.1.C). Cereals are the most important crop produced in the area, but recently maize cultivation has gained importance. Erosion and sedimentation processes are mainly concentrated in the foothills and river systems (Vandam 2014). The latter are at some locations severely incised, with incision probably dateable to the retreat of the lake in the Pleistocene (Vandam 2014).

Three consecutive intensive survey seasons were conducted in the Burdur Plain by the Sagalassos Survey Team, from 2010 to 2012, which built on the outcomes of previous extensive surveys from our project and others (e.g., Waelkens et al. 2000; Özsait 1991). The area that we selected to conduct our research was the southwest corner of the plain area, as few archaeological sites were known in that area and its landscape well represented the entire plain area. The goal of the intensive survey was twofold: First, it aimed to further the investigation of the western peripheral zones of the territory of Sagalassos. By comparing the occupation history of the Burdur Plain to that of Sagalassos and its immediate vicinity, we intended to explore the nature and scope of the contacts between these areas. Furthermore, we wanted to investigate the influence the city had on this outlying area, especially from around 200 BCE onward, when the territory of Sagalassos started to expand (Poblome et al. 2013). The second aim of the survey was to investigate the still poorly understood regional context of the Late Prehistoric settlements known so far in the area. Sites such as Hacılar (Mellaart 1970) and Kuruçay (Duru 1994) are considered to have played a major role in the prehistoric settlement history of the region and even Turkey at large, but it was unknown what the surrounding human landscape looked like.

Dereköy Highlands

In comparison to the Burdur Plain, the Dereköy Highlands might be deemed as "marginal," not in terms of distance to the ancient city of Sagalassos but rather due to their ecological characteristics. The landscape of the Dereköy Highlands contrasts greatly with the Burdur Plain. The area is dominated by moderate to steep mountains (ca. 1,300–1,700 m; some peaks reach above 2,000 m), plateaus, and narrow river valleys (1,000 masl) that have cut into the hills (Figure 16.1.D). Most of the hills are covered with dense vegetation of mainly *Quercus coccifera*, *Juniperus* shrubs, and *Pinus* trees until 1,600 m when the flanks start to become bare. The hills themselves are currently exploited chiefly by shepherds, while parts of the valleys and the low to moderate slopes are under cultivation by farmers (mainly cereals and to a lesser extent maize, alfalfa, and walnut trees), especially in the vicinity of the modern villages. From a geological point of view the research area can be considered as complex. It consists mainly of deposits of the upper Cretaceous limestone and a Miocene sandstone and siltstone component from the Bey Dağları Massif, but Oligocene flysch deposits and Senonian ophiolite of the Lycian nappe do occur as well (Degryse et al. 2008). The valleys, on the other hand, are mainly characterized by quaternary alluvial and slope deposits (Degryse et al. 2008). In comparison to other parts of Burdur Province, the Dereköy Highlands have a limited amount of permanent fresh water sources. The Ağlasun Çayı runs in the Ağlasun Valley, and springs can be found only in the northern extent where the permeable limestone formation meets the more impermeable ophiolites and flysch deposits. In other areas temporary wash systems that are active in spring and autumn can be found. Previous geomorphological surveys in landscapes similar to the Dereköy Highlands in Burdur Province, as well as our observations in the research area, suggest that these are very active with much slope erosion, mass movements, and sedimentation (Paulissen et al. 1993; Six 2004; Van Loo et al. 2017).

In 2016 and 2017 the Sagalassos Archaeological Research Project initiated two intensive survey campaigns in the Dereköy Highlands. With this survey we want to focus our research on previously underexplored landscape units in the highlands. By doing so we want to investigate when and how communities operated in these landscapes in terms of subsistence, mobility, and resource exploitation. Furthermore, we want to test to what extent our current patterns in occupation history (based on intensive lowland survey in intermountainous plains and valleys and extensive surveys) in the region hold up. We wish to answer the question of how these areas were integrated within the larger socioeconomic system and how this may have changed through time.

Survey Methodology

The surveys of the Burdur Plain and the Dereköy Highlands had a similar goal: to document all human activity, including small and less visible sites. Therefore, the survey methodology for each differs only to a limited extent. However, since we had to meet the varying topographies and visibilities of the highlands, we decided to integrate some different survey methods into our Dereköy Highlands survey design. Both intensive surveys were designed from a siteless methodology perspective (Dunnell and Dancey 1983; Kaptijn 2009) in which through a total collection strategy (with the exception of counted tile fragments) and subsequent material study, spatial patterns in artifact distribution across the landscape were documented. Site boundaries were determined by the artifact fall-off patterns. The survey teams consisted of four to six fieldwalkers (varying per season) who were spaced 20 m from one another and prospected transects of 1 m wide. The archaeological finds for each 50 m segment of the surveyed transects were bagged together, referred to as plots (Figure 16.2.A). For each plot the visibility was graded (0 to 5, with 5 being perfect visibility). The spacing distance of the fieldwalkers and the collection per plot of 50 sq m allowed us to track changes in artifact densities in detail while covering a considerable amount of terrain each day. In the Burdur Plain almost the entire expanse of the survey area could be surveyed using this methodology, except for a few slopes and hilltops that were extensively surveyed. The Dereköy-Hisar region provided surprisingly good visibility and accessibility, so the same intensive tract-walking survey could be conducted in ca. 85 percent of the fields. If the visibility and accessibility of the selected fields were limited, a two-stage survey method was implemented to ensure the intensive exploration of these areas (similar to Düring and Glatz 2015). The first stage consisted of a modified version of our systematic tract-walking survey using undulating transects (Banning 2002:91–92, 77). The surveyors remained spaced at intervals of about 20 m, but they walked in less strictly linear transects that allowed them to move toward areas of better visibility and to circumvent obstacles in the landscape (Figure 16.2.B). If artifact concentrations were identified, we organized a second stage gridded survey to acquire detailed information about the concentrations (Figure 16.2.C). In these cases, grids of 10 × 10 or 5 × 5 m were laid out, in which the surveyor could collect all material and count all tiles within a three-minute time period.

The aim was to get a representative sample of landscapes in both research areas. Therefore, we selected fields in all different landscape units present in the research areas: valleys, uplands, hill spurs, hills, isolated plateaus, among others. In addition, based on our ongoing results in the field, we selected new zones during the campaign and explored locations that

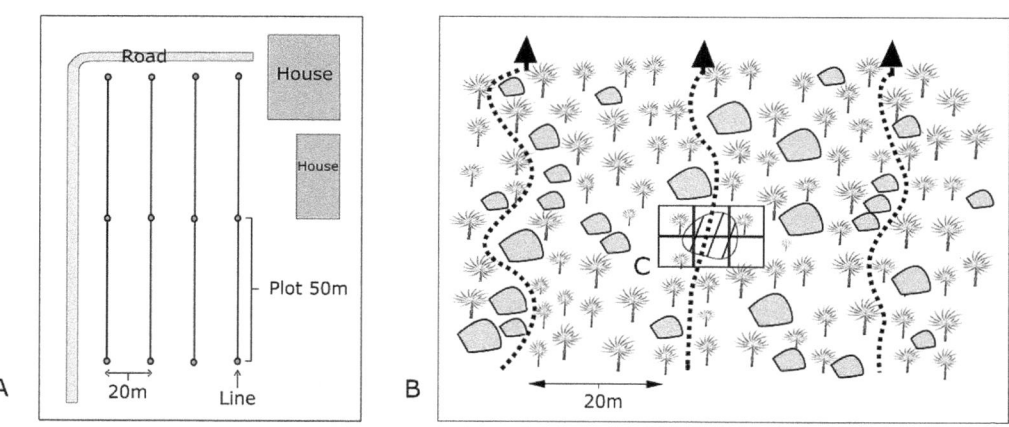

Figure 16.2. Applied survey methodology in the Burdur Plain and Dereköy Highlands. In addition to our tract-walking surveying method (A), an undulating transect walking (B) and gridded survey (C) were implemented within the Dereköy Highlands in areas with less visibility.

were pointed out by local inhabitants. Lastly, it was attempted to survey fields as continuously as possible to avoid having highly investigated "islands" within a larger research area, which would make the surveyed areas less representative. A total of 8.2 sq km (6.8% of the total area) in the Burdur Plain was intensively surveyed over three seasons and about 5.02 sq km (6.1% of the total area) in the Dereköy Highlands over two seasons.

RESULTS

The survey projects were very productive and identified a wide range of new sites in the Burdur Plain and the Dereköy Highlands. A comparison between the two survey datasets reveals some interesting patterns that we want to highlight here.

First, the differences in the number of collected artifacts per study region is noticeable. One might assume that less artifacts can be found in the highlands in comparison to the lowlands, but the opposite was true. In two seasons in the highlands 17,224 pottery sherds were collected, which gives a general sherd density of 3.6 sherds per plot (50 sq m). For the Burdur Plain, the numbers are lower: 10,535 sherds, resulting in a lower density of 1.8 sherds per plot (50 sq m). A similar pattern can be seen in the total numbers of the other material categories (see Table 16.1). Only ground stones were particularly more abundant in the Burdur Plain than in the Dereköy Highlands: seventy-five versus six (see Table 16.1). The higher numbers of artifacts in the highlands reflects a higher number of identified sites as well: twenty-five versus sixty.[1] Since we are dealing with a smaller investigated area in the Dereköy Highlands, we can clearly state that the site density is much higher compared to the Burdur Plain.

Second, a higher off-site pattern can be observed in the pottery distribution of the Dereköy Highlands (Figure 16.3). In the Burdur Plain the sites resemble isolated islands of high artifact densities in an almost empty plain where no or little other sherds occurred. The central part of the survey area, for instance, proved to be very scarce with artifacts. Off-site

TABLE 16.1. OVERVIEW OF THE TOTAL NUMBER OF COLLECTED (OR COUNTED; TILES) ARTIFACTS PER MATERIAL CATEGORY AND SITES

Material Category	Burdur Plain	Dereköy Highlands
Pottery sherds	10,535	17,224
Tiles	5,168	9,255
Lithic artifacts	417	2,286
Ground stones	75	6
Glass sherds	33	65
Metal	6	43
Production waste	33	974
Site Numbers	25	60

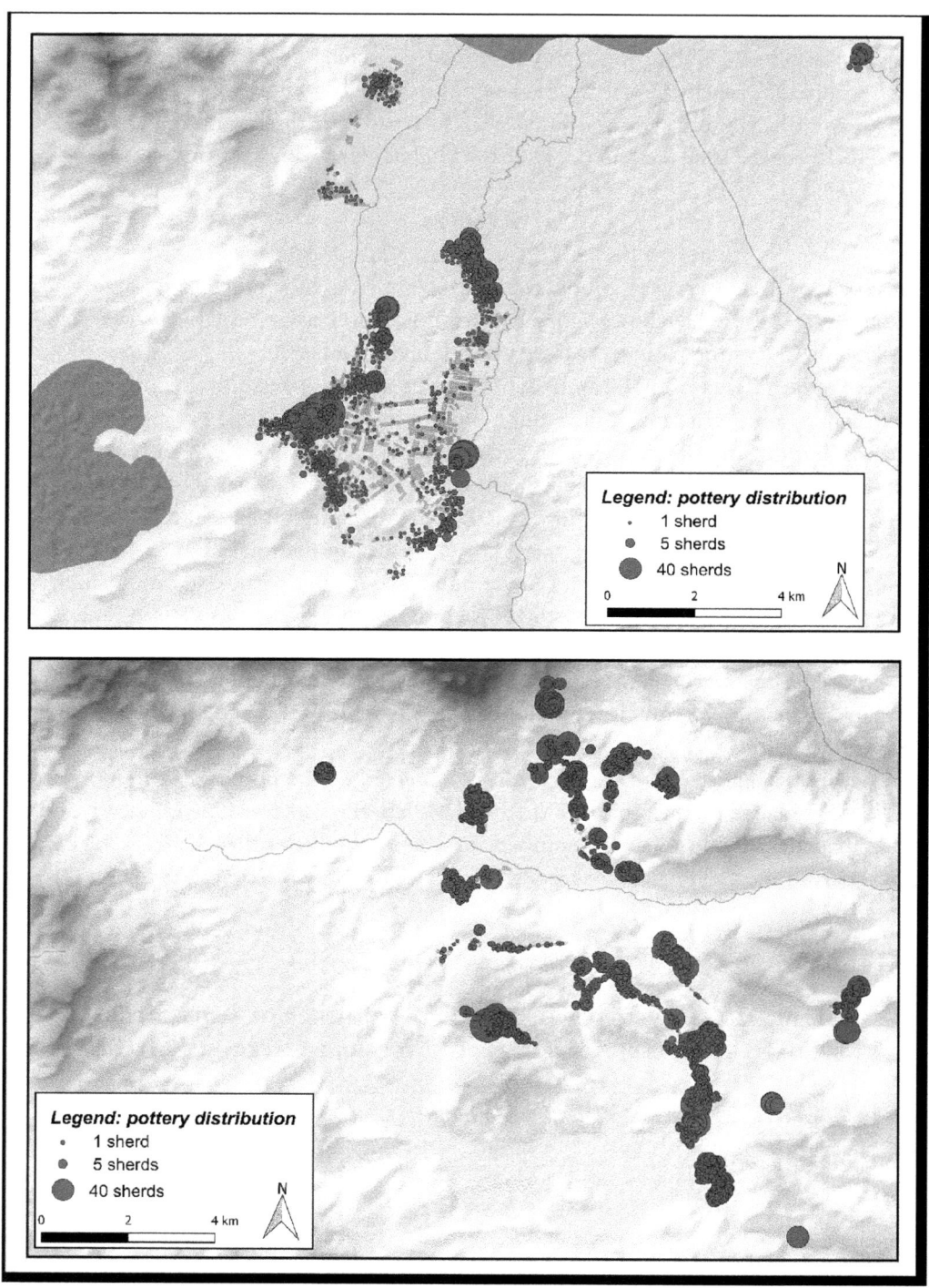

Figure 16.3. Artifact distributions of the Burdur Plain (*above*) and the Dereköy Highlands (*below*).

densities were on average 0.4 sherds per 100 sq m in the Burdur Plain, while site densities reached as high as 23 sherds per 100 sq m, with higher off-site densities observable in closer proximity to the sites. The Dereköy Highlands, on the other hand, reveals a higher and continuous distribution of pottery, 2.2 sherds per 100 sq m. Only a few small areas in the Ağlasun Valley for instance revealed little to no artifacts.

Third, the chronology of collected artifacts (and sites) between the Burdur Plain and Dereköy Highlands reveals dissimilarities. As illustrated in Figure 16.4, there are certain periods that are far better represented in either the lowlands or the highlands. For instance, the late antique and Late Ottoman artifacts were particular dominant in the highlands and occurred in much lower numbers in the lowlands. The same is true for all the lithics from different Paleolithic phases in the Dereköy Highlands. Evidence of early prehistoric farmers[2] is well represented in the Burdur Plain and other plain areas of Burdur Province, while it is currently missing in the highlands. However, our results do not only demonstrate dissimilarities, but during certain periods we see, to a large degree, connectivity between the high- and lowlands, for example, the influx of Late Chalcolithic period sites in both areas and the overall poor representation of sites during certain periods such as the Roman Imperial period.

Lastly, the variety of site types that occur in the survey areas is noteworthy as well. A wide range of sites have been identified within the highlands: flat open-air settlements (ranging from farms and villages to secondary centers), hunter-gatherer activity sites, church sites, cave sites, (lithic and metal) production sites, hilltop sites, and pastoral structures such as sheds and animal pens. In contrast, the Burdur Plain revealed a much more limited range of sites, with characteristic mounded sites (which are missing in the highlands), flat open-air settlements (ranging from farms and villages to secondary centers), cemeteries, and hilltop

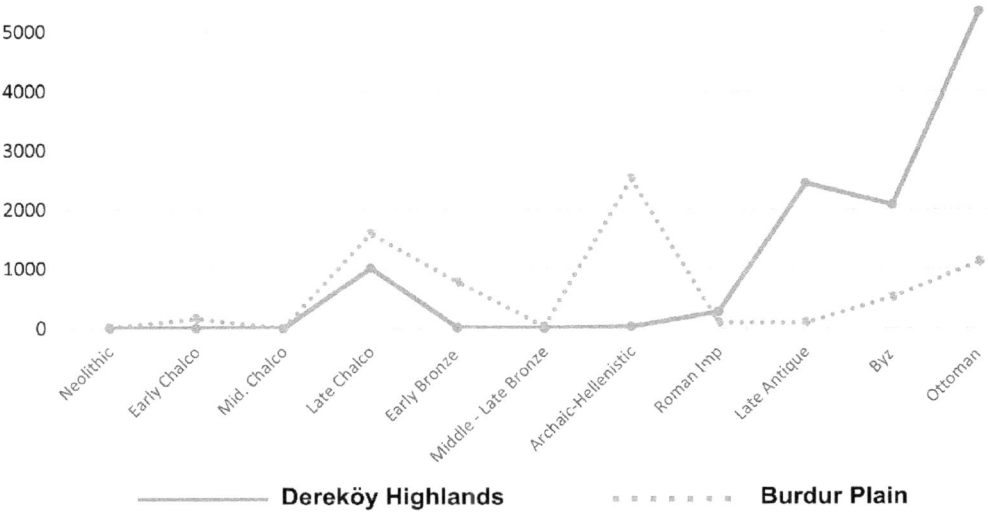

Figure 16.4. Distribution of the chronology of the collected sherds from the Dereköy Highlands and Burdur Plain.

sites situated around the plain area. It is thus clear that different types of sites can be found in different landscapes.

Discussion

The comparison between the survey results from the Burdur Plain and Dereköy Highlands illustrates clear archaeological discrepancies. The question remains of how these can be explained, which factors played a role in the survey outcomes, and how they varied in scale and importance through time. Additionally, we must discuss whether the survey outcomes reflect past patterns or to what extent they are related to survey research issues such as visibility and preservation. We believe that the interpretation of the presented survey outcomes cannot be approached straightforward, and that there was an interplay of factors.

Micro-regional Ecologies, Resources, and Subsistence Strategies

As mentioned the Western Taurus Mountains consist of a mixture of landscapes with a very heterogeneous geology and environmental variations. This means that we are dealing with diversity in hydrology, vegetation, and topography and thus varying ecological potentials even within one region. This is not only visible nowadays but must also have been the case in the past, as is indicated by the geomorphological and paleoenvironmental data that the Sagalassos Project has collected over the last thirty years. For example, palynological evidence has demonstrated that the three adjacent valleys of Ağlasun, Gravgaz, and Bereket simultaneously supported vastly different vegetation at certain periods in time, including the start of the Beyşehir Occupation Phase (henceforth, BO-Phase) when we see a rebound in deciduous and evergreen oak, a major deforestation followed by intensive arboriculture, and the appearance of a human induced shrub-steppe, respectively (Bakker et al. 2012; Kaniewski 2007). Hence, the ecological differences between the Burdur Plain and the Dereköy Highlands can most likely be seen as a primary explanation for the different archaeological patterns attested in the survey outcomes. The environment can act as a major push/pull factor for communities and may even elucidate why during some periods certain areas were avoided. However, when areas with specific ecological characteristics are used in a sustainable way, they can become extremely interesting to live in and/or to exploit, both within lowlands and highlands.

It can be argued that environmental circumstances in the Burdur Plain are ideal per se for farmers as there is a large amount of flat, high-quality arable land, plus easy access to fresh water sources. In a mountainous region such as Burdur Province, flat land that is not prone to erosion is rare. Generally, slopes with an inclination greater than 30 percent are considered unsuitable for crop cultivation (Van Velthuizen et al. 2007). Figure 16.5 shows that large tracts of land flat enough to cultivate are relatively scarce. It is therefore not surprising that we attested, in both excavations and surveys, communities that were engaged in mixed farming (plant cultivation and animal husbandry). Both prehistoric and historic settlements were located on the valley bottoms, close to the edge of the plain or along the

Figure 16.5. Slope inclination map with indication of suitable farming land. Note the wide variety across the territory of ancient Sagalassos (black line).

streams with a clear preference toward water sources and fertile land (Vandam and Kaptijn 2015). The importance of these environmental factors has also been demonstrated by a multivariate analysis (Vandam et al. 2013). The material culture of the surveyed and excavated sites also indicates a reliance on crop cultivation, with the high number of grinding stones and sickle blades, and in the case of the excavated sites, a high number of jars with stored cereals and pulses in them (e.g., Mellaart 1970; Vandam and Kaptijn 2015). The studies on the botanical and faunal remains from these prehistoric settlements in the Burdur Plain and similar plains in the area further support the mixed-farming subsistence lifestyle of lowland communities (De Cupere et al. 2017). The fact that the Burdur Plain communities were involved in these farming activities might explain why we identify mounded sites in plain areas: they form ideal settlement locations for crop cultivators. Furthermore, constant occupation at one location is interesting for early farmers, as yields increase through fertilization (Jones 2005). That being said, intensive use for too long leads to depletion of the soil eventually.

The highlands of Dereköy tell a different story as they provide a whole different range of resources that also must have appealed to people. Open areas of fertile land are scarce and only occur in small pockets in the mountains and within the river valleys. The current lack of early farmers in our survey outcomes in this area might be related to this fact, and perhaps can also be explained by past environmental conditions. The pollen data from the eastern extent of the Ağlasun Çayı, 5 km west of our survey research area, indicates that the valley floor during the Early Holocene was particular wet (Bakker et al. 2012), and perhaps even too wet for early agriculture. Later, in the late antique and Byzantine periods, however, the arable lands in the highlands were cultivated, and we have evidence of a productive landscape (Vandam et al. 2019a). In the survey we have picked up a sharp rise in rural population residing in small, isolated farms and farming villages. The many locally produced amphorae and (counterweight and screw) presses identified at the sites indicate that these people were engaged in wine/oil production, which considering the altitude is not a given (Poblome et al. 2008; Vermoere et al. 2003). The fact that this changing settlement system and an increased specialization took place during late antiquity in the Dereköy Highlands fits well with the current understanding of this period. We believe that they might be understood as responses to major socioeconomic changes (e.g., reorganization of the provinces and central responsibilities in the area; Poblome 2014) In the Bereket Valley, an intramontane valley located between the Burdur Plain and Dereköy Highlands, this specialization might be visible in the shift away from mixed farming and a specialized focus on pastoral activities only (Kaptijn et al. 2013). The fact that we do not observe this in the Burdur Plain might have to do with its location within the territory of Sagalassos (see the section on connectivity and proximity).

Despite the limited amount of arable lands, the highlands are rich in other valuable resources, such as flint nodules and iron ore (minerals: magnetite and hematite; Degryse et al. 2003), that lay on the surface at many locations in the highlands. The many (lithic and metal) production sites from different periods in the Dereköy survey area illustrate that people exploited these local resources throughout time. The combination of the expansive terrain of rich hunting grounds and the abundant flint resources explain chiefly why we attested so many Paleolithic hunter-gatherer activity areas. Additionally, the hills must have provided excellent grazing terrain during later periods, as is evidenced in the pollen records by the expansion/recovery of oak woodlands during the BO-Phase in Ağlasun, which were presumably used as grazing areas for pigs (Bakker et al. 2012), and multiple periods of strong expansion of meadow steppe-type species during the post-BO-Phases in Bereket and Gravgaz leading up to the present day (Kaniewski et al. 2007; Vermoere et al. 2003). For the Late Ottoman period especially, it seems that the highlands were exploited by shepherds. Many Late Ottoman field stone structures and animal pens/enclosures have been identified during the intensive survey. Possibly related to these activities is the high off-site density in the highlands for this period, particularly since it mainly comprised water jug fragments. For the older periods it was not evidenced that a similar pastoral subsistence strategy was being pursued in our research area (see the section Research Areas), which fits the idea that the modern vertical transhumance strategy does not go far back in time, but rather as has been illustrated pastoralism in Anatolia has taken many forms through time (Hammer and Arbuckle 2017). Lastly, limestone and timber can be considered as important recourses that must have been exploited in the hills especially in Roman times when large-scale building activity occurred due to its scarceness in the plain areas. Evidence of past stone quarrying occurs in close distance to historical sites and still occurs nowadays in the highlands but on a much larger scale, forming an enormous threat to the preserved archaeology. In contrast to other areas of Burdur Province, the Dereköy Highlands have limited accessibility to secure and permanent fresh water sources, which must have been a challenge for past communities. Prehistoric and production sites tend to cluster around temporary washes fed by rain/snow melt water, and for the later periods we have evidence of constructed wells (late antique/Byzantine period) to get access to groundwater and cisterns (Late Ottoman) to collect rainwater. Nowadays, shepherds still use these ancient features in addition to large water tanks that are brought up high into the hills.

It is clear that both lowlands and highlands were generally very rich in resources, and that they were not exploited in the same way across time and space.

Connectivity and Proximity

The connectivity and proximity of the Burdur Plain and the Dereköy Highlands with ancient Sagalassos and other regional poles of attraction can also help determine the local archaeology, and must be considered as another explanatory factor. It can, for instance, shed light on why an increase or decrease of human activity took place during certain historical periods. Burdur Plain is located at the western extent of Sagalassos's administrative territory. The distance between the city of Sagalassos and this area is as much as two days of walking (for an average walker following the path of least effort) (Figure 16.6). Its remote location vis-à-vis Sagalassos might be one of the main reasons why we have small numbers of Roman artifacts in the Burdur Plain survey, despite the fact that the plain area was well connected with the southern Mediterranean coastal area and northeastern extent of Pisidia, including Pisidian Antioch, through the Augustan Via Sebaste (Mitchell 1993; Talloen in press). The fact that this area was a border zone might also be part of the explanation why so few Roman artifacts were found. Eight identical boundary markers, most of them not in their original location today but once probably having stood along the Via Sebaste, all carry inscriptions that demarcate the border and describe a border correction during the reign of Nero. The inscription reads that the land to the right of the stone belongs to Sagalassos, while the area

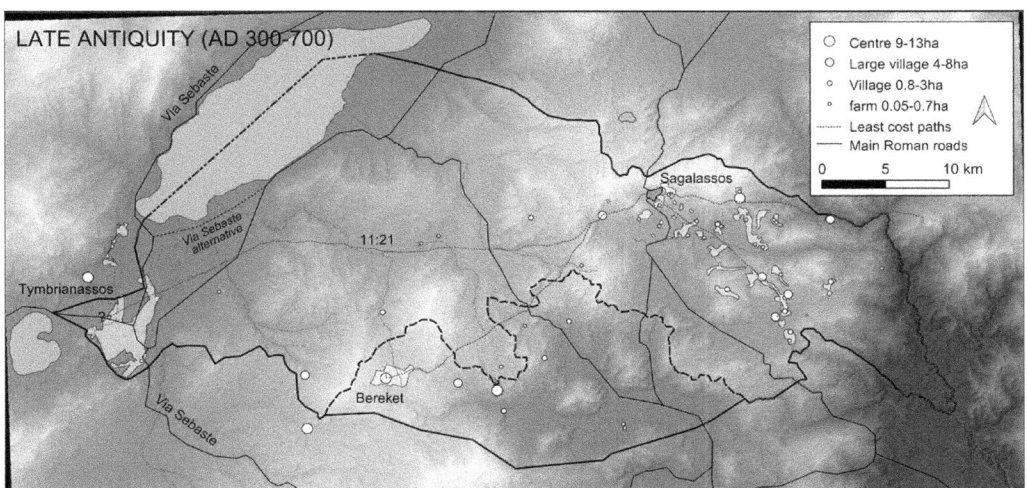

Figure 16.6. Calculated least-cost path from the Burdur Plain to Sagalassos with the main late antique secondary centers.

to the left belongs to the imperial estate of Tymbrianassos, a fifth of which also belongs to Sagalassos (Ramsay 1886:129; Waelkens et al. 2000:171–172, 175–176). However, the fact that we found a limited amount of Roman material on the survey does not mean that the area was completely abandoned. In the modern provincial town of Burdur (e.g., Burdur museum inscriptions: Horsley and Kearsley 2007; Istasyon/Burdur Höyük: Mellaart 1954; Waelkens et al. 2000:21, 151) and the smaller modern villages (especially Düğer), Roman architectural remains have been found, which potentially indicate Roman predecessors at these locations. Furthermore, an important decree of the governor of Galatia dated around 14–19 AD, concerning a claim for transport assistance, was found in Burdur (Mitchell 1976).

The Dereköy area is located much closer to Sagalassos, between two and three hours walking (Figure 16.7), which could have had an influence on site densities and site locations within the area. Three hours walking distance is considered to be the maximum people will travel to a marketplace, as this allows traveling back and forth and conducting business in a single day (Bintliff 2008). The entire Dereköy Highland region may therefore have been focused on Sagalassos for the trading of their surplus. However, the presence of larger villages at rather regular intervals and a secondary center, Düldül Yüzü (at an altitude of 1,500 m; Vandam et al. 2018), suggests that people could also have focused on these larger sites for their more frequent needs (Figure 16.7). From our long-term survey work it has become clear that

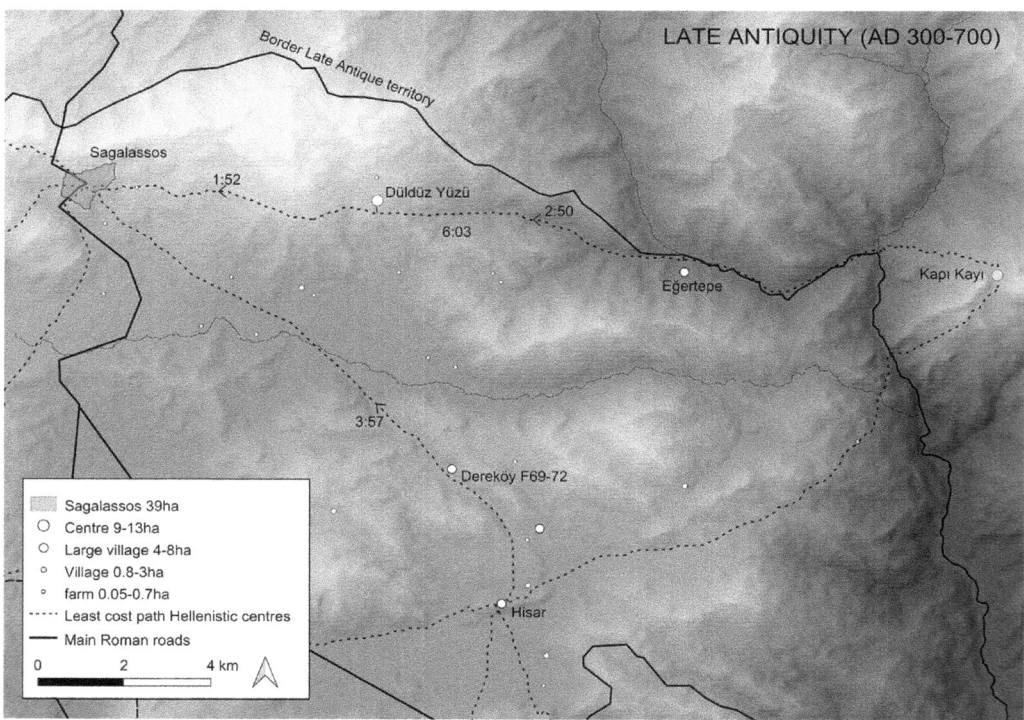

Figure 16.7. Calculated least-cost paths from the surrounding ancient centers to Sagalassos. Many of the newly identified sites in the Dereköy Highlands were founded along these paths.

the 1,200 sq km large territory of Sagalassos during the Roman period was organized around secondary sites for many practical reasons. These sites were often large (between 8 and 12 ha), monumental, and had economically strategic positions as markets for their surroundings, just like Düldül Yüzü. A least-cost path analysis between Sagalassos and neighboring ancient cities such as Kremna, Belören/Keraia, and Kapı Kaya illustrated that Düldül Yüzü, as well as several other settlements, were set on the predicted paths/routes between these sites (Figure 16.7). Most of the sites actually date back to the late antique and Byzantine periods when, as mentioned, we observed an increasing rural population with the development of an agriculturally productive landscape. This development contrasts sharply with the limited number of Roman Imperial sites in the highlands. During this period we have found mainly a cluster of small farmsteads in close vicinity to Sagalassos itself (Vanhaverbeke et al. 2009)

Preservation and Surface Visibility

In the Dereköy Highlands we have identified significantly more artifacts than in the Burdur Plain, which can to a certain extent be explained by the difference in fragmentation rates and the poor preservation of artifacts from the former. Although the collected sherds have not been studied specifically on their fragmentation (i.e., average sherd weight per unit), we have indications that the attested patterns might affect our absolute survey numbers as well. It was notable that most of the sherds of the Dereköy Highlands were particularly small, weathered, and occasionally covered with moss/algae, which indicated that they have been lying on the surface for a certain period of time. These sherds were, thus, in a much worse state when compared to the Burdur Plain materials, which have often been recently plowed out of the ground. In addition, during the material study it became clear that we were dealing with large differences in the locally produced pre-Roman ceramics (e.g., Late Chalcolithic and Iron Age) between both areas, which fits within the outcomes of a recent comprehensive analytical pottery study (Braekmans et al. 2017). Due to the different clay properties, clay pastes, and firing practices, the pre-Roman local pottery from the Dereköy Highlands had softer fabrics with lots of inclusions and thus is a more easily breakable material than the ones from the Burdur Plain.

Related to this and what should be taken into account considering general survey numbers is the overall visibility of the investigated fields. It has been illustrated that poor surface visibility can cause lower numbers of collected artifacts (e.g., Terrenato and Ammerman 1996). As mentioned during both surveys the visibility was scored in a similar way: ranging from 0–5, with 5 being perfect visibility. A comparison of the visibility reveals that the Dereköy Highlands had in general poorer visibility. The Burdur Plain survey had a good to excellent visibility, as about four of five of the surveyed plots were rated with a score between 3 and 5. For the Dereköy Highlands, on the other hand, the majority of the visibility was rated between 2 and 3 (64%), with significantly less fields being scored above 3 than in the Burdur Plain (ca. 50%; see Table 16.2). This comparison indicates that surface visibility can be excluded as an important explanatory factor for the higher artifact numbers in the Dereköy Highlands. It rather suggests that even more finds would have been identified if the visibility would have been better in the highlands.

TABLE 16.2. THE PERCENTAGE OF SURVEYED AREA PER VISIBILITY SCORE

Visibility	Percentage of Surveyed Area in the Burdur Plain	Percentage of Surveyed Area in the Dereköy Highlands
0	9%	2%
1	3%	9%
2	9%	33%
3	28%	31%
4	40%	23%
5	11%	2%

GEOMORPHOLOGICAL PROCESSES

Geomorphological processes determine to a great extent the site recovery and thus directly the survey results (Banning 2002; Terrenato and Ammerman 1996). The dissimilarities in landscape between the Burdur Plain and Dereköy Highlands result in different geomorphological processes that take place at different rates, which doubtless is also reflected in our survey outcomes. Furthermore, human impact on the landscape has contributed not only to the shifting of land use patterns over time but also to the visibility and mobility of the archaeological materials. Modern and historical deforestation, particularly in the highland areas, has resulted in much of the topsoil from the hillslopes shifting to the valley bottoms (Van Loo et al. 2017), taking artifacts with it and contributing to the obscuring of sites on both ends.

No detailed geomorphological studies have been conducted in the Burdur Plain or the Dereköy Highlands themselves. However, general observations were made by geomorphologists from our project in the research area (see the section on research areas) and some conclusions can be made related to our archaeological survey results. Next to the fact that the Dereköy Highlands are particularly interesting for hunter-gatherers from an ecological perspective, the high recovery rate of Paleolithic artifacts in this area is also determined by local geomorphological processes such as erosion. Prior to our survey the oldest archaeological materials in Burdur Province were dated to the Epipaleolithic and Neolithic, which were found in plain areas and river valleys (Vandam 2019). During our highland survey various isolated Middle Paleolithic artifacts were collected as well as one large concentration on a plateau. This concentration was identified in the channels of a gully system that has cut into underlying deposits, up to 8 m deep (Figure 16.8). Since the materials were particularly fresh in nature it seems that the artifacts have only been washed out fairly recently. Without this erosive process, the materials would still be covered, which explains why until this point we only found them in very active landscapes. This means that we cannot exclude the presence of older and/or other hunter-gather communities in other parts of the landscape in the area, where we do not have these processes. However, as mentioned, the Burdur Plain is only fairly recently exposed through the retreat of Burdur Lake, which makes older Paleolithic occupation in this area unlikely.

Figure 16.8. Middle Paleolithic lithic artifacts were discovered in areas (e.g., Field 117) with active erosion process.

The river valleys within the Dereköy Highlands and the plain area of the Burdur Plain, on the other hand, seem to be prone to similar concealing processes, which indicates that some specific sites are underrepresented in our survey outcomes. A sediment core taken on the eastern end of the Ağlasun River valley, 7 km eastward of our highland research area, illustrated an infill of 8.5 m over the last 8,500 years (Six 2004:108–135). However, this infill was not seen in all cores of the river valley; especially toward our research area less material was deposited (Six 2004:108–135). Through our attempt to make a transect across the Dereköy Highlands, it became clear that the river sedimentation is high in an area of 100 to 300 m on either side of the river, as no artifacts were found in that area. A clear increase of the artifact densities was identified toward the foothills. However, in some foothills large colluvium deposits have been observed (Six 2004). Therefore, we can argue that sites that focused specifically on floodplains and foothills are underrepresented in the settlement history. Similarly, this can be argued for the Burdur Plain as well since sites were identified at the edge of the plain where colluvial deposits have been observed. At one specific location in the foothills, which was leveled for agricultural purposes, an Early Chalcolithic site was discovered about 60 cm to 1 m below the present surface. Sedimentation processes within the plain area are less well known, but the fact that many prehistoric artifacts were recovered in the area suggests a good site recovery in general. The rivers within the plain area have cut into the Pleistocene lacustrine deposits rather severely. The occurrence of Chalcolithic sites on old riverbanks from different rivers confirms that these sites were established after this incision process took place, which perhaps continued further onward later (Vandam et al. 2019b).

Conclusions

To conclude, this chapter has aimed to stress the importance of differentiation and contextualization of archaeological research in a mountainous region. It is clear that mountain ranges cannot be considered as singular entities and that they can comprise a huge variety of landscapes, ecology, and even archaeology. In this case study we focused on the Western Taurus Mountains where these varieties occurred on a microscale. For many years the main focus of our survey research was on intermountain valleys and plain areas, but by relocating our research area toward the highlands it became clear that these areas have great archaeological potential as well. Therefore, we can question to what extent these landscapes were truly marginal, and whether they were recognized as such in ancient times. The richness of resources within the highlands were exploited from early on, but how these landscapes were used and viewed by past communities varied enormously through time. The complex relationship illustrated between the archaeologies of different landscapes highlights the key importance of contextualizing both lowlands and highlands to gain a better understanding of the bigger picture.

Acknowledgments

This research was supported by the Belgian Programme on Interuniversity Poles of Attraction, the Research Fund of the KU Leuven, and the Research Foundation Flanders–FWO. The Burdur Plain survey was supported by a Methusalem grant of the Flemish Government received by Prof. Dr. Marc Waelkens. This work would not have been possible without the help and hard work of all the participants of the Burdur Plain and Dereköy archaeological surveys. We are grateful to the Ministry of Culture and Tourism of the Republic of Turkey, and its representatives, for the survey permission and aid during the fieldwork campaigns. Finally, we would like to express our gratitude to Dr. Arnau Garcia-Molsosa and Prof. Dr. Peter Biehl for inviting us to the tenth IEMA visiting scholars conference and for giving us a good idea of why Buffalo is called the city of good neighbors.

Notes

1. Including previously known sites in both research areas.
2. Mainly in the form of large visible höyük/tell sites.

References

Bakker, J., E. Paulissen, D. Kaniewski, V. De Laet, G. Verstraeten, and M. Waelkens 2012 Man, Vegetation and Climate during the Holocene in the Territory of Sagalassos, Western Taurus Mountains, SW Turkey. *Vegetation History and Archaeobotany* 21(4–5):249–266.

Banning, E. B. 2002 *Archaeological Survey: Manuals in Archaeological Method, Theory and Technique.* Springer, New York.

Bintliff, J. L. 2008 Considerations on Agricultural Scale-Economies in the Greco-Roman World. In *Feeding the Ancient Greek City*, edited by R. Alston and O. M. V. Nijf, 17–31. Peeters, Leuven.

Braekmans, D., P. Degryse, B. Neyt, M. Waelkens, and J. Poblome 2017 Reconstructing Regional Trajectories: The Provenance and Distribution of Archaic to Hellenistic Ceramics in Central Pisidia (Southwest Turkey). *Archaeometry* 59(3):472–492.

De Cupere, B., D. Frémondeau, E. Kaptijn, E. Marinova, J. Poblome, R. Vandam, and W. Van Neer 2017 Subsistence Economy and Land Use Strategies in the Burdur Province (SW Anatolia) from Prehistory to the Byzantine Period. *Quaternary International* 436:4–17.

Degryse, P., P. Muchez, M. Sintubin, A. Clijsters, W. Viaene, M. Dederen, P. Schrooten, and M. Waelkens 2008 The Geology of the Area around the Ancient City Sagalassos. In *Sagalassos VI: Geo- and Bio-Archaeology at Sagalassos and in Its Territory*, edited by P. Degryse and M. Waelkens, 17–24. University Press, Leuven.

Degryse, P., P. Muchez, S. Six, and M. Waelkens 2003 Identification of Ore Extraction and Metal Working in Ancient Times: A Case Study of Sagalassos (SW Turkey). *Journal of Geochemical Exploration* 77(1):65–80.

Dunnell, R. C., and W. S. Dancey 1983 The Siteless Survey: A Regional Scale Data Collection Strategy. *Advances in Archaeological Method and Theory* 6:267–287.

Düring, B. S., and C. Glatz 2015 *Kinetic Landscapes: The Cide Archaeological Project 2009–2011: Surveying the Western Turkish Black Sea Region*. De Gruyter Open, Warsaw.

Duru, R. 1994 *Kuruçay Höyük I: 1978–1988 kazılarının sunuçları neolitik ve erken kalkolitik çağ yerleşmeleri, Türk Tarih Kurumu yayınları 44*. Türk Tarih Kurumu Basımevi, Ankara.

Hammer, E. L., and B. S. Arbuckle 2017 10,000 Years of Pastoralism in Anatolia: A Review of Evidence for Variability in Pastoral Lifeways. *Nomadic Peoples* 21(2):214–267.

Horsley, G. H. R., and R. A. Kearsley 2007 *Greek and Latin Inscriptions in the Burdur Archaeological Museum: Regional Epigraphic Catalogues of Asia Minor V*. The British Institute at Ankara, London.

Jones, G. 2005 Garden Cultivation of Staple Crops and Its Implications for Settlement Location and Continuity. *World Archaeology* 37(2):164–176.

Kaniewski, D., E. Paulissen, V. De Laet, K. Dossche, and M. Waelkens 2007 A High-Resolution Late Holocene Landscape Ecological History Inferred from an Intramontane Basin in the Western Taurus Mountains, Turkey. *Quaternary Science Reviews* 26(17–18): 2201–2218.

Kaptijn, E. 2009 *Life on the Watershed: Reconstructing Subsistence in a Steppe Region Using Archaeological Survey: A Diachronic Perspective on Habitation in the Jordan Valley*. Sidestone Press, Leiden.

Kaptijn, E., J. Poblome, H. Vanhaverbeke, J. Bakker, and M. Waelkens 2013 Societal Changes in the Bereket Valley in the Hellenistic, Roman and Early Byzantine Periods: Results from the Sagalassos Territorial Archaeological Survey 2008 (SW Turkey). *Anatolian Studies* 63:75–95.

Kıs, M., O. Erol, S. Senel, and M. Ergin 1989 Preliminary Results of Radiocarbon Dating of Coastal Deposits of the Pleistocene Pluvial Lake of Burdur, Turkey. *Journal of Islamic Academy of Sciences* 2(1):37–40.

Mellaart, J. 1954 Preliminary Report on a Survey of Pre-Classical Remains in Southern Turkey. *Anatolian Studies* 4:175–240.

Mellaart, J. 1970 *Excavations at Hacılar*. 2 vols. Edinburgh University Press, Edinburgh.

Mitchell, S. 1976 Requisitioned Transport in the Roman Empire: A New Inscription from Pisidia. *Journal of Roman Studies* 66:106–131.

Mitchell, S. 1993 *Anatolia: Land, Men, and Gods in Asia Minor*. Vol. 1. Oxford University Press, Oxford.

Özsait, M. 1991 Nouveaux sites contemporains de Hacilar en Pisidie Occidentale. *Anatolia Antiqua* 1:59–118.

Paulissen, E., J. Poesen, G. Govers, and J. De Ploey 1993 The Physical Environment at Sagalassos (Western Taurus, Turkey): A Reconnaissance Survey. In *Sagalassos II: Report on the*

Third Excavation Campaign of 1992, edited by M. Waelkens and J. Poblome, 229–247. University Press, Leuven.

Poblome, J. 2014 The Economy of the Roman World as a Complex Adaptive System: Testing the Case in Second to Fifth Century CE Sagalassos. In *Structure and Performance in the Roman Economy: Models, Methods and Case Studies—Collection Latomus*, vol. 350, edited by E. Paul and V. Koenraad, 97–140. Peeters, Leuven.

Poblome, J., D. Braekmans, M. Waelkens, N. Fırat, H. Vanhaverbeke, F. Martens, E. Kaptijn, K. Vyncke, R. Willet, and P. Degryse 2013 How Did Sagalassos Come to Be? A Ceramological Survey. In *Festschrift for Levent Zoroğlu*, edited by M. Tekocak, 175–186. AKMED, Antalya.

Poblome, J., M. Corremans, P. Bes, K. Romanus, and P. Degryse 2008 It Is Never Too Late . . . The Late Roman Initiation of Amphora Production in the Territory of Sagalassos. In *Euergetes, Festschrift für Prof. Dr. Halek Abbasoğlu zum 65: Geburtstag*, edited by I. Delemen, S. Çokay-Kepçe, A. Özdizbay, and O. Turak, 1001–1012. Suna-İnan Kıraç Akdeniz Medeniyetleri Araştırma Enstitüsü, Antalya.

Price, S. P., and B. Scott 1991 Pliocene Burdur Basin, SW Turkey: Tectonics, Seismicity and Sedimentation. *Journal of Geological Society* 148(2):345–354.

Ramsay, W. M. 1886 Notes and Inscriptions from Asia Minor (III). *American Journal of Archaeology and of the History of the Fine Arts* 2(2):123–131.

Six, S. 2004 Holocene Geomorphological Evolution of the Territory of Sagalassos. PhD thesis, University of Leuven, Leuven.

Talloen, P. in press The Road to Salvation: Travel and the Sacred along the Imperial Road in Pisidia. In *Pathways of Communication: Roads and Routes in Anatolia from Prehistory to Seljuk Times*, edited by L. Vandeput. Cambridge University Press, Cambridge.

Terrenato, N., and A. J. Ammerman 1996 Visibility and Site Recovery in the Cecina Valley Survey, Italy. *Journal of Field Archaeology* 23(1):91–109.

Van Loo, M., B. Dusar, G. Verstraeten, H. Renssen, B. Notebaert, K. D'Haen, and J. Bakker 2017 Human Induced Soil Erosion and the Implications on Crop Yield in a Small Mountainous Mediterranean Catchment (SW Turkey). *CATENA* 149:491–504.

Van Velthuizen, H., B. Huddleston, G. Fischer, M. Salvatore, E. Ataman, F. O. Nachtergaele, M. Zanetti, and M. Bloise 2007 *Mapping Biophysical Factors That Influence Agricultural Production and Rural Vulnerability: Environment and Natural Resources Series no. 11*. Food & Agriculture Org., Rome.

Vandam, R. 2014 Everybody Needs Good Neighbors: Exploring Late Prehistoric Settlement Strategies and Socioeconomic Behavior in the Burdur Plain, SW Turkey. PhD thesis, University of Leuven, Leuven.

Vandam, R. 2019 Exploring the Culture Landscape of Neolithic (6500–6100 BC) Hacılar, SW Turkey: A Typical Nucleated Settlement Pattern or Potentially Biased? In *Social and Economic Changes in the Second Half of the 7th Millennium in the Near East*, edited by A. Marciniak, 181–204. Lockwood Press, Atlanta.

Vandam, R., and E. Kaptijn 2015 Living in the Burdur Plain: Reconstructing Human Subsistence Diachronically (6500–200 BC). In *Pisidian Essays in Honour of Hacı Ali Ekinci*, edited by H. Metin, A. Polat-Becks, R. Becks, and M. Firat, 165–176. Ege Yayınları, Istanbul.

Vandam, R., E. Kaptijn, N. Broothaerts, B. De Cupere, E. Marinova, M. Van Loo, G. Verstraeten, J. Poblome 2019a "Marginal" Landscapes: Human Activity, Vulnerability, and Resilience in the Western Taurus Mountains (Southwest Turkey). *Journal of Eastern Mediterranean Archaeology and Heritage Studies* 7(4): 432–450.

Vandam, R., E. Kaptijn, and B. Vanschoenwinkel 2013 Disentangling the Spatio-environmental Drivers of Human Settlement. *PLoS ONE* 8(7, e67726):1–11.

Vandam, R., B. Mušič, and I. Medarič I. 2019b Contextualizing Kuruçay Höyük: Assessing the Unexplored Late Chalcolithic Landscape Near the Beginning of Early Social Complexity in SW Turkey. *Journal of Field Archaeology* 44(1):1–19.

Vandam, R., P. Talloen, Y. Zenger, and J. Poblome 2018 Düldül Yüzü: The Exploration of a Secondary Center in the Territory of Sagalassos. *News Bulletin on Archaeology from Mediterranean Anatolia* 16:180–187.

Vanhaverbeke, H., J. Poblome, M. Waelkens 2009 The Archaeological Intensive Suburban Survey Near Sagalassos. *Araştırma Sonuçları Toplantısı* 26(3):173–175.

Vermoere, M., L. Vanhecke, M. Waelkens, and E. Smets 2003. Modern and Ancient Olive Stands Near Sagalassos (Southwest Turkey) and Reconstruction of the Ancient Agricultural Landscape in Two Valleys. In *Global Ecology and Biogeography*, 217–235. Wiley-Blackwell.

Waelkens, M., E. Paulissen, H. Vanhaverbeke, J. Reyniers, J. Poblome, R. Degeest, W. Viaene, J. Deckers, B. De Cupere, W. Van Neer, H. A. Ekinci, and M. O. Erbay 2000 The 1996 and 1997 Surveys in the Territory of Sagalassos. In *Sagalassos V: Report on the Survey and Excavation Campaigns of 1996 and 1997*, edited by M. Waelkens and L. Loots, 17–216. Leuven University Press, Leuven.

Yıldırım, Ü., and M. Uysal 2011 Changes in the Coastline of the Burdur Lake between 1975 and 2010. In *Proceedings of the International Symposium on Environmental Protection and Planning: Geographic Information Systems (GIS) and Remote Sensing (RS) Applications* edited by M. Ayvaz, 7–12. ISEPP, Izmir.

CHAPTER SEVENTEEN

Developing a Systematic Approach to the Archaeological Study of Mountain Landscapes

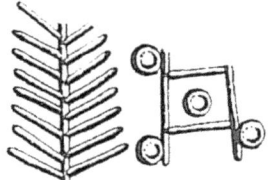

The Raganello Basin Experience

Martijn van Leusen, Wieke de Neef, and Jan Sevink

Abstract *Between 2011 and 2014 the authors investigated in detail a selection of protohistoric surface scatters and their surroundings in the Maddalena upland basin (600–1,000 masl). Part of the Raganello River basin in the southern Apennines (northern Calabria region, Italy), this area had previously been archaeologically surveyed by the University of Groningen Institute of Archaeology between 2005 and 2008. The new and interdisciplinary investigations consisted of geophysical surveys and geoarchaeological and pedological studies. We here primarily use the work conducted at site RB73 to illustrate how depositional, postdepositional, and current land use processes result in the present expression of a surface scatter or "site" as recorded in the archaeological field survey, demonstrating that long-term slope processes in the flysch geology of typical Apennine upland valleys have a fundamental impact on the preservation and appearance of the archaeological record. We argue that confidence in our theoretical and practical understanding of this record remains unjustified in the absence of carefully designed, integrated geoarchaeological and geophysical work.*

Introduction

The Groningen Institute of Archaeology has been active in northern Calabria (Italy) since 1990, when excavations at the Iron Age hilltop sanctuary, settlement, and necropolis of Timpone Motta di Francavilla Marittima were begun under the direction of Prof. Marianne Kleibrink (Kleibrink 2006).[1] While these excavations have continued in later years under Prof. Peter Attema of the GIA, and lately under Dr. Jan Jacobsen of the Carlsberg Glyptotek in Copenhagen, systematic fieldwalking surveys of the surrounding landscape began in 2000. Directed by one of us (Van Leusen), these initially focused on the areas within 5 km of the excavation, covering the foothills on either side of the Raganello River. In 2005–2008 these surveys were extended as a formal stratified landscape sampling survey of the whole Raganello River basin in three transects crossing the river and covering the uplands and mountains (the third main landscape zone, the coastal plain, is unsuitable for surveying due to its thick overburden of Late Holocene sediments; Attema et al. 2010:100–103; Van Leusen 2015).

In geological terms, the Raganello basin is situated in the southern Apennines, which consist of Mesozoic and Cenozoic sedimentary rocks of the Ligurid and Sicilid sedimentary basins (Santoro et al. 2009). Due to continued regional uplift, the Raganello River, its tributaries, and other streams have extensively dissected the landscape, resulting in canyons, steep slopes, and screes. Middle to Late Quaternary marine deposits form the Sibaritide coastal plain and its inland extensions (Fuchs 1980), and the interplay between regional tectonic uplift and glacio-eustatic changes has resulted in a series of marine terraces reaching elevations of around 500 masl. The older and higher terraces are severely dissected and sometimes barely recognizable; they are loosely described as the "foothills" zone.

Over a period of fifteen years, teams from the GIA have conducted fieldwalking surveys in the Raganello basin as part of four successive research programs: the Regional Pathways to Complexity program (RPC, 1997–2001), the Raganello Archaeological Project (RAP, 2002–2005), the Hidden Landscapes Project (HLP, 2005–2010), and the Rural Life in Protohistoric Italy Project (RLP, 2010–2015). The results of the initial surveys in the foothill zone have been published as part of the comparative landscape studies of the Regional Pathways to Complexity Project (Attema et al. 2010). In the period 2005–2008 these surveys were extended as part of the HLP research program to cover two transects across the upper Raganello valley. While systematic intensive surveys were in practice largely limited to accessible agricultural fields within these transects, we also investigated less accessible locations. Already since the late 1990s the caving club Gruppo Speleologico "Sparviere" (GSS, directed by Antonio Larocca) assisted our teams by reporting, and then reinvestigating with us, remote locations where protohistoric pottery had been encountered. We regard this collaboration as extremely important to us because these sites tend to be located in the nonagricultural, and very often nearly inaccessible, parts of the uplands and mountains, and they therefore provide information complementary to that of our own surveys.

Since 2005, attention shifted to landscape formation processes and how they affect our ability to record archaeological remains. Feiken (2014; cf. Van Leusen and Feiken 2007) studied overall gradation (erosion and sedimentation) processes and slope profiles in the upper Raganello basin, and in the latest research program (the RLP, 2010–2015) we have focused on the natural and anthropogenic geomorphological processes happening within single landscape units and at the scale of individual sites (i.e., over distances of hundreds to tens of meters) in order to understand site formation and postdepositional processes and their effects on the detection of protohistoric artifact scatters. These processes are described and explained by Sevink et al. (2016).

The main objective of the RLP was the in-depth investigation of a representative sample of the 160 protohistoric surface scatters mapped in the earlier RAP/HLP surveys. After classifying these scatters according to their material assemblage and landscape zone (De Neef 2016:82–92), the RLP team investigated representative examples from six site classes by detailed archaeological resurveys, magnetic-based geophysical techniques, and geopedological surveys involving intensive manual coring. We used a combination of invasive and noninvasive approaches to investigate the selected sites: intensive fieldwalking surveys and geophysical surveys as noninvasive approaches, corings and test pits as invasive approaches. The latter were needed to compensate for the limitations of the former: even intensive fieldwalking survey often does not provide more than a very accurate map of undiagnostic sherds on the surface, and in few cases can geophysical anomalies be interpreted confidently without supporting evidence. In such cases corings and test pits can often provide information leading to an understanding of the stratigraphy on and around sites and of the causes of geophysical anomalies, as well as allow us to obtain good samples for dating, ecology, and the study of soils and archaeological materials. However, our aim was always to conduct the minimum amount of invasive research: if enough information about the character and current state of an archaeological site can be obtained by noninvasive means, then no further invasive study should be necessary.

The particular landscape unit of interest here is the "upland undulating sloping land" (UUSL) of the Maddalena basin, which is confined between two limestone dominated ranges and is a geomorphologically active landscape with various slope processes including mass movements. Its geology is dominated by loamy marls with yellowish brown to orange yellow soils, depending on the extent of soil development. The fine texture of the dense marls inhibits percolation of water, so groundwater exudes in the contact zone between the more permeable limestone and the marl. The instability of the marls leads to an irregular topography with common landslides and mudflows. The marls hold intercalated bands of harder rock including shale, phyllite, and rarely iron-rich quartzitic sandstone, and there are incidental outcrops of ophiolite. Sometimes huge boulders and blocks of limestone debris deriving from the nearby limestone ranges also protect the marl against erosion, thus standing out as ridges and producing a very irregular relief. Bands of more erosion resistant rock locally result in relatively flat areas with similar less eroded soils and with accumulation of colluvium. Soil depth is primarily related to the amount of colluvial material deposited on top of a more or less eroded soil in the bedrock. In particular the western limestone range is bordered by large debris slopes and fans that extend into the marl uplands and are composed of poorly sorted and very coarse limestone debris. We will return to these debris slopes later on.

We will first discuss in detail the case of site RB73, which was one of the surface scatters randomly selected to represent the UUSL landscape type. We will then "zoom out" to include other sites in this sample, and conclude with lessons learned and implications for regional settlement and land use models.

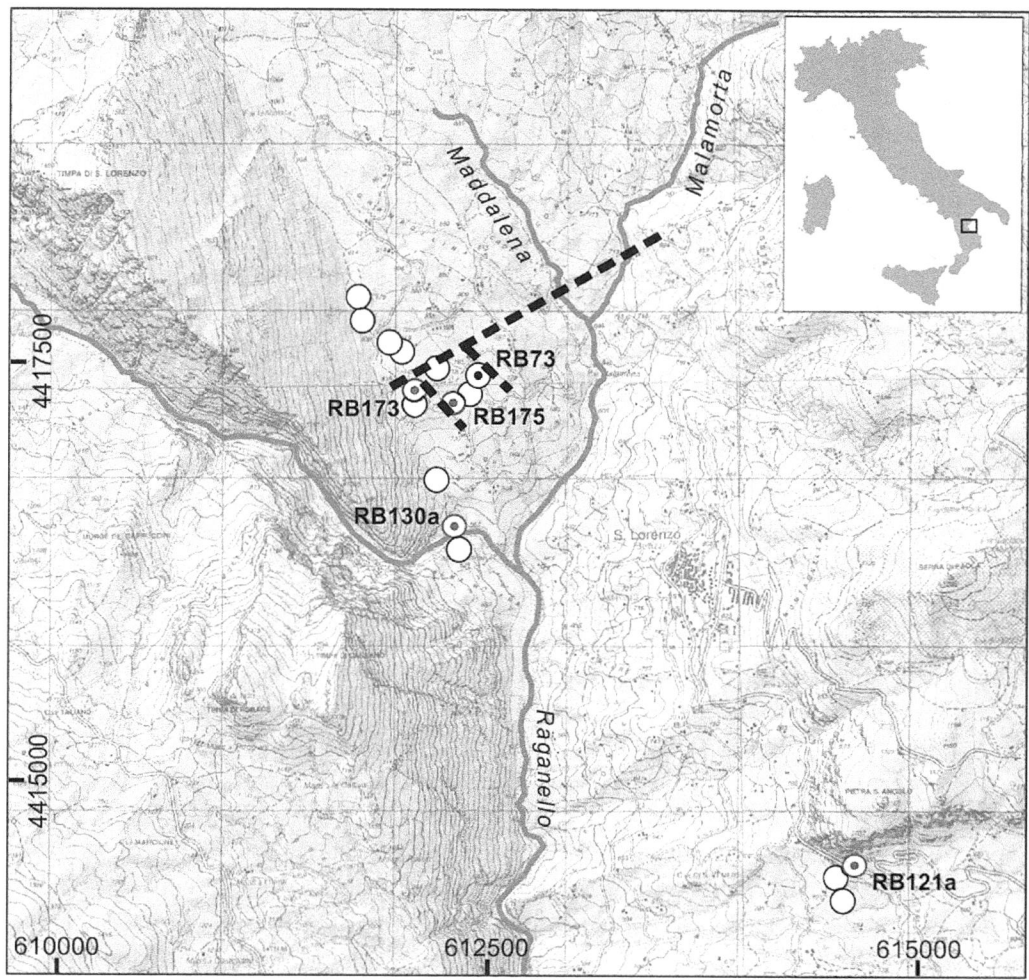

Figure 17.1. Topography and morphology of the Maddalena basin, with locations of coring transects and (selected) protohistoric sites.

The Case of Site RB73

To demonstrate the effects of this active landscape on archaeological detectability, as well as the learning curve the team had to undergo, we turn to site RB73. This is a small concentration of protohistoric handmade pottery recorded during a systematic fieldwalking survey in 2005 on a local flat in a tilled field, just above an agricultural terrace bank (Figure 17.2). Following total collection, the scatter assemblage consisted of 27 poorly preserved sherds, totaling 265 g, which we were not able to date more precisely than "protohistoric" (the term we use to indicate the Bronze and Iron Ages in Italy). Dispersed off-site material was recorded in other parts of the field, including pottery from historical phases.

Figure 17.2. Protohistoric scatter RB73 after the initial survey in 2005—field photo, survey map, assemblage photo.

Following the inclusion of RB73 in our sample of sites to be investigated in greater detail, in spring 2013 Sevink and MSc student Michael den Haan performed a detailed geopedological transect study, during which they noted an unnatural landform ("mound") requiring further investigation. This study showed that the depth and complexity of the archaeological stratigraphy vary sharply across the field, with clear and deep archaeological layers in some locations including near the mound. In one of these corings, moreover, they found an intercalated thin tephra layer that, in view of the general dating of the pottery scatter, was first thought to be the Avellino pumice dating from around 2 ka BC. However, subsequent radiocarbon dating of charcoal collected from this coring would show that the tephra must have originated from the Vesuvian eruption of AD 79 (Sevink et al. 2016), which had never been recorded so far south on land.

In the same campaign of spring 2013, our team member Kayt Armstrong conducted a magnetic gradiometry survey using a Bartington Grad601 dual sensor array recording at 0.125 m point distance, and a magnetic susceptibility survey to detect MS contrasts at the soil surface (Figure 17.3; these and other results of the geophysical studies conducted by the RLP are being prepared for publication by Armstrong and Van Leusen [forthcoming] but have been partly published in De Neef 2016, De Neef et al. 2017, and De Neef et al. 2018). The gradiometer data do not show any constructed features but they do show a sinuous anomaly, running from top to bottom across the field. The initial interpretation of this anomaly was that it might be due to the local variation in bedrock geology that is to be expected in a flysch geology, or that it might be a filled gully.

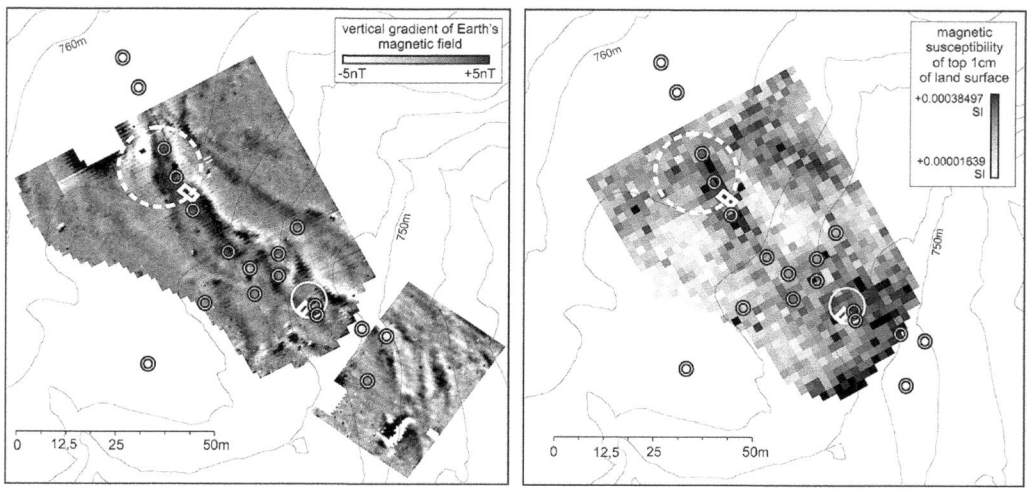

Figure 17.3. Results of the magnetic gradiometer and magnetic susceptibility surveys conducted in 2013, after De Neef et al. 2017, fig. 11. Locations of scatter, mound, and corings indicated.

To understand these rather puzzling results, in autumn 2013 we opened two 4 × 2 m test pits. The first pit was excavated on the southern slope of the mound, next to the coring with the Pompeii tephra; the second was excavated at the location of the protohistoric surface scatter. Results were surprising (Figure 17.4:C, D). Pit 1 showed a deep tilting stratigraphy, with strata dating at least from the Bronze Age to the Roman period. Near the top of the section are two layers dated by pottery to the Hellenistic-Roman Imperial period (De Neef 2016:417; De Neef et al. 2018:168), with an intercalated thin layer of volcanic tephra. What little pottery of these periods had been recorded in the 2005 survey had at that time been ignored as general "background noise," but new observations of roof tile and building stone on the surface now suggested a substantial Classical site must have been close by. The lower, still tilting layers contained animal bones and pottery generically datable to the Metal Ages. Pit 2 showed a tilting stratigraphy including several protohistoric archaeological deposits interpreted as occupation layers. This explains the presence of the surface scatter as a locally plowed-out outcropping of one of these layers: the archaeological material in these layers consists of poorly preserved handmade pottery, similar to that found in the surface scatter. As we did not reach sterile soil or rock in the 2013 season, pit 2 was reopened and deepened to 1.8 m—the maximum reach of our small mechanical excavator—in 2014. Throughout the section anthropogenic layers were documented, and charcoal from the bottom of the pit was dated to the Early Bronze Age; even earlier but unexplored deposits may well be present.

Using the combined results of their geopedological studies in 2013, Sevink and Den Haan drew up a hypothetical reconstruction of the stratigraphy of the field, in which the presence of the original scatter RB73 was explained as deriving from mixed colluvial and

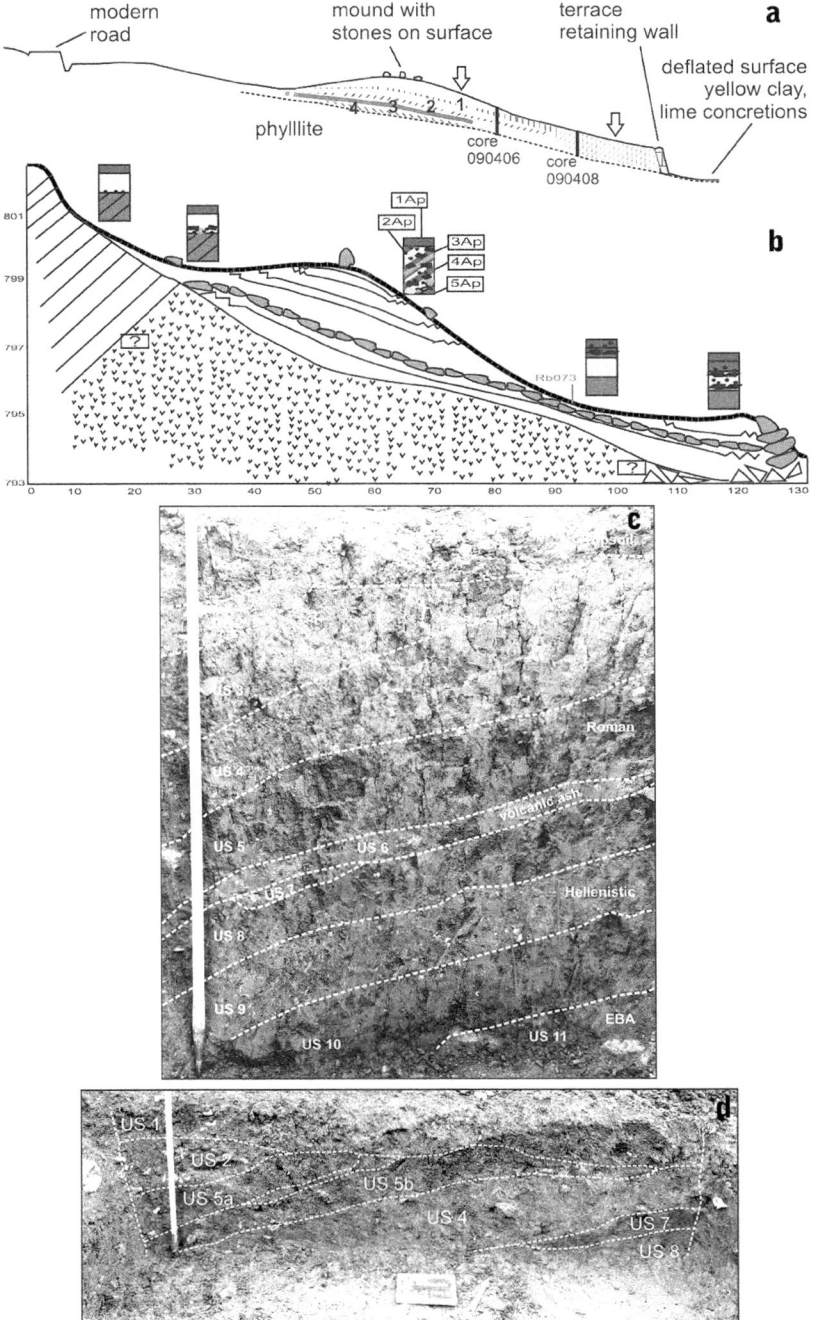

Figure 17.4. Section drawings across the mound and lower terrace bank based on our understanding of the situation in late 2013 (A, B). A: interpretation by De Neef, original drawing; B: interpretation after Sevink et al. 2016, fig. 39. Locations of 2013/2014 test pits indicated by block arrows. Sections of the two test pits showing tilted stratigraphy (C, D). After De Neef 2016, figs. A80 and A82.

anthropogenic deposits downslope of the "mound" (Figure 17.4:B; Sevink et al. 2016:53–56). De Neef arrived at a similar reconstruction (Figure 17.4:A) but showed the archaeological strata as not confined to the "mound." Clearly, the issue of how the mound itself was formed and how it might relate to the filled depression or gully running through the field (as suggested by the tilting layers, the varying depth-to-C of the corings, and the geomagnetic results) was still unresolved. Moreover, there was still no proof in the form of systematic corings for the interpretation of the anomaly as a depression or gully. Therefore, in 2015, Sevink and MA student Nikolaas Noorda conducted a detailed geopedological survey, involving about sixty corings and bringing the total to about eighty-five corings. At the same time, De Neef also conducted a new and higher resolution gradiometer survey of the whole field, using more sensitive Foerster sensors and an interval of only 5 cm between readings (De Neef et al. 2017:167 and fig. 7). Recently, a full multidisciplinary paper on the site was published (Sevink et al. 2020). An overview of the major results is presented here:

1) The new magnetometry resulted in a clearer and more complete image of the sinuous anomaly, resolving some vague features of the 2013 dataset into positive circular anomalies of a size and strength that indicate that they may be pits dug during the later phases of gully infill.

2) Depth to hard rock of the combined set of new and earlier corings was found to correlate quite well with the new geophysical data: a branching sinuous depression runs down the field, reaching up to about 4 m depth and filled with anthropogenic deposits, and an anthropogenic cover of more limited thickness is present throughout the study area.

3) The massive archaeological deposits consist of a series of occupation layers containing abundant pottery, bone, and charcoal, dating back to at least the Chalcolithic/EBA as shown by 14C datings of charcoal in its lower strata.

4) The upper strata date from the Late Imperial Roman period and contain a distinct tephra layer from the Pompeii eruption. In lower, presumably early second millennium BC strata, volcanic material was encountered that based on its isotopic composition and radiocarbon age could be identified as tephra from the Vesuvian AP2 eruption (ca. 1700 cal yr BP).

The dating evidence at RB73 now indicates that the site has been occupied, possibly with interruptions, from at least the Late Copper Age to the Early Imperial period. Debris (pottery, bones, charcoal) from nearby habitations, mixed with soil, over time filled a deep natural gully with sloping layers and outside this gully covered the original land surface—thus contributing to the general pottery "background noise" recorded in the 2005 survey. The gully must have remained in existence, at least in part, until the latest occupation phase since even the upper, Roman layers clearly tilt down toward the center of the gully. For the earlier (prehistoric) occupation phases at least we now think that the availability of a reliable year-round source of water, originating from the springs at the boundary between the limestone ranges and the marls, was what attracted settlers to this and similar locations in the upland. Modern parallels demonstrate the continued importance of such places for "irrigated gardening" and local food provision in the study area (Figure 17.5, inset). Small basins are constructed to collect and store the water, and wells may have been dug to reach the water table in the driest season. Given the sharpness of the round positive anomalies identified in 2015, these must date from the latest use phases, by which time most of the

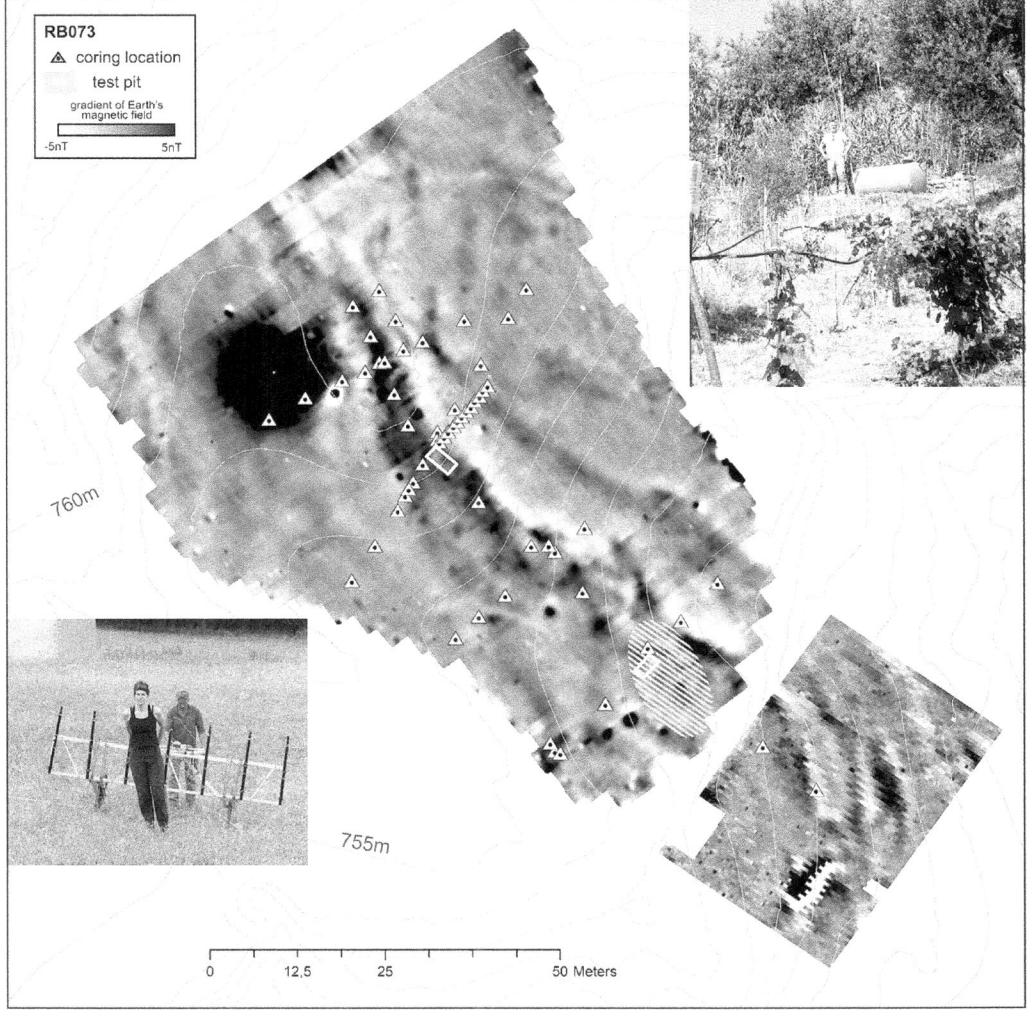

Figure 17.5. Additional gradiometer and coring data collected in 2015 indicate the presence of an erosional gully, in existence since at least the EBA and still not completely filled by settlement debris in the Early Imperial period. Inset (*top right*): A modern parallel to the protohistoric situation at RB73 is shown here, with spring water buffered in the basin at the top of the slope used to irrigate garden crops in the foreground.

gully had been filled in; it is probable that they represent wells but this can only be confirmed by further coring or excavation.

As mentioned before, geological processes in this landscape generate springs at locations where groundwater is forced to the surface, but over centuries and millennia these also lead, in combination with human land management activities, to modifications of its morphology and drainage network. The current topography and morphology suggest, in fact, that another spring-fed stream may have run through the same field until relatively recently and was only diverted when, in the 1950s, some of the mule paths were converted to tarmac roads.

Broader Context: Other Sampled Sites in the Uplands

What does the case of site RB73 tell us about the preservation and detection of archaeological remains in relation to the more general physical geographical description of the upland undulating sloping land (UUSL)? RB73 demonstrates to us that the presence, size, finds density, and modern setting of small undiagnostic protohistoric pottery scatters in this landscape type in no way indicate the presence of a deep and complex long-duration archaeological stratigraphy. Depositional and postdepositional histories have conspired to hide the late prehistoric landscape from us. How many other undiagnostic scatters would, on more intensive scrutiny, turn out to be only the tip of such an iceberg?

Our random site sample from the UUSL contained two more such scatters: RB173 and RB175, both provisionally dated to Middle Bronze Age 1–2 on the basis of the pottery fabrics (pers. comm. F. Ippolito, Jan. 18, 2019). At site RB173, which within an area of a little over 1 ha contains at least five identifiable pottery scatters, previous intensive manual coring had already revealed the presence of archaeologically relevant deposits (Feiken 2014:136–139). Since even with additional corings we were not able to construct convincing profiles out of this dataset (De Neef et al. 2018), we can only explain the extreme variability between the corings as reflecting a situation similar to that at site RB73, with cracks and gullies in the natural bedrock filled with deposits from nearby habitations (Sevink et al. 2016:53). At site RB175, our manual coring detected archaeological layers at depths between 1 to 2 m, some 20 m away from the original surface scatter (see Figure 17.6:A). As with RB73, this archaeological deposit was preserved in this location by later aggradation behind a drystone terrace wall, which put it beyond the reach of the modern plow, but also beyond that of our gradiometer sensors. The same archaeological deposits appear to be present much more superficially just downslope of that same terrace wall, where the lack of aggradation (and probably some plow erosion) had failed to produce a protective layer (Sevink et al. 2016:50–51).

Taken together, these cases strongly suggest that slope processes are the dominant factor in determining how much of the protohistoric landscape in the UUSL is presented to our eyes and instruments. Surface scatters are meaningful in the sense that they indicate locations where more extensive archaeological deposits are brought to the surface by natural

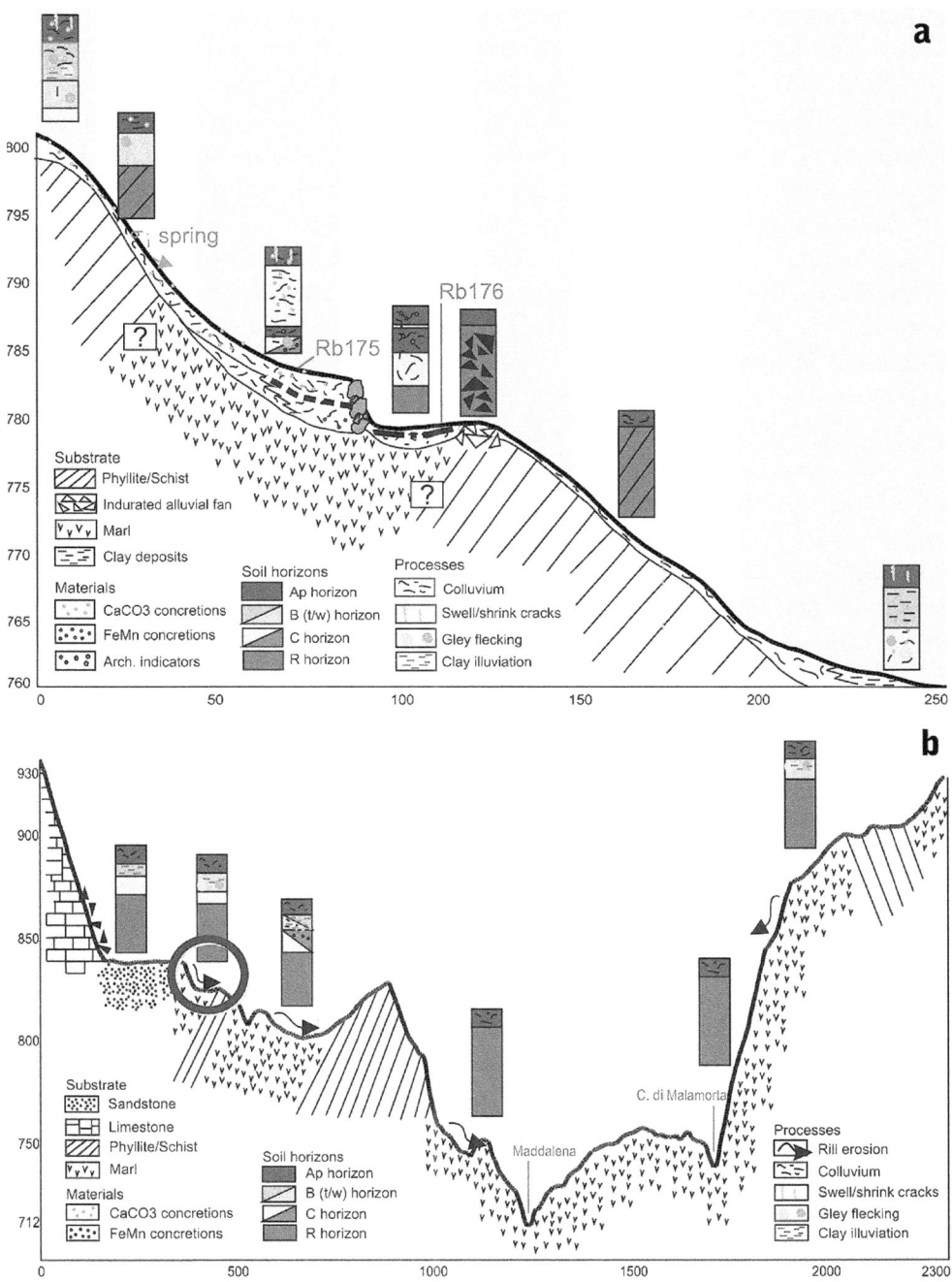

Figure 17.6. Cross section showing slope processes and soils around site RB175 (A). Landscape-scale coring transect through the Maddalena upland, showing diverse composition of flysch basin fills, resulting in different relief and soils (B). Source Sevink et al. 2016, figs. 32–34.

and anthropogenic processes, but they cannot be equated to individual "sites" in the sense of habitations without further supporting evidence. The overall diverse geological composition of the flysch basin fills in this landscape, documented in a landscape-scale coring transect (Figure 17.6:B), is expressed in variations in the relief, soils, and vegetation. Stands of oak, a valuable source of pig fodder, are limited to outcrops of sandstone; farms and other significant constructions are located on the more resistant phyllite outcrops.

Another significant landscape type of the uplands is formed by the limestone debris slopes and cones that form at the foot of the major massifs. Often considered unpromising, or even dangerous due to continuing rock falls, we included this landscape type in our surveys and recorded many protohistoric scatters in them. We investigated two of those, RB121a and RB130a, as part of our random site sample. Here we found that neither magnetometer survey nor coring was able to provide useful assistance: the terrain strewn with rock does not allow the collection of continuous geophysical data over any substantial distance, and corings, despite many attempts, never penetrate more than 0.5 m before hitting a rock. We were therefore greatly surprised that a test pit sunk at RB130a showed the presence of a 1.40 m deep archaeological stratigraphy, consisting of three distinct MBA occupation phases with some later (probably Byzantine) disturbance (De Neef 2016:124–125). Similar deep stratigraphies were later attested at RB121a as well, with finds indicating that occupation began already in the Neolithic (De Neef et al. 2018).

The gradation history of this landscape type is very different from that of the UUSL: aggradation is mostly in the form of episodic rock falls since very little fine sediment derives from the overlying limestones, and localized erosion derives exclusively from disturbance by goat tracks and human activities such as gravel extraction and road construction. We believe early settlers were attracted to this landscape type because with no substantial forest growth it was relatively accessible, well drained, in a superior topographic position with respect to the surrounding landscape, and, in winter, heated by the nearby massive limestone. We may imagine a small, possibly seasonal, settlement in both locations, each with several huts constructed on artificially leveled plots around the foot of the debris slope. The fine lime-rich sediment between the rocks, deriving from the overlying slopes, inhibits bacterial degradation of wastes, so in addition to being undisturbed by recent agricultural degradation these sites offer a superior perspective for paleoecological study. However seemingly unpromising, poor and weathered surface pottery scatters must therefore in many cases indicate substantial well-preserved settlement evidence.

Discussion

The examples discussed previously demonstrate how the gradational history of whole landscape units, and its effect on the archaeological record, can be assessed in a systematic manner. The results of our in-depth study, based on a random sample of surface sites, allow us to conclude with confidence that the small undiagnostic pottery scatters recorded in large numbers by standard modern systematic fieldwalking surveys are just the "tip of the iceberg." Site RB73 turned out to harbor a deep stratigraphy, including periods (Chalcolithic–EBA) for which no open-air upland sites were previously known in the study area. The original scatter RB73 can now be recognized for what it is: the plowed-up "top" of one of the tilting fills of a gully whose presence in the modern landscape had been completely obliterated. The unpromising landscape unit of debris slopes turned out to hide some of the earliest, and very well-preserved, habitations in the whole of the Raganello watershed basin. A picture of late prehistoric Apennine upland settlement is therefore beginning to emerge, in which certain landscape niches (south/east facing limestone debris slopes for warmth/shelter/control; reliable summer water sources for vegetable plots) are preferred.

From a methodological point of view it may be noted that for the research described here a truly multidisciplinary approach is needed, because no single prospection method is foolproof, and a geologist's understanding of the scales and rates at which geomorphological processes occur must be married to an archaeologist's understanding of cultural deposits and activities. Multidisciplinary research, however, requires significant and sustained effort from all specialists involved—not just to communicate effectively about mental models, questions, and interpretations but also to be prepared to question those same models and interpretations if they conflict with those of others, and/or with the evidence.

Besides the "conflict of disciplinary loyalty" encountered by multidisciplinary research teams, another conflict of loyalty arises when socioeconomic models long established in the archaeological community are challenged by new evidence. Long tradition, reinforced by the Italian system of academic "schools," has tended to fossilize the protohistoric settlement system models constructed since the 1970s by the Italian protohistorian Renato Peroni (Peroni and Trucco 1994) for Metal Age south Italy. Peroni's model for developments in the Final Bronze Age in the Sibaritide, for example, in which a significant reduction in the number of tribal territories takes place by the end of the Recent Bronze Age (Figure 17.7), was based on general theoretical models supplemented by what limited field data were available in the late 1980s. Part of his argument was that large storage vessels (so-called dolia) are only to be found in a few central places, where they attest to the redistribution functions of these tribal central places. At the time, however, knowledge of the settlement distribution in the region was severely limited and biased by the selective study of "suitable" hilltop locations in the foothill zone. Essentially no data were available for the uplands and mountains, where the effort to locate sites would have been much greater, or for the coastal plain, where the evidence lies inaccessible beneath several meters of later sediments.

In Peroni's model the uplands and mountains are regarded as of marginal significance only, and given the state of evidence at the time this might have been true if the bulk of the population/political power really resided in the foothills or in the lowland; but since only confirmatory evidence was ever sought for this model the possibility of refutation remained unexplored. Our research now indicates that the archaeological record of the uplands and mountains has been severely underestimated, so new and alternative settlement and land use models for late prehistory and early protohistory should at least allow for the possibility that uplands and mountains were not peripheral parts of the human landscape (a possibility further explored by Ippolito 2016 and by the recent Pollino Archaeological Landscape Project: Attema et al. 2019; De Neef et al. 2021). Although at this point we can do no more than

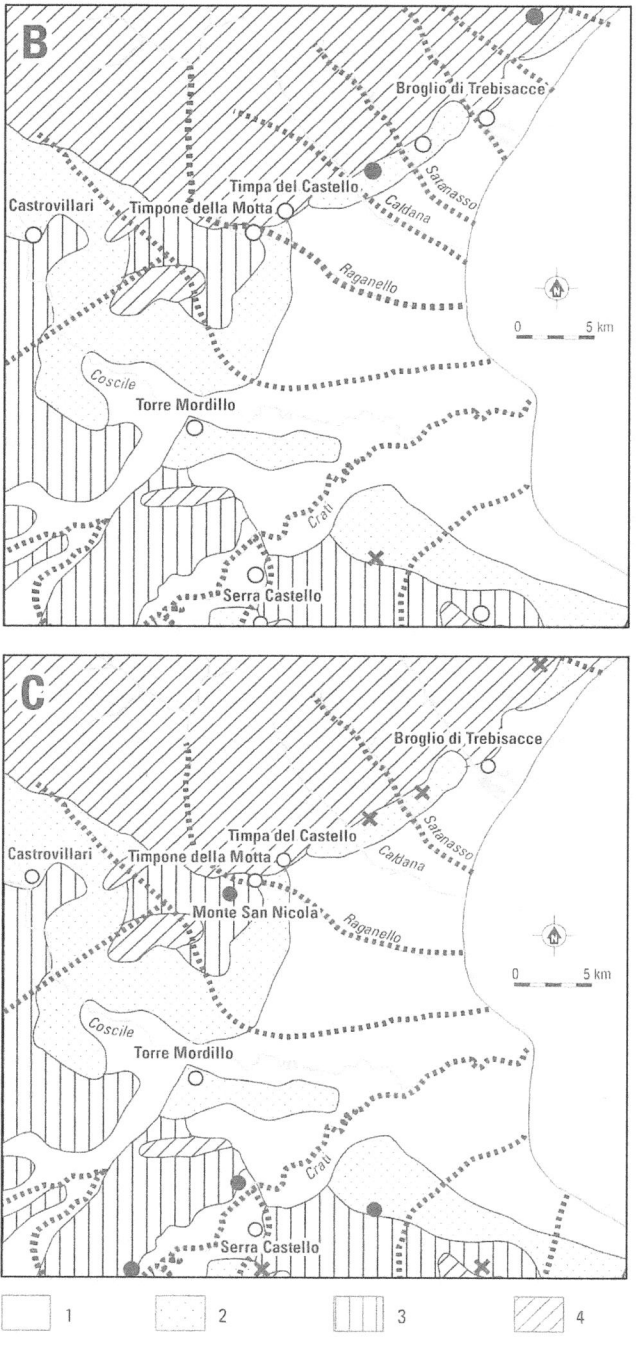

Figure 17.7. Peroni's models for the Recent and Final Bronze Age settlement in the Sibaritide (after Peroni and Trucco 1994, figs. 229 and 232). A significant reduction in the number of tribal territories takes place in the northern half of the area by the end of the Recent Bronze Age. Closed circle: new site; open circle: site continuing from previous period; cross: abandoned site.

speculate, we believe it is worthwhile to build location models in which the accessibility and natural resources of the landscape in the Mid-Holocene play a major role. While we believe that Peroni himself would have had no problem abandoning any model or theory if the evidence were against it, the fact that more than one generation of Italian archaeologists has been raised on his unopposed models has caused them to assume an air of infallibility. The simple fact that, in addition to the hilltops in the foothill zone identified as central places by Peroni himself, nearly all the other available hilltops in our study area have now been proved to hold significant archaeological sites strongly argues for the revision of his model and for a renewed focus on pre- and protohistoric land use and settlement in the uplands and mountains.

A final issue to be addressed here is the implications of our research for sustainable heritage management and tourism in the region. In mountainous areas such as ours, the pressures of agriculture and construction tend to be much less than in coastal plains and river valleys, so these threats to the archaeological record are generally less urgent and overwhelming to heritage managers. In the absence of any monumental archaeological remains, however, heritage managers and local authorities are struggling to make any significant use of archaeology in cultural tourism. We believe, however, that there are good possibilities to develop sustainable heritage tourism by combining natural and cultural heritage resources in one package: tourist trails (both day trips and multistage hiking trails) could be designed to make use of the stunning natural beauty, plant and animal life, and visible remains of preindustrial lifeways such as threshing floors and drove roads, while at the same time informing about the invisible historical and archaeological dimensions of the landscape.

Acknowledgments

The Hidden Landscapes and Rural Life research programs were fully funded by the Netherlands National Foundation for Scientific Research NWO (grant nos. 276-61-002 and 360-61-010). Permissions for invasive fieldwork were arranged with the Soprintendenza per i beni archeologici della Calabria and individual landowners, with the kind help of the mayors and municipal staff of the *comuni* of Civita, Cerchiara di Calabria, San Lorenzo Bellizzi, and Francavilla Marittima.

Note

1. During production of this volume, relevant results and discussions have also been published elsewhere (De Neef et al. 2018; Sevink et al. 2020; Van Leusen and De Neef 2018). These publications extend and reinforce the arguments put forth here.

References

Armstrong, K. L., and P. M. van Leusen forthcoming *Rural Life in Protohistoric Italy: Geophysical Studies*. Raganello Basin Studies 3. Barkhuis, Groningen.

Attema, P. A. J., G.-J. Burgers, and P. M. van Leusen 2010 *Regional Pathways to Complexity: Settlement and Land-Use Dynamics from the Bronze Age to the Republican Period*. Amsterdam Archaeological Studies 15. Amsterdam University Press, Amsterdam.

Attema, P., A. Larocca, and W. de Neef 2019 Questioning the Concept of Marginality: Early Modern Ethnography and Bronze Age Archaeology of the Foothills and Uplands of the Raganello Basin (Northern Calabria, Italy). *Journal of Eastern Mediterranean Archaeology and Heritage Studies* 7(4):482–502.

De Neef, W. 2016 Surface–Subsurface: A Methodological Study of Protohistoric Settlement and Land Use in Calabria (Italy). Doctoral thesis, University of Groningen.

De Neef, W., K. Armstrong, and M. van Leusen 2017 Putting the Spotlight on Small Protohistoric Pottery Scatters in Northern Calabria (Italy). *Journal of Field Archaeology* 42(3): http://dx.doi.org/10.1080/00934690.2017.1332930.

De Neef, W., A. Larocca, and P. Attema 2021 Archaeology Meets Ethnography: Mobility in the Foothills and Uplands of the Pollino Range (Calabria) during the Bronze Age and Late Modern Period. In *Dal Pollino all'Orsomarso: Ricerche Archeologiche fra Ionio e Tirreno*, edited by G. Mittica, C. Colelli, A. Larocca, and F. Larocca, 363–381. Analecta Romana Instituti Danici, Supplementum 56. Edizioni Quasar, Roma.

De Neef, W., P. M. van Leusen, K. Armstrong, B. Ullrich 2018 Between a Rock, a Gully, and a Hard Place: Archaeological Prospection of Metal Age Remains in the Uplands of the Raganello Basin (Calabria, Italy). In *Funde in der Landschaft: Neue Ergebnisse archäologischer Prospektion*, edited by C. Wolhlfahrt and C. Keller, 159–170. Materialien zur Bodendenkmalpflege im Rheinland 26. LVR-Amt für Bodendenkmalpflege, Bonn.

Feiken, H. 2014 Dealing with Biases: Three Geo-archaeological Approaches to the Hidden Landscapes of Italy. Doctoral thesis, University of Groningen. http://hdl.handle.net/11370/6e34dad1-0a06-454c-b6c7-d1f3ce61285f.

Fuchs, F. 1980 Quartäre Küsten und Flussterrassen in der Umrahmung des Golfs von Tarent (Süd-Italien). *Catena* 7:27–50.

Ippolito, F. 2016 Before the Iron Age: The Oldest Settlements in the Hinterland of the Sibaritide (Calabria, Italy). Doctoral thesis, University of Groningen.

Kleibrink, M. 2006 *Oenotrians at Lagaria Near Sybaris, a Native Proto-urban Centralised Settlement*. A Preliminary Report on the Excavation of Timber Dwellings on the Timpone della Motta near Francavilla Marittima (Lagaria), Southern Italy (London 2006). Accordia Research Institute, London.

Peroni, R., and F. Trucco (eds.) 1994 *Enotri e Micenei nella Sibaritide*. Istituto per la storia e l'archeologia della Magna Grecia, Taranto.

Santoro, E., M. E. Mazzella, L. Ferranti, A. Randisi, E. Napolitano, S. Rittner, and U. Radtke 2009 Raised Coastal Terraces along the Ionian Sea Coast of Northern Calabria, Italy, Suggest Space and Time Variability of Tectonic Uplift Rates. *Quaternary International* 206:78–101.

Sevink, J., M. den Haan, and P. M. van Leusen 2016 *Soils and Soil Landscapes of the Raganello River Catchment (Calabria, Italy)*. Raganello Basin Studies 2. Barkhuis, Groningen.

Sevink, J., W. De Neef, M. A. di Vito, I. Arienzo, P. A. J. Attema, E. E. van Loon, B. Ullrich, M. Den Haan, F. Ippolito, and N. Noorda 2020 A Multidisciplinary Study of an Exceptional Prehistoric Waste Dump in the Mountainous Inland of Calabria (Italy): Implications for Reconstructions of Prehistoric Land Use and Vegetation in Southern Italy. *The Holocene* 30(9):1310–1331. Doi 0959683620919974.

Van Leusen, P. M. 2015 Predicting and Detecting Protohistoric Remains in the Raganello Basin: Methodological Studies 2006–2015. In *Predicting Prehistory: Predictive Models and Field Research Methods for Detecting Prehistoric Contexts—Proceedings of the International Workshop Grosseto (Italy), September 19–20, 2013*, edited by G. Pizziolo and L. Sarti, 123–132. MILLENNI Studi di archeologia preistorica 11. Museo e Istituto Fiorentino di Preistoria, Florence.

Van Leusen, P. M., and H. Feiken 2007 Geo-archeologie en Landschapsclassificatie. *Tijdschrift voor Mediterrane Archeologie* 37:6–16.

Van Leusen, M., and W. de Neef 2018 On the Trail of Pre- and Protohistoric Activities around San Lorenzo Bellizzi: Geo-archaeological Studies of the University of Groningen, 2010–2015. In *Il Pollino: Barriera naturale e crocevia di culture—Giornate internazionali di archeologia, San Lorenzo Bellizzi, 16–17 aprile 2016*, edited by C. Colelli and A. Larocca, 39–47. Richerce 12. Dipartimento di Studi Umanistici, Università di Calabria, Rende.

CHAPTER EIGHTEEN

Agropastoralism in a Dispersed Village, Mountain Economy

Results of the Shala Valley Project, Northern Albania

Michael L. Galaty

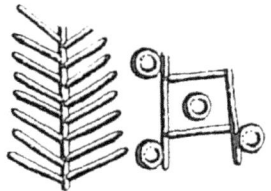

Abstract   *The Shala Valley Project (SVP) was a five-year, regional ethnoarchaeological project focused on the Shala Valley of northern Albania. Shala is located in the Bjeshkët e Namuna ("Accursed") mountains and is home to the Shala "tribe" (Alb.* fis*). Northern Albania is the only place in Europe where tribal groups, with origins in the Late Medieval period, survived intact into the twenty-first century, with chiefs, councils of elders, feuds, and an oral customary law code. The SVP conducted intensive archaeological, architectural, and ethnographic surveys throughout all of Shala, with a particular focus on the village of Theth. One particularly interesting result of the project was an ability to investigate mountain agropastoralism systematically, through time. The agropastoral economy of Shala depends on a so-called dispersed, that is, nonnucleated, village system. Houses are organized into "neighborhoods" that, in Theth, are on average 700 m apart. Theth's village system and built environment reflect complex networks of reciprocal labor, which support an agropastoral lifestyle, but also reinforce a kinship-based sociopolitical system, centered on ideologies of honor and hospitality. When such ideologies break down, feuds ensue. Dispersed village systems represent one particular adaptive response to life in a mountainous landscape. Nucleation represents another, taken by the prehistoric inhabitants of Theth, who occupied a Bronze–Iron Age hill fort called Grunas. Identification of dispersed versus nucleated village systems in the archaeological record may therefore signal agropastoral economies, particular ideological systems, or both. Both settlement models are applied to Mycenaean Greek sites, with interesting results.*

The Shala Valley Project (SVP) was a regional ethnoarchaeological project focused on the Shala Valley of northern Albania (Figure 18.1). Shala is located in the Bjeshkët e Namuna ("Accursed") mountains and is home to the Shala "tribe" (Alb. *fis*) (Figure 18.2). Four one-month, summer fieldwork seasons were conducted, from 2005 to 2008, during which teams of archaeologists, architectural historians, and ethnographers surveyed 1,000 fields, documented 580 structures, and interviewed 36 heads of household (Galaty et al. 2013:17) (Figure 18.3).[1] Ten archaeological sites were identified and further explored, leading to test excavations at several, including a previously unknown prehistoric hill fort, called Grunas (SVP Site IAS 006; see Galaty et al. 2013, chap. 10). In addition, historical records in various countries, including Albania, Austria, England, Turkey, the United States, and the Vatican, were searched for references to Shala and the wider region. The data thereby collected allowed us to paint a vivid picture of life in Shala through time, and particularly for the past six hundred years, during which the tribal system formed and grew. Finally, the oral customary law code of the Albanian mountains, the *Kanuni i Lekë Dukagjinit* (The Code of Lekë Dukagjini), attributed to a fifteenth-century chieftain, Lekë Dukagjini (1410–1481), and not transcribed and published until 1933, by Fr. Shtjefën Gjeçov, a Franciscan priest, is a remarkable document and resource that records in great detail all of the

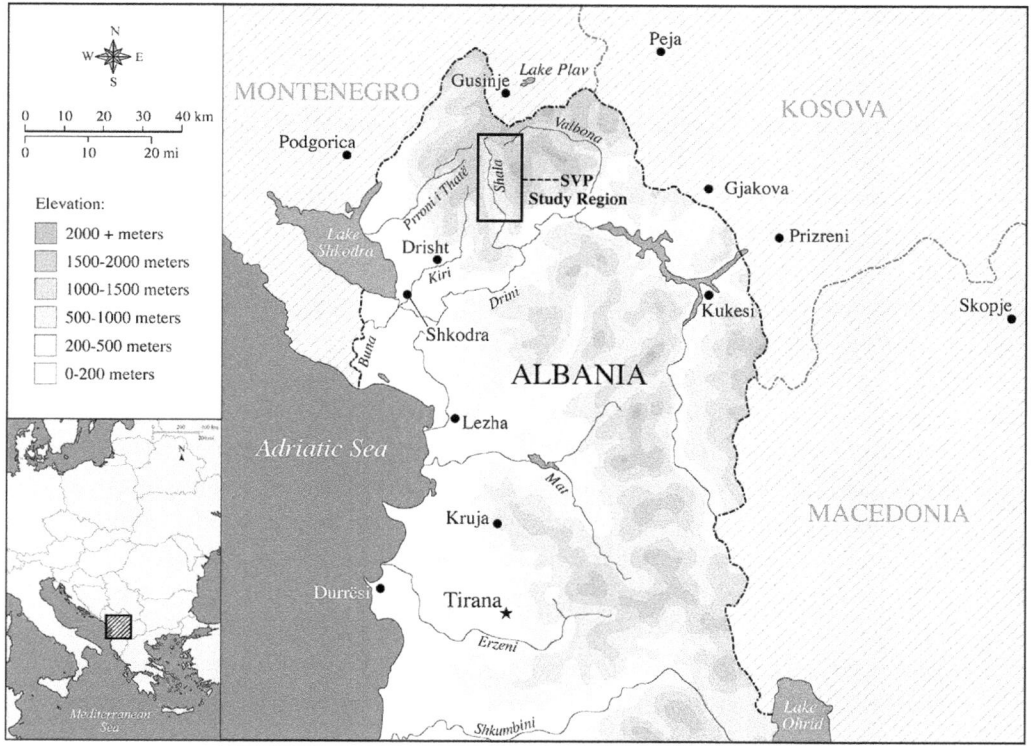

Figure 18.1. Modern northern Albania and surrounding countries showing major cities, rivers, lakes, and the SVP's study region. Map by Jill Seagard.

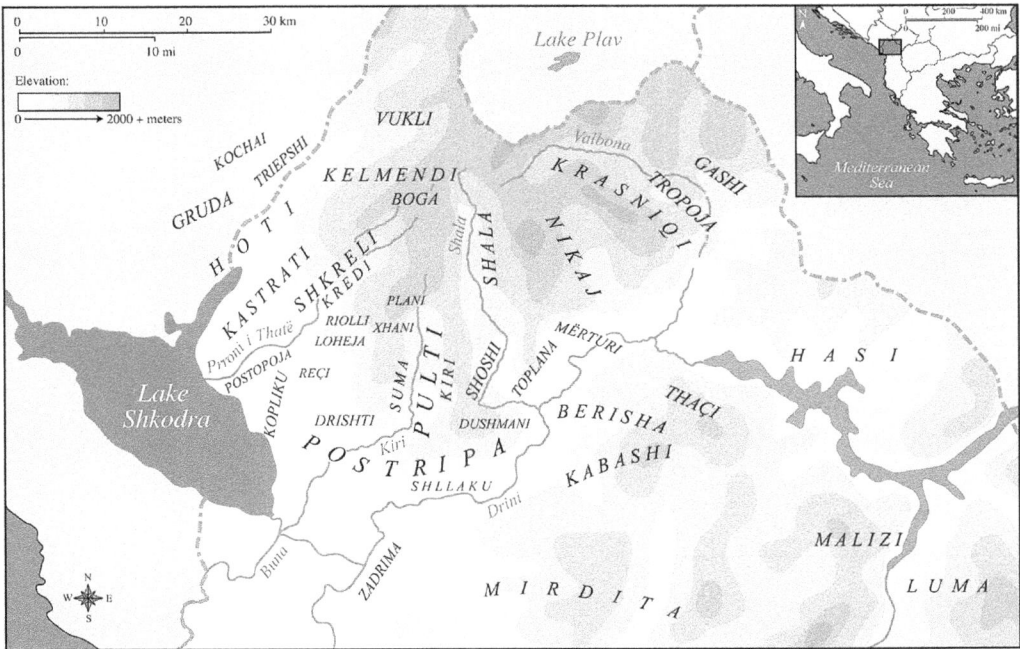

Figure 18.2. Northern Albanian tribal territories. Map by Jill Seagard.

rules meant to determine social relationships and regulate behavior within the tribal system. The ideological basis for the *Kanun* is the concept of honor (*nder*). Men (and thus families) were constantly measured, one against the other, in terms of how much honor they had accrued and by what means. For example, a man who owed blood in a feud, who was "in blood" (*ne gjak*), experienced a net loss of honor until the debt had been paid. Similarly, a man who did not extend proper hospitality (*mikpritja*) to guests, either because he was poor or stingy, was dishonored.

One interesting result of our work was the ability to describe the functioning of Shala's political economy in great detail, particularly when considered together with the *Kanun*. The Albanian *fis* is a textbook example of a tribe, in the classical, anthropological sense of the term (Parkinson 2002). Tribal social segments are nested and decomposable, kinship is traced through the male line, residence is patrilocal, and marriage exogamous (Galaty et al. 2013, chap. 5). Moreover, tribal segments are spatially configured and map onto village neighborhoods (*mëhalla*, or *lagja* in the local idiom). Each neighborhood is composed of large, defensible stone houses and their associated outbuildings, terraces, and fields (Figure 18.4). Houses were designed to accommodate large, extended families, including a patriarch (*zot i shpi*, "the lord of the house"), his wife (who ran the household), all of his sons, and their wives and children. The boundaries separating tribes, villages, neighborhoods, and family lands are carefully marked and dutifully maintained. Shala tribal territory encompasses ca. 200 sq km, ranging in elevation from 724 m at valley bottom in Theth, to 2,694

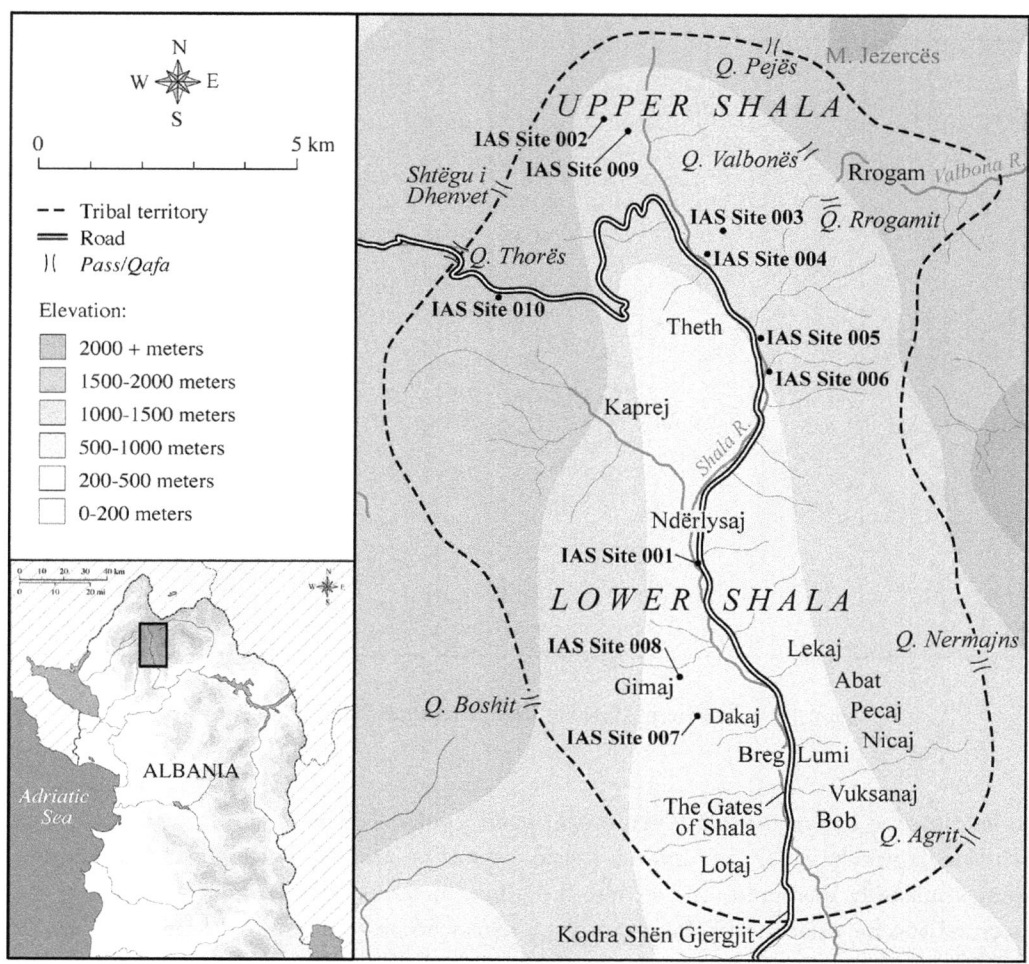

Figure 18.3. Villages, roads, rivers, and sites of Shala identified by the SVP. Map by Jill Seagard.

m at the top of Mount Jezercë, the highest peak in the Bjeshkët e Namuna. The elevation at the southernmost end of Shala at Lotaj is 300 m. Average annual rainfall totals 2,291 mm and snow can reach depths of 3 m or more (Galaty et al. 2013:109, 114).

The focus of this chapter will be the village of Theth, located at the north end of the valley (see, again, Figure 18.3). Theth proper includes ten neighborhoods (Figure 18.5). In 2005, we surveyed 338 fields in Theth, recorded 460 structures, and interviewed 26 heads of household (Galaty et al. 2013:17). Of the 460 structures recorded, 136 were houses (Galaty et al. 2013:124). SVP ethnographers found that those who live in Theth all descend from a single male ancestor, Ded Nika, who arrived in Theth between nine and twelve generations ago, depending on the patriline being counted (Galaty et al. 2013:56). In 1918, when the Austrians conducted a census of Albania, there were 769 individuals living in Theth, all of

Figure 18.4. Houses and terraces, looking south down the valley of the Shala River. The Ulaj and Kolaj neighborhoods are in the foreground, Grunas neighborhood in background. Photo by Ann Christine Eek.

whom were Roman Catholic (Seiner 1922:26). Until 1991, when Albania's socialist government fell, all residents of Shala, including Theth, lived there year-round.

The people of Shala practice mixed-village farming (Halstead 1990), based on irrigation and cultivation of New World crops, maize in particular, and short-distance vertical transhumance (Galaty et al. 2013, chap. 6). Most households own cows and pigs, and a small herd of sheep and goats, never larger than fifty head (Galaty et al. 2013:110–111). Sheep and goats are kept in barns over the winter and taken to nearby pastures during summer. Summer pastures are owned and maintained by families, who construct temporary structures there called *stani*. Most *stani* are to be found at elevations of 1,000–1,500 m.

Theth's built environment reflects expansion through time, as households grew and families split, through a process called the "separation of brothers," which is described in great detail in the *Kanun* (Book Four: Marriage, Chapter Seven: Division of Property, Gjeçov 1989: 46–51). SVP architectural historians were able to track this process of extensification by carefully analyzing and dating houses (Galaty et al. 2013, chap. 7). The result of extensification was a "dispersed" settlement system, similar to the one described by Stone (1991) for the Kofyar of Nigeria. Theth's system of neighborhoods, spread out along the length of the upper valley (see, again, Figure 18.5), represents one particular adaptive response to the subsistence requirements of a mountainous environment, primarily a shortage of good land, but also recapitulates the tribal ideological system. Men needed

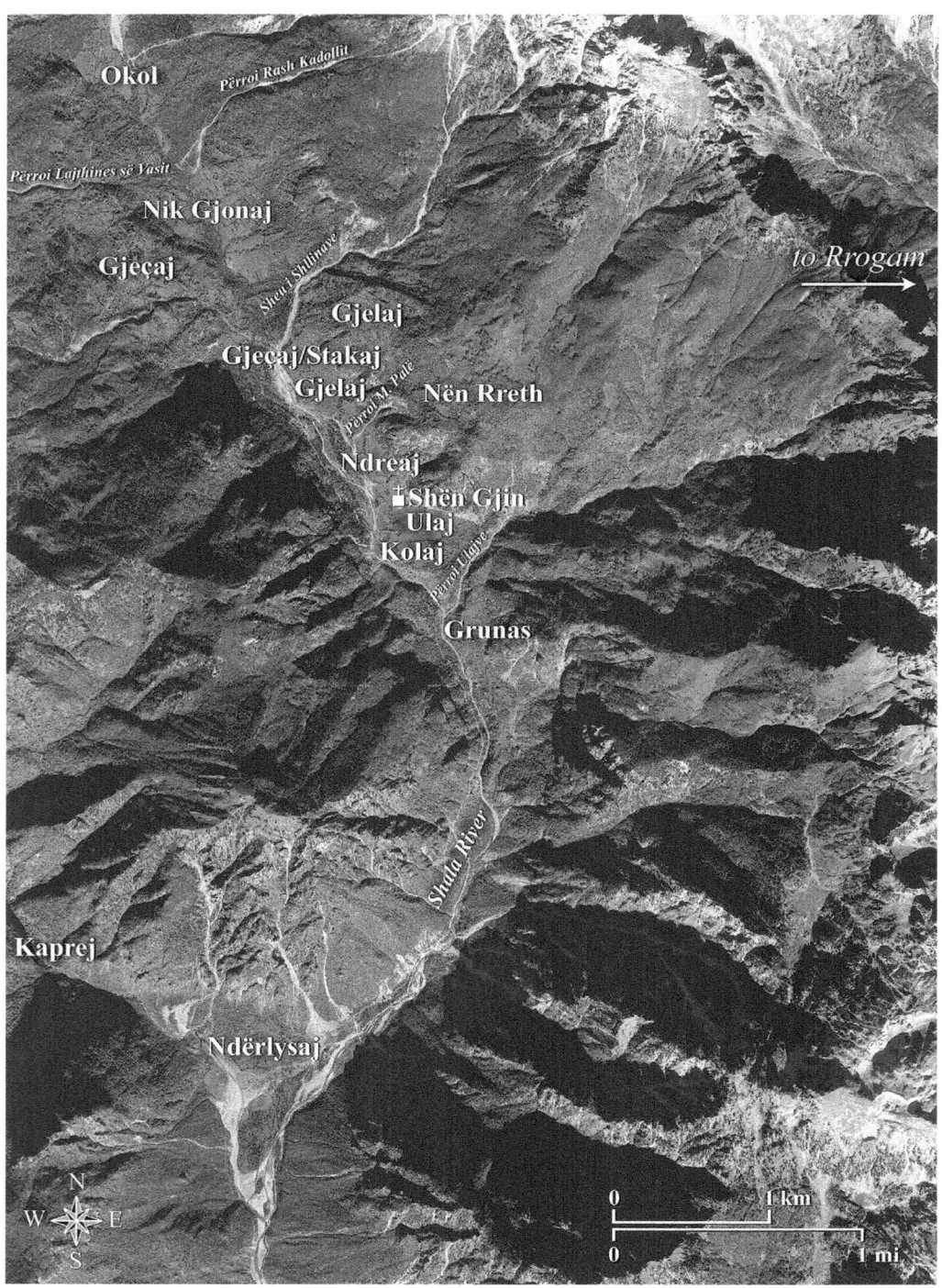

Figure 18.5. Satellite image of Theth with streams, neighborhoods, and churches marked. Map by Jill Seagard.

periodic help from members of other kinship groups, who lived in other neighborhoods, for example, at harvest time, and to mow grass, construct houses, fix irrigation canals, and build and repair terraces. In return for their labor, hosts provided food and drink to their guests—including meat and *raki* (a strong "brandy" made from fermented grapes or plums), as well as coffee, sugar, white (versus corn) bread, salt, and tobacco, all of which had to be acquired in distant market towns—and a place to sleep if need be, in ways prescribed by the *Kanun* (Book Eight: Honor, Chapter Eighteen: Social Honor, XCVI: "The Guest," Gjeçov 1989:132–134). This network of reciprocal labor exchanges tied groups of men together across kinship, and neighborhood, lines, but also served as a primary venue for discussing and measuring honor. The worst offense possible, according to the *Kanun*, was that aimed at a guest: "An offense against a father, a brother, and even a cousin without heirs may be forgiven, but an offense against a guest is not forgiven" (Book Eight: Honor, Chapter Eighteen: Social Honor, XCVII: "Violation of Hospitality," Gjeçov 1989:136).

In what remains of this chapter, I describe the dispersed village system of Theth in more detail and draw comparisons to both the Kofyar (see earlier discussion) and to the mountain landscapes and kinship systems of Europe. Furthermore, I compare the settlement system of modern Theth to that of prehistoric Theth. Despite an identical mountainous landscape, similar climate, and similarly harsh environment, the Bronze–Iron Age occupants of Shala maintained very different, highly nucleated settlement systems. Prehistoric nucleation betrays not only a very different subsistence system but perhaps different ideological concerns as well. Using Theth as an analog, careful analysis of prehistoric settlement systems in mountain environments may allow archaeologists to infer something about past social structures, political-economic organization, and associated belief systems. I provide several examples, drawn from the archaeological record of Mycenaean Greece.

Theth's Dispersed Village System

Of the ten neighborhoods of Theth, the three oldest—Ndreaj, Kolaj, and Ulaj—surround the Church of Saint John (Figure 18.5). The farm fields encompassing the church produced concentrations of late medieval pottery not found elsewhere in Theth (with the exception of one medieval sherd found in Okol) (Galaty et al. 2013:194–196). By contrast, early modern pottery was found in five neighborhoods, the above four plus Grunas and Gimaj (Galaty et al. 2013:194–196). Finally, modern pottery was collected in large numbers throughout all of Theth (Galaty et al. 2013:194–196). Archaeological survey data thereby support the architectural data, described briefly earlier, demonstrating steady growth in neighborhood and overall village size, as brothers separated and new land was brought under cultivation. Growth was not dendritic, emanating from a single point source, that is, the vicinity of the church; rather, lineage segments, and with them neighborhoods, grew from various discrete nodes as lineage/neighborhood founders sequentially occupied the upper valley's best, flattest land. For this reason, younger neighborhoods are found on the steepest land (see Table 18.1), requiring greater numbers of terraces, and on the west side of the valley, which receives the least amount of sunlight, especially during short winter days (e.g., Gjeçaj). Newly established

Table 18.1. Spatial Statistics Related to Theth Neighborhood Size and Configuration

Neighborhood	Size (ha)	Number of Houses	Ave Slope	Ave Distance Between Structures	
Ulaj	14,29	22	7,4	52,42	
Kolaj	6,94	11	8,4	62,83	
Grunas	12,23	7	8,6	106,36	
Ndreaj	15,68	12	10,4	106,66	
Nik Gjonaj	64,81	16	11,7	69,36	
Okol	29,71	19	12.0	67,28	
Gjeçaj	92,31	20	13,5	108,78	
Stakaj	2,18	3	15,1	60,81	
Nën Rreth	9,99	4	18,6	238,71	
Gjelaj	70,32	22	19,7	68,57	
Average	31,85	13,6	11,34	94,18	
				78,12	(with Nën Rreth removed)

Average distance between each neighborhood and all others: **1580.40**
Average distance between each neighborhood and its two closest neighborhoods: **717.66**
(measured from the center of each neighborhood)
Average distance between each neighborhood and its two closest neighborhoods: **161.58**
(measured from the closest edge of each neighborhood)

households in younger neighborhoods tend, therefore, to be disadvantaged in various ways compared to well-established households in older neighborhoods, and thus perhaps more dependent on systems of reciprocal labor. Eventually all of Theth's neighborhoods merged, such that each neighborhood now has at least one contiguous neighborhood. Neighborhoods are connected by a system of sunken paths, called *shtegs*. Older neighborhoods possess more complex path systems, based on network analysis (see Galaty et al. 2013:137–139).

Stone's (1991:344) study of a "dispersed settlement system" in the mountains of Nigeria, among the Kofyar, found an agricultural landscape and economy composed of *ungwa*, that is, neighborhoods, roughly equivalent to Theth's *lagja*, and supported by shared reciprocal labor agreements across *ungwa* lines, including expectations of hospitality (primarily eating and the drinking of beer). *Ungwa* were configured such that no man walked more than 700 m in a given day to a different *ungwa* to work any other man's land. Because we had mapped every house in Theth as well as neighborhood boundaries, we could test Stone's rule. Theth's average neighborhood size is 31.85 ha and the average distance between houses is about 100 m (Galaty et al. 2013:124; see Table 18.1). The average distance between each neighborhood and all other neighborhoods is 1,580 m (Galaty et al. 2013:124; see Table 18.1). The average distance between each neighborhood and the closest two neighborhoods is 717 m (Galaty et al. 2013:124; see Table 18.1). Theth thereby conforms well to Stone's (1991) mathematical definition of a dispersed settlement system.

One important factor driving Theth's process of expansion and dispersion was steady population growth through time, which we tracked using a combination of baptismal records, censuses, and travelers' reports (Galaty et al. 2013:77–79). Northern Albania represents well the so-called "Balkan" (or "Mediterranean") marriage pattern: patrilocal, exogamous "joint" families, led by patriarchs, composed of several confederated households, headed by multiple sons/brothers, all of whom were encouraged to marry as soon as possible and try to have as many children as possible, male children in particular (Kaser 1992, 1994). This can be contrasted to the so-called "Alpine" (or "European") marriage pattern: bilateral "stem" (i.e., nuclear) families, composed of single households, in which the oldest son/brother is allowed to marry first, and the others later, if finances allow (Viazzo 1989). The former encourages systems of partible inheritance (cf. the *Kanun*'s "separation of brothers"), whereas the latter encourages impartible inheritance (Kaser 2002) (and, interestingly, illegitimacy, which is unheard of in Albania; viz., there is no Albanian word for "bastard"). A corollary result of joint family structures and partible inheritance would appear to be dispersed village systems, like that in Theth. By contrast, Kaser (1992, 1994) links the Balkan marriage system to traditions of pastoralism with Illyrian (i.e., prehistoric) roots.

THETH'S PREHISTORIC NUCLEATED VILLAGE SYSTEM

Grunas was the last of Theth's neighborhoods to be surveyed by SVP field teams, at the tail end of the 2010 season. It is the southernmost of Theth's neighborhoods (not counting Ndërlysaj, a late extension) and is characterized by extremely large terraces at its southern extremity (Figures 18.5 and 18.6). The terraces are positioned just below a large waterfall and redirect its waters, rendering the landform usable (Figure 18.7). As it turns out, these terraces—which are much larger than all other terraces elsewhere in Theth—were constructed sometime after about 1000 BC, at the end of the Late Bronze Age (Galaty et al. 2013:202). The SVP conducted three years of excavation at the Grunas site (2006–2007). It sits atop a sheer cliff, at a choke point in the valley, separating south from north Shala, and was surrounded on three sides by a (now collapsed) fortification wall. It was therefore highly defensible and an ideal location from which to control movement back and forth through the mountains. Archaeobotanical and -faunal analyses indicate a dependence on wheat (which appears to have been brought to the site from elsewhere) and sheep/goats, and seasonal (i.e., summer) exploitation (Galaty et al. 2013:221–227). Grunas was occupied until just prior to the Roman conquest, when it was abandoned.

Unlike its modern occupants, the prehistoric occupants of Theth appear to have maintained a highly nucleated settlement system, based at Grunas. Archaeological survey recovered only two prehistoric potsherds elsewhere in Theth, near the caves at Okol (Galaty et al. 2013:170). Likewise, in south Shala, prehistoric settlement was nucleated at the hill fort of Dakaj (Galaty et al. 2013:173–177). Prehistoric nucleation can be attributed to several factors. First, there was a clear interest in collective defense and control of movement, which

Figure 18.6. Largest, westernmost terrace wall at Grunas. Photo by Ann Christine Eek.

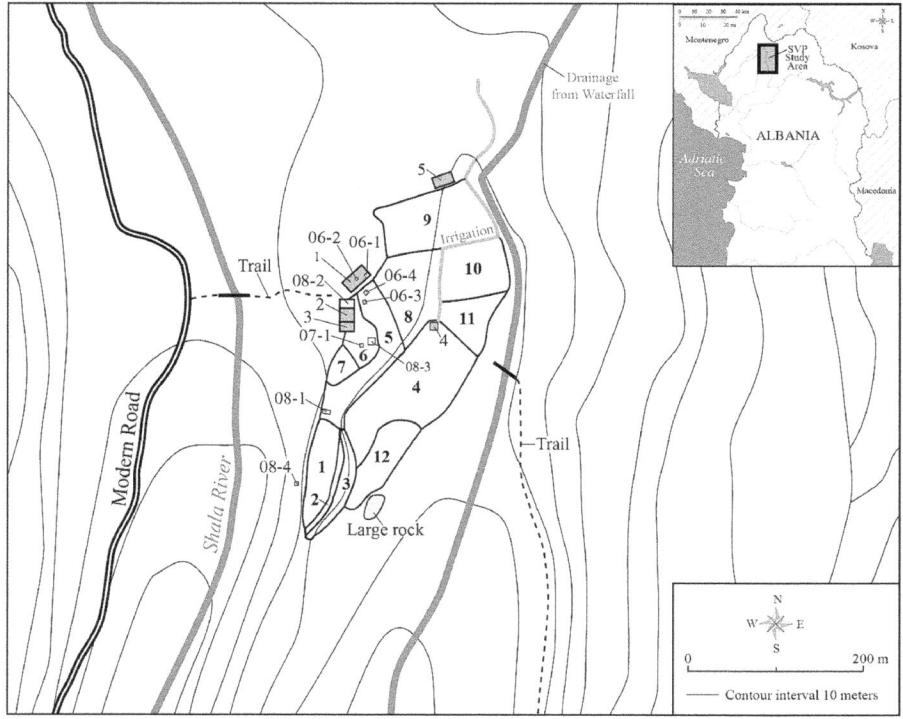

Figure 18.7. Site of Grunas. Dashed numbers indicate excavation units; individual terraced platforms enumerated in boldface; single-digit numbers not in boldface refer to individual structures. Map by Christopher T. Fisher and Jill Seagard.

the hill fort at Grunas certainly allowed. The Shala Valley provided subsidiary access to metal-rich Kosovo for those following the so-called Lissus-Naissus Road, along the Drin River (Galaty et al. 2013:67–69). Having arrived in Shala and cleared Dakaj and Grunas, travelers would have surmounted the Qaf Peja (the Peja Pass) near Mount Jezercë, crossing into what is now Montenegro, then on to Peja, Kosovo, via the Rugova Valley. Those who built Grunas perhaps did so to monitor and regulate travel through the valley, back and forth from coast to interior. Second, the modern occupants of Shala grow New World crops, like maize and potatoes, which are well adapted to mountain climates and are easily storable, facilitating year-round settlement. Growing these crops allowed and encouraged the modern dispersed settlement system documented by the SVP, but they were not (obviously) available during prehistory. Finally, northern Albania's prehistoric sociopolitical system was less developed than that of modern northern Albania and most probably did not depend on highly complex systems of reciprocal labor. Systems of reciprocal labor exchange can, however, be inferred for the Mycenaeans and may have been prerequisites for the kind of palace-dominated state-level systems of political economy that evolved in Late Bronze Age southern Greece but not in prehistoric Albania (Galaty et al. 2016).

Theth versus Mycenaean Pylos

The Mycenaean "Palace of Nestor" is located in Messenia, southwest Greece, near Pylos, on a ridge called Ano Englianos (Davis 1998). The landscape is characterized by gently rolling hills leading up to a mountain range, dominated by Mount Aigaleon, with an elevation of ca. 1,000 m. The palace was built sometime around 1300 BC and sits midway between the mountains and the sea, at an elevation of 150 m. It was excavated by Carl Blegen, beginning in 1939, who discovered 1087 Linear B tablets, which document the economic activities of palatial administrators. Halstead (e.g., 2007) has described the Mycenaean regional agricultural system in great detail, based on archaeological and textual evidence. The Mycenaean diet was based on the Mediterranean triad of olives, wheat, and wine, supplemented by some meat from sheep/goats, cattle, and pigs. The Mycenaean settlement system, however, is not easily characterized as either nucleated or dispersed, but comparison to modern and prehistoric Theth provides an interesting sense of scale and context.

The Pylos Regional Archaeological Project (PRAP) documented an almost continuous pottery scatter along the Englianos ridge, from the palace to the large coastal "port" site of Romanou (Bennet 2007), a distance of ca. 5 km. The palace and its inferred lower town occupied ca. 21 ha at the northeast end of the ridge (Bennet 2007). Theth is almost exactly the same length and breadth as this settlement corridor, as demonstrated when a map of Theth is scaled, transposed, and overlaid on a satellite photo of the region (Figure 18.8). As such, the Mycenaean settlement pattern, as exemplified by Pylos, might be best characterized as "dispersed," or potentially so. It is certainly far less nucleated than prehistoric Theth, and all of northern Albania for that matter, where nucleated settlement at hill forts was the norm. The Mycenaeans did not possess New World crops, so some other factor must explain their propensity for extensification. I assert that Mycenaean dispersion may point to the existence of reciprocal labor arrangements that were similar in scale and organization to

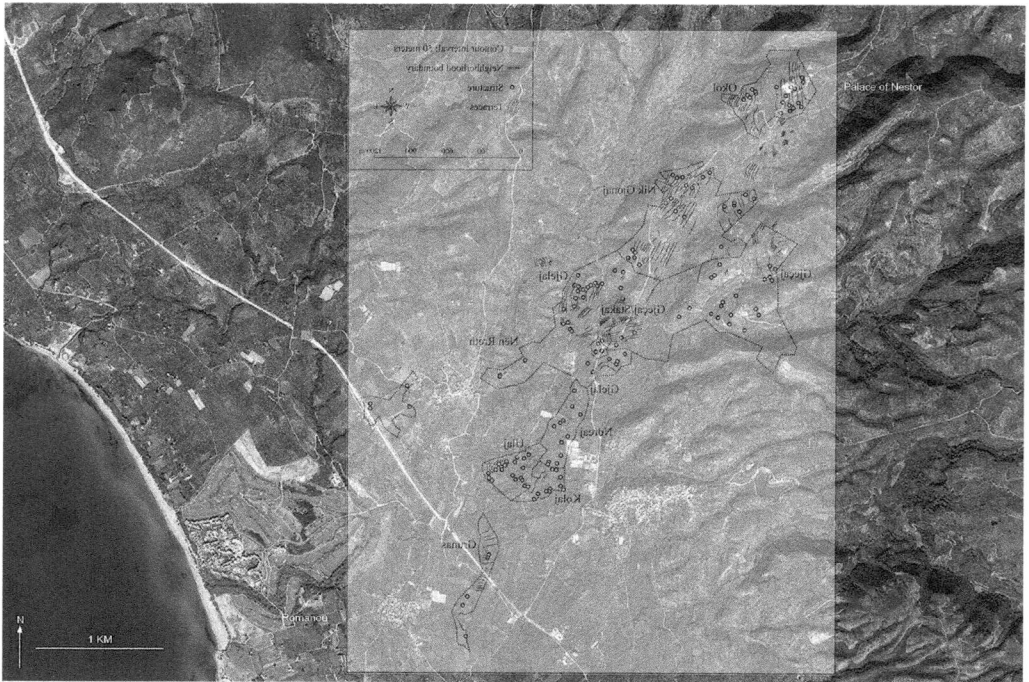

Figure 18.8. Theth transposed and overlaid on a satellite image of Pylos, from the palace to the coast. Map by Michael L. Galaty.

those created in modern Theth, to accompany the political economy outlined in the *Kanun*. Furthermore, given the data from modern Theth, we might also infer a "Balkan" marriage pattern and systems of partible inheritance for the Mycenaeans.

Very few Mycenaean houses have been excavated. That said, there are several good examples from the site of Nichoria, a secondary center affiliated with the palace located on the other side of the Aigaleon range, near Kalamata (McDonald and Wilkie 1992). Mycenaean houses are typically characterized as being rather small, perhaps meant to accommodate nuclear families. However, when a typical joint-family house from Theth (see Galaty et al. 2013:118–121), which currently accommodates upward of ten people—three brothers, who did not separate, and their families, as well as grandma and grandpa—is scaled and compared to a typical Mycenaean house from Nichoria (McDonald and Wilkie 1992:384), they are found to be quite similar in size and configuration, though it is unclear whether that from Nichoria possessed upper floors (Figure 18.9). In the past in Theth, such houses sometimes accommodated as many as fifty people, or more. Thus, it is perhaps misleading to assume Mycenaean stem as opposed to joint families based on house size alone.

Using Theth as an analog for Mycenaean Pylos, we might reconstruct a dispersed settlement system, one in which labor was traded between families or extended kinship groups, across "neighborhood" lines. If Stone's (1991) rule held for Ano Englianos, as it did for

Agropastoralism in a Dispersed Village, Mountain Economy 355

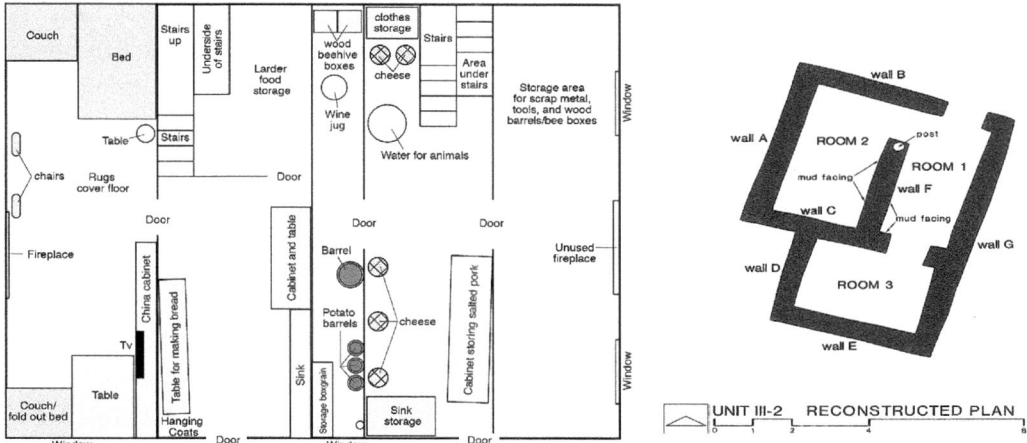

Figure 18.9. Scaled comparison of Structure 221, ground floor, in Theth, a large joint-family house (line drawing by Jill Seagard), to a Late Helladic IIIA2 house from Unit III-2, Nichoria (McDonald and Wilkie 1992:384). The latter image is used by permission of University of Minnesota Press.

Theth, there may have been as many as five to ten neighborhoods or interacting village segments that worked the agricultural lands between the palace and the coast. As was the case in Theth, hospitality obligations likely accompanied Mycenaean labor exchanges, helping to explain the apparent Mycenaean fascination with "feasting" (Wright 2004). With state formation, this system of reciprocity and commensal feasting would have been co-opted by the palace, laying the basis for palatial administration of a "redistributive" economy (Galaty et al. 2016). A similar process of state formation did not occur in Albania, in part because "Illyrian" settlement systems were not dispersed in ways that encouraged or required reciprocity of the kind that evolved later, in late medieval Theth. Theth's (and Pylos's) settlement and marriage systems were not responses to the challenges of long-distance, transhumant pastoralism in mountain environments, as adduced by Kaser (1992, 1994); rather, they facilitated very specific forms of political-economy, backed by complex systems of ideology.

Conclusion: Mountain Ideological Systems

Albania broke from the Ottoman Empire in 1912 and a parliamentary state was established. One of the main threats to the young Albanian nation came from the northern tribes, which continued to assert their independence, just as they had under the Ottomans. Eventually, Ahmet Zogu (1895–1961), a tribal chieftain from Mati, seized controlled of the government and in 1928 was crowned Zog I, King of the Albanians (reigned 1928–1939). He accelerated the policy of tribal destabilization, a process completed after World War II, under Enver Hoxha and the socialists. First, the Albanian government sought to open up the mountains by building roads (Vickers 1999:119). The road to Theth, for example, was completed in 1934 (Galaty et al. 2013:72). Easier access to the mountains took away the tribes' most potent weapon: their isolation. Second, the government sought to ban private ownership of guns (Vickers 1999:117). Without guns, the tribes could not defend themselves, but, perhaps more importantly, they could not pursue blood feuds, one key source of honor. Third, the borders were closed. The people of Theth could no longer cross the Qaf Peja and access traditional market towns in Montenegro and Kosovo. Alternatively, travel to Shkodra in Albania was a more difficult journey, often through enemy territory. Without easy access to markets, the prestige goods needed to meet hospitality requirements could not be acquired, another major blow to the system of honor dictated by the *Kanun*. Additionally, because hospitality underpinned reciprocal labor agreements, when these faltered, the agropastoral economy suffered as well, causing starvation and migration. The deleterious effects of tribal destabilization were described by Red Cross captain William Warfield, in a 1919 letter accessed by SVP historians in the Red Cross Archives in Washington, DC:

> At present, the serious problem in the mountains is the inaccessibility of the market towns. . . . All the valleys leading away from Lake Scutari have been cut off by the frontier troubles from the natural markets. Notably the people of Klementi, Nikai, Shala, Grashi, and Grasnichi are likely to be in serious difficulty not later than the month of May on account of the closing of the Montenegrin frontier, the destruction of the market of Gusinje [in Montenegro] and the isolation of Djakova [in Kosovo].[2]

He closed his report by noting that if relief were not sent to the mountains soon, "there will be an increase in unrest on the frontier and probably bands will be formed to engage in armed attempts to secure food" (Galaty et al. 2013:73). The chaos described by Warfield represents a geopolitical humanitarian failure in the aftermath of World War I, which is why the Red Cross was in the Albanian mountains to begin with, but also reflects the overall breakdown of the tribal ideological system. Thus, as archaeologists, we should not underestimate the power of ideology to effect sociocultural change, including in prehistoric times.

Northern Albania's prehistoric settlement system, which was highly nucleated at hill forts, like Grunas, is marked by incredible stability. The Projekti Arkeologjik i Shkodrës (PASH; i.e., the Shkodra Archaeological Project), an intensive survey of the Shkodra Plain and surrounding foothills, directed by myself and Lorenc Bejko of the University of Tirana, from 2010–2014 (preliminary reports in Galaty et al. 2018, 2019; Galaty and Bejko in press), found that the first hill forts in the region were likely established as early as the Late–Final Neolithic, sometime after about 4000 BC, and, unlike Grunas, were never really abandoned. An extensive settlement system, focused on the plains, did not materialize until as late as the early medieval period, beginning about AD 600. The nucleated pattern thus persisted in northern Albania for almost five thousand years. This can be contrasted to the Mycenaean settlement system, which I have characterized as dispersed, or extensive. The Mycenaean states, which had formed sometime around 1300 BC, collapsed in dramatic fashion a short one hundred years later. The Palace of Nestor was burned to the ground and the region of Pylos was almost fully depopulated (Davis 1998).

As was the case with northern Albania in the aftermath of World War I, the collapse of Pylos may have been "geopolitical" too, linked to the wider collapse of the Eastern Mediterranean world system (Cline 2015). But there may have been an ideological component, as well. The system of reciprocity that the palace appropriated probably predated state formation by a good length of time (Galaty et al. 2016). Certainly, there are references in Linear B to regional officials and village councils (the *damoi*) that are eerily similar to those outlined in the *Kanun*. If leaders of Mycenaean households, including the palace, lost access to prestige goods as the Eastern Mediterranean world-system imploded (see Galaty 2017), and systems of reciprocity and hospitality (i.e., feasting) wavered, the dispersed settlement system may have become a lability, in various ways. In the absence of nucleation, raising a communal defense would have been difficult. But a greater liability may have been underlying ideologies that promoted conflict over cooperation, particularly when honor was a stake. Echoes of Mycenaean reciprocity—whether exchanges of women, exchanges of weapons, or exchanges of blood through feuds—are certainly found in Homer. Similar echoes still sound in the northern Albanian mountains today, where the *Kanun* is alive and well, and agropastoral mountain economies hang in the balance. And yet, the most recent feud in Theth (in 2012) was not about resources, like land or water for irrigation; rather it was caused by a violation of patrilocal marriage rules. Such is the staying power of ideology. Like mountains, beliefs are slow to move, and when they do, earthquakes ensue.

Acknowledgments

I would like to thank Arnau Garcia-Molsosa for the invitation to attend the mountain landscapes conference at IEMA. It was good to see old friends and make new ones. Thanks, as well, to the people of Theth, Albania. Without their help and patience, this chapter could not have been written.

Notes

1. All project data, including notebooks, photos, drawings, database files, geospatial data, and redacted interview transcripts, are available for download from the Archaeology Data Service: http://archaeologydataservice.ac.uk/archives/view/svp_mellon_2009/.
2. Red Cross Central File, 1917–1934, Stack 130, Row 77, Compartment 20, Shelf 2–3, Boxes 899–902, Folder 899.08 "Reports." United States National Archive and Research Administration, College Park, Maryland.

References

Bennet, J. 2007 Pylos: The Expansion of a Mycenaean Palatial Center. In *Rethinking Mycenaean Palaces II: Revised and Expanded Second Edition*, edited by M. L. Galaty and W. A. Parkinson, 29–39. Monograph 60. UCLA Cotsen Institute of Archaeology Press, Los Angeles.

Cline, E. H. 2015 *1177 B.C.: The Year Civilization Collapsed*. Princeton University Press, Princeton.

Davis, J. L. (ed.) 1998 *Sandy Pylos: An Archaeological History from Nestor to Navarino*. University of Texas Press, Austin.

Galaty, M. L. 2017 Prestige-Goods Economies: The Prehistoric Aegean and Modern Northern Highland Albania Compared. In *Regional Approaches to Society and Complexity*, edited by A. R. Knodell and T. P. Leppard, 75–93. Equinox Books, Sheffield.

Galaty, M. L., and L. Bejko (eds.) in press *Archaeological Investigations in a Northern Albanian Province: Results of the Projekti Arkeologjik i Shkodrës (PASH)*. Two volumes. University of Michigan Museum of Anthropological Archaeology Press, Ann Arbor, MI.

Galaty, M. L., L. Bejko, and S. Deskaj 2019 Projekti Arkeologjik i Shkodrës (PASH) 2010–2014: Preliminary Results of a Regional Archaeological Survey of the Shkodër Region. In *Proceedings of the Sixième Colloque International sur l'Illyrie Méridionale et l'Épire dans l'Antiquité, Tirana, Albania, May 20–23, 2015*, edited by J. L. Lamboley, L. Përzhita, and A. Skenderaj, 47–56. De Boccard, Paris.

Galaty, M. L., L. Bejko, S. Deskaj, R. Yerkes, S. Allen, and R. Bolus 2018 Landscape Archaeology in Northern Albania: Results of the 2014 Field Season of the Projekti Arkeologjik i Shkodrës (PASH). In *Landscapes of Southeastern Europe*, edited by L. Mirosevic, G. Zaro, M. Katic, and D. Birt, 35–48. Lit Verlag, Berlin.

Galaty, M. L., O. Lafe, W. E. Lee, and Z. Tafilica (eds.) 2013 *Light and Shadow: Isolation and Interaction in the Shala Valley of Northern Albania*. Monumenta Archaeologica 28. UCLA Cotsen Institute of Archaeology Press, Los Angeles.

Galaty, M. L., D. Nakassis, and W. A. Parkinson 2016 Introduction to Reciprocity in Aegean Palatial Societies: Gifts, Debt, and the Foundations of Economic Exchange. *Journal of Mediterranean Archaeology* 29(1):61–70.

Gjeçov, Shtjefën 1989 *Kanuni i Lekë Dukagjinit* [The Code of Lekë Dukagjini]. Translated by Leonard Fox. Gjonlekaj, New York.

Halstead, P. 1990 Present to Past in the Pindhos: Diversification and Socialization in Mountain Economies. *Revista di Studi Liguri* 61(1–4):61–80.

Halstead, P. 2007 Toward a Model of Palatial Mobilization. In *Rethinking Mycenaean Palaces II: Revised and Expanded Second Edition*, edited by M. L. Galaty and W. A. Parkinson, 66–73. Monograph 60. UCLA Cotsen Institute of Archaeology Press, Los Angeles.

Kaser, K. 1992 The Origins of Balkan Patriarchy. *Journal of Modern Greek Studies* 8:1–39.

Kaser, K. 1994 The Balkan Joint Family Household: Seeking Its Origins. *Continuity and Change* 9(1):45–68.

Kaser, K. 2002 Inheritance and Family Forms in Eastern Europe. *History of the Family: An International Quarterly* 7(3):311–314.

McDonald, W. A., and N. C. Wilkie (eds.) 1992 *Excavations at Nichoria in Southwest Greece, Vol. II: The Bronze Age Occupation*. University of Minnesota Press, Minneapolis.

Parkinson, W. A. (ed.) 2002 *The Archaeology of Tribal Societies*. International Monographs in Prehistory, Ann Arbor, MI.

Seiner, F. 1922 *Ergebnisse der Volkszählung in Albanien, in dem von Österr.-Ungar: Truppen 1916–1918 besetzten Gebiete*. Höler-Pichler-Tempsky A.-G., Vienna.

Stone, G. D. 1991 Agricultural Territories in a Dispersed Settlement System. *Current Anthropology* 32:343–353.

Viazzo, P. P. 1989 *Upland Communities: Environment, Population and Social Structure in the Alps since the Sixteenth Century*. Cambridge University Press, Cambridge.

Vickers, M. 1999 *The Albanians: A Modern History*. I. B. Tauris, London.

Wright, J. C. (ed.). 2004 *The Mycenaean Feast*. American School of Classical Studies at Athens Press, Princeton.

Chapter Nineteen

The Inka Landscape of Cusco and the Watanay Valley

Territorial Patterns in Andean Cities

José Alejandro Beltrán-Caballero and Ricardo Mar

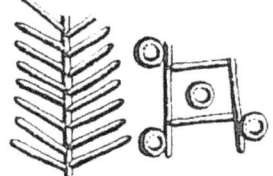

Abstract *In Inka times Cusco was the center of a hierarchic system of settlements of different sizes and with different functions. A dense network of roads that had as axes the four main branches of Qhapaq Ñan joined the settlements with the ceremonial center located in the high part of the Watanay valley. This set was fed by a system of terraces and channels, base of the intensive agriculture in the valley. The symbolic appropriation of this territory was based on the maintenance of hundreds of* wakas—*or sacred places—that gathered the population during the important days marked by the calendar. Investigations carried out during the last years along the Watanay valley from Angostura to Saqsaywaman have allowed us to gather the necessary information to approach the Inka landscape and to reconstruct the urban system of the Inka capital.*

Introduction

The abrupt high-altitude valleys that offered great seasonal rainfall are one of the ecological systems that in the Americas generated specific settlement strategies. In the Andes, the natural shortage of arable land due to the steep slope of the valleys demanded not only large, terraced works but the construction of a system of canals for irrigation and/or water evacuation during the rainy season. However, the changes in altitude offered an important advantage: different natural ecosystems nearby. The simultaneous control of several of these ecosystems made the Andean communities capable of producing complementary food resources.

In the Peruvian case, the Andes are a region of contrasts. From the deserts of the coast stretched at sea level, it is just a day to reach the view of the snowy peaks from the highlands of the mountain range at 4,000 m high. Mountains are the solution of continuity to a variety of different landscapes and ecosystems. Such a complex natural environment demanded an extraordinary effort of adaptation for the survival of human groups. As we will see more broadly in the case of Inka Cusco, the integration of channels, terraces, settlements, and systems was given under the premise of maintaining the balance with the natural environment.

Cusco is one of the most surprising cities of America. Its pre-Hispanic past, the superposition of different historical periods in its built tissue, and its importance as a precolonial and still living urban compound is only comparable with Tenochtitlan, currently Mexico City. Traditionally the idea of Inka Cusco as a city is related to the space limited by the two canalized streams: the rivers Saphi and Tullumayo (Bauer 2004; Gasparini and Margolies 1977). A settlement placed on the hillside that forms the head of the valley, in the highest part of the top basin of the Watanay River, which was just the representative or ceremonial center. Now we know that an extensive network of settlements exceeded the limit of these two rivers to extend over the valley slopes occupying what is now the modern city of Cusco (Agurto 1980; Farrington 2013; Niles 1987).

This dispersed territorial organization of the ancient city was well known thanks to the works of Santiago Agurto (1980) and Susan Niles (1987). However, the rich archaeological documentation generated in the last thirty years, both about the historic city and its immediate surroundings, has not yet been integrated in the reconstruction of the cultural landscape that completely transformed the valley in Inka time. This has been the aim of the project Cusco: A New Vision of the Inka City (see the acknowledgments).

Based on the architectural study of the historical center of contemporary Cusco (Beltrán-Caballero et al. 2011; Beltrán-Caballero and Mar 2014), our project has made possible not only to reconstruct the layout of the Inka representative center, which extends between the Tullumayo and Saphi Rivers, but also, and for the first time ever, propose a virtual image of the Inka city (Figure 19.1). Inka walls visible today in the streets of Cusco were already documented by Agurto in 1980 and Paredes in 1999. These walls constitute the perimeter of some of the enclosures in which the Inka city was organized and are the first key to study the urban form of the representative center. Besides these Inka walls we have numerous excavations within current city blocks and the extensive documentation prepared by the Gerencia del Centro Histórico of Municipalidad del Cusco that has given us fundamental information to reconstruct an image of the Inka city that lies beneath the modern city. The study of the spatial and volumetric configuration of architectural compounds that were part of this center has provided a better understanding of the architectural and urban strategies that conditioned its design (Bouchard 1983; Kendall 1985; Protzen 2005). Buildings and open spaces should reflect the sacred character of the settlement and transmit the great idea of a place built to honor the gods (Figure 19.2).

The archaeological evidence of Inka remains collected from Angostura to the top of Saqsaywaman, in particular that related to water management and the establishment of agricultural terraces, has provided the keys to understanding the transformation of the nat-

The Inka Landscape of Cusco and the Watanay Valley 363

Figure 19.1. Aerial view of the virtual image of the ceremonial center of Inka Cusco with Saqsaywaman compound (*foreground*), San Blas agricultural terraces (*top left*), and the ceremonial center between the Tuyumayo and Saphi Rivers (*top right*). For the first time ever we have an image that brings us closer to what could be the capital of the Tawantinsuyu and its interpretation. Drawing by R. Mar and J. A. Beltrán-Caballero.

ural environment in the Watanay Valley. Colonial sources, while presenting some contradictions, allow us to attribute this transformation to Pachacuti Inka Yupanqui, the great Inka ruler (Rostworowski 2001). Due to the fact that most of the valley is now covered by modern buildings, it has been necessary for the study of ancient Inka landscape to develop an archaeological map integrating all kinds of evidence, comparing these data, and completing the layout of the system through the rich documentation of 1956 aerial photos (see the following section on the 1956 DIRAF aerial photographs).

The same process has been carried out to study the historical center. Thanks to this it has been possible to verify that the construction of the city during the colonial and republican periods (sixteenth–nineteenth centuries) relied directly on the ancient terraces. Frag-

Figure 19.2. Virtual view of some of the most representative compounds of the ceremonial center: Hatun Rumiyoq (*foreground left*), Awkaypata square (*foreground right*), Hatunkancha (*center*), and Cusikancha and Korikancha compounds (*background*). Drawing by R. Mar and J. A. Beltrán-Caballero.

ments of the ancient retaining walls have been preserved inside the modern buildings that form the different neighborhoods. Evidently, the old walls have been repaired and reconstructed many times as a result of four hundred years of urban life. However, the structure of the walls and the stones used in their construction denote that the blocks produced in Inka times have been reused again and again.

The 1956 DIRAF Aerial Photographs

In 1956 the DIRAF (Dirección de Aerofotografía de la Fuerza Aérea del Perú) did a low-altitude flight over the Watanay Valley taking a series of high-resolution photographs covering the entire length of the river basin. The great quality of the original photos has allowed us to produce a document in which we identify, document, and study the evidence and the archaeological remains that in 1956 were still part of the valley. These photographs were taken before the great urban expansion that caused the earthquake of 1950. Thanks to this it is possible to draw terraces, canals, and roads, identify agricultural fields, or locate reservoirs that no longer exist due to modern construction that has extended all over the valley, destroying or hiding the elements of Inka times.

Naturally, the image transmitted by these photographs corresponds to the agricultural system that existed in 1956 in the surroundings of Cusco. It was a cultural landscape that had its base in the Inka configuration, but transformed by five centuries of colonial and republican history. By identifying all the impressions and footprints that can be recognized in the photographs it has been possible to notice the characteristics of agricultural terraces and their water supply and drainage systems. They are the oldest elements of the system (Inka) that were still largely intact in 1956 below the later modifications that took place in these fields throughout the last five centuries.

Data for the Study of the Transformation of the Valley

Terraces, Channels, and Settlements in the Cusco Valley

To understand what the founding of the Inka capital involved it is necessary to begin with the geological history of the valley (Beltrán-Caballero et al. 2011). At the end of the Pleistocene the melting of the glaciers led to the formation of a large lake called Lake Morkil, which occupied the entire length of the valley (Córdoba 1986, 1987; Gregory 1916). The lake was drained when the cap that contained it eroded in the area called Angostura (Figure 19.3). There remained only a series of wetlands in the lower part of the valley whose continuous water supply was facilitated by the geological setting of the region. The head of the valley is the limit of the Chinchero geological formation (Mendivil and Dávila 1994), a calcareous substrate that is crossed by a dense karst network feeding numerous springs that flow into the Watanay Valley's high north slope. These springs along with the rainwater gave rise to the torrents and mountain rivers that descended from the hillside and fed the wetlands, a situation that persisted for millennia until the Inkas, converted into a regional power, undertook the complete transformation of the valley (Beltrán-Caballero et al. 2011).

The archaeological information collected allows us to talk about the strategies followed by the Inkas to transform the natural condition of the valley (Kendall 1992, 2013). As in other places (Regal Matienzo 2005), the first concern was channeling the streams for managing rainwater and drainage of wetlands (Figure 19.4). Then, the topography of the valley was changed with the construction of terraces that allowed the creation of new agricultural land and protection of the existing soil. These are two complementary actions that appear regularly on the implementation of Inka agricultural strategies (De la Torre and Burga 1986; Kendall 2013; Nickel 1982). Rising agricultural areas by rehabilitating wetlands sustained a balanced population growth in the valley (Earls 1981). But it was also necessary to organize an irrigation system consisting of canals and reservoirs well known in Cusco since the work of Jeanette Sherbondy (1979, 1982, 1986, and 1987). In the Andes these actions marked the Inka will to promote advanced agriculture (Covey 2006; Earls 1998). In addition, an extensive network of hierarchical settlements was built, accompanied by several hundred sacred sites—or *wakas*—one of the functions of which was the symbolic control of the anthropic landscape (Kaulicke 2001; Van de Guchte 1990; Zuidema 1964, 1983). A dense set of roads, part of the Qhapaq Ñan system, integrated all elements in a unitary tissue (Amado 2005; Floerke and Amado 2013; Hyslop 1984). In short, all these

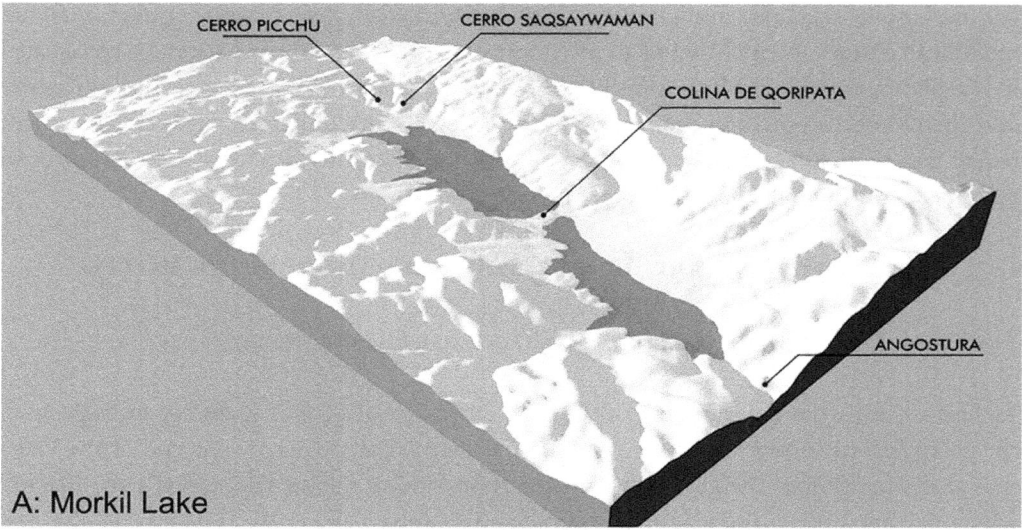
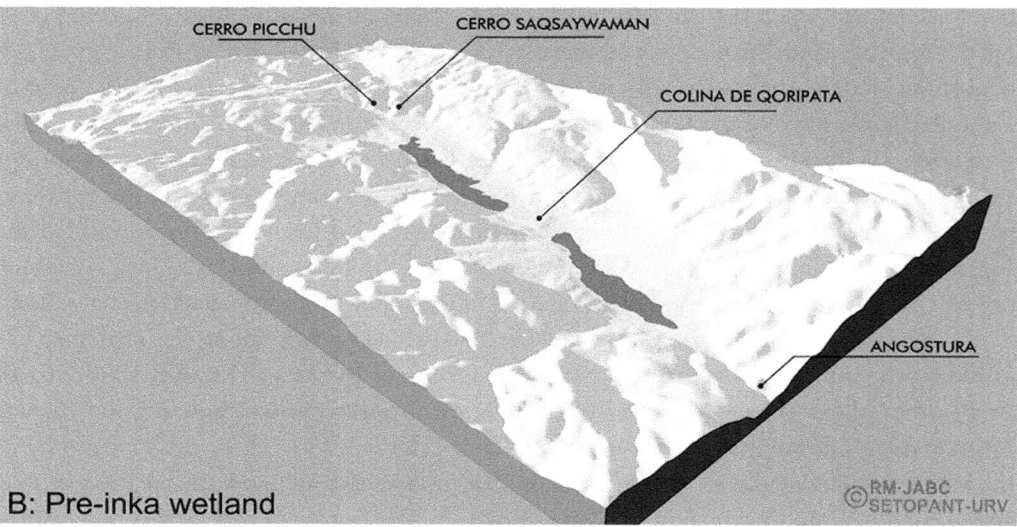

Figure 19.3. Evolution of Cusco Valley before the Inka expansion, drawing by R. Mar and J. A. Beltrán-Caballero. A. Extension of the valley covered by Morkil Lake. Formed at the end of the Pleistocene after the last glaciation, the lake emptied at some point due to the collapse of the cap that contained it at Angostura. As a result, a number of lagoons/wetlands remained as the last vestiges of the great lake. B. Perimeter of the two main wetlands. The refounding of Cusco as the imperial capital accomplished by Pachacuti required their drainage and desiccation.

complementary actions were thought to make possible the establishment of a large population and were part of the measures that accompanied the refounding of Cusco as a great state capital and center of Tawantinsuyu (Figure 19.5).

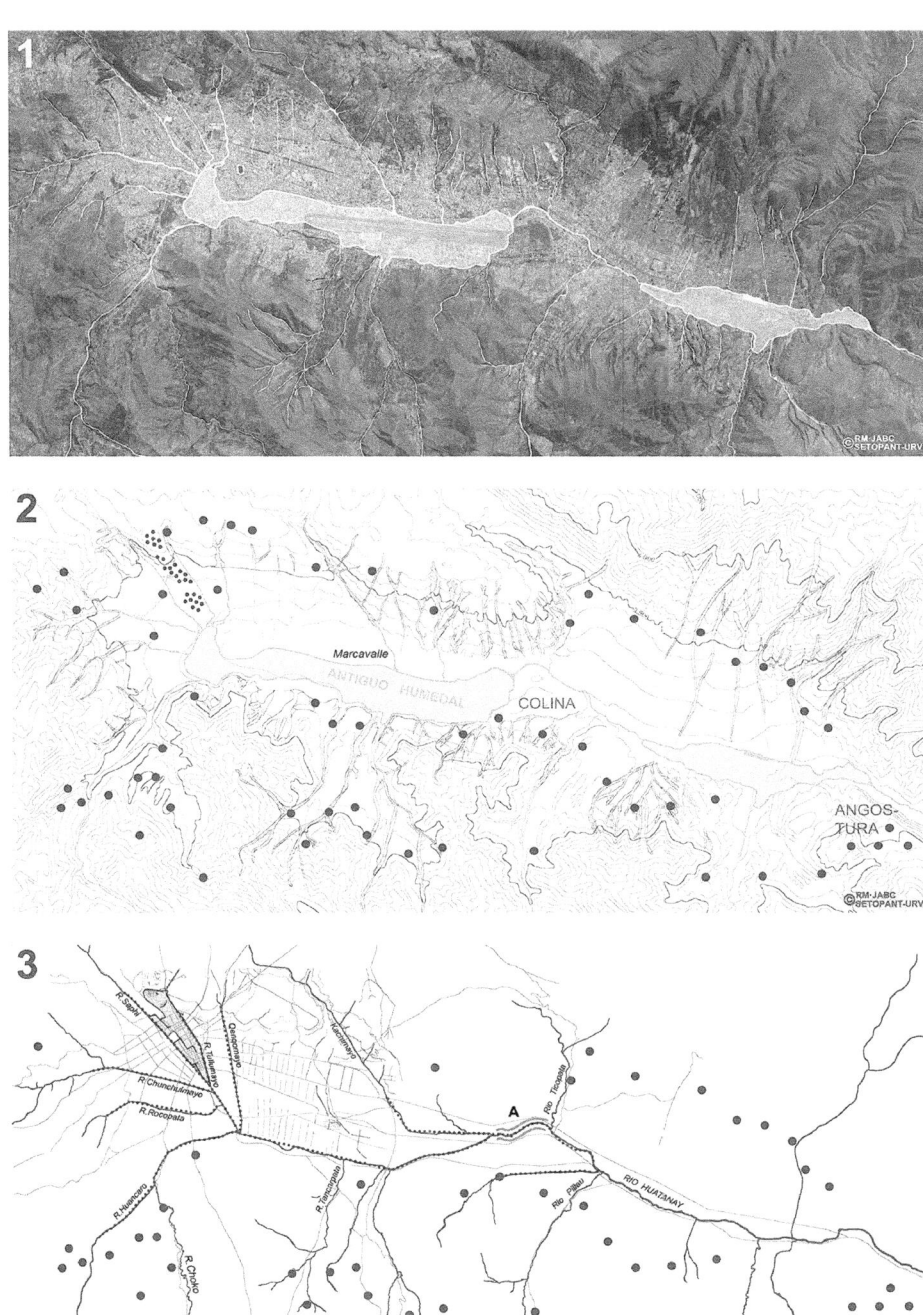

Figure 19.4. 1. Reconstruction of wetlands in pre-Inka times. 2. Distribution of the sixty main *killke* (pre-Inka) settlements published by Bauer (2004:Figure 8.4). 3. Courses of rectified rivers, new Inka channels for drying up wetlands, road system, and ceremonial center of the Inka capital. Drawing R. Mar and J. A. Beltrán-Caballero.

Figure 19.5. Roads, terraces, canals, *wakas*, and settlements in the great capital of Tawantinsuyu, drawing by R. Mar and J. A. Beltrán-Caballero. The idea of Cusco as a constellation of settlements was described by Santiago Agurto over thirty years ago (Agurto 1987:80–81). The road network organized both neighborhoods of the city and the surrounding towns. Agurto drew as a "puma" shape the politico-religious center settled between the Saphi and Tullumayo Rivers. This was surrounded by a buffer zone without buildings and peripheral settlements described by Garcilaso de la Vega.

Channels and Management of Rainwater

It is well known that the Tullumayo and Saphi Rivers cross the city by Inka rectilinear layout channels. In today's urban space they flow through the ground, serving as support to the principal east-west axes of movement in the downtown. Actually, all stream courses that descended to the valley (Saphi, Tullumayo, Chunchulmayo, Wanqaro, etc.) were modified to control the movement and disposal of rainwater (Beltrán-Caballero et al. 2011; Herrera and Ali 2009; Regal Matienzo 2005). Some sections of these channels have been disabled and replaced by modern ducts as in the case in Limaqpampa Square (Benavente 2009).

Looking at the layout of the six modified torrents we see that they radially converge to a point at the foot of the southern slope of the valley. This is where the Watanay River begins. Its position in respect to the axis of the valley is atypical due to is displacement to the south, and in some points it cuts the base of the slope. These circumstances allow us to identify the current riverbed as a huge artificial canal. The most likely reason for its construction was to prevent water from the slopes from feeding the wetland formed after the collapse of the prehistoric lake (Beltrán-Caballero et al. 2011; Beltrán-Caballero 2013). While the

Watanay River was created, channel streams of the northern slopes of the valley were artificially driven to the area of San Sebastián where they emptied into the Watanay River.

The Drainage of the Wetland and Adjacent Crop Fields

Considered as a whole the new hydraulic infrastructure radically cuts the water supply to the wetland to expand the area intended for agriculture. However, this enterprise was not enough to channel rainwater. As usual in the draining of marshes (Seligmann and Bunker 1993) it is necessary to build a complementary drainage system to control the excess of water in the new fields. Archaeology has documented sporadically some of these channels (Ardiles 1986). However, photographs from 1956 show the full extent of the system. It appears associated with a group of retaining walls built to protect the new agricultural soils. The retaining walls extend surrounding the old swamp.

Many Inka elements have disappeared, buried or destroyed by the expansion of the contemporary city. However, the 1956 aerial photographs combined with current cartographic documentation allow us to reconstruct the layout of the canals, dams, and terraces that supported agricultural exploitation in the grounds that extend today among Collasuyu Avenue and the current airport. It is possible to distinguish two topographic units that match the current streets of this neighborhood: the former wetland and the gently sloping fields around it (Figure 19.6).

The first topographic unit corresponds to the western sector of the airport with adjacent neighborhoods (Los Sauces, Urbanización Kennedy, and Calle Jorge Chávez). It forms an almost horizontal surface around 3,250 masl. The northern limit of this flat area matches the actual curved path of Tupac Amaru Avenue. In 1956 aerial photos we see that before the modern opening of this avenue there was a retaining wall with the same layout whose curved shapes show us without doubt its Inka origin. Throughout this area the water table crops out a few feet deep. In addition, some geological surveys carried out for the construction of modern foundations have documented recent lacustrine bottom silts (Beltrán-Caballero et al. 2011:327, note 43). The most likely conclusion is that this horizontal field corresponded to former wetland and was surrounded by a retaining wall that matches the current path of Tupac Amaru Avenue. This interpretation is further confirmed by the network of channels that appears on aerial photos parallel to each other and perpendicular to Watanay riverbed.

In the lower areas of this sector surface channels were combined with an underground drainage system. Archaeological excavations at the Urbanización Kennedy—located beside the airport—have documented an extensive network of small channels (40 x 40 cm and 50–80 m long) buried 1.5 m deep (Ardiles 1986). This underground system displays the scale of the work undertaken to drain the wetland and the optimization of new agricultural areas. The construction technique of the channels allows us to say that these are works of the Inka period (Ardiles 1986:82).

The second topographic unit is the gently sloping lands surrounding the ancient wetland. Indeed, the current topography of the urbanized land shows that beyond Tupac

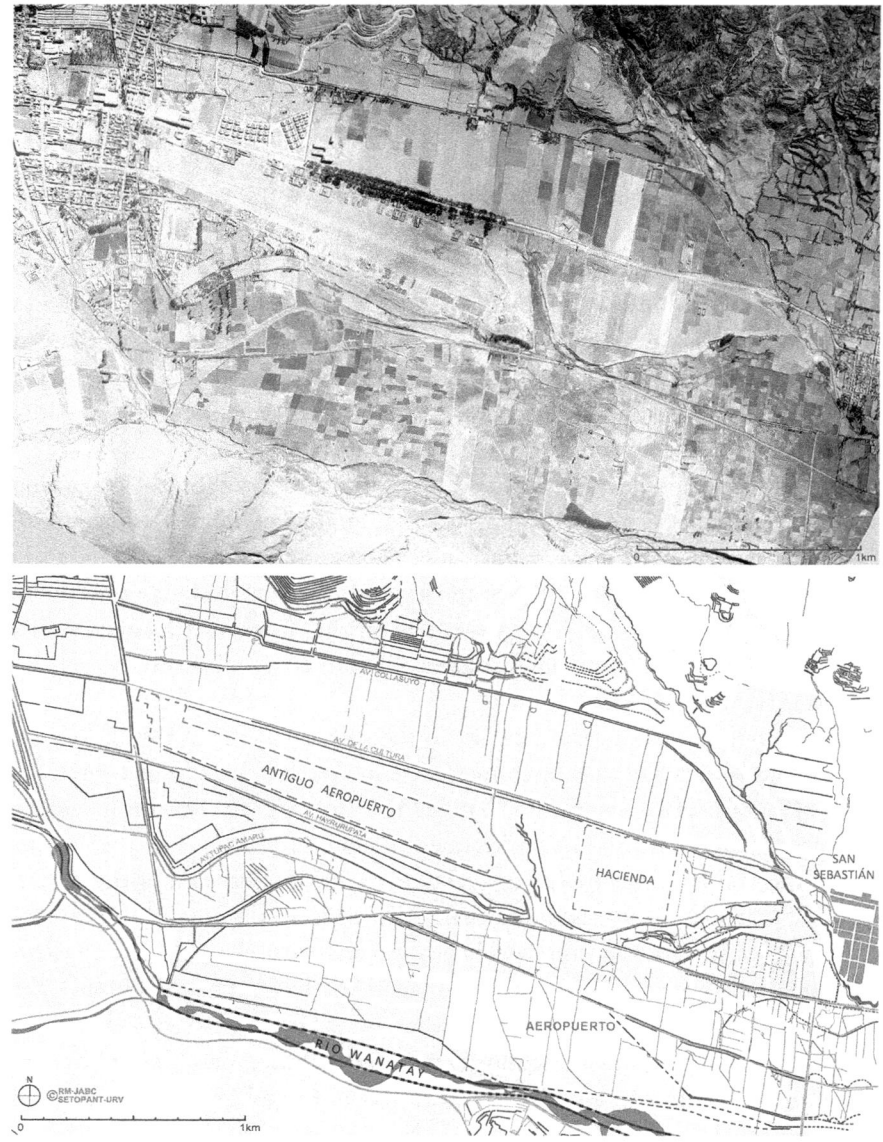

Figure 19.6. DIRAF aerial photos of 1956 of the valley of Cusco have allowed drawing the slopes and platforms that distributed agricultural fields. They coincide with the position of Inka retaining walls, not always well preserved, and their relation with Inka roads. If we complete the layout of the retaining walls (dashed lines), a system of curved terraces like that known in Urubamba Valley in Pisac and Ollantaytambo is drawn. In 1956 the valley lands had a complex irrigation system consisting of canals and reservoirs. The more complicated and irregular paths are the most modern. It is also possible to identify a system of regular layout of parallel channels that define elongated crop fields too. It is a unitary system that extends from the Avenida Collasuyu to the Watanay River. Its layout is conditioned by Inka roads and the retaining walls of the terraces. Both circumstances show that the remains of the original Inka irrigation system were partially preserved until 1956. Drawing by R. Mar and J. A. Beltrán-Caballero.

Amaru Avenue (the old limit of wetland) the sloping land rises northward to conclude with a modern rectilinear street layout: Huayruru Pata Avenue, an ancient Inka road (Amado 2005; Floerke and Amado 2013). In 1956 aerial photos, this slope appears supported on a series of retaining walls parallel to the Tupac Amaru Avenue curved path. By their form and layout missing retaining walls can only be interpreted as Inka constructions: a complex curved path that was projected on the ground from the drawing of large arc segments; "waves" existing in different places of the Urubamba Valley (Hyslop 1990). The entire lower valley of Pisac—which was susceptible to flooding and where the colonial city was placed—was modeled on Inka times with a system of high curvature walls that still remains on the ground. Another example is Patallacta, where large curve terraces also model the base of the valley protecting the main settlement.

The Great Central Plain: The Area of Avenida de la Cultura

The position of Huayruru Pata Avenue sets the limit of the hillside supported by the curved walls and the beginning of an extensive elongated plain (3 x 1.5 km) that reached to Collasuyu Avenue. Its slope was so soft that it could be rectified without walls. The Avenida de la Cultura crosses this sector longitudinally and served in Inka times as a main arterial road. These fields received a lot of water from the gullies of the northern slope. The channels used for drainage and evacuation are clearly identified in aerial photographs of 1956, which allows reconstructing the regular network formed. It draws elongated path crop fields perpendicular to the Avenida de la Cultura. These elements of the old Inka landscape have disappeared under current developments.

Given the size and complexity of the works for the desiccation of this great wetland and managing their new farmland, the most likely conclusion is that the management of Watanay Valley was the great laboratory test that allowed the Inkas to apply strategies for land management and transformation of the environment on a large scale (Kaulicke et al. 2003).

Between San Blas District and Kachimayo River

For its specific morphology the valley of Cusco is a closed ecosystem. Therefore, in addition to draining the wetland and organizing the flatlands of the valley floor, an integrated management required the complete transformation of the northern slope. This is a steep mountain slope shaped by a series of natural streams extending between the upper district of San Blas and the ravine of the Kachimayo River. Their banks descended on the plains of the valley and the streams finally flowed into the large wetland. Photographs of 1956 show the dense network of terraces, many of them now missing, that extended along several kilometers.

Agricultural terraces and retaining walls served to transform this natural terrain and organize the slope. They also integrate in the layout the rich archaeological documentation that allows us to locate the position of great religious centers—generated around rocks seen as sacred landscape features (*wakas*) that should be important religious centers: Mesa

Redonda-Pachatosa, Patallacta, Huayracpunco, and Teteqoca (Bauer 1998; Gullberg 2009; Van de Guchte 1990)—drawing the network of Inka roads and setting up the position and the name of some ancient towns (Figures 19.7 and 19.8).

The Topography of San Blas District

San Blas district (Figure 19.7) appears currently covered by colonial and republican buildings that have preserved much evidence of ancient Inka terraces and roads. The area follows the Tullumayo River layout. Its south boundary is an Inka road that matches the street Chiuanpata. It is remarkable the regularity of the rectangular platforms developed in parallel to the course of Tullumayo River. They form a system of staggered "boxes" at both sides of the river. On the west side (ceremonial center) they extend along the streets Siete Borreguitos, Ladrillos, Siete Culebras, and Hatunrumiyoq.

In San Blas district (on the eastern slope) the width of the first line of platforms is 5 m; the second at some points reaches 7 m; and the third, which takes place only in the lower part of the neighborhood, can reach 8 m. If we consider the slope of the terrain in some cases, these platforms should reach 5–7 m in height, a topographical situation corresponding to the steep slope of modern buildings currently open onto Tuyumayo Street near the *waka* Sapantiana.

Indeed, all buildings of Tullumayo Street on the side of San Blas district open onto this street by rectangular, narrow, and elongated rooms corresponding to the shape of the first of the terraces. These spaces are closed by a retaining wall holding a second row of rooms located at a higher elevation. Although in many cases retaining walls have been removed to make space for modern buildings, we have sufficient buildings with stepped sections to reconstruct the old profile of Inka terraces flanking this bank of Tullumayo River.

The sector of San Blas can be subdivided depending on its topographical features. A first platform served to sustain an extensive "Triangular Terrace," roughly horizontal. Its northern end begins near the *waka* Sapantiana the height at which the Tullumayo River enters in the city. Here it has been documented is an ancient water spring associated with a reservoir and some remains of Inka walls with numerous reused lithics. This large triangular area continues east to reach the present church of San Blas. Here it is common to situate the temple of the god of lightning (Illapa) where the mummy of Pachacuti was found (Sarmiento 1988 [1572]:155) and where according to Bernabé Cobo (1964 [1653]:54) infant sacrifices were made. This area corresponded to Toqokachi neighborhood, although we hardly have archaeological evidence: a male burial (Bejar 1976) and Inka ceramic on the surface (Morris 1967; Paredes 1999).

Another sector of platforms extends over the polygonal area demarcated by Recoleta and Lucrepata Streets. Some of the Inka retaining walls have been preserved between blocks of modern urbanization. From these remains it is possible to reconstruct the geometry of the zigzag terraces that during Inka times allowed distributing rectangular platforms within a larger triangular space. This system ended in the Qenqomayo River currently channeled and that runs along the Callejon Retiro (Figure 19.7).

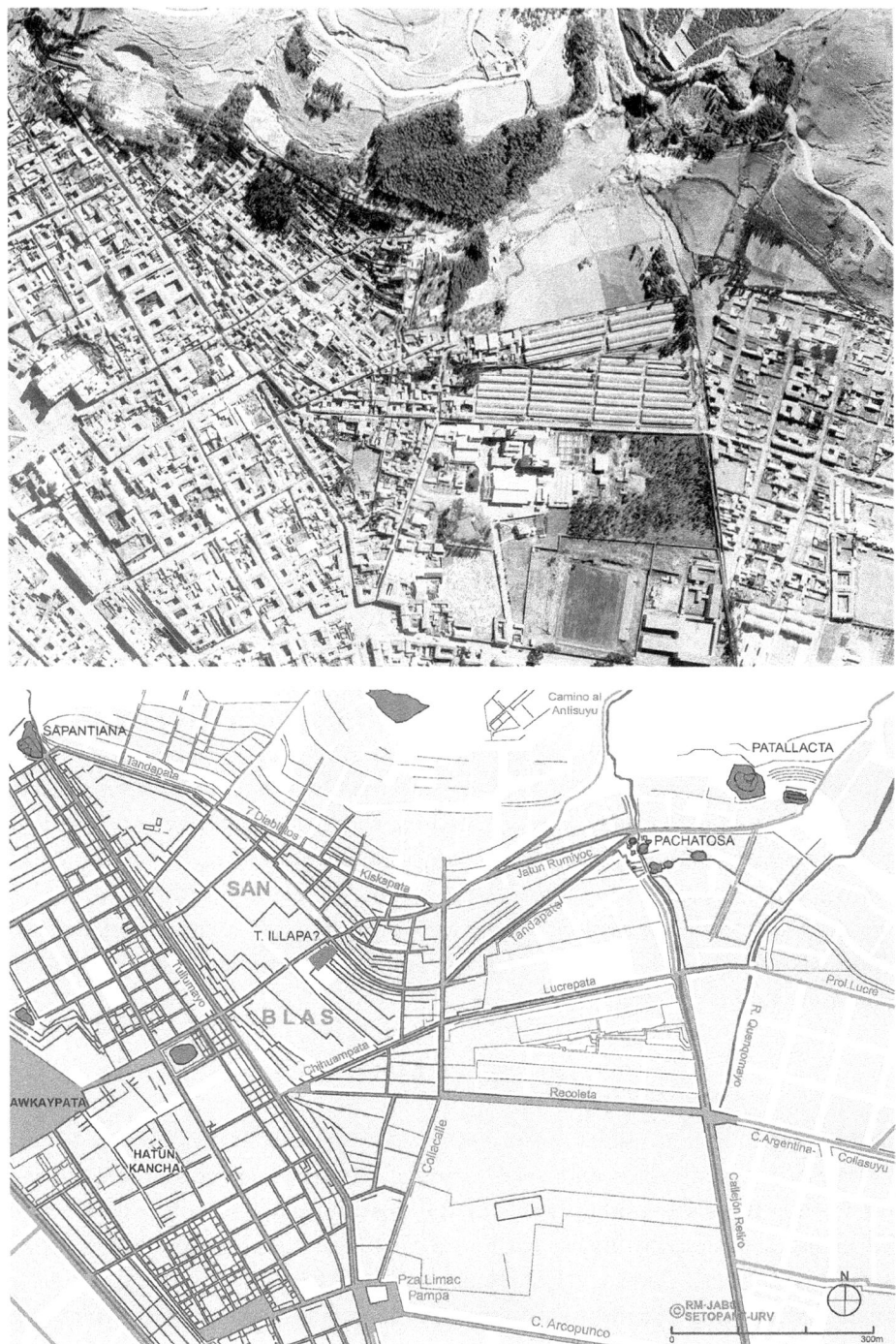

Figure 19.7. Aerial photograph between San Blas and Qencomayo River in 1956 (DIRAF) and its interpretation in a drawing by R. Mar and J. A. Beltrán-Caballero. *Wakas*, roads, terraces, and Inka planning from Illapa temple (San Blas) to Patallacta.

Terraces from Pachatosa to Hayraq Punco

The topography of the hillside allows two distinct natural areas to be distinguished (Figure 19.8). The upper part (3,300–3,500 masl) is a strip of steep slope eroded by water channels descending from the highlands extending northeast of Saqsaywaman and includes Qenqo, Laqo, and Sirenaqocha archaeological sites. The lower part (3,200–3,300 masl) is a smooth slope inclined plane that ends in Collasuyu Avenue. The topographical differences between these two areas determined the application of two different architectural strategies.

The steepest part of the slope—natural curved shapes produced by soil erosion—was stabilized by a dense sequence of terraces adapted to the contours. Photos of 1956 show a sequence with twenty stepped terraces. The whole terrace system begins at the top of San Blas and continues without interruption along 3 km to reach Kachimayo River and the town of Salinas. As we approach, San Blas's topography allowed combining straight with curved sections; some sectors come to be in the form of an authentic zigzag (Figure 19.7). The latest twist in the terraces occurs at the top of San Blas. Ancient terraces are located between existing streets Tandapata and Kiskapata. From this point terraces continue straight to gradually disappear when they reach the ancient Inka road whose origin is the *waka* Sapantiana (Siete Diablitos-Kiskapata).

The lower part of the slope was much more regular and gentler and extended to the current Collasuyu Avenue. It was organized by groups of large rectangular platforms supported by retaining walls whose heights adapted to different terrain slopes. Depending on its orientation, several subsystems of platforms or terraces can be recognized.

Down Collasuyu Avenue another sector of terraces begins after crossing the river Qencomayo and extends over two miles until reaching the Kachimayo riverbed (Figure 19.8). It consists of a series of elongated platforms—some nearly 250 m in width—parallel to the avenue. The best preserved walls—more than 100 m in length and 2 m in height—are holding the platforms in the sections behind the university, the Garcilaso de la Vega School, and Cuzqueña brewery. The current road was built on a large Inka retaining wall that at some point reaches 10 m high.

Inka Landscape Management

The new layout of the ceremonial center and its suburbs, wetland desiccation and management of the surrounding fields, and construction of the terraces described between San Blas and Kachimayo River were only part of the transformation of the valley. We have archaeological evidence to describe the occupation of the highlands north of Saqsaywaman from the subbasin of Chacan River until Kachimayo River. Also at the south side of the valley, combined with farming systems, were built settlements and storage systems that go until the gates of the valley in Angostura.

In fact, the most spectacular case of organic association between settlements and agricultural systems occurred in San Jerónimo area at the northeast corner of the valley. The extraordinary conservation of Patapata and Larapa terraces allows us to assess the importance of the works undertaken by the Inkas to transform this vast plain with gentle slopes.

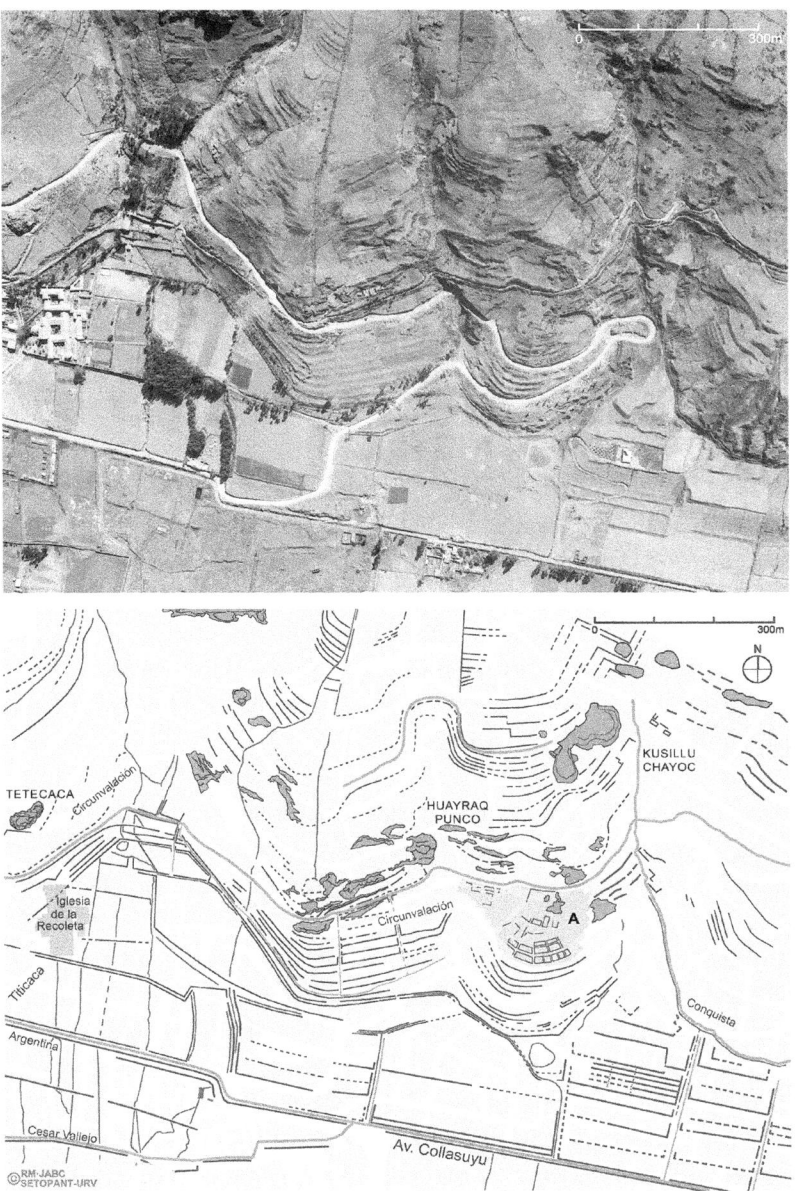

Figure 19.8. Aerial photography from 1956 DIRAF flying (*top*), and its interpretation in a drawing by R. Mar and J. A. Beltrán-Caballero. Between the neighborhood of San Blas and Kachimayo River an extensive network of agricultural terraces stretched. Retaining walls were prolonged over several kilometers forming an integrated layout with the old roads and some large sacred rocks (*wakas*) that were the focus of several religious centers. Inka builders transformed the upper part of the slope using curved terraces adapted to the terrain. Curved terraces start at the top of San Blas and continue, following a wavy line along 3 km to reach Kachimayo River and the town of Salinas. Aerial photographs make it possible to reconstruct a sequence with twenty stepped terraces. In 1956 photographs it is possible to identify an Inka settlement of polygonal enclosures surrounded by curved platforms (*left*, A).

There were built a great set of zigzag terraces supported by only orthogonal path retaining walls. By its size it is comparable to the most important examples in the Sacred Valley or Chinchero plateau (Colqa terraces and Saywiti). These agricultural lands are still in use and are irrigated and drained by an intricate network of canals dating back to Inka times.

On the terraces between San Blas and Kachimayo it is sufficient to overlap the road system (Amado 2005; Floerke and Amado 2013) to realize that each subsystem of terraces was built following the orientation of the adjacent roads:

A) Tandapata-Siete Diablitos-Kiskapata is an Inka road that begins in the *waka* Sapantiana and served to position the terraces of the northern part of San Blas.

B) Kiskapata Street links to Jatunrumiyoc, an Inka road leading to *waka* Mesa Redonda (identified with the *waka* Pachatosa; Bauer 1998:79).

C) The Inka road that begins at the end of Tandapata Street reached Laqo religious site and Antisuyu main road after crossing at least four *wakas*. This road began in the top of the square of San Blas, the probable location of Illapa temple. The end of this road continued straight, leaning on powerful walls, to head to Pachatosa and again in a straight line toward the *waka* Patallacta. From there the road reached the *waka* Kusilluchayoc, finally reaching the Laqo temple.

D) This relationship is also recognized in Lucrepata, an Inka road whose extension after crossing the river Qenqomayo (Callejon Retiro) goes straight to the *waka* Teteqoca and from there ascends toward the *waka* Huayraqpunco.

In turn, roads related the large *wakas* of the sacral landscape. All we have cited (Sapantiana, Pachatosa, Patallacta, Teteqoca, Huayraqpunco, Kusilluchayoc . . .) are today large blocks of emerging rocks in the landscape related to buildings whose traces are still preserved in the rock surface. Before their destruction by the "extirpators of idolatries" should be impressive milestones in the landscape (Van de Guchte 1990; Zecenarro 2001). Its position on the natural topography (Bauer 1998; Zuidema 1964) determined the layout of the secondary roads and these in turn set the guidelines for the layout and orientation of the terrace systems.

Unfortunately we know only some of the holy places that focused the symbolic appropriation of the territory. Bernabé Cobo listed springs, lagoons, and in some cases just places on the territory as points where the Andean religion was focused. We need to understand the construction of this anthropic landscape as a complex process in which the perception of supernatural places had to play a relevant role. Do not forget that other expressions of nature whose role in this process is more difficult to pin down must also have their role. This is the case with some views to sacred mountain, particularly the far, eternally snowcapped *apus* (Zecenarro 2003), or lines that draw the movement of the stars in the sky (Urton 1981), that must also provide guidelines for a sacred appropriation of the territory.

As we have shown in the previous examples, this valley located high in the Andean region, with excellent agricultural potential, fed by seasonal rains and numerous natural sources, was totally transformed by Inka rulers, particularly by Pachacuti. The objective was to settle there the great urban structure intended to be the center of the new power that was emerging in the region (Covey 2006). The great transformation of the valley was thought to support a dense population that would maintain the center and capital of the Tawantinsuyu. We know for colonial sources that it involved the settlement of a large population. The famous quote from Sancho de la Hoz refers to the one hundred thousand houses dispersed throughout the valley. This fact was verified by Santiago Agurto (1980) from a hypothetical distribution of the known Inka settlements, their surface, and their density of occupation. For some of these settlements we have partial archaeological data (Farrington 2013; Niles 1987). The description of the twelve districts surrounding the capital by Garcilaso de la Vega is still the most complete information about the names and locations of some of these populations.

As we have seen the territorial organization was based on the road network—main, secondary, and ceremonial—of the Qhapaq Ñan and supported in the network of *wakas*. We know the four main branches of Qhapaq Ñan born at Awkaypata Square and the streets of the representative center built between Tullumayo and Saphi Rivers. In Andean thought, people could be dispersed across the territory, however a ceremonial center (Von Hagen and Morris 1998) was needed to serve as a framework for festivals large enough to accommodate crowds when the calendar indicated (Zuidema 2010). This place also had to serve as the new state administrative center and seat of religious and political power. It was precisely in order to start operating from new bases that Pachacuti reorganized the distribution of populations of the valley (Miño 1994; Zecenarro 2001). This involved the construction of urban aggregates in the valley and the ceremonial center, which should serve to focus the entire system (Figure 19.9).

Conclusion

Cusco and the Idea of the City in the Andes

The occupation of the valley in Inka times used a model we can called "dispersed." Talking about the city of Cusco is talking about a particular way to materialized human settlements in the Andes. To understand how this urban structure works as a unity our first problem is to establish the limits and boundaries of its territory, a problem that has been studied from very different perspectives. Configured as a dispersed urban aggregate located in a very anthropized landscape Cusco went far from the closed traditional city models studied by archaeological research. The terminology used to refer to the "city" and its periphery reflects the idea of a much more "closed" space related to urban traditions of the ancient world in

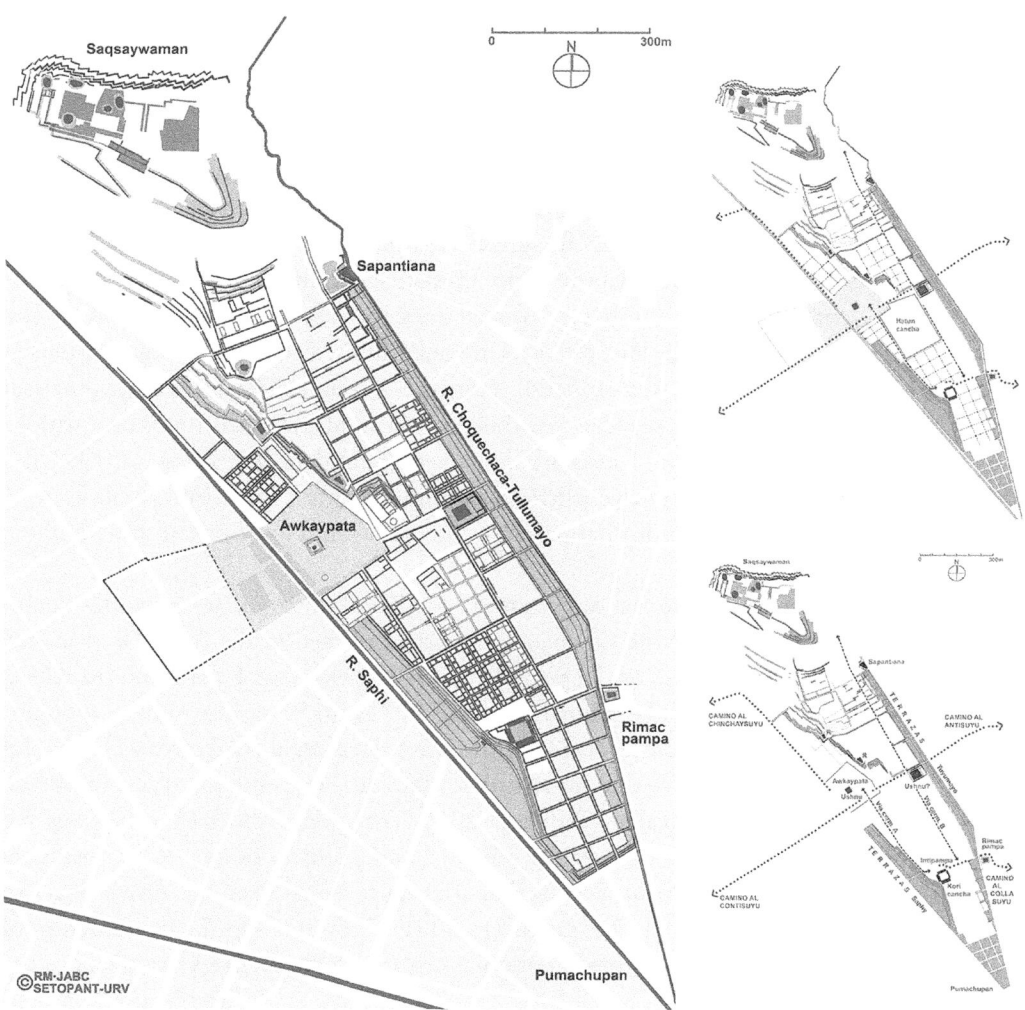

Figure 19.9. Reconstruction of the urban layout of the ceremonial center of Cusco between Saphi and Tullumayo Rivers. Drawing by R. Mar and J. A. Beltrán-Caballero.

the Middle East and the Mediterranean region. There the idea of the city wall as a defensive frontier of religious value arises from the perception of the natural environment as a hostile territory. The interior of the city takes its primary value as an ordered space compared to the outside tidy chaos (Rykwert 1985). This is an idea that does not fit and even clashes sharply with the patterns of settlement found in the Andes and the complex integration strategies with the environment developed by American cultures (Von Hagen and Morris 1998).

As previously mentioned, traditional studies believe that the Inka city lay between the channeled Saphi and Tullumayo/Choquechaca Rivers from their confluence in Pumachupan until the slopes of the hill of Saqsaywaman. It is true that the remains of Inka buildings have a higher density under the colonial buildings of the historic center of Cusco.

In this high point of the valley head they formed a dense urban tissue. It was the symbolic heart of the entire network: a functional and ceremonial center of something we can define as an outspread urban system.

In the last thirty years the archaeological map has been enriched with numerous findings (buildings of all types, roads, streets, *wakas*, terraces, canals, and reservoirs) that allow a more complete image of the settlements that were part of the ancient Inka capital (Niles 1987; Zecenarro 2001). Although is not possible to reconstruct the whole system, data allow us to define the territory in some of its main urban features. We can talk about a peripheral system of settlements to the ceremonial center, a first ring that lay until the end of the valley in Angostura. Settlements such as Kallachaca, Inkilltambo, or Choquequirao Pukio are excellent evidence of the skill and ingenuity with which the Inka transformed the landscape to the last corner of the valley. Terracing to stabilize slopes required not only a sophisticated technique but also in-depth knowledge of the dynamics of the environment (Kendall and Chepstow-Lusty 2006). Inkilltambo is a great example of an extensive system of agricultural terraces built on both slopes of a secondary valley (Figure 19.10). A ceremonial complex was organized in several levels around a carved rock. Some buildings were used as residences and others were destined for the storage of products. This site extends almost 0.5 km along the course of the Kachimayo River.

Figure 19.10. Virtual reconstruction of Inkilltambo. Drawing by R. Mar and J. A. Beltrán-Caballero.

But the urban aggregate radio could extend even outside the strict confines of the valley. In this sense some authors consider the city as a territorial system further comprising Yucay Valley, Chinchero plateau, and the head of the Cusco basin (Brisseau 1981:17). A large region of sixty miles in diameter, where Cusco would be the main ceremonial complex surrounded by successive rings of settlements increasingly distanced from each other as we move away from the center (Miño 1994). Some important ceremonies, such as the "Situa" or the expulsion of ashes ritual, allow us to realize that the Tawantinsuyu capital was conceived as a large territory extending, on one side, from the Vilcanota Valley to the Apurimac Valley, on the other. In some sense, the "extended" Cusco mingled with the heartland of Inka power and it was the final result of the complex management strategies of the natural environment accomplished for millennia in the Andean region (Von Hagen and Morris 1998).

The "dispersed" pattern of territory occupation defined the characteristics of the city and its parts. We know that clay models were made to plan the great works; however, the layout of the main urban elements had to be progressively implemented in the field. Built infrastructure has enabled us to establish a possible sequence where channels lead us to terraces and crop fields, crop fields are linked to the settlements where farmers lived, and eventually settlements contextualize the road network facing territorial accessibility. Water was one of the main factors in the beginning of this sequence. In Inka culture an obvious symbolic interest in capturing and using water always existed. But water was the blood of the sacred peaks—the *apus*—and therefore the flow of life too (MacLean 1986). Both aspects, one practical and the other religious, were combined with the extraordinary ability demonstrated by the Inkas to intervene in the landscape.

Cusco and the Transformation of the Natural Environment

To justify the transformation of the natural environment and especially its exploitation, the prior preparation of myths and metaphorical narratives that explain the symbolic value that had the most significant natural features was required (Niles 1999). So fountains, lakes, large rocks, and of course mountains took on a supernatural value linked to the past of different social groups (*ayllus*). A large rock could be a petrified group ancestor and a source could have been miraculously discovered by other more or less historical ancestors (Sherbondy 1982). As the land (Pachamama) could not be possessed, rights of use were linked to the mythical justifications the group could present. Naturally, each *ayllu* should keep worship in *wakas* located in the lands and channels these groups guarded and maintained. This shows how the last purpose of the mythical-religious system settled on the territory was to control the farmland and the sources of water needed for irrigation.

We can imagine that the radical transformation of Watanay Valley reflected ultimately new power relationships within the social structure of the Inkas by blood with people considered Inka by privilege and even with the subjected peoples who had just entered into the orbit of a new Andean regional power. In turn, we would like to think that maybe Cusco was the laboratory where many strategies were tested that would then be adopted elsewhere beyond Watanay basin. In Cusco we have examples of some of the highest terraces built (the wall behind the buildings on Suecia Street is a good example), the longest and deepest canals that cross an Inka population center, renovation of large tracts of wetland, and a complex network of main and secondary roads that link the vast system of peripheral settlements and infrastructure support. The process undertaken of reorganization of the existing elements and the construction of new development is of such complexity that it only could be carried out by an overview and an iron will.

If we just consider the way settlements took form in the millennia of Andean urban history (Canziani 2009) we could understand that the growth of the city meant the projection on the territory of a mesh of constructed hierarchical places. The population of the ceremonial center moved to the productive periphery, following the rhythm of the celebrations of the calendar. In this context it does not make much sense to oppose the defined and protected city with the surrounding agricultural area. This situation becomes very apparent when trying to define the limits of Cusco as a city capital of Tawantinsuyu.

Acknowledgments

This chapter is part of the project Cusco: A New Vision of the Inka City, a cooperative project between San Antonio Abad University (Cusco) and Rovira i Virgili University (Tarragona), with funding from AECID (Spain) and with the support of the National Museum of the American Indian–Smithsonian Institute (NMAI–SI, Washington), the Municipality of Cusco, and the Dirección Desconcentrada de Cultura de Cusco, Peruvian Ministry of Culture (2012–2016). The SETOPANT research group (Seminar of Ancient Topography—URV/www.setopant.com) is the axis that articulates the proposal: to use the tools provided by archaeology of architecture, archaeological excavation, and archaeology of territory and landscape in the study of human settlements.

The main objective of this project is to propose a coherent image of the old city, reconstructing the Inkas' cultural landscape along the Watanay Valley, which includes both "Puma City" and the suburbs surrounding it. The virtual reconstruction of the Inka ceremonial center that extends beneath the streets of the colonial city is part of the results of this work. This 3D model is currently part of the exhibition *The Great Inka Trail: Engineering of an Empire* that takes place in the NMAI in Washington.

Among the many professionals who are part of this project we want to highlight the work and untiring support of Dr. Ramiro Matos, curator of the Smithsonian Institution. Among the collaborators from Cusco we want to acknowledge the support of archaeologists Luz Marina Monroy who has documented the first phases of occupation of the valley (formative period), key to the reconstruction of the environment in the Inka period, and María Eugenia Muñiz who reviewed the excavation memories from the files of the Dirección Desconcentrada de Cultura de Cusco; the historian Donato Amado who has reviewed the information of the historical archives of Cusco for the reconstruction of the road system in Watanay Valley; the geologist José Carlos Ramírez who provided a geological report on the morphological formation stages of the valley; the architect Crayla Alfaro, manager of the Office of the Historic Center of Cusco.

Finally, special thanks to Dr. Josep Maria Palet (ICAC) who has followed the trajectory of this research.

References

Agurto, S. 1980 *Cusco: La traza urbana de la ciudad Inca*. UNESCO, Instituto Nacional de Cultura del Perú, Cusco.

Agurto, S. 1987 *Estudios acerca de la construcción, arquitectura y planeamiento inkas*. Cámara Peruana de la construcción, Lima.

Amado, A. 2005 Sistema vial andino en el valle de Cusco. In *Qhapaq-Ñan del Tawantinsuyu* 1:7–23.

Ardiles, P. 1986 Sistema de drenaje subterráneo prehispánico. In *Alpanchis* 27:75–97.

Bauer, B. S. 1998 *The Sacred Landscape of the Inka: The Cuzco Ceque System*. University of Texas Press, Austin.

Bauer, B. S. 2004 *Ancient Cuzco: Heartland of the Inka*. University of Texas Press, Austin.

Bejar, R. 1976 Un entierro en T'oqokachi. In *Revista del Museo Nacional de Lima* 42:145–155.

Beltrán-Caballero, J. A. 2013 Agua y forma urbana en la América Precolombina: el caso del Cusco como centro del poder inka. PhD dissertation, Universitat Politecnica de Catalunya, Barcelona.

Beltrán-Caballero, J. A., and R. Mar 2014 Territorio y ciudad en el Cusco Inka: La construcción del paisaje inka en el valle del Watanay. In *El Urbanismo Inka del Cusco: Nuevas Aportaciones—Arqueología y Arquitectura en la capital del Tawantinsuyu*, 23–55. Municipalidad del Cusco, Cusco-Washington-Tarragona.

Beltrán-Caballero, J. A., R. Mar, and D. Zapater 2011 Medio natural y gestión de recursos hidráulicos en América: la fundación del Cusco. In *Aquae sacrae: agua y sacralidad en la Antigüedad*, 313–341. Universitat de Girona, Girona.

Benavente, P. 2009 Rescate de un muro fino de la plaza Limacpampa. In *Saqsaywaman* 9:203–222. Instituto Nacional de Cultura Región Cusco, Cusco.

Bouchard, J. F. 1983 *Contribution a l'étude de l'architecture inka*. Les Editions de la MSH, Paris.

Brisseau, J. 1981 *Le Cuzco dans sa région*. In *Travaux De l'Institut Français d'Etudes Andines*, Tome XVI. Institut français d'études andines, Lima.

Canziani, J. 2009 *Ciudad y territorio en los Andes: contribuciones a la historia del urbanismo prehispánico*. Fondo Editorial de la Pontificia Universidad Católica del Perú, Lima.

Cobo, B. 1964 [1653] *Historia del Nuevo Mundo*. Biblioteca de Autores Españoles. Madrid.

Córdoba, M. E. 1986 *Estudio Geológico de la Ciudad del Cusco*. Cusco.

Córdoba, M. E. 1987 *Geología del Cusco*. Cusco.

Covey, R. A. 2006 *How the Inkas Built Their Heartland: State Formation and the Innovation of Imperial Strategies in the Sacred Valley, Peru*. University of Michigan Press, Ann Arbor.

De la Torre, C., and M. Burga (eds.) 1986 *Andenes y camellones en el Perú andino*. Consejo nacional de ciencia y tecnología, Lima.

Earls, J. 1981 Ecorregulación y ordenamiento del mundo en dos culturas andina. *Ideología*:7–36. Ayacucho.

Earls, J. 1998 *The Character of Inka and Andean Agriculture*. Departamento de Ciencias Sociales, Pontificia Universidad Católica del Perú, Lima.

Farrington, I. 2013 *Cusco: Urbanism and Archaeology in the Inka World*. University Press of Florida, Gainesville.

Floerke, K., and D. Amado 2013 *Cusco Valley Inka Road Survey*. Poster presented in the Congreso de Andeanistas, University California Berkeley, February 2013. Berkeley.

Gasparini, G., and L. Margolies 1977 *Arquitectura Inka*. Centro de Investigaciones Históricas y Estéticas. Facultad de Arquitectura y Urbanismo. Universidad Central de Venezuela, Caracas.

Gregory, H. E. 1916 A Geologic Reconnaissance of the Cuzco Valley. In *American Journal of Science* 41(241):1–100.

Gullberg, S. R. 2009 The Cosmology of Inka Huacas. PhD thesis, James Cook University, Townsville.

Herrera, A., and M. Ali 2009 Paisajes del desarrollo: la ecología de las tecnologías andinas. In *Antipoda* 8:169–173, Bogotá

Hyslop, J. 1984 *The Inka Road System*. Academic Press, Orlando.

Hyslop, J. 1990 *Inka Planning Settlement*. University of Texas Press, Austin.

Kaulicke, P. 2001 La función cultural de las obras hidráulicas en el tiempo de los inkas. In *Boletín de la Sociedad Geográfica de Lima* 114:64–86.

Kaulicke, P., et al. 2003 Agua, ancestros y arqueología del paisaje. In *Boletín de Arqueología PUCP* 7:27–56.

Kendall, A. 1985 *Aspects of Inka Architecture: Description, Function and Chronology, Part 1 and 2*. BAR International Series 242. Archaeopress, Oxford.

Kendall, A. (ed.) 1992 *Arqueología y Desarrollo Rural: Infraestructura agrícola e hidráulica pre-hispánica—Presente y futuro*. The Cusichaca Trust, Asociación Gráfica Educativa, Lima.

Kendall, A. 2013 Applied Archaeology in the Andes: The Contribution of Pre-Hispanic Agricultural Terracing to Environmental and Rural Development Strategies. In *Humans and the Environment: New Archaeological Perspectives for the Twenty-First Century*, edited by M. I. J. Davies and F. N. M'Mbogori, 153–170. Oxford University Press, Oxford.

Kendall, A., and A. Chepstow-Lusty 2006 Cultural and Environmental Change in the Cuzco Region of Peru: Rural Development Implications of Combined Archaeological and Palaeoecological Evidence. In *Kay Pacha: Cultivating Earth and Water in the Andes*, edited by P. Dransart, 185–197. BAR International Series 1478. Archaeopress, Oxford.

MacLean, M. 1986 Sacred Land, Sacred Water: Inka Landscape Planning in the Cuzco Area. PhD dissertation, Department of Anthropology, University of California, Berkeley.

Mar, R., and J. A. Beltrán-Caballero 2015a El conjunto arqueológico de Saqsaywaman (Cusco): una aproximación a su arquitectura. In *Revista Española de Antropología Americana* 44:9–38.

Mar, R., and J. A. Beltrán-Caballero 2015b The Urbanism of Inka Cusco. In *Catálogo de la exposición The Great Inka Road*, 25–34. NMAI–Smithsonian Institution, Washington, DC.

Mar, R., and J. A. Beltrán-Caballero 2015c Visualizing Cusco: Archaeology of Architecture in the Inka Capital—Planning and Construction. In *Engineering the Inka Empire: A Symposium on Sustainability and Ancient Technologies*. Washington, DC.

Mendivil, S., and D. Dávila 1994 *Geología de los Cuadrángulos de Cuzco y Livitaca*. Instituto Geologico Minero y Metalurgico, Lima.

Miño, L. 1994 *El manejo del espacio en el imperio inka*. FLACSO sede Ecuador, Quito.

Morris, C. 1967 Storage in Tawantinsuyu. PhD dissertation, University of Chicago.

Nickel, C. 1982 The Semiotics of Andean Terracing. In *Art Journal* 42(3):200–203.

Niles, S. 1987 *Callachaca: Style and Status in an Inka Community*. University of Iowa Press, Iowa.

Niles, S. 1999 *The Shape of Inka History: Narrative and Architecture in an Andean Empire*. University of Iowa Press, Iowa.

Paredes, M. 1999 Registro informatizado de restos prehispánicos en el centro histórico de Cusco, diagnóstico e interpretación. PhD dissertation, Departamento de Arqueología, Universidad de San Antonio Abad, Cuzco.

Protzen, J. P. 2005 *Arquitectura y construcción inkas en Ollantaytambo*. Fondo editorial de la PUCP, Lima.

Regal Matienzo, A. 2005 [1970] *Los trabajos hidráulicos del Inka en el antiguo Perú*. Instituto Nacional de Cultura de Perú, Lima.

Rostworowski, M. 2001 *Pachacutec Inka Yupanqui*. Série Historia Andina, vol. 23. Instituto de Estudios Peruanos, Lima.

Rykwert, J. 1985 *La Idea de Ciudad: Antropología de la forma urbana en el Mundo Antiguo*. Hermann Blume, Madrid.

Sarmiento de Gamboa, P. 1988 [1572] *Historia de los Inkas*. Miraguano Ediciones, Madrid.

Seligmann, L., and J. Bunker, S. G. 1993 An Andean Irrigation System: Ecological Visions and Social Organization. In *Irrigation at High Altitudes: The Social Organization of Water Control Systems in the Andes*, edited by W. P. Mitchell and D. Guillet, 203–232. Society for Latin American Anthropology Publication Series 12. American Anthropological Association, Washington, DC.

Sherbondy, J. E. 1979 Les réseaux d'irrigation dans la géographie politique de Cuzco. In *Journal de la Société des Américanistes* 66:45–66.

Sherbondy, J. E. 1986 Los ceques: Código de canales en el Cusco Inkaico. In *Allpanchis* 27:39–60. Instituto de Pastoral Andina, Cuzco.

Sherbondy, J. E. 1987 Organización hidráulica y poder en el Cuzco de los inkas. In *Revista Española de Antropología Americana* 17:117 ss.

Sherbondy, J. E. 1982 The Canal Systems of Hanan Cuzco. PhD dissertation, Department of Anthropology, University of Illinois, Urbana-Champaign.

Urton, G. 1981 *At the Crossroads of the Earth and the Sky: An Andean Cosmology*. University of Texas Press, Austin.

Van de Guchte, M. 1990 *Carving the World: Inka Monumental Sculpture and Landscape*. Michigan University Microfilms, Ann Arbor.

Von Hagen, A., and C. Morris 1998 *The Cities of the Ancient Andes*. Thames and Hudson, New York.

Zecenarro, B. G. 2001 *Arquitectura Arqueológica en la Quebrada de Thanpumach'ay*. Municipalidad Provincial del Cusco, Cusco.

Zecenarro, B. G. 2003 Apus tutelares y asentamientos del Cusco Preinka. In *Boletín de Arqueología PUCP* 7:387–405.

Zuidema, T. 1964 *The Ceque System of Cuzco: The Social Organization of the Capital of the Inka*. E.J. Brill, Leiden.

Zuidema, T. 1983 Hierarchy and Space in Inkaic Social Organization. In *Ethnohistory* 30(2):49–75.

Zuidema, T. 2010 *El calendario inka: tiempo y espacio en la organización ritual del Cuzco—la idea del pasado* Fondo Editorial del Congreso del Perú, Lima.

Chapter Twenty

On the Supposed Marginality of Mountain Areas

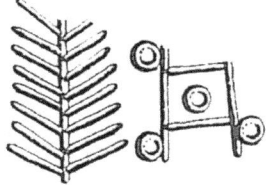

Hèctor A. Orengo

Abstract *This chapter presents an attempt to analyze the idea of isolation of mountain environments. This isolation is often indirectly related to backwardness (often disguised as traditionalism or conservativism) and marginality, also reflected in mentions to risk or the frontier character of mountain areas. In my discussion I try to make manifest perceptions that most authors do not consider they hold and put them forward for open debate, which may eventually result in a more balanced understanding of mountain areas. This discussion is, therefore, subjective and based on my own experience.*

I draw from both archaeological and contemporary examples of European mountain communities to argue that these conceptions are artifacts of a) our current global economic setting, b) our urban modern lifestyles, which often limit our understanding of mountain economy and practices, and c) our biased approach in terms of time, space, or study topic to the archaeology and history of these areas.

I conclude that mountain communities were always well integrated within their physical, social, and economic settings. Mountain areas offer sufficiently different and diverse environments to count with particular resources that are complementary to those found in lowland areas. The modification and exploitation of these environments have generated important innovations and specialized knowledge that have permitted mountain communities not just to be perfectly adapted to their particular socioeconomic settings but to develop successful economies during the last millennia.

INTRODUCTION

I would like to start this text thanking Dr. Arnau Garcia-Molsosa for the invitation to present a paper at the IEMA conference at Buffalo and to author one of the chapters in this book. To write a chapter for this volume is a unique opportunity to reflect on issues that do not usually fit in journals, which are more focused on specific case studies or periods.

The IEMA conference provided an excellent forum where interdisciplinary experts in mountain human–environment relations presented not just their research but more or less directly their research conceptions. It was fecund ground to compare different traditions, geographies, and approaches and this chapter stems from my thoughts during these sessions and some others with a similar focus, as well as my own work on European mountains. This chapter is therefore an attempt to contrast my own experience with the perceptions exhibited during the talks, and in particular with the idea of isolation of mountain environments. This isolation is often indirectly related to backwardness (often termed as traditionalism or conservativism) and marginality, also reflected in mentions to the frontier character of mountain areas. This is by no means a conception particular to the IEMA conference (nor to most of the papers presented there) but one that has subtly permeated meetings and conference sessions dealing with the archaeology of mountain areas since I started working in this subject back in 2004.

In this chapter I argue from an explicit European perspective that these conceptions are artifacts of our urban modern lifestyles, our often limited understanding of mountain economy and practices and our biased approach in terms of time, space, or study topic to the archaeology and history of these areas. This chapter aims to analyze these conceptions and open a, hopefully, fruitful debate that may eventually result in a more balanced understanding of mountain areas.

ISOLATED MOUNTAINS

The isolated character of mountain areas has often been related to difficulties in accessing them. By definition they do not present ports that open them to the sea with all its connection possibilities (although many ports are relatively accessible to mountain ranges). They also have fewer roads than the lowlands as they need to adapt to the topography of the terrain. These, therefore, are neither straight nor follow a straight, wide, or particularly even route and their slope hinders the use of wheeled transport. We assume that, as is the case today, these roads were little transited in the past. This is not a misguided assumption as mountains have today low population densities in comparison to lowlands and, except in a few cases, they do not host large urban centers. They are not just difficult to reach and move through, but they also have other characteristics that contribute to visualize mountains as inhospitable areas. A harsher climate than that of the lowlands, with high mountains being inaccessible half of the year due to snow cover, their vegetation cover that ranges from dense shrub and forests to continuous grasslands at higher altitudes, has also contributed to marginalize and characterize these spaces as pastoral, in opposition to agricultural landscapes that have a weighty bibliography backing their "civilizing" nature.

However, mountains can be considered as constituting folded surfaces and, if "unfolded," their areas would significantly increase. Verticality allows mountains to integrate highly diverse environments in relatively small spaces, multiplying the resources reachable in shorter distances. It is also important to note that in previous periods the movement might have had a lower cost for people accustomed to such environments. What to us might look like insurmountable barriers to locals are everyday environments with no particular restriction. I clearly remember how while we were struggling to excavate cheese production structures in Perafita Valley (Andorran Pyrenees) at 2,200 masl the area's shepherd remarked how local women from Les Escaldes used to walk up the valley to collect fresh milk during the milking season twice a day, a walk implying a height difference of 1,000 m.

Despite the difficulties involving wheeled transport, mountain communities used to maintain a network of well-trodden paths and stone roads that today are invisible or difficult to find due to the expansion of forests and vegetation, and lack of maintenance. Even when only earthen paths existed these could have maintained an intense mule traffic as the volume of Andorran contraband toward France and Spain attests since the eighteenth century to a degree that by the mid-nineteenth century was considered as forming a basis of the Andorran economy (Bertran i Soler 1847:247). The particular intensity of Andorran contraband is the fruit of particular socioeconomic and historic factors but serves well to illustrate how, despite the supposed limited availability of roads fit for transport, many paths were used in high-mountain settings to transport large quantities of produce for a long period of time. More so when taking into account that the main roads (easier to control) were not used for such traffic and the fact that the trips were made during the night and, therefore, the paths must have been accessible for loaded mules.

Backward, Conservative, and Marginal Areas

It is nowadays difficult to find an explicit mention of the backwardness of mountain areas as this can be understood, with reason, as negative and backward itself. However, there are a series of assumptions and tags pinned to mountain areas, such as that of conservative, marginal, or traditional that in my opinion implicitly refer to this concept and are a fruit of our modern urban lifestyle.

Cretan mountain society is very interesting in this respect. Mountain communities there are formed by, as a *Telegraph* reporter put it (Freeman 2008), a "feisty, independent people" in "remote, clan-dominated areas, where the first loyalty is to family, not government." Indeed, one of the points usually made about these areas is their independence from authority and the maintenance of old traditions based on manly honor and blood, and their love for guns, clearly advertised by the bullet holes in many signposts in the area. Mediators or *mesites* are prestigious individuals that are required to intervene in cases of conflict. They very successfully manage to avoid bloodshed and prevent the intervention of police and the legal system (Chereji 2018; Tsantiropoulos 2008). Indeed, the assiduous visitor to Crete willing to go beyond summer resorts would have heard about the warring state of affairs between mountain villages and Cretan police, which prevents the latter from accessing these areas. The fact that the mountainous areas of Crete are one of the largest producers of cannabis in Europe,[1] a good reason to impede police access, is rarely mentioned in these romanticized accounts of Cretan rebellious mountains. Mountains are today a focus of less investment than areas where more population concentrates or more productive activities develop, this has facilitated the preservation of more traditional activities and customs despite the fact that these traditions used to be also part of lowland communities. The modern lack of investment or development in conjunction with the maintenance of traditional sociocultural systems has found fertile ground for the development of alternative, even illegal, activities. It is worth noting that the same socioeconomic situation that preserves practices such a blood feuds in mountain areas that can be considered backward has also facilitated the development of a production activity that is not just fully a part of current society but integrated in international economic networks.

In the mountain village of Tor (Catalan Pyrenees) another tale-telling case developed a few years back. The mountain of Tor is strategically situated in the frontier with Andorra between the ski stations of Pal and Arinsal just below a mountain pass joining the Andorran and Catalan territories. In 1896 the heads of the thirteen houses of Tor signed an agreement to co-exploit the natural resources of this mountain. In order to be a member of this association it was necessary to own property in Tor, to be living in the village, and to be head of a family. By the 1970s the harsh living conditions (no water, electricity, or phone are available there) have left the village uninhabited, although Josep Montané, Pepe, head of the Sansa family, made a point of going there often to accomplish the society's conditions. In 1976 Rubén Castañer, an Andorran developer, was contacted by Pepe with plans to develop the mountain with a ski station that would join Pal and Arinsal stations in what would be the largest ski station and winter resort in the Spanish Pyrenees. This renewed a long-lived conflict between Josep Montané and Jordi Riba, "el Palanca," head of the Riba family and horse breeder, which opposed the development of the mountain, resulting in the deaths of two workers of el Palanca by bodyguards of Castañer in 1980. In 1995 Pepe was declared as the only owner of the mountain, but five months later he was found dead in his house in Tor with a wire around his neck and clear signs of violence.

The case had important media coverage with multiple news, podcasts, documentaries, and two books.[2] In these the landscape is described as pristine, natural, stunning, and its beauty is set off against the horrifying nature of crime. Epithets such as penury, marginal, and isolated repeat constantly in this coverage, but in reality, the crimes were very much related to modern economic concerns, connectivity and development. Although Tor mountain might seem to be very isolated, it stands at the center of many interests. Apart from the interest of Josep Montané, Rubén Castañer, and several Andorran, French, and British investors to create a massive ski and winter resort in the area, according to data gathered by Porta (2005), Tor has been considered an ideal point to open a new frontier with Andorra, as the other two frontier passes are usually saturated; however, Tor mountain is also an important route for contrabandists that constantly move large quantities of tobacco, but allegedly also weapons, other goods, and people from Andorra to Spain. The deaths and conflict in Tor are ironically more related to its connectivity than its isolation; the confluence of incompatible extraneous interests in the area represented by local people with their own interests in mind is ultimately the cause of the tragedy. The marginality of this area is an artifact of our preconceptions as we tend to think that a small place at high altitudes is disconnected from modern society. Crimes such as the ones described in Tor, moved by very current economic interests, also happen in cities and lowland settlements on an everyday basis but they are simply not regarded as extraordinary enough to excite interest. The contrast between our idealized concept of a natural, pure mountain environment inhabited by hardy people and the horrifying crime facilitated by penury and marginality make these deeds news and contribute to picturing mountain areas as isolated and backward.

In fact, much of this backwardness of mountain areas, with their late adoption of many innovations, is starting to be disproved by archaeological data. Only recently new excavation and paleoenvironmental data (Bahn 1983; Bertranpetit and Vives 1995; Ejarque 2013; Ejarque et al. 2010; Gassiot et al. 2017; Llovera 1986; Miras et al. 2007 and 2010; Orengo 2010; Orengo et al. 2014; Palet et al. 2007 and 2017; Servera et al. 2013; Yáñez 2005) have disproved, as Gassiot et al. (2017) put it, the "non-explicit consensus" that the neolithization process in mountain areas was later and less intensive than that of the lowlands. Equally interesting is the fact that high-mountain pastures, a defining trait of the highest supraforestal zones, at least in the Pyrenees are not natural but a result of human-controlled burning as early as the Middle Neolithic (Ejarque 2013; Ejarque et al. 2010). So much for this idealized scenario of pristine mountains.

Risky Environments?

Much has also been written in relation to risk perception in mountain environments (e.g., Walsh 2005). It seems to me, however, that these environments are not particularly risky to those who inhabit and know them well. Activities, as in other areas, are strictly regulated by the period of the year and the exigencies of the particular socioeconomic system in place, and these regulations tend to reduce risk factors considerably. When dealing with mountain environments risk should be interpreted more in relation to particular social or economic contexts than to environmental settings. In fact, mountain areas have often been considered a refuge in troubled times or by persecuted groups. Mountains, for example, concentrated the remains of republican forces and persecuted republican sympathizers (e.g., Morín et al. 2004), who formed into guerrillas and/or hid from the repressive fascist Francoist Civil Guard and police forces after the fall of the legitimate government of Spain. Again, the conception of risk is, in my opinion related to our urban lifestyles and lack of environmental knowledge. In this regard, it is curious to see how in the context of high-mountain excavations how differently mountain and lowland people react to the same situations. Summer thunderstorms in the high mountains are dangerous phenomena and few lowland people are aware that a lightning strike can kill not just whatever it hits but everything in a radius of around a hundred meters in wet grasslands. Mountain shepherds are well aware of this, and that this can cost them a whole flock and their own lives, and they look for shelter as soon as it is clear that a storm is in the making, while lowland people can wait until the storm is at hand and select inadequate shelter, unaware of the danger. Many other examples come to mind, such as our incapacity of food procurement in mountain settings or the way in which we react to grazing animals, disregarding the dangers of calving cattle or male horses, which are a cause of increasing concern for weekend excursionists in the Pyrenees. Ironically, while lowland people are generally unaware of mountain dangers, they seem to keep a vague general conception of the danger and inhospitality that mountain settings present. It is perhaps because of this unawareness that lowlanders tend to suffer more accidents, which helps to recreate the myth of mountains' inhospitality. Mountains' harsher climate, in particular, has played a leading role in this. However, our high-resolution paleoenvironmental and archaeological data for the eastern Pyrenees shows that rather than a decrease, high-mountain occupation and exploitation witnessed an important increase during the Little Ice Age (Ejarque 2013; Orengo et al. 2014), as it is known, the cold period around AD 1150–1550 (Mateo and Gómez 2004).

One of the characteristic situations I have found in my own ethnoarchaeological work is the way in which experienced agropastoralists look at me when I pose entirely legitimate (to me) questions about the use of agropastoral structures or the development of their work. They seem to be assessing if I am trying to test them or joke at them. Their staring only abates when they have fully considered the possibility that a lowland academic can also be a complete ignorant. For them many of the questions I am truly interested to elucidate have obvious answers that they would have not bothered to mention if I would have not specifically asked about them. Indeed, much of the most interesting information I have come across has been delivered by pursued chance comments rather than as a consequence of my direct questioning, and I am always left with the feeling that I lack questions more than answers. Such is the extent of our ignorance of traditional practices; such is the space that we, at least partially, fill with our preconceptions.

Frontier Nature of Mountain Areas

Linked to these conceptions is the "frontier" character of mountain areas. Applied to this context, frontier seems an ambiguous term (see Leveau and Palet 2010 for an interesting discussion of the Roman mountain frontiers and their perception). Mountains being invariably large areas, this term does not seem to be related to a well-delineated line in space nor a set of disputed lines separating areas with different administrative, legal, institutional, and sociocultural organizations. In this context, frontier seems to be more related to far-west iconography of no-man's-land, where productive activities and settlements are unstable and there is a factor of risk related to disputes between communities living at both sides of it.

It is true that the difficulty of movement (particularly with armies) and the ease of defense and hiding of mountain areas makes mountains fertile ground for guerrillas or highwaymen, as we commented in the particular case of the Spanish antifascist resistance. However, these kinds of frontiers are always temporary until a victory or agreement between the parts in conflict is achieved, and it would be wrong to put forward a characterization that is only valid during short periods of time. In fact, leaving aside the romantic adventurous view of the frontier, frontiers tend to be not just well-delimited natural areas but also areas of resources so important that they cannot be renounced by any of the communities living on both sides of them. A good example of this is rivers, often used as frontiers in the Greek and Roman classical period. Barcino, the Roman colony from which modern Barcelona developed, like many other classical cities, had its limits at the Llobregat and Besós Rivers, which provided invaluable resources to the inhabitants on both sides of them. The Évros River (currently Maritsa) marks the frontier between Bulgaria and Greece and Turkey and Greece at different parts of its route while the eponym river Ebro in Spain acts as a frontier of several administrative divisions alongside its course. This might explain the long duration of frontiers, even those of relatively small communities. Examples in lowland areas are abundant. The limits of the towns around the Albufera lagoon in Valencia (Figure 20.1), an important provider of resources for local communities, adapt and elongate to provide access to the lake to all of them. Many of the medieval town borders in the Baix Camp and Tarragonés regions, around the Roman capital of Tarraco, follow ancient Roman paths (Palet and Orengo 2011) probably to assure that both communities had unhindered access to the mobility and communication that these roads represented.

Although borders in mountains are more difficult to trace, the Garraf mountain range presents an interesting case study. Four large pastoral enclosures were studied and dated in the Garraf (Figure 20.1). From these, Marge del Moro, dated to the third century AD, was located at the border between Begues and Vallirana; Puig dels Avençons, dated to the sixth century AD, at the border between Begues and Olesa de Bonesvalls; and the biggest of these enclosures, which has two phases of use, one during the Bronze Age and the second during the Early Iron Age (and was probably in use at later stages), is located at the exact point of confluence of the limits between the populations of Begues, Olesa de Bonesvalls, Olivella, and Avinyonet del Penedès (Orengo and Palet 2018). It is worth noting how the town limit of Avinyonet del Penedès elongates, as in the case of the borders of the towns surrounding the Albufera lagoon, to give access to this particular enclosure, and by extension to the important resources that might have linked to it. In Andorra it is common to find between the medieval documentation complaints that groups from a different community have displaced the stones marking the commons limits to increase their pastures (Orengo 2010).

Borders and frontiers can be marginal and dangerous in dangerous times but they also serve to delimit precious resources to which several communities need access. With this discussion about borders I introduce a new topic, that of the economic importance of mountain areas.

Economic Importance

In a recent conference session on mountain economies, mountain resources were divided into rocks or stones, minerals, pigments, and wood. To these, most discussants would add

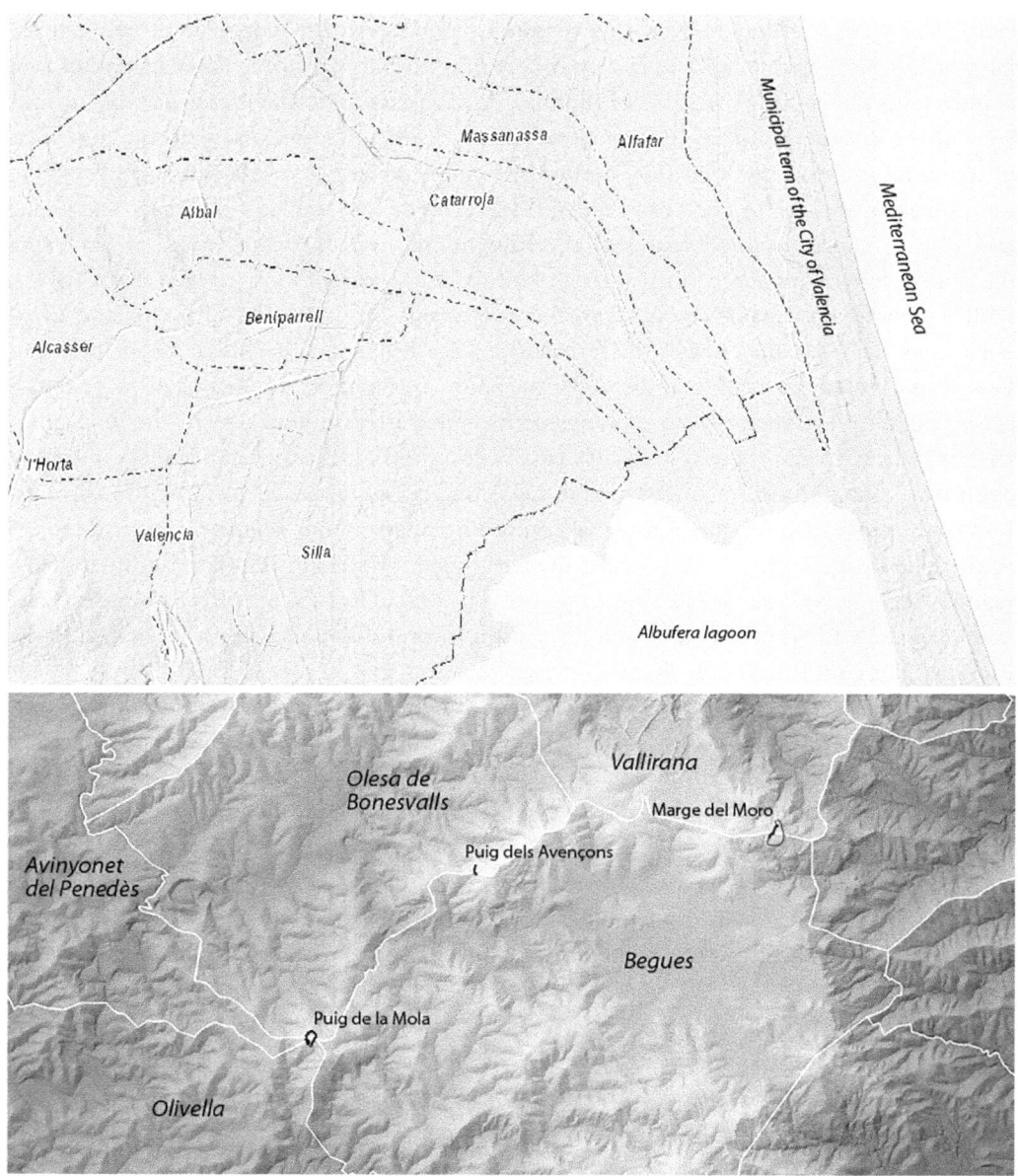

Figure 20.1. Territorial boundaries around the Albufera coastal lagoon (Valencia) and in the Garraf mountain range (Barcelona).

pastures in relation to their allegedly pastoral economic focus. It is true that those are the most evident natural resources found in mountain environmental settings, but agriculture is also present in terraces and sediment accumulation areas. I would argue, therefore, that the big difference in terms of resources between lowlands and mountains is therefore reduced to sea resources. Salt, in particular, is an important resource in high-mountain pastoral economies given the low mineralization of water there, which, nonetheless, can also be produced in mountain environments through saline water sources of which we have many examples in the Pyrenees.

From these resources a rather large amount of products can be derived, for which we only know about or can identify archaeologically a small part. Many of these can also be produced in lowlands, so, in my opinion, what makes a real difference is the capacity of the environment coupled with the particular socioeconomic context. For example, in the Madriu-Perafita-Claror Valleys (Andorra) an intensive activity of pitch extraction from pine trees from the second to the seventh century AD was identified (Orengo et al. 2013). This research also linked the production of pitch to that of charcoal, which was probably employed for the smelting of iron ore in kilns, such as those documented in the nearby Cadí Range at a similar height during the same period (Palet et al. 2010). The interesting fact about these data is that the production of pitch was using local techniques, just as that identified in the Massif Central in France, which was using pre-Roman materials (e.g., Trintignac 2003). This production was clearly not a Roman innovation; local populations producing pitch and charcoal were using their own traditional practices to respond to the new demand for iron and pitch brought by their integration into the Roman economic sphere. These could have been produced in lowland territories but not at such a large scale given the availability of ore and forest resources. It is the particular Roman economic context coupled with the large availability of certain resources and the experience exploiting them that create the opportunity for these mountain products to be exported over large distances. The importance of pitch in Andorra is also mentioned in a document dated to AD 860[3] (Baraut 1988) in which King Charles II "the Bald" confirms to Urgell his right to receive the tithe of the iron and pitch produced in Andorra. Since these were the only taxable industries of Andorra, they must have involved an important production. Ironically, the payment of a tithe for the produced pitch has been interpreted (Oliver 1998) as an indirect way to tax sheep, as these were marked using pitch. This is a good example of how the economic orientation of mountain areas tends to be interpreted following preconceived beliefs, even if, as in this case, it requires reinterpreting a straightforward document using complicated arguments to highlight the pastoral focus of this mountain area.

In a similar manner, the famous *perna cerretana*, which appears in the Latin sources, most significantly in Diocletian's Edict concerning the Sale Price of Goods, as an expensive pork ham exported from this same area (the Cerretania region included the area of Andorra) should be understood (Orengo et al. forthcoming) as a mountain commodity produced using traditional methods that was exported to the extremes of the empire as a luxury product.

Discussion: Mountains in Their Socioeconomic, Cultural, and Historical Context

Products such as iron, pitch, stone, charcoal, specific types of meat, cheese, ice and snow, lime, and quartzite are specific or can be produced at a larger scale in mountain ranges. This is an important distinction as it can mark the level of economic buoyancy of these areas depending on the particular socioeconomic situation of the period.

In periods like the Roman when a certain economic integration of the different territories of the empire propitiated large-scale production for extraregional trade, those territories with large availability of certain resources specialized and intensified their production. This can be seen in the particular focus on pitch and iron in the aforementioned Andorra example, products that were abundant in the area. Mountains during these periods were not isolated but wholeheartedly integrated within large-scale socioeconomic networks given their particular production types and the ease with which with they could produce them. This fairly compensated for the supposed isolation of these territories or the difficult access.

During the Middle Ages mountain resources continued to be perfectly integrated within their larger socioeconomic context. In Andorra the continuing production of iron and pitch during the ninth and tenth centuries, probably the only taxed products of the area, was indicative of trade and not just local and regional consumption. Pastoral produce was not taxed because it was probably directed toward local and regional consumption. This was perhaps related to the fact that most other communities, also in the lowlands, had their own pastoral production and therefore they would not invest in obtaining goods that they could produce themselves. Pastoralism in Andorra starts to be integrated in extraregional economic networks at a later stage, precisely when sheep rearing starts being a large-scale business for wool production. Between the eleventh and twelfth century transhumance movements start and the conflicts between the large monasteries of Santes Creus and Poblet in the lowlands for the rights of mountain pastures at this early moment (Vilà i Valentí 1991) illustrate well the economic value of these areas. Sheep transhumance increases its importance with the grouping of flocks coming from not just monasteries but landowners and towns during the twelfth and fourteenth centuries and so does the value of mountain pastures. At this moment we start finding multiple conflicts in the Andorran documentation for the right to exploit mountain pastures, which become an important economic resource for the community until the twentieth century, as the increasing population pressure and urbanization, drainage of coastal wetlands, agricultural expansion, and industrialization progressively reduced available pasture space in the lowlands and increased demand for animal produce. Iron and charcoal in Andorra continued to be important Andorran exports throughout this period (Codina 2005), particularly with the advent of industrialization, which required enormous amounts of both. This little economic history of Andorra serves to exemplify how these high-mountain valleys were never isolated from their socioeconomic context but tightly integrated. Interestingly, the nature of this integration changed with the particularities of the period, but specific products, such as iron and charcoal, continued being exported with more or less intensity.

The concentration of population and crop production in the lowlands, in particular coastal plains in eastern Spain, is an interesting concept that deserves further comment. As coastal wetlands were systematically drained from the seventeenth century onward, coastal ranges were deforested and population concentrated, lowlands were increasingly exploited for crop production and habitation. This process was, of course, exaggerated around large habitation nuclei. Cities became less self-sufficient, with important requirements that could only be provided by mountain areas. As a natural consequence of this process involving demand for and availability of produce, the value of locally produced crops decreased while that of mountain products increased. Many of those were absolutely necessary for the maintenance of urban lifestyle, such as ice for the transport and preservation of produce; charcoal and iron for the making of tools; timber, stone, and lime for construction; and, of course, wool, cheese, milk, and meat (Ejarque and Orengo 2009; Garcia-Molsosa 2013). While city populations were dependent on mountain resources, mountain nuclei were relatively self-sufficient through the use of terraces for crop production. Farmhouses in these areas increased their size during the modern period beyond that of any equivalent in the lowlands to become real production centers. Ironically, it is in part their "isolation" and low population density in combination with the particularity of the environment that renders their products such valuable resources.

It can be argued that people conducting these mountain industries were nonetheless underprivileged and had little access to the revenues of this trade. Indeed, many of the owners of mountain exploitations could have been living in cities. In any case, most people living in cities during the modern period were also quite low positioned in the social scale. It is only during the twentieth century with the important innovations on transport that allowed intercontinental trade that mountain resources have stopped being essential for lowland populations and investment in these areas decreased, leading often to depopulation. In my opinion this is, together with our ignorance of the diversity and value of mountain products, the basis for many allusions to and half-expressed opinions on the marginality of mountain landscapes. The nature of mountain–lowlands relations during the twentieth century is also a product of a socioeconomic context and does not form an intrinsic part of the character of mountain areas. As archaeologists and historians, we should better appreciate the value of context. Mountains continue to adapt to their historical and economic context today and the rise of mountain tourism, mountain sports, cannabis production or contraband, and, why not, mountain archaeology is proof of this evolving relation that forms a historical continuum in an integrated society.

Concluding Remarks

This chapter has tried to argue that mountain communities were always perfectly integrated within their environment. Their knowledge and know-how allowed them to modify it to their own needs, exploit it successfully, and live according to their own expectations without any looming sense of risk. Isolation, marginality, backwardness, traditionalism, or conservativism are necessarily subjective terms that are mostly held by outside observers and cannot be applied to mountain areas in general without a careful analysis of the particular socioeconomic and cultural factors of the period and area under study. Even then these terms can only refer to the particular topic being analyzed. Under such contextualization these concepts can also be applied to many lowland and coastal areas under particular situations and historical contexts. Mountain areas offer sufficiently different and diverse environments to count with particular resources (or in larger quantities) that are complementary to those found or produced in lowland areas. Their exploitation has generated important innovations and particular adaptations that have permitted mountain communities not just to feel comfortable within their environments but to develop successful economies during the last millennia. Our own socioeconomic background, which allows the obtention of resources that could only be found in mountains in the past, from long-distance sources has undermined the conception of mountains as wealthy. This joins to the fact that most researchers working today on mountains are strangers to them (even more so when past mountain societies are concerned) and may perceive them as alien, uncomfortable, poor, difficult, and/or risky. Together these factors are, in my view, responsible for these misconceptions.

This brief text is necessarily subjective, based on my own experience and observations working in European mountain areas and therefore partial in time and space. This is somehow unavoidable as here I am trying to deal with sometimes fuzzy concepts arising from the general constructs formed by our society's collective imaginary. With it I try to make manifest perceptions that most authors do not consider they hold and put them forward for open examination. Hopefully, it will contribute to highlight the enormous value of mountain areas for both past and future societies.

Notes

1. A selection of news reports referring to Cretan cannabis production: http://www.balkanalysis.com/blog/2005/08/29/cretan-drug-lords-defend-fields-with-land-mines-albanian-armed-guards/; http://www.ekathimerini.com/33862/article/ekathimerini/news/crete-drug-lords-in-police-battle; https://www.telegraph.co.uk/news/worldnews/europe/greece/2207277/Drug-dealing-shepherds-set-up-Crete-crime-empire.html; https://www.independent.co.uk/news/world/europe/greek-police-retreat-after-ambush-by-cretan-drug-gangsters-5329103.html; http://www.ekathimerini.com/221076/article/ekathimerini/news/police-destroy-cannabis-plants-in-crete.
2. A selection of these include: https://elpais.com/diario/2004/03/28/domingo/1080449559_850215.html; http://www.ccma.cat/tv3/alacarta/30-minuts/tor-la-muntanya-maleida/video/196447331/; http://www.ccma.cat/catradio/tor/tots/; http://lacampanaeditorial.com/llibre-267/; https://www.pageseditors.cat/ca/l-home-de-tor.html.
3. The document in fact indicates that the tithe on pitch was previous to this date as it only intends to confirm a right already in place. The continued taxation of iron and pitch after this date should also be assumed as the tithe right was confirmed in multiple documents until, at least, the tenth century.

References

Bahn, P. 1983 *Pyrenean Prehistory: A Palaeoeconomic Survey of the French Sites*. Aris & Phillips, London.
Baraut, C. 1988 *Cartulari de la vall d'Andorra, segles IX–XIII*. Vol. 1. Conselleria d'Educació i Cultura del Govern d'Andorra, Andorra la Vella.
Bertran i Soler, T. 1847 *Itinerario descriptivo de Cataluña*. Impremta de Olivares H., Barcelona.

Bertranpetit, J., and E. Vives (eds.) 1995 Muntanyes i població: El passat dels Pirineus des d'una perspectiva multidisciplinària. In *I Simposi de Poblament dels Pirineus*. Centre de Trobada de les Cultures Pirinenques, Andorra la Vella.

Chereji, C. R. 2018 Mediating Blood Feuds in the Cretan Mountains. https://www.mediate.com/articles/raduc1feud.cfm. Accessed June 20, 2018.

Codina, O. 2005 De fer et de laine: Economie et société des vallées Andorranes de 1575 à 1875. Unpublished doctoral dissertation, University of Perpignan.

Ejarque, A. 2013 *La alta montaña pirenaica: génesis y configuración holocena de un paisaje cultural—Estudio paleoambiental en el valle del Madriu-Perafita-Claror (Andorra)*. BAR International Series 2507. Archaeopress, Oxford.

Ejarque, A., Y. Miras, S. Riera, J. M. Palet, and H. A. Orengo 2010 Testing Micro-regional Variability in the Holocene Shaping of High Mountain Cultural Landscapes: A Palaeoenvironmental Case Study in the Eastern Pyrenees. *Journal of Archaeological Science* 37(7):1468–1479.

Ejarque, A., and H. A. Orengo 2009 Legacies of Change: The Shaping of Cultural Landscapes in a Marginal Mediterranean Range, Garraf Massif, Northeastern Spain. *Oxford Journal of Archaeology* 28(4): 425–440.

Freeman, C. 2008 Drug-Dealing Shepherds Set Up Crete Crime Empire. *Telegraph*, June 28. https://www.telegraph.co.uk/news/worldnews/europe/greece/2207277/Drug-dealing-shepherds-set-up-Crete-crime-empire.html. Accessed June 20, 2018.

Garcia-Molsosa, A. 2013 Arqueologia dels paisatges culturals del massís del Montseny: Dinàmiques històriques de la prehistòria a l'Edat Mitjana. Unpublished PhD thesis, Institut Català d'Arqueologia Clàssica, Rovira i Virgili University.

Gassiot Ballbè, E., A. Rodríguez, D. Antón, L. Obea Gómez, M. Quesada Carrasco, and S. Díaz Bonilla 2017 The Beginning of High Mountain Occupations in the Pyrenees: Human Settlements and Mobility from 18,000 cal BC to 2000 cal BC. In *High Mountain Conservation in a Changing World*, edited by J. Catalan, J. M. Ninot, and M. M. Aniz. Advances in Global Change Research 62. Springer.

Leveau, P., and J. M. Palet 2010 Les Pyrénées romaines, la frontière, la ville et la montagne: L'apport de l'archéologie du paysage. *PALLAS* 82:171–198.

Llovera, X. 1986 La Feixa del Moro (Juberri) i el Neolític Mig-Recent a Andorra. *Tribuna d'Arqueologia*:15–24.

Mateo, M., and A. Gómez 2004 La Pequeña Edad del Hielo en Andorra: episodios morfogenéticos y su relación con la producción de cereales en Europa. *Boletín de la Sociedad Española de Historia Natural (Sección Geológica)* 99:173–183.

Miras, Y., A. Ejarque, H. A. Orengo, S. Riera, J. M. Palet, and A. Poiraud 2010 Prehistoric Impact on Landscape and Vegetation at High Altitudes: An Integrated Palaeoecological and Archaeological Approach in the Eastern Pyrenees (Perafita Valley, Andorra). *Plant Biosystems* 144(4):946–961.

Miras, Y., A. Ejarque, S. Riera, J. M. Palet, H. A. Orengo, and I. Euba 2007 Dynamique holocène de la végétation et occupation des Pyrénées andorranes depuis le Néolithique ancien, d'après l'analyse pollinique de la tourbière de Bosc dels Estanyons (2180 m, Vall del Madriu, Andorre). *Comptes Rendus Palevol* 6(4):291–300.

Morín, J., B. Díaz, R. Barroso, M. Escolà, M. López, A. Pérez-Juez, R. Recio, and F. Sánchez 2004 Arqueología de la Guerrilla Antifranquista en Toledo. La 14.ª División de la 1.ª Agrupación del Ejército de Extremadura y Centro. *Bolskan* 21:181–188.

Oliver, J. 1998 El delme de la pega de la Seu d'Urgell a Andorra en els inicis del domini feudal del pastoralisme pirinenc. *Annals del Centre de Barcelona* 1996:157–168.

Orengo, H. A. 2010 Arqueología de un paisaje cultural pirenaico de alta montaña: Dinámicas de ocupación del valle del Madriu-Perafita-Claror (Andorra). Unpublished doctoral dissertation, Institut català d'Arqueologia Clàssica–Universitat Rovira i Virgili.

Orengo, H. A., and J. M. Palet 2018 *Memòria científica de les activitats realitzades en el marc del projecte "Els orígens del pastoralisme intensiu i la creació de paisatges culturals al nord-est de la Península Ibèrica."* Project report delivered to the Department of Culture of the Generalitat de Catalunya.

Orengo, H. A., J. M. Palet, A. Ejarque, Y. Miras, and S. Riera 2013 Pitch Production during the Roman Period: An Intensive Mountain Industry for a Globalised Economy? *Antiquity* 87(337):802–814.

Orengo, H. A., J. M. Palet, A. Ejarque, Y. Miras, and S. Riera 2014 The Historical Configuration of a UNESCO World Heritage Site: The Cultural Landscape of the Madriu-Perafita-Claror Valley. *Archeologia Postmedievale* 17(2013):333–343.

Orengo, H. A., A. Ejarque, Y. Miras, S. Riera, and J. M. Palet Forthcoming The Perna Ceretana: A Mountain Ham Exported Internationally as a Luxury Product during the Roman Period.

Palet, J. M., and H. A. Orengo 2011 The Roman Centuriated Landscape: Conception, Genesis and Development as Inferred from the Ager Tarraconensis Case. *American Journal of Archaeology* 115(3):383–402.

Palet, J. M., A. Ejarque, Y. Miras, S. Riera, I. Euba, and H. A. Orengo 2007 Formes d'ocupació d'alta muntanya a la Vall de la Vansa (Serra del Cadí—Alt Urgell) i la vall de Madriu-Perafita-Claror (Andorra): estudi diacrònic de paisatges culturals pirinencs. *Tribuna d'Arqueologia* 2006:229–253.

Palet, J. M., H. A. Orengo, A. Ejarque, I. Euba, Y. Miras, and S. Riera 2010 Formas de paisaje de montaña y ocupación del territorio en los Pirineos orientales en época romana: estudios pluridisciplinares en el valle del Madriu-Perafita-Claror (Andorra) y en la Sierra del Cadí (Cataluña). *Bollettino di Archeologia online* 1:67–79.

Palet Martínez, J. M., A. Garcia-Molsosa, H. A. Orengo Romeu, and T. Polonio Alamino 2017 Els espais altimontans pirenaics orientals a l'Antiguitat: 10 anys d'estudis en arqueologia del paisatge del GIAP-ICAC. *Treballs d'Arqueologia* 21:77–97.

Porta, C. 2005 *Tor, tretze cases i tres morts*. La Campana Editorial, Barcelona.

Servera, G., Y. Miras, S. Riera, R. Julià, P. Allée, H. A. Orengo, S. Paradis-Grenouillet, and J. M. Palet 2013 Tracing the Land Use History and Vegetation Dynamics in the Mont Lozère (Massif Central, France) during the Last 2000 Years: The Interdisciplinary Study Case of Countrasts Peat Bog *Quaternary International* 353:123–139.

Trintignac, A. 2003 La production de poix dans la cité des Gabales (Lozère) à l'époque gallo-romaine. *Revue Archéologique de Picardie* 1/2:239–248.

Tsantiropoulos, A. 2008 Collective Memory and Blood Feud: The Case of Mountainous Crete. *Crimes and Misdemeanours: Deviance and the Law in Historical Perspective* 2(1):60–80.

Vilà i Valentí, J. 1991 Evolució històrica de la transhumància a Catalunya. *Treballs de la Societat Catalana de Geografia* 25:63–72.

Walsh, K. 2005 Risk and Marginality at High Altitudes: New Interpretations from Fieldwork on the Faravel Plateau, Hautes-Alpes. *Antiquity* 79:289–305.

Yáñez, C. 2005 El Neolític. In *Història d'Andorra*, edited by E. Belenguer, 51–76. Edicions 62, Barcelona.

Contributors

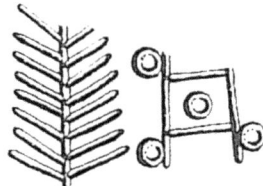

Andrey B. Belinskiy, OOO Nasledie
José Alejandro Beltrán-Caballero, Seminar of Ancient Topography, Rovira i Virgili University
Robert H. Brunswig, Department of Anthropology, University of Northern Colorado
Florian Couderc, Université Toulouse 2 Jean-Jaurès, CNRS, UMR 5608, TRACES
Michael R. Coughlan, Institute for a Sustainable Environment, University of Oregon
Felipe Criado-Boado, Institute of Heritage Sciences (Incipit), Spanish National Research Council (CSIC)
Cecilia Dal Zovo, Institute of Heritage Sciences (Incipit), Spanish National Research Council (CSIC)
Wieke de Neef, University of Ghent
Ana Ejarque, ISEM, CNRS, Université de Montpellier
Daniela Festi, Institute for Interdisciplinary Mountain Research, Austrian Academy of Sciences
Michael L. Galaty, Museum of Anthropological Archaeology, University of Michigan
Arnau Garcia-Molsosa, Institute for European and Mediterranean Archaeology, State University of New York at Buffalo
Emilie Gauthier, Laboratoire Chrono-environnement, UMR6249/CNRS, Université de Franche-Comté, Besançon
Mercourios Georgiadis, Catalan Institute of Classical Archaeology
Ted L. Gragson, Department of Archaeology, University of Georgia and Université de Toulouse
Eva Kaptijn, Erfgoed Gelderland
Dmitrij S. Korobov, Institute of Archaeology, Russian Academy of Sciences
Marlène Lavrieux, Institut des Sciences de la Terre d'Orléans (ISTO), UMR 7327 CNRS, Université d'Orléans and Department of Environmental Sciences, University of Basel
Mélanie Le Couédic, ITEM, Université de Pau et des Pays de l'Adour
Paul M. Ledger, CNRS, Université Clermont Auvergne, GEOLAB and Department of Archaeology, Queen's College, Memorial University of Newfoundland
David S. Leigh, Department of Archaeology, University of Georgia

Ricardo Mar, Seminar of Ancient Topography, Rovira i Virgili University
Michela Mariani, School of Geography, University of Nottingham
Lene Melheim, Museum of Cultural History, University of Oslo
Yannick Miras, CNRS, UMR 7194, Histoire Naturelle de l'Homme Préhistorique, Département de Préhistoire, Muséum National d'Histoire Naturelle, Institut de Paléontologie Humaineand CNRS, Université Clermont Auvergne, GEOLAB
Franco Nicolis, Archaeological Heritage Office of the Autonomous Province of Trento
Klaus D. Oeggl, Department of Botany, University of Innsbruck
Hèctor A. Orengo, Catalan Institute of Classical Archaeology (ICAC)
Josep M. Palet, Catalan Institute of Classical Archaeology (ICAC)
Jeroen Poblome, Sagalassos Archaeological Research Project, Department of Archaeology, KU Leuven
Tania Polonio, Catalan Institute of Classical Archaeology (ICAC)
Christopher Prescott, The Norwegian Institute in Rome, University of Oslo
Andreas Putzer, South Tyrol Museum of Archaeology
Sabine Reinhold, Eurasia Department of the German Archaeological Institute
Santiago Riera, Seminar of Researches and Studies on Prehistory, University of Barcelona (SERP-UB)
Ana Ruíz-Blanch, Institute of Heritage Sciences (Incipit), Spanish National Research Council (CSIC)
Jan Sevink, Institute for Biodiversity and Ecosystem Dynamics (IBED), University of Amsterdam
Phillips Stevens Jr., Department of Anthropology, State University of New York at Buffalo
Pawel Valde-Nowak, Institute of Archaeology, Jagiellonian University
Ralf Vandam, Sagalassos Archaeological Research Project, Department of Archaeology, KU Leuven and Department of Art Sciences and Archaeology, Vrije Universiteit Brussel
Martijn van Leusen, University of Groningen
Patrick T. Willett, Sagalassos Archaeological Research Project, Department of Archaeology, KU Leuven, Department of Anthropology, State University of New York at Buffalo

Index

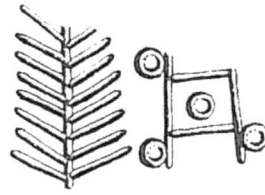

Aaron, 47
Abobeira (Serra da), 24
Abraham, 38
Adirondack Mountains, 43
Aegean (region), 10, 78–79, 81–83, 303
Ağlasun valley, 307, 311–314, 319
Agunbek (site), 157
Agung, mount, 37, 47
Ahmet Zogu, 355
Aigaleon, Mount, 353–354
Aigols Podrits (site), 185–186
Alagir gorge, 156, 161
Albufera lagoon (València), 391–392
Alpide or Alpine-Himalayan orogenic belt, 154
Alpine, 4–5, 11, 14, 95–97, 100, 118, 130, 132, 141–142, 146, 181, 198, 351; alpine (or "european") marriage pattern, 351; alpine-subalpine ecotone, 100; archaeology, 154; cabin, 133; communities, 119; environment, 139, 141; front (First World War), 148; high-alpine 111, 118–120, 156, 211; pastoral economy, 154; pastoral systems, 117–118; pre-alpine, 267; valley communities, 144
Alps, 10–11, 23, 96–98, 119, 131, 133, 139, 141–142, 147, 153–154, 156, 180, 192, 212, 262, 264; Austrian, 153; central, 3, 119, 172; eastern alps, 3, 11, 117–119, 147; French, 133; high, 10; Italian, 212; southern, 142; swiss, 96–98, 131, 133; western, 180, 192
Alta-Kautokeino dam, 199, 203
Altan Shiree (site), 65
Altar, 40, 47, 58, 65, 80
Amber, 211
Amelestoy (site), 285, 289–290, 297
Anatolian or Central Plateau, 303
Andes, 19–20, 26, 32, 39, 46, 361–362, 365, 377–378; central, 3, 21; high, 68; northern, 3
Animals, 29, 44, 46, 51, 63, 82, 88, 100, 153, 162–163, 165–166, 168–169, 233, 281, 339, 394; domesticated, 10, 95–96, 104, 106–107, 157, 160, 209–210, 221, 248, 278; herbivores, 101, 198, 220–222, 280; ungulate, 118–119; wild 29, 63, 81, 107, 156, 198
Anitkythera island, 86
Ano Englianos mountain ridge, 353–354
Antchologuia (site), 290, 295–297
anthropocene, 28, 254, 294

antiquity, 7–8, 11, 179, 186, 191–193, 214, 288, 314; late 179, 186, 191–193, 311–317
antler, 201, 205, 211
Apennines, 3, 12, 325–326, 337
Apurimac valley, 380
arable lands, 12, 234, 269, 312–314, 361
Araxes river valley, 155, 157
Arboriculture, 312
Arctic Circle, 198, 219, 221
Årdal (mountains), 207–208, 210
Arukhlo (site), 155
Atacameños/Lincan Antai, 21
Auge, The Duke of, 139–140
Auvergne mountains, 253, 255–256, 260, 262–264, 266–267, 270, 274
Avalanches, 127, 150
Aydat lake (site), 257, 259–261, 264, 266–267
ayios yeoryios sto vouno (site), 78, 81–83, 85–88
Aymara, 21

baal/hadad, 46
Babia Góra massif, 238
Bachama culture, 44
backwardness, 385–387, 389, 395
Baden Culture, 104, 245–246
baetyl, 87–88
Bagargi (site), 285, 289–290
Baga Shiree (site), 63
Balkan marriage system, 351, 354
Barbanza, sierra de, 24–27
Barcino (site), 391
Bargari (site), 297
Basque, 282, 290
Bata, 44
Bavarian Forest, 236–237, 247
bear, 156, 211
Behastoy (site), 285, 289–290, 297
Bell Beaker culture, 211
Belören/Keraia (site), 317
Bereket valley, 312, 314
Besakih, 37, 47
Beskidy mountains, 94, 104–107, 234, 237–238, 242–246

Besós river, 391
Bey Dağları Massif, 307
Beyşehir Occupation Phase (BO-Phase), 312, 314
Białka river, 102
Biały Dunajec river, 102
Biesiadki (site), 105, 242
Bieszczady mountains, 105–107
Birkenmajer, K., 235
bison, 101, 103
Bjeshkët e Namuna mountains, 343–344, 346
Black Elk, 42
Black Forest, 234, 236, 248
blood feuds, 345, 356–357, 388
Bogd Khan Uul mountain, 57
bone; animal, 82, 87, 95, 157, 165–166, 172, 201, 205, 209, 211, 248, 330, 332; carved 101; human, 83, 223, 290, 297
Borobudur temple, 40
Boz Çayı river, 306
Breheimen, 203
bronze, 34; or early iron, 290
Bronze Age, 10, 13, 23–24, 31–32, 56, 79, 89, 100, 184, 186, 206–212, 253, 255, 293–294, 328, 343, 349, 351, 391; Early, 104, 106–108, 133, 139, 142, 179, 192, 265–267, 270, 330, 332–334; Late, 58–59, 64–65, 86, 117–118, 120, 124, 127, 129–130, 133–134, 139, 144, 146, 153, 155, 159–162, 164, 167–170, 208–209, 268, 355, 337–338, 351, 353; Middle, 86, 130, 133, 139, 142, 159–160, 164–165, 266, 268, 288–290, 334, 336
Buddhism, 38, 40, 54, 64; buddhist stupas, 23, 47, 58, 65
büğdüz Çayı river, 306
Bükk culture, 105
Burdur plain, 303–319
burial, 29, 58, 81, 89, 104, 159–161, 165, 241, 245, 372; cremation, 289–290; ground, 46, 83–85; khirigsuur, 23, 58–59, 65; monuments, 51–161; mounds, 55–57, 68, 70, 159–161, 165
burning, 190, 239, 278, 281, 286–290, 389

Burustolia (site), 296–297
Byzantine, 313, 315, 317, 321, 336
Bølling/Allerød Interstadial (Late Glacial) warming, 101

cableway, 148
Cadí mountain range, 180–181, 183–184, 188, 190–193, 393
Campo Lameiro (site), 24
campsite, 12–13, 54–55, 58, 61–65, 95–98, 100–104, 106–107, 162–163, 165, 246, 391
  hunting, 96, 103–104, 114; *seater,* 222; *stani,* 347
caribou, 223
Carpathians, 3, 11, 106; foothills, 240, 242; polish, 235–237, 244–246; Western, 10, 93–94, 100, 102, 104–105, 108, 111–113, 115, 236, 250
Carrowmore (site), 24
Caspian sea, 57, 155
Castro Lupario (site), 29
Çatal Höyük (site), 46
cattle, 29, 45–36, 104, 133, 157–158, 160–161, 165–166, 168, 204, 206, 211, 221–223, 239, 247–248, 347, 353, 390
Caucasus; central, 157, 160, 166; greater, 154–158, 160; lesser, 155, 160, 170; North, 3, 11, 153, 156–157, 160–161, 165, 169–170; Northwest, 97, 157; Russian, 96; South, 155–158, 160, 165
cave, 40, 97–104, 156–157, 184, 200, 206–207, 210–211, 311, 351; Mortuary-Cave, 290, 297; sacred, 79–80
cemetery, 24, 153, 160–161, 166, 169, 311
Cerdanya valley, 180, 184, 191–192, 393; *perna cerretana,* 393
Pork, 393
ceremonial center, 361–363, 367, 372, 374, 377–381
Cergowa Mount, 237
Chacan River, 374
chaîne des puys, 253, 255–257, 261
Chalcolithic, 266, 319, 332; late, 311, 317
Cham Group, 237

Chantemerle (site), 266
Charcoal, 102, 120, 122, 142, 160, 184–185, 188, 245, 257, 262, 284–286, 289, 329–330, 332; accumulation, 277–282, 288–289, 291–292; mounds, 183; production, 11, 186, 191–193, 393–395
Charles II "The Bald" (King), 393
chicken, 82, 221
Chinchero plateau, 365, 376, 380
Chobareti (site), 155, 160
Choquechaca river, 378
Choquequirao Pukio (site), 379
Chunchulmayo (river), 368
Cmi (site), 155–156, 161
Coma del Freser valley, 180, 183, 185
Coma de Vaca valley, 180, 183–185, 191
Coma de Vaca I (site), 186–187
comb production, 205
contraband, 387–389, 395
copper age, 120, 332
Corded Ware Culture, 106, 237–238
Corent (site), 257–258, 262, 264, 268–269
cosmology, 19, 38–39, 46, 51, 54, 56–57, 59–61, 64–65
Cova del Catau de l'Ós (site), 184
Crete, 78–83, 85–86, 88, 387–388
Cusco (site), 12, 361–366, 368–370, 378, 380–381
Czarny Dujanek (site), 102

Dąbrówka (site), 244
Dachstein region, 133
Dairy production, 133, 168–169, 207, 247, 290–293; cheese, 144, 193, 200, 387, 393, 395; milk, 144, 183, 188, 193, 222, 387, 395; strainers, 144–145
Dakaj (site), 351, 353
dam, 198–199, 203–204, 369
Danube river, 46
deer, 59, 104, 142, 156, 211
deities/gods, 20–21, 29, 32, 37–40, 44–48, 56, 59, 79–82, 86, 88, 362, 372
Dereköy Highlands, 303–319
Devesa do Rei (site), 31, 33

Diné (Navajo), 40
Diocletian's edict, 393
Dogs, 221
Domeyko mountain range, 21
Don river, 157
Dosso Rotondo (site), 142–145, 147
Dovrefjell (site), 205
Dovre mountains, 205
Drahanovice (site), 245
drinking cups, 82, 87
Drin river, 353
Drymonas, Mount, 78, 86
Düğer Çayı river, 306
düldül yüzü (site), 316–317
Dunajec river, 102, 240, 242, 246
Durfeld (site), 247
Dzdaghi (site), 155
Dzdzuna Klde (site), 156
Dzud-zuna (site), 155

Eka Dasa Rudra festival, 47
Ekashevsk (site), 165
Elbrus, Mount, 155, 161
elk/moose, 101, 104, 198
Els Estanys (site), 186
enclosure, 120, 153, 157, 163, 183–188, 191, 240, 314, 391; corral, 55, 63; pens, 222, 311, 314; sheepfolds, 225
Eneolithic, 157–160
Enveig mountain, 192
Epigravettian, 99
Epipaleolithic, 318
Erik the Red, 220, 222
Espinasse fen (site), 257–259, 261–262, 264, 267–268
Ethnicity, 197, 200, 202, 213, 282
European Landscape Convention, 141
Evans, Arthur, 45
Évros river, 391

farming, 11, 14, 93, 96, 104–107, 156–157, 183, 192, 197, 210, 219–222, 225–226, 235–236, 239, 260, 269–273, 278, 306–307, 312–313, 321, 347, 349, 374; mountain, 153, 160, 168–170, 198, 200, 206–207
farmsteads, 16, 81, 83, 198, 211, 220, 222–223, 226, 273, 282, 311, 314, 317, 336, 349, 371, 380, 395; summer farms/shielings, 144, 200, 202, 204, 207–208
feud, 343, 345, 356–357, 388
figurine, 80, 82, 87, 103
Finail Valley, 133
Finisterre, 29
Finsevatn lake, 201
fishing, 95, 98, 200, 207, 211, 222–223, 227, 236
Fløyrlivatn (site), 198, 203
fodder, 5, 95, 119, 156, 221–222, 225, 240, 267, 336; winter, 165, 167–168, 239
Fodio, Usman dan, 44
Fontalba (site), 187, 191
Fontanille (site), 266
forest, 5, 42, 93, 102, 132–133, 144, 154, 158, 165–166, 180, 197, 204, 227, 248, 336, 386–387; alpine, 192; beech, 256, 260; clearances, 8, 11, 96, 98, 105–106, 124, 127, 130, 142, 147, 156, 179, 182, 184–186, 188, 190–193, 198, 209, 222, 239, 253, 255, 260, 262, 266–268, 277–283, 286–289, 293–294, 312, 318, 389, 394; coniferous, 234, 256; deciduous, 234–236, 239, 305, 312; mountain, 11, 106, 127, 260, 266–267; oak, 260, 314; pine, 120–121, 124, 127, 181, 185–186, 188; pine, 181; subalpine forests, 124, 179
forestry, 11, 13–14, 147, 156, 179, 181, 183, 187–188, 190–191, 201, 209, 280, 314, 391–395
fowl, 211
Frattesina (site), 146
Frazer, J. G., 46
Fuji, Mount, 47
Funnel Beaker Culture (FBC), 105–106, 206, 237, 245

Galician Massif, 3
Galileo Galilei, 47

Gallia Narbonense (Roman Province), 192
Garcilaso de la Vega, 368, 377
Garðar Igaliku (site), 222
Garraf Massif, 391–392
Gegenii Ovoo (site), 65
Gergovie (site), 261
glacier, 5, 8, 10, 96, 101, 109. 117, 132–133, 148, 188, 197–198, 201, 204, 212
goat, 63, 81–82, 104, 118, 157–158, 165, 168, 170, 206, 209, 211, 221–223, 336, 347, 351, 353
Gobi-Altai mountains, 10, 23, 51, 53, 58, 61–62, 66
Goleró (site), 188, 190
Gravgaz valley, 312, 314
grinding: facilities, 165; stones, 157, 167, 313
Grotte du Noisetier (site), 97
Grunas (site), 343–344, 347, 349–353, 356
Gumbashi pass (site), 160, 162
Gwari, 44
Gwoździec (site), 105

Hacılar (site), 306
Hallstatt (site), 7, 153–154
Hannibal, 147
Hardangerjøkulen glacier, 201
Hardangervidda mountain plateau, 197, 199, 201, 203–208, 210, 213
Harz forest, 93, 234
Hellenistic period, 85, 330
heritage, 2, 53–54, 65, 183, 193, 199, 203–204, 270–271; cultural, 5, 14, 51, 66, 89, 141, 180, 197, 226, 339; heritagization, 14, 180; immaterial, 56; technological, 144; UNESCO World Heritage, 181, 256
Herod, 29
heroe, 40, 43–44
hides, 101, 211
hiking, 42–43, 200–201, 339
Himalayas, 23–24, 38, 57
Hispania Tarraconense (Roman Province), 192
Holocene, 3, 124, 235, 254, 257, 288, 290; early, 23, 96–98, 103, 156, 198, 313; late 195, 245, 276, 326

Horns of consecration (Minoan cultic symbols), 45, 80, 87
horse, 101, 103, 133, 165–166, 168, 170, 221, 388, 390
Hoxha, Enver, 355
Hoz, Sancho de la, 377
hunter-gatherers, 10, 13, 96, 100, 102, 156, 200–201, 206, 210–211, 219, 311, 314, 318
hunting, 93, 96–98, 101, 103–104, 118, 106, 142, 144, 156, 198, 205, 207, 209, 211–212, 222–223, 234, 244, 314; seasonal, 102, 200, 206
hut/cabin, 133, 148, 183–184, 186–188, 191, 201, 206, 208–209, 284, 311, 336
Hvalsey (site), 223
hydraulic infrastructure, 369
hydroelectric power development, 5, 8, 197–199, 203–204, 207–208, 211, 213–214

Ibarrandoua (site), 283, 285–286, 288, 290–293, 295–297
ibex, 142
ice patch archaeology, 10, 197–198, 200, 204, 211–214
Igaliku (site), 220–222, 224–225
Ihitsaga (site), 283, 286–288, 291–294, 296–297
Ikh Bod Uul (IBU) Mountain, 10, 23, 51–66
Ilicino, mount, 29
Illapa (God), 372; temple, 372–373, 376
inka, 12, 19, 21, 361–381; empire (Tawantinsuyu), 363, 366, 368, 377, 380–383; pre-Inka, 367
Inkilltambo (site), 379
inselbergs, 37–38, 44
Inuit, 220, 223, 226
Iria Flavia (site), 29
iron age, 13, 23–24, 31, 58, 64, 69, 75, 122, 127, 130, 176, 184, 186, 207, 217, 253, 255, 268, 293–294, 317, 325, 328, 340, 343, 349; early, 70, 73, 124, 133, 152–153, 161, 169, 173, 209–210, 272, 290, 391; late, 133, 205, 288, 290
irrigation, 119, 123, 154, 222, 305, 333, 349, 357, 361, 365, 370, 376, 380

Isaac, 38
Isaiah, 42
Istasyon (site), 316
Iulia Libica (site), 191–192

Jaça del Mig (site), 191
Jaroszowice (site), 243
Jasło-Krosno basin, 105–106
Java island, 40
Jezercë, Mount, 346, 353
Jotunheimen mountains, 200
Juktas, Mount, 37, 45, 80–81, 90
Jupiter, 29

Kabardinka (site), 162–169
Kachimayo river, 371, 374–376, 379
Kailas mount, 38–39
Kallachaca (site), 379
Kalvebeitet (site), 209
Kamiennik, Mount, 105, 244
Kanuni i Lekë Dukagjinit (The Code of Lekë Dukagjini), 344–345, 347, 349, 351, 354, 356–358
Kapı Kaya (site), 317
Kastri (site), 78, 81–82
Katafygadi cave (site), 78, 83–85
Khun Tolgoi (site), 65
Killke culture, 367
King, Marthin Luther Jr., 37, 42
Kislovodsk basin, 157, 159–161, 165, 169–170
Kjølskarvet (site), 198
Klady necropolis (site), 160
Knossos (site), 37, 45, 47, 80–81
Koban (site), 153, 155, 161, 169
Kofinas peak sanctuary (site), 80
Kofyar, 347, 349–350
Kondratowa valley, 107
Kotis (site), 155–156
Kraków-Częstochowa upland, 101, 104
Kremna (site), 317
Kura-Araxes culture, 160
Kura river, 155, 157
Kuruçay (site), 306
Kusilluchayoc (site), 376

Kvikne (site), 198
Kvitingkjølen (site), 212
Kythera island, 3, 10, 77, 81–83, 87–89

Lac du Puy (site), 257–258, 262, 264, 268
La Chomette (site), 266
Laerdal valley, 200, 203
Lagaun mire (site), 120–122, 124, 126–127, 130, 132–133
Lalinde-Gönnersdorf culture, 103
Laqo temple (site), 374, 376
Lavarone Luserna plateau, 146
Layat (site), 265
Lazarianika grave (site), 84
Lepenski Vir (site), 46
Leska peak (site), 10, 77–78, 81–90
Lessini mountains, 141
Likancabur mountain, 21
Limagne plain, 253, 255–257, 261, 265–266
linear, 82, 104–105, 110–111, 118, 162–163, 165–167, 240–242, 249, 308, 353, 357
Linear Band pottery culture (LBK), 104–105, 110–111, 163, 165–167, 240–244, 246
Lithic industry, 87, 94–98, 101–102, 104–107, 141–142, 144, 157, 165, 170, 198, 205, 211, 240, 243–244, 246, 309, 311, 314, 319, 372; axes, 104, 205–206, 236–239, 242, 245–247; bifaces, 207, 209; obsidian, 105; sickle, 144, 313; stone vessels, 80, 82–83, 209
Little Ice Age, 223, 226, 390
livestock, 144, 147, 165–168, 179, 183–188, 191–193, 221, 224, 226, 240, 248, 281, 286, 290, 394
Llobregat river, 391
Łoniowa (site), 104–105, 240–242
Luserna Pletz von Mozze (site), 143, 146, 152

Machu Pichu (site), 7
Maddalena basin, 325, 327–328, 335
Madriu-Perafita-Claror valleys (MPCV), 180–181, 183–184, 186, 188–189, 191, 193–194, 387, 393, 397

Magdalenian, 108; Epi-Magdalenian, 102–103; late, 96–97, 99–104, 110, 113–115
Makwada, 44
Maleas cape, 86
Malta (site), 295, 297
Marcy, Mount, 43
Marge del Moro (site), 391
Massif Central, 3, 11, 255, 393
Maszycka cave (site), 100
Maykop culture, 159–160
Mediterranean, 12, 141, 179, 193, 268–270, 315, 353, 357–378
megalithism, 24–25, 27, 32, 34; cromlech, 290, 297; dolmen, 261, 297; menhir, 261
Mermigkari, Mount, 82–86, 89
Meru, mount, 40
Meshoko (site), 155, 157–158
Mesolithic, 46, 96, 98–99, 103, 133, 141–142, 198, 235, 237; late, 206
Messenia (site), 353
metallurgy, 7, 13, 87, 144, 160–161, 170, 198, 207, 211, 235, 264, 309, 311, 391; copper, 139, 144, 146–147, 156, 211, 236; iron, 183, 185–186, 190–192, 202–205, 314, 393–395; mining, 11, 54, 95, 100, 147, 154, 156, 160–161, 166, 179, 181, 183, 191–192, 227
Middle Ages, 8, 11, 30, 47, 140, 147, 179, 192, 205, 201, 207–208, 218, 221–226, 269, 290, 292–294, 391, 394; Early, 30, 75, 187, 191, 193, 215, 356; late, 343, 349, 355
Millagate (site), 285, 289–290, 297–298
Minoan, 10, 87–88; linear A, 82
Moadalen valley, 210–211
Modern Age, 20, 206, 210
Mousterian; late, 96–97, 99
Montané, Josep ("Sansa"), 388
Morkil lake, 365–366
Moses, 38, 42
mountain; communities, 4, 6–7, 12–13, 156, 160, 385, 387, 395–396; economy, 6–7, 154, 166–167, 170, 385–386, 391; high, 8, 11, 13–14, 23, 51, 53–54, 60–61, 64–66, 83, 96, 98–100, 104, 106, 139, 147, 153–154, 156, 161, 165–166, 170, 179–180, 183–184, 186, 188, 190–193, 202, 386–389, 392, 394; low, 93, 100, 108; middle, 11, 93, 96–97, 99–100, 102–103, 106–107, 156–158, 233–237, 239, 241–243, 245–249, 251, 260, 278–279; pass, 59, 160, 162, 184, 248, 353, 388; sacred mountains, 9, 20–21, 24, 26, 28, 32, 34, 37–43, 45, 47–57, 59, 61, 63, 65–69, 71, 73, 75, 81, 361, 365, 368, 371–377, 379–380
Mount Moriah, 38
mule, 334, 387
mustelids, 211
Mycenaean, 146, 343, 349, 353–357; linear B, 353, 357
Mylopotamos, 84, 89
myth, 20–21, 23, 26, 31–32, 37–38, 40, 44, 78, 200, 202, 380

Neanderthal, 96–97
Neolithic, 10, 28, 32, 46, 93, 96, 100, 108, 117–122, 124, 130–131, 133–134, 142, 156–159, 201, 208, 212, 220, 234–239, 245, 253–254, 264, 268, 277–278, 287, 318, 336–337; Early neolithic, 104–105, 179, 184, 192, 210, 233, 240, 242, 246, 262, 266, 287; Late/Final, 98, 106–107, 184–186, 198, 206–207, 209–211, 233, 239–240, 242, 246–247, 261, 265–267, 356; Middle, 105, 179, 184–185, 192, 198, 205, 242, 260–263, 270, 389
Nero, 315
Nichoria (site), 354–355
Nieznajowa (site), 237
Nika, Ded, 346
Noisetier (site), 97
Novosvobodnaya-Klady (site), 155, 160
Nowa Biała (site), 102–103
Núria valley, 180, 183–184
Nyset-Steggje valleys, 199–200, 203–204, 207–208, 210–211

Obłazowa cave (site), 103
O Castriño de Conxo (site), 31

Oglio river, 133
Ollantaytambo (site), 370
Olympus, Mount, 26, 40
Orawa-Nowy Targ (Podhale) Basin, 102–104
Orog Nuur lake, 52–53, 58, 61
Orris de la Torbera de Perafita (site), 184
Ortles Cevedale massif, 147–148
Ossau valley, 192
Ottoman period, late, 311, 314–315
Ötzi, mummy of, 7, 117, 121, 139, 141
Ötztal mountains, 120, 130, 134
ovoo cairns, 23, 57–60, 64–65

Pachacuti Inka Yupanqui, 363, 372, 377
Pachamama, 44, 380
Pachatosa, Waka (site), 374, 376
Paio, 29
Palace of Nestor (site), 353, 356
Paleolithic, 13, 142, 235, 237, 311, 314; late/upper 10, 102–103, 111, 114–115; middle 110, 113, 318–319
Paps of Anu mount, 38
pastures, 8, 11, 14, 54, 93, 96, 102, 104, 118, 142, 144, 147, 154, 156, 181, 185, 201, 208, 221–222, 224, 235, 240, 247–248, 256, 259–260, 262, 266–267, 278–281, 289, 278, 286, 288, 293–294, 314, 386, 390–392, 394; alpine, 9–10, 13, 58, 59–61, 65, 97, 117, 119–121, 124, 127, 133–134, 163, 179, 184, 186, 188, 192, 282
summer, 5, 106–107, 157, 167–168, 204, 278, 347
pasture activities, 121, 123, 131
pasture activity, 118, 123, 144
pasture indicators, 117–120, 122–124, 127, 130–134
pasturing, 19, 38–39, 61, 63, 65, 95, 101, 117–118, 124, 127, 133, 144, 153–154, 157–158, 162–163, 165–169, 179, 182–186, 200–201, 205, 222–224, 239–240, 260, 262, 266, 280–282, 286, 288, 294, 312, 314, 347, 390, 393–395; overgrazing, 54, 219, 224, 279; proxies/indicators, 13–14, 119–120, 122–123, 130–132, 134, 206,

267; seasonal, 11, 96, 103–107, 191–192, 198, 208, 240, 248, 278
peat bog, 8, 10, 111–112, 118, 182, 242–245, 250, 398
Penaud mire (site), 121–122, 124–125, 130, 133
Petit Beaulieu (site), 266
Pic d'OrhyY, 277–279, 287, 290, 294
Pico Sacro, 28–32
Pieniny mountains, 235
pig, 157–158, 221, 223, 314, 336, 347, 353
pilgrimage, 28, 60, 77, 80, 83–85, 88–89
Pindo, mount, 29
Pindus Mountains, 29, 96–97
Pista (site), 295–297
pitch/resine, 186, 188, 190–192, 193, 211, 393–394; kilns, 188–189
Piz (Peak) Giumela, 148
Planells de Perafita (site), 184, 188
Pleistocene, 96–97, 100–103, 108, 111–116, 235, 257, 306, 319, 321, 366
Pleta de les Bacives (site), 184, 188
Pliny the Elder, 190–191
Podczerwone (site), 102
Podhale basin, 93, 101–105, 107
Pokunsyrt (site), 163
Pontus Mountains, 155, 303–304
Popocatepetl volcano, 47
Poprad-Matejovce (site), 240
pottery, 8, 82, 85, 87, 90, 104–105, 110–111, 133, 135, 142, 156, 174, 184, 186–187, 191, 233, 239–242, 249, 290, 309, 311, 317, 326, 328–330, 332, 334, 336–337, 340, 349, 353; cooking, 82, 87, 186–187, 191
Pradell (site), 188, 190–191
Prehistoric, 353
early prehistoric, 271, 311
late prehistoric, 51, 55–58, 60–62, 65, 306, 322, 334, 337
Prehistory, 8, 10–14, 23–24, 31, 49, 64, 95–96, 107–108, 121, 124–126, 128–129, 133, 140, 142, 146, 153–154, 161, 186, 200, 202, 205–206, 211, 235–237, 239, 244,

246, 253–255, 260, 263–264, 269–270, 283, 289–291, 312–314, 319, 332, 343–344, 349, 351, 353, 356, 368; late, 23, 58, 337
Presena glacier (site), 151
prestige goods, 356–357
Preuschen, Ernst, 146
protohistory, 23, 31–32, 144, 147, 253, 255, 269–270, 325–330, 333–334, 336–337, 339
Ptolomeus, 191
Puig dels Avençons (site), 391
Puigmal massif, 187, 191
Punta Cadini (site), 148
Punta Linke (site), 14, 143, 148–150
Puntsag Ovoo hill (site), 59, 65
Puy de Dôme, 256
Puy de la Vache volcano, 257
Puy de l'Enfer volcano, 257
Puy Lassolas volcano, 257
Pylos (site), 353–357
Pyrenees, 186, 190, 262, 264, 393, 397; Catalan, 5, 179–181, 267, 387–390; French, 96–97; high, 179, 186, 193–194, 263; Western, 3, 11–12, 192, 277–278

Qaf Peja pass, 353, 356
Qencomayo river, 372–373, 376
Qenqo Laqo (site), 374
quarries, 96–97, 198, 203, 314
Quechua, 21
Queen Lupa, 29
Queyriaux (site), 261
Quimal peak, 21

Racha region, 166
Raganello river basin, 325–326, 337
Ramosch-Mottata (site), 133
Ransyrt (site), 162
reindeer, 101, 103–104, 198, 201, 204–205
religion, 32, 37–41, 43–44, 48, 52, 62, 79, 81, 380; religious architecture, 40, 269; sites, 371, 375–378
Rioni river, 155
Rishikesh valley, 24

ritual, 20, 30–32, 51, 56–57, 59–60, 62, 64–65, 77, 79, 80–81, 83–85, 87–89, 154, 161, 380; sites, 37, 40, 45–47, 83, 162
Riu dels Orris (site), 189–190
road, 6, 61, 77, 80, 83–85, 88–89, 121, 165, 187–188, 200–201, 203–204, 214, 233, 242, 256, 326, 334, 336, 339, 346, 350, 353, 355, 364, 370–376, 386–387; network, 89, 192, 367–368, 377, 379–381, 383; qhapaq ñan, 19, 361, 365, 377; roman, 140, 391; silk, 62; *Via Sebaste,* 315
rock art, 23–24; engraved, 30–32, 47, 63–65, 133, 379
Rocky Mountains, 3, 8, 93–94
Rofenhöfe, 118
Roman, 31, 127, 141, 179, 186–188, 190–193, 205, 207, 269–270, 314–316, 351, 390–391, 393–394; Imperial period, 311, 317, 332–333
Romanou (site), 353
romanticism, 7, 41, 197, 200, 388, 391
Rotmoos climatic fluctuations, 118
Rugova valley, 353
Røldal-Suldal, 203

Saami, 41, 199–200
sacrifice, 38, 47, 82, 372; animal, 87–88
Sagalassos (site), 304–306, 313–317
Saint James the Apostle, 29, 31–32
Sakdrisi (site), 155
Sakrsisi (site), 160
salt, 95, 156, 170, 349, 392; flats, 21; mines, 160; springs, 107
sanctuaries, 20, 32, 133; peak, 10, 77–89; 325; shrine, 46–47, 80, 86
Sandomierz basin, 101, 103–104
San Francisco peaks, 40
San Pedro de Atacama, 21
Santiago de Compostela, 28–29, 31
Sapantiana Waka (site), 372, 376
Saphi river 362–363, 368, 377–378
scandinavia mountains, 2–3, 8, 10, 197
Schlandraun valley, 120, 127
Schnals valley, 120, 134

Schwarzboden mire (site), 120–122, 127–128, 130, 133
Schwarzwald mountains, 93
Scutari lake, 356
seal, 223
Secale, 259
Sedano (site), 24
sedentism, 153, 157–158, 160, 170, 233, 245, 254
Segre river upper valleys, 186, 190
Shala valley, 343–347, 349, 351, 353, 356
sheep, 46, 104, 118, 156–158, 165–166, 168, 206, 209, 211, 219–226, 291, 293, 347, 351, 353, 393–394
shepherd, 83, 93, 106–107, 133, 141, 200, 239, 245, 248, 286, 294, 307, 314–315, 387, 390; herder, 53, 55, 60–61, 63–66, 168, 248, 290
Shiva, 38, 47
Shivling, Mount, 38
shrub, 11, 224, 227, 280, 282, 307, 312, 386; clearance, 106
Sibaritide region, 326, 337–338
Sinai, Mount, 38
Sioni-Tsopi culture, 158
Sirenaqocha (site), 374
Skawa river valley, 243–244
Ski, 6, 40–41, 150, 212, 388
Skrivarhelleren (site), 199, 203, 207, 210
Sognefjord, 197, 199, 207
Sowin, 7 (site), 101
Spisko-Gubalowskie foothills, 102–103
steppe, 23, 51–52, 61, 154–157, 160, 165–166, 305, 314
Strabo, 191
Strane pod Tatrami (site), 240
Sumtangen (site), 201–203, 205
Świderian culture, 102–104

Tainaron cape, 86
Tarraco (site), 391
Tatra mountains, 104, 116, 235; high, 10, 93, 100–101, 105, 107, 240; low, 240; National Park, 93–95, 99–108; Northern, 102

Taunus mountains, 234
Taurus mountains, 12, 155, 320; Western, 3, 303–305, 312
Taygetos, Mount, 86
Tenochtitlan (site), 362
tent, 101–104
terrace, 5, 11, 82, 154, 345, 347, 349, 351, 392, 395; agricultural, 87, 168–169, 328, 334, 352, 361–365, 368–376, 379–380
Ter valley, 179–181, 183–184, 186, 191–193, 196
Teteqoca, waka, 372, 376
textile working, 207, 211–212
Theth village, 343, 345–351, 353–356
Timpanogos, Mount, 41
timpone motta (site), 325
Torbera de Perafita I (site), 184
Tor village, 388–389
tourism, 5–7, 47, 144, 214, 339, 395
trade, 98, 105, 141, 170, 188, 193, 205, 207, 223, 268–270, 316, 354, 394–395
traditionalism/conservativism, 64, 385–387, 395
transhumance, 10, 13, 19, 23, 56, 58, 60–62, 65, 93, 95–97, 99–111, 113–115, 118, 120–121, 130, 133–134, 141, 153–154, 161, 179, 191–193, 198, 200, 222, 233, 240, 249–250, 286, 290, 292, 314, 347, 355, 394
Traostalos (site), 80
Treskavac, Mount, 46
Trialei Plateau (site), 165
tribe, 38–39, 343–345, 355–356
Tsona Klde (site), 155–156
Tullumayo river, 362, 368, 372, 377–378
Tunulliarfik fjord (Eiriksfjord), 222
Tuyn Gol river, 53
Tuyumayo river, 363
Tworkowa (site), 105
Tyin lake, 203, 211
Tymbrianassos estate, 316

Uluru (Ayers Rock), 44
United Nations Agenda, 21 4–6

Unakozovskaya (site), 155
Urubamba valley, 370–371
Urutlekrǎi (site), 207–209
Usman dan Fodio, 44
Uszwica river, 242
Uztarbe (site), 285, 289–290, 297

Valcamonica, 23–24, 133
Val dei Mocheni (valley), 146
Val di Cembra, 146
Valley of Lakes, 52, 58, 61, 66
Val Venosta/Vinschgau valley, 120, 130–131, 141
Vansa, La, valley, 180
Vent Valley, 120, 141
Vernagt lake, 120–123, 127, 129–130, 132–134
Vesuvian eruption, 329, 332
Veyre river, 253, 255, 257
Vézolle (site), 261
Vezzena plateau, 146
Vilcanota valley, 380
Vistula river, 99, 104–105

Wanqaro river, 368
Wasatch mountain range, 41
Watanay river valley, 361–365, 368–371, 377, 379–383
wells, 62, 314, 333–334

wetlands, 182, 365–369, 371, 374, 381, 394
White Mountains, 86
Wilczyce (site), 104
Wiśnicz foothills, 104–105, 241–242
Witow I (site), 102
wool, 200, 211, 394–395; loom weight, 133
woolly mammoth, 101
woolly rhinoceros, 101
world war: First World War/Great War, 10, 14, 139, 142, 147–150, 198, 356–357; Second World War, 198, 202, 213, 355
worship, 38–40, 56, 88, 380

younger dryas, 96, 98, 102
Yucay Valley, 380

Zagli Barzond (site), 155, 161
Zagórze (site), 245
Zagros massif, 155
Zaisan hill (site), 57
Zakros (site), 80
Zamok (site), 155, 157
Zawoja-Przysłop (site), 238
Żerków (site), 105, 242
Zion, Mount, 41
Zogu, Ahmet/Zog I, King of the Albanians, 355
Zuma rock, 44

www.ingramcontent.com/pod-product-compliance
Ingram Content Group UK Ltd.
Pitfield, Milton Keynes, MK11 3LW, UK
UKHW050544150426
5217IPUK00026B/2066